NARRATIVE

FICTION

An Introduction and Anthology

NARRATIVE

FICTION

An Introduction and Anthology

KELLEY GRIFFITH

University of North Carolina at Greensboro

Harcourt Brace College Publishers

Fort Worth   Philadelphia   San Diego   New York   Orlando   Austin   San Antonio
Toronto   Montreal   London   Sydney   Tokyo

Editor in Chief	Ted Buchholz
Acquisitions Editor	Stephen T. Jordan
Developmental Editor	Helen Triller
Project Editor	Angela Williams
Production Manager	Jane Tyndall Ponceti
Senior Book Designer	Serena Barnett Manning
Permissions Editor	Van E. Strength

Address for Editorial Correspondence
Harcourt Brace College Publishers, 301 Commerce Street, Suite 3700, Fort Worth, TX 76102

Address for Orders
Harcourt Brace and Company, 6277 Sea Harbor Drive, Orlando, FL 32887
1-800-782-4479, or 1-800-433-0001 (in Florida)

Credits and acknowledgments begin on page 647.

ISBN: 0-15-500155-8

Library of Congress Catalogue Number: 92-76097

Printed in the United States of America

4 5 6 7 8 9 0 1 2 3 054 9 8 7 6 5 4 3 2 1

For Saralyn

Preface

After teaching Introduction to Fiction courses for many years, I began to realize that my colleagues and I were omitting many great works of fiction. Like most instructors in introductory courses, we taught short stories and novels. But why, I wondered, weren't we teaching the *Iliad* or the *Odyssey*? Or *Sir Gawain and the Green Knight*? Or European fairy tales? As I thought about these questions further, I realized that we were excluding not just Western works but non-Western works as well. Why weren't we teaching the oral fiction of tribal cultures, or the *Shahnama,* or the *Mahabharata,* or *The Tale of Genji*? Weren't they fiction too?

The short story and novel are, of course, rewarding and important forms of fiction, but they are relatively recent genres, the novel springing up in the early eighteenth century and the short story in the early nineteenth century. They are, furthermore, Western genres, evolving out of and reflecting the scientific, industrial, urban, and rationalistic aspects of modern Western culture. An unfortunate result of focusing only on the short story and the novel in introductory courses is that we privilege Western fiction over the fiction of the rest of the world. Perhaps unintentionally, we leave students with the impression that the "best" forms of fiction are modern and Western. Another consequence is that we deny ourselves and our students the opportunity to explore the rich heritage of fiction from times and cultures other than our own.

The purpose of *Narrative Fiction: An Introduction and Anthology* is to provide a gateway to *all* of the world's fiction. To address that purpose, I have tried to do two things in this book. The first is to create an anthology of works from different parts of the world that can be enjoyed, analyzed, and studied for themselves. Equally important, I have tried to establish a *framework* for exploring fiction, a framework that extends its usefulness beyond the works contained here. Although many frameworks are possible for the study of fiction, the one I have chosen for this book is the study of genres.

The genres framework has a number of advantages for the teaching of fiction. One is flexibility. If instructors would like to study a genre more thoroughly, they need only supplement the works already in *Narrative Fiction: An Introduction and Anthology* adding perhaps an entire collection of tales; another epic, romance, or novel; or a selection of short stories from a particular region. If instructors want to extend the range of this book, they may do so by adding more genres. The genres discussed here are commonplace in world literature, but there are many other genres of fiction, both Western and non-Western, that are worthy of study.

Another advantage of a genres approach is that it gives readers the opportunity to explore fiction that is interesting and meaningful to them. Such fiction often exists within genres other than the best known or most "respectable" genres. These might include popular genres such as science fiction, western, detective, spy, romance, and gothic. But they might also include genres that are unique to particular cultures or groups of people. They might even include genres that are amalgams of several artistic media, such as cartoons, films, and television programs.

The genres framework, finally, makes fiction itself an object of study. Most people who teach only the short story and the novel—at least the instructors I know—usually teach some of the elements of fiction (plot, characterization, theme, and so forth) and move on to close readings of individual works. Rarely do they bring up the cultural conditions that produced the short story and novel, or how fiction functions in society, or why people enjoy the kinds of fiction they do, or even what fiction is and how it may be different from nonfiction. But a genres approach almost inevitably raises these kinds of questions. Indeed, these are the very kinds of questions that have been central to the enormous amount of critical and theoretical work done on narrative in the past thirty years. A genres approach to fiction makes it possible to incorporate much of that work into our teaching.

Narrative Fiction: An Introduction and Anthology should be useful for almost any level of the study of fiction. In introductory courses, instructors can make this book the entire focus of the course, using only the material contained within it. They can also make it the basic textbook, supplementing it with other readings. In more advanced courses, instructors can use *Narrative Fiction: An Introduction and Anthology* as a starting point for an extended study of the nature, cultural contexts, and functions of fiction.

The book has been organized for a progressive study of narrative fiction. The first chapter is an introduction to the elements of fiction. Following the discussion of each element are "Questions for Analyzing . . ." to help readers think about how the elements work in any fictional text. The succeeding chapters focus on well-known genres of fiction. The chapters are arranged in roughly chronological order, starting with the earliest genre, myth, then moving to epic, tale, romance, narrative poetry, and concluding with the most recent genres, the short story and the novel. Each of these chapters includes an introduction to the genre, a selection of works that illustrate the genre, and "Questions for Study" after each selection that help students think about what they have read. All of the genre chapters conclude with a brief list of works for further reading.

Acknowledgments

I am grateful to the many people who have helped me with this book. The following reviewers have provided me with stimulating suggestions: Oliver Billingslea, Auburn University; Helen M. Casey, SUNY–Delhi College of Technology; Katherine Golden, Skidmore College; William Goldhurst, University of Florida; Katherine Keller, University of Central Florida; M. Gilbert Porter, University of Missouri; Michael Rose, Lane Community College; and Mary Ann Wilson, University of Southwestern Louisiana. My editors Bill McLane, Stephen Jordan, and Helen Triller have not only encouraged me in this project but have made invaluable contributions to it. Finally, I am deeply grateful to my family for their kind support and gracious care.

Contents

NARRATIVE

FICTION

An Introduction and Anthology

Chapter One

Introduction to Narrative Fiction

You may be familiar with the famous story that frames the Arabian collection of tales *The Thousand and One Nights*. Once upon a time, the story goes, a king from "the lands of India and China" discovers that his wife is unfaithful. He immediately kills her and her lover and embarks on a savage vendetta against women. He marries one virgin after another and kills each on her wedding night. In time, the king asks Shahrazad (or Scheherazade, as she is sometimes called) to be his bride. Much to the bewilderment of her family, she agrees. But she has a trick up her sleeve. On her wedding night she begins to tell the king a story. Just when she reaches the climax, she stops and refuses to finish until the next day. The spellbound king, in order to hear the rest of each story, puts off killing her. And so it goes for 1001 nights, nearly three years. During this time Shahrazad bears the king three children, gains his love, and saves her life.

The story of Shahrazad is a testament to the power of stories. "Tell me a story" is a plea we associate with children, but the plea is universal among people of nearly all age groups, historical periods, and cultures. So potent are stories that many cultures continue to believe they have magical powers and treat them with the care and respect often reserved for sacred objects.

Stories permeate our experience. Each of our lives is a story. We review it, add to it, and tell it. Each of our families is a story. We hear it told and retold as we grow up. Our society is a web of stories. We listen to them at school, at social gatherings, at holiday festivals. Our games and entertainments are based on stories. Our religions are structured by cosmic stories that give meaning and direction to our lives. In short, we cannot escape the influence of stories. To be human is to think and communicate with stories.

The subject of this book is the most familiar kind of story, narrative fiction. A **story** is a series of events that occur in time. A **narrative** is a telling of a story, a recounting of events in a temporal sequence. The distinguishing characteristic of narrative is the presence of a teller. The "teller" can be any medium through which a story is revealed. Images in a film, cartoon, or painting, movements in a dance, sounds of musical instruments—all of these can tell stories. In this book, however, we focus on narratives that use language, especially written language, as their medium of communication. Although the dividing line between nonfictional and fictional narrative is sometimes hard to discern, in general **narrative fiction** recounts events that have not happened, or that some people, at least, believe have not happened. When we read nonfictional narratives, such as diaries, autobiographies, biographies, and histories, we assume that the events contained in them have happened. When we read fictional narratives—like folktales, epics, romances, short stories, and novels—we know or believe that the events did not occur.

This book is an invitation to study the whole range of fictional narrative. It focuses on some of the most enduring kinds or genres of narrative. The first of these is the earliest and perhaps most influential genre of narrative, myth. Following the chapter on myth are chapters on other ancient and venerable narrative genres: epic, tale, romance, and narrative poetry. The concluding chapters feature the most popular genres of our time, the short story and the novel.

Why, we might ask, should we study so many kinds of narrative fiction? Few people seem to write epics, tales, fables, or narrative poems anymore. And myths may seem like something from the very distant past, irrelevant to us. Why not study just the short story and novel?

The assumption underlying this book is that we enhance our enjoyment and knowledge of literature by reading many kinds of narratives rather than just a few kinds. By reading more than just the short story and novel, we become familiar with great narratives from the past. The short story and novel are recent forms of fiction, emerging only within the last 250 years. Other forms of fiction are much older and more numerous, and they are products of rich cultural traditions. By looking beyond the short story and novel, we extend our interest to all time periods. We place the short story and novel within an evolving narrative tradition. And we unlock a treasure trove of great narratives, including anonymous folk narratives and works by authors like Homer, Vergil, Ovid, Dante, Boccaccio, Chaucer, Malory, Shakespeare, Coleridge, and Tennyson.

Another reward of looking beyond the short story and novel is that we can explore cultures outside the boundaries of Western culture. People in non-Western cultures, of course, have in recent times written short stories and novels. But the short story and novel are not only recent forms of literature, they are Western forms. They represent Western ways of thinking and communicating. Other kinds of narrative, like myth, legend, and tale, are more typical of non-Western cultures and are part of those cultures' past and present. Myths, for example, express religious beliefs and cultural traditions. Legends record history. Tales provide entertainment. When we study such narrative forms, they become gateways to cultures different from our own.

A third benefit of studying many kinds of narrative fiction is that they open our eyes to the role narrative plays in our own society. The short story and novel may be the most respected narrative fiction of the literary establishment, but the older narrative forms continue to survive in our own culture. Scholars of myth, for example, tell us that *all* cultures, even modern, industrial ones, have mythologies. Myths are so embedded in our assumptions and our communications that they often guide and control us even though we may not be aware of them. Other narrative forms such as fables, parables, and tales are also all around us. They may not be as respected by the literary establishment as are short stories and novels, but they are part of popular culture. So-called urban legends—a kind of oral folktale—are widespread throughout the United States. They often provide the plots for many popular television shows and films. Indeed, television and film have taken over the role of storyteller in our society. They tell stories that have qualities similar to those of folk narratives. Many of the written narratives found on drugstore and supermarket paperback racks are not quite short story or novel but rather more like earlier forms of narrative, the tale and romance. By analyzing other forms of narrative, we can study the powerful appeal of popular narrative and its place in our culture.

There are many ways to approach the narratives printed in this book. You may want simply to read them for entertainment. But you may want, also, to study them and probe their importance to the authors and societies that produced them, to our society, and to you personally. The two approaches discussed in this chapter should help you make such a study. They provide ways of thinking about narrative. To "think about" something means, in part, to raise questions about it and to try to answer them. Raising questions is often the hardest part of thinking. You have to know where to look in order to find the questions. One of the best ways to find questions is to analyze the object of study—in this case, narrative. The two approaches presented here are both analytic. **Analysis** means to separate something into its elements so you can examine their relationship to one another and to the whole. Once you know what the elements are, you can look for them and ask questions about how they work and what they contribute to the whole. Here we discuss ways of analyzing two "wholes" related to narrative: the narratives themselves and the kinds or genres of narratives.

ANALYZING INDIVIDUAL NARRATIVES

Let's say that you have just read a narrative. Perhaps you enjoyed it, perhaps not. Whatever your reaction, you want to understand the narrative better. How can you do that? For most readers, the best place to start is with the narrative itself. You may not want to look at *every* aspect of the narrative, but you will want at least to think about certain aspects of it, things that caught your eye. What things? In order to answer that question, to begin thinking about a particular narrative, you need to know something about narrative form.

In one sense, the form of a specific narrative is everything that makes up that narrative, everything that makes it unique. In another sense, the form of a narrative consists of the elements that are common to all narratives. All narratives contain conventions or devices that make up a kind of "grammar" or system of communication. These conventions include elements such as plot, characterization, theme, and point of view. The way these conventions are *used* in a particular narrative accounts for its uniqueness. Familiarity with the conventions of narrative allows us to think about why a specific narrative creates the effects it does, what it seems to mean, and how it is similar to and different from other narratives. If we like one narrative but not another, thinking about the conventions of each should help us understand our preference. If a narrative puzzles us, knowing something about how narrative conventions communicate ideas should help us get at the work's possible meanings.

The following discussion offers brief definitions of elements common to all narrative fiction. Each definition is followed by a set of questions that should be useful in analyzing a particular narrative and should lead you to think of your own questions.

The Elements of Narrative

Language

The medium of the narratives in this book is language. Authors try to use language in such a way that it fits their subject matter and affects their audience in predictable ways. Authors employ many devices to achieve these ends—variations in syntax (sentence structure), diction (word choice), sound qualities (rhyme and rhythm), figurative language (metaphor, simile), levels of diction (archaic, genteel, slangy, profane), and dialogue.

We can enjoy the language of a work for its own sake. But a work's language is important, as well, for its relationship to other elements in the narrative. When characters speak, authors fashion a language that reflects the characters' backgrounds, attitudes, and traits. Authors also use language to establish the tone of the narrative. No matter who the narrator is, whether the author, a character in the story, several characters, or someone outside the story, the narrative has a tone. **Tone** is the narrator's attitude toward the narrative's subject matter. The tone may, for example, be sarcastic, friendly, sad, angry, or indignant. Language, furthermore, affects the way we experience the narrative—the pace of the narrative and the ease with which we hear and read it. When the language is complicated by devices that require concentrated thought, like distorted syntax, unusual diction, and elaborate figures of speech, the pace at which we experience the narrative is slower than if the language is easily and immediately clear. Language, in fact, pervades all the elements of the narrative and provides a way of understanding them.

QUESTIONS FOR ANALYZING LANGUAGE

1. What characterizes the language of the work? Why does the author use this kind of language?

2. What do we learn about the characters from the way they use language?

3. What is the tone of the narrative? How does the language communicate that tone?

Theme

Theme is the ideas in the work. It is the comments the work seems to make about the real world. Of all the elements of narrative, theme may be the most satisfying to explore, because it helps us discover meaning in the work.

When studying a work's themes, be sure to distinguish them from the work's subjects. A **subject** is something the work is about, such as love, fate, justice, bravery, or loss. A **theme** is what the work says about a particular subject: Love demands commitment, fate is often fickle, justice is elusive, bravery requires self-sacrifice, loss is unavoidable. You can tell subject from theme by the way each is stated. A subject can be stated in a word or a phrase, but a theme must be stated in one or more complete sentences.

When analyzing theme, think of the narrative as a form of rhetoric. **Rhetoric,** simply put, is the art of persuasion. Almost all narratives, in one way or another, are rhetorical. Authors want to persuade us of something. In general, they want to persuade us that the fictional worlds they create are believable or, at least, compelling enough to capture our imagination. More specifically, they want to persuade us that certain ideas about the real world are true. Our task as interpreters of theme is to spot the rhetorical devices that communicate the work's ideas.

One such device is the binary opposition. A **binary opposition** is two opposing or contradictory forces or ideas: love vs. hate, sacred vs. profane, good vs. evil, honor vs. dishonor, order vs. chaos. Works of literature rest upon at least one set of binary oppositions but more likely upon many sets of binary oppositions. The biblical story of Adam and Eve (see p. 32), for example, has many binary oppositions: Man vs. woman, humankind vs. serpent, humankind vs. God, serpent vs. God, paradise vs. the world outside of paradise. Authors will often use binary oppositions to persuade us that one idea or group of ideas is better than another. They do this by having one of the opposing forces of a binary opposition "win" over the other. Thus in the Adam and Eve story, "God" (and all the qualities associated with God) wins over the "serpent" (and all the qualities associated with the serpent).

Another rhetorical device is symbolism. Broadly speaking, a **symbol** is something that represents something else. The word *tree,* for example, is a symbol for the object "tree." But in literature, a symbol is an object that has meaning beyond itself. The object is concrete and the meanings are abstract. Light, for example, is a concrete phenomenon that in Western culture traditionally symbolizes abstract qualities like knowledge, spirituality, and purity. The seasons also have traditional symbolic values; winter is associated with death and spring with rebirth. Colors can be symbolic: red (passion, anger), white (purity), green (growth, nature, rebirth). Authors often use symbols to communicate ideas. At the beginning of Dante's *Divine Comedy,* for example, the protagonist has wandered off the "straight path" into a "dark wood." The wood is "savage and stubborn," a "bitter place." The protagonist does not know how he got there, only that he had "become so sleepy at the moment when [he] first strayed, leaving the path of truth." Dante makes clear that the path, the wood, and the protagonist's sleep are symbols. The path symbolizes Christian faith and morality, the sleep symbolizes the protagonist's departure from them, and the dark wood symbolizes his psychological and theological state of despair and alienation.

Authors communicate ideas not just through specific elements like binary oppositions and symbolism but also in their overall development of characters and control of the action of the story. Snow White, for example, is selfless, kind, generous, and sympathetic with the gentle aspects of nature. The witch is egotistical, controlling, possessive, and leagued with the violent aspects of nature. The author—in this case the various tellers of the Snow White tale—uses Snow White's triumph over the witch to signal that the qualities and values associated with her are more desirable than those associated with the witch.

The themes of a work may be difficult to pin down or to state simply. Even the ideas presented in works like "Snow White," which may at first glance seem fairly simple, can be surprisingly complex. One set of binary oppositions may be supplemented, even contradicted, by others. In modern fiction, especially, opposing forces may each have admirable as well as unadmirable qualities. The author's choice of which side wins may seem arbitrary. Or the author may allow neither side to win decisively, in which case we must decide for ourselves which side is better. Some narratives may contain direct statements of theme, as is the case with many fables and parables. But in most narratives, subject and theme are implicit rather than explicit. When themes seem obscure or complex, as, for example, in the works of modern authors like Franz Kafka and Anton Chekhov, the best we can do is pay tribute to the author's complex vision of life and try to identify the rhetorical devices that signal the author's ideas.

QUESTIONS FOR ANALYZING THEME

1. What are some of the subjects of the work? (What does the work seem to be about?)

2. What are some of the themes of the work? (What does the work seem to say about its subjects?)

3. What binary oppositions does the author establish in the work? What values or qualities seem to be represented by each binary opposition? Which binary opposition seems most important? Which seems to contain and control the others or most of the others? Are the binary oppositions clearcut or complicated by contradictory qualities? For example, is one side of the opposition clearly good and the other clearly evil, or does each side contain good and bad qualities? Which side seems to win out over the other? Do you agree with the author's choice of which side wins?

4. What symbols, if any, does the author seem to use? What do they seem to communicate about the meaning of the work?

5. Are the themes of the work difficult to identify? Do the themes seem contradictory?

6. What worldview does the work represent? Is the work, for example, pessimistic or optimistic about the conditions of life? Are the characters happy with their lives? Do they strive for goals they find meaningful? How successful are they in solving their problems? Does the work seem to show that life can have purpose and order?

Plot

Broadly defined, **plot** is the succession of events of the narrative or what happens. When someone asks you to tell them the plot of a narrative, they usually want you to recount the events. But plot is not just the events of a narrative; more accurately, it is the author's arrangement and selection of the events. There is a difference, then, between story and plot. **Story** is the chronological sequence in which the events occur. Plot is the author's arrangement of the events of the story. The two arrangements—the chronological sequence and the author's arrangement— are usually different. At the beginning of a detective story, for example, the author lets us see that a murder has been committed, but we do not know who the murderer is. As the detective uncovers clues, we learn about the events that led up to the murder. Finally, when the murderer is exposed, we can reconstruct the entire sequence of events in chronological order.

Plot is different from story also in the way the author selects the events of the narrative. In a story, events need have no logical relationship except that they occur one after the other. An example would be a sequence of events in which a cat runs into the living room, then a dog, and then a cook holding a meat cleaver. A story would present these events with no explanation of why one occurs after the other. In a plot, however, events are connected by a logical relationship of cause and effect. A plot would show that the cat runs into the room *because* the dog is chasing it. The cook runs into the room *because* she is chasing the dog. She is chasing the dog *because,* in chasing the cat, the dog has overturned the meat on the chopping block.

Few narratives are without plot. It is hard to imagine a narrative whose events are totally unrelated to one another or are not arranged in some pleasing or purposeful order. But some narratives have less plot than others. Folk tales and romances, for example, tend to have less plot, or less complicated plots, than short stories and novels.

What qualities does plot give to a narrative? First, authors use plot to engage us emotionally. Narratives in which one thing happens after another for no apparent reason would be very boring. Authors, therefore, often engage readers' interest by means of an exciting plot device, conflict. Plots depict characters in conflict with one another, with their environment, and within themselves. When characters conflict with other people or with things, the conflicts are *external.* Examples of external conflicts are physical battles, struggles with natural phenomena like storms and disease, and verbal arguments. When characters debate within themselves, the conflicts are *internal.* Characters who are torn between doing one thing and another, who harbor warring personalities, or who struggle to discover the truth about something are all experiencing internal conflicts. Conflicts in a narrative can be intense, as in adventure tales, or so understated as to seem almost nonexistent. In creation myths, for example, the divinity may seem to bring forth new life effortlessly, but the implicit conflict is between chaos (the state of the cosmos before creation) and order (the new creation). In general, the more intense the conflicts, the more the plot will stir our emotions and elicit our immediate interest in the circumstances of the narrative.

Another plot device that engages us emotionally is the author's arrangement of events. Most narratives follow a pattern: Conflicts are established at the beginning, intensified throughout the middle, brought to a climax near the end, and dissolved in a brief conclusion. Within this pattern, many variations are possible. The plot can be loose and rambling, as in some folk narratives, or intricate and tightly woven, as in most short stories. Authors may present incidents in chronological order or relate them in flashbacks. They may vary the pace of the action, so that one part of the narrative moves quickly, with lots of action, and another part moves more slowly. Usually the pace of the narrative picks up as it moves toward the end.

A second quality that plot gives narratives is meaning. Authors use plot to communicate ideas. By setting up conflicts, authors imply concepts. On the concrete level of action, the primary opposition in a narrative is represented by a protagonist and an antagonist. The **protagonist** is the main character. Sometimes there is more than one protagonist, but typically just one. The protagonist is in conflict with one or more antagonists. The **antagonist** may be a person or persons but may be other things, such as forces of nature, hostile divinities, or psychological traits that cause emotional or intellectual conflicts within the protagonist.

On the abstract level of ideas, the protagonist and antagonist represent concepts and values. Although the author, for the sake of realism, may give the protagonist some unappealing qualities, he or she usually wants us to root for the protagonist. Our allegiance is based on our approval of the "good" qualities associated with the protagonist. If the protagonist, for example, is a "hero" or "heroine," he or she possesses qualities we admire—bravery, cleverness, energy, loyalty, unselfishness, patriotism. Sometimes we may not admire the protagonist. A narrative may be a study in monstrosity, as are some of Edgar Allan Poe's stories. In such a case, the protagonist seems despicable, and we want to see him or her defeated in the end. Or we may profoundly disagree with the author's values and despise a protagonist the author thinks admirable. But our allegiance to *either* side of the conflict is based on our identity with the values of the side we prefer.

Another plot device authors use to convey values is the ending. Endings resolve plot conflicts. When we finish a narrative, we may feel that the ending is exactly right and could have been no other way. But this feeling of rightness obscures the other choices the author had for ending the plot. To engage our interest, authors have to keep us guessing about how the conflicts might be resolved. We have to believe that more than one resolution is possible. Even when we know in advance how the plot will turn out, authors intrigue us with the possibility that the story could end differently. When authors choose endings, they make value judgments. They give one set of values priority over another. Knowing this gives us the freedom to disagree with the author's choice of an ending. We may prefer, instead, an ending that seems more in keeping either with the values present in the narrative or with our own. Nineteenth-century authors, for example, often felt compelled to impose "happy" endings on their plots. But sometimes those endings seem forced. We might prefer other endings that seem justified by details in the narrative.

QUESTIONS FOR ANALYZING PLOT

1. Does the narrative seem to have much plot? How does the presence or absence of plot devices affect your enjoyment or understanding of the narrative?

2. How are the events in the narrative arranged? Are they in chronological order? Does the author use flashbacks? Flashforwards? How, if at all, does the plot depart from strictly chronological order? Why does the author arrange the events in this way?

3. What is the pace of the narrative? Does the pace change? Why does the author establish a particular pace or change the pace?

4. What are the key events? What seems to cause them? A character? Natural forces? Accident? What values or psychological traits lead characters to do what they do?

5. What are the main conflicts of the narrative? Which are external, which internal?

6. What causes the conflicts? What effects do the conflicts have?

7. How are the conflicts resolved?

8. Who are the protagonists? Who or what are the antagonists? In what ways are they in conflict?

9. What values and qualities seem attached to opposing sides of conflicts? What values and qualities does the protagonist have? What values and qualities does the antagonist have? How does the author make one set of values seem more appealing than another?

10. What choices about ideas and values does the ending seem to communicate? Which side of a conflict seems to "win" and what implications does that victory have for the themes of the narrative? Can you see the possibilities for other endings? If so, how would they affect the themes of the narrative?

Characterization

Characters are the actors in a narrative, and **characterization** is the author's presentation and development of characters. Characters are usually human beings, but sometimes they are supernatural or otherworldly figures, like gods, goddesses, angels, demons, fairies, giants, witches, and mermaids. Sometimes they are animals, as in fables and folktales. Usually, even though such characters are nonhuman, they nonetheless have human characteristics. They speak, reason, and act like human beings. But authors may use nonhuman characters to represent qualities and actions that are inexplicable to human understanding— unmotivated evil, for example, or awesome, mysterious power, like the power of nature or of God.

There are two general kinds of character, simple and complex, and thus two levels of psychological complexity in narratives. **Simple characters,** sometimes called **flat characters,** have only one or two personality traits and are easily identifiable as stereotypes—the miser, the country bumpkin, the naive optimist, the hard-driven businessman, the jealous spouse. Simple characters abound in folk narratives, like fairy tales and fables, but most narratives have at least some simple characters. **Complex** (or **round**) **characters** have numerous, sometimes conflicting, personality traits. It may be difficult to pinpoint with certainty why they do what they do, what their goals are, what their values and philosophy are, why they are the way they are. Complex characters typically appear in realistic narratives like the short story and novel. Since a narrative must focus so much attention on a complex character to make him or her credible, there are fewer complex characters in works of literature than simple characters. Rather, one complex character is usually surrounded and partly defined by a number of simple characters.

Narratives that feature only simple characters tend to emphasize ideas or exterior action. In thematic narratives—those whose main purpose is to relay ideas—the characters have just enough traits to make the ideas clear: the greedy king, the faithful Christian, the lazy servant, the chaste wife, the prodigal son. In action narratives, like spy fiction and sentimental melodrama, the simple characters are functions of plot. They have just enough traits to establish conflicts and set the story in motion: the inept father, the vulnerable heroine, the cruel villain, the noble hero.

Narratives that feature complex characters focus less on action and obvious "morals" and more on the values, thoughts, and feelings of the characters. Complex characters are more like real people than simple characters. They experience a broad range of emotions, fall into confusion, exhibit good and bad qualities, and make mistakes. Narratives with complex characters, therefore, shift the "action" from outside the characters to inside their minds. These narratives involve us in the drama of social, moral, and psychological choices. Will Elizabeth, despite her misconceptions, hasty conclusions, and inner turmoil, marry Darcy? Will Clyde, in spite of his respect for human life, murder Roberta, who thwarts his ambitions for status and luxury? As readers, we participate in the mental struggles of complex characters.

Characters who remain the same throughout a work are **static** characters. Characters who change—that is, who alter their beliefs and patterns of behavior— are **dynamic** characters. Usually, complex characters change and simple characters remain the same, but not always. Odysseus in the *Odyssey* is a fairly complex character, but although he goes through many harrowing, heartrending, exhausting experiences, he never changes. The prodigal son, in the parable told by Jesus, is a simple character. His experiences are only briefly described, but he changes. An event that often signals a character's change is an epiphany. An **epiphany** is a character's recognition of the truth about himself or herself and about the nature of his or her circumstances. Usually this recognition is overwhelming and climaxes a long period of anguish and misunderstanding. Despite the great length of the *Odyssey*, Odysseus never has an epiphany. But in the brief parable of the prodigal son, the protagonist experiences a powerful epiphany that changes his life.

Characterization is one of the most appealing aspects of narrative fiction. We enjoy narratives because we like the characters. We care about what happens to them. Why do we? One reason is that we empathize with the situations that threaten or challenge them. When we read Poe's "The Pit and the Pendulum," we suffer the same sense of entrapment and peril the protagonist does, and we struggle with him as he tries to escape. Another reason is that we may identify with traits—status, activities, personality, looks—that make the characters seem like ourselves or like people whose lives appeal to us. Reading fiction, then, becomes a vicarious participation in lives that seem glamorous. But perhaps the most important reason we like certain characters is because we share their values. They believe and do the "right" things and are in conflict with characters or forces that are "wrong." Our empathy arises from a commitment to ideas that are important to us. We want those ideas and the characters who hold them to win out in the end.

QUESTIONS FOR ANALYZING CHARACTERIZATION

1. Which are the simple characters in the narrative? What are their traits? How are the simple characters used to generate conflict and move the action forward? What concepts, if any, do the simple characters seem to represent? How do the simple characters help create the work's themes?

2. Which are the complex characters? What makes them more complex than simple characters? What has caused them to be the way they are? What motivates them? What are their goals? What, if anything, is contradictory or difficult to understand about them? Do they fully understand themselves? What problems confront them? Why are they successful or unsuccessful in solving their problems?

3. Which characters change? How do they change? What seems to cause them to change? What epiphanies, if any, do they experience?

4. Which characters do you like? Which do you dislike? Why?

5. What values and ideals do the characters seem to represent? What values and ideals seem to "win" at the end?

Setting

Authors of narratives place ("set") their characters and events in a "world," in a locale, time, and culture. **Setting,** then, is comprised of the physical, temporal, and cultural details of the narrative's world. As with the other elements of narrative, setting plays an important part in communicating the themes of the narrative.

The **physical aspect** of the setting includes all of the places where the action takes place—the forest, the castle, the field of war, the town, the room. The physical setting includes also the objects—furnishings, natural phenomena, artifacts—located in these places. In addition, the physical setting includes the natural laws that govern the material world. In a realistic narrative, we expect the laws of nature to be the same as in the real world. But in fantastic narratives, the laws of nature are different. Animals speak, human beings fly, swords have miraculous properties. Authors present the physical setting through sensuous description— the way it smells, tastes, feels, sounds, and looks. The sensuous details about a house would include the taste and smell of the food, the sounds of household machines, the intensity of the light, the feel of the furniture.

The temporal aspect of the setting consists of three things: time period, length of time, and perception of time. The time period includes seasons of the year and times of day. The season of Charles Dickens's "A Christmas Carol"—winter, Christmas—provides it with its major themes. Dickens, furthermore, divides the action between day (Scrooge's miserliness, the misery of the poor) and night

(Scrooge's dreams, his guilty conscience, his imagined death). When Scrooge awakens, it is morning, a time of rebirth and new opportunities. Time period also includes the historical era. Leo Tolstoy's novel *War and Peace* is set during Napoleon's invasion of Russia in 1812, Margaret Mitchell's novel *Gone with the Wind* is set during the American Civil War, Jane Austen's novels are set during the late eighteenth century and early nineteenth century. Some narratives are set in remote or inaccessible time periods. Creation myths, for example, often take place in a physical environment (the cosmos) and a time (pre-history, pre-creation) that no human being has ever experienced. Still other works may have universal settings; they could be anywhere, anytime. When narratives are set in the present, however, we almost always expect them to be realistic—to match the typical and probable happenings of real life.

Length of time in a narrative is closely related to perception of time. Length of time is the amount of time actually covered by the events of the narrative. The biblical account of creation, for example, covers seven days. The epic poem *Beowulf* contains almost the entire life of its hero, Beowulf. The perception of time is the way a character or the reader feels about how quickly or slowly time seems to pass. Even if the length of time is brief, a character's perception or our perception may be that the time passes very slowly. Scrooge's Christmas Eve is only one night long, but he feels as if he has lived through a lifetime. And so do we, because Dickens uses Scrooge's dreams to fill us in on the details of his past and his possible future.

Two narrative devices influence perception of time: summary narration and scenic narration. In **summary narration,** the narrator briefly relates (sums up) events and directly states how much time is passing. The narrator might say, for example, that "Henry Arnold spent ten years as a servant in the Argive palace. His life was difficult there, because he never had enough to eat and his employers were rude and inconsiderate." In **scenic narration,** the narrator describes an event in so much detail that the account takes about as long to read as it would to occur in real life. A scene in Henry Arnold's life at the palace might detail his experience of hunger—the meager serving of food for his supper, the gnawing pains in his stomach later that evening, his futile attempt to steal food from the kitchen. Another scene might feature a dialogue between Henry and Lady Argive, in which she rudely and unfairly accuses him of something he did not do.

Summary narration and scenic narration have different effects on the reader. Summary narration gives us intellectual distance from the events. Authors frequently use summary narration to tell us what the events mean. In contrast, scenic narration is more vivid. It allows us to experience the events firsthand, as if we were present on the scene. Scenic narration involves us more emotionally. We may even find a scene confusing and have to puzzle out its meaning without the help of a narrator's interpretation, just as we must when we witness scenes in real life. Summary and scenic narration also affect our perception of time. Summary narration speeds up the passage of time, scenic narration slows it down. A summary narration of Henry's ten-year stay may take only a few sentences, but a scenic narration of that same time period would take much, much longer. In fact, it would take so much longer that few authors rely solely on scenic narration. More often, they alternate between summary and scenic narration, speeding up the time here, slowing it down there.

Setting, finally, includes cultural environment, the patterns of behavior and beliefs that dominate the society in which the characters live. Family relationships, moral values, political systems, class structures, gender roles, race relations—all are part of cultural environment. Societies gain coherence through codes that govern meaning and behavior. The clothes people wear, their furniture, their child-rearing practices are directed by cultural codes. Authors of fictional narratives may not overtly identify these codes, but they refer to them indirectly. As readers of narratives, we are challenged to uncover the cultural codes that are implicit in the author's representation of settings and characters. In the thirteenth-century Germanic epic *The Nibelungenlied,* for example, we see that clothes are important to this culture. The characters place a high value, both monetary and emotional, on clothes and pay careful attention to the kinds of clothes they wear for particular occasions. Our task as readers is to try to understand why clothes were so important to these people and how they relate to other prominent practices of their society, such as courtship, marriage, and warfare.

Because a society dominates its inhabitants so greatly, cultural setting is one of the most important sources of conflicts in narratives. A narrative may describe, for example, a society in which boys are allowed to go to school but girls are expected to stay home. Another narrative may present a society in which all citizens are expected to believe a particular religious or political doctrine. Characters in such narratives often feel constricted by their cultural environment and rebel against it. Or even if they want to conform, they may find it difficult to do so. Perhaps they feel torn between two competing loyalties—lover vs. parents, family vs. country, one child vs. another, personal happiness vs. duty. Perhaps they grow beyond the narrow worldview of their society and want to escape. Perhaps they breach a cultural taboo and want to avoid the consequences. Perhaps the society to which they give allegiance betrays them.

Setting affects us emotionally and intellectually. It affects us emotionally because it is a major factor in a work's atmosphere. The **atmosphere** of a narrative is the emotional reaction that we or the characters have to the world of the narrative. Authors create atmosphere through a combination of devices, including language, pace of action, and description of setting. Gothic stories are famous for making us feel vulnerable and afraid. Their settings are claustrophobic, unstable, and threatening. We feel that at any minute something will leap out or the floor will cave in or we will stumble into our worst nightmare. Atmosphere need not, however, be overpowering. It can be calm and subtle, like the feeling of orderliness and rationality that pervades Jane Austen's novels.

Setting affects us intellectually by providing potential sites of meaning in the narrative. A physical location, for example, takes on significance by its association with certain values and practices (a house in which greed and selfishness have destroyed a family, a tree under which a character experiences enlightenment). A season or time of day symbolizes certain attitudes: morning (hope), midnight (despair), Easter (rebirth), winter (death). A scene may force us to dwell on the impact of particular values and practices—the destructiveness of racism, the efficacy of patience. Most encompassing of all, a society or period in history can be the focus of the author's condemnation or approval. In *Candide* Voltaire satirizes the foolish and cruel practices of nearly all the societies of the Western world.

QUESTIONS FOR ANALYZING SETTING

1. What characterizes the physical setting of the narrative? If there are several physical settings, how are they different?

2. To what senses does the author appeal in order to establish the physical setting? What general impression does the physical setting make?

3. When does the narrative take place—what historical period, what season of the year, what time of day? How does the time period affect the characters and the action? How does it relate to the characters' attitudes?

4. How much time passes during the narrative?

5. In what ways does the author slow down and speed up our impression or the characters' impression of the passage of time?

6. What characterizes the society depicted in the narrative? What cultural codes are reflected by details of setting and by the characters' actions and beliefs? How does society influence the characters? What are the rewards of conforming, the punishments of not conforming? Are the characters happy or unhappy with this society? What conflicts does the society create? How are these conflicts resolved?

7. What is the atmosphere of the narrative? If the atmosphere changes, how does it change? What seems to be the author's purpose in making such changes?

8. What values are associated with physical objects or places? What is the author or narrator's attitude toward the time period of the setting? When the author uses scenic narration, what does he or she seem to emphasize? Does the author seem to approve of the society he or she depicts?

Point of View

Point of view is the position from which the story is told. It is also the position from which the reader or hearer experiences the story. The phrase "point of view" means literally the physical place from which we see what is going on. But point of view establishes more than just a visual perspective. It also helps determine our emotional and intellectual relationship to the places, characters, and events of the narrative. Think how we would react, for example, if we could see an automobile accident from two different places, from, say, a second-floor window and from inside the automobile. From inside the automobile, we would feel shocked, disoriented, threatened, and out of control. We would react emotionally rather than intellectually. From the second-floor window, however, we might feel startled at first, but we would also feel removed from the accident. We could see it as a whole, and we could even begin to make judgments about its causes. That is, we could impose an intellectual order on a sequence of events that to someone directly involved would seem like chaos.

A key question about point of view, then, is, through whose eyes or thoughts do we experience the story? There are four points of view that authors can adopt, four positions from which we can experience the narrative. The first is the **omniscient** point of view. In this position, the narrator seems to have complete knowledge of everything that happens in the narrative, including facts about the physical location, the history of the society, and all the characters' actions and thoughts. The word *omniscient* means all-knowing, so in the omniscient point of view we experience the story from the position of a godlike narrator who surveys all of the action from a remote place. Omniscient point of view is similar to watching the automobile accident from a second-floor window in the company of a wise and experienced commentator. The narrator (commentator) would tell us what occurs on the ground and what goes on in the minds of the participants, but the narrator would also give us the detachment and understanding of a second-floor observer. The narrator might show us or say, for example, that as shaken up as the participants feel, the accident is not so bad—no one is in real danger.

The second point of view is **limited omniscient.** The limited omniscient point of view is like omniscient except for one thing: the narrator provides access (limits himself or herself) to the mind of only one character. This character is almost always the protagonist. The limited omniscient point of view, then, gives us two positions from which to experience the story: that of one of the characters and that of the narrator. Our experience of the story varies with the emphasis placed on these two positions. At one extreme, the narrator is nearly omniscient, telling us what the main character knows and does not know. We would, for example, view the automobile accident from the safety of the second-floor window but still know some of the thoughts of one of the participants. At the other extreme, the narrator virtually disappears, so that everything or nearly everything we learn filters through the mind of the protagonist. In this case, we would experience the automobile accident only from inside the automobile, through the perception of a participant. Usually, however, the limited omniscient point of view takes a position somewhere between these two extremes. The narrator would allow us to share a participant's experience of the automobile accident but would also pull us back to see and understand the accident in a larger context.

The third point of view is **first person.** In this point of view, the author pretends to disappear altogether and leaves the task of telling the story to one of the characters. The narrator uses the first-person pronoun, "I," and tells the story to other characters or to us, as if we were in the story too. The first-person point of view is the most like a real-life telling of a true story. Omniscient and limited omniscient narrators have access to information that no real person can have. But first-person narrators know only what real people can know. Like us, they learn what other people think only by what they do or say. Like us, they find out what happens only by reading or hearing about it or by experiencing it. Like us, they often lack a detached and comprehensive understanding of events. The first-person narrator's state of mind determines our emotional reaction to the story. If a narrator tells about his or her automobile accident right after it happens, the account will be more confused and turbulent than it will weeks later, when the narrator has collected more information and calmed down.

The fourth point of view is the **objective** or **dramatic.** In this point of view, the narrator remains outside the characters' minds and refrains from comment about the meaning of the events. It is "objective" because it denies us access to the unspoken thoughts—the subjectivity—of the characters. It is "dramatic" because it presents the action as if it were a stage play viewed by us from the audience. But a more accurate analogy can be made to film. The narrator is like the camera through whose lens we see the action of the film. The narrator makes no evaluative comments but only presents facts. The narrator, furthermore, may choose to show us facts from many different positions, much like the camera angles used in a film. We might, for example, see the automobile accident from distant as well as close-up perspectives: an overhead view of the whole accident; a ground view of windows smashing, hubcaps popping off, fenders caving in; an interior view of people thrown about and injured. We might learn how people react to the accident, but only through what they do and say out loud. Since the narrator makes no evaluative comments about the action, we are left to make sense of it on our own.

Point of view is crucial to our understanding of the work's meaning. Authors use narrators to relay information and to express opinions. As readers, we need to question the reliability of the narrator. Can we rely on the narrator to give us correct information? Can we rely on the narrator to make sound judgments? We can approach these questions by focusing on the author. Does the *author* think the narrator is reliable? Establishing an equivalence of author with narrator may be speculative on our part, but the narrative is, after all, the author's creation. It is a vehicle for the author's ideas. If the narrator seems to speak for the author, the narrator should be reliable. Another approach to assessing the narrator's reliability is to focus on ourselves. Do *we* think the narrator is reliable? Even if the narrator seems to speak for the author, do we trust either one?

Consider how we might apply these questions to each of the four points of view. For the most part, the omniscient narrator speaks for the author. Some omniscient narrators, like the narrator of Henry Fielding's *Tom Jones,* seem something like fictional characters. But no omniscient narrator is exactly like the author. An omniscient narrator may, for example, speak strongly for marital fidelity when the author is, in real life, a rakehell philanderer. Nonetheless, the narrator, for the time of the narrative, speaks for the author and is in this sense "reliable." We may, however, have other reasons for finding the omniscient narrator unreliable. We may disagree with the author's values or spot inconsistencies in the author's facts and opinions. The narrator of *The Nibelungenlied,* the thirteenth-century German epic, for example, condemns the murder of the hero Siegfried in the first half. He calls it "treachery" and "cowardice" (Siegfried is stabbed in the back). But in the second half of the epic he praises Siegfried's murderers as "heroes" and condemns Siegfried's wife for seeking their punishment. Which judgment should we accept?

The other three points of view make it more difficult to assess authors' opinions of narrators. In all three—limited omniscient, first-person, and objective—the author seems absent from the narrative and makes no direct commentary on it. Authors nonetheless communicate opinions about their narrators. They generate sympathy or antipathy for narrators by having them conform to or differ with the readers' values, by having other characters make comments about the narrators, and by resolving conflicts for or against the narrators.

Consider as an example the point of view of Robert H. Abel's recent short story "New Line," which is limited omniscient. An omniscient narrator shares the task of narration with the mind of (thoughts of) the protagonist. The protagonist is a child abuser; he has sexually molested his daughter. The omniscient narrator, who seems to speak for the author, never says he disapproves of the protagonist, but we sense the author's disapproval from the way the protagonist lives (he is irresponsible, he is violent, his emotions are often out of control) and from the disapproval expressed by other characters who know him well. Abel resolves the conflicts by having the protagonist admit his guilt (in his thoughts, to us) and plan to leave town to avoid a court appearance. By the end of the story, we have learned to mistrust the protagonist's truthfulness and moral judgments. Our distrust rests on Abel's assumption that we will disapprove of parents who sexually molest their children. But what if an author celebrates a narrator whose values we abhor—say, a highly efficient member of the Gestapo at Auschwitz. Then we would distrust both the narrator and the author.

QUESTIONS FOR ANALYZING POINT OF VIEW

1. What is the point of view of the narrative? Sometimes authors will use more than one point of view in a work (omniscient, for example, mixed with first-person). Is there more than one point of view in the work? If so, how are the various points of view different? How do they affect the way you react to the narrative?

2. If the author uses an omniscient point of view, what judgments does the narrator make about the setting, characters, and events? What does the narrator say, if anything, about the meaning of the work? Which characters' minds are open to the reader? How do those characters' experience of the events of the story differ?

3. If the author uses a limited omniscient point of view, to which character's thoughts do we have access? To what extent is the narrative filtered through the mind of that character? Wholly? Partly? To what extent does the omniscient narrator narrate the story? Do the omniscient narrator and the protagonist dif-

fer in the ways they understand or evaluate the details of the narrative? What is the narrator's attitude toward the protagonist? What does the omniscient narrator seem to think of the protagonist?

4. If the author uses a first-person point of view, what motivates the narrator to tell the story? To whom does the narrator tell the story? What is the narrator's outlook on life? What are the narrator's opinions about the places, events, and characters?

5. If the author uses an objective point of view, from what angles of vision do we experience the events of the story? What details provide insight into the qualities and thoughts of the characters?

6. How reliable is the narrator? Do you trust the narrator to give a truthful account of the facts? Would the author agree with the narrator's opinions? How do you know? Do you agree with the narrator's values and judgments?

ANALYZING THE GENRES OF NARRATIVE FICTION

It is a cold, rainy night. You are home for vacation. Everyone else in the house has gone to bed. You have been saving Sue Grafton's latest detective thriller for just such a time. Perfect. You settle in for three hours of uninterrupted escape. Of course, the book need not be a detective thriller. Maybe it is a gothic romance, or a work of science fiction, or a horror tale. And maybe you do not even care who the author is. You just picked the book off the shelf because it belongs to a particular kind of fiction. Your friends like this kind of fiction. You like it too.

Whenever you read a work just because it belongs to a particular kind of literature, as in this imaginary scene, you have succumbed to the pleasures of genre. **Genre** is a French word that means "type" or "kind." Literary genres are kinds of literature. Each literary genre is defined by conventions that mark it as distinct from other genres. **Conventions** are regular ways of doing things, "rules" that govern how things are done. The three broadest literary genres are drama, poetry, and narrative fiction. But these genres subdivide into other genres, such as tragedy and comedy (for drama) and elegy, ode, sonnet, and pastoral (for poetry). Narrative fiction can be classified in many ways, but the genres represented in this book are persistent and well-known. They are myth, epic, tale, romance, narrative poetry, short story, and novel. These genres cut across national and time boundaries and can be illustrated by many works of literature.

Genres are a prominent feature of literature. Authors always craft their works according to the conventions of established genres. Authors may change the conventions of a genre somewhat, rebel against them, and thus move their works toward the formation of new genres. But such change is usually evolutionary and slow. One reason is that readers are as dependent on genres as authors. We could not understand a work of literature unless we had some knowledge of its genre. When we begin to read a work, we recognize it as belonging to a certain genre and we expect it to abide by the conventions of that genre. If it does not, we become disoriented and impatient. Narrative fiction, for example, is a genre of literature. We learn to recognize and enjoy fiction because we become familiar with its conventions. Most of us learn these conventions as children, when we hear stories read to us, when we watch television, when we go to movies. We may not be fully conscious of the conventions of fiction, but we immediately sense when any of them are absent.

Knowing about the genres of literature gives us insight into individual works, the cultures from which they come, and the appeal works have for readers, including ourselves. There are many approaches to studying literary genres, but three seem especially useful. The first is to analyze the conventions of the genre. The second is to analyze the cultural context of the genre. The third is to analyze how the conventions of genres are used in individual works.

Conventions of Genres

What are the genres of narrative fiction? How can we tell them apart? Answering these questions is not always easy. Genres overlap. Their rules change. Authors vary in their use of generic conventions. Identifying genres, then, is not an exact science. But we know that genres exist because when we read lots of narratives we find it easy to group them by similarities. We can begin a study of narrative genres by reading or experiencing enough narratives to group them according to distinctive conventions. These conventions can be found in at least three places.

The first place is the elements of fiction (language, theme, plot, and so forth). Authors' use of these elements determines most of the conventions of a genre. A genre like gothic or horror, for example, features particular kinds of characters (obsessive villains, psychotic aristocrats, vulnerable "normal" people), settings (decayed mansions, maze-like tunnels, stormy weather), and actions (supernatural happenings, violent attacks, climactic upheavals). These uses of narrative elements of fiction make gothic horror easily distinguishable from other genres, like the western, or science fiction, or the comic novel of manners.

The second place is the relationship of the genre to reality. Conventions establish the degree to which genres reflect the real world. We can locate genres somewhere between two poles, with realism at one extreme and fantasy at the other. Genres that belong near the realism pole are more like real life. Genres that belong near the fantasy pole are less like real life.

Two genres that belong at the realistic pole are the novel and the short story. Novels and short stories typically represent life as it really is. In fact, some novels and short stories are so realistic that they are indistinguishable from nonfictional narratives. We have no way of knowing, for example, that Daniel Defoe's novel

Robinson Crusoe is fictional except that Defoe tells us it is. The events that Crusoe, the first-person narrator, recounts are unusual but plausible. This illusion that the narrative is similar to or even the same as real life is a distinguishing characteristic—a convention—of these two genres. Another convention of realistic narratives is that their worldview typically incorporates all the aspects of real life, including its unpleasantnesses and difficulties. Realistic narratives, as a result, can seem pessimistic and gloomy. Stephen Crane's novel *The Red Badge of Courage,* for example, is an attack on the romantic belief that war is glamorous. Crane's protagonist suffers from the harshness of war and achieves only a limited and impermanent victory over it.

Other genres, like fairy tale and romance, belong near the fantasy pole. Unrealistic conventions—miraculous animals, perfect characters, shimmering castles—easily distinguish fantasy from realistic genres. Fantasy genres, furthermore, gloss over the harsh aspects of life: the hero and heroine look wonderful, overcome all obstacles, and live happily ever after. Still other genres, like epic and fable, belong somewhere between the two poles of realism and fantasy. Homer's *Odyssey* uses conventions of fantastic events and characters, but it also offers a plausible presentation of Bronze Age Greece and a frank appraisal of human difficulties.

A third place for identifying conventions is the function genres serve within a society. The uses a society assigns genres are conventions that help distinguish one genre from another. The characteristics of folktale, for example, often seem the same as those for myth. Folktale and myth are distinguishable, however, by their function. Myths are typically used in religious rituals, told only at certain times of year, and restricted to certain groups of people. Folktales, on the other hand, are told anytime and enjoyed by everyone. In our society, short stories and novels are considered to be "serious," often studied in university courses for aesthetic qualities and depth of thought. Contemporary romances, on the other hand, such as westerns and spy thrillers, are considered to be "fun." They are read for entertainment and escape. The dividing line between "serious" fiction and "fun" fiction may at times be blurry. But when we can identify such social functions, they become part of the conventions of a genre.

QUESTIONS FOR ANALYZING THE CONVENTIONS OF GENRES

1. What genres of narrative fiction are you familiar with? Which ones do you enjoy? Why? Which ones do not appeal to you? Why?

2. How do elements of fiction distinguish a genre from other genres? What characterizes the physical locations? When are the narratives usually set? Do the plots follow the same pattern? Do the same types of characters keep turning

up in narrative after narrative? Are the themes the same? Is the point of view the same? Do these narratives feature a similar kind of language? Are there catch phrases (like "once upon a time") that identify a particular genre?

3. What relationship to the real world does a genre have? Do the works of a genre reflect the real world? How so? How do they not reflect the real world?

4. What function does the genre seem to have in society? Can you determine the social function from evidence in the works? If not, what can you learn about the cultural function of the genre from sources outside the work, like biographies, histories, and anthropological studies?

Cultural Context of Genres

Genres are cultural phenomena. No single author creates a genre. Rather, genres emerge from the work of many authors. A genre is like a language. It is a code made up of the bits and pieces of a culture. Only those people who share the culture can understand the genre. The culture may be very small, encompassing only a few people, like a tribe isolated in the South American rain forest, or it may be very large, embracing millions of people, like Western culture, Oriental culture, Islamic culture. The genre we call fiction is itself a product of culture. It may seem universal to us, but only because its conventions have become familiar to many cultures, not just one or two. A culture could conceivably have no fiction. If so, its members would find fiction baffling.

Studying genres necessarily means examining the culture from which they come. Even if we dutifully note all of the formal conventions of a genre—like its uses of language, character, plot, and so forth—we have only succeeded in learning the mechanical details of the genre's "grammar." We still do not know what the genre means, how it achieves that meaning, or why it is important. The key to discovering these things is always through a study of the culture that valued and enjoyed it.

As an example of how genres represent cultures, consider detective fiction, which became a recognizable genre in the West during the nineteenth century. The detective hero is a convention of detective fiction. Scholars contend that the earliest fictional detectives, like Edgar Allan Poe's Dupin and Sir Arthur Conan Doyle's Sherlock Holmes, reflect nineteenth-century Europe's enormous respect for science. These detectives are dispassionate, rigorously analytical, and brilliant. Holmes is in fact a scientist and has published treatises on a variety of topics relating to forensic science. Another convention of nineteenth-century detective fiction is its setting, almost always the great industrial cities, which were by-products of nineteenth-century capitalism. These cities, with their maze-like streets and their heterogeneous populations, were perfect environments for intrigue and crime. Dupin works in Paris, Holmes in London. A third convention of detective fiction is the crime, almost always a murder or threat of murder. The pursuit and punishment of the murderer upholds a central value of nineteenth-century culture, respect for the individual. The murderer destroys the individual's most valuable possession, life itself. A final convention is the institutions the crime threatens to destroy. The murderer threatens valued institutions that people in the nineteenth century held dear—the family, boards of trade, governmental agencies, universities. The detective, by capturing the murderer, purges these institutions of those who would corrupt and destroy them.

Other genres reflect their own cultural contexts. The epic reflects the classical world's faith in cosmic harmony, national solidarity, and heroic deeds. The chivalric romance reflects the medieval fascination with romantic love, religion, and courtly behavior. European fairy tales, a product of oral folk tradition, reflect the economic and class status of peasants during the Middle Ages. The short story and novel, arising in the eighteenth and nineteenth centuries, reflect a modern faith in individualism and empirical observation. Some recent authors claim to be moving beyond the short story and novel toward new genres, as yet unnamed, that reflect new cultural conditions.

There are at least two ways to study the cultural context of genres. The first is to look within the works for information about cultures. Individual works, of course, often give a wealth of information about the cultures from which they come. The *Odyssey,* for example, speaks volumes about the religious beliefs, the family relationships, the methods of warfare, and the attitude toward work of the ancient Greeks. Since genres are not works but rather frameworks for works, they do not themselves give information. But their conventions point to cultural concerns and patterns of behavior. The conventions of Homeric epic—the hero, the battles, the hero's encounters with parents and wife, the interactions of gods and human beings—reveal that nearly everything in ancient Greek culture centered on war. The conventions of medieval romance, in contrast, suggest different obsessions: warfare, yes, but also proper behavior of men toward women and decorum at court.

A second way of studying the cultural context of genres is to look outside the works for information about cultures. Disciplines like history, philosophy, religious studies, and anthropology supply such external evidence. External evidence helps us understand what functions genres served in a culture, and it clarifies and complements internal evidence. Reading historical studies about ancient Greece, for example, pinpoints how accurately Homer's epics reflect Greek society during the Bronze Age. Such studies give us details about the Greeks that he does not. They correct any liberties he takes with facts.

QUESTIONS FOR ANALYZING THE CULTURAL CONTEXT OF GENRES

1. When was the genre popular? What cultural conditions seem to be responsible for its popularity?

2. When did the genre cease to be popular? Why did people lose interest in it?

3. What cultural conditions does the genre reflect? What do particular conventions of the genre tell us about aspects of society?

Individual Works and Genres

Usually when we read a work of fiction, especially a work we expect to enjoy, we do not think about its genre. This is true because we are already familiar with the genre, at least unconsciously. We just read and enjoy. But recognizing how works conform to genres is a tool for analyzing works, especially the meanings of works. Genres, as we have said, reflect the interests, patterns of behavior, environments, and values of particular cultures. When authors compose according to the rules of a genre, they inevitably make those rules part of the work.

At least two issues are relevant to the study of how genres influence the meaning of individual works. The first is the extent to which a work does and does not conform to the conventions of its genre. Works that rigidly conform, like many folktales, dutifully incorporate the expected meanings of the genre. For folktales, that meaning may be something like the belief or hope that poor people can transcend their lowly status through pluck, luck, shrewdness, and marriage. Works that depart from the conventions often challenge the expected meanings of the genre. A folktale, then, might take a slightly different path to show that poor people are, after all, limited in their social mobility no matter what they do. A kind of fiction that flagrantly challenges the traditional meanings of genres is parody. A **parody** keeps all or most of the conventions of a genre except for one, the nature of the subject matter. Usually parodies are comic, so the change in attitude toward subject matter moves from serious to frivolous. A famous example is Alexander Pope's "The Rape of the Lock." Pope imitates well-known conventions of epic but instead of featuring subject matter of cosmic or national importance, he focuses on something silly and trivial.

Genres affect the meanings of works in a second way. Authors often import conventions from one genre into another and thereby let us know that the qualities and meanings we associate with one genre are now applicable within the present work. This borrowing from and reference to conventions from other genres is called **intertextuality.** Many of the short stories in this book are examples of intertextuality. Both Joyce Carol Oates in "Where Are You Going, Where Have You Been?" and Elizabeth Bowen in "The Demon Lover" imitate aspects of the medieval ballad and particularly one ballad, "The Demon Lover." Bernard Malamud in "The Magic Barrel" and D. H. Lawrence in "The Rocking-Horse Winner" include conventions of the fairy tale. Shirley Jackson's "The Lottery" resembles a fable. These authors work within the short story genre, but by bringing in conventions from other genres, they subvert our expectations and channel our understanding of what their works mean.

Another kind of intertextuality is the inclusion of archetypes in a work. An **archetype** is a convention—a kind of character, plot pattern, place, symbol—that recurs in many works of literature. Archetypes are often highly visible conventions of genres. An example of an archetype common to Western culture is the hero's journey to a low place. This archetype is a recognizable convention of myth, epic, folktale, and romance. When heroes journey downward—into the underworld, into caves, into dark, damp, snakey places—they experience painful and troubling ordeals. Demonic or mysterious forces test their integrity, strength, and commitment. Some heroes, when they touch bottom, begin to master their antagonists and start on a journey upward, back to health and stability. But other heroes never come back. They wander aimlessly, lost in seemingly endless passageways, not knowing where they are going, desperately wishing to escape back to the light. Many protagonists of myth, epic, and romance make the journey downward: Ishtar in Babylonian myth, Odysseus in the *Odyssey,* Aeneas in the *Aeneid,* Jesus in Christian tradition, Dante in *The Divine Comedy.* This archetype appears in several of the works in this book, including Nathaniel Hawthorne's "Young Goodman Brown" and T. Coraghessan Boyle's "Greasy Lake." The opposite archetype is the hero's journey to high places, where he or she experiences exaltation and transcendence.

QUESTIONS FOR ANALYZING INDIVIDUAL WORKS AND GENRES

1. To what genre does the work seem to belong?

2. How does the work conform to the conventions of the genre? What patterns and values traditionally associated with the genre does the work exhibit?

3. How does the work depart from the conventions of the genre? What emotional effect do these departures have on the reader? Is the reader, for example, frustrated or pleasantly surprised? What implications for the meaning of the work do the departures have?

4. What conventions from other genres and what archetypes does the author seem to incorporate into the work? How do these conventions and archetypes influence your enjoyment of the work and your understanding of its meaning?

The following chapters invite you to enjoy and analyze individual works and to explore their relationship to the genres and cultures that gave rise to them. These chapters, each of which focuses on a well-known narrative genre, are arranged in roughly chronological order. Myth, for example, precedes the short story and the novel. But the chapters are also arranged by affinity. Myth and epic have a close affinity, because mythic characters, settings, and stories appear in many epics. Tale and romance, narrative poetry and short story, and short story and novel form other closely allied pairs. We begin, then, with the most profound and influential form of narrative, myth.

Chapter Two
Myth

INTRODUCTION

We often think of the term *myth* as meaning something untrue. We might hear someone say, "It is a myth that President Reagan could speak Chinese." And when we think of the narrative genre called myth we may think of it as including fictional stories, untrue stories, like the Greek and Norse myths that children often devour along with other tales of fantasy and enchantment.

But the kind of story that scholars of literature and culture call **myth** is quite different from these popular meanings. Laurie Honko, the Finnish folklorist, defines myth as

> a story of the gods, a religious account of the beginning of the world, the creation, fundamental events, the exemplary deeds of the gods as a result of which the world, nature and culture were created together with all the parts thereof and given their order, which still obtains.[1]

According to Honko and other scholars, myth has five basic characteristics:

First, myths are considered to be true stories about sacred events. Mythic accounts, therefore, are authoritative and must be accepted on faith. The Greek myths, for example, may seem like fanciful stories to us, but before Christianity replaced Greek and Roman religion in Europe, many people believed them to be literally true.

Second, myth offers a comprehensive understanding of the nature of the universe and of our place in it. For this reason, the most important myths in a religious

---

[1] "The Problem of Defining Myth," *Sacred Narrative: Readings in the Theory of Myth*, ed. Alan Dundes (Berkeley: University of California Press, 1984) 49.

system are cosmogonic myths, myths of creation. Creation myths explain and verify the order of the world. Before creation, there was chaos; after creation there was order. This order is reflected in everything about the way the world now is: geographical features, physical traits of animals, social structures, moral codes, religious beliefs, ritual practices, taboos, the cycle of life (birth, maturity, death). Creation myths explain how these things came about and why. The setting of creation myths is primordial—the first time and place, when life as we know it came into being. Not all myths of a religious system are about creation, but all of them confirm the universal order established at creation. Taken together, they account for the total order of everything, including where we as a species fit in, where we as a cultural group fit in, and where we as individuals fit in.

Third, all or some of the actors in myth are divine. A myth may recount the deeds of just one god, like the one god in Hebrew myth, or of many gods, like the divinities in Greek myth. The gods may inhabit a setting that is remote or different from earth as we know it, like the primordial cosmos of creation myths. Or the setting may be the ordinary world, where the gods visit and exert their extraordinary powers.

Fourth, myth serves as model. Because myth establishes the underlying order of all reality, it provides a model for human behavior. It is not only the basis for ethics, the rules that govern right and wrong actions, but for practical actions, such as those having to do with surviving in the natural world. Myths tell us that because the world was created in a certain way, people should *therefore* behave in certain ways. The laws stated in the first five books of the Hebrew Bible, for example, are based upon the order of the universe established by God at creation. At creation, God gave humankind special responsibilities that were later codified in Hebrew law.

Finally, myth occurs in association with religious ritual. Rituals are the ceremonies in which people express their religious faith and beliefs. Rituals communicate myths. They do so either verbally, by means of narratives, or theatrically, by means of dances, songs, and images. But rituals also have power. They have power to remind people of their religious beliefs and reinforce their commitment to them. And rituals have supernatural power. Some people believe that rituals actually recreate the original events of the myths and transfer them to the present. Many Christians hold, for example, that the wine and bread used during the ritual of Holy Communion actually become the blood and body of Jesus. Communion thus reenacts the death and resurrection of Jesus and gives renewed life to the individual who participates in the ritual. Communion is the most important Christian ritual because the death and resurrection of Jesus is a "new creation," a creation myth that supplants or complements the stories of creation at the beginning of the Hebrew Bible. Because of their ostensible power, religious rituals are often performed on special occasions. In some cultures, for example, creation rituals were performed when the crops had just been planted and when a new ruler began to reign. These rituals transferred the explosive power of the first creation to the new crops and the new ruler.

This scholarly definition of myth would seem to place myth at odds with the subject matter of this book, narrative fiction. If myth is "true," can we categorize it as fiction? Many people, for example, insist that the myths from the Hebrew Bible printed in this collection are literally true, that they are historical fact, not "fiction."

Myth, however, does belong in a consideration of fiction. One reason is that religious myths are often viewed as fictional. People who, for whatever reason, refuse to believe the tenets of a religion will categorize its myths as fiction. Or even if people believe in a religion, they may reject the historical accuracy of its myths and believe instead that the myths are thematically rather than literally true. That is, although the myths may not recount historical events, they, like other works of fiction, offer profound insights into the human condition. Most people, for example, no longer believe in the literal truth of Greek myths but find their thematic and psychological implications fascinating.

Another reason why myth is important to the study of fiction is that authors often imitate the features of myth. Myth, therefore, has become more than just a religious phenomenon. It has become a literary genre as well. Just as authors can imitate other genres of fiction—like fable, romance, and epic—they can imitate the conventions of myth. By duplicating the conventions of myth, like primordial settings, godlike characters, and battles between the forces of good and evil, authors can create works of fiction that have the shape of myth. Recent authors of fantasy fiction, like J. R. R. Tolkien, rely heavily on these conventions for their fictional creations. Authors also use the conventions of myth to focus attention on the same kind of questions raised by myths—fundamental questions about human existence, such as those about nature, sexuality, ethics, death, the origins of culture, and the purposes of life. An example of such a work is Herman Melville's novel *Moby Dick*. Moby Dick, the white whale, is godlike in his power and knowledge. Captain Ahab's quest for Moby Dick is really a religious quest for answers to questions that only God can answer.

A third reason why myth belongs in a study of fiction is that works of fiction often serve some of the functions of myth. Like religious myths, which embody the religious beliefs of a culture, works of fiction can become "secular" myths. Large numbers of people see them as representing ideas that pertain to their society's history and values. One explanation of the enormous popularity of Mary Shelley's gothic romance *Frankenstein* is that it has become a kind of "myth" of the aspirations, successes, and failures of our own scientific and technological culture. A similar secular myth is the American western. In its seemingly endless variations, it has become a creation myth about the United States. It takes us back to the "frontier," the primordial time of the founding of the nation, the source of our most important moral and political values.

Despite these fictional manifestations of myth, myth, more than any other literary genre, is a phenomenon of culture. Cultures are networks of belief systems that almost spontaneously give rise to stories—"myths"—that embody them. If we are alert to their presence, we can see them all around us—in political ideologies, like Marxism, fascism, democracy, in theories about ethnic groups and races, in beliefs about sexuality and gender. Space exploration, for example, has inspired a secular mythology. The beliefs that underlie this mythology have been eloquently stated in the writings of the Jesuit paleontologist Teilhard de Chardin, most notably in his book *The Phenomenon of Man.* Evolution, according to Teilhard, has moved from simple to increasingly complex and "higher" life forms, climaxing with the most complex of all, the human brain. Evolution, furthermore, is a "progress" that combines intellectual and technological advancement with a conscious and unconscious yearning for spiritual growth. At the moment, Teilhard holds, space exploration is the next key step toward the ultimate goal of evolution, a coalescence of spirit (God, ultimate knowledge) and matter (human beings in their now limited and flawed state). This belief, then, assumes that there is a spiritual force somewhat akin to "God," that there is a cosmic plan with humankind at its center, and that technology is the measure of progress. We may not have read any philosophical arguments for these beliefs like Teilhard's books, but probably many of us ascribe in some vague way to them—space exploration is the new "frontier," we will learn important things from it, "out there" in the vastness of space lies a spiritual force or, at least, wiser and more advanced life forms that will lead us away from our self-destructive ways toward social and emotional peace. The "mythical" expression of this set of beliefs can be seen in numerous fictional works, such as science fiction narratives, television shows, and films like the *Star Trek* series, *2001, The Day the Earth Stood Still, E. T., Close Encounters of the Third Kind,* and the *Star Wars* saga. But true stories, like accounts of astro-scientists and astronauts, can also become part of the space exploration myth. Myth, in other words, combines "fact" with literary forms to represent an encompassing narrative that many people believe to be true.

The myths contained in this chapter are almost all related to religious systems of belief. The one exception is the account of creation by Lucretius, which is a secular myth. These selections come from a number of different cultures: Hebrew, Middle Eastern, ancient Greek, Asian, African, and Native American. The versions printed here are as close in time to their actual use as possible. They are not, in other words, summaries of myths by modern authors but rather versions produced by people who lived in the cultures that used them.

In the headnotes to each myth we indicate the approximate date they were first written down. For traditional stories—that is, stories that emerge from an oral tradition of anonymous authorship—we indicate when the stories were first collected. These stories, however, are almost always much older than their collection dates. This selection only begins to represent the enormous variety of myth throughout the world, but it does exhibit some of the conventions of myth. And although these myths appear out of their cultural and religious context, they can be understood and appreciated on their own merit. They are grouped under three recurrent and thought-provoking patterns of myth: creation, the fall, and resurrection. These themes recur in much of the world's literature, including some of the works contained elsewhere in this book.

MYTHS OF CREATION

Creation myths deal with the very beginning of things. They are the most profound kind of myth. They are used to speculate about the intersection of the unknown and the known. They seem to exist in all cultures. They establish the most important and basic truths: the nature of reality, the place that all things occupy in the scheme of reality, and the value of all things. They often also account for longstanding cultural practices, such as rituals and moral precepts. Of all the myths, creation myths have the most influence over what people believe and how they conduct their lives.

ANCIENT PALESTINE

Yahweh Creates the World in Six Days (Genesis 1:1-2:4)

The Hebrews were a nomadic people belonging to the Semitic lan-guage group who migrated to Palestine around the third or second mil-lenium B.C. Abraham, the founder of the Hebrew people, migrated to Palestine in about 1500 B.C. At some point in their history, the Hebrews rejected the polytheistic religion that dominated the Middle East and embraced a belief in one god, whose name in ancient Hebrew was "Yahweh." This name is mysterious, since it was spelled only with con-sonants ("YHVH"), but it seems to have some connection with the Hebrew verb "to be" or "to happen." The first book of the Hebrew Bible, Genesis, begins with two different accounts of Yahweh's cre-ation of the world. The first version, Genesis 1:1-2:4, is the most recent, written down about 500 B.C. The second, Genesis 2:4-25, is much older, written down about 900 B.C. Both accounts existed in oral tradi-tion long before they were put in writing.

1   In the beginning when God created the heavens and the earth, [2] the earth was a formless void and darkness covered the face of the deep, while a wind from God swept over the face of the waters. [3] Then God said, "Let there be light"; and there was light. [4]And God saw that the light was good; and God separated the light from the darkness. [5] God called the light Day, and the darkness he called Night. And there was evening and there was morning, the first day.

6 And God said, "Let there be a dome in the midst of the waters, and let it sep-arate the waters from the waters." [7]So God made the dome and separated the waters that were under the dome from the waters that were above the dome. And it was so. [8]God called the dome Sky. And there was evening and there was morn-ing, the second day.

9 And God said, "Let the waters under the sky be gathered together into one place, and let the dry land appear." And it was so. [10]God called the dry land Earth, and the waters that were gathered together he called Seas. And God saw that it was good. [11]Then God said, "Let the earth put forth vegetation: plants yielding seed, and fruit trees of every kind on earth that bear fruit with the seed in it." And it was so. [12]The earth brought forth vegetation: plants yielding seed of every kind, and trees of every kind bearing fruit with the seed in it. And God saw that it was good. [13]And there was evening and there was morning, the third day.

14 And God said, "Let there be lights in the dome of the sky to separate the day from the night; and let them be for signs and for seasons and for days and years, [15]and let them be lights in the dome of the sky to give light upon the earth." And it was so. [16]God made the two great lights—the greater light to rule the day and the lesser light to rule the night—and the stars. [17]God set them in the dome of the sky to give light upon the earth, [18]to rule over the day and over the night, and to separate the light from the darkness. And God saw that it was good. [19]And there was evening and there was morning, the fourth day.

20 And God said, "Let the waters bring forth swarms of living creatures, and let birds fly above the earth across the dome of the sky." [21]So God created the great sea monsters and every living creature that moves, of every kind, with which the waters swarm, and every winged bird of every kind. And God saw that it was good. [22]God blessed them, saying, "Be fruitful and multiply and fill the waters in the seas, and let birds multiply on the earth." [23]And there was evening and there was morning, the fifth day.

24 And God said, "Let the earth bring forth living creatures of every kind: cattle and creeping things and wild animals of the earth of every kind." And it was so. [25]God made the wild animals of the earth of every kind, and the cattle of every kind, and everything that creeps upon the ground of every kind. And God saw that it was good.

26 Then God said, "Let us make humankind[1] in our image, according to our likeness; and let them have dominion over the fish of the sea, and over the birds of the air, and over the cattle, and over all the wild animals of the earth, and over every creeping thing that creeps upon the earth."

[27]So God created humankind in his image,
in the image of God he created them;
male and female he created them.

28 God blessed them, and God said to them, "Be fruitful and multiply, and fill the earth and subdue it; and have dominion over the fish of the sea and over the birds of the air and over every living thing that moves upon the earth." [29]God said, "See, I have given you every plant yielding seed that is upon the face of all the earth, and every tree with seed in its fruit; you shall have them for food. [30]And to every beast of the earth, and to every bird of the air, and to everything that creeps in the earth, everything that has the breath of life, I have given every green plant for food." And it was so. [31] God saw everything that he had made, and

---

[1]The Hebrew word for humankind or "man" is *Adam*.

indeed, it was very good. And there was evening and there was morning, the sixth day.

2   Thus the heavens and the earth were finished, and all their multitude. ² And on the seventh day God finished the work that he had done, and he rested on the seventh day from all the work that he had done. ³ So God blessed the seventh day and hallowed it, because on it God rested from all the work that he had done in creation.

4 These are the generations of the heavens and the earth when they were created.

Questions for Study

1. What was the universe like before creation? What new order does creation bring about?

2. In what sequence are things created? Does the sequence suggest a hierarchy of values?

3. What is God's relationship or connection with nature?

4. What oppositions does the myth establish?

5. What authority and responsibility does God give humankind?

Yahweh Creates Adam and Eve (Genesis 2:4-25)

4 In the day that the LORD God made the earth and the heavens, ⁵ when no plant of the field was yet in the earth and no herb of the field had yet sprung up— for the LORD God had not caused it to rain upon the earth, and there was no one to till the ground; ⁶ but a stream would rise from the earth, and water the whole face of the ground— ⁷ then the LORD God formed man from the dust of the ground, and breathed into his nostrils the breath of life; and the man became a living being. ⁸ And the LORD God planted a garden in Eden, in the east; and there he put the man whom he had formed. ⁹ Out of the ground the LORD God made to grow every tree that is pleasant to the sight and good for food, the tree of life also in the midst of the garden, and the tree of the knowledge of good and evil.

10 A river flows out of Eden to water the garden, and from there it divides and becomes four branches. ¹¹ The name of the first is Pi´shon; it is the one that flows around the whole land of Hav´i·lah, where there is gold; ¹² and the gold of that land is good; bdellium and onyx stone are there. ¹³ The name of the second river is Gi´hon; it is the one that flows around the whole land of Cush. ¹⁴ The name of the third river is Tigris, which flows east of Assyria. And the fourth river is the Euphrates.

15 The LORD God took the man and put him in the garden of Eden to till it and keep it. And the LORD God commanded the man, "You may freely eat of every tree of the garden; [17] but of the tree of the knowledge of good and evil you shall not eat, for in the day that you eat of it you shall die."

18 Then the LORD God said, "It is not good that the man should be alone; I will make him a helper as his partner." [19] So out of the ground the LORD God formed every animal of the field and every bird of the air, and brought them to the man to see what he would call them; and whatever the man called every living creature, that was its name. [20] The man gave names to all cattle, and to the birds of the air, and to every animal of the field; but for the man there was not found a helper as his partner. [21] So the LORD God caused a deep sleep to fall upon the man, and he slept; then he took one of his ribs and closed up its place with flesh. [22] And the rib that the LORD God had taken from the man he made into a woman and brought her to the man. [23] Then the man said,

> "This at last is bone of my bones and flesh of my flesh;
> this one shall be called Woman,
> for out of Man this one was taken."

24Therefore a man leaves his father and his mother and clings to his wife, and they become one flesh. [25] And the man and his wife were both naked, and were not ashamed.

Questions for Study

1. How is this story different from the preceding one?

2. What was the universe like before creation?

3. What is the sequence in which things are created?

4. What are the implications for the status of males and females in this myth? What does the myth seem to say about marriage? What does "one flesh" mean?

5. What is the meaning of nakedness?

6. What privileges and responsibilities do human beings have?

ANCIENT GREECE

The Creation of the Gods
(Hesiod, Theogony)

Greek mythology developed on the Greek peninsula during the Mycenaean era (c. 1600 to 1100 B.C.) and the so-called Greek Dark

Ages (c. 1100 to 800 B.C.), which began with the fall of Mycenae and ended with the rediscovery of writing. As the Greeks expanded their economic and military power throughout the Aegean Sea, they also spread their religion. The earliest written versions of Greek mythology are by two great poets, Homer and Hesiod. Both belonged to a group of professional poets called "rhapsodes" whose calling was to recite poems for sacred and social occasions. Homer composed his epics, the *Iliad* and the *Odyssey,* around 750 B.C. Hesiod lived about the same time as Homer but probably composed his accounts of the gods somewhat later.

Unlike Homer, whose interest in the gods lies mainly in how well they fit into the plots of his epics, Hesiod is concerned with the theological implications of the gods. In the *Theogony* he identifies and classifies the gods, mainly through genealogy (who gave birth to whom) and function (what each god does). Like Homer, he begins his account with a prayer to the muses, the goddesses of poetry. In his account of creation the main actors are Chaos (the first "being"), Earth, Heaven (Earth's son and consort, god of the sky), Earth and Heaven's children (the Titans), Cronus (one of the Titans), and Aphrodite (Heaven's daughter, goddess of love). Mount Olympus is the dwelling place of the gods.

*H*ail, children of Zeus! Grant lovely song and celebrate the holy race of the deathless gods who are for ever, those that were born of Earth and starry Heaven and gloomy Night and them that briny Sea did rear. Tell how at the first gods and earth came to be, and rivers, and the boundless sea with its raging swell, and the gleaming stars, and the wide heaven above, and the gods who were born of them, givers of good things, and how they divided their wealth, and how they shared their honors amongst them, and also how at the first they took many-folded Olympus. These things declare to me from the beginning, ye Muses who dwell in the house of Olympus, and tell me which of them first came to be.

Verily at the first Chaos came to be, but next wide-bosomed Earth, the ever-sure foundation of all the deathless ones who hold the peaks of snowy Olympus, and dim Tartarus[1] in the depth of the wide-pathed Earth, and Eros [Love], fairest among the deathless gods, who unnerves the limbs and overcomes the mind and wise counsels of all gods and all men within them. From Chaos came forth Erebus[2] and black Night; but of Night were born Ether[3] and Day, whom she conceived and bare from union in love with Erebus. And Earth first bare starry Heaven, equal to herself, to cover her on every side, and to be an ever-sure abiding-place for the blessed gods. And she brought forth long Hills, graceful haunts of the goddess-Nymphs who dwell amongst the glens

---

[1] *Tartarus.* The lower part of the underworld.   [2] *Erebus.* The upper part of the underworld.
[3] *Ether.* The upper atmosphere.

of the hills. She bare also the fruitless deep with his raging swell, Pontus, without sweet union of love. But afterwards she lay with Heaven and bare deep-swirling Oceanus, Coeus and Crius and Hyperion and Iapetus, Theia and Rhea, Themis and Mnemosyne and gold-crowned Phoebe and lovely Tethys. After them was born Cronus the wily, youngest and most terrible of her children, and he hated his lusty sire.

And again, she bare the Cyclopes, overbearing in spirit, Brontes, and Steropes and stubborn-hearted Arges, who gave Zeus the thunder and made the thunderbolt: in all else they were like the gods, but one eye only was set in the midst of their foreheads. And they were surnamed Cyclopes (Orb-eyed) because one orbed eye was set in their foreheads. Strength and might and craft were in their works.

And again, three other sons were born of Earth and Heaven, great and doughty beyond telling, Cottus and Briareos and Gyes, presumptuous children. From their shoulders sprang an hundred arms, not to be approached, and each had fifty heads upon his shoulders on their strong limbs, and irresistible was the stubborn strength that was in their great forms. For of all the children that were born of Earth and Heaven, these were the most terrible, and they were hated by their own father from the first. And he used to hide them all away in a secret place of Earth so soon as each was born, and would not suffer them to come up into the light: and Heaven rejoiced in his evil doing. But vast Earth groaned within, being straitened, and she thought a crafty and an evil wile. Forthwith she made the element of grey flint and shaped a great sickle, and told her plan to her dear sons. And she spoke, cheering them, while she was vexed in her dear heart:

"My children, gotten of a sinful father, if you will obey me, we should punish the vile outrage of your father; for he first thought of doing shameful things."

So she said; but fear seized them all, and none of them uttered a word. But great Cronus the wily took courage and answered his dear mother:

"Mother, I will undertake to do this deed, for I reverence not our father of evil name, for he first thought of doing shameful things."

So he said: and vast Earth rejoiced greatly in spirit, and set and hid him in an ambush, and put in his hands a jagged sickle, and revealed to him the whole plot.

And Heaven came, bringing on night and longing for love, and he lay about Earth spreading himself full upon her. Then the son from his ambush stretched forth his left hand and in his right took the great long sickle with jagged teeth, and swiftly lopped off his own father's members and cast them away to fall behind him. And not vainly did they fall from his hand; for all the bloody drops that gushed forth Earth received, and as the seasons moved round she bare the strong Furies and the great Giants with gleaming armor, holding long spears in their hands, and the Nymphs of the ash trees. And so soon as he had cut off the members with flint and cast them from the land into the surging sea, they were swept away over the main a long time: and a white foam spread around them from the immortal flesh, and in it there grew a maiden. First she drew near holy Cythera, and from there, afterwards, she came to sea-girt Cyprus, and came forth an awful and lovely goddess, and grass grew up about her beneath her shapely feet. Her gods and men call Aphrodite, and the foam-born goddess and rich-crowned Cytherea, because she grew amid the foam, and Cytherea because she reached Cythera, and Cyprogenes because she was born in billowy Cyprus, and member-loving because she sprang from the members. And with her went Eros, and comely Desire followed her at her birth at the first and as she went into the assembly of the gods. This honor she has from the beginning, and this is the portion allotted to her amongst men and undying gods,—the whisperings of maidens and smiles and deceits with sweet delight and love and graciousness.

But these sons whom he begot himself great Heaven used to call Titans (Strainers) in reproach, for he said that they strained and did presumptuously a fearful deed, and that vengeance for it would come afterwards.

Questions for Study

1. How is this account of creation different from and similar to the account in the Hebrew Bible?

2. What relationship do the gods have to nature and natural forces?

3. What qualities do the gods represent?

4. What oppositions does this myth establish?

5. What role does sexuality play in the creation of the universe? How are gender and family relationships important?

6. What "order" emerges from creation?

ANCIENT ROME

The Universe Is Created from Atoms (*Lucretius,* On the Nature of the Universe)

Little is known about Titus Lucretius Carus (96?-55 B.C.) except that he lived in Rome during the turbulent events of the first century B.C. and that he was a follower of the Greek philosopher Epicurus (c. 342-270 B.C.). Epicurus believed that the highest good was serenity of the soul and the absence of mental and physical pain. Lucretius's *On the Nature of the Universe (De Rerum Natura)* is a poem about the physical nature of the universe. In it he develops a number of Epicurean ideas. He attacks religion as false beliefs, mere superstitions that serve only to generate fear. He also presents Epicurus's theory that all matter is made up of atoms, tiny particles that are invisible and indivisible. In Book Five, Lucretius gives an account of creation and the evolution of human life. This account resembles other creation myths but with one major difference: No divine beings are present or have anything to do with creation. Rather, creation simply happens.

Next I shall describe how combinations of matter
created the earth and heaven and the ocean depths,
and the courses of the sun and moon. For surely
the atoms did not take their places by volition,
nor did they place themselves by sharp intelligence,   5
nor did they agree what movements to produce,
but many elements in many different ways,
bombarded with blows and carried along by their own weight,
from time immemorial, have been wont to move and meet
in various ways, and try out all the permutations   10
that they were able to produce by coming together.
And so it happens that, after being dispersed for ages,
attempting every sort of motion and conjunction,
at last those atoms come together whose combination
can form the first-beginnings of all great things we know: 15
the earth, the sea, the sky, and the races of living creatures.
        At that time the sun's bright disc was not to be seen
soaring on high with ample light, nor the constellations
of the heavens, nor sea nor sky nor earth nor air,
nor any of the things we see and know today;   20
but a strange wind and a newly-gathered mass of atoms
of every sort, whose discord brought a mighty conflict
of intervals and pathways and connections and weights,
and blows and impacts, and many motions and conjunctions;
due to the different shapes and variations of form,   25
they could not all remain locked in the combinations
or make the necessary motions when combined.
Then they began to be sorted out, and like combined
with like, so that the world began to take its shape,
and the main parts began to arrange themselves in order: 30
the lofty heavens were separated from the earth,
the ocean found its proper place, spread out with its waters,
the pure ethereal fires of heaven were set apart.
        In the first place, all the particles of earth
being heavy and interlocked, conglomerated   35
in the middle and took for themselves the lowest places;
and the more closely they were packed and came together,
the more they squeezed out all the elements of sea
and stars and sun and moon and ramparts of the world.
For these are made of smoother and of rounder atoms,   40
much smaller than the elements that make up earth.
And so, by breaking out from the fine pores and channels
of the parts of earth, at first the flaming ether
lightly lifted itself from the mass, taking fire with it;
very much the same as we have often seen,   45

when in the early morning the golden beams of the sun
are all aglow with the dawn on the dew-bespangled grass,
and lakes and ever-flowing rivers exhale a vapor
until the earth itself appears at times to steam;
and all these vapors come together in the air   50
and weave a cloudy texture underneath the sky.
In the same way, then, the light and volatile ether
with body coalesced and curved round on all sides
was widely diffused on every side and in all directions,
and thus it enveloped the other parts in a close embrace.   55
There followed the beginnings of the sun and moon,
whose spheres revolve in the upper air between the two,
and neither earth nor ether could claim them for their own,
as they were neither heavy enough to settle down,
nor light enough to glide aloft to the upper regions,   60
and yet they remain between, whirling like living bodies,
and thereby forming parts of the whole universe,
just as in our own bodies, certain parts
are stationary, while other parts are free to move.
Now, therefore, when these elements were once withdrawn,   65
suddenly the earth sank down where the deep blue sea
extends, and flooded the depression with salty waves.
And day by day, the more the tide of ether, and rays
of the sun compressed the earth and made it solid
with frequent blows on every side from the outer edges,   70
so that it was shrunk and condensed on its own center,
the more the salty sweat, squeezed out of its own body,
oozed out and increased the fluid levels of the sea,
and the more the particles of heat and air
slipped out through the tiny pores and flew away,   75
thereby increasing the shining temples of the sky.
So the plains settled and lofty mountains grew more steep,
for, of course, the rocky crags could not sink down,
nor could every part subside to the same degree.
    So it was that the earth became compact and solid   80
and all the muddy sediment of the world came together
of its own weight, and settled at the bottom, like dregs.
Then sea and air and fiery ether itself remained
all pure and unalloyed—one lighter than the other,
and ether, lightest and most volatile of all,   85
floats aloft above the windy air and breezes,
nor does it mingle its pure substance with the winds;
it leaves the lower regions to be tossed about
by violent storms and spun around by whirling tempests,
while it glides on in a steady course with its own fires;   90

for the ether gently flows with unchanging course,
just as the Euxine flows with never-changing tides,
keeping an even current with its gliding motion.

Questions for Study

1. How is this "secular" myth different from and similar to other creation myths?

2. What exists before creation?

3. What causes creation?

4. What order is established by creation?

5. What oppositions does this account establish?

6. In what ways is Lucretius's account "fictional"? Is it less fictional than the religious creation myths?

ANCIENT INDIA

Creation Out of the Void (The Rig-Veda)

Hindu is the Persian word for "Indian," and Hinduism is, simply stated, the religion of India. It is an ancient religion that has undergone many changes and exists in many forms. Hindu myths, therefore, vary from age to age. The oldest Hindu myths occur in the *Rig-Veda* (Veda is the Indian word for scripture and the title *Rig-Veda* means scriptures or hymns of praise), a collection of hymns to various gods. Some of these hymns are possibly as old as 4000 B.C.; the *Rig-Veda* itself was compiled about 1200 B.C. Although the *Rig-Veda* mentions some thirty-three gods, its system of gods and theological concepts is much simpler than in later Hindu writings. Its hymns are characterized by a sense of wonder and joyousness. The account of creation printed here is one of the most famous passages from all Hindu scripture.

   1 Then neither Being nor Not-being was,
     Nor atmosphere, nor firmament, nor what is beyond.
     What did it encompass? Where? In whose protection?
     What was water, the deep, unfathomable?

2 Neither death nor immortality was there then,
No sign of night or day.
That One breathed, windless, by its own energy:
Nought else existed then.

3 In the beginning was darkness swathed in darkness;
All this was but unmanifested water.
Whatever was, that One, coming into being,
Hidden by the Void,
Was generated by the power of heat.

4 In the beginning this [One] evolved,
Became desire, first seed of mind.
Wise seers, searching within their hearts,
Found the bond of Being in Not-being.

5 Their cord was extended athwart:
Was there a below? Was there an above?
Casters of seed there were, and powers;
Beneath was energy, above was impulse.

6 Who knows truly? Who can here declare it?
Whence it was born, whence is this emanation.
By the emanation of this the gods
Only later [came to be].
Who then knows whence it has arisen?

7 Whence this emanation hath arisen,
Whether [God] disposed[1] it, or whether he did not,—
Only he who is its overseer in highest heaven knows.
[He only knows,] or perhaps he does not know!

Questions for Study

1. What existed before creation?

2. Who or what was the creator? What characterizes the creator?

3. What is the sequence in which things are created?

4. What provides the energy for creation? From whence does this energy come?

5. What oppositions does this myth establish?

6. What is the narrator's attitude toward creation?

[1]Or, 'created'.

AFRICA

Bumba Creates the World (Bushongo)

Although religion in sub-Saharan Africa (the non-Muslim part of Africa) varies from tribe to tribe, it nonetheless has many common elements. Religion touches every aspect of tribal life and is closely associated with nature. The Africans believe that the spiritual dwells within and controls the minute phenomena of nature—animals, trees, plants, lakes, streams, rock formations. The supreme deities are usually associated with the sky (male) and the earth (female). Much of African religious practice centers on ancestor worship. Unlike Hebrew, Greek, and Hindu myths, African myths exist almost entirely in an oral tradition. Many African myths have been written down, but usually by non-African collectors of folklore rather than Africans themselves. African myths, therefore, are much less thought of as "literature" than those in cultures where writing is important. They are also more closely associated with ritual and cultural practices. Most African creation myths deal with tribal origins rather than the origin of the universe, but the story printed here is an exception.

This story is from the Bushongo people, a subgroup of the Bantus, who live in the tropical rain forest along the Congo River in Zaire. The story was first collected in 1910.

*I*n the beginning, in the dark, there was nothing but water. And Bumba was alone.

One day Bumba was in terrible pain. He retched and strained and vomited up the sun. After that light spread over everything. The heat of the sun dried up the water until the black edges of the world began to show. Black sandbanks and reefs could be seen. But there were no living things.

Bumba vomited up the moon and then the stars, and after that the night had its own light also.

Still Bumba was in pain. He strained again and nine living creatures came forth: the leopard named Koy Bumba, and Pongo Bumba the crested eagle, the crocodile, Ganda Bumba, and one little fish named Yo; next, old Kono Bumba, the tortoise, and Tsetse, the lightning, swift, deadly, beautiful like the leopard, then the white heron, Nyanyi Bumba, also one beetle, and the goat named Budi.

Last of all came forth men. There were many men, but only one was white like Bumba. His name was Loko Yima.

The creatures themselves then created all the creatures. The heron created all the birds of the air except the kite. He did not make the kite. The crocodile made serpents and the iguana. The goat produced every beast with horns. Yo, the small fish, brought forth all the fish of all the seas and waters. The beetle created insects.

Then the serpents in their turn made grasshoppers, and the iguana made the creatures without horns.

Then the three sons of Bumba said they would finish the world. The first, Nyonye Ngana, made the white ants; but he was not equal to the task, and died of it. The ants, however, thankful for life and being, went searching for black earth in the depths of the world and covered the barren sands to bury and honor their creator.

Chonganda, the second son, brought forth a marvelous living plant from which all the trees and grasses and flowers and plants in the world have sprung. The third son, Chedi Bumba, wanted something different, but for all his trying made only the bird called the kite.

Of all the creatures Tsetse, lightning, was the only troublemaker. She stirred up so much trouble that Bumba chased her into the sky. Then mankind was without fire until Bumba showed the people how to draw fire out of trees. "There is fire in every tree," he told them, and showed them how to make the firedrill and liberate it. Sometimes today Tsetse still leaps down and strikes the earth and causes damage.

When at last the work of creation was finished, Bumba walked through the peaceful villages and said to the people, "Behold these wonders. They belong to you." Thus from Bumba, the Creator, the First Ancestor, came forth all the wonders that we see and hold and use, and all the brotherhood of beasts and man.

Questions for Study

1. What exists before creation?

2. How is this myth similar to and different from other accounts of creation?

3. In what sequence are things created?

4. What power and authority do human beings have?

5. What order emerges from creation? How is the created universe linked together into a harmonious whole?

NORTH AMERICA

Earth-Initiate Creates the World (Maidu)

There are many differences in the religious beliefs and practices of the native tribes of North America, but there are also common elements. Native American religion typically consists of a worship of nature. Not only is nature sacred but so too are supposedly "practical" activities that relate to nature, such as hunting, fishing, building, making clothes, planting, and playing. The Native American view of time is also conditioned by reverence for nature. Native Americans think of time as cyclical, like the days, months, and seasons, rather than linear. They believe that words have sacred power and that myths are not just stories about sacred events but, under certain circumstances, actually become the events. Like African myths, Native American myths remain an oral rather than a written tradition.

This story comes from the Maidu people, who lived in northern California, near the Nevada border. Their religion, the Kuksu cult (from *Kuksu*, the first human being), features secret societies made up of several members each. The story was first collected in 1902.

*I*n the beginning there was no sun, no moon, no stars. All was dark, and everywhere there was only water. A raft came floating on the water. It came from the north, and in it were two persons,—Turtle and Father-of-the-Secret-Society. The stream flowed very rapidly. Then from the sky a rope of feathers was let down, and down it came Earth-Initiate. When he reached the end of the rope, he tied it to the bow of the raft, and stepped in. His face was covered and was never seen, but his body shone like the sun. He sat down, and for a long time said nothing. At last Turtle said, "Where do you come from?" and Earth-Initiate answered, "I come from above." Then Turtle said, "Brother, can you not make for me some good dry land, so that I may sometimes come up out of the water?" Then he asked another time, "Are there going to be any people in the world?" Earth-Initiate thought awhile, then said, "Yes." Turtle asked, "How long before you are going to make people?" Earth-Initiate replied, "I don't know. You want to have some dry land: well, how am I going to get any earth to make it of?" Turtle answered, "If you will tie a rock about my left arm, I'll dive for some." Earth-Initiate did as Turtle asked, and then, reaching around, took the end of a rope from somewhere, and tied it to Turtle. When Earth-Initiate came to the raft, there was no rope there: he just reached out and found one. Turtle said, "If the rope is not long enough, I'll jerk it once, and you must haul me up; if it is long enough, I'll give two jerks, and then you must pull me up quickly, as I shall have all the earth that I can carry." Just as Turtle went over the side of the boat, Father-of-the-Secret-Society began to shout loudly.

Turtle was gone a long time. He was gone six years; and when he came up, he was covered with green slime, he had been down so long. When he reached the top of the water, the only earth he had was a very little under his nails: the rest had all washed away. Earth-Initiate took with his right hand a stone knife from under his left armpit, and carefully scraped the earth out from under Turtle's nails. He put the earth in the palm of his hand, and rolled it about till it was round; it was as large as a small pebble. He laid it on the stern of the raft. By and by he went to look at it: it had not grown at all. The third time that he went to look at it, it had grown so that it could be spanned by the arms. The fourth time he looked, it was as big as the world, the raft was aground, and all around were mountains as far as he could see. The raft came ashore at Ta´doiko, and the place can be seen to-day.

When the raft had come to land, Turtle said, "I can't stay in the dark all the time. Can't you make a light, so that I can see?" Earth-Initiate replied, "Let us get out of the raft, and then we will see what we can do." So all three got out. Then Earth-Initiate said, "Look that way, to the east! I am going to tell my sister to come up." Then it began to grow light, and day began to break; then Father-of-the-Secret-Society began to shout loudly, and the sun came up. Turtle said, "Which way is the sun going to travel?" Earth-Initiate answered, "I'll tell her to go this way, and go down there." After the sun went down, Father-of-the-Secret-Society began to cry and shout again, and it grew very dark. Earth-Initiate said, "I'll tell my brother to come up." Then the moon rose. Then Earth-Initiate asked Turtle and Father-of-the-Secret-Society, "How do you like it?" and they both answered, "It is very good." Then Turtle asked, "Is that all you are going to do for us?" and Earth-Initiate answered, "No, I am going to do more yet." Then he called the stars each by its name, and they came out. When this was done, Turtle asked, "Now what shall we do?" Earth-Initiate replied, "Wait, and I'll show you." Then he made a tree grow at Ta´doiko,—the tree called Hu´kimtsa; and Earth-Initiate and Turtle and Father-of-the-Secret-Society sat in its shade for two days. The tree was very large, and had twelve different kinds of acorns growing on it.

After they had sat for two days under the tree, they all went off to see the world that Earth-Initiate had made. They started at sunrise, and were back by sunset. Earth-Initiate travelled so fast that all they could see was a ball of fire flashing about under the ground and the water. While they were gone, Coyote and his dog Rattlesnake came up out of the ground. It is said that Coyote could see Earth-Initiate's face. When Earth-Initiate and the others came back, they found Coyote at Ta´doiko. All five of them then built huts for themselves, and lived there at Ta´doiko, but no one could go inside of Earth-Initiate's house. Soon after the travellers came back, Earth-Initiate called the birds from the air, and made the trees and then the animals. He took some mud, and of this made first a deer; after that, he made all the other animals. Sometimes Turtle would say, "That does not look well: can't you make it some other way?"

Some time after this, Earth-Initiate and Coyote were at Marysville Buttes. Earth-Initiate said, "I am going to make people." In the middle of the afternoon he began, for he had returned to Ta´doiko. He took dark red earth, mixed it with water, and made two figures,—one a man, and one a woman. He laid the man on his right side, and the woman on his left, inside his house. Then he lay down himself, flat on his back, with his arms stretched out. He lay thus and sweated all the afternoon and night. Early in the morning the woman began to tickle him in the side. He kept very still, did not laugh. By and by he got up, thrust a piece of pitch-wood into the ground, and fire burst out. The two people were very white. No one to-day is as white as they were. Their eyes were pink, their hair was black, their teeth shone brightly, and they were very handsome. It is said that Earth-Initiate did not finish the hands of the people, as he did not know how it would be best to do it. Coyote saw the people, and suggested that they ought to have hands like his. Earth-Initiate said, "No, their hands shall be like mine." Then he finished them. When Coyote asked why their hands were to be like that, Earth-Initiate answered, "So that, if they are chased by bears, they can climb trees." This first man was called Ku´ksu; and the woman, Morning-Star Woman.

When Coyote had seen the two people, he asked Earth-Initiate how he had made them. When he was told, he thought, "That is not difficult. I'll do it myself." He did just as Earth-Initiate had told him, but could not help laughing, when, early in the morning, the woman poked him in the ribs. As a result of his failing to keep still, the people were glass-eyed. Earth-Initiate said, "I told you not to laugh," but Coyote declared he had not. This was the first lie.

Questions for Study

1. What exists before creation?

2. How is earth important as a source of creation? What implications does this have for the order that emerges from creation?

3. What characterizes Earth-Initiate?

4. What is the sequence in which things are created?

5. What roles do the nonhuman characters other than Earth-Initiate seem to play? What do they represent?

MYTHS OF THE FALL

Myths of creation tell about the unknown and perhaps unknowable power that brought the universe into existence. Stories of the fall deal with us, with humankind. Their authors ask fundamental questions about our identity and purpose: What are our capabilities and limits? Why are we the way we are? Why do we suffer pain and trouble? What are our obligations? A prominent feature in many stories about the first people is a "paradise" from which the troubling aspects of human life are absent. In this paradise people work very little, they are untroubled by pain and death, and they live in harmony with nature and one another. Put another way, they enjoy the orderliness of the new creation. But something happens—perhaps the breaching of a taboo—that causes them to "fall" from this new state of orderliness to the state we occupy now. Stories of the fall, then, ponder the painful realities of human existence and speculate about their causes. Some stories focus only on the most mysterious and troubling fact of human existence, death. Others are broader in scope and include such troubles as disease, natural disasters, and human cruelty. Whatever their focus, these myths all seem to bemoan our present fate and yearn for a return to a time when we were secure, healthy, and at one with the force or forces that gave us life.

ANCIENT PALESTINE

Adam and Eve Are Expelled from Eden (Genesis 3:1-24)

These two stories in the Hebrew Bible immediately follow the account of creation found on p. 30. The first written version of these stories dates from about 900 B.C.

3   Now the serpent was more crafty than any other wild animal that the LORD God had made. He said to the woman, "Did God say, 'You shall not eat from any tree in the garden'?" ²The woman said to the serpent, "We may eat of the fruit of the trees in the garden; ³ but God said, 'You shall not eat of the fruit of the tree that is in the middle of the garden, nor shall you touch it, or you shall die.'" ⁴ But the serpent said to the woman, "You will not die; ⁵ for God knows that when you eat of it your eyes will be opened, and you will be like God, knowing good and evil." ⁶ So when the woman saw that the tree was good for food, and that it was a delight to the eyes, and that the tree was to be desired to make one wise, she took of its fruit and ate; and she also gave some to her husband, who was with her, and he ate. ⁷ Then the eyes of both were opened, and they knew that they were naked; and they sewed fig leaves together and made loincloths for themselves.

8 They heard the sound of the LORD God walking in the garden at the time of the evening breeze, and the man and his wife hid themselves from the presence of the LORD God among the trees of the garden. ⁹ But the LORD God called to the man, and said to him, "Where are you?" ¹⁰ He said, "I heard the sound of you in the garden, and I was afraid, because I was naked; and I hid myself." ¹¹ He said, "Who told you that you were naked? Have you eaten from the tree of which I commanded you not to eat?" ¹² The man said, "The woman whom you gave to be with me, she gave me fruit from the tree, and I ate." ¹³ Then the LORD God said to the woman, "What is this that you have done?" The woman said, "The serpent tricked me, and I ate." ¹⁴ The LORD God said to the serpent,

> "Because you have done this,
> cursed are you among all animals
> and among all wild creatures;
> upon your belly you shall go,
> and dust you shall eat
> all the days of your life.
> ¹⁵ I will put enmity between you and the woman,
> and between your offspring and hers;
> he will strike your head,

and you will strike his heel."
¹⁶To the woman he said,
"I will greatly increase your
pangs in childbearing;
in pain you shall bring forth children,
yet your desire shall be for your husband,
and he shall rule over you."
¹⁷And to the man he said,
"Because you have listened to
the voice of your wife, and have eaten of the tree
about which I commanded you,
'You shall not eat of it,'
cursed is the ground because of you;
in toil you shall eat of it all the days of your life;
¹⁸thorns and thistles it shall bring forth for you;
and you shall eat the plants of the field.
¹⁹By the sweat of your face
you shall eat bread
until you return to the ground,
for out of it you were taken;
you are dust,
and to dust you shall return."

20 The man named his wife Eve, because she was the mother of all living. ²¹And the LORD God made garments of skins for the man and for his wife, and clothed them.

22 Then the LORD God said, "See, the man has become like one of us, knowing good and evil; and now, he might reach out his hand and take also from the tree of life, and eat, and live forever"—²³ therefore the LORD God sent him forth from the garden of Eden, to till the ground from which he was taken. ²⁴ He drove out the man; and at the east of the garden of Eden he placed the cherubim, and a sword flaming and turning to guard the way to the tree of life.

Questions for Study

1. What characterizes life before the fall?

2. What kind of knowledge do Adam and Eve get by eating from the Tree of Knowledge?

3. What does nakedness symbolize?

4. Why does Yahweh expel Adam and Eve from the Garden? What does this act suggest about the nature of Yahweh?

5. What are the consequences of the fall?

6. Who or what is to blame for the fall?

The First Murder (Genesis 4:1-16)

4   Now the man knew his wife Eve, and she conceived and bore Cain, saying, "I have produced a man with the help of the LORD." ²Next she bore his brother Abel. Now Abel was a keeper of sheep, and Cain a tiller of the ground. ³In the course of time Cain brought to the LORD an offering of the fruit of the ground, ⁴and Abel for his part brought of the firstlings of his flock, their fat portions. And the LORD had regard for Abel and his offering, ⁵but for Cain and his offering he had no regard. So Cain was very angry, and his countenance fell. ⁶The LORD said to Cain, "Why are you angry, and why has your countenance fallen? ⁷If you do well, will you not be accepted? And if you do not do well, sin is lurking at the door; its desire is for you, but you must master it."

8 Cain said to his brother Abel, "Let us go out to the field." And when they were in the field, Cain rose up against his brother Abel, and killed him. ⁹Then the LORD said to Cain, "Where is your brother Abel?" He said, "I do not know; am I my brother's keeper?" ¹⁰And the LORD said, "What have you done? Listen; your brother's blood is crying out to me from the ground! ¹¹And now you are cursed from the ground, which has opened its mouth to receive your brother's blood from your hand. ¹²When you till the ground, it will no longer yield to you its strength; you will be a fugitive and a wanderer on the earth." ¹³Cain said to the LORD, "My punishment is greater than I can bear! ¹⁴Today you have driven me away from the soil, and I shall be hidden from your face; I shall be a fugitive and a wanderer on the earth, and anyone who meets me may kill me." ¹⁵Then the LORD said to him, "Not so! Whoever kills Cain will suffer a sevenfold vengeance." And the LORD put a mark on Cain, so that no one who came upon him would kill him. ¹⁶Then Cain went away from the presence of the LORD, and settled in the land of Nod, east of Eden.

Questions for Study

1. Why does Yahweh reject Cain's offering but not Abel's?

2. Why does Cain kill Abel?

3. What is Cain's punishment?

4. How is this story related to the story of Adam and Eve's expulsion from Eden?

Prometheus Tricks Zeus (Hesiod, Theogony*)*

In Hesiod's account of creation in the *Theogony* (c. 700 B.C.), the stories about the first human beings follow immediately after those about the creation of the gods (see p. 33). After Cronus defeats his father, Heaven, Cronus reigns over creation with his sister and consort Rhea. Their son Zeus leads his siblings in a revolt against Cronus and the other Titans. Zeus wins with the help of Prometheus, son of Iapetus, one of the Titans. Hesiod gives no account of the creation of humankind, but elsewhere in Greek mythology Prometheus and his brother Epimetheus are cited as the creators of humankind. Epimetheus, whose name means "afterthought," is dimwitted and harmful to humankind. Prometheus, whose name means "forethought," is shrewd and helpful. In the first of the following stories recorded by Hesiod, Prometheus tricks Zeus into accepting the least desirable part of the ox as a sacrifice from human beings, leaving the best part for human beings to eat. In the second story, Prometheus steals fire and gives it to human beings. In retaliation for both of these deeds, Zeus gives humankind Pandora, whose name means "the gift of all" (that is, the gift of all the gods) and later punishes Prometheus.

Now Iapetus took to wife the neat-ankled maid Clymene, daughter of Ocean, and went up with her into one bed. And she bare him a stout-hearted son, Atlas: also she bare very glorious Menoetius and clever Prometheus, full of various wiles, and scatter-brained Epimetheus who from the first was a mischief to men who eat bread; for it was he who first took of Zeus the woman, the maiden whom he had formed. But Menoetius was outrageous, and far-seeing Zeus struck him with a lurid thunderbolt and sent him down to Erebus because of his mad presumption and exceeding pride. And Atlas through hard constraint upholds the wide heaven with unwearying head and arms, standing at the borders of the earth before the clear-voiced Hesperides; for this lot wise Zeus assigned to him. And ready-witted Prometheus he bound with inextricable bonds, cruel chains, and drove a shaft through his middle, and set on him a long-winged eagle, which used to eat his immortal liver; but by night the liver grew as much again everyway as the long-winged bird devoured in the whole day. That bird Heracles, the valiant son of shapely-ankled Alcmene, slew; and delivered the son of Iapetus from the cruel plague, and released him from his affliction—not without the will of Olympian Zeus who reigns on high, that the glory of Heracles the Theban-born might be yet greater than it was before over the plenteous earth. This, then, he regarded, and honored his famous son; though he was angry, he ceased from the wrath which he had before because Prometheus matched himself in wit with the almighty son of Cronus. For when the gods and mortal men were divided at Mecone, even then Prometheus was forward to cut up a great ox and set portions before them, trying to befool the mind of Zeus. Before the rest [humankind] he set flesh and inner parts thick with fat upon the hide, covering them with an ox paunch; but for Zeus he put the white bones dressed up with cunning art and covered with shining fat. Then the father of men and of gods said to him:

"Son of Iapetus, most glorious of all lords, good sir, how unfairly you have divided the portions!"

So said Zeus whose wisdom is everlasting, rebuking him. But wily Prometheus answered him, smiling softly and not forgetting his cunning trick:

"Zeus, most glorious and greatest of the eternal gods, take which ever of these portions your heart within you bids." So he said, thinking trickery. But Zeus, whose wisdom is everlasting, saw and failed not to perceive the trick, and in his heart he thought mischief against mortal men which also was to be fulfilled. With both hands he took up the white fat and was angry at heart, and wrath came to his spirit when he saw the white ox-bones craftily tricked out: and because of this the tribes of men upon earth burn white bones to the deathless gods upon fragrant altars. But Zeus who drives the clouds was greatly vexed and said to him:

"Son of Iapetus, clever above all! So, sir, you have not yet forgotten your cunning arts!"

So spake Zeus in anger, whose wisdom is everlasting; and from that time he was always mindful of the trick, and would not give the power of unwearying fire to the ash-tree race[1] of mortal men who live on the earth.

Questions for Study

1. What characterizes Zeus? What is contradictory or inconsistent in Zeus's characterization?

2. What is Zeus's attitude toward humankind?

3. What characterizes Prometheus? What is Prometheus trying to achieve?

4. Why does Zeus choose the bad portion of the meat?

Prometheus Steals Fire
(Hesiod, Works and Days)

This account of the creation of Pandora appears in Hesiod's *Works and Days* (c. 700 B.C.). Hesiod's father was a well-to-do farmer. In the *Works and Days* Hesiod accused his brother Perses of cheating him out of most of his inheritance by bribing the wealthy "barons" of their

---

[1] *ash-tree race.* Hesiod refers to human beings as ash-tree people, possibly from a belief that they originated from ash trees.

homeland. Hesiod wrote *Works and Days* to his brother, urging him to settle their differences and avoid laziness. Most of the book instructs Perses about the work a good farmer should do on each day of the year. Work is necessary, Hesiod says near the beginning, because Prometheus stole fire for humankind and Zeus created Pandora. Hesiod tells the story of Pandora in the *Theogony,* but this version is more detailed and complex. The god who creates Pandora is Zeus's lame son, Hephaestus, the god of craftsmanship.

*P*erses, lay up these things in your heart, and do not let that Strife who delights in mischief hold your heart back from work, while you peep and peer and listen to the wrangles of the court-house. Little concern has he with quarrels and courts who has not a year's victuals laid up betimes, even that which the earth bears, Demeter's grain. When you have got plenty of that, you can raise disputes and strive to get another's goods. But you shall have no second chance to deal so again: nay, let us settle our dispute here with true judgment which is of Zeus and is perfect. For we had already divided our inheritance, but you seized the greater share and carried it off, greatly swelling the glory of our bribe-swallowing lords who love to judge such a cause as this. Fools! They know not how much more the half is than the whole, nor what great advantage there is in simple food.

For the gods keep hidden from men the means of life. Else you would easily do work enough in a day to supply you for a full year even without working; soon would you put away your rudder over the smoke, and the fields worked by ox and sturdy mule would run to waste. But Zeus in the anger of his heart hid it, because Prometheus the crafty deceived him; therefore he planned sorrow and mischief against men. He hid fire; but that the noble son of Iapetus stole again for men from Zeus the counsellor in a hollow fennel-stalk, so that Zeus who delights in thunder did not see it. But afterwards Zeus who gathers the clouds said to him in anger:

"Son of Iapetus, surpassing all in cunning, you are glad that you have outwitted me and stolen fire—a great plague to you yourself and to men that shall be. But I will give men as the price for fire an evil thing in which they may all be glad of heart while they embrace their own destruction."

So said the father of men and gods, and laughed aloud. And he bade famous Hephaestus make haste and mix earth with water and to put in it the voice and strength of human kind, and fashion a sweet, lovely maiden-shape, like to the immortal goddesses in face; and Athene to teach her needlework and the weaving of the varied web; and golden Aphrodite to shed grace upon her head and cruel longing and cares that weary the limbs. And he charged Hermes the guide, the Slayer of Argus, to put in her a shameless mind and a deceitful nature.

So he ordered. And they obeyed the lord Zeus the son of Cronus. Forthwith the famous Lame God moulded clay in the likeness of a modest maid, as the son of Cronus purposed. And the goddess bright-eyed Athene girded and clothed her, and the divine Graces and queenly Persuasion put necklaces of gold upon her, and the rich-haired Hours crowned her head with spring flowers. And Pallas Athene bedecked her form with all manner of finery. Also the Guide, the Slayer of Argus, contrived within her lies and crafty words and a deceitful nature at the will of loud thundering Zeus, and the Herald of the gods put speech in her. And he called this woman Pandora, because all they who dwelt on Olympus gave each a gift, a plague to men who eat bread.

But when he had finished the sheer, hopeless snare, the Father sent glorious Hermes, the swift messenger of the gods, to take it to Epimetheus as a gift. And Epimetheus did not think on what Prometheus had said to him, bidding him never take a gift of Olympian Zeus, but to send it back for fear it might prove to be something harmful to men. But he took the gift, and afterwards, when the evil thing was already his, he understood.

For ere this the tribes of men lived on earth remote and free from ills and hard toil and heavy sicknesses which bring the Fates upon men; for in misery men grow old quickly. But the woman took off the great lid of the jar with her hands and scattered all these and her thought caused sorrow and mischief to men. Only Hope remained there in an unbreakable home within under the rim of the great jar, and did not fly out at the door; for ere that, the lid of the jar stopped her, by the will of Aegis-holding Zeus who gathers the clouds. But the other countless plagues wander amongst men; for earth is full of evils and the sea is full. Of themselves diseases come upon men continually by day and by night, bringing mischief to mortals silently; for wise Zeus took away speech from them. So is there no way to escape the will of Zeus.

Questions for Study

1. What was life like before the fall? What are the consequences of the fall?

2. What causes the fall?

3. What is the gods' attitude toward humankind?

4. What themes about gender does this story develop?

5. How is this story similar to and different from the story of the fall in the Hebrew Bible (see p. 46)?

6. What is the importance of Hope?

AFRICA

The Origin of Death (Amazulu)

The Amazulu peoples of South Africa are ancestor worshippers. They believe that their first ancestor, the first human being, was the creator of all life. His name, Unkulunkulu, means "the most ancient man." Stories about the coming of death because of a misdelivered message are common in African mythology. This story reflects a long-standing Amazulu hatred of the chameleon and especially the lizard. The story was first collected in 1884.

*U*nkulunkulu was the first man. We do not know his wife; and the ancients do not tell us that he had a wife.

We hear it said, that Unkulunkulu broke off the nations from Uthlanga [a reed].

It is said he sent a chameleon; he said to it, "Go, Chameleon, go and say, Let not men die." The chameleon set out; it went slowly; it loitered in the way; and as it went, it ate of the fruit of a tree, which is called Ubukwebezane.

At length Unkulunkulu sent a lizard after the chameleon, when it had already set out for some time. The lizard went; it ran and made great haste, for Unkulunkulu had said, "Lizard, when you have arrived, say, Let men die." So the lizard went, and said, "I tell you, It is said, Let men die." The lizard came back again to Unkulunkulu, before the chameleon had reached his destination, the chameleon which was sent first; which was sent, and told to go and say, "Let not men die."

At length it arrived and shouted, saying, "It is said, Let not men die!" But men answered, "O! we have heard the word of the lizard; it has told us the word, 'It is said, Let men die.' We cannot hear your word. Through the word of the lizard, men will die."

Questions for Study

1. What causes death? Whose "fault" is it?

2. What does the mixed-up message suggest about the order (or disorder) of life?

NORTH AMERICA

Coyote Brings Death to Humankind (Maidu)

This story, collected in 1902, is the continuation of the Maidu creation myth on p. 42. Ku'ksu is the first man. Coyote is a godlike figure who is present at the creation of humankind.

*B*y and by there came to be a good many people. Earth-Initiate had wanted to have everything comfortable and easy for people, so that none of them should have to work. All fruits were easy to obtain, no one was ever to get sick and die. As the people grew numerous, Earth-Initiate did not come as often as formerly, he only came to see Ku´ksu in the night. One night he said to him, "To-morrow morning you must go to the little lake near here. Take all the people with you. I'll make you a very old man before you get to the lake." So in the morning Ku´ksu collected all the people, and went to the lake. By the time he had reached it, he was a very old man. He fell into the lake, and sank down out of sight. Pretty soon the ground began to shake, the waves overflowed the shore, and there was a great roaring under the water, like thunder. By and by Ku´ksu came up out of the water, but young again, just like a young man. Then Earth-Initiate came and spoke to the people, and said, "If you do as I tell you, everything will be well. When any of you grow old, so old that you cannot walk, come to this lake, or get some one to bring you here. You must then go down into the water as you have seen Ku´ksu do, and you will come out young again." When he had said this, he went away. He left in the night, and went up above.

All this time food had been easy to get, as Earth-Initiate had wished. The women set out baskets at night, and in the morning they found them full of food, all ready to eat, and lukewarm. One day Coyote came along. He asked the people how they lived, and they told him that all they had to do was to eat and sleep. Coyote replied, "That is no way to do: I can show you something better." Then he told them how he and Earth-Initiate had had a discussion before men had been made; how Earth-Initiate wanted everything easy, and that there should be no sickness or death, but how he had thought it would be better to have people work, get sick, and die. He said, "We'll have a burning." The people did not know what he meant; but Coyote said, "I'll show you. It is better to have a burning, for then the widows can be free." So he took all the baskets and things that the people had, hung them up on poles, made everything all ready. When all was prepared, Coyote said, "At this time you must always have games." So he fixed the moon during which these games were to be played.

Coyote told them to start the games with a foot-race, and every one got ready to run. Ku´ksu did not come, however. He sat in his hut alone, and was sad, for he knew what was going to occur. Just at this moment Rattlesnake came to Ku´ksu, and said, "What shall we do now? Everything is spoiled!" Ku´ksu did not answer, so Rattlesnake said, "Well, I'll do what I think is best." Then he went out and along the course that the racers were to go over, and hid himself, leaving his head just sticking out of a hole. By this time all the racers had started, and among them Coyote's son. He was Coyote's only child, and was very quick. He soon began to outstrip all the runners, and was in the lead. As he passed the spot where Rattlesnake had hidden himself, however, Rattlesnake raised his head and bit the boy in the ankle. In a minute the boy was dead.

Coyote was dancing about the home-stake. He was very happy, and was shouting at his son and praising him. When Rattlesnake bit the boy, and he fell dead, every one laughed at Coyote, and said, "Your son has fallen down, and is so ashamed that he does not dare to get up." Coyote said, "No, that is not it. He is dead." This was the first death. The people, however, did not understand, and picked the boy up, and brought him to Coyote. Then Coyote began to cry, and every one did the same. These were the first tears. Then Coyote took his son's body and carried it to the lake of which Earth-Initiate had told them, and threw the body in. But there was no noise, and nothing happened, and the body drifted about for four days on the surface, like a log. On the fifth day Coyote took four sacks of beads and brought them to Ku´ksu, begging him to restore his son to life. Ku´ksu did not answer. For five days Coyote begged, then Ku´ksu came out of his house, bringing all his beads and bear-skins, and calling to all the people to come and watch him. He laid the body on a bear-skin, dressed it, and wrapped it up carefully. Then he dug a grave, put the body into it, and covered it up. Then he told the people, "From now on, this is what you must do. This is the way you must do till the world shall be made over."

About a year after this, in the spring, all was changed. Up to this time everybody spoke the same language. The people were having a burning, everything was ready for the next day, when in the night everybody suddenly began to speak a different language. Each man and his wife, however, spoke the same. Earth-Initiate had come in the night to Ku´ksu, and had told him about it all, and given him instructions for the next day. So, when morning came, Ku´ksu called all the people together, for he was able to speak all the languages. He told them each the names of the different animals, etc., in their languages, taught them how to cook and to hunt, gave them all their laws, and set the time for all their dances and festivals. Then he called each tribe by name, and sent them off in different directions, telling them where they were to live. He sent the warriors to the north, the singers to the west, the flute-players to the east, and the dancers to the south. So all the people went away, and left Ku´ksu and his wife alone at Ta´doiko. By and by his wife went away, leaving in the night, and going first to Marysville Buttes. Ku´ksu stayed a little while longer, and then he also left. He too went to the Buttes, went into the spirit house, and sat down on the south side. He found Coyote's son there, sitting on the north side. The door was on the west. Coyote had been trying to find out where Ku´ksu had gone, and where his own son had gone, and at last found the tracks, and followed them to the spirit house. Here he saw Ku´ksu and his son, the latter eating spirit food. Coyote wanted to go in, but Ku´ksu said, "No, wait there. You have just what you wanted, it is your own fault. Every man will now have all kinds of troubles and accidents, will have to work to get his food, and will die and be buried. this must go on till the time is out, and Earth-Initiate comes again, and everything will be made over. You must go home, and tell all the people that you have seen your son, that he is not dead." Coyote said he would go, but that he was hungry, and wanted some of the food. Ku´ksu replied, "You cannot eat that. Only ghosts may eat that food." Then Coyote went away and told all the people, "I saw my son and Ku´ksu, and he told me to kill myself." So he climbed up to the top of a tall tree, jumped off, and was killed. Then he went to the spirit house, thinking he could now have some of the food; but there was no one there, nothing at all, and so he went out, and walked away to the west, and was never seen again. Ku´ksu and Coyote's son, however, had gone up above.

Questions for Study

1. What is life like before the fall? What are Earth-Initiate's intentions for humankind?

2. What characterizes Coyote? Why does he want to bring death to people? Is he malicious? Does he know what he is doing? What does he learn?

3. What hopes does the story hold out for humankind?

MYTHS OF RESURRECTION

According to myths of the fall, the apparent end of the human story is death. But myths of resurrection hold out the hope that death is not, after all, the end or the ultimate limitation. Death, these myths claim, can be transcended. Myths of resurrection complete a cycle, represented in the organization of this chapter, that begins with order (creation), moves to the rupture of order (the fall), and concludes with the return to order (resurrection).

Myths of resurrection have many different points of departure. Some refer to the cycle of death and rebirth that occurs in nature, especially the seasonal regeneration of the earth. In others death is seen as symbolic. States of moral defeat, of despondency, of disease, of ignorance are like "death" but can be overcome. Some myths deal only with the individual's fate, others with the fate of a tribe or nation, and still others with the fate of all people. Among the best-known myths in Western culture are those about a god who dies and is then resurrected. The stories of the Egyptian god Osiris, the Greek god Dionysus, and the Christian divinity Jesus are examples.

Myths of resurrection point to a future life. A frequent subject of these myths is the apocalypse, the cosmic cataclysm at the end of the time in which the righteous will be rewarded and the wicked punished. Another subject is the "paradise" where the righteous people will go after death. But even when myths of resurrection speak of the future, they seem also to hint, at least, about how we should live our lives now.

MESOPOTAMIA

The Flood (from the Epic of Gilgamesh*)*

The Sumerians created the world's first civilization in Mesopotamia, the fertile region between the Tigris and Euphrates rivers in what is now

Iraq. The Sumerian era lasted from about 3200 B.C. to about 2000 B.C. The Sumerians were conquered by the Old Babylonians, who were in turn conquered by the Assyrians, whose empire lasted from roughly 1300 B.C. until 612 B.C. The story of the Flood, a natural disaster that wiped out nearly all human beings, goes back to Sumerian civilization and perhaps even further back than that. The story of the Flood is an almost universal myth. Even landlocked cultures have stories of the Flood. Since the Tigris and Euphrates rivers flooded often, the story may have been based on a real event. The account printed here is from the *Epic of Gilgamesh,* which is an amalgamation of stories from Sumerian, Old Babylonian, and Assyrian cultures. It was first written down in Babylonia about 1800 B.C. Gilgamesh was possibly a real person, a Sumerian king who ruled about 2600 B.C. In the *Epic of Gilgamesh* he is a semi-divine but mortal hero who, depressed about the death of a friend, goes in search of eternal life. After many adventures he arrives at the dwelling of Utnapishtim, who survived the Flood and was granted immortality by the gods. In Utnapishtim's account of the Flood, the gods attempt to destroy all people but lose their resolve and grant the earth and humankind a new life.

The chapter printed here is Utnapishtim's account of the Flood. The key gods in this story are Enlil (the supreme god), Ishtar (queen of heaven, goddess of love and war), Shamash (god of the sun), and Ea (god of wisdom, creator and benefactor of humankind).

"**Y**ou know the city Shurrupak [Utnapishtim said to Gilgamesh], it stands on the banks of Euphrates? That city grew old and the gods that were in it were old. There was Anu, lord of the firmament, their father, and warrior Enlil their counsellor, Ninurta the helper, and Ennugi watcher over canals; and with them also was Ea. In those days the world teemed, the people multiplied, the world bellowed like a wild bull, and the great god was aroused by the clamor. Enlil heard the clamor and he said to the gods in council, 'The uproar of mankind is intolerable and sleep is no longer possible by reason of the babel.' So the gods in their hearts were moved to let loose the deluge; but my lord Ea warned me in a dream. He whispered their words to my house of reeds, 'Reed-house, reed-house! Wall, O wall, hearken reed-house, wall reflect; O man of Shurrupak, son of Ubara-Tutu; tear down your house and build a boat, abandon possessions and look for life, despise worldly goods and save your soul alive. Tear down your house, I say, and build a boat. These are the measurements of the barque as you shall build her: let her beam equal her length, let her deck be roofed like the vault that covers the abyss; then take up into the boat the seed of all living creatures.'

"When I had understood I said to my lord, 'Behold, what you have commanded I will honor and perform, but how shall I answer the people, the city, the elders?' Then Ea opened his mouth and said to me, his servant, 'Tell them this: I have learnt that Enlil is wrathful against me, I dare no longer walk in his land nor live in his city; I will go down to the Gulf to dwell with Ea my lord. But on you he will rain down abundance, rare fish and shy wild-fowl, a rich harvest-tide. In the evening the rider of the storm will bring you wheat in torrents.'

"In the first light of dawn all my household gathered round me, the children brought pitch and the men whatever was necessary. On the fifth day I laid the keel and the ribs, then I made fast the planking. The ground-space was one acre, each side of the deck measured one hundred and twenty cubits, making a square. I built six decks below, seven in all, I divided them into nine sections with bulkheads between. I drove in wedges where needed, I saw to the punt-poles, and laid in supplies. The carriers brought oil in baskets, I poured pitch into the furnace and asphalt and oil; more oil was consumed in caulking, and more again the master of the boat took into his stores. I slaughtered bullocks for the people and every day I killed sheep. I gave the ship-wrights wine to drink as though it were river water, raw wine and red wine and oil and white wine. There was feasting then as there is at the time of the New Year's festival; I myself anointed my head. On the seventh day the boat was complete.

"Then was the launching full of difficulty; there was shifting of ballast above and below till two thirds was submerged. I loaded into her all that I had of gold and of living things, my family, my kin, the beasts of the field both wild and tame, and all the craftsmen. I sent them on board, for the time that Shamash had ordained was already fulfilled when he said, 'In the evening, when the rider of the storm sends down the destroying rain, enter the boat and batten her down.' The time was fulfilled, the evening came, the rider of the storm sent down the rain. I looked out at the weather and it was terrible, so I too boarded the boat and battened her down. All was now complete, the battening and the caulking; so I handed the tiller to Puzur-Amurri the steersman, with the navigation and the care of the whole boat.

"With the first light of dawn a black cloud came from the horizon; it thundered within where Adad, lord of the storm was riding. In front over hill and plain Shullat and Hanish, heralds of the storm, led on. Then the gods of the abyss rose up; Nergal pulled out the dams of the nether waters, Ninurta the war-lord threw down the dykes, and the seven judges of hell, the Annunaki, raised their torches, lighting the land with their livid flame. A stupor of despair went up to heaven when the god of the storm turned daylight to darkness, when he smashed the land like a cup. One whole day the tempest raged gathering fury as it went, it poured over the people like the tides of battle; a man could not see his brother nor the people be seen from heaven. Even the gods were terrified at the flood, they fled to the highest heaven, the firmament of Anu; they crouched against the walls, cowering like curs. Then Ishtar the sweet-voiced Queen of Heaven cried out like a woman in travail: 'Alas the days of old are turned to dust because I commanded evil; why did I command this evil in the council of all the gods? I commanded wars to destroy the people, but are they not my people, for I brought them forth? Now like the spawn of fish they float in the ocean.' The great gods of heaven and of hell wept, they covered their mouths.

"For six days and six nights the winds blew, torrent and tempest and flood overwhelmed the world, tempest and flood raged together like warring hosts. When the seventh day dawned the storm from the south subsided, the sea grew calm, the flood was stilled; I looked at the face of the world and there was silence, all mankind was turned to clay. The surface of the sea stretched as flat as a roof-top; I opened a hatch and the light fell on my face. Then I bowed low, I sat down and I wept, the tears streamed down my face, for on every side was the waste of water. I looked for land in vain, but fourteen leagues distant there appeared a mountain, and there the boat grounded; on the mountain of Nisir the boat held fast, she held fast and did not budge. One day she held, and a second day on the mountain of Nisir she held fast and did not budge. A third day, and a fourth day she held fast on the mountain and did not budge; a fifth day and a sixth day she held fast on the mountain. When the seventh day dawned I loosed a dove and let her go. She flew away, but finding no resting-place she returned. Then I loosed a swallow, and she flew away but finding no resting-place she returned. I loosed a raven, she saw that the waters had retreated, she ate, she flew around, she cawed, and she did not come back. Then I threw everything open to the four winds, I made a sacrifice and poured out a libation on the mountain top. Seven and again seven cauldrons I set up on their stands, I heaped up wood and cane and cedar and myrtle. When the gods smelled the sweet savor, they gathered like flies over the sacrifice. Then, at last, Ishtar also came, she lifted her necklace with the jewels of heaven that once Anu had made to please her. 'O you gods here present, by the lapis lazuli round my neck I shall remember these days as I remember the jewels of my throat; these last days I shall not forget. Let all the gods gather round the sacrifice, except Enlil. He shall not approach this offering, for without reflection he brought the flood; he consigned my people to destruction.'

   "When Enlil had come, when he saw the boat, he was wrath and swelled with anger at the gods, the host of heaven, 'Has any of these mortals escaped? Not one was to have survived the destruction.' Then the god of the wells and canals Ninurta opened his mouth and said to the warrior Enlil, 'Who is there of the gods that can devise without Ea? It is Ea alone who knows all things.' Then Ea opened his mouth and spoke to warrior Enlil, 'Wisest of gods, hero Enlil, how could you so senselessly bring down the flood?

> Lay upon the sinner his sin,
> Lay upon the transgressor his transgression,
> Punish him a little when he breaks loose,
> Do not drive him too hard or he perishes;
> Would that a lion had ravaged mankind
> Rather than the flood,
> Would that a wolf had ravaged mankind
> Rather than the flood,
> Would that famine had wasted the world
> Rather than the flood,
> Would that pestilence had wasted mankind
> Rather than the flood.

It was not I that revealed the secret of the gods; the wise man learned it in a dream. Now take your counsel what shall be done with him.'

   "Then Enlil went up into the boat, he took me by the hand and my wife and made us enter the boat and kneel down on either side, he standing between us. He touched our foreheads to bless us saying, 'In time past Utnapishtim was a mortal man;

henceforth he and his wife shall live in the distance at the mouth of the rivers.' Thus it was that the gods took me and placed me here to live in the distance, at the mouth of the rivers."

Questions for Study

1. What causes the Flood?

2. How do the gods participate in the creation of the Flood? What forces do the gods represent?

3. What is the gods' attitude toward humankind? What conflicts do they have with one another? How does their attitude toward the Flood change? Why?

4. What are the signs of new life?

5. Do human beings do anything to bring about new life?

6. How is this account of the Flood similar to and different from the one in the Hebrew Bible (Genesis 6-8)?

AFRICA

Obatala's Farm at Abeokuta (Yoruba)

The Yoruba people live in southwestern Nigeria, in the rain forest along the Niger River. Several of their cities, notably Ife and Benin, are large and hundreds of years old. In this myth Obatala, the creator of humankind, is one of the *orisha,* the gods. Other gods are Olorum, the sky god and chief deity, Eshu, the god of uncertainty, and Orunmila, the god of divination. This story was first collected in 1973.

*O*batala owned a farm at a place named Abeokuta, where the city by that name still stands. When Obatala apportioned land in the beginning, after creating humans, he kept the most barren and stony share for himself. His farm at Abeokuta was more rock than soil, and everyone asked, "How can crops be grown at such a place?" But because Obatala was a great orisha the crops he planted grew abundantly among the stones. People observed that while they had to work hard from morning until night to grow enough to eat, Obatala's farm was always green even though he worked only a little. Whether there was much rain or none, whether he tended his fields often or rarely, there was never a lack of grain or yams.

People began to speak of it. They were resentful. They said, "What kind of a person can Obatala be? He gives us portions of land that begrudge us our food, while he keeps for himself a portion that grows more than he can eat." After a while they were saying, "How long are we to suffer with such a tyrant?" In time they spoke such words as, "If we had Obatala's land we would be fortunate. How can we obtain it?"

They forgot that Obatala had created land over the watery wastes and that he had made the first human beings. They said, "It is time to be rid of Obatala. Let us destroy him." But they did not know how to do it. They discussed the matter for many days, until one man proposed that Obatala be killed by stones. They agreed that stones should be rolled down on Obatala from a hill near his farm.

They went to the top of the hill where some enormous stones were resting. When Obatala passed by on the way to his fields they dislodged the stones and sent them rolling downward. Obatala was battered by the stones. His body was broken into many pieces and scattered across the land.

The word went from one place to another that Obatala had been destroyed by envious men. The orisha Eshu received the news. He was saddened. He went to Abeokuta to verify the story. When he found it was true he went up to the sky and reported the tragedy to Olorun. Olorun sent Orunmila to find Obatala's body and bring it back. Orunmila went to Abeokuta. He searched for a long time, gathering all the pieces of Obatala's body, and he carried them back to the sky so that Olorun could give life to Obatala again.

Olorun gave Obatala's parts life, but each part became a separate orisha. Instead of one Obatala there were numerous gods created out of his fragments. These orishas came to be called Orisha-Nla. Each one was less than Obatala, but all together they were the sum of Obatala, so that Obatala lived on in another form. This truth came to be understood by humans. Even now many men call Obatala by the name Orisha-Nla, and this name recalls the evil deed carried out at Abeokuta.

Questions for Study

1. What characterizes Obatala, the creator of humankind?

2. Why do human beings want to kill him?

3. What brings about his resurrection? What form does it take?

4. What meaning does this story have for human beings? How is this myth similar to other myths about gods who are killed and resurrected?

TIBET

Life after Death (The Tibetan Book of the Dead)

Buddhism was founded by a prince named Siddhartha who was born in northern India about 560 B.C. After a royal upbringing, he renounced his family and underwent a period of religious devotion that climaxed with a spiritual revelation one night under a tree. He began teaching, and by the time of his death, at age eighty-one, he had established a large community of followers. The term *buddha* means "one who has awakened," or one who knows the *dharma,* the basic truth of things. According to Buddhist teaching, anyone can become a buddha, but buddhas are extremely rare. It takes many lifetimes of spiritual discipline to achieve the blameless life of a genuine buddha. Someone who strives for buddhahood is a *bodhisattva* ("one on the path to awakening"). The bodhisattva's goal is to change the nature of his or her *karma,* the cumulative effect of one's deeds over many lifetimes, so that the good deeds finally outweigh the bad. Siddhartha was the first buddha, and he claimed to have lived many previous lives as a bodhisattva. Buddhist scriptures vary widely in their teachings but focus largely on the attitudes and disciplines needed to gain a correct understanding of reality. Buddhism has spread throughout the world but is especially dominant in the Far East.

    The Tibetan Book of the Dead, compiled about A.D 1400, is a Buddhist treatment of life after death. The myth reprinted here deals with the fate of "you" rather than a god or semi-divine hero. It recounts the path that a bodhisattva will follow after death.

This is what the Lama reads to the dying person:

Preamble

I now transmit to you the profound teachings which I have myself received from my Teacher, and, through him, from the long line of initiated Gurus. Pay attention to it now, and do not allow yourself to be distracted by other thoughts! Remain lucid and calm, and bear in mind what you hear! If you suffer, do not give in to the pain! If restful numbness overtakes you, if you swoon away into a peaceful forgetting—do not surrender yourself to that! Remain watchful and alert!

    The factors which made up the person [the dying person] are about to disperse. Your mental activities are separating themselves from your body, and they are about to enter the intermediary state. Rouse your energy, so that you may enter this state self-possessed and in full consciousness!

I. The moment of death, and the clear light of Pure Reality

First of all there will appear to you, swifter than lightning, the luminous splendor of the colorless light of Emptiness, and that will surround you on all sides. Terrified, you will want to flee from the radiance, and you may well lose consciousness. Try to submerge yourself in that light, giving up all belief in a separate self, all attachment to your illusory ego. Recognize that the boundless Light of this true Reality is your own true self, and you shall be saved!

Few, however, are those who, having missed salvation during their life on earth, can attain it during this brief instant which passes so quickly. The overwhelming majority are shocked into unconsciousness by the terror they feel.

The emergence of a subtle body

If you miss salvation at that moment, you will be forced to have a number of further dreams, both pleasant and unpleasant. Even they offer you a chance to gain understanding, as long as you remain vigilant and alert. A few days after death there suddenly emerges a subtle illusory dream-body, also known as the "mental body." It is impregnated with the after-effects of your past desires, endowed with all sense-faculties, and has the power of unimpeded motion. It can go right through rocks, hills, boulders, and walls, and in an instant it can traverse any distance. Even after the physical sense-organs are dissolved, sights, sounds, smells, tastes, and touches will be perceived, and ideas will be formed. These are the result of the energy still residing in the six kinds of consciousness, the after-affects of what you did with your body and mind in the past. But you must know that all you perceive is a mere vision, a mere illusion, and does not reflect any really existing objects. Have no fear, and form no attachment! View it all evenmindedly, without like or dislike!

II. The experience of the spiritual realities

Three and a half days after your death, Buddhas and Bodhisattvas will for seven days appear to you in their benign and peaceful aspect. Their light will shine upon you, but it will be so radiant that you will scarcely be able to look at it. Wonderful and delightful though they are, the Buddhas may nevertheless frighten you. Do not give in to your fright! Do not run away! Serenely contemplate the spectacle before you! Overcome your fear, and feel no desire! Realize that these are the rays of the grace of the Buddhas, who come to receive you into their Buddha-realms. Pray to them with intense faith and humility, and, in a halo of rainbow light, you will merge into the heart of the divine Father-Mother, and take up your abode in one of the realms of the Buddhas. Thereby you may still at this moment win your salvation.

But if you miss it, you will next, for another seven days, be confronted with the angry deities, and the Guardians of the Faith, surrounded by their followers in tumultuous array, many of them in the form of animals which you have never seen in the life you left. Bathed in multicolored light they stand before you, threatening you and barring your passage. Loud are their voices, with which they shout, "Hit him! Hit him! Kill him! Kill him!" This is what you have to hear, because you turned a deaf ear to the saving truths of religion! All these forms are strange to you, you do not recognize them for what they are. They terrify you beyond words, and yet it is you who have created them. Do not give in to your fright, resist your mental confusion! All this is unreal, and what you see are the contents of your own mind in conflict with itself. All these terrifying deities, witches, and demons around you—fear them not, flee them not! They are but the benevolent Buddhas and Bodhisattvas, changed in their outward aspect. In you alone are the five wisdoms, the source of the benign spirits! In you alone are the five poisons, the source of the angry spirits! It is from your own mind therefore that all this has sprung. What you see here is but the reflection of the contents of your own mind in the mirror of the Void. If at this point you should manage to understand that, the shock of this insight will stun you, your subtle body will disperse into a rainbow, and you will find yourself in paradise among the angels.

III. Seeking rebirth

But if you fail to grasp the meaning of what you were taught, if you still continue to feel a desire to exist as an individual, then you are now doomed to again re-enter the wheel of becoming.

The judgment

You are now before Yama, King of the Dead. In vain will you try to lie, and to deny or conceal the evil deeds you have done. The Judge holds up before you the shining mirror of Karma, wherein all your deeds are reflected. But again you have to deal with dream images, which you yourself have made, and which you project outside, without recognizing them as your own work. The mirror in which Yama seems to read your past is your own memory, and also his judgment is your own. It is you yourself who pronounce your own judgment, which in its turn determines your next rebirth. No terrible God pushes you into it; you go there quite on your own. The shapes of the frightening monsters who take hold of you, place a rope round your neck and drag you along, are just an illusion which you create from the forces within you. Know that apart from these karmic forces there is no Judge of the Dead, no gods, and no demons. Knowing that, you will be free!

The desire for rebirth

At this juncture you will realize that you are dead. You will think, 'I am dead! What shall I do?' and you will feel as miserable as a fish out of water on red-hot embers.

Your consciousness, having no object on which to rest, will be like a feather tossed about by the wind, riding on the horse of breath. At about that time the fierce wind of karma, terrific and hard to bear, will drive you onwards, from behind, in dreadful gusts. And after a while the thought will occur to you, 'O what would I not give to possess a body!' But because you can at first find no place for you to enter into, you will be dissatisfied and have the sensation of being squeezed into cracks and crevices amidst rocks and boulders.

The dawning of the lights of the six places of rebirth

Then there will shine upon you the lights of the six places of rebirth. The light of the place in which you will be reborn will shine most prominently, but it is your own karmic disposition which decides about your choice. The rays of lights which will guide you to the various worlds will seem to you restful and friendly compared with the blinding flash of light which met you at first.

If you have deserved it by your good deeds, a white light will guide you into one of the heavens, and for a while you will have some happiness among the gods. Habits of envy and ambition will attract you to the red light, which leads to rebirth among the warlike Asuras, forever agitated by anger and envy. If you feel drawn to a blue light, you will find yourself again a human being, and well you remember how little happiness that brought you! If you had a heavy and dull mind, you will choose the green light, which leads you to the world of animals, unhappy because insecure and excluded from the knowledge which brings salvation. A ray of dull yellow will lead you to the world of the ghosts, and, finally, a ray of the color of darkish smoke into the hells. Try to desist, if you can! Think of the Buddhas and Bodhisattvas! Recall that all these visions are unreal, control your mind, feel amity towards all that lives! And do not be afraid! You alone are the source of all these different rays. In you alone they exist, and so do the worlds to which they lead. Feel not attracted or repelled, but remain evenminded and calm!

Reincarnation

If so far you have been deaf to the teaching, listen to it now! An overpowering craving will come over you for the sense-experiences which you remember having had in the past, and which through your lack of sense-organs you cannot now have. Your desire for rebirth becomes more and more urgent; it becomes a real torment to you. This desire now racks you; you do not, however, experience it for what it is, but feel it as a deep thirst which parches you as you wander along, harassed, among deserts of burning sands. Whenever you try to take some rest, monstrous forms rise up before you. Some have animal heads on human bodies, others are gigantic birds with huge wings and claws. Their howlings and their whips drive you on, and then a hurricane carries you along, with those demonic beings in hot pursuit. Greatly anxious, you will look for a safe place of refuge.

Everywhere around you, you will see animals and humans in the act of sexual intercourse. You envy them, and the sight attracts you. If your karmic coefficients destine you to become a male, you feel attracted to the females and you hate the males you see. If you are destined to become a female, you will feel love for the males and hatred for the females you see. Do not go near the couples you see, do not try to interpose yourself between them, do not try to take the place of one of them! The feeling which you would then experience would make you faint away, just at the moment when egg and sperm are about to unite. And afterwards you will find that you have been conceived as a human being or as an animal.

Questions for Study

1. What actions should the dying person take to gain paradise?

2. What stages does the dying person go through on the way to paradise?

3. What can go wrong? What are the barriers to paradise? What causes them?

4. What is illusion? What is reality?

5. What characterizes paradise?

ANCIENT PALESTINE

The New Jerusalem (Revelation 21-22:5)

Christianity centers on the life and teachings of Jesus of Nazareth, who was born about 6 B.C. and was crucified about A.D 27. Nazareth was a town in middle Palestine. The story of Jesus is recorded primarily in the opening books of the Christian Bible, the four gospels. Jesus was a Jew who drew many of his teachings from the Hebrew Bible. The most influential interpreter of Jesus's life and teachings was Paul, whose writings consist of letters written to Christian congregations in Rome and the Middle East. Paul held that Jesus was resurrected after his death and went to heaven. Jesus was the anointed one—messiah (Hebrew), christ (Greek)—prophesied in the Hebrew Bible, come to save all people. Through Jesus's resurrection, Paul says, all people who believe in his divinity and follow his teachings will gain eternal life and will dwell with Jesus in heaven.

The Book of Revelation is the last book in the Christian Bible. The narrator—the "I"—of the book is John from the island of Patmos (in the Aegean Sea), who claims to have been given a vision of the end of time. The Book of Revelation is John's prophetic account of Jesus's return to earth to punish the wicked and reward the good. John sees his account as parallel to the creation story in Genesis: Jesus's second coming will be a new creation, similar to the first. John of Patmos was probably the author of the book, about A.D 95, during a time of widespread persecution of Christians by the Roman emperor Domitian. Revelation recounts the apocalyptic upheavals that will precede the return of Jesus at the end of time. The passage reprinted here occurs at the end of the book. It describes the paradise—the New Jerusalem— that Christians will inherit. Paradise will begin with the marriage of Christ, the lamb, with his bride, the New Jerusalem.

21   Then I saw a new heaven and a new earth; for the first heaven and the first earth had passed away, and the sea was no more. [2] And I saw the holy city, the new Jerusalem, coming down out of heaven from God, prepared as a bride adorned for her husband. [3] And I heard a loud voice from the throne saying,

> "See, the home of God is among mortals.
> He will dwell with them as their God;
> they will be his peoples,
> and God himself will be with them;
> [4] he will wipe every tear from their eyes.
> Death will be no more;
> mourning and crying and pain will be no more,
> for the first things have passed away."

5 And the one who was seated on the throne said, "See, I am making all things new." Also he said, "Write this, for these words are trustworthy and true." [6] Then he said to me, "It is done! I am the Alpha and the Omega, the beginning and the end. To the thirsty I will give water as a gift from the spring of the water of life. [7] Those who conquer will inherit these things, and I will be their God and they will be my children. [8] But as for the cowardly, the faithless, the polluted, the murderers, the fornicators, the sorcerers, the idolaters, and all liars, their place will be in the lake that burns with fire and sulfur, which is the second death."

9 Then one of the seven angels who had the seven bowls full of the seven last plagues came and said to me, "Come, I will show you the bride, the wife of the Lamb." [10] And in the spirit he carried me away to a great, high mountain and showed me the holy city Jerusalem coming down out of heaven from God. [11] It has the glory of God and a radiance like a very rare jewel, like jasper, clear as crystal. [12] It has a great, high wall with twelve gates, and at the gates twelve angels, and on

the gates are inscribed the names of the twelve tribes of the Israelites; [13] on the east three gates, on the north three gates, on the south three gates, and on the west three gates. [14] And the wall of the city has twelve foundations, and on them are the twelve names of the twelve apostles of the Lamb.

15 The angel who talked to me had a measuring rod of gold to measure the city and its gates and walls. [16] The city lies foursquare, its length the same as its width; and he measured the city with his rod, fifteen hundred miles; its length and width and height are equal. [17] He also measured its wall, one hundred forty-four cubits [1] by human measurement, which the angel was using. [18] The wall is built of jasper, while the city is pure gold, clear as glass. [19] The foundations of the wall of the city are adorned with every jewel; the first was jasper, the second sapphire, the third agate, the fourth emerald, [20] the fifth onyx, the sixth carnelian, the seventh chrysolite, the eighth beryl, the ninth topaz, the tenth chrysoprase, the eleventh jacinth, the twelfth amethyst. [21] And the twelve gates are twelve pearls, each of the gates is a single pearl, and the street of the city is pure gold, transparent as glass.

22 I saw no temple in the city, for its temple is the Lord God the Almighty and the Lamb. [23] And the city has no need of sun or moon to shine on it, for the glory of God is its light, and its lamp is the Lamb. [24] The nations will walk by its light, and the kings of the earth will bring their glory into it. [25] Its gates will never be shut by day—and there will be no night there. [26] People will bring into it the glory and the honor of the nations. [27] But nothing unclean will enter it, nor anyone who practices abomination or falsehood, but only those who are written in the Lamb's book of life.

22   Then the angel showed me the river of the water of life, bright as crystal, flowing from the throne of God and of the Lamb [2] through the middle of the street of the city. On either side of the river, is the tree of life with its twelve kinds of fruit, producing its fruit each month; and the leaves of the tree are for the healing of the nations. [3] Nothing accursed will be found there any more. But the throne of God and of the Lamb will be in it, and his servants will worship him; [4] they will see his face, and his name will be on their foreheads. [5] And there will be no more night; they need no light of lamp or sun, for the Lord God will be their light, and they will reign forever and ever.

Questions for Study

1. What characterizes this paradise? What images and symbols help describe its qualities?

2. What moral practices are necessary to attain this paradise? What practices prevent people from attaining it?

3. What is the nature of the divinity who inhabits this paradise? How is he described?

---

[1]That is, almost seventy-five yards.

The Ghost Dance at Wounded Knee (Brule Sioux)

After the defeat of General George Armstrong Custer by the Sioux at Little Big Horn in Montana in 1876, the United States Army drove the Sioux onto reservations, where they became impoverished and disheartened. But in 1890 a new Native American religion emerged, the Ghost Dance religion, which featured a belief that the earth, including white people, would be destroyed and Native American ancestors— the ghosts—would return to set up a new Native American age. Fearing a renewed Native American uprising, the white agent at the Pine Ridge Reservation in South Dakota called in the army to suppress a ghost dance. At Wounded Knee Creek, eighteen miles from the reservation, the army opened fire on defenseless men, women, and children, killing 250 of them. The following story was narrated by Dick Fool Bull in 1967 and 1968.

*T*his is a true story; I wish it weren't. When it happened I was a small boy, only about six or seven. To tell the truth, I'm not sure how old I am. I was born before the census takers came in, so there's no record.

When I was a young boy, I liked to stick around my old uncle, because he always had stories to tell. Once he said, "There's something new coming, traveling on the wind. A new dance. A new prayer." He was talking about *Wanagi-wachipi,* the ghost dance. "Short Bull and Kicking Bear traveled far," my uncle told me. "They went to see a holy man of another tribe far in the south, the Piute tribe. They had heard that this holy man could bring dead people to life again, and that he could bring the buffalo back."

My uncle said it was very important, and I must listen closely. Old Unc said:

> This holy man let Short Bull and Kicking Bear look into his hat. There they saw their dead relatives walking about. The holy man told them, "I'll give you something to eat that will kill you, but don't be afraid. I'll bring you back to life again." They believed him. They ate something and died, then found themselves walking in a new, beautiful land. They spoke with their parents and grandparents, and with friends that the white soldiers had killed. Their friends were well, and this new world was like the old one, the one the white man had destroyed. It was full of game, full of antelope and buffalo. The grass was green and high, and though long-dead people from other tribes also lived in this new land, there was peace. All the Indian nations formed one tribe and could understand each

other. Kicking Bear and Short Bull walked around and saw everything, and they were happy. Then the holy man of the Piutes brought them back to life again.

"You have seen it," he told them, "the new Land I'm bringing. The earth will roll up like a blanket with all that bad white man's stuff, the fences and railroads and mines and telegraph poles; and underneath will be our old-young Indian earth with all our relatives come to life again."

Then the holy man taught them a new dance, a new song, a new prayer. He gave them sacred red paint. He even made the sun die: it was all covered with black and disappeared. Then he brought the sun to life again.

Short Bull and Kicking Bear came back bringing us the good news. Now everywhere we are dancing this new dance to roll up the earth, to bring back the dead. A new world is coming.

This Old Unc told me.

Then I saw it myself: the dancing. People were holding each other by the hand, singing, whirling around, looking at the sun. They had a little spruce tree in the middle of the dance circle. They wore special shirts painted with the sun, the moon, the stars, and magpies. They whirled around; they didn't stop dancing.

Some of the dancers fell down in a swoon, as if they were dead. The medicine men fanned them with sweet-smelling cedar smoke and they came to life again. They told the people, "We were dead. We went to the moon and the morning star. We found our dead fathers and mothers there, and we talked to them." When they woke up, these people held in their hands star rocks, moon rocks, different kinds of rocks from those we have on this earth. They clutched strange meats from star and moon animals. The dance leader told them not to be afraid of white men who forbade them to dance this *Wanagi-wachipi.* They told them that the ghost shirts they wore would not let any white man's bullets through. So they danced; I saw it.

The earth never rolled up. The buffalo never came back, and the dead relatives never came to life again. It was the soldier who came; why, nobody knew. The dance was a peaceful one, harming nobody, but I guess the white people thought it was a war dance.

Many people were afraid of what the soldiers would do. We had no guns any more, and hardly had any horses left. We depended on the white man for everything, yet the whites were afraid of us, just as we were afraid of them.

Then when the news spread that Sitting Bull had been killed at Standing Rock for being with the ghost dancers, the people were really scared. Some of the old people said: "Let's go to Pine Ridge and give ourselves up, because the soldiers won't shoot us if we do. Old Red Cloud will protect us. Also, they're handing out rations up there."

So my father and mother and Old Unc got the buggy and their old horse and drove with us children toward Pine Ridge. It was cold and snowing. It wasn't a happy ride; all the grown-ups were worried. Then the soldiers stopped us. They had big fur coats on, bear coats. They were warm and we were freezing, and I remember wishing I had such a coat. They told us to go no further, to stop and make a camp right there. They told the same thing to everybody who came, by foot, or horse, or buggy. So there was a camp, but little to eat and little firewood, and the soldiers made a ring around us and let nobody leave.

Then suddenly there was a strange noise, maybe four, five miles away, like the tearing of a big blanket, the biggest blanket in the world. As soon as he heard it, Old Unc burst into tears. My old ma started to keen as for the dead, and people were running around, weeping, acting crazy.

I asked Old Unc, "Why is everybody crying?"

He said, "They are killing them, they are killing our people over there!"

My father said, "That noise—that's not the ordinary soldier guns. These are the big wagon guns which tear people to bits—into little pieces!" I could not understand it, but everybody was weeping, and I wept too. Then a day later—or was it two? No, I think it was the next day, we passed by there. Old Unc said: "You children might as well see it; look and remember."

There were dead people all over, mostly women and children, in a ravine near a stream called Chankpe-opi Wakpala, Wounded Knee Creek. The people were frozen, lying there in all kinds of postures, their motion frozen too. The soldiers, who were stacking up bodies like firewood, did not like us passing by. They told us to leave there, double-quick or else. Old Unc said: "We'd better do what they say right now, or we'll lie there too."

So we went on toward Pine Ridge, but I had seen. I had seen a dead mother with a dead baby sucking at her breast. The little baby had on a tiny beaded cap with the design of the American flag.

Questions for Study

1. How are the historical circumstances that produced this myth similar to those that produced the Christian myth of the New Jerusalem? How is the content of this myth similar to and different from that of the myth of the New Jerusalem?

2. What characterizes this paradise?

3. How does this paradise contrast with the actual circumstances of the Sioux after 1876?

FOR FURTHER READING

Campbell, Joseph. *Hero with a Thousand Faces.* New York: Pantheon Books, 1949. Campbell became well-known for his treatises on myth. This book deals with the hero myth as it appears in many cultures.

Dundes, Alan, ed. *The Flood Myth.* Berkeley: U of California P, 1988. Dundes collects in this book Flood myths from around the world along with scholarly articles about them.

Dundes, Alan, ed. *Sacred Narrative: Readings in the Theory of Myth.* Berkeley: U of California P, 1984. Dundes's introduction and the scholarly essays in this collection explain many different approaches to the study of myth.

Eliade, Mircea, ed. *From Primitives to Zen: A Thematic Sourcebook of the History of Religions.* New York: Harper & Row, 1967. Eliade, a great scholar of myth, reprints and categorizes here myths from all over the world.

Erdoes, Richard, and Alfonso Ortiz, eds. *American Indian Myths and Legends.* New York: Pantheon Books, 1984. This is a comprehensive anthology of Native American narratives.

Feldmann, Susan, ed. *African Myths and Tales.* New York: Dell, 1963. Feldmann's introduction to this anthology is a thoughtful survey of African narrative.

Hamilton, Edith. *Mythology.* New York: New American Library, 1942. Hamilton retells Greek, Roman, and Norse myths. Her introduction discusses the nature of Greek myths and points to written sources.

Hinnells, John R., ed. *A Handbook of Living Religions.* New York: Penguin, 1984. The essays in this book provide introductions to the religions from which most of the world's myths come.

Hooke, S. H. *Middle Eastern Mythology.* Baltimore: Penguin, 1963. Hooke provides a scholarly treatment of Mesopotamian, Egyptian, Hebrew, and Christian myth, among others.

Patai, Raphael. *Myth and Modern Man.* Englewood Cliffs, NJ: Prentice-Hall, 1972. Patai discusses the secular myths that pervade modern society.

Pokagon, Simon. "Indian Superstitions and Legends." *The Forum.* 35 (July 1898), 618-29. Reprinted in *Native American Folklore in Nineteenth-Century Periodicals.* Ed. William M. Clements. Athens, Ohio: Swallow Press and Ohio UP, 1986. Pokagon, a college-educated Native American, describes the beliefs and myths of his own tribe. He weighs the differences between white and Native American religion.

Sproul, Barbara C., ed. *Primal Myths: Creating the World.* San Francisco: Harper & Row, 1979. Sproul's introduction to this anthology of creation myths is an excellent discussion of the nature of myth. Her headnotes to the many myths included here contain information about the cultures from which the myths come.

Chapter Three
The Epic

INTRODUCTION

An **epic** is a long narrative poem that gives an account of heroic deeds. There are two kinds of epic—*folk epic* and *literary epic.* **Folk epics** originate as oral works. They may at some point be written down but first exist in oral form. **Literary epics** are written imitations of folk epics.

Folk epics typically come from and reflect a preliterate society dominated by a powerful, warlike nobility. They celebrate a long-past heroic age in which kings and great national heroes conducted themselves nobly in military exploits. The purpose of folk epics is to preserve the order of society by extolling traditional values. These values have to do largely with proper behavior in battle, but they also pertain to such social matters as class distinctions, relations between the sexes, and even forms of entertainment.

We do not know the names of the poets who composed the surviving oral epics. But their place in society and methods of composition were similar to those of the poets in ancient Greece. In the so-called Dark Ages of Greece (c. 1150 until 800 B.C.) poets belonged to groups something like craft guilds. They composed their works using traditional stories, recited their compositions at sacred and social occasions, and passed them on from generation to generation. Probably at about the middle of the eighth century B.C., one of these poets, the person we know as Homer, combined stories from the oral tradition into two great works, the *Iliad* and the *Odyssey.* It is possible that Homer was illiterate and that he intended his compositions to be recited over a period of several days. It is likely that he composed his epics at just about the time that writing was rediscovered in Greece and someone immediately wrote them down. Probably each of the folk epics that has survived, from whatever country, came into existence through the efforts of one person, who drew upon a longstanding oral tradition to fashion a single great work, which someone then put into writing.

The form of the ancient epics was determined in part by the needs of the poets. They composed in poetry, which is much easier to memorize than prose. And poetry, because it contains musical devices like onomatopoeia, rhythm, and alliteration, is more pleasing to the ear than prose. Epic poets also used narrative formulas they could insert at will during oral presentations. Such formulas consisted of certain words, phrases, descriptions, and short narratives. We can easily spot them in Homer because he repeats them throughout his epics. Every time he describes the sun rising, he uses some variation of the phrase "Dawn comes early, with rosy fingers." And in the *Odyssey,* he repeats the story of Penelope's tapestry enough times and with so little variation that we recognize it as a set piece, to be inserted in the narrative at opportune moments.

Apart from poetic devices, which vary from culture to culture, the epic has a number of distinctive characteristics. It combines three kinds of narrative: myth, legend, and folktale. A **myth** is a religious story about gods and events that represent the fundamental order of the universe. A **legend** is a story about historical beings who lived in the distant past. Legends may include exaggerations and fictional material, but the characters are thought to have actually lived and to have performed many of the deeds described in the legend. A **folktale** is a short, usually fictional, narrative that belongs to an oral tradition and is told for entertainment. In an epic, the characters and events of myth overlap with those of legend. Interspersed among this material may be folktales, which the characters tell one another for entertainment. The ancient Greeks believed that Agamemnon, Hector, Priam, Achilles, Odysseus, and all the other human participants in the Trojan War really did exist, but in Homer's narratives about them, gods and goddesses influence and interrelate with them.

The heroes and heroines of folk epic are human but nonetheless far superior to average people. They are enough like us that we can identify with them, but they are superior in their skills, bravery, social position, strength, and physical attractiveness. These heroes and heroines, furthermore, take part in events of national, international, and even cosmic importance. Their deeds, needless to say, display all of their heroic qualities to advantage, especially their prowess in battle. The setting of epics is vast in scope. It sometimes encompasses all horizontal space—the entire known geographical world—and all vertical space—from heaven above to hell below. Epics have philosophical depth. They raise disturbing questions about the nature of life and provide few if any easy answers to them. Who, for example, are the forces or divine beings who govern the universe? What is their relationship to us? By what plan or logic do they govern? What is justice? How should the unjust be punished and the just rewarded? Homer's epics show the gods to be capricious and arbitrary, inflicting great suffering and turmoil on mortals, but he makes no attempt to explain why. Epics, as a result, often lack "happy" endings. They sometimes conclude with the heroes defeated, the nation in ruins, the future bleak.

The narrators of folk epics present themselves as all-knowing and completely trustworthy. They take us to the far reaches of the cosmos and give us access to characters' activities and thoughts. They seem trustworthy because they usually have a quasi-divine status. They are not merely masters of traditional stories but act as conduits through which the gods speak. Homer begins his epics by asking the gods (the muses) to help him tell the stories, as if he cannot do it without their help. The language of epic—poetry—not only gives dignity and grandeur to its characters and events but reflects the divine inspiration that epic poets were believed to have had.

Literary (or written) epic is different from folk epic in that its authors do not draw from an oral tradition but consciously imitate the style and formulas of the great surviving folk epics. Authors of literary epics make them more tightly integrated than oral epics by eliminating devices—like repeated stories and phrases—that are useful for oral delivery but unnecessary for reading. Literary epics also have more obvious themes than oral epics. Like folk epics, they include troubling issues, but these issues are resolved more directly and neatly. European authors of literary epics, such as Vergil, Dante, and Milton, imitated the more superficial conventions of Homer's epics. They typically opened with a statement of theme and an invocation of the muse. They began their epics *in medias res* ("in the middle of things") and related important events by means of flashbacks. They included other Homeric conventions such as the catalog (an extended list of armor, weapons, warriors, ships, and armies), the "epic" simile (an elaborately developed analogy), and the long formal speech (delivered by one or more of the characters, often in an assembly in which the participants debate fundamental issues). The limitation of literary epics is that they sometimes seem contrived. They may contain many of the more obvious conventions of folk epics but often lack the vigor and substance of the earlier form.

The earliest folk epics were composed by the Sumerians and take place during a heroic age that existed sometime before 3000 B.C. The Babylonian *Epic of Gilgamesh* (c. 2700 B.C.), derived from Sumerian narratives, tells the story of Gilgamesh, King of Uruk, half human and half divine, who quests for and loses the chance to become immortal. Homer's *Iliad* and *Odyssey,* perhaps the best-known folk epics, were composed around the eighth century B.C. Other folk epics include the *Mahabharata* (Indian, about 1000 B.C.), *Beowulf* (English, A.D. 700-900), the *Cid* (Spanish, twelfth century), the *Song of Roland* (French, twelfth century), and the *Nibelungenlied* (German, thirteenth century). Three great literary epics are Vergil's *Aeneid* (30-19 B.C.), Dante's *The Divine Comedy* (A.D. 1300-21), and Milton's *Paradise Lost* (1667).

Beowulf

In the fifth century A.D. Germanic tribes from northern Europe—the Angles, Saxons, and Jutes—invaded the British Isles; ultimately these groups became the dominant groups there. The anonymous author of

the folk epic *Beowulf* was a descendent of those invaders. He probably lived in the eighth century A.D., although some scholars place him
as late as the tenth century. He was a Christian who fashioned his
poem from a long-standing oral tradition of Germanic epic poetry. This
tradition dealt with the heroic activities of Germanic tribes before they
had been converted to Christianity. Although the author weaves Christian references into his material, the pagan beliefs and practices of the
characters in the poem dominate its value system and atmosphere.

The characters in *Beowulf* belong to tribes that lived in Denmark
and Sweden. Some of the characters, like Beowulf and the monsters,
are fictional, but others were real people, whose actions are recorded
in legends, contemporary accounts, and archeological finds. Hygelac
defeated Ongentheow about A.D. 510. Ingeld married Freawaru about
518. Hygelac was killed in a raid in the Rhineland about 521. Hrothgar
died about 525. Heorot was burned to the ground about 520. And
Onla invaded Geatish territory and killed Heardred about 533. The relative certainty of these dates allows scholars to place the time of the
action in *Beowulf* in the sixth century A.D.

Beowulf offers many challenges to our interpretive skills. At first
glance, it seems like a fairly straightforward story. It tells how Beowulf
fights and slays three monsters and thereby establishes his heroic
stature. *Beowulf* can be understood and enjoyed purely on this level of
heroic action. But a careful reading shows *Beowulf* to be a dense and
complicated story, a quality that makes the epic thematically richer
than if it were solely about a hero's struggle against monsters. One
complicating factor is in the third episode—Beowulf's fight against the
dragon—which occurs decades after the first two episodes. *Beowulf* is
by then an old man. He is very different from the Beowulf who kills
Grendel and Grendel's mother, and the outcome is different. As we
read this episode, we are challenged to compare it with the earlier ones
and to figure out why the author included it.

A further complication in *Beowulf* is the conflict between the
author's Christian beliefs and the pagan beliefs of the characters in the
story. There are two "gods" in *Beowulf*. One is the Christian god of justice and mercy; the other is the pagan god, an amorphous deity or force
that the characters refer to as "Fate." (The Old English word for "fate"
is *wyrd*.) These two gods seem very different. And the values of the two
religions are different as well. Christianity urges peace, humility, and
reconciliation; the pagan religion inspires boastfulness, heroism in battle, and revenge. The ultimate reward for the Christian is heaven; the
reward for the pagan hero is treasure and fame. We wonder why the
author mixes these different religious systems. Does he intend a
Christian criticism of the Germanic pagan culture? Is Beowulf himself
an object of criticism? Does the whole poem lead to a Christian message? Or are the Christian elements basically meaningless?

The most confusing element of *Beowulf* is the flashbacks and flashforwards to tribal and intertribal events. These stories are hard to understand. The author assumes that we already know them, and therefore introduces them abruptly, incompletely, and out of chronological order. It is hard to keep the names and events straight, to remember what happened when and to whom. But the tribal history in *Beowulf* is important. It serves as a commentary on the main story. You can easily understand and enjoy the three accounts of Beowulf's heroic fights with the monsters, but those who take the trouble to connect the apparently "extra" material to the Beowulf story will discover a rich tapestry of themes. The translator has placed the digressions about tribal history and the allusions to the Bible in italics, so that you can spot when the narrative departs from the main story. The summary of action and the genealogical tables on pp. 160–162 will help you sort out people and events.

The key tribes in *Beowulf* are the Danes, the Geats, and the Swedes. The Danes dwell on a large island called Zealand (the location of present-day Copenhagen). This is the tribe of which Hrothgar is chief or "king." Across a narrow strait from Zealand is Weathermark (the southern tip of Sweden), where the Geats (Beowulf's tribe) live. When Beowulf sails to Denmark to help Hrothgar, Hygelac (Beowulf's uncle) is the king of the Geats. Ultimately Beowulf becomes king of the Geats. The Swedes live to the north of the Geats. The Danes are linked to the Swedes by marriage (Hrothgar's sister married Onla, the king of the Swedes at the beginning of *Beowulf*). The Geats have a longstanding feud with the Swedes that will apparently continue after Beowulf's death.

The cultural practice that governs tribal relationships in *Beowulf* is the duty to avenge the killing of a kinsman. Germanic custom assumed that if one's kinsman was slain, then one either had to kill the slayer or exact a *wergild* ("man gold" or "man price") from him in the form of an appropriate treasure. This duty held true even if the death was accidental. The result was that anytime one tribe fought another and someone was killed, unless a *wergild* was paid, the desire for revenge would smolder, sometimes for years, until warfare broke out anew. The tribes tried to assuage warlike passions through political marriages, but to little avail. The backdrop of *Beowulf,* then, is a seemingly endless cycle of killing, revenge, and counter-revenge. Readers can get a sense of this melancholy state of affairs without necessarily understanding all the details of tribal relationships. The cumulative effect of these details is a pervasive sense of doom, especially in the final episode of the poem.

Beowulf is written in Old English, a Germanic language that is the basis for modern English but that is incomprehensible to speakers of modern English without careful study. The poetic form of *Beowulf*

consists of a series of lines each of which contains four stressed syllables. Each line is divided into two parts by a strong pause (caesura), so
that each half of the line has two stressed syllables. The number of
unstressed syllables varies from line to line. The line is "bound"
together by alliteration: the initial consonant of the third stressed syllable rhymes with the initial consonant of one or both of the first two
stressed syllables. In modern English, such a line would look something like this:

Germanic epic poetry in its oral form was recited by a *shope* or bard
who accompanied his recital by the rhythmic strumming of a lyre.

Marijane Osborn's translation of *Beowulf*, reprinted here,
attempts to provide a readable version of the poem and yet retain some
of the poetic characteristics of the original. All versions of *Beowulf* are
based on one tenth-century manuscript, located in the British Museum.
There is no other source for the poem.

> What of the Spear-Danes° in days of yore?
> We have heard of the glory of the great folk-leaders,
> how those athelings° did arduous deeds!
>
> Often Shield Shefing shattered the courage
> 5   of troops of marauders by taking their mead-seats.
> He terrified those nobles—long after the time
> he appeared as a foundling. Comfort for that fate
> came when he grew and prospered in glory
> until those who lived in the neighboring lands
> 10 over the whale's road° had to obey him,
> yield him tribute. Yes—a good king!
>
> Later a boy was born to Shield,
> a young lad in his house, the hope of the Danes,
> whom God had sent them, perceiving their need,
> 15 how they had suffered with no king to sustain them
> for far too long. The Lord of Life,

---

[1]*Spear-Danes. Beowulf* opens with a thumbnail sketch of Hrothgar's ancestry. (See the genealogical table on p.
160.) The founder of Hrothgar's tribe was Shield (the Danes are called the "Shieldings," meaning "sons of Shield").
His son was a Beowulf (not the hero of the poem), and Beowulf's son was Halfdane, Hrothgar's father. We get
glimpses of the unhappy future of the Danes later in *Beowulf* (see ll. 2020-69). The Danes are referred to variously
as Spear-Danes, South-Danes, East-Danes, North-Danes, West-Danes, Bright-Danes, etc.
[3]*athelings.* Noblemen.
[10]*whale's road.* The sea.

the Wielder of Glory, gave worldly honor
to Shield's son among the South-Danes.
Beowulf was famous—his glory spread far.
20   Thus a young warrior should strive to be worthy:
giving freely, while still in his father's care.
In later days, then, friends will leap
to stand beside him when strife comes—
companions will serve him. By praiseworthy deeds
25   a man shall prosper among people everywhere.
Shield, when old and his hour had come,
turned away into the Lord's protection.
His loving companions carried him out
to the ocean's edge as he had ordered
30   when still he could speak as the Shielding's lord;
long had that dear prince ruled in the land.
Shining in the harbor, a ring-prowed ship
stood icy and eager, the atheling's vessel.
There they laid their beloved lord,
35   their giver of rings, that glorious man,
on the deck by the mast among many treasures,
fine things from foreign lands.

Never was ship more nobly adorned
with battle weapons and garments of war,
40   with blades and with byrnies!° On his breast they laid
many a gift that would go with him
in his far wanderings over the waves.
They girded him round with ancient gold
more generously on that final journey
45   than those folk did who set him adrift
alone on chill seas when only a child.
At the last they set up a golden standard
high over his head, then let the waves have him—
gave him to the sea. Their hearts were sad
50   and mournful their minds, for men cannot know,
neither hall-councillors nor heroes under Heaven,
how to say what hands received that cargo.

1. Ancient Beginnings

Then in the strongholds the son of Shield,
Beowulf the Dane, grew dear to his people

40*byrnies.* Coats of mail. Mail is a cloth-like armor woven of small metal links.

55   as a famous king when his father, in dying,
had gone from the land. Late in life
he sired Halfdane, who held the proud Shieldings
until gray with age, a grim old warrior.
Four sons and daughters he fathered all told,
60   and brought them up to be great rulers:
Heorogar and Hrothgar and Halga the Good,
and an excellent daughter, who was Onla's queen,
beloved wife of the Swedish war-king.

Then Hrothgar was granted glory in battle,
65   success in the field, which ensured that his friends
obeyed him eagerly, until that band grew
to a mighty troop. It came to his mind then
that he would command that a huge mead° building
be made for his warriors, a mighty hall
70   which the sons of men should hear of forever.
And he would apportion out to his people
all that God had given him,
except for shared lands and the lives of men.
I have heard that then through the whole world
75   craftsmen of many kinds were ordered
to make that place fair. In due course it befell
that Hrothgar's pride and joy was completed,
the greatest of halls. He named it Heorot—
his word was law throughout the land.
80   He kept his vow and gave rings of value
as banquet treasures. The building towered
high and wide-gabled—awaiting the hostile
leap of flames. But it was a long time yet
before the sword-hatred of a son-in-law
85   should wake to avenge a wicked slaughter.

In these days a spirit who dwelt in darkness
was growing more agonized in his anger
each time that he heard the joy in the hall
ring out anew. The round-harp hummed,
90   the clear song of the *shope.*° He sang who knew well
about the ancient beginnings of men.
He said the Almighty made the world,
the shining plain encircled by water,
exulting set out the sun and moon

---

[68]*mead.* An alcoholic beverage made of water, honey, malt, and yeast.
[90]*shope.* An Old English word for poet or bard.

95   as lamps to give light to land dwellers,
      and fairly adorned the fields of earth
      with limbs and leaves. Then he made life
      for every kind of creature that moves.
      And so the lordly ones lived in delight
100   and happy ease, until One began
      to perform evil deeds, a fiend from Hell—
      that grim spirit was called Grendel!

105   *Long he lived mournful in demon's lair*
      after the Creator had cast out Cain°
      and all his kindred for the killing of Abel—
      the Lord everlasting avenged that blow!
      No joy had Cain in that jealous feud
110   *when the Maker had driven him far from mankind.*
      From his loins were born the uncanny beings,
      giants and orcs and evil elves,
      and also the titans who long contended
      against God. He gave them their due!

2. The Coming of Grendel

115   The fall of night brought Grendel forth
      to see how the Danes, with their drinking done,
      had gone to rest in that gabled hall.
      He found there, sleeping after the feast,
      a band of warriors, quite unaware
120   of the woes of men—so the vengeful monster,
      grim in his wrath, was ready at once
      to rage upon them! From rest he plucked
      thirty thanes, and, thrilled with his plunder,
      darted away to his own den,
125   making for home with a sackful of murder.

      When dawn came, the light of day
      revealed Grendel's skill at slaughter;
      and then festivity turned to woe—
      sad songs in the morning. Mighty Hrothgar,
130   that famous ruler, wrapped in anguish,
      wept at the death of his warrior-thanes.°

---

[106]*Cain.* According to the biblical account (Genesis 4.1-16), Cain's murder of his brother Abel was the first murder, a result of Adam and Eve's sin. See p. 48 for the account.
[131]*warrior-thanes.* Sworn followers of the king.

Others found the monster's footprints,
a signature that foretold a strife
too long, too difficult. And without delay,
135   the next night, indeed, he began anew
with more killing, and had no qualms
about that feud—he was too fixed on it!
Then he who sought a sleeping place
somewhere else was easy to find—
140   in the women's bowers. For who would brave
the violence of that new hall-vassal
once he had seen it?

They kept themselves then
at a safer distance away from the demon,
and Grendel ruled and raged against mankind,
145   alone and evil, until empty stood
the best of houses. That was a hard time,
twelve long winters of bitter woe.
The king of the Danes had to endure
this cruel affliction, and it became
150   as familiar to the sons of men
as a well-known song, that Grendel waged
war against Hrothgar, with hateful attacks
and murderous forays for many a season,
a permanent feud. He wanted no peace.
155   To stop killing the Danish kindred
or settle with gold was no goal of his—
no hall-lord had any reason to hope
for bright compensation from that slayer's hand!
No, that demon, that dark death-shadow,
160   leapt out upon young and old alike,
a hideous ambush! In darkness he held
the misty moors. Men cannot know
whither such hell-wights bend their ways!
Thus mankind's foe carried on the feud.
165   That fiend in exile often performed
ghastly deeds; and he dwelt in Heorot,
the gold-decked hall, in the dead of night
(but close to that gift-throne he could not come,
draw nigh the lord's treasure, nor know his love).
170   To the lord of the Danes his dwelling there
was heart-breaking torment. Others took
more active council: they cast about
in secret to discover what could be done
to stem the tide of sudden attacks.

175 At times they vowed in idol-tents
       to sacrifice, in ancient phrases
       seeking aid from the slayer of souls°
       in their deep sorrow.
            Such was their wont,
       the hope of the heathens; in their hearts they thought of
180 *Hell below. They knew not the Lord,*
       the Judge of Deeds, or how to rejoice
       in trusting God, the Protector in Heaven,
       the Wielder of Glory. Woe be to him
       who because of strife must shove his soul
185 *to the heart of the fire! He cannot hope*
       for help or change, ever. Happy is he
       who may seek out the Lord on his last day
       and ask for peace in the Father's embrace!

3. Beowulf Goes to the Land of the Danes

       Despite his wisdom, Halfdane's son
190 could not stop turning over his troubles
       in that painful time, or suppress his worry—
       the strife was too cruel that had stricken his people,
       a grim persecution, the greatest night-terror.
       But Grendel's deeds were told to a Geat
195 in his far homeland, to Hygelac's thane.°

       He was the mightiest man in the world
       in those long ago days of this fleeting life,
       and noble of purpose. He ordered prepared
       a goodly ship, and said he would go
200 over the swan's road to seek out Hrothgar,
       knowing that prince had need of men.
       His wise friends did not find fault
       with him for that daring, though he was dear to them;
       indeed, they encouraged him, casting lots
205 for his coming venture, and the valiant fighter
       chose from among the Geatish champions
       the bravest he could find. Then Beowulf went forth
       as one of fifteen, a sea-crafty warrior
       who showed them, by landmarks, the way to his ship.
210 The moments passed; the men waited.

---

[177] *slayer of souls.* The devil.
[195] *thane.* Sworn follower.

When the vessel was well afloat on the waves
they clambered aboard beside the cliff
where the currents whirled, carrying treasures
into that hold, handsome weapons
215   and splendid armor. Then they cast off
on a willing journey in their ship of wood.

Thrust by the wind over billowing waves,
it flew through the foam as free as a bird,
and sailed so far by the following day
220   that sailors perched in that twisted prow
could make out the shining shapes of land:
bright seacliffs, broad headlands,
then sharp rocky crags. They had crossed the ocean;
the voyage was over. Eagerly now,
225   they leapt ashore to anchor their ship,
their ring-mail° singing as they moved around.
But they paused to give their thanks to God
for an easy passage on the perilous sea.

From the high sea wall someone was watching;
230   the Shielding whose task was to guard that shore
saw them lift their shields from the side of the ship,
ready for battle. Bursting with curiosity,
wondering what kind of men these were,
Hrothgar's sentinel leapt to his saddle,
235   rode down to the shore, and shook his spear
in a mighty fist, though his words were formal:
"Who are you, coming here in armor,
a band of men in byrnies, steering
your high-keeled ship down the ocean streets,
240   across the water? Look, I have watched here
at this land's end for a long time
to make certain that no sea-invader
would disembark on the Danish shore,
and never have warriors borne weapons here
245   more openly! Nor do you offer
any sign of the elders' consent.
And never in the world have I seen a more noble
man in armor tower above others
than him in your midst; that is no mere hall-thane
250   made proud with weapons—may his appearance
never prove false! But now, inform me

226*ring-mail.* Mail.

of your kindred before you come any farther
on Danish soil—you might be spies!
Listen to me, sea-faring men
255   far from your homes, I have one thought,
and here it is: you had better hurry
and tell me clearly where you have come from!"

4. His Reply to the Sentinel's Challenge

The leader among them made his reply,
wisely unlocked his hoard of words:
260   "You are looking at men from the land of the Geats;
we are Hygelac's hearth companions.
My father, familiar to men everywhere,
was a noble prince whose name was Edgetheow.
He lived many winters before passing away,
265   aged and honored; the elders who offer
advice to kings recall him well.
With friendly intent we have come very far
to seek your lord, the son of Halfdane,
guide of his people. Give us advice!
270   How shall we approach your proud leader
to make known our mission? There can be nothing
secret about it, for surely you know
whether it is true, as we have been told,
that among the Danes some dire being
275   shows hatred by his deeds in the dead of night;
uncannily hostile, he causes terror
with a grim corpse-hunger! I have come to Hrothgar
to offer help with an open heart,
to aid that good king in overcoming
280   the fiend—if change from this evil affliction
can ever grant him relief again—
and then his burning cares will be cooler;
or else he will have to endure forever
a life of distress, so long as there stands
285   the best of houses in its high place!"

The sentinel spoke where he sat before them,
brave on his warhorse: "Words and deeds
are two things that an intelligent man
must learn to assess if he means to succeed.
290   I hear you tell me that you intend

loyal service to the Shielding's lord.
Come then, with your weapons; I will show you the way.
Moreover, my thanes will be ordered to guard
your freshly tarred ship, to shield it well
295   against all marauders while it rests by the shore—
until the time comes that its coiled prow
is launched on the currents to carry you back
across the waves to Weathermark,
along with those brave men you have brought
300   who have the luck to survive with their lives!"
Then he turned his horse. Behind them remained
the roomy vessel bound by a rope,
lying at anchor.

　　Likenesses of boars
above their cheekplates, bright with gold,
305   shone wondrously, warlike shapes
keeping guard over life. The Geats hurried,
marching together until they could glimpse
that great timbered hall with its golden roof.
No building there was in all the world
310   more famous than this ruler's fortress—
its light shone out over many lands!

Pointing the way to that warriors' hall,
the sentinel instructed them
how to approach it, then turning his horse,
315   bade them farewell in a few words:
"Now I must go. May God almighty
hold you with honor and keep you unharmed
in your brave venture. Back to the sea
I must go to keep watch against invaders."

5. The Road to Heorot

320   Down the wide path paved with stone
the men walked together. Their byrnies gleamed;
the hand-locked rings in that hardy armor
sang as the warriors went along
the road to the hall. When they arrived there,
325   tired from seafaring, they set down their shields,
wondrously strong, against the wall,
then sank to the bench. Again their byrnies
rang out in song, and the spears stood
all together where the Geats had placed them,

330   an ash-grove with iron-gray leaves. Those athelings
       had worthy weapons!

           Then a warrior came out
       to inquire of the strangers what their kindred was.
       "Whence do you bring those brilliant shields,
       gray sarks° and grim masked helmets,
335   and all those iron spears? I am Hrothgar's
       official spokesman, and may I say
       that I've never seen a troop more bravely attired?
       I suspect neither exile nor piracy
       will have prompted your coming, but courage and pride
340   have led you to Hrothgar."

           Their leader answered,
       selecting his words in a lordly manner,
       strong under his helmet: "We are Hygelac's
       boon companions. Beowulf is my name.
       I wish to tell Halfdane's son himself,
345   that noble ruler, the nature of
       the cause that brings me, if he will accord us
       the honor of approaching such a princely man."

       Wulfgar spoke; a high-ranking Wendel,°
       his clever mind was known to many,
350   along with his prowess in war, and his wisdom:
       "I shall inquire of our king,
       the friend and lord of the Danish folk
       and their giver of rings, about granting you
       leave to approach him, our famous leader,
355   and I shall return at once to tell you
       whatever it pleases him to reply."
       Quickly he strode to where the king
       sat inside, with his silver hair
       shining among friends; before his shoulder
360   Wulfgar, according to noble custom,
       stood, and spoke freely to his friendly lord:
       "We have visitors who have voyaged far
       to come here, sir, seafaring Geats.
       The leader of these athelings
365   is called Beowulf, and they request
       permission to enter, that they might hold speech
       with my noble lord. Do not deny them

334*sarks*. Mail coats.
348*Wendel*. Geat. Wendel is an area in Sweden.

a kindly answer, O gracious king!
In war equipment they appear worthy
370 of our esteem. Indeed, that earl
did well who guided these warriors hither."

6. Beowulf's Request

Hrothgar spoke, lord of the Shieldings:
"Beowulf? I knew him when he was a boy.
His father was Edgetheow. For his fealty
King Hrethel gave him the Geatish princess,
375 his own daughter, to adorn his home.
Now his son comes seeking our friendship.
Already those who rove the seas
bearing our courtesy gifts to the Geats,
bright treasures of gold, tell tales of him,
380 that he has the might of thirty men
in the grip of his hand. Perhaps holy God
has sent him to us as a sign of hope
for the West Danes—would this were true!—
against Grendel's horror. To that good man
385 I shall offer gifts to honor his courage.
Go now, quickly, tell them to come in
and see how good kinsmen gather together.
Say also these words: their coming is welcome
to the Danish people!"

Turning to the door,
390 Wulfgar spoke from just inside:
"My master, the lord of the Danes, commands me
to say he knows your noble lineage,
and invites you, who have so bravely ventured
across the waves, to be welcome here.
395 You may enter, in all your war-equipment,
even your helmets, to approach Hrothgar;
but let your shields and those dangerous shafts
await out here the result of your words."
Beowulf arose then, and around him his men,
400 a notable troop; he entrusted some
with guarding the weapons while he went inside.
They marched together as the messenger led them
under Heorot's roof. The hardy warrior
went in his helmet to stand on the hearth,
405 where his byrnie sparkled as he spoke

(that battle-net linked with a smith's lively skill):
"Health to Hrothgar! I am Hygelac's
kinsman and thane. Many things I have done
that are famous already. This affair of Grendel
410   was related to me in my own land
by travelers, who told us that this timbered hall,
the best of buildings, made for brave men,
stands empty and useless when the evening light,
fair in the heavens, fades from the sky.

415   "My own kinsmen and the wisest of the councillors,
and the best among us, O mighty Hrothgar,
persuaded me that I should seek you
because they knew my enormous strength,
and had seen my courage that time when I came
420   bloody from a fight where I captured five
of our huge enemies in a hard battle,
then killed, by night, a number of sea monsters,
totally crushed them—they had courted trouble!—
avenging the Geats. Now it is Grendel's turn.
425   Now I should like to hold, alone,
a meeting with that monster, if you will permit me.
Chief of the Danes, champion of the Shieldings,
I ask one boon (do not forbid me!):
Allow me, noble lord of warriors,
430   protector of the folk, now I have come so far,
to attempt alone, with only my troop,
this brave company, to cleanse Heorot!

"And because I gather that Grendel rashly
spurns all weapons, I also wish
435   (in order to please my own dear prince
Hygelac, and make him proud of me)
to lay aside my shining sword
and yellow shield, and show that demon
a fight to the death, foe against foe,
440   with my grip alone! Then he who loses
must give himself up to the judgment of God.

"But if that fiend should win the fight
in this place of battle, I think that upon
the Geats he will feed . . . as on Danish folk
445   he has often been sated. So you need not consider
where to hide my head, for he will have me
dripping with blood, if death takes me.

He will bear me away, his mouth watering,
to taste my flesh, tearing it ruthlessly,

450   staining the moors. So do not distress
yourself concerning my body, but send
this best of byrnies, if battle takes me,
to Hygelac, for it is Hrethel's heirloom,
the work of Wayland, that I wear on my breast,

455   the finest of garments. Fate goes as it must!"

7. Hrothgar's Acceptance

Hrothgar spoke, lord of the Shieldings:
"Both from duty, my friend Beowulf,
and a sense of kindness you have come to us.
Your father started the greatest of feuds

460   when by his own hand he slew Heatholaf
among the Wylfings; the Geats were wary
of defending their friend with a feud in the offing,
so he came away to the kingdom of the Danes,
overseas to the Shieldings, and they sheltered him.

465   All this happened when, as a youth,
I had just come to power in the jewelled kingdom,
the bright stronghold of the Danes. My brother
Heorogar had died, a son of Halfdane
born before me; he was better than I!

470   But I settled that feud by sending gifts
to the Wylfings over the water's ridge.
I sent them treasures, and he swore me oaths.

"Hard it is to say from my heart
to any man what misery,

475   what havoc Grendel has wrought with his hatred,
what harm he has done us. My dear hall-troop
of warriors has waned; *wyrd*° has swept them
into Grendel's power. But God may easily
deprive that desperate foe of deeds!

480   Often it has been that able men
have boasted loudly over their beer
that they would defy the fiend's attack
with fierce blades, and hold the hall—
and then in the morning there would only remain

485   the marks of their blood on this noble building,
the planks of the benches painted with gore,

---

477 *wyrd.* Fate.

the hall, with their lives. Of loyal men
I would have the fewer when that fight was done . . .

"Sit now to the feast and unfetter your thoughts,
490   pledge great deeds as your mood may prompt you!"
Then room was made in that friendly mead-hall
for all the Geats to sit together
on the drinking benches, and those doughty men
went to their places. A thane was watchful
495   of their every need, and from the ale-vessel
poured shining liquid. At times the shope
sang in the hall, and happiness reigned
over all that gathering of Danes and Geats.

8. Unferth's Taunt

Unferth spoke; the son of Edgelaf,
500   who sat at the feet of the Shielding lord,
unbound his battle-runes.° Beowulf's voyage
and his noble venture rankled enormously,
for Unferth begrudged any greatness in others,
and found it offensive if they earned more fame
505   under the heavens than he himself—:
"Are you that Beowulf who strove against Breca
across the sea in a swimming contest,
where the two of you recklessly risked your lives
on the high seas for a heedless boast?
510   They say that nobody could dissuade you,
neither friend nor foe, from that fruitless act
of wilful pride. You swam through the water,
arching your arms through the ocean currents,
weaving the waves, drawing hand after hand,
515   gliding on the sea; then suddenly the billows
swelled in a storm, and you struggled there
for seven nights. But Breca outswam you;
he had more strength. And a morning dawned
when the tide had hurled him on the Heatho-Raemes' shore.
520   He went on home then, a hero to his people
in the land of the Brondings where he belonged,
and was soon entrusted with treasure and kingdom
in that mighty fortress. In his match against you,
Breca entirely fulfilled his boast.
525   I wonder if you will not come off the worse

501*unbound his battle-runes.* Began to speak brusquely.

in this venture, too (though you have prevailed
in many grim battles), if you dare to remain
waiting in this hall for a whole night."
Beowulf spoke, the son of Edgetheow:

530 "Well, Unferth, my friend, being full of beer,
you have much to say about my swim
with Breca! But truly I tell you this:
my strength was greater against the sea
and the angry waves than any other man's.

535 The two of us vowed, being very young—
we were both only boys when we made this boast—
to venture out on the wild ocean
and dare to risk our lives. And we did it!
As we breasted the waves, we held naked blades

540 fiercely in our hands to defend ourselves
against the great whales. Breca could not gain
any distance from me in that mighty current
through the speed of his stroke, nor did I wish to spurt
away from him, so together in the waves

545 we swam for five nights, until swept asunder
by the swelling waters of the coldest weather,
as night grew dark and a wind from the north
turned wildly against us.

       "The rough waves
aroused the fury of the great fishes,

550 and there my hand-locked mail helped me;
my byrnie defended me from those foes,
where, woven for battle, it lay on my breast
adorned with gold. Drawing me down,
a fierce monster held me fast

555 in his ugly grip. But it was granted
that I should touch that beast with the tip
of my blade, and the storm of battle destroyed
the huge sea-creature through my hand . . .

9. Credentials of Courage

"Those predators, pressing in upon me,

560 harassed me sorely. But I served them well
and justly with my jewelled sword.
At their feast below those foul spoilers
had little pleasure; they had planned to partake
of me, at their banquet on the ocean bottom!

565 But the following morning they were flotsam, lying
along the shore, put to sleep by my blade,
hurt so severely that voyagers
have never since been hindered in sailing
their ships on those seas. From the east shone
570 God's bright beacon; the billowing waves
grew calm, and then I saw cliffs ahead,
a windy land. *Wyrd* often saves
the undoomed hero if his courage holds!

"In the end my sword appeared to have slain
575 nine sea-beasts. Never have I heard of
a harder night battle under heaven's vault,
nor a man more forlorn among the waves;
but I survived the violent clutch
of those foes, and weary from the fight was swept
580 by the flooding tides onto Finnmark° shores,
left high and dry.

"I have not heard
that you have brandished your flashing blade
in battles so wild. Breca has never,
nor indeed, either of you, yet done
585 anything comparable in the way of conflict
with the blood-gleaming sword—I do not boast overmuch—
though one must remember your brother's murder,
and he your own kinsman! For that deed, Hell
will claim you someday, clever though you are.

590 "I say to you truly, son of Edgelaf,
that demon would never have done so many
crimes so insulting to your king,
such harm in Heorot, if your own heart
were half so brave as you yourself boast;
595 he has found out that he need not fear
an avenging storm of violent blades,
the feuding swords of the brave Shieldings.
He takes his toll, sparing none
of the Danish people, takes his pleasure,
600 puts them to death and expects no reprisal
from the Danes of the Spear. But soon enough
I shall show him the strength and courage
of a Geatish warrior! And whoever wishes
can go bravely to mead after tomorrow's

---

580 *Finnmark.* Lapland.

605   morning light shines for men,
       when the radiant sun rises in the south!"
       Then Hrothgar, the giver of rings, was glad.
       The brave old chieftain of the Bright Danes,
       the leader of those people, who had longed for help,
610   had faith in Beowulf's firm resolution.
       When the jesting of heroes rose joyously
       and words were winsome, Wealtheow came forth,
       Hrothgar's queen, mindful of kinship.
       That gold-laden lady, greeting the men,
615   handed the cup around the hall,
       first to the lord who guarded that land,
       the dear home of his people. She bade him take pleasure
       in his drink from the cup, and the noble king
       gladly partook of the shining goblet.
620   Then the Helming° lady went through the hall
       to young and old, letting each man use
       the cup in his turn, until the time came
       that the ring-laden queen in courtesy
       bore the mead-cup to Beowulf.
625   She greeted the prince, and piously thanked God
       that the course she desired had come to pass—
       that now she could count on someone for comfort
       from the wicked deeds.

      The fierce warrior
       accepted the cup that the queen held out.
630   He drank, and then, sonorous, inspired by the challenge,
       Beowulf spoke, Edgetheow's son:
       "I resolved, when first I set out to sea,
       when I boarded that ship with my band of men,
       that I would fully perform the wish
635   of your people, or fall in the fight, caught fast
       in that horrible claw. I shall behave
       with fitting courage, or my final day
       shall come to meet me in this mead-hall!"
       The woman liked well those noble words
640   of the Geat's pledge; gold-laden she went
       to sit in splendor beside her lord.
       Then, as before, the sounds were fair
       inside that hall, the warriors happy,
       their tales brave, until the time came
645   that Halfdane's son wanted to seek
       his evening rest; he knew that the enemy

620*Helming.* Wealtheow's tribe, the Helmings.

had longed to do battle in that high building
from the time they had seen the sun's first light
until nightfall lengthened across the land
650 and shadows came moving in dark shapes
under the clouds.

The company all rose.
Hrothgar the king spoke to his hero,
offering Beowulf the best of luck,
and rule of his wine-hall, saying these words:
655 "I have never entrusted to another man,
so long as I have been able to lift my shield,
lordship in this hall but to you alone.
Take now and hold the best of houses,
remember fame, hold fast to valor,
660 watch against the foe! You shall want for nothing,
if you come through alive from this deed of courage!"

10. The Watch for Grendel

Then out from Heorot Hrothgar went,
the lord of the Shieldings, with his loyal thanes;
the old warrior wanted to seek his wife,
665 his consort Wealtheow, and the comfort of bed.
Men soon discovered that the King of Glory,
in special dispensation, had set a hall-watch
against Grendel, a guard against giants.
In his great strength the prince of the Geats
670 trusted fully—and in God's friendship.
That warrior removed his woven mail-coat,
the helmet from his head, and handed his sword,
the finest iron blade, to a friendly thane,
bade him take care of that battle gear.

675 Then Beowulf, before he climbed into his bed,
reflected on some of his former words:
"I take no less pride in my martial prowess,
in my hardy fighting, than Grendel in his.
Thus with the sword I shall not slay him,
680 kill him with that weapon, though I certainly could;
he would not understand how to strike back
with blade against shield, though he is brave enough
in his wicked strength. So this night we abstain
from the sword altogether, if Grendel dares seek

685 a war without weapons, and then wise God,
the holy Lord, on whichever hand
seems fitting, will assign the victor's fame."

Putting his face to the pillow, the warrior
began to rest, and around him many
690 a brave man sank to sleep in the hall.
Not one of those thanes thought for a moment
that he would live to return to his beloved
home, his kindred, and the hall he was raised in;
they had been told that death had taken
695 very many before them in that mead-hall,
too many good Danes. But the Maker granted
that the fight of the Weathergeats would be woven
with battle victory, that they would vanquish
their strange foe through the strength of one,
700 through his own power. Truly, forever,
mighty God has ruled mankind;
this is known.

In the night he came—
the shadow walker! The warriors slept
who were trusted to guard that gabled hall,
705 all but one. This was known also:
that Grendel could not, when God did not wish it,
draw them under the demon shadow.
But one man lay there, watchful, and waiting
in anger for the enemy and the outcome of that fight.

11. The Fight with Grendel

710 From the moor there came, under misty cliffs,
Grendel striding; he bore God's wrath.
The monster of evil had it in mind
to hunt for his dinner in that high hall!
Under the masses of cloud he moved
715 until he could glimpse the gleams of gold
that marked those timbers. That was not the first time
that he had visited Hrothgar's home,
but never before had he found in that place
a fiercer welcome, or warriors more fiery!
720 To the hall he came, huge and striding,
doomed, without joy. At once the door
sprang from its hinges at the touch of that hand.
He burst open the building's mouth,

cruel in his rage, and quickly then
725 he stepped across the colored floor,
moving in fury, as from his eyes
there leapt a horrible light like a flame.

Within that mead-hall he saw many men,
kinsmen, sleeping calmly together,
730 loyal companions. Then his heart leapt up:
that terrible demon intended to tear
each comrade's life, before daylight came,
away from his body. The thought of a banquet
made his mouth water. But *wyrd* would not
735 let him enjoy that taste any longer
after that night.

The noble kinsman
of Hygelac watched to see how the wicked
predator meant to plan his attack.
That loathsome demon would not delay;
740 like a flash, he snatched up the first of his quarry,
a sleeping man, and slit him open,
bit his body, gulped down his blood,
swallowed huge morsels, immediately
had devoured each part of his victim's corpse
745 to his fingers and toes!

Again he stepped forth,
nearer now, clutched at the next with his claw,
stirred from his rest a stronger man!
As the demon reached out, the other grasped him,
and grimly sat up against that arm.
750 And then that cruel fiend first discovered
that he had never met, throughout middle earth,
in any warrior in all the world,
a mightier grip. In his heart he grew
greatly afraid—but he could not flee.
755 His single thought was to slip into darkness,
back among his devils; those earlier days
of gluttony here were gone forever.

High of courage, Hygelac's kinsman
remembered his evening's speech, stood up,
760 gripped fast against him; fingers burst;
Grendel was desperate to get away,
but the prince came closer. The monster in panic

felt like swinging free if he could,
then breaking for the fen, but he knew that his fingers
765   were caught in that grip. That was a dismal call
for the harmful fiend, that he paid to Heorot!

The hall thundered, sounding to the thanes
who lived in that place hideously like
the pleasure of men who were merry on ale.
770   Both were furious. The floor boomed.
Then it was a wonder that the noble wine-hall
held out so well against those warriors,
that it did not fall. But it was made fast
within and without with iron bands
775   designed by a clever smith. From the sill
at the floor of the building where those fierce ones fought
benches lavish with gold sprang loose.
No wise man among the Shieldings
had ever expected that anyone
780   could break that beautiful antlered building
or pull it apart, unless pulsing flames
were to swallow it up.

The sound roared out,
gaining in frenzy, pouring out fear
for all of the Danes, for each of those
785   who heard that wailing come through the wall,
the mournful tune of God's antagonist,
his song, not of victory—the slave of Hell
bemoaning his fate. He held him fast
who was the mightiest man in the world
790   in those long ago days of this fleeting life.

12. The Quelling of Grendel

For nothing in the world did Beowulf want
to let that killer escape alive,
nor did he consider that Grendel had served
any useful purpose! A daring youth
795   from the band of warriors came slashing about
with his ancient sword; he wanted to save
the life, if he could, of his noble leader.
And others joined him, just as brave,
but unaware when they drew their weapons—
800   intending to hew Grendel down between them,

to get at his life—that none of the greatest
iron blades over all the earth,
not any sword at all, could ever touch him;
he had cast a spell on all cutting edges,
805   making them harmless. Yet his departure,
in those long ago days, from this fleeting life,
would be grippingly painful, and that grim spirit
would be forced to descend to the fires of the damned.

Then he who had perpetrated such horrors,
810   so many crimes against mankind,
the fiend who was waging a permanent feud
with God, found that his garment of flesh
would no longer serve him, for the noble kinsman
of Hygelac had gripped him hard by the hand
815   (each was loathsome to the other alive),
and was pulling his body to pieces, cracking
his shoulder wide open. Sinews sprang out
and the body burst apart! Beowulf was victor,
and the demon Grendel in his death-throes
820   sought only to flee far into the wilds
to his joyless den, for there was no doubt,
he knew, that his life, the number of his days,
was done. For all the Danes, that conflict
had been settled according to their desire:
825   he who had come from so far had cleansed
Hrothgar's hall, and from hateful intrusions
had rescued it.

He revelled in his deed,
in the work of that night, for nobly had he
fulfilled his pledge. The prince of the Geats
830   had entirely undone the distress of the Danes
that had bound them up in endless brooding
and caused them, of sad necessity,
to endure such sorrow. The clear sign of this
came when that hand was placed by the hero
835   with arm and shoulder, all in one piece,
Grendel's whole grip, up under the gable.

13. An Appropriate Tale

Then in the morning many a warrior
hastened to that gift hall, as I have heard;

noble men came from far and near,
840   from all over the land, to look on that marvel,
the foe's huge footprints. His fall seemed
no cause for regret to any of the councillors
who looked on the tracks of the loser of that fight
and saw how weary of mind he was
845   as he made his way thence. To the monsters' tarn,
fated and fleeing, he bent his way.
The water there was welling with blood,
a terrible surf that was swirling up
in burning waves of hot battle gore.
850   Joyless, forlorn and despairing of life,
he hid his doomed and heathen soul
in the harboring fen. There Hell took him.

Afterwards the troop of old companions
and the younger men, too, turned to pleasure,
855   warriors riding away from the pool,
glorious on their horses. The heroic deed
of Beowulf was spoken of, and many men said
that north or south between the two seas,
across the whole earth, there existed no other
860   warrior so brave, more worthy of rule,
under the vast vault of the heavens!
Yet their own prince, Hrothgar, they did not disparage
by such regard, for he was a good king.
At times those riders gave free rein
865   to their roan stallions, let them race,
let them leap forth where the turf seemed fair,
in a test of speed. At times the king's thane,
a splendid man who remembered old songs
and kept them in his mind along with many
870   long ago sayings, began linking his words,
binding them together. Soon he began
to recite with discernment Beowulf's success,
and skillfully to adapt an appropriate story,
mingling his words.

He said all there was
875   that he had heard of about the heroic
deeds of Sigemund,° the strange things that happened
on the wide travels of that son of Waels—

---

[876]*Sigemund.* The narrator compares Beowulf favorably with the legendary Norse hero Sigemund. The original
audience for *Beowulf* would have immediately recognized the parallel of Sigemund's fight with the dragon to
Beowulf's (in the final episode of the poem). In the thirteenth century German epic the *Nibelungenlied,* Sigemund
is the father of the hero Siegfried. Fítela is Sigemund's nephew.

feuds and crimes that few men
would have heard about, if there had not been
880   Fítela with him in later frays,
when Sigemund would say to his sister's son
something of such feats as they fought together,
always companions in the play of swords;
they killed many giants.

To Sigemund came
885   the glory due him after his death,
for that hero had slain a mighty serpent,
the guardian of a hoard. Under the gray stone
the atheling's son descended alone
on that fearsome deed, Fítela not with him.
890   It was granted, however, that his gleaming sword
should strike through that dragon to stand in the wall
quivering, and the beast was destroyed by that blow!
So fearlessly had the warrior performed
that now he could enjoy the hoard of jewels
895   at his own leisure. He loaded his boat.
Wael's son carried that glimmering wealth
into the hold; and the hot beast shrivelled.

In deeds of prowess (for which he prospered),
Sigemund was the most famous of warriors,
900   *of protectors or fighters, among all folk*
since King Heremod's° glory declined
with his might and his courage. Among the Jutes
Heremod was betrayed by his own retainers
to men who killed him. Keen were the sorrows
905   *that had long oppressed him, and to his people*
he had grown to be the greatest of burdens.
Many a warrior mourned his exploits,
lamenting for those days when he had believed
that Heremod could not fail as a cure for affliction,
910   *that he would thrive as a prince among thanes*
in his father's pattern, ruling the people
and the kingdom's wealth, its fortress and warriors,
the country of the Shieldings. The kinsman of Hygelac,
Beowulf, became a help to his comrades
915   *and to all, but hatred took hold of the other.*

---

901 *King Heremod.* In this digression, the poet compares Beowulf to Heremod, a former king of Denmark. Beowulf is different from Heremod, who began his reign with great promise but became increasingly melancholy and murderous. Later in the poem, Hrothgar lists some of Heremod's misdeeds (ll. 1709-22).

At times, racing down the yellow roads,
they matched their horses. Then the morning light
moved on, and many a man of valor
hastened to that high hall to see
920 the curious trophy; likewise the king,
the keeper of the hoard, came from his wife's house.
He walked along firm in his warrior's glory,
known well to be best, and his queen walked with him
across the meadow with an escort of maidens.

14. Hrothgar and the Hand

925 Hrothgar spoke—he went to the hall,
stepped onto the raised place and looked at the roof
adorned with gold, and at Grendel's hand—:
"For this great sight may we give our thanks
to God Almighty! I have endured many
930 afflictions from Grendel, but the Keeper of Glory
can always work wonder after wonder.

"It was not long ago that I gave up hope,
gave up expecting ever to experience
relief from misery, when marked with blood
935 the best of houses stood humbled by horrors—
a far-reaching woe to the men of wisdom,
for they had lost trust in their power to protect
the stronghold of the folk from foes like demons
and wicked spirits. But now this warrior
940 through the might of God has managed the deed
that none of us earlier could have ever
contrived with our wits. Indeed, that woman
who bore, according to noble custom,
such a son, if still she lives,
945 well may declare that wise God
blessed that birth!

"Now, good Beowulf,
I should like to claim you as my own kinsman,
a son in my heart. Hold well, henceforth,
to our new relationship. You shall know no lack
950 of precious things where I wield power.
I have often granted a gift from the hoard
to honor less worth in a lowlier warrior,
weaker in battle. Now, Beowulf, you
have performed such feats that your fame will live
955 forever and ever. May ancient God

grant you always the grace that he grants you now!"

Beowulf spoke, the son of Edgetheow:
"With kindly intent we came to perform
that deed of valor, to meet with the demon
960 and test the strength of that fearsome stranger.
Yet I wish you had seen him stretched out in death
before your own eyes, in all his trappings!
I meant to bind him immediately
onto his deathbed with a dreadful grip
965 so that under my hand he would lie there, openly
struggling for his life—unless he escaped,
weakened though he was. But the Lord did not want me
to stop him from leaving with his life intact:
I could not hold onto him hard enough—
970 he was too strong. But he had to forsake
his hand, his arm, and his whole shoulder,
to save himself and seek escape.

"That destitute being did not thereby
purchase relief for a longer life
975 haunted by his sins, for his wound holds him
tight in the clutch of terrible pain,
a woeful bond; there he must wait,
that guilty demon, for the Great Judgment,
what Heaven's King decides to decree."
980 Then Edgelaf's son Unferth was altogether
a quieter man in vaunting his courage
when the athelings saw the other's skill
displayed high up: the enemy's hand
with its fearful fingers. In front of each one
985 stood a strong nail very like steel,
the talon of the heathen warrior's hand,
a horrible spike. Everyone said
that no iron blade of noble valor
could ever have touched him, that no trusty sword
990 could have harmed that bloody hand of battle!

15. The Banquet

Then all hands were called to Heorot
to make that hall beautiful. Many were the men
and women, too, by whom that wine-house
was adorned for its guests. Golden shone
995 the weavings on the walls, scenes of wonder
for every person who looked thereon.

That bright interior had been broken to rubble,
though tightly bound in bands of iron;
hinges had sprung open, and only the roof
1000   was intact when the demon turned away,
marked with his deeds, to make his flight,
desperate for life. Death is not easy
to hide away from, try it who will!
For those with souls, by necessity,
1005   must pass, each one, to the place prepared
for all who inhabit human lands,
where the body falls asleep in its narrow bed
after the banquet.

    Then came the hour
when Hrothgar, the son of Halfdane, decided
1010   that he wanted to sit at the feast himself.
I have never heard of a noble band
comport themselves better in their ring-giver's presence.
Brilliant in their fame, they sank to the benches,
rejoiced at the banquet. Joining in their pleasure
1015   with many a cup of mead in that hall
were two bold kinsmen toasting together,
Hrothgar and Hrothulf. Heorot within
was filled with friends; few were the Danes
who gave any thought then to thickening plots.

1020   Hrothgar presented a golden standard
to Beowulf the Geat, to honor his greatness,
and with that banner a helmet and byrnie;
and then many saw a magnificent sword
borne in to the hero. Beowulf drank
1025   from the cup in the hall; no cause had he
for shame before friends at that treasure-sharing!
I have not heard of many great kings who have made
four golden gifts in friendlier wise
to another man on the ale bench!
1030   Spanning that helmet a crest stood high,
twisted with wires to protect the head
from blows without, so that no hard blade
could wound the warrior who was wearing it
into a fight against violent foes.
1035   The king of athelings then ordered that eight
stallions bright with golden bridles
be led through the hall. On one of those horses
was a fine saddle, finished with gems;

1040 it had been the king's own battle seat
when Hrothgar had wished to test his hand
at sword-play. Never was that warrior known
to retreat from the front when corpses fell!

By now the lord of the Ingwines° had lavished
upon the Geat a goodly share
1045 of horses and jewels, and he wished him joy of them.
Thus the hoard guardian honored that hero
with such a bounty of stallions and wealth
that no one can find a fault in his kindness
who holds to the truth of that treasure-giving.

16. Hildeburh's Sorrow

1050 Once again, to each princely warrior
who had braved the sea paths with Beowulf,
Hrothgar gave marvellous gifts on the mead-bench,
heirloom treasures. Then he ordered yet more:
that the man° should be honored with gold whom earlier
1055 Grendel had slaughtered, as he would have slain
more Geats and Danes, had not wise God
and that warrior's courage conquered *wyrd*.
The Lord ruled then the lives of men,
as still he does. Thus understanding
1060 and prudence are best, for much must be borne
of good and ill, by anyone
who dwells in this world in these difficult days.
Singing° and music swelled together
in the presence of Hrothgar, Halfdane's war prince;
1065 *the harp had been strummed to many a story*
when the king's shope began to declaim
a formal hall tale in front of the mead-bench,
about Finn's men when disaster befell them,
and that Danish hero, Hnaef of the Shieldings,
1070 *who was destined to fall in Frisian slaughter.*
Truly, Hildeburh had cause to protest

[1043]*Ingwines*. The Danes.

[1054]*the man*. The Geat warrior killed by Grendel. Hrothgar compensates the Geats for the warrior's death by paying *wergild* ("man gold"). The *wergild* is both a payment and an honor.

[1063]*Singing*. This digression (ll. 1063-1215) includes the shope's account of the so-called Finn Episode and Wealtheow's reaction to it. Rather than tell a story about a hero's victory, which would seem appropriate for this festive occasion, the shope recounts a family tragedy. Because the author assumes his audience's familiarity with the story, the shope's account is fragmentary and confusing to modern readers. But the Finn Episode is told in another Old English manuscript, which makes it possible to provide a summary of the episode and a genealogical table that fill in the gaps of the shope's version (see p. 160).

the good faith of the Jutes. Guiltless, she found herself
deprived of her loved ones at that play of shields—
one son, one brother; wounded by the spear,
1075   they sank to their deaths. That was a sad woman!

Hardly without cause did Hoc's daughter
bemoan her fate when morning came,
when under the sky she could clearly see
the murdered corpses of those she had cared for
1080   most dearly in the world. War also took
all Finn's thanes, save only a few,
so that he was not able in any way
to press Hengest to a fight in this place
or dislodge those Danes who were still alive
1085   with the prince's friend.

           So the Frisians offered
a compact of peace; they would clear out completely
a second hall and its ruling high seat,
which the Shielding warriors could share with the Jutes;
and at the ring-giving the Frisian ruler
1090   would honor the Danes every day,
offering treasures to Hengest's troop—
just as many of those jewels and weapons
of plated gold as he would give
to deck out the Frisians in their drinking hall.
1095   Then they swore on either side
to keep the peace. To Hengest, the king
promised with undisputed zeal
that he would protect that dwindled troop
with honor and wisdom, and that no man would
1100   weaken their pact with words or deeds;
and no malicious tongues were allowed
to mention the fact that the Danes were following
their chieftain's slayer, having no other choice.
If anyone dared with audacious speech
1105   to remind the Danes of that deadly hatred,
then the sword's edge would settle it!

The pyre was made ready and precious gold
carried from the hoard. The hardiest warrior
of all the Shieldings was laid there, shining,
1110   where all could see the blood-stained sarks,
the iron-hard boar-helmets, overlaid
with glittering gold, and many good men

who had died of their wounds. What warriors had fallen!
Then Hildeburh said that her own son
1115   should be laid beside Hnaef, and left to the flames;
his corpse should be burnt beside his kinsman,
at his uncle's shoulder. Then singing, she
lamented her sorrow. The warrior ascended;
the hugest of fires wound up to the heavens,
1120   howling by the mound. Heads were consumed;
gashes burst open and the blood sprang out
through bitter wounds. Soon the blaze,
greediest of spirits, had swallowed the dead
of both peoples; their power had vanished.

17. Hengest's Revenge

1125   The Shieldings went forth to find themselves dwellings;
lamenting their friends, they looked around Frisia
for house and high fortress, for Hengest was forced
to remain with Finn through a mournful winter.
He cast no lots, yet kept on thinking
1130   of home, though he could not cross the ocean
on his serpent-prowed ship, for the sea was swollen
with mighty storms; it strove with the wind.
Then winter locked the waves in icy bonds
until spring weather brought warmth again—
1135   as still it does. The dazzling seasons
keep their proper times.

When the winter had passed
and the land was fair, a longing to go
took hold of that thane. But he gave more thought
to wreaking vengeance than to riding the seas,
1140   to bringing about a bitter meeting
that he had in mind for the men of the Jutes.
The choice of revenge, then, was very easy,
when Hunlafing° laid upon his lap
"Light of Battle," that best of blades,
1145   whose edges were known to the Jutish nobles.

Then cruel were the swords that struck down the king,
Finn the brave-hearted, in his own house,
for Guthlaf and Oslaf° had greatly complained

1143*Hunlafing.* Apparently the son of Hunlaf, a Danish warrior killed in the first battle with the Frisians.
1148*Guthlaf and Oslaf.* Brothers to Hunlaf.

of being attacked after weary traveling—
1150 *and held Finn to blame. The fiery heart*
cannot be subdued; that hall was dyed
red with friends' lives, and the ruler lay
slain among his troop, and the queen was taken.
The Shielding warriors bore to their ship
1155 *the ancient treasures that Finn had protected*
in his coffers at home—all they could carry
of the precious ornaments. And over the sea paths
they took his lady to the land of the Danes,
led her to her people.

The lay was sung,
1160 *the minstrel's tale, and mirth started up again;*
the revels increased as cup-bearers came
pouring the wine. Then Wealtheow came forth
in her golden necklace where the king and his nephew
sat nobly together, still known for their friendship,°
1165 *each true to the other. And there sat Unferth*
at the feet of those princes; they praised and trusted
his great courage, though to his kinsmen
he had done little service at the play of swords.

The lady spoke: "Take this cup, my lord,
1170 *giver of rings, gold-friend to men!*
Be joyful, and speak with generous words
of kindness to the Geats, in your kingly way.
Be gracious, and remember them with those gifts
from near and far that fill your coffers.
1175 *I have been told that you wish to take*
this man for your son. But the bright mead-hall,
Heorot, is cleansed. Hand out while you hold them
the kingdom's rewards, but leave to your kinsmen
folk and rule when you must go forth
1180 *to discover your fate.*

"O friend of the Shieldings,
I know that my gracious Hrothulf will guard
our children with honor, if you are chosen
before your nephew to make your way forth
from life in this world. I expect he will wish
1185 *to repay our sons with special goodness*

1164*still known for their friendship.* A reference to future discord among the Danes, with Unferth as a likely traitor or at least a catalyst for trouble.

if he recalls all the kindnesses
that we showed to him when he was young."

She went along the bench then, to where her boys were,
Hrethric and Hrothmund, and the sons of heroes,
1190   *all the youths together; there sat the Geat,*
Beowulf himself, between those two brothers.

18. The Ring-Giving

Bearing the mead cup, the queen bid Beowulf
in courteous words to partake of that wine,
and his worth was acknowledged with noble treasures:
1195   two arm rings, a corselet, and a golden collar—
the greatest torque I have ever heard tell of.

No,° I have not heard of a finer hoard treasure
under the heavens since Hama made off
with the Brosinga mene° to that bright city
1200   *(precious figures in a princely setting);*
he turned from Eormenric to eternal gain.
Hygelac of the Geats, Swerting's grandson,
flaunted that collar on his final campaign,
when he strove to protect beneath his standard
1205   *the booty he had won—but* wyrd *took him.*
Because of his pride he had courted trouble,
a feud with the Frisians. On the flowing waves
powerful Hygelac transported that treasure
of fabulous wealth—to fall under his shield.
1210   *Then three things passed into Frankish power:*
his life, his war-gear, and that wondrous collar.
Less noble were the fighters who, after the feud,
plundered that corpse on the field of carnage—
of havoc for the Geats.

But applause had greeted
1215   *the tale of Hama, and then in the hall*

1197*No.* This digression (ll. 1197-1214) explains the origin of the necklace Wealtheow gives Beowulf, and at the same time gives a flash-forward to Hygelac's (Beowulf's uncle's) ill-fated raid on the Frisians. It is the first of four references to this raid. Hygelac initiated the raid and was killed in it. See the summary and genealogical tables on pp. 161–162 to place this raid in the chronological context of Geatish history. The "I" of line 1197 is the narrator. According to Norse legend, the adventurer Hama robbed Eormenric, the king of the East Goths, of the necklace. Hama's turn to "eternal gain" may have been a renunciation of earthly wealth in favor of life as a monk. We learn later (ll. 2172-74) that Beowulf gives the necklace to Hygelac's queen, Hygd, who apparently gave it to Hygelac to wear during the Frisian raid.
1199*mene.* Necklace.

Wealtheow spoke: "Wear this collar,
dear Beowulf, well; let it bring you luck,
and the corselet, too, from the common treasure.
May you show your power, and to these young Shieldings

1220   grant your favor, and I'll not forget you!
You have fought so well that far and near,
forever and ever, men will honor you
as widely as that home of the winds, the sea,
encircles the land. As long as you live,

1225   be happy, young man; with many gifts
I shall recall your deeds. Be kind
to my sons in everything, blessed atheling!

"Here each warrior is true to the other,
disposed to be generous, loyal to his prince.

1230   They are harmonious and courteous men—
having drunk from my cup, they do as I bid!
She returned to her seat and the banquet continued.
They feasted and drank, unwary of the doom,
the twisting fate determined of yore,

1235   that would strike among them long before morning!
Hrothgar, their leader, went away to his house
to seek his bed. Within that high building
the athelings kept watch, as often before.

They cleared the benches and laid down bolsters,

1240   fluffed up feather-beds. (But one of those friends
lay down on his couch a doomed man!)
They had hung their shields above their heads,
bright on the wall, and over each bench
ready to hand they set their steep helmets

1245   that towered in battle, and their ring-mail byrnies,
their magnificent spears. Such was their custom:
they always kept fit and ready for a fight
at home or afield, eager to help
whenever their lord might look to them

1250   in need. That was truly a noble people!

19. Grendel's Mother Comes

They fell asleep. One man paid sorely
for his evening's rest, as often had happened
when Grendel came to dwell in that gold-hall,
evilly, until an end came to that:

1255   after crimes against others he was killed himself!

But then it was seen that still there lived
another monster, marking time
after Grendel's death, the demon's mother,
a witch of the sea, resenting her sorrow,
1260   one who was wont to dwell underwater
in the cold streams *after Cain sent*
a sharp blade through his own brother,
his father's offspring; he set forth then, fated,
proscribed for his murder from life among men,
1265   *to dwell in the wastelands. From his loins awoke*
the demons of wyrd; *Grendel was one of them,*
that hateful foe who had found at Heorot
a man awake and waiting for the fight.
The horrible being laid hold of Beowulf,
1270   *but he remembered his mighty strength,*
the ample gift that God had given him,
and counted on support and comfort from the Prince
who rules on high. Thus he wrestled
that monster from Hell. Humiliated, then,
1275   *mankind's foe went joyless to find*
a place to die in. And that demon mother,
with her heart as heavy as a hanged man, wanted
to venture to Heorot to avenge her son's death.

She came then to Heorot; in that hall the Danes
1280   were fast asleep. A change of fortune
befell them as she entered—and yet the force
of Grendel's mother amounted to less
than his by as much as a woman's might
is shadowed by the strength of a sword-bearing man—
1285   when that fine weapon forged with the hammer,
the blade with a pattern emblazoned with blood,
strikes out at the boar above the helmet.

Then damascened° blades were drawn in the hall,
the swords hanging over the seats, and many
1290   shields held fast in men's fists were raised;
but helmets were forgotten when horror came upon them,
and byrnies left aside.

    That sea witch wanted
to escape with her life when she was discovered,
but she carried off in her cruel grip
1295   a noble warrior when she went to the fen.

1288*damascened.* Ornamented with wave-like patterns.

He was the dearest of Hrothgar's companions,
his truest supporter between the two seas,
a noble shield-warrior of great renown,
whom she took from his bed. Beowulf was not there,

1300   for after the gift-giving he had been guided
to another building for the rest he had earned.
A cry rose in Heorot. She reached for the claw,
taking down that hand from its bloody height.
Sorrow was renewed in the homes of the Shieldings:

1305   that was no bargain, when on both sides
they paid for their feuding with the lives of friends!

Savage was the hatred of that hoary old warrior
when they told him about his best of thanes,
and he knew his dearest companion was dead!

1310   Beowulf was quickly bidden to come
to Hrothgar's dwelling; it was break of day.
Nobly he moved among his men,
a champion among warriors, to where the king waited,
wondering if God would ever grant him

1315   a change from this time of terrible woe.
Along the floor walked the worthy fighter
among his thanes—the whole hall thundered—
until he came before the king
and hailed him, asking if he had had

1320   a pleasant night, as he had planned.

20. Grendelsmere

Hrothgar spoke, the Shielding's protector:
"Ask not about pleasure. Sorrow is renewed
for the Danish people. Ashere is dead,
the elder brother of Yrmenlaf,

1325   my confidant and advisor in council,
my shoulder companion, with whom I would parry
the blades that threatened to smite our boar-helmets,
protecting each other. As Ashere was,
such a man ought an atheling be!

1330   "A demon wandering in darkness slew him
by night in Heorot, and I know not whither
that creature has borne away her catch,
anticipating feasting. She avenged that fight
of night before last when you laid on Grendel,

1335 grappling him hard, with hostile intent,
when for far too long he had torn and depleted
the folk of my hearth. He fell in battle,
and now there comes to avenge her kinsman
a second mighty slayer of men,
1340 who goes very far in her fury for vengeance
as many a thane may often think
when in great distress he grieves for his treasure-giver,
weeping in his heart. Now that hand lies low
which once gave worthy rewards to you all!

1345 "But there is a tale that the country folk tell,
and hall-councillors, too—I have heard it myself.
They say they have sometimes spotted two
such huge monsters who walk the moors,
wanderers from elsewhere. One was formed,
1350 so far as the most discerning could see,
in a woman's likeness; the second one
shared her exile in the shape of a man,
except he was huger than anyone human!
The folk who dwelt there in olden days
1355 named him Grendel, but nobody knows
his sire, or whether other spirits
were spawned before him.

        "In a secret land
they dwell, among wild fells, wolf-slopes,
windy headlands where a waterfall
1360 hurtles down through the mist into darkness
under the fells. Not far away
in miles lies hidden that lonely mere°
overhung by trees covered in hoar-frost,
a deep-rooted wood that shadows the water.
1365 They say every night there appears a strange
fire on the lake!—And no man lives
so wise as to know that water's depth.
Though the stag of the heath, pressed hard by hounds,
should make for the forest with his mighty antlers,
1370 put to flight from afar, he will forfeit his life
on the shore rather than swim in that lake
to protect his head. Not a happy place!
There the wind stirs up sudden storms
where clashing waves ascend to the clouds

1362*mere.* Sea.

1375 and the sky presses down, dark and smothering,
weeping from above.

"Now once more you
alone can save us, but you have never seen
that fearful place where you may find
the surly demon. Seek if you dare!
1380 I shall honor you for taking that on,
just as before, in jewels and gold,
worthy treasures, if you come away."

21. Creatures of the Mere

Beowulf spoke, Edgetheow's son:
"Grieve not, wise ruler! Rather should a man
1385 avenge his friend's murder than mourn him too much.
Death comes to all. Let him who is able
achieve in the world what he wants of glory
and fame among men before he must die—
for the atheling, that is afterwards best!
1390 Arise, great king, let us go quickly
to mark the track of Grendel's mother.
She will not escape under cover, I swear,
to the darkest cavern, or the depths of the sea,
or the wild forest, go where she will!
1395 For a day only endure with patience
the weight of your sorrow—I know you will."
The gray-haired king leapt up, thanking God,
the mighty Sky-Lord, for what that man said.

Then a horse was bridled for Hrothgar,
1400 a stallion with braided mane. In splendor
the king rode, followed by his band on foot
carrying shields. The spoor was clear
as it wound along the path through the woods,
then over the waste land, and onward she had gone
1405 over mirky moorlands, making off
with the corpse of the best of all the comrades
who made their home in Hrothgar's hall.
That son of princes picked his way
over steep cliffs that were loose with stone,
1410 along narrow footpaths and unknown trails,
precipitous mosses where monsters dwelt.
With a certain few he spied out the land,
going before so that others could follow,

when suddenly he came to a stand of trees
1415   bending across gray blocks of stone,
a dismal wood. Dark beneath
lay a stagnant and bloody lake.
To all the Danes it was hard to endure,
a difficult thing for many a thane,
1420   for each of those friends, when on the edge
of that stony cliff they came upon it—
Ashere's head.

     The water welled hotly
as they looked at the lake. Then loud and clear
the war horn sang out, and those walkers found
1425   boulders to sit on, where they could see
many a wondrous serpent winding
through shallows, or lying on rocky ledges—
such creatures of the deep as often, near dawn,
will show themselves to passing ships,
1430   a horrid meeting!

     They hurried away,
snapping and angry at the bright sound
of the pealing horn. A prince of the Geats
shot at one of those swimming monsters
so hard with his arrow that the point drove home
1435   to score on its life; then on that lake
he dawdled at swimming, when death was on him!
With a hooked javelin they hemmed him in;
as he bled out his life they thrust a boar-spear
under his scales and drew him to shore,
1440   a wondrous serpent. With awe the warriors
looked on this thing that lived in the mere!

Recklessly Beowulf readied himself
in his coat of mail, carefully woven
and finely adorned, which would dare to enter
1445   that lake; this byrnie would protect his body
so that no malicious monster's claw
could dig in his breast or endanger his life.
And the shining helmet hurling its light
through the depths of that tarn would protect his head;
1450   made worthy with jewels, through the surging waters
the encircling bands would shine as they did
in days long ago, when a great smith wrought it
and set about it the shapes of boars

so that no sharp blade could wound him in battle.
1455 And the last helper was not the least.
Hrothgar's *thule*° lent it to him—
a hilted sword whose name was *Hrunting*.
Among the highest of inherited treasures,
that iron blade, hardened in blood,
1460 was fretted with serpent-marks; never had it failed
any warrior who wound his fist
hard upon it, in perilous quest
or fierce battle. That was not the first time
that it had to perform a courageous feat!

1465 Indeed, Unferth, the son of Edgelaf,
said little about that strength he had boasted of
earlier at beer, when he lent his blade
to a better warrior; he did not wish
to risk his own life in that turbid lake
1470 with a noble feat. There he lost fame,
renown for courage. Not so the other,
once he had readied himself for war!

22. The Encounter with the Sea-Hag

Beowulf spoke, Edgetheow's son:
"Consider now, great son of Halfdane,
1475 wise leader and gold-friend of warriors,
now that I'm ready, think of those things
we spoke of earlier: if in your service
I should lose my life, you said you would like
to perform the office of father to me.
1480 Be, then, a guardian to my band of warriors,
my brave companions, if battle takes me.
And the riches you gave me for honor and glory,
dear Hrothgar, convey them to Hygelac,
so that the lord of the Geats may look
1485 upon that gold and priceless treasure
and know that I found a munificent
giver of rings, who was grateful to me.
Let Unferth have that ancient heirloom,
my wave-marked sword, known widely to men
1490 for its hard blade. With Hrunting I
shall hew myself glory or death shall have me!"
After these words the prince of the Weathergeats

1456*thule.* Orator.

turned away with courage, not caring at all
to wait for an answer. The waters swallowed him.

1495   Part of the day had already passed
before he reached that unfathomed bottom.
At once that ravenous hag who had ruled
those flooding waters for fifty years
discovered, slavering, that some strange human
1500   was diving down to her demon lair.
She grappled with him, gripping him tight
with terrible claws, but she could not harm
his body, for the ring-mail wrapped it around.
Unable to get at the Geat through his sark
1505   or penetrate it with her piercing talons,
the sea-hag, clutching him, swam to the bottom,
dragging that prince to her dismal home
in a manner that, no matter how brave he was,
he could reach no weapon. Harassing him,
1510   many a curious creature of the depths
broke its tusks against his byrnie;
monsters pursued him.

    Then the warrior perceived
that now he stood in a strange battle-hall,
where no water was getting him wet
1515   and the swirling tarn could never touch him
because of the roof. He saw ruddy flames,
a blaze of firelight shining brightly.
And then the hero saw that hag,
the incredible mere-witch, and cut a great swathe
1520   through the air with his blade, holding nothing back,
so that crashing on her skull the ring-marked sword
sang out greedily. Then her guest found out
that his gleaming blade would not bite
or harm her, no, that heavy sword
1525   failed him at need. Many a fight
had it endured, often driven
through a fated man's helmet; that time was the first
for that gleaming treasure that its glory faded.

Now Hygelac's nephew, keen for renown,
1530   was resolute; and in a rage
he hurled that sword, with its shining marks
and steel blade, so it struck the ground
and lay there, still. He trusted his strength,

the might of his grip. Thus a man shall do
1535 when he hopes to gain some lasting glory
for his deeds in battle: he does not fear death!

Then by the shoulder Beowulf seized
Grendel's mother—the Geat was now
furious, and had few qualms about fighting—
1540 and swung her, hard, so she smashed to the floor!
Promptly she paid him back for that pass,
closing upon him with a clammy embrace,
and, weary, that strongest of warriors stumbled;
catching his foot, he went crashing down.
1545 She straddled her hall-guest and drew her *sax,*
a gleaming knife; she wanted to get
vengeance for her child. But on his chest
lay the woven sark; that saved his life
with iron rings that blunted both point and blade.
1550 Edgetheow's son would have ended his days
there under the pool, the prince would have perished,
except he was helped by his woven sark,
that hard net of war—and by holy God,
who brought him victory in that battle.
1555 The Ruler of the Skies decided it rightly,
with ease, when Beowulf stood up again.

23. Cleansing the Tarn

He saw before him a fabulous blade
among other armor, an ancient sword
worthy of a warrior, the choicest of weapons—
1560 except it was mightier than any other man
could bear into battle but Beowulf,
heavy and ornate, the handwork of giants.
The daring champion of the Shieldings dived
for that radiant hilt, raised it high,
1565 despairing of his life, lunged angrily,
slashing down hard through the skin of her neck,
breaking the vertebrae, the blade vanishing
through her. Fated, she fell to the floor.
The warrior rejoiced, lifting his weapon.
1570 The flame leapt up and light poured out,
shining as bright as the sun in heaven,
the sky's candle. He cast an eye
around him, then walked along the wall,
holding that weapon high by the hilt

1575   with a single purpose. That sword was still useful
to that prince of warriors, for he wished to repay
Grendel for many a remorseless attack
that the demon had made on the men of the Danes,
more often, by far, than that one occasion
1580   when he had slain Hrothgar's hearth companions
asleep in their beds, and eaten, slavering,
fifteen men of the Danish folk,
and carried another such number away—
hideous booty! Beowulf well
1585   had paid him back, to the point that now
he saw Grendel lifeless, lying on his bed
a foul corpse, as the fight at Heorot
had earlier decreed. That corpse sprang apart
when Beowulf dealt it a final blow,
1590   hacking off Grendel's monstrous head.

At this, the thoughtful thanes who stood
watching by the lake with wise Hrothgar
saw the tarn grow turbulent
and the water bubbling up with blood.
1595   The gray-haired elders spoke together,
saying they did not expect to see
the brave warrior come back again
to hail their king. The water-hag,
many men thought, had murdered him.
1600   So at the ninth hour the noble Shieldings
gave up waiting; the gold-friend of the warriors
turned toward home. But their guests, sick at heart,
sat there, staring at the lake and hoping,
but not expecting, to see their noble
1605   friend once more.

     Forming icicles
of iron, that blade, hot with the blood
of monsters, was melting. It soon diminished
entirely, wondrously, like the winter ice
when the Father loosens the bonds of frost,
1610   unwinding the water ropes, he who holds rule
over times and seasons; that is the true God.
The prince of the Weathergeats did not wish
to take more of the treasures (though he saw many there)
than Grendel's head and with it the hilt
1615   adorned with jewels; the damascened blade
had vanished entirely; the venomous blood
of those hideous creatures was that hot!

Then he came away who had accomplished
the fall of those demons, diving up
1620   through the clearing pool; all that expanse
of waters was cleansed when the wandering fiend
passed away from life and this fleeting world.

The leader of the Sea Geats made for land,
swimming bravely, revelling in his booty,
1625   the mighty burden that he had brought with him.
His thanes approached him, thanking God,
glad to see their prince again,
rejoicing that Beowulf was safely back.
They lifted his helmet from his head
1630   and loosened his byrnie. The lake subsided
in low ripples laced with blood.
Light-hearted, the men went marching along
the path which crossed the perilous moor
to the well-trodden road. Away from the cliff,
1635   bold as kings, they carried that head,
loathsome to each of those loyal thanes,
fierce as they were. It took four warriors
to stagger under the bloody stake
on which to Heorot they bore that head.
1640   Then all fourteen of them, fierce and brave,
striding along the stone-paved path,
suddenly came to the king's bright hall;
their prince marched with them, proud among his warriors.

That prince of thanes, well worthy of praise,
1645   brave of deed and destined for glory,
came inside and saluted the king.
Behind him by its knotted hair was borne
that demon's head, where the nobles were drinking—
monstrous for them and that woman among them
1650   to see, yet a wonder, and they watched it, aghast.

24. The Giant Sword-Hilt

Beowulf, son of Edgetheow, spoke:
"O King, this treasure comes from the sea.
Gladly we give you this golden hilt
that you gaze on here, for the glory of the Shieldings.
1655   I barely survived with my life that venture
under the water. It was hard work,

a battle where I would have been
taken at once—but God protected me.
In that encounter I could accomplish
1660   nothing with Hrunting, though it is a noble blade;
but the Ruler of Men enabled me
to see hanging, huge on the wall,
this ancient sword (often he aids
one who is friendless), so I drew the weapon
1665   and swung it hard when I had the chance
to kill that demon. Then the damascened blade
melted when immersed in the monsters' blood,
the hottest of battle gore. I took that hilt
away from the foe in fitting vengeance
1670   for wicked deeds, the deaths of the Danes.

I promise you now that by night in Heorot
you may sleep without sorrow among your warriors;
and, lord of the Shieldings, you need no longer
be afraid, for the folk of your hearth—
1675   that any of the thanes, young or old,
will endanger his life there, as he did before."

Then into the hands of gray-haired Hrothgar
was given the giants' golden hilt,
the ancient artifact. After the fall
1680   of devils, this work of wondersmiths went
to the prince of the Danes—and from this world passed
grim-hearted Grendel, God's adversary,
guilty of murder, and his mother also.
That hilt was kept by the best of kings
1685   who had ever held sway between the two seas,
or dealt out gold in Danish lands.
Hrothgar spoke—he looked on the hilt,
that ancient heirloom. *Upon it was etched*
the long ago beginnings of strife
1690   *when the fierce giants were slain in the flood.°*
It swept them away, a tribe estranged
from the Ruler eternal; as retribution
he sent upon them the surging waters.
And on that sword-guard, in shining gold,
1695   *graceful runes were correctly engraved,*
saying for whom that choicest of swords
had first been made, with its twisted markings

1690*the flood.* This digression alludes to the biblical account of the Flood (Genesis 6-9).

shaped like serpents. Then the wise king spoke
(he was Halfdane's son), and all fell silent:

1700   "Of this man let me say, I who administer
truth and justice throughout our tribe
as guardian of our people, reflecting on the past—
that he was well born! Beowulf, my friend,
before me I see fame, spreading far

1705   through the whole world—yours! Steadily you hold
your strength with discernment. You will see how I show
that friendship we spoke of. And to your own folk
you shall become an abiding comfort,
a help to your people.

      "Heremod° was not so

1710   to Edgewela's sons, to the Honor-Shieldings.
He did *not* turn out as the king they needed,
but took to killing his Danish kinsmen,
furiously slaughtering his friends at the table,
his own companions, until in the end

1715   he turned to his death in solitude,
though God had granted him great strength,
exalting him above other men.
But a blood-thirsty mood grew up in his breast,
and from his gold-hoard he gave no rings

1720   to honor the Danes, and he dwelt without gladness,
so that even he suffered distress from that strife—
destroying his kinsmen. Understand from this
the virtue of giving! This advice I offer you
wise from many winters.

      "A wonder it is

1725   how mighty God in great generosity
grants discernment to all sorts of men—
and lands, and rank. He rules all things.
At times he allows to wander in delight
the wilful thoughts of a well-born man:

1730   All the joys men can have he has in his hall,
and he holds the trust of protecting his people.
God grants him such power in his part of the world
—a large kingdom—that he cannot, in his lack
of discernment, foresee an end to it.

1735   He lives in luxury, not hindered in the least

1709*Heremod.* See ll. 898-915 for the first allusion to Heremod.

by illness or age; no evil sorrow
shadows his heart, no strife anywhere
draws the hateful blade—for him the world
wends to his will. He knows nothing worse . . .

25. *"Change Always Comes"*

"Until, within him, arrogance
1740 waxes and grows, and the watcher slumbers
who guards the soul; that sleep is too fast,
bound up in cares, and the killer nigh,
waiting to shoot wickedness from his bow.
1745 Then in that man's breast a bitter arrow
strikes under his guard, the sinister promptings
of a spirit accursed. He cannot shield himself.
What he has had for so long now seems too little.
He lusts after gain, and gives no more
1750 the gold rings of honor; he overlooks
even the beginnings of his own glory,
the gifts which God gave him at first.
And in the end it always transpires
that the feeble flesh declines and fails
1755 until fated, it falls. Then someone else
inherits the rings and hands them out recklessly;
he has no qualms about coffers of gold.

"Shield yourself from conflict with sin,
dear Beowulf, by choosing what is better:
1760 that which endures. Do not be arrogant
now that your power is at its peak—
for a time only, for all too soon
sickness or the blade will snatch your life,
or the fire's assault, or the sweep of the waves,
1765 or brandished sword, or soaring arrow,
or terrible old age . . . or your eye's brightness
will fail and darken, until suddenly death
has overpowered you, noble prince!

"So it was for me. I wielded power
1770 for fifty years, defending the Danes
with spear and sword against assaults
from many a tribe of this middle earth,
so effectively that I knew of no foe
under the heavens. Then look! In my own hall

1775 change came upon me when Grendel appeared,
      affliction after feasting when the ancient foe
      came on his endless visits to cause me
      immeasurable grief. Thanks be to God
      that I have lived now long enough
1780 to be able to look at that loathsome head
      with my own eyes, at the end of the ancient feud!

      "Now, go to your bench, enjoy the banquet
      prepared in your honor; we shall pass
      much treasure between us by the time morning comes!"
1785 Glad at heart, the Geatish prince
      went back at once as the wise king bade
      to his place on the bench; and the pleasures of feasting
      with those welcome guests began anew
      in the hall of the Danes. Shadows darkened
1790 around the warriors. At last all rose,
      for the old king with the ashen hair
      longed for his bed, and Beowulf, too,
      felt an enormous need for rest,
      triumphant but weary. At once a hall-thane
1795 courteously offered to accompany him
      to the visitors' quarters, and with great devotion
      he looked after everything that in those days
      a seafaring thane might be thought to need.
      The generous hero lay in a hall
1800 that arched high and golden; the guest slept there
      until the black raven blithely announced
      a joyous daybreak. When the jewel of the sky
      thrust back the shadows, the Geatish thanes
      were up and ready, anxious to fare
1805 home to their folk. Far was the journey,
      and the visitor eager to board his vessel.

      Then Beowulf bade that Hrunting be borne
      to Unferth; he told him to take back his sword,
      an excellent weapon, and that he wanted
1810 to thank him for the loan of a loyal friend
      skilled in warfare; in no way did his words
      find fault with that weapon. That was a fine warrior!
      And then the athelings were anxious to go,
      ready in their armor. Honored by the Ring-Danes,
1815 Beowulf walked forward to the raised floor
      where Hrothgar was, and he hailed him.

26. Taking Leave

Beowulf spoke, Edgetheow's son:
"We seafarers now have this to say:
having come from afar, we are eager to fare
1820   home to our king. Here we have been
royally entertained; you have treated us well.
If there is any way in this world I may earn
more of your love and esteem, my lord,
by heroic deeds, than I already have,
1825   you need only call me and I shall come.

"And if I discover from across the sea
that neighboring tribes are treating you ill
(as monsters did to the Danes for a time),
a thousand or more brave thanes I shall bring
1830   to help at your need. I know that Hygelac,
lord of the Geats and leader of the folk,
young though he is, will urge me on
in words and deeds, to assist you well
as a friend, with esteem and force of weapons,
1835   where you have need of noble warriors.

"If Hrethric himself, as the son of a prince,
determines to go to the home of the Geats,
he will find friends there. Faraway lands
are good to visit, if a man has valor."

1840   Hrothgar spoke to him in answer:
"Wise God himself must send those words
into your heart; I have never heard
a young man speak with more discernment.
You are strong in prowess and in presence of mind
1845   and wise in speech. I consider it likely,
if it comes to pass that a spear pierces
Hrethel's son, Hygelac your prince,
or a blade takes him off in battle, or illness
destroys him, and you are still alive,
1850   the Geats will not find a better friend
than you to choose as their champion and king,
as guardian of their hoard, if you wish to hold
that kingdom of kinsmen.

"Your courage pleases me
better the longer I know you, dear Beowulf;

1855   you have so performed that these two folk,
       the Danes and the Geats, shall have peace together
       and conflict shall rest, those hostile encounters
       and feuds which once afflicted our people.
       So long as I guard this land and its coffers,
1860   treasure shall pass between us, fine gifts
       of greeting shall cross the gannet's bath.°
       The craft with twisted prow shall carry
       tokens of esteem. I tell you, these people
       are disposed to be firm both in feud and friendship,
1865   blameless, according to the customs of old."

       Then in that hall Halfdane's son
       again gave him treasures, twelve good things,
       and said with these gifts he should go home safely
       to his own dear kinsmen, but come again soon.
1870   Bending to kiss his friend, the king,
       the leader of the Shieldings, laid his hand
       on Beowulf's neck. Tears blinded
       the gray-haired old man, whose immense wisdom
       led him to expect what he wanted least:
1875   that never again would they meet, two gallant
       companions in council. The prince was so dear
       that Hrothgar could not withhold a sigh,
       though as a stern Shielding he shut in his heart
       how very much he cared for that man,
1880   locked it in his breast.

          Proudly, Beowulf
       strode through the grassy meadows, glittering,
       a warrior in gold. His ship awaited
       its lordly owner, riding at anchor.
       Often on that journey, generous Hrothgar
1885   was acclaimed for his gifts. That was a king!—
       blameless entirely, until his strength
       was taken by age; it destroys many men.

27. Homeward over the Sea

       The brave young Geats came striding together
       onto the shore, their ring-mail shining,
1890   hand-woven sarks. The sentinel saw them

[1861] *gannet's bath.* The sea.

approach as before, but felt it improper
rudely to hail such guests from his high
post on the rocks, so he rode down to greet them,
saying how welcome they would seem to their friends
1895   in the handsome byrnies they were wearing home.
Still on the sand, the spacious vessel
with twisted prow was loaded with treasures,
horses and battle-gear. The mast towered high
over Hrothgar's gifts from the Danish hoard.
1900   When Beowulf granted a gilded sword
to the Shielding who had guarded his ship, that man
was accounted a treasure the worthier by his comrades
who drank in the mead-hall.

    The land of the Danes
was left behind when they launched their ship
1905   upon the deep waters. Whipping by the mast
was the sail secured by a rope, and the craft
crashed through the waves, impelled by the wind,
swept onward, unhindered, over a sea
that foamed at its prow. Fleetly it crested
1910   wave after wave, until well-known cliffs
of the Geatish shore could be glimpsed from afar,
distant headlands. Then, driven by the breeze,
that gleaming vessel glided ashore.

Down to the harbor that guard came hurrying
1915   who for weeks had been anxiously scanning the waves
for any sign of those sorely-missed travelers.
Securely he anchored their ample ship
with ropes to the shore, lest the raging seas
should carry away that winsome craft.
1920   Then Beowulf commanded that the mighty treasure
be fetched from the hold. Those hardy companions
did not have to go far to find their king,
Hygelac, Hrethel's son, waiting at home
in his fortress by the sea-wall, among his friends.

1925   The building was splendid, the king very bold,
sitting high in his hall, Queen Hygd very young,
but wise and accomplished, though the winters were few
that this daughter of Haereth had dwelt in that castle.
She was never known to be niggardly
1930   in her generous gifts to the Geatish people—

whereas Thryth° had been more than miserly
before she became an excellent queen!

None of her friends had dared to face her
except her own lord, or dared to look her
1935   *straight in the eye, but that she would consider him*
ripe for the strangler's rope, drawn tight
by fists around his neck, then followed
by a blade descending on him, poor suspect;
the damascened sword clears up all doubt!
1940   *Such is not a suitable custom*
for a lady to practice, lovely though she be,
for a peace-weaver, killing a man on the pretext
that he has accosted her uncouthly.

Offa stopped that. At ale men told
1945   *of the following consequence: she had become*
far less vindictive and dangerous
from the first moment that she had set foot,
glimmering with gold and the grace of high birth,
on Offa's threshold, thinking to wed him.
1950   *On her father's advice she had ventured the voyage*
over pale green seas to the prince's hall,
and there on the throne, famed for good things,
she well enjoyed both her generous life
and the love in her heart for that lord of heroes,
1955   *for he was accounted, I have heard it said,*
the best and truest between the seas
of all the immense kindred of mankind;
Offa of the spear was widely respected
in gifts and in war. With wisdom he ruled
1960   *over his country, and he fathered Eomer,*
who flourished to be a support to his friends,
but grim in battle, Garmund's grandson!

28. Beowulf's Tale

Brave with his men came Beowulf
striding across the wide sands
1965   of the Geatish shore. From the south was shining
the candle of the world, the sun, as they came

[1931] *Thryth.* This digression (ll. 1931-62) recounts the story of the cruel Thryth, who becomes a good queen when she marries Offa. Offa was king of the Angles in the fourth century. The narrator seems to establish an opposition between the cruel Thryth and the kindly Hygd.

to the fortress where they knew that their noble lord,
the young king Hygelac, a hard man in battle
(who had ordered the slaying of Ongentheow°),
1970   was giving out rings. To this ruler the news
of the hero's return was quickly told,
that into the courtyard Beowulf was coming,
bearing his linden shield, alive,
hale from his fight, to the Geatish hall.

1975   At once they made room for the warriors, like guests
in their own home, as Hygelac bade,
and Beowulf, the victor, sat down on the bench
across from his kinsman. In courteous speech
Hygelac welcomed his friend with words
1980   both earnest and hearty, while Hygd the queen
moved through that building with a vessel of mead.
Loving her people, she passed the cup
to each warrior's hand, and in that high hall
the king began to question his friend,
1985   urging him to tell (as curiosity tore at him)
what fine adventures the Sea-Geats had found.

"What befell you, Beowulf my friend,
on that sudden journey that you resolved on,
seeking a fight far over the seas,
1990   a battle in Heorot? Could you help at all
to defeat the sorrow of Hrothgar, that famous
king of the Danes? Because of his grief
I sighed myself, having little desire
that my friend should go, no faith in that venture,
1995   entreating you to leave that monster alone
and to let the South Danes settle for themselves
their war with Grendel. Thanks be to God
that I see you at home now, safe and sound."

Beowulf spoke, Edgetheow's son:
2000   "I shall keep no secret, Hygelac my king,
about that battle between us two,
me and Grendel, when we met together
in Hrothgar's hall, that place where he had
formerly caused such cruel sorrow
2005   for all the Shieldings. But I avenged them
so well that in all the world not one

1969 *Ongentheow.* With Beowulf's return home, the poet introduces a new tribal feud, that between the Geats and the Swedes. This feud becomes increasingly prominent as the poem moves toward conclusion. Here Hygelac is called the slayer of Ongentheow, the Swedish king, but the real slayer, we learn later, was Eofor, one of Hygelac's warriors. See the summary of events and genealogical tables on pp. 161-162.

of Grendel's kindred, that greedy race
that dwells in the clutches of malice, has cause
to boast of that fight at midnight. When first
2010   I arrived at that ring-hall to visit its ruler,
he showed me at once (or as soon as he knew
what my purpose was) to a warrior's seat
suitably near to his own son.

"All were high-spirited. Never have I seen
2015   in any hall under Heaven's vault
more pleasure at mead. At times that pledge
of peace to her people, the queen, would pass
among the young men to rally them, making
presents of twisted rings. At times
2020   it was Hrothgar's daughter who handed around
the ale-vessel to each in turn.
I heard those warriors who sat in the hall
call her Freawaru° when they thanked her for
some precious gift. She is promised,
2025   fresh and golden, to Froda's son.
It is her father, the Shieldings' friend
and king, who has planned this, counting on it
to settle a painful feud, with the priceless
gift of his daughter. But it is doubtful
2030   that warriors will leave their spears for long
when a prince has fallen, though the bride be fair!

"Little may it please the Heathobards' lord
or his people to see a prince of the Danes
enter their hall with that elegant lady,
2035   *honored by the elders, and on him shining*
an ancient sword, a ring-marked heirloom
a treasure once held by the Heathobards
in the past, when they had the power to keep it . . .

29-30. The Fated Hall

"Until they squandered in desperate shield-play
2040   *their own lives and their loved ones' too.*
Then when he sees the ring on that sword
an old spear warrior will speak out,
remembering slayings—his mood is savage—

2023*Freawaru.* Beowulf predicts (ll. 2023-69) events that the author and his audience knew had already taken place. Hrothgar married his daughter Freawaru to Froda's son, Ingeld, in an attempt to settle an old feud with Ingeld's tribe, the Heathobards. But this marriage failed to prevent renewed warfare between the two tribes.

and grim in his heart will begin to test
2045 *the younger man's courage, recalling him*
to thoughts of war by saying these words:
'My lord, look well upon that weapon.
Is it not the blade your father bore,
glorious in his helmet, gripping it tight,
2050 *wielding it splendidly when the Danes slew him?*
The proud Shieldings won, when Withergyld
lay dying among our fallen men.
Now here the son of one of those slayers
comes jubilant with his jewelled treasure
2055 *into the Heathobards' hall, displaying*
that weapon which you by rights should wear!'

"Thus he incites him, saying such words
at each opportunity, until the time comes
when Freawaru's thane, for his father's deeds,
2060 *must fall, blood-drenched from the biting sword,*
a forfeit, and the slayer will get away free
with his life, for well he knows his own land.

"Then on both sides the pledge will be broken,
the oath of friendship, when desire for feud
2065 *wells up in Ingeld, and after his grief,*
cooler will be his love for his queen.
I count the less, then, on loyalty,
sincere friendship without deceit,
from the noble Danes.

"Now I shall speak°
2070 *more about Grendel, so that you may imagine,*
O giver of treasures, when we came to grips,
what happened to me. When Heaven's gem
had vanished from the sky, the violent guest
came angry in the evening to seek us out
2075 *where as yet unharmed we guarded the hall.*
Grim was the fate that befell Handscio
in that sudden battle; the belted warrior
was the first to die. That famous thane
fell prey to Grendel, who gulped him down,
2080 *his entire body. But the bloody-toothed slayer*
thought only of slaughter, and did not the sooner
want to go out again, empty-handed,

2069*Now I shall speak.* This digression (ll. 2069-2143), Beowulf's account of his victory over Grendel and Grendel's mother, is different in tone and some details from the narrator's account.

from that high hall. He put out his hand,
eager to test my strength, and took
2085 *firm grip on me. A glove hung from him,*
gaping and strange, cleverly strengthened
with bands of ornament, adorned all over,
with devilish skill, with dragon pelts.
The wicked ravager wanted to thrust
2090 *me in there, guiltless, one of many,*
but it dawned on him that he could not do this
when I sprang to my feet in an angry stance.

"It would take too long to tell how I gave
requital to that killer for every crime,
2095 *how I, my lord, brought honor to all*
the Geatish folk. He got away,
enjoying his life for a little longer,
but he had to relinquish his right hand
to escape from Heorot, and crawl away humbled
2100 *to his dismal end in the depths of the mere.*

"Well did the friend of the Shieldings reward me
for that hard battle with the brightest treasures
of delicate gold, after day had come
and we had sat down to the warriors' feast.
2105 *There were stories and songs. The astute old Shielding*
gave us tales from long ago.
At times he stroked the joyous strings
of the round-harp, at times he narrated a story
that was sad and true, or a tale of wonder,
2110 *recounted correctly according to custom.*
And then, at times, the intrepid old king,
crippled with age, would begin to recall
his former strength, and would heave a sigh
when, ancient of years, he remembered his youth.

2115 *"Thus in that hall for the whole day*
we took our pleasure, until once more
night came to men. Then Grendel's mother
was ready at once for her wicked revenge.
Sorrowful she came. Her son had been taken
2120 *by death—and the war-hate of the Weathergeats.*
Vengeful she came, and boldly she killed
a warrior, and life sped away from Ashere,
a wise old councillor of the Shielding clan,
and when morning came they could not carry
2125 *their death-weary friend to do him honor*

on the funeral pyre with a flaming brand,
for her fiendish embrace had borne away
his body to the depths of the black tarn!

"To Hrothgar that sorrow was the hardest to bear
2130 *of all that had fallen upon his folk,*
and at his wits' end he asked me once more
(evoking your name) to perform valor,
to put my life at risk in that pool
in a bid for glory and for bright reward.

2135 *"As you know, I found that terrible foe,*
the witch who guarded those surging waters,
and for a while it was doubtful which
would win, but the water welled with blood
when I hacked off her head in that battle-hall
2140 *with an ancient blade. In agony, she*
gasped out her last; my own life was still
unmarked by fate, and with many fine things
the warriors' protector acknowledged my worth.

31. The Dragon Awakes

"Thus in accordance with custom lived
2145 the king of the Danes, who gave me no cause
to feel neglect, for he gave me treasures
equal to the honor that I had earned.
To convey them to you, my valiant Hygelac,
was my first wish, to show my good will,
2150 for all my happiness lies in your hands.
I have few close kinsmen but you, my king."

He bade them bring in the boar head-piece,
the helmet of battle, the frost-gray byrnie
and the gleaming sword, and then he spoke:
2155 "That wise king, Hrothgar, rewarded me
with this noble byrnie, but he wanted you to know
the details of whose bright heritage it was.
He said that his elder brother had owned it
and worn it to battle, yet Hrothgar did not wish
2160 to pass it on to his princely son,
proud Heoroward, though he held him dear.
Now all this is yours to use as you will!"

And then I heard that four swift horses,

matched bays of apple brown,
2165 were added to this bounty. Beowulf granted
a huge treasure of horses and war-gear
to his king—and thus should a kinsman do,
not weave nets to trap another,
designing his death in secret. To Hygelac
2170 Beowulf was ever loyal in battle,
and each was thoughtful for the other's welfare.
I heard that he gave to Hygd that necklace,
so wondrously made, that Wealtheow the queen
had given to him, together with three
2175 of the supple steeds in their glorious saddles.
She, too, was more glorious, with that gift on her breast.

Thus Edgetheow's son revealed himself
to be worthy and brave; renowned for his battles,
he aspired to glory. Never did he strike
2180 at a dear companion in a drunken rage,
or know such anger—for he was nourished
by God's own gift, the greatest strength
of all humankind. He was humble as a youth,
and his Geatish comrades had thought him a coward,
2185 nor had the lord of those hearth companions
wished to acknowledge his worth on the mead-bench;
they believed that his spirit was lax and slothful,
unfit for an atheling! But, destined for fame,
the prince saw time reverse such opinion.

2190 Now Hygelac, famous for fighting, commanded
that one of his father's heirlooms be fetched,
a treasure of gold. Among the Geats
no sword was known more noble than this!
He laid it formally in Beowulf's lap
2195 and added to that gift a great estate
of seven thousand hides,° with hall and throne.
They both, in that Geatish realm, had birthright
to land and privilege, but more of the latter
fell to him who was higher of rank.
2200 Vast were the battles that then developed
in later days, after the death
of Hygelac the king. From behind bright shields
shining swords hewed down his son
Heardred, sought out by invading Swedes
2205 where he stood courageous among his ranks

2196*hides.* A "hide" varies according to time and place; sometimes it is as much as 120 acres.

in the midst of the fray. They had marked him for slaughter.
The broad kingdom came then to Beowulf
who ruled it well for fifty winters
(a noble old guardian of his native land,
2210   wise king to the Geats), until One began—
a dragon!—to rule in the dark of night.

High on the heath he guarded a hoard
inside a stone barrow. Down to it steeply
ran a secret way, and into it wandered
a man who by accident came on that ancient
2215   heathen treasure, and took in his hand
a priceless goblet. Though beguiled by a thief
who came while he slept, the dragon concealed
nothing of his wrath. The neighboring warriors
2220   and farmers found out how great was his fury!

32. Strife Comes Anew

The man had not wished to enter the worm's hoard!°
He who performed this fatal act
was a low-born servant in distress,
fleeing from a master's flogging
2225   for some misdeed. He needed shelter
and went inside, but at once he saw
something that made him sick with horror.
There was no mistaking the strangeness that lurked
deep in the rock. The wretch was terrified!
2230   Yet still he reached out for more disaster—
and clutched the cup.

        A king's ransom
of ancient treasure lay in that earth-house.
Once, long ago, a noble warrior
had given the matter grave thought
2235   before he hid that vast inheritance,
dear to his people. Death had taken them,
all but him, at some earlier time,
and left him alone of that lofty race,
a friendless guardian of fabulous wealth.
2240   He felt that his own days would be too few
to enjoy those riches. The barrow stood ready,

2221 *worm's hoard. Worm* is an archaic word for dragon.

newly built above the waves
at the edge of a cliff, with no easy access.
Inside it he carried a kingdom's bounty,
2245   priceless rings and plated gold,
a worthy hoard! Then he said these words:

"Keep, earth, now that kings may not,
this treasure of ours! From you we took it
in the beginning—then grievous strife,
2250   death in battle, took each of my brave
and noble kinsmen who had known such joy
in the gabled hall. Who now remains
to brandish the sword or burnish the cup
that we drank from together? They all have gone.
2255   And from the high crown of the helmet crumble
the plaques of gold; the polishers sleep
who were wont to brighten that mask of battle.
And the cloak of mail that endured the clash
of iron swords biting over the shield—
2260   it rusts on the wearer, no longer a ring-shirt
proud to wander the traveler's ways
by a hero's side. No more will the harp
sing happy songs, nor will the good hawk
swoop through the hall, nor the swift stallion
2265   stamp in the doorway. Death has sent out
many of the living from the land of men!"
Thus one man sang his words of woe
alone, for his lost ones. Sadly he lingered
days and nights until death's flood
2270   swept over his heart.

    The hoard was found
standing open by that old dawn fiend,
he who burning seeks out barrows,
the smooth evil dragon who soars through the night
surrounded by flame, striking fear
2275   into hearts below. He always looks
for a hoard in a mound, and for many years
will guard heathen gold. Little good does it do him!
This time it was for three hundred winters
he had kept that hoard with a huge craftiness
2280   in its treasure mound, until one man
humiliated him. That man carried
the cup to his lord, begging for deliverance
at his hands from the whip. Thus the hoard was exposed,
the treasure diminished, when mercy was given

2285 to the churl, empty-handed, for his lord was enchanted
by this golden vessel of long ago—

Then the dragon awoke and strife came anew!
He snaked along that surface of stone
and found a footprint. The foe had stepped
2290 all too close to his evil head.
Thus may a man not marked by fate
survive with ease many a venture
by the grace of God! But the hoard's guardian
moved along eagerly, hoping to meet
2295 the thief who had sorely disturbed his sleep.
Blazing with wrath, he blasted around
outside the barrow; no one could be seen
in all that waste. But the thought of war
had stirred him up, and at times he struck inward,
2300 seeking his cup, and he saw again
how someone had tampered with his treasure,
disturbed his gold. That guardian waited
impatiently for the day to pass;
by the time night fell his fury was boundless!
2305 He wished to pay back with a billow of flame
his dear cup's theft. Day drew to a close
as the dragon wished, and he did not wait,
lingering on that cliff ledge, but leapt up with fire,
a coil of flame! A cruel beginning
2310 that was to the folk. Far worse was the end:
they paid for that gold with their giver of rings.

33. The Hall-Burning

The fiend began to spit out flame,
to burn the bright buildings, pouring from above
a stream of fire that men fled from, aghast—
2315 that hostile sky-worm sought to leave
nothing alive. The leaping fury
of his wicked malice was widely seen,
how he hunted and hated the Geatish folk,
intent on harm. Then back to his hoard,
2320 to his secret den, he would shoot before daybreak,
having fanged those people about with fire,
with peaks of flame. He put his trust
in his home to protect him—that hope proved false!

The horrible news was quickly made known

2325   to Beowulf, that in burning flames
        his home, the best of halls, had perished,
        the gift-throne of the Geats. That brought the gravest
        despair to his heart, the heaviest thoughts,
        for he feared that he might have offended God,
2330   bitterly angered him, possibly broken
        some ancient law. With a long sigh,
        he mulled over such dark imaginings—
        as was not his custom. The coiling dragon
        had destroyed from outside that island of safety,
2335   the people's fortress, with fire; for that
        the prince of the Weathergeats planned revenge.
        The protector of warriors, the lord of the troop,
        commanded his smith to make of iron
        an ornate shield, for well he knew
2340   that a shield of wood could offer no shelter
        against flame. That good old atheling,
        who for years had held the wealth of the hoard,
        was doomed to encounter the end of his days
        in this fleeting life, along with the dragon.
2345   The prince of rings despised absolutely
        the thought of advancing with all his thanes
        in a great force seeking a solitary flyer;
        he did not fear his fight with the dragon
        or take much account of that creature's strength,
2350   for he had braved many great battles,
        passing safely through difficult straits
        from the day that he, alone, had cleansed Heorot
        and crushed to death the demon strength
        of that loathsome clan.

            Nor was that the least
2355   *of his encounters where Hygelac° was killed,*
        the princely friend of the Geatish people,
        Hrethel's son, slain on Frisian soil
        by a blood-thirsty sword in a mighty battle,
        beaten down by the blade. Beowulf survived
2360   *that slaughter by means of his skill in swimming,*
        taking with him thirty trophies
        when he launched himself alone on the sea.
        Of little value were the Hetwares' victory
        taunts at Beowulf as they bore down

[2355] *Hygelac.* In this second digression on Hygelac's raid on the Frisians (ll. 2354-79), Hygd offers Beowulf the king-ship after Hygelac is killed. Beowulf rejects the offer in deference to Hygelac's son, Heardred. See the summary of the feud between the Swedes and the Geats on p. 162 for a clarification of what happens when. The first reference to the Frisian raid (ll. 1197-1214) focuses on the necklace Hygelac wears.

2365   *with their wooden shields, for few there were*
        who left him, able to limp back home!

        After that battle Edgetheow's son
        swam to his people across the sea.
        There Hygd offered him hoard and kingdom,
2370   *rings and throne, for she did not think*
        that her noble son could hold the ancestral
        hall against strangers when Hygelac was dead.
        But even in need the thanes could not
        find any means of persuading that man
2375   *to be high king over Heardred's head,*
        the son of his lord, or to rule his land.
        Instead, he supported the young prince
        among the folk with friendly advice
        until he was older. Then two exiles°
2380   *sought Heardred out, the sons of Ohtere*
        rebelling against his brother, Onla,
        the best of kings who gave kindly treasures
        betokening honor between the two seas,
        a famous prince. That was fatal to Heardred.
2385   *For hospitality, Hygelac's son*
        received a mortal blow from the sword.
        Then Onla left for his own land
        when Heardred lay dead, and he allowed
        Beowulf to hold that royal hall
2390   *and rule the Geats. That was a good king!*

34. The Father's Lament

        But Beowulf did not forget that battle,
        the fall of his lord, in later days,
        when Eadgils, the other son, sought his aid.
        He helped him with an army, with warriors and weapons,
2395   *across the wide ocean. Then Eadgils avenged*
        his cold exile: he slew his king!
        Thus valiantly Beowulf had survived
        battles and feuds and bitter fights,
        each dangerous quest, until that day
2400   when he had to confront the fiery worm.

[2379] *two exiles.* Eanmund and Eadgils, sons of the Swedish king, Ohtere. The narrator's account of the death of Heardred and of Beowulf's coming to the throne (ll. 2379-96) is the first of four accounts of the feud between the Geats and the Swedes. It is chronologically the last episode in the feud. See the summary of events and genealogical tables for an orderly presentation of this feud. The other accounts are Beowulf's (ll. 2472-2509), the narrator's story about Wiglaf's father (ll. 2602-19), and the messenger's account (ll. 2922-3007).

The ruler of the Geats strode forth in rage,
one man among twelve, to seek that monster.
He had found by then the reason for that feud,
the baleful slaughter, for someone had brought
2405 the fabulous cup to the hands of his king,
and he who had wakened the hideous strife
now made in that troop the thirteenth man,
a fearful captive. Trembling, he was forced
to show the way, and he went unwilling
2410 to where he alone knew the earth-hall lay,
the underground barrow, close to the ocean,
the pounding waves. Wondrous ornaments
filled it within, and a frightful custodian,
primed for war, held those precious things
2415 beneath the earth. That treasure was not
an easy bargain for anyone to get!

The king sat down at the top of the cliff
and turned to face the friends from his hearth.
The heart of the lord of the Geats was heavy,
2420 his mind restless and ready for the slaughter,
wyrd very near, waiting to seek
his soul's hoard, and to wrest asunder
his life from his body. Not for long now
would that warrior's life be wound with flesh!
2425 *Beowulf spoke,*° *Edgetheow's son:*
"I endured in my youth many dangerous battles,
violent encounters; I recall them well.
I was only seven when I was received
by Hrethel, the ring-lord, from my father's hand.
2430 *He cared for me and treated me kindly*
with gold and feasting, a friendly kinsman.
I was not any less beloved to him
in his athelings' hall than his own sons,
Herebald and Hathcyn and my dear Hygelac.

"Untimely prepared for that eldest prince
2435 *was the bed of death by a kinsman's deed,*
when Hathcyn struck down Herebald
with a bright arrow from his horn-tipped bow:
he missed his mark and murdered his kinsman,
2440 *shot his own brother with a bloody dart—*

---

²⁴²⁵*Beowulf spoke.* In this digression, Beowulf speaks of his childhood (ll. 2425-34), of Hathcyn's accidental killing of Herebald (ll. 2434-71), and of the war between the Geats and the Swedes (ll. 2471-2509)

unaccountably, a sorrowful crime
that could not be paid for, painful to the heart,
a valiant life that must go unavenged,
a miserable thing—as for an old man°
2445   *who can only stand by when his boy is riding*
young on the gallows, and a grieving lament
is all he can say, for his own son hangs there
as food for the ravens, and old and infirm
he cannot offer any help at all.

2450   *"Then every morning reminds him again*
of his boy's dying, and he does not wish for
another son who will guard the ancestral
hall and fortune, when the first has been
exposed to death through some evil deed.
2455   *Sadly he sees in his son's dwelling place*
a wine-hall empty—the wind has ceased—
a round-harp bereft—the rhythms sleep—
a hale youth in darkness. There is no harp-thrum there,
no songs in the wine-courts as once there were.—

35. Beowulf's Attack

2460   *"Then he goes to his couch and begins to chant,*
alone, for his lost one. All too large
seem house and lands.

"Such was the heaviness
the lord of the Geats felt after the loss
of his son; he could not right that slaughter
2465   *by punishment, or even permit*
the relief to himself of hating the slayer
for his violent deed, though he was not dear to him.
That sorrow weighed so sorely upon him
that he gave up life's joys, and chose God's light.
2470   *But he gave to his sons, as a good man does,*
his landed wealth, when he passed away.

"Then again there was war between the Weathergeats
and the Swedish folk across the sea—

[2444]*as for an old man.* Beowulf offers an analogy to explain Hrethel's feeling about Hathcyn's accidental killing of Herebald. According to Germanic law, relatives of criminals could not seek retribution or *wergild* for the execution of their ken. Hrethel, then, is like a father whose son has been executed. He is filled with despair not just because of the absence of his son but because he can take no action.

hard battles after Hrethel died.
2475   *Ongentheow's men were mighty and bold,*
active warriors, who did not want
to sue for peace, but at Sorrowhill
fell on the Geats and slaughtered them fiercely.
My kinsmen were valiant; they avenged all that
2480   *by strenuous fighting, and I have found*
that the Swedish leader bought his life
at a high price. But to Hathcyn, now king
of the Weathergeats, that war proved fatal.
I recall that Hygelac avenged Hathcyn.
2485   *A blade struck down his brother's slayer;*
though Ongentheow launched an attack upon Eofor,
the Geat split open the old Scylfing's°
masked helmet. His hand remembered
many a battle, and did not hold back
2490   *the killing blow.*

   "I, too, requited
the gifts of my prince, as was most proper,
with my bright sword on that battle field;
he had given me the holdings and the hall I was born in.
He had no reason to seek a courageous
2495   *man of less might from among the Gifthas*
or the Danes of the Spear, or the Swedes themselves,
to buy loyalty there, for keen was my longing
to stand with my king in every conflict,
to show my love so long as this sword
2500   *endures, which so often has given me aid;*
it fell to me in my fight with Dayraven,°
the Huga, whom I slew with my bare hands.
He did not manage to bring to his master
that bright adornment, the Danish necklace,
2505   *from Hygelac's body, for in that battle*
he fell, bearer of the Frisian standard—
and not by the sword; beneath my grip
his body broke. But now the blade
that shines in my hand shall fight for this hoard!"

2510   In brave words Beowulf vowed
his last deed: "I have endured
many a battle, yet again I must,
as wise guardian of the Geats, seek conflict

2487*Scylfing's.* Swede's.
2501*Dayraven.* The Frisian (Hugan) killer of Hygelac. Lines 2501-08 make up the third reference to Hygelac's fatal raid on the Frisians.

with that murderous dragon, if he dares
2515   to come to me out from his earthen hall."

Then final words he spoke to his friends,
standing there masked in their shining helmets:
"I would bear no sword or weapon to that battle
if I knew another way to fight that worm,
2520   to carry out my boast with honor
and come to grips, as I did with Grendel.
But this time I fear hot battle fumes,
dragon breath and deadly venom,
so I'll fight the beast with shield and byrnie,
2525   and I shall not flee a foot's space
from that barrow's guardian. But what *wyrd,* and God,
decree, will happen. My spirits are high,
and I need no boast to inspire me now.

"Wait here above, my byrnied warriors,
2530   shining in your armor, to see which of us shall
better survive this violent quarrel
down on the cliff side; and remember, this quest
is not within anyone else's power
but mine alone, to match him in strength
2535   and quell him nobly. With courage I shall
gain that gold, or grim will be
the defeat that claims the life of your friend!"

Helmeted and fierce, the brave fighter
rose with his shield; in his shining byrnie,
2540   trusting in his solitary strength, he went
clambering down the stones, no cowardly man!
Then he who had ventured on violent battles,
when manly virtue had counted for much
in the clash of tribesmen, came upon
2545   an arch of stone standing in the wall
through which a fiery stream came flowing
out from the mound, nor could any brave man
pass without burning to penetrate
deep to that hoard through that dragon flame.

2550   Then the Weathergeat let a single word
burst out in fury from his breast;
stout-hearted, he stormed, and through the gray stone
that bright and vivid voice resounded.
Hate was awakened! When the hoard's guardian
2555   heard human speech, there remained no space

to ask for friendship, for billowing forth
from beneath the gray stone came noxious smoke
from the monster's hot breath. The barrow thundered!
On the cliff's ledge the Geatish lord
2560   swung his shield to face that stranger.
This fired the heart of the fearsome serpent
with battle fury. Already Beowulf
had drawn his sword, an heirloom shining
with tempered edges. Terror came
2565   raging at each enemy from the other!

The prince took his stand behind his steep
and curving shield, as the dragon coiled
abruptly together. Beowulf waited.
The gleaming worm came at him; gliding
2570   smooth in its flames, it sped to its fate.
But the time that Beowulf's shield protected
his life and limb was less than he hoped for
when first he had thought of having it forged
to wield in that battle—for *wyrd* did not
2575   decree him victory. But his valiant hand
had swung the sword, and down it struck,
so hard against those gleaming scales
that the bright edge blunted against the bone.
It bit less nobly than its king had need of
2580   in such bitter straits!

    Then the barrow's guardian,
enraged after that ferocious swing,
spat out flames that billowed far
around the battle. Beowulf did not
boast of his victory, for his naked blade,
2585   that weapon so long a willing companion,
had failed him at need. That famous son
of Edgetheow did not find his journey easy
when it came to leaving the land of his kinsmen:
against his wishes he would have to go
2590   to a dwelling elsewhere—as all are doomed
to take their leave of this fleeting life.

Then again those enemies clashed together.
The guardian of the hoard took heart, his breast
swelling with rage, and the erstwhile ruler
2595   found himself trapped in the heart of the fire!

Not at all did those champions so carefully chosen
from his comrades leap up to stand by their leader,
valiant in the fight, no, they fled to the woods
to save their lives—except one, whose sorrow
2600   tore at his heart. The ties of kinship
can never be ignored by a noble man!

36. Wiglaf

He was called Wiglaf, Weohstan's son,°
a beloved shield warrior, a Shilfing prince
of Swedish kindred. He saw that his king
2605   was suffering from the heat beneath his helmet,
and recalling those good things he had granted him—
the wealthy home of the Wagmunding clan
and every folk right his father had owned—
he could not restrain himself from stretching
2610   for his lindenwood shield and his lambent sword.

That sword was famous to folk as the heirloom
of Eanmund the Swede, Ohtere's son
who was slain as he stood on Geatish soil,
killed by Weohstan. To his Shilfing kinsman
2615   *Weohstan took those battle trophies,*
helmet and byrnie and ancient blade,
and Onla granted him Eanmund's gear,
his nephew's armor, saying nothing
about the slaying of his brother's son.
2620   *For many years Weohstan kept that weapon*
and the byrnie, bright treasures, until his son
could perform such deeds as his father did.
Then among the Weathergeats Weohstan gave him
that priceless war-gear when he passed away,
2625   *a wise old fighter.*

This was the first time
that the young champion had had a chance
to stand in battle beside his lord.
His courage did not fail, nor his father's heirloom
falter at that fighting, as the fiend discovered
2630   later, when they came to clash together.

2602*Weohstan's son.* See the summary of events on p. 162 for Weohstan's part in the feud between the Geats and
Swedes. The digression (in italics, ll. 2611-25) is the third reference to the war between the Geats and the Swedes.

Wiglaf spoke, saying many words
of censure to his friends. His heart was sad:
"I remember that time, drinking our mead
in the lofty hall, when we promised our lord
2635   who was giving us weapons of gold to engage us,
that we would repay him for that precious gear
if need occurred, requite him in action
for helmet and sword. Such was the reason
that we were the men whom he chose from his warriors
2640   for this venture, remembering our vaunted worth
at the giving of weapons. He had thought we were
eager to wear helmets and hurl our spears.
Our lord had planned to do this alone;
the protector of the Geats undertook it without us,
2645   he who had gained the greatest glory
among men for his deeds, but the day has come
that Beowulf needs the combined strength
of all his warriors.

"Let us go to his aid,
and help our leader lapped round by that heat,
2650   by those grim flames! God knows
that I should prefer the fire to devour
my body with my lord than to live without helping him!
A shameful thing if we bore home shields
after this fight, unless we first
2655   had felled the foe to save our friend,
our generous prince. It is not a just
return for his bounty that alone of the band
he should suffer affliction, and fall in battle.
For myself, I shall share my shield and helmet,
2660   byrnie and sword with Beowulf!"
As he waded then in his shining war-gear
through the deadly smoke, he said to his lord:
"My king and kinsman, this is your calling.
In the days of your youth you swore that you
2665   would never give up your noble purpose
so long as you lived! My lord, single-minded,
you must now try to protect your life
with all your might. I shall help you!"

After those words, the angry worm
2670   launched his attack for a second time.
Brilliant and shining in sheets of flame

and waves of fire he sought his foes,
burning Wiglaf's shield to the boss!
Not even his byrnie could offer him aid,
2675   so the brave youth dived beneath his dear
kinsman's iron shield, when his own
was gone in the blaze. Then again the king
remembered valor, and swung his mighty
blade with great strength, so it struck down hard
2680   on the beast's head—and broke apart!

Nagling was the name of that noble sword,
but it failed at battle. Beowulf was not granted
success with any blade of iron;
his hand was too strong. No sword could help him.
2685   They tell me his swing would overtax
the mightiest blade when he brandished it,
and in battle he was none the better for it.

Then to the attack for the third time
rushed the fierce fire-drake, intent on his feud,
2690   charging at that hero when he saw his chance,
raging with fire, gripping him around
the neck with his terrible fangs! And now
Beowulf's life-blood drenched his body!

37. The Slaying of the Dragon

Then at need, I heard, Wiglaf made known
2695   at his king's side his strength and courage,
the hardy keenness that was his heritage.
He did not heed that dragon's head
but burnt his hand in helping his kinsman,
striking a little lower down
2700   so that his sword went slicing into
that fearsome beast, and the billowing flames
began to diminish. Then the lord of the Geats
came to his senses, remembered the *sax*
beneath his mail, and drawing that knife,
2705   plunged the blade in the dragon's belly!
They felled the beast; combining their strength,
the two noble kinsmen had cut him down
both together. Thus should a man be,
a thane at need!

> To Beowulf that
>
> 2710 marked the last of his mortal victories,
> of his deeds in this world, for that wound the dragon
> had given him began to grow,
> to fester and burn, and soon he found
> that within his breast a bitter poison
> 2715 was welling up. The old warrior
> sat down to think (and deep were his thoughts)
> on a seat by the wall, observing how the work
> of giants, great arches of jutting stone,
> supported that ancient place with pillars.
> 2720 Then with cool water gentle Wiglaf
> began to refresh his failing lord,
> to lave away the blood, and loosen
> the helmet from that weary head.
> Beowulf spoke, despite the pain
> 2725 of his dreadful wound, for he knew full well
> that he had played out his allotted portion
> of pleasure on earth; that was all passed away,
> and death had come incalculably near:
>
> "Now I would give my battle gear
> 2730 to my heir, had I been granted any
> son of my flesh to safeguard my memory
> beyond my life. For fifty years
> I have kept these people safe; no king
> dwells among neighboring tribes who dares
> 2735 to seek me out with brandished swords
> and terrify us. In my time I abided
> what fate would bring, held fast to my own,
> sought no strife nor swore unrightfully
> vows unkept. Because of all this
> 2740 I take pleasure, even now in pain from my wounds,
> that the Ruler of Men has little reason
> to accuse me of the murder of kinsmen
> when life leaves my body.
>
> "Now quickly, go look
> at the hoard that is stacked beneath that gray stone,
> 2745 now that the dragon lies dead, dear Wiglaf,
> sorely wounded, bereft of his wealth.
> Hurry, so that I may have the time
> to admire that treasure, that mound of gold
> and ruddy jewels, and then the more gently

2750   in sight of that brilliance I may abandon
        the life and lordship I have held for so long."

38. The Treasure in the Mound

        I heard that Wiglaf, Weohstan's son,
        on hearing these words of his wounded lord,
        obeyed him, and went in his ring-mail byrnie,
2755   woven for battle, into that barrow.
        There the young prince, as he passed along
        the bench, saw many a jewelled brooch,
        and gold things glittering all over the ground,
        wondrous weapons hanging high on the wall
2760   in the den of that dragon, the old dawn flyer,
        and drinking goblets, their polishers gone,
        sockets agape where garnets had been,
        and helmets rusty with age, and rings
        twisted with cunning. Easily may treasure,
2765   gold in a mound, overpower the mind
        of anyone human, heed it who will!

        He also saw hovering, high over the hoard,
        a golden banner, the greatest of woven
        wonders, and from it a light poured forth,
2770   showing him further along the floor
        the glowing wealth. But no glimpse of the dragon
        was there to be seen, for the sword had destroyed him.

        Then those riches, I heard, were ransacked by
        one man alone, who laid in his arms
2775   all that he wished of that giant-wrought wealth,
        goblets and dishes, and the golden banner,
        that brightest of beacons. The old lord's blade
        with its edges of iron had earlier slain
        him who had guarded those heaps of gold
2780   for a long time with the terror of fire
        hot before the mound, surging up murderously
        at the darkest hour—until he died.
        Wiglaf was in the wildest haste
        to get back with the treasures, tormented by
2785   the question of whether he would come upon
        his prince alive, the Weathergeats' lord
        whom he had left dying for his deed of courage.

Bearing that fabulous wealth, he found
his leader bloody, that life at the ebb.
2790   Then Wiglaf, once more, caressed him with water
to soothe him, until the spear of his words
burst through his breast, and Beowulf spoke,
in pain, looking upon the gold:

"For all this magnificence I must needs
2795   give words of thanks to the wise Lord,
eternal God, for this gold I see,
for letting me gain such a gift of wealth
for my dear people before my death!
I have traded my life for these splendid treasures;
2800   they will fulfill the needs of the folk—
I, their lord, may be here no longer.
After the pyre ask them to build me
a mound shining above the shore
at Whalesness, high and whitely gleaming,
2805   to remember me by, and for seafaring men
to speak of as Beowulf's barrow, whenever
they see it from a distance when driving their ships
on the misty paths of the perilous seas."

That bold leader then lifted from his neck
2810   his golden necklace, and gave it to Wiglaf
with his blade and byrnie and the brilliant helmet,
and commanded the youth to use them well:
"You are the last of our Wagmunding° line;
wyrd has lured all the others away,
2815   my courageous kinsmen, called to the death
of athelings, and I must go after them!"
Those were the last words from the old lord's
heart, before having to taste the hostile
flames of the pyre, but his soul went forth
2820   to find the judgment of the just.

39. Wiglaf's Words

Sick at heart the young man saw
his dearest friend painfully faring
beyond his reach, stretched there on a rock
at the end of life. The slayer, also,

2813*Wagmunding.* Beowulf and Wiglaf's family name.

2825 lay there dying; that terrible dragon
was curved like a bow, though bent no longer
to hold the guardianship of the hoard
in wicked bitterness, for the blade had deposed him.
That hammer's legacy, hard and sharp,
2830 had cut him down in his coiling attack,
and now he lay dead near the barrow door—
no more to arch through the still air of midnight,
to float through the heavens flaunting his riches,
a sight to remember!—for he sank to earth,
2835 a sky-demon quelled by the strength of that hand.
Indeed, I have heard that rare is the hero
(though he were daring in every deed)
who would not have failed in such a feat—
braving the venom of dragon breath
2840 or running his hands through that golden hoard,
if he came upon its fiery keeper
awake in the cave! To Beowulf was
a king's ransom of gold requited;
but man and monster had met the end
2845 of this fleeting life.

It was not long then
before the traitors slunk out from the trees,
all ten together, having broken their troth,
not daring to acknowledge their lord's great need
for their spears in battle. Bright in their armor,
2850 but shamefully bearing their shields, they came
forward to the place where their prince lay dead,
and regarded Wiglaf. Wearily he sat,
as a comrade should, near his lord's shoulder,
trying to revive him, to no avail.
2855 Much as he cared to, he could not manage
to keep life burning in the breast of his king,
nor move the Lord's will in any manner,
for God in justice and judgment had ordered
the day and its deeds, as he always does.

2860 And then from Wiglaf those craven warriors
found rough words ready for their return!
Thus he spoke, the son of Weohstan,
sadly to those friends he had formerly loved:
"This must be told, for it is the truth.
2865 Beowulf gave you gold and byrnies for battle,

the warriors' armor you are wearing now.
When on the mead-bench you sat making merry,
he would pass a helmet to a hall companion,
or a byrnie, or whatever he could find that was beautiful
2870 from home or afar to honor his friends—
a loyalty that was completely lost,
thrown away on thanes like you!

"When war came upon him, the king of our people
had no cause to boast of his battle companions!
2875 Yet the God of Victories helped him avenge
his life by his own hand when high deeds were needed.
And I, in my own way, tried to offer
protection at battle, indeed attempted
to persevere beyond my power,
2880 and the deadly foe seemed the feebler for it.
After I struck him, the flames less strongly
flowed from his jaws. But defenders too few
stood by our king when strife came upon him.

"Now giving of treasure to honor your troth
2885 must end, and your kinsmen, because of you,
must lose their right to enjoy this land
and the comfort of living among loyal friends,
when the athelings hear how men will harken
far and wide to your defection,
2890 your inglorious deed. Death is better
to every warrior than life without honor!"

40. Hygelac's Arrogance

He ordered then that the outcome of the fight
be announced above, where the shield-bearing nobles
had sat, sad in mind, all morning, all day,
2895 waiting, expecting one of two things:
the return of their lord, or the last day
of his dear life. Little did that man
who rode up to the headland hide his news;
his voice rang out with all the truth:

2900 "Now gone is our joy, our generous prince!
The lord of the Geats lies on his deathbed,
stretched out in slaughter by the serpent's deed!
Endlong beside him his enemy lies
slain by the *sax*. With the sword our king

2905 could find no way of wounding that monster,
the wicked destroyer. Now Wiglaf, the son
of Weohstan, sits in watch over Beowulf,
one man beside his friend who is slain,
keeping guard with a grieving heart
2910 over friend's head and foe's.

   "Now° our people may find
   that the time has come for an era of trouble,
   when the Franks and the Frisians hear of the fall
   of our strong king. Hard was the strife
   destined for the Hugas when Hygelac's fleet
2915 *of proud ships sailed for Frisian shores;*
   the Hetwares repelled him with superior might
   and brought it about that the king in his byrnie
   should not survive to divide his loot
   with his fighting men, but fell among them!
2920 *Since that victory, the Merovingian*
   king of the Franks has denied us all kindness.

   "Nor do I expect we can count on peace
   or good faith from the Swedes, for when Ongentheow slew
   Hathcyn, the son of Hrethel, in battle
2925 *at Ravenswood, it was widely known*
   that arrogance had prompted the Geatish people
   to join in that feud of the Shilfing folk.
   They had launched an attack upon Ongentheow's troops,
   but fiercely he had returned their foray,
2930 *cut down the ruler of the Geats, and rescued*
   his lady, Onla and Ohtere's mother,
   a gaunt old woman stripped of her gold.
   Grimly he pursued his Geatish foes,
   but they found a refuge in Ravenswood
2935 *(with difficulty, for their leader was dead).*

   "Then the king surrounded those wretched few
   whom the sword had left, and promised them sorrow
   all night long, saying when the light
   of day revealed them, vengeful blades
2940 *would hack down some, while others would hang*
   high on the gallows as a game for the crows!
   But dawn brought help and relief; they heard

2910*Now.* In this final digression of the poem, the messenger (ll. 2897-99) gives the fourth account of Hygelac's raid on the Frisians (ll. 2910-21) and continues with the fourth account of the war between the Geats and Swedes (ll. 2922-3007).

the sound of Hygelac's well-known horn,
his trumpet of war, as hot on their tracks
2945 *their lord came to save his beleaguered band.*

41. Feud in Ravenswood

"Then the bloody swathe of the Swedes and the Geats,
the track of their slaughter, was readily seen,
how they stirred up feud and strife between them.
Wise old Ongentheow went with his kinsmen,
2950 *grimly, to seek the safety of his fortress,*
a good stronghold on higher ground.
He had heard much of Hygelac's valor
and did not have faith in his own defences—
that he had the power to parry the attack
2955 *of the Geats, or to save the Swedes' bright gold,*
or their women and children. So in Ravenswood he went
to seek his refuge. But the Geats pursued
the Swedes, and Hygelac's banners were seen
flashing victoriously over the fields
2960 *when his men pressed forward to harry that fortress.*

"There the silver-haired king of the Swedes
was brought to bay with a shining blade,
and that mighty ruler had to submit
to the angry judgment of Eofor the thane.
2965 *Wulf, his brother, had struck the old warrior*
so fiercely that the blood jetted forth from the veins
under his hair. But the old Shilfing,
never afraid, with a far more vicious
onslaught, had quickly requited that thrust
2970 *in the time it took him to turn around.*
Then Wulf was unable to raise his weapon
to repay the old king for the powerful blow
that had cut right through the crest of his helmet.
He began to waver, wet with blood,
2975 *and dropped to his knees—but he was not doomed yet!*
He recovered in the end, though the wound nearly killed him.
Eofor the brave, seeing his brother
lying still on the ground, raised high his sword,
a jewelled weapon wrought by giants,
2980 *and struck past his shield at that Shilfing helmet*
across from him, killing the king of the Swedes!
At last the Geats turned to attend their fallen.
They raised up those wounded who were able to walk,

and took them to join in the jubilant victory.
2985 *Eofor the thane took King Ongentheow's*
royal byrnie, robbing him also
of hilted sword and shining helmet;
he bore these accoutrements of the king
to his prince, Hygelac, who promised him
2990 *fitting reward among the warriors.*

"He did as he said; Hrethel's son
acknowledged that battle with noble treasures
when they all came home. To Wulf and Eofor
he granted homesteads of a hundred thousand
2995 *hides of land, and a hoard of rings.*
No one could blame him, they had been so brave.
Then he gave to Eofor his only daughter
as wife, to grace a worthy dwelling.

"That is the feud and the conflict of foes,
3000 *the enmity of thanes, that leads me to think*
that the men of Sweden will seek us out
when they hear of Beowulf's latest battle—
how that hero has fallen, who formerly held
our hoard and kingdom against the hatred
3005 *of vengeful lords, a valiant leader*
who honored his warriors, and altogether
behaved nobly!

"Now haste is best.
Let us go to look on the king of the Geats,
and carry our giver of golden rings
3010 to his lofty pyre. What burns with our lord
shall not be meager, for there is the mighty
hoard of gold so grimly bought,
and paid for at last with his own life,
fabulous treasures. The flames must devour them,
3015 the fire embrace them, with none held back
to be worn by a warrior, or a beautiful woman
who graces her neck with a gleaming jewel.
Sad must she go, bereft of gold,
to pace, alone, down alien paths,
3020 now that our lord has passed beyond laughter,
harp song and happiness. Now shall the hand
of the warrior on many cold mornings grasp
for his ashen spear; not at all shall singing
rouse him from dreams, but the dark raven,

3025 eager for thanes, will call out many things,
asking the eagle how well he ate
when with the cruel wolf he plundered corpses!"

Many and true were the terrible things
that messenger said; not much did he gild
3030 his facts or words. Then the warriors,
with grief-stricken faces, rose to their feet
to see the harrowing sight at Eaglesness.
On a sandy ledge of the cliff they saw,
lying on his deathbed, the lord who once
3035 had given them rings; now he had reached
the end of his life. But the lord of battles,
that warrior of the Geats, died a wondrous death!—
for also they beheld, hard by their king,
the amazing creature whom he had killed,
3040 his mortal foe. That huge fire-drake,
a horrible monster scorched black with the heat
of his own flames, lay fifty feet long,
stretched out on the sand. By night he had sprung
in joy to the skies, then sailed back down
3045 to seek his den. He was now quite dead,
never more to coil in his earthy cave.

Nearby stood cups and beautiful goblets;
plates lay there, and precious swords
eaten through by rust. For a thousand winters
3050 they had been buried in the bosom of the earth.
Once that mighty hoard had been woven
around with a spell,° so that its splendor
could not be disturbed by anyone tampering
with all its gold, unless God himself,
3055 the High King of Victories, revealed the power
of opening the hoard to whom he wanted,
to whatever man seemed meet to him.

42. The Rifling of the Hoard

Clearly the dragon was doomed to fail
in wickedly trying to keep the treasure
3060 hidden in darkness! Indeed, that guardian
struck down his foe, but that feud was well

3052*spell.* The person who buries the treasure, called by critics the Last Survivor, does not mention a spell or curse on the treasure (ll. 2231-2266). This spell has apparently caused the downfall of everyone who has tried to own the treasure, including the Last Survivor's tribe and the dragon.

and quickly avenged.

Where the man of valor
shall meet his death as ordained by fate
is always a mystery, when he may no longer
3065 live with his kinsmen in the lofty hall.
So it was for Beowulf, when ready for battle
he approached the mound. How his departure
from the world would occur, he could not foresee.
Those long-ago princes who placed that treasure
3070 in the ground until doomsday had cursed it grimly,
saying that he would be guilty of sin,
bound by the worship of wicked idols,
tormented by greed, who touched that gold.
(*He*° was not wracked by gold-fever. Rather
3075 had he wished it granted by the owner's good will!)

Wiglaf spoke, the son of Weohstan:
"Often the will of one man brings
exile to many, as it does to us.
We could not persuade our noble king,
3080 protector of the Geats, to take our advice
not to meet that guardian of the mound,
but to let him lie where he had for so long,
dwelling in his lair until the world's last days.
But Beowulf held to his high destiny,
3085 and the hoard is won. That *wyrd* was too harsh
that prompted thither the prince of our land!

"When it was granted that I might go
inside that barrow and see all around,
an entrance by no means easily won
3090 to that earthen house, in haste I took
as much with my hands as I could hold,
and bore that burden of brilliant treasure
outside to my king. He was still alive then,
wise and aware, an old man wearily
3095 speaking in sorrow. He wished me to say
farewell, and to bid you to build a mound
where the pyre was, as high as his deeds were heroic,
a beacon as great as of men he had been
the worthiest of warriors in all the world,
3100 so long as he had been granted life
for the giving of rings.

3074*He.* Beowulf, who, unlike previous owners of the treasure, was not motivated by greed in his attempt to
recover the treasure.

"Now let us go
to gaze once more on the gold in the mound,
at those shining treasures. I will show you the way,
so that you may have the joy of beholding
3105   that abundant wealth. Let the bier be made ready
quickly, by the time that we have returned,
so that we can carry our beloved king,
our dear prince, to the place where he
must rest in the keeping of the High Ruler."

3110   That brave young warrior, Weohstan's son,
commanded those nobles to announce to others,
to hall-lords and fighters, that they should fetch
wood for the pyre and bring it to the place
where the king would lie. "For the leaping flame
3115   now must devour the noblest of men,
who has often stood in a shower of iron,
a blizzard of arrows impelled by the bow
over the shield-wall, feather-clad shafts
obediently aiding the flight of the barb."
3120   Carefully, then, Wiglaf culled
seven of the best from Beowulf's band
of Geatish thanes, and in gleaming armor
the eight warriors went together
beneath that dark roof. Wiglaf raised
3125   a flaming torch as he went in front.
Lots were not cast for whom should carry
that gold away, now that no guardian
gave any thought to those precious things
that were left in the mound. Little did those men
3130   who heaped up the treasure so hastily
have scruples at fetching it out! And the fire-drake—
they shoved him over the cliff, let the shining
waves enfold him, take him away!
They loaded a wagon with all the wealth
3135   of countless treasures, and carried their lord,
their white-haired king, to Whalesness.

43. Lament for Beowulf

The Geatish people prepared for him
a huge pyre high on the headland,
splendidly hung with helmets and shields
3140   and shining byrnies, as he had bidden.
The lamenting warriors then laid their lord,

their mighty prince, in the midst thereof,
and a few were assigned to set alight
that fire on the cliff top. A cloud of woodsmoke
3145 rose up dark from the roaring flame
encircled with weeping—the wind subsided—
until the blaze had broken that bone-house,
hot within.

      Sad at heart,
the last companions mourned for their prince,
3150 and a woman with her hair bound up bewailed
the passing of Beowulf. In a song of despair
and suffering, she told of sorrows to come,
of how she feared greatly days of grief,
many a raid of ravaging warriors,
3155 the shame of slavery. Heaven swallowed the smoke.

Then they raised for the ruler of the Weathergeats
a mound on the hilltop, high and broad,
to be seen from afar by seafaring men,
a warrior's beacon, built in ten days.
3160 Around the ashes of that atheling
they set an enclosure so fairly designed
that the wisest men should find it worthy,
and they placed in the mound the precious treasure
of rings and jewels from the ravaged hoard,
3165 the twisted gold they had taken earlier.
They let the earth hold that princely hoard,
left it in the ground, where still it lies,
as useless to men as it was of yore.

Then around the barrow rode the bravest
3170 of the sons of athelings, twelve in all,
expressing their sorrow and mourning their prince,
wishing to declare what that warrior was like.
They chanted of his courage, acclaiming his deeds
and his generous manhood—as it is meet
3175 that a man should salute his lord in words
and love him in his heart, when at last he must
go forth from his failing cloak of flesh.

And thus the Geatish people grieved
at the death of their prince: his hearth companions
3180 said that he was, of the world's rulers,
the kindest of men and the gentlest of kings,
the most loving to his people, the most longing for esteem.

GENEALOGICAL TABLES AND SUMMARIES OF EVENTS

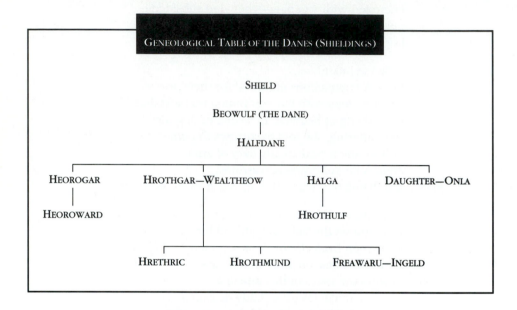

GENEOLOGICAL TABLE OF THE DANES (SHIELDINGS)

SHIELD

BEOWULF (THE DANE)

HALFDANE

HEOROGAR   HROTHGAR—WEALTHEOW   HALGA   DAUGHTER—ONLA

HEOROWARD   HROTHULF

HRETHRIC   HROTHMUND   FREAWARU—INGELD

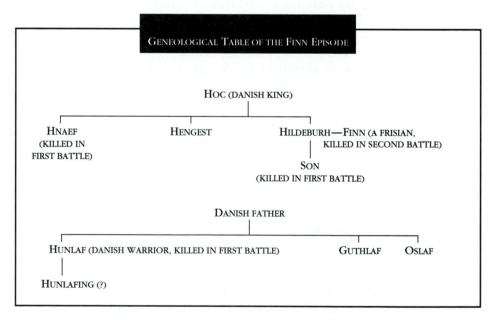

GENEOLOGICAL TABLE OF THE FINN EPISODE

HOC (DANISH KING)

HNAEF   HENGEST   HILDEBURH—FINN (A FRISIAN,
(KILLED IN   KILLED IN SECOND BATTLE)
FIRST BATTLE)   SON
                                       (KILLED IN FIRST BATTLE)

DANISH FATHER

HUNLAF (DANISH WARRIOR, KILLED IN FIRST BATTLE)   GUTHLAF   OSLAF

HUNLAFING (?)

Summary of the Finn Episode

Hildeburh, the daughter of Hoc, a Dane, is married to Finn, a Frisian or Jute. Her brother Hnaef leads a party of Danes to pay an ostensibly friendly visit to her and Finn. All goes well until one evening an argument leads to violence. Many are killed. When Hildeburh surveys the scene the next morning she finds that among the dead are her brother Hnaef and her son. Finn lacks the forces to expel the Danes, and the Danes cannot return home because of the winter weather. Hildeburh's brother Hengest becomes chief of the Danish party and strikes a truce with Finn. The tribes live in peace through the winter, but when spring comes, the son and brothers (Guthlaf and Oslaf) of one of the killed Danes, Hunlaf, urge Hengest to revenge Hunlaf's death. The Danes attack the Jutes, kill Finn, and take Hildeburh back to Denmark.

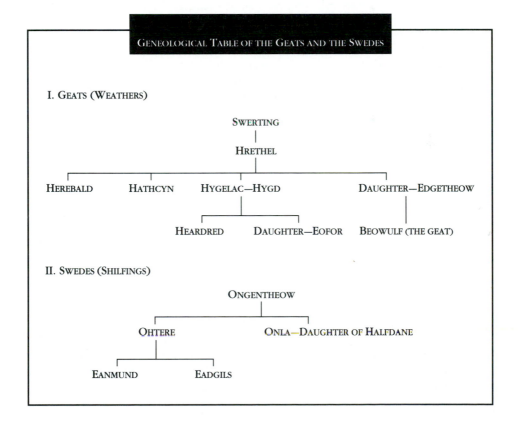

GENEOLOGICAL TABLE OF THE GEATS AND THE SWEDES

I. GEATS (WEATHERS)

SWERTING
|
HRETHEL

HEREBALD   HATHCYN   HYGELAC—HYGD   DAUGHTER—EDGETHEOW

HEARDRED   DAUGHTER—EOFOR   BEOWULF (THE GEAT)

II. SWEDES (SHILFINGS)

ONGENTHEOW

OHTERE   ONLA—DAUGHTER OF HALFDANE

EANMUND   EADGILS

Summary of the Feud Between the Geats and the Swedes

The history of the relationship between the Geats and Swedes covers a period extending from Beowulf's childhood to the probable continuation of the feud after his death. When Beowulf is seven, King Hrethel (his grandfather) adopts him and rears him as a son (ll. 2425-34). A family tragedy occurs when Hrethel's son Hathcyn accidentally kills his brother Herebald. The impact of the tragedy is doubled because Hrethel cannot exact revenge or *wergild* from his own son. Hrethel dies of sorrow, leaving the throne to Hathcyn (ll. 2435-71). Sweden apparently initiates the feud with the Geats (ll. 2472-78). In a battle near Ravenswood, the Swedish king Ongentheow kills Hathcyn, and the Geatish warrior Eofor kills Ongentheow. Hygelac becomes king of the Geats and gives his daughter in marriage to Eofor (ll. 2472-89, 2922-98).

Hygelac initiates a raid on the Frisians (in northern Germany). The Geats are driven back, and Hygelac is killed. Beowulf heroically escapes back to Weathermark. The four references to this raid are lines 1197-1215, 2354-79, 2490-2509, and 2910-21. Hygelac's queen, Hygd, offers Beowulf the throne, but he rejects the offer. Instead, he counsels Hygelac's young son Heardred until Heardred can assume the kingship (ll. 2354-79).

In the meantime, conflict breaks out in the Swedish royal family. Ongentheow is succeeded by his older son, Ohtere, who dies and is succeeded by his brother Onla. Details in *Beowulf* are sketchy, but Onla apparently usurps the throne. Ohtere's sons Eanmund and Eadgils flee Sweden and take refuge in the Geatish court. In retaliation, Onla attacks the Geats and kills Heardred. During the same raid, Weohstan (serving with the Swedes) kills Eanmund. Onla withdraws, leaving Beowulf as king of the Geats (ll. 2379-90, 2602-25).

There are three principle accounts of the Geatish-Swedish wars: the narrator's (ll. 2379-96), Beowulf's (ll. 2472-2509), and the messenger's (ll. 2922-3007). A fourth, very brief account is the narrator's story of Wiglaf's father's career (ll. 2602-19).

As king, Beowulf establishes peace through strength in battle. He attacks the Swedes, kills Onla, and places Eadgils on the Swedish throne (ll. 2391-96). He attacks the Frisians and avenges Hygelac's death (ll. 2490-2509). After this, Beowulf seeks no further feuds, and no neighboring tribes dare attack him (ll. 2729-39). Peace reigns for fifty years until the dragon ravages Geatish villages (ll. 2200-11). Wiglaf joins Beowulf to fight the dragon. Wiglaf's father Weohstan fought with the Swedes against the Geats (he killed Eanmund and was rewarded by Onla), but later switched loyalties to the Geats (ll. 2602-25). Weohstan and Wiglaf, it turns out, are members of Beowulf's family, the Wagmundings (ll. 2813-16). After Beowulf's death, the messenger speculates that the Frisians and the Swedes will renew their feuds with the Geats (ll. 2910-3007).

Questions for Study

1. Beowulf, when considered over the full extent of his career, is a complex character. What are his traits? How does he change? What does he fight for?

2. What constitutes heroism in *Beowulf?* Who are the heroes? What sets them apart from others? How is Beowulf unique as a hero? How, for example, is he different from Unferth?

3. What characterizes the monsters against whom Beowulf fights? Where do they live and why do they live there? What qualities or realities do they possibly symbolize? What is Beowulf's attitude toward them? What are the monsters' attitudes toward themselves? What is the narrator's attitude toward them?

4. In what ways is treasure important to the characters and society depicted in *Beowulf?* Of what does "treasure" consist? What is considered valuable about it?

5. Where does the author manifest his Christian beliefs? How do they conflict with the pagan beliefs of the characters? What meaning do they give to the poem?

6. A number of women appear in the predominately masculine world of *Beowulf*—Wealtheow, Hildeburh, Thryth, Freawaru, among others. What is the role of women in this society? How do these particular women illustrate that role? What do they experience? What must they think and feel about the events recounted in the epic?

7. What is the relationship between the story of Beowulf's fight against the monsters and the other stories in the poem: stories told for entertainment (the Sigemund story, the Finn Episode, the story about Thryth's marriage to Offa) and the stories about tribal history (Freawaru's marriage to Ingeld, the Frisian raid, the Swedish-Geatish wars)?

8. Is there a method in the way the poet presents the other stories? Why, for example, doesn't he give the historical background all in one place, say at the beginning? Why does he put the stories or fragments of them where he does?

9. How are the three main sections of *Beowulf*—Grendel, Grendel's mother, the dragon—different? Is there a meaningful change or progression from one to another? How are they similar?

10. What is the attitude toward death in *Beowulf?* How are funerals conducted? How do they contribute to the epic qualities of the poem? What specific funerals are most important?

11. The person who gathered and buried the treasure that the dragon defends is known as the Last Survivor. How is his story parallel to Beowulf's?

12. In what ways does *Beowulf* illustrate the transitory nature of human existence?

13. How are the digressions on Cain and Abel (ll. 105-14 and 1688-99) relevant to the themes of the poem? Why does the poet place them where he does?

FOR FURTHER READING

Abercrombie, Lascelles. *The Epic.* Freeport: Books for Libraries Press, 1969. Abercrombie's book, first published in 1914, is a brief, readable discussion of the epic.

Bowra, C. M. *Heroic Poetry.* New York: St. Martin's Press, 1966. Bowra, a well-known scholar, provides a thorough study of the epic.

Bruce-Mitford, Rupert. *The Sutton Hoo Ship-Burial.* 2 vols. London: British Museum Publications, 1975. Bruce-Mitford gives descriptions and photographs of the Sutton Hoo treasures, excavated in 1939 in England. The excavation uncovered a complete ship and its contents dating from the Anglo-Saxon period. The ship, armor, weapons, and other artifacts provide a window into the world of *Beowulf.*

Gardner, John. *Grendel.* New York: Knopf, 1971. Gardner's novel retells the Beowulf story from the monster's point of view with Grendel as the narrator.

Oinas, Felix J., ed. *Heroic Epic and Saga: An Introduction to the World's Great Folk Epics.* Bloomington: Indiana UP, 1978. The essays in this book are by various scholars and provide introductions to the world's great epics and epic traditions, including African and Asian as well as European. Alain Renoir's essay on *Beowulf* is an excellent brief discussion of the cultural context, artistic techniques, and critical interpretations of the poem.

Merchant, Paul. *The Epic.* London: Methuen, 1971. Merchant gives a short overview of the epic from ancient to modern times. He includes a comparison of *Beowulf* to the *Iliad.*

Yu, Anthony C., ed. *Parnassus Revisited: Modern Critical Essays on the Epic Tradition.* Chicago: American Library Association, 1973. This collection features scholarly essays on the nature of epic, the role of the poet narrator, techniques of narration, and the epic hero.

Chapter Four
The Tale

INTRODUCTION

The tale is the most universally loved of all forms of narrative. Throughout the world it gives pleasure to young and old. It is at least as old as myth. Before the invention of the electronic media, it was the prime form of entertainment. It continues to be culturally important, especially in societies that favor an oral tradition of narrative over a written or electronic tradition. And although in industrial societies the short story has supplanted the tale as a more prestigious form of fiction, the short story evolved from the tale, and the tale continues to be composed and enjoyed.

The **tale** is a relatively short story whose main purpose is to entertain and whose material and form are usually traditional. A narrative is "traditional" when it has no known authorship and when it has been told enough times that its subject matter and form remain basically the same from telling to telling. Myths are often traditional, too, but they are different from the tale because their function is different. Myths account for and verify the order of the universe and are closely associated with sacred ritual. But although the tale can be used for instruction, it has no sacred or ritualistic function. Its main purpose is to entertain.

Traditional tales are usually called "folktales," but folktales are not the only kind of tale. Another kind is the "literary tale." Literary tales have identifiable authors, who either retell traditional stories or make up their own. Whether or not their material is original, as long as they retain the form of the traditional tale, their work is clearly a "tale." Even in folktales the hand of a teller may be visible. A teller can be true to the tradition and yet include or leave out material at will. But the authors of literary tales, like Chaucer, are more likely to use literary conventions, like versification, symbolism, intricate plotting, and elaborate settings more fully and self-consciously than tellers of folktales, who are mainly trying to remain true to a tradition.

Most tales have certain characteristics in common. First, the plot of a tale relies heavily upon action. We are more interested in what will happen next than in where the action occurs or what the characters are like.

Second, in longer tales the plot is usually episodic. One episode follows another, and these episodes often have little to connect them except that the same characters take part in them. A plot device that often links episodes is the "road." Characters set off on a journey and have adventures along the way. Tales, of course, need not be episodic. Some are intricately plotted, so that all the events are tied together, often in unexpected ways. Such careful construction is more evident in literary tales than in folktales. But, as in all tales, the interest lies in the action rather than in other elements. The climax of the plot occurs when the protagonists overcome the last barriers to their happiness. "Happiness" usually consists of marriage and newfound wealth.

Third, the events that take place in a tale typically are implausible. Actions occur because of miraculous or unusual circumstances, characters suddenly reverse opinions and intentions, accident and coincidence determine what happens. Fourth, characters are thinly developed; we rarely get enough information about them to think of the characters as individuals. They seem like cardboard props who exist mainly to further the action. We know them as "the prince," "the princess," "the witch," or "the youngest son." We learn that they are "beautiful," "ugly," "mean," or "good." But we know little more about them than that. We do not learn how they feel, except that they are in love, distressed, afraid, or lonely. In the tale, we probably do not want to know more. Characters in tales experience extreme distress. Knowing little about them gives us enough intellectual distance to enjoy the action.

Fifth, details of setting in a tale are minimal. The place of the action is vaguely indicated: "a forest," "the desert," "along the river," "a castle," "a hamlet." On those infrequent occasions when the action occurs in a real place, we may get more information, but it relates only to the immediate action at hand. The time of the action is usually the remote past—"once upon a time" or "many years ago." The world of the tale may be realistic, conforming to the laws and the probabilities of the real world, or fantastic, featuring marvels never witnessed by real people. Tales sometimes combine realism and fantasy. Like Dorothy in *The Wizard of Oz,* the hero or heroine may leave a realistic world and enter a fantasy world featuring forests, a castle, or the sea.

This chapter includes selections from four famous kinds of tale: fable, fairy tale, trickster tale, and literary tale. As with the myths in Chapter 2, the headnotes indicate when the stories were first written or collected. Traditional stories—stories coming from an oral tradition of anonymous authorship—almost always predate their first printing by many years.

FABLE

A **fable** is a brief, simple story that usually makes some point about the human condition. Fables are a seemingly universal kind of narrative. They occur in the literary traditions of most of the world's cultures. The fables included in this chapter are two of the best-known kinds, animal fables and parables.

Animal fables feature animals as characters who act like human beings and whose actions often illustrate certain unpleasant realities of human experience. Since the most famous author of animal fables in the West is Aesop, we are accustomed to seeing morals stuck onto the ends of animal fables. But the morals were added by editors; the stories themselves are much older. Many animal fables seem on the surface, at least, to serve other purposes than just pointing to a moral. Some are explanatory. They establish the origin of natural phenomena, such as the leopard's spots and the zebra's stripes. Other animal fables are jokes, meant to elicit laughter. But under the surface of most animal fables lies some commentary about human life. A common topic of animal fables, for example, is the use and abuse of power. The protagonists of animal fables often must come to terms with forces and individuals who are more powerful than they are.

Unlike animal fables, parables almost always feature human beings as characters. Parables are less playful than animal fables, and they are more severely restricted to their themes. Even when animal fables point to an obvious moral, they often include extra details of setting and characterization, details that are not necessarily related to the moralistic meaning of the fable. But every detail in parables is usually tied to a message. Animal fables, furthermore, are often comic; parables almost never are. Animal fables, therefore, are likely to be more entertaining purely as story than parables.

The origin of the word **parable**—the Greek *paraballein,* "to compare"— reveals its method. Parables are analogies to real-life experiences, or, at least, to what might happen in real life. Those television commercials that dramatize what can happen on trips when we fail to take traveller's checks are a kind of parable. Great teachers, like Socrates, Jesus, and the Buddha, used parables to illustrate their beliefs. Parables, then, are more philosophical than fables. They teach personal morality and proper attitudes toward such things as property, religion, life, and death.

As old as fables are, they continue to be a popular form of story. Modern writers often blend the methods of fables with those of more recent forms of narrative. The American writer James Thurber (1894-1961) wrote wry animal fables that reflect the absurdity of modern life. George Orwell's *Animal Farm* (1945) is a novel-length animal fable about totalitarian government. And the Czechoslovakian Franz Kafka (1883-1924) wrote bizarre, dreamlike short stories and novels that seem like elaborate parables. In addition to written narrative, other media, like film and television, revitalize old fables and produce new ones for popular consumption. Parables are especially prominent, for example, during political campaigns.

AESOP

The Wolf and the Lamb

Aesop was a legendary Greek who supposedly lived sometime in the sixth century B.C. He was believed to be the author or at least the teller of many fables, and years after his death, collections of fables were attributed to him. The fables that we know as "Aesop's fables" are based on medieval Latin texts. The Greek versions of them have been lost, and Aesop himself probably never wrote them down.

*O*nce upon a time a Wolf was lapping at a spring on a hillside, when, looking up, what should he see but a Lamb just beginning to drink a little lower down. "There's my supper," thought he, "if only I can find some excuse to seize it." Then he called out to the Lamb, "How dare you muddle the water from which I am drinking?"

"Nay, master, nay," said Lambikin; "if the water be muddy up there, I cannot be the cause of it, for it runs down from you to me."

"Well, then," said the Wolf, "why did you call me bad names this time last year?"

"That cannot be," said the Lamb; "I am only six months old."

"I don't care," snarled the Wolf; "if it was not you it was your father;" and with that he rushed upon the poor little Lamb and—

Warra warra warra warra warra—

ate her all up. But before she died she gasped out—

"ANY EXCUSE WILL SERVE A TYRANT."

Questions for Study

1. What details characterize the wolf and the lamb?

2. What line of reasoning does the wolf use as the basis for his attack on the lamb? Why does the wolf even bother with logic? Why does he not simply attack the lamb? What does this tale seem to be saying about the nature of aggressors?

3. To what real-life situations might this tale apply?

4. Are there other morals that this tale seems to illustrate?

AESOP

The Dog and the Wolf

A gaunt Wolf was almost dead with hunger when he happened to meet a House-dog who was passing by. "Ah, Cousin," said the Dog. "I knew how it would be; your irregular life will soon be the ruin of you. Why do you not work steadily as I do, and get your food regularly given to you?"

"I would have no objection," said the Wolf, "if I could only get a place."

"I will easily arrange that for you," said the Dog; "come with me to my master and you shall share my work."

So the Wolf and the Dog went towards the town together. On the way there the Wolf noticed that the hair on a certain part of the Dog's neck was very much worn away, so he asked him how that had come about.

"Oh, it is nothing," said the Dog. "That is only the place where the collar is put on at night to keep me chained up; it chafes a bit, but one soon gets used to it."

"Is that all?" said the Wolf. "Then good-bye to you, Master Dog."

"BETTER STARVE FREE THAN BE A FAT SLAVE"

Questions for Study

1. How is the wolf in this tale different from the wolf in the previous one? What details differentiate the wolf from the dog?

2. What is the dog's attitude toward the conditions of his life?

3. In spite of the moral attached to the end of this tale, is it possible to be sympathetic to the dog?

4. To what real-life situations might this tale apply?

The Blue Jackal (The Panchatantra)

This fable comes from *The Panchatantra,* a famous collection of Far Eastern fables assembled in India around the early fourth century A.D. In some versions of the Hindu religion, Indra is the chief god, governing rain and thunder.

Once there lived in a forest an old jackal. He could not always get enough to eat, not being very good at hunting. One day he wandered into a neighboring city in search of food. Some fierce city dogs saw him and, barking furiously, gave chase. In fear and desperation the jackal ran helter-skelter. Ultimately he stumbled into the back-yard of a washerman. There was a vat of indigo there, and into it jumped the jackal.

And in the nick of time, too! For soon the pack of hounds were on the spot. But the jackal was hidden in the indigo vat, and the dogs did not see him. Frustrated, they went away, yelping furiously.

The jackal then came out and slunk away into the forest. The other animals saw him in amazed terror.

"What is this blue animal we see?" they asked one another. "We have not seen his like before. He must have been sent by the king of heaven, by Indra himself, to rule over us."

The jackal heard them and seized the opportunity. Mounting a mound he said, "O inmates of the forest! Listen to me! I have indeed been sent by Indra, as some of you have guessed, to rule over you. Therefore, obey me now and carry out my orders."

And he was so self-assured that the animals believed him, without any exception.

And so the jackal became their king. He made the lion his prime minister, the tiger the lord-in-waiting, the elephant the doorkeeper, the monkey the bearer of the royal umbrella, and so on. But he had his fellow jackals beaten and driven away. The other animals all hunted for him and laid the kill before him for the first morsels.

And so the blue jackal lived in glory. One day, however, he heard in the distance the yell of a pack of jackals. At once he thrilled to the sound. His whole body quivered with joy. He gave a return howl in piercing tone.

No sooner had he done so than the lion and the tiger and the other animals perceived that a jackal had made a fool of them and that they had been his servants. In rage and anger they pounced on him. The poor jackal made vain efforts to flee, but could not. He was torn to pieces by his irate erstwhile subjects. So ended the life of the blue jackal.

Pretend to be more than what you are, and you will come to a sorry end.

Questions for Study

1. How is this jackal characterized? What are his attitudes toward himself, his station in life, and the other animals? How do his attitudes change?

2. Why does he chase all the other jackals away when he becomes king?

3. Does the narrator seem sympathetic to the jackal? Does the narrator seem to want us to be sympathetic to the jackal?

4. To what real-life situations might this tale apply?

5. What morals other than the one given might be drawn from this tale?

The Blind Men and the Elephant

Buddhist parables appear throughout the Buddhist scriptures and are attributed to Siddhartha (the Buddha) or his followers. The purpose of the parables was to instruct people in religious and ethical principles as well as matters of common sense. This parable was supposedly told by Siddhartha himself when he was in residence in Sāvatthi, an ancient city in India. He tells the parable as a commentary on some "heretic" monks who have recently come to the city. These heretics could not agree with one another about religious doctrine and were constantly fighting and arguing. The conclusion of the parable is Siddhartha's application of it to the heretics.

*I*n olden times, in this very city of Sāvatthi, there was a certain king. And that king ordered a certain man: "Come, my man, assemble in one place all the men in Sāvatthi who are blind from birth." "Yes, your majesty," said that man to that king. And when, in obedience to the king's command, he had laid hands on all the men in Sāvatthi who were blind from birth, he approached that king. And having approached, he said this to that king: "Your majesty, the blind from birth in Sāvatthi are assembled for you." "Very well! Now let the blind men feel of the elephant." "Yes, your majesty," said that man to that king. And in obedience to the king's command he let the blind men feel of the elephant, saying: 'This, O blind men, is what an elephant is like.'"

Some of the blind men he let feel of the elephant's head, saying: "This, O blind men, is what an elephant is like." Some of the blind men he let feel of the elephant's ears, saying: "This, O blind men, is what an elephant is like." Some of the blind men he let feel of the elephant's tusks, saying: "This, O blind men, is what an elephant is like." Others he let feel of the trunk, saying the same. Others he let feel of the belly, others of the legs, others of the back, others of the member, others of the tail, saying to each and to all: "This, O blind men, is what an elephant is like."

Now when that man had let the blind men feel of the elephant, he approached that king. And having approached, he said this to that king: "Your majesty, those blind men have felt of the elephant; do as you think fit."

Then that king approached those blind men. And having approached, he said this to those blind men: "Blind men, have you felt of the elephant?" "Yes, your majesty, we have felt of the elephant." "Tell me, blind men, what is an elephant like?"

The blind men who had felt of the elephant's head, said: "Your majesty, an elephant is like a water-pot." The blind men who had felt of the elephant's ears, said: "Your majesty, an elephant is like a winnowing-basket." The blind men who had felt of the elephant's tusks, said: "Your majesty, an elephant is like a plowshare." Those who had felt of the trunk, said: "An elephant is like a plow-pole." Those who had felt of the belly, said: "An elephant is like a granary." Those who had felt of the legs, said: "An elephant is like pillars." Those who had felt of the back, said: "An elephant is like a mortar." Those who had felt of the member, said: "An elephant is like a pestle." The blind men who had felt of the elephant's tail, said: "Your majesty, an elephant is like a fan."

And they fought among themselves with their fists, saying: "This is what an elephant is like, that is not what an elephant is like"; "This is not what an elephant is like, that is what an elephant is like." And thereat that king was delighted.

"Precisely so, O monks, the heretics, the wandering ascetics, are blind, without eyes; know not good, know not evil; know not right, know not wrong. Knowing not good, knowing not evil, knowing not right, knowing not wrong, they quarrel and brawl and wrangle and strike one another with the daggers of their tongues, saying: 'This is right, that is not right'; 'This is not right, that is right.'"

Questions for Study

1. What is Siddhartha's moral? Does he give hints about how to achieve true knowledge?

2. What other morals might this story illustrate?

3. What does "blindness" symbolize? What does the elephant symbolize?

4. Why is the king delighted by the outcome of his experiment?

5. To what real-life situations might this tale apply?

The Good Samaritan (Luke 10:25-37)

Like the Buddha, Jesus, the founder of the Christian religion, used parables to teach his doctrines. "The Good Samaritan" and "The Prodigal Son" are perhaps the best known of Jesus's parables. Samaritans were Jews who had intermarried with gentiles and had incorporated elements of pagan religion into their religious practice. Pure-blooded Jews, like the members of Jesus's audience, treated Samaritans with contempt. As a result, there was much enmity between the Jews of Jesus's day and Samaritans. Priests and Levites were religious officials associated with the Jewish temple in Jerusalem. A *denarius* (singular for *denarii*) was the standard wage for one day's work. Both "The Good Samaritan" and "The Prodigal Son" are contained in the Gospel of Luke, which was written c. A.D. 90.

10   25 Just then a lawyer stood up to test Jesus. "Teacher," he said, "what must I do to inherit eternal life?" ²⁶ He said to him, "What is written in the law? What do you read there?" ²⁷ He answered, "You shall love the Lord your God with all your heart, and with all your soul, and with all your strength, and with all your mind; and your neighbor as yourself." ²⁸ And he said to him, "You have given the right answer; do this, and you will live."

29 But wanting to justify himself, he asked Jesus, "And who is my neighbor?" ³⁰ Jesus replied, "A man was going down from Jerusalem to Jericho, and fell into the

hands of robbers, who stripped him, beat him, and went away, leaving him half dead. [31] Now by chance a priest was going down that road; and when he saw him, he passed by on the other side. [32] So likewise a Levite when he came to the place and saw him, passed by on the other side. [33] But a Samaritan while traveling came near him; and when he saw him, he was moved with pity. [34] He went to him and bandaged his wounds, having poured oil and wine on them. Then he put him on his own animal, brought him to an inn, and took care of him. [35] The next day he took out two denarii, gave them to the innkeeper, and said, 'Take care of him; and when I come back, I will repay you whatever more you spend.' [36] Which of these three, do you think, was a neighbor to the man who fell into the hands of the robbers?" [37] He said, "The one who showed him mercy." Jesus said to him, "Go and do likewise."

Questions for Study

1. What is the moral of this tale?

2. Why does Jesus make his protagonist a Samaritan?

3. What details distinguish the Samaritan from the priest and the Levite?

4. Does this tale have a real-life application outside of a Christian context?

The Prodigal Son (Luke 15:11-32)

The context for this parable is a sermon in which Jesus tells one parable after another. The prodigal's association with pigs is significant. Pigs were held in low esteem by Jews because they are forbidden as food in the Hebrew Bible.

15   11 Then Jesus said, "There was a man who had two sons. [12] The younger of them said to his father, 'Father, give me the share of the property that will belong to me.' So he divided his property between them. [13] A few days later the younger son gathered all he had and traveled to a distant country, and there he squandered his property in dissolute living. [14] When he had spent everything, a severe famine took place throughout that country, and he began to be in need. [15] So he went and hired himself out to one of the citizens of that country, who sent him to his fields to feed the pigs. [16] He would gladly have filled himself with the pods that the pigs were eating; and no one gave him anything. [17] But when he came to himself he said, 'How many of my father's hired hands have bread enough and to spare, but here I am dying of hunger! [18] I will get up and go to my father, and I will say to him, "Father, I have sinned against heaven and before you; [19] I am no longer worthy to be called your son; treat me like one of your hired hands.'' [20] So he set off and went to his father. But while he was still far off, his father saw him and was filled with compassion; he ran and put his arms around him and kissed him. [21] Then the son said to him, 'Father, I have sinned against heaven and before you; I am no longer worthy to be called your son.' [22] But the father said to his slaves, 'Quickly, bring out a robe—the best one—and put it on him; put a ring on his finger and sandals on his feet. [23] And get the fatted calf and kill it, and let us eat and celebrate; [24] for this son of mine was dead and is alive again; he was lost and is found!' And they began to celebrate.

25 "Now his elder son was in the field; and when he came and approached the house, he heard music and dancing. [26] He called one of the slaves and asked what was going on. [27] He replied, 'Your brother has come, and your father has killed the fatted calf, because he has got him back safe and sound.' [28] Then he became angry and refused to go in. His father came out and began to plead with him. [29] But he answered his father, 'Listen! For all these years I have been working like a slave for you, and I have never disobeyed your command; yet you have never given me even a young goat so that I might celebrate with my friends. [30] But when this son of yours came back, who has devoured your property with prostitutes, you killed the fatted calf for him!' [31] Then the father said to him, 'Son, you are always with me, and all that is mine is yours. [32] But we had to celebrate and rejoice, because this brother of yours was dead and has come to life; he was lost and has been found.'"

Questions for Study

1. Why does the brother react so hostilely to his father's treatment of the returning prodigal? Does the tone of the tale invite sympathy for the brother?

2. Why does the father react so positively to the prodigal son?

3. What is the moral of this tale? Does the tale have a real-life application outside a Christian context?

Tortoise and Dove (Basotho)

This fable, collected in 1964, comes from the Basotho people, who dwell in the Lesotho mountain region of southern South Africa. The collector and translator of the tale retain the repetitions and sounds that are characteristic of Basotho storytelling.

*I*t was in the days of the big hunger. There was a big famine in the land, and Tortoise had no more food left to eat. He walked around the little bushes and hunted,

hunted, hunted around for something to put inside his stomach. He hunted, but he found nothing. And so he pulled his head and his little legs under his shell, for he was afraid he might die of hunger.

Now Tortoise is a man who always walks alone. He has no father or mother to take care of him. He has no wife or children who can work for him. So now he would have to die alone, he thought. He lay down with his hungry stomach. *Tu-u-u-u.*

Dove, who sat high up in a tree, saw how Tortoise was hunting for food. She also saw that he found nothing. Nothing at all. And she felt very sorry for him when she saw him lying there so quietly. She sang to him: *Coor-coor, coor-coor,* but he did not put his head out of his shell.

"Tortoise, big man, why don't you go to the other side of the river? I fly there every day, and there is plenty of food."

Tortoise stuck his head out from under his shell and listened to what Dove had to say.

"Keep quiet, woman!" he shouted. "How can that food help me if there is a stream of water between me and the food?"

"But you can swim through, big man," she said.

"I am not a fish that I can swim," said Tortoise.

"Why don't you fly over the river?"

"Because I am not a bird. Where are my wings?"

Tortoise wept over the plentiful food on the other side of the river. He wept because he was so hungry he was afraid he might die.

Dove wept with him. *Coor-coor, coor-coor, coor-coor!*

Then she had a plan.

"Tortoise," she said. "Find a dry stick, and bite on one end."

"I don't eat sticks, Mother," said Tortoise sadly.

"It is not for you to eat," said Dove. "I will take the other end of the stick in my mouth and fly over the water with you."

"That is a fine plan, Mother," said Tortoise.

"Yes, it is a fine plan," agreed Dove. "But you must not talk to Fish if he rises from the water to talk to you."

"No, I will not," Tortoise promised.

And then they did as they had planned. *Yoalo, yoalo.* Tortoise found a dry stick and bit on one end, and Dove bit on the other end, and they flew out over the water. Dove flew over the water, and Tortoise hung below her on the other end of the stick.

Au, but that was a strange business! Fish could not believe what he saw. He looked, he looked, he looked, but he could not understand it at all. He was astonished, for he had never in his life seen a tortoise high up in the sky.

"You, fellow," said Fish, with his mouth full of water. "I never knew that you could fly! If I did not see this with my own eyes, I would not believe it!"

Tortoise became angry with Fish.

"What do you think?" he asked. "And why should I not be able to fly?"

But before he could finish speaking he fell *twaaah!* right into the water. He had let go of the stick when he argued with Fish, and Dove flew away with only the stick in her mouth.

She came back again to see whether Tortoise would come out of the water. She flew to and fro over the water to see whether Tortoise might come out higher upstream, or whether he might come out of the water lower downstream. But no, there was no sign of him. She kept on flying, she kept on flying with the stick in her mouth, but to no avail. Tortoise stayed under the water. He did not come up again.

Then she went to lay the little stick down on her nest. But her heart remained black, it would not lie down, because of the big man who had fallen in the water. She wept over him: *Coor-coor, coor-coor, coor-coor . . .*

Every day. Every day. Until this very day.

And she keeps on hunting for Tortoise. She keeps the stick in her mouth. She wants to give it to Tortoise again so that she can lift him out of the water as soon as he shows his head.

But Tortoise will never come out of the water again. No, he will not, because he found plenty of food under the water on the river bed. Much more food than there ever was on the ground and under the trees. He will never come out of the water again. He will stay there.

And this is how Tortoise became Turtle. And here the story comes to an end.

Questions for Study

1. The teller of this fable places no moral at the end. What might the moral or morals be?

2. What details characterize Tortoise and Dove? What is Dove's attitude toward Tortoise?

3. This fable has a happy ending. What unhappy ending might it have had?

4. To what real-life situations might this tale apply?

The Dogs Hold an Election (Brule Sioux)

> This fable, from the Lacota peoples of the Great Plains region of the United States, is an example of how folk narrators can adapt traditional forms of the tale to reflect contemporary circumstances. The fable was narrated by Lame Deer in 1969.

We don't think much of the white man's elections. Whoever wins, we Indians always lose. Well, we have a little story about elections. Once a long time ago, the dogs were trying to elect a president. So one of them got up in the big dog convention and said: "I nominate the bulldog for president. He's strong. He can fight."

"But he can't run," said another dog. "What good is a fighter who can't run? He won't catch anybody."

Then another dog got up and said: "I nominate the greyhound, because he sure can run."

But the other dogs cried: "Naw, he can run all right, but he can't fight. When he catches up with somebody, what happens then? He gets the hell beaten out of him, that's what! So all he's good for is running away."

Then an ugly little mutt jumped up and said: "I nominate that dog for president who smells good underneath his tail."

And immediately an equally ugly mutt jumped up and yelled: "I second the motion."

At once all the dogs started sniffing underneath each other's tails. A big chorus went up:

"Phew, he doesn't smell good under his tail."

"No, neither does this one."

"He's no presidential timber!"

"No, he's no good, either."

"This one sure isn't the people's choice."

"Wow, this ain't my candidate!"

When you go out for a walk, just watch the dogs. They're still sniffing underneath each other's tails. They're looking for a good leader, and they still haven't found him.

Questions for Study

1. What is the moral of this tale?

2. How is the tale comic?

3. What does the tale suggest about the history and circumstances of Native Americans?

FRANZ KAFKA

Before the Law

Franz Kafka (1883-1924) was born into a German-speaking Jewish family in Czechoslovakia. His fiction, most of which was not published during his lifetime, bespeaks a sense of alienation and anxiety that seems to have arisen from his family and religious circumstances. Almost all of his fiction has a parable-like quality. Kafka published "Before the Law" as a separate work during his lifetime and incorporated it into his novel *The Trial,* which was published after he died. The protagonist of *The Trial* is charged with unspecified crimes, makes an unsuccessful quest to discover what the crimes are, and is executed. "Before the Law" is a "literary" rather than a folk fable. The author imitates the form of the fable to express personal and perhaps cultural meanings. Kafka's dreamlike fiction, however, lends itself to many interpretations.

*B*efore the law stands a doorkeeper. To this doorkeeper there comes a man from the country and prays for admittance to the Law. But the doorkeeper says that he cannot grant admittance at the moment. The man thinks it over and then asks if he will be allowed in later. "It is possible," says the doorkeeper, "but not at the moment." Since the gate stands open, as usual, and the doorkeeper steps to one side, the man stoops to peer through the gateway into the interior. Observing that, the doorkeeper laughs and says: "If you are so drawn to it, just try to go in despite my veto. But take note: I am powerful. And I am only the least of the doorkeepers. From hall to hall there is one doorkeeper after another, each more powerful than the last. The third door-keeper is already so terrible that even I cannot bear to look at him." These are diffi-culties the man from the country has not expected; the Law, he thinks, should surely be accessible at all times and to everyone, but as he now takes a closer look at the door-keeper in his fur coat, with his big sharp nose and long, thin, black Tartar beard, he decides that it is better to wait until he gets permission to enter. The doorkeeper gives him a stool and lets him sit down at one side of the door. There he sits for days and years. He makes many attempts to be admitted, and wearies the doorkeeper by his importunity. The doorkeeper frequently has little interviews with him, asking him questions about his home and many other things, but the questions are put indiffer-ently, as great lords put them, and always finish with the statement that he cannot be let in yet. The man, who has furnished himself with many things for his journey, sac-rifices all he has, however valuable, to bribe the doorkeeper. The doorkeeper accepts everything, but always with the remark: "I am only taking it to keep you from think-ing you have omitted anything." During these many years the man fixes his attention almost continuously on the doorkeeper. He forgets the other doorkeepers, and this first one seems to him the sole obstacle preventing access to the Law. He curses his bad luck, in his early years boldly and loudly; later, as he grows old, he only grumbles to himself. He becomes childish, and since in his yearlong contemplation of the door-keeper he has come to know even the fleas in his fur collar, he begs the fleas as well to help him and to change the doorkeeper's mind. At length his eyesight begins to fail, and he does not know whether the world is really darker or whether his eyes are only deceiving him. Yet in his darkness he is now aware of a radiance that streams inextin-guishably from the gateway of the Law. Now he has not very long to live. Before he dies, all his experiences in these long years gather themselves in his head to one point, a question he has not yet asked the doorkeeper. He waves him nearer, since he can no longer raise his stiffening body. The doorkeeper has to bend low towards him, for the difference in height between them has altered much to the man's disadvantage. "What do you want to know now?" asks the doorkeeper; "you are insatiable." "Everyone strives to reach the Law," says the man, "so how does it happen that for all these many years no one but myself has ever begged for admittance?" The doorkeeper recognizes that the man has reached his end, and to let his failing senses catch the words roars in his ear: "No one else could ever be admitted here, since this gate was made only for you. I am now going to shut it."

Questions for Study

1. What does the "Law" seem to represent?

2. What does the gate represent? Who or what are the gatekeepers?

3. How does the protagonist change? How does the doorkeeper change?

4. Should the protagonist have acted in a different way?

5. What morals can be drawn from this parable?

6. To what real-life situations might this parable apply?

JAMES THURBER

The Moth and the Star

The American humorist James Thurber (1894-1961) was born in Ohio and worked there as a newspaper reporter before going to New York, where he worked and wrote for *The New Yorker*. Thurber's literary fables, collected in *Fables for Our Time* (1940), reflect many of the complexities and perplexities of twentieth-century life.

A young and impressionable moth once set his heart on a certain star. He told his mother about this and she counseled him to set his heart on a bridge lamp instead. "Stars aren't the thing to hang around," she said; "lamps are the thing to hang around." "You get somewhere that way," said the moth's father. "You don't get anywhere chasing stars." But the moth would not heed the words of either parent. Every evening at dusk when the star came out he would start flying toward it and every morning at dawn he would crawl back home worn out with his vain endeavor. One day his father said to him, "You haven't burned a wing in months, boy, and it looks to me as if you were never going to. All your brothers have been badly burned flying around street lamps and all your sisters have been terribly singed flying around house lamps. Come on, now, get out of here and get yourself scorched! A big strapping moth like you without a mark on him!"

The moth left his father's house, but he would not fly around street lamps and he would not fly around house lamps. He went right on trying to reach the star, which was four and one-third light years, or twenty-five trillion miles, away. The moth thought it was just caught in the top branches of an elm. He never did reach the star, but he went right on trying, night after night, and when he was a very, very old moth he began to think that he really had reached the star and he went around saying so. This gave him a deep and lasting pleasure, and he lived to a great old age. His parents and his brothers and his sisters had all been burned to death when they were quite young.

    Moral: Who flies afar from the sphere of our sorrow is here today and here tomorrow.

Questions for Study

1. Why does the moth keep striving to reach the star? What is the moth's family's reaction to his striving?

2. What is the meaning of Thurber's moral?

3. What other morals might be drawn from this tale?

4. What is humorous about this fable?

5. In what ways are the moth and his parents like real people? What does the star symbolize? What does the flame symbolize?

JAMES THURBER

The Rabbits Who Caused All the Trouble

Within the memory of the youngest child there was a family of rabbits who lived near a pack of wolves. The wolves announced that they did not like the way the rabbits were living. (The wolves were crazy about the way they themselves were living, because it was the only way to live.) One night several wolves were killed in an earthquake and this was blamed on the rabbits, for it is well known that rabbits pound on the ground with their hind legs and cause earthquakes. On another night one of the wolves was killed by a bolt of lightning and this was also blamed on the rabbits, for it is well known that lettuce-eaters cause lightning. The wolves threatened to civilize the rabbits if they didn't behave, and the rabbits decided to run away to a desert island. But the other animals, who lived at a great distance, shamed them, saying, "You must stay where you are and be brave. This is no world for escapists. If the wolves attack you, we will come to your aid, in all probability." So the rabbits continued to live near the wolves and one day there was a terrible flood which drowned a great many wolves. This was blamed on the rabbits, for it is well known that carrot-nibblers with long ears cause floods. The wolves descended on the rabbits, for their own good, and imprisoned them in a dark cave, for their own protection.

When nothing was heard about the rabbits for some weeks, the other animals demanded to know what had happened to them. The wolves replied that the rabbits had been eaten and since they had been eaten the affair was a purely internal matter. But the other animals warned that they might possibly unite against the wolves unless some reason was given for the destruction of the rabbits. So the wolves gave them one. "They were trying to escape," said the wolves, "and, as you know, this is no world for escapists."

Moral: Run, don't walk, to the nearest desert island.

Questions for Study

1. What similarities and differences are there between this fable and Aesop's "The Wolf and the Lamb" (p. 168)?

2. What is the animals' attitude toward the wolves? The rabbits?

3. What does Thurber suggest about the thought processes and motivations of creatures like the wolves?

4. What is the meaning of Thurber's moral? What other morals might be drawn from this fable?

5. Thurber called his fables "fables for our time." How does this fable reflect the historical circumstances of the 1930s?

FAIRY TALES

The English expression **fairy tale** is a misnomer, because fairies rarely appear as characters in fairy tales. The German word **Märchen,** which means "a little tale, a brief story," more accurately characterizes the fairy tale. But even though the fairy tale rarely features fairies, it nonetheless projects a dreamlike world in which the miraculous is so "real" that characters take it for granted.

The fairy tale has other characteristics as well. A structuring device in fairy tales is repetition. The repetitions in European fairy tales follow a predictable pattern of threes: three tasks, three adventures, three trips to the ball. The tone of most fairy tales is light and playful, yet events are violent and painful. Frequently fathers are absent or reticent, leaving the females to fend for themselves. Heroes and heroines are usually outcasts and victims who aspire to transcend their lowly status. They are young, innocent, vulnerable, isolated, but ideally beautiful and good. They typically have a reverence for nature. As a result, nature—trees, animals, weather—aids them. Either from carelessness or innocence, they break taboos, and thus have to extricate themselves from seemingly hopeless situations.

They face radical loss—of loved ones, home, property, limb, reputation, life. Yet by means of pluck and luck, they win satisfying rewards. Central to the plot of most fairy tales is the love story. Usually one of the lovers is either lower class or disguised as lower class and aspires to marry royalty. The happy ending, standard in fairy tales, almost always takes the form of marriage, wealth, and high station.

The fairy tale is, strictly speaking, a European phenomenon. Some folklorists claim, furthermore, that it is a literary phenomenon. They distinguish between "folktales," which belong to an oral folk tradition, and "literary" tales, like fairy tales, which have been recast by writers. The best known writers of fairy tales, Charles Perrault, the brothers Grimm, and Hans Christian Andersen, drew their tales from folk tradition but often altered the tales for literary or thematic purposes. Their tales, then, may resemble oral folktales but are not quite the same, either. They were writing for an educated middle-class audience whose expectations were different from those of the "folk." But whatever the source of fairy tales, whether from writers or a folk tradition, they seem distinguishable as a narrative genre. Many tales from outside Europe, furthermore, seem to share enough of these elements to be classifiable as "fairy tales." Reprinted here, then, are two European "literary" fairy tales and one African folktale that shares many of the features of the European fairy tale.

CHARLES PERRAULT

Little Thumb

Charles Perrault (1628-1703) was a French lawyer, poet, and literary critic. He is best known today as the author of the *Tales from the Past,* also known as *Tales of Mother Goose,* published in 1697. Perrault claimed to have composed the tales for the amusement of his children, but perhaps because fairy tales had become the rage in the French court at the time, he prefaced the book with a letter to the niece of the king, Louis XIV, in which he dedicates the book to her and claims that his tales are morally instructive. Some of his tales—"Cinderella," "Bluebeard," and "Sleeping Beauty"—are among the most famous in the world. Perrault seems to have relied on folk material for his tales and retained the simplicity of oral folk delivery. But he seems also to have changed and embellished the tales for his own purposes. It is probably impossible to know which parts of the tales came from folk tradition and which parts came from Perrault's invention. The folk elements, however, such as the details about daily life, seem to represent a world of peasant experience that was at least as old as the Middle Ages.

*O*nce upon a time there was a woodcutter and his wife, who had seven children, all boys. The eldest was but ten years old, and the youngest only seven.

They were very poor, and their seven children were a great source of trouble to them because not one of them was able to earn his bread. What gave them yet more uneasiness was that the youngest was very delicate, and scarce ever spoke a word, which made people take for stupidity that which was a sign of good sense. He was very little, and when born he was no bigger than one's thumb; hence he was called Little Thumb.

The poor child was the drudge of the household, and was always in the wrong. He was, however, the most bright and discreet of all the brothers; and if he spoke little, he heard and thought the more.

There came a very bad year, and the famine was so great that these poor people resolved to rid themselves of their children. One evening, when they were in bed, and the woodcutter was sitting with his wife at the fire, he said to her, with his heart ready to burst with grief:

"You see plainly that we no longer can give our children food, and I cannot bear to see them die of hunger before my eyes; I am resolved to lose them in the wood to-morrow, which may very easily be done, for, while they amuse themselves in tying up bundles of twigs, we have only to run away and leave them without their seeing us."

"Ah!" cried out his wife, "could you really take the children and lose them?"

In vain did her husband represent to her their great poverty; she would not consent to it. She was poor, but she was their mother.

However, having considered what a grief it would be to her to see them die of hunger, she consented, and went weeping to bed.

Little Thumb heard all they had said; for, hearing that they were talking business, he got up softly and slipped under his father's seat, so as to hear without being seen. He went to bed again, but did not sleep a wink all the rest of the night, thinking of what he had to do. He got up early in the morning, and went to the brookside, where he filled his pockets full of small white pebbles, and then returned home. They all went out, but Little Thumb never told his brothers a word of what he knew.

They went into a very thick forest, where they could not see one another at ten paces apart. The woodcutter began to cut wood, and the children to gather up sticks to make bundles. Their father and mother, seeing them busy at their work, got away from them unbeknown and then all at once ran as fast as they could through a winding by-path.

When the children found they were alone, they began to cry with all their might. Little Thumb let them cry on, knowing very well how to get home again; for, as he came, he had dropped the little white pebbles he had in his pockets all along the way. Then he said to them, "Do not be afraid, my brothers—father and mother have left us here, but I will lead you home again; only follow me."

They followed, and he brought them home by the very same way they had come into the forest. They dared not go in at first, but stood outside the door to listen to what their father and mother were saying.

The very moment the woodcutter and his wife reached home the lord of the manor sent them ten crowns, which he had long owed them, and which they never hoped to see. This gave them new life, for the poor people were dying of hunger. The woodcutter sent his wife to the butcher's at once. As it was a long while since they had eaten, she bought thrice as much meat as was needed for supper for two people. When they had eaten, the woman said:

"Alas! where are our poor children now? They would make a good feast of what we have left here; it was you, William, who wished to lose them. I told you we should repent of it. What are they now doing in the forest? Alas! perhaps the wolves have already eaten them up; you are very inhuman thus to have lost your children."

The woodcutter grew at last quite out of patience, for she repeated twenty times that he would repent of it, and that she was in the right. He threatened to beat her if she did not hold her tongue. The woodcutter was, perhaps, more sorry than his wife, but she teased him so he could not endure it. She wept bitterly, saying:

"Alas! where are my children now, my poor children?"

She said this once so very loud that the children, who were at the door, heard her and cried out all together:

"Here we are! Here we are!"

She ran immediately to let them in, and said as she embraced them:

"How happy I am to see you again, my dear children; you are very tired and very hungry, and, my poor Peter, you are covered with mud. Come in and let me clean you."

Peter was her eldest son, whom she loved more than all the rest, because he was red haired, as she was herself.

They sat down to table, and ate with an appetite which pleased both father and mother, to whom they told how frightened they were in the forest, nearly all speaking at once. The good folk were delighted to see their children once more, and this joy continued while the ten crowns lasted. But when the money was all spent, they fell again into their former uneasiness, and resolved to lose their children again. And, that they might be the surer of doing it, they determined to take them much farther than before.

They could not talk of this so secretly but they were overheard by Little Thumb, who laid his plans to get out of the difficulty as he had done before; but, though he got up very early to go and pick up some little pebbles, he could not, for he found the house-door double-locked. He did not know what to do. Their father had given each of them a piece of bread for their breakfast. He reflected that he might make use of the bread instead of the pebbles, by throwing crumbs all along the way they should pass, and so he stuffed it in his pocket. Their father and mother led them into the thickest and most obscure part of the forest, and then, stealing away into a by-path, left them there. Little Thumb was not very much worried about it, for he thought he could easily find the way again by means of his bread, which he had scattered all along as he came; but he was very much surprised when he could not find a single crumb: the birds had come and eaten them all.

They were now in great trouble; for the more they wandered, the deeper they went into the forest. Night now fell, and there arose a high wind, which filled them with fear. They fancied they heard on every side the howling of wolves coming to devour them. They scarce dared to speak or turn their heads. Then it rained very hard, which wetted them to the skin. Their feet slipped at every step, and they fell into the mud, covering their hands with it so that they knew not what to do with them.

Little Thumb climbed up to the top of a tree, to see if he could discover anything. Looking on every side, he saw at last a glimmering light, like that of a candle, but a long way beyond the forest. He came down, and, when upon the ground, he could see it no more, which grieved him sadly. However, having walked for some time with his brothers toward that side on which he had seen the light, he discovered it again as he came out of the wood.

They arrived at last at the house where this candle was, not without many frights; for very often they lost sight of it, which happened every time they came into a hollow. They knocked at the door, and a good woman came and opened it.

She asked them what they wanted. Little Thumb told her they were poor children who were lost in the forest, and desired to lodge there for charity's sake. The woman, seeing them all so very pretty, began to weep and said to them: "Alas! poor babies, where do you come from? Do you know that this house belongs to a cruel Ogre who eats little children?"

"Alas! dear madam," answered Little Thumb (who, with his brothers, was trembling in every limb), "what shall we do? The wolves of the forest surely will devour us to-night if you refuse us shelter in your house; and so we would rather the gentleman should eat us. Perhaps he may take pity upon us if you will be pleased to ask him to do so."

The Ogre's wife, who believed she could hide them from her husband till morning, let them come in, and took them to warm themselves at a very good fire; for there was a whole sheep roasting for the Ogre's supper.

As they began to warm themselves they heard three or four great raps at the door; this was the Ogre, who was come home. His wife quickly hid them under the bed and went to open the door. The Ogre at once asked if supper was ready and the wine drawn, and then sat himself down to table. The sheep was as yet all raw, but he liked it the better for that. He sniffed about to the right and left, saying:

"I smell fresh meat."

"What you smell," said his wife, "must be the calf which I have just now killed and flayed."

"I smell fresh meat, I tell you once more," replied the Ogre, looking crossly at his wife, "and there is something here which I do not understand."

As he spoke these words he got up from the table and went straight to the bed.

"Ah!" said he, "that is how you would cheat me; I know not why I do not eat you, too; it is well for you that you are tough. Here is game, which comes very luckily to entertain three Ogres of my acquaintance who are to pay me a visit in a day or two."

He dragged them out from under the bed, one by one. The poor children fell upon their knees and begged his pardon, but they had to do with one of the most cruel of Ogres, who, far from having any pity on them, was already devouring them in his mind, and told his wife they would be delicate eating when she had made a good sauce.

He then took a great knife, and, coming up to these poor children, sharpened it upon a great whetstone which he held in his left hand. He had already taken hold of one of them when his wife said to him:

"What need you do it now? Will you not have time enough to-morrow?"

"Hold your prating," said the Ogre; "they will eat the tenderer."

"But you have so much meat already," replied his wife; "here are a calf, two sheep, and half a pig."

"That is true," said the Ogre; "give them a good supper that they may not grow thin, and put them to bed."

The good woman was overjoyed at this, and gave them a good supper; but they were so much afraid that they could not eat. As for the Ogre, he sat down again to drink, being highly pleased that he had the wherewithal to treat his friends. He drank a dozen glasses more than ordinary, which got up into his head and obliged him to go to bed.

The Ogre had seven daughters, who were still little children. These young Ogresses had all of them very fine complexions; but they all had little gray eyes, quite round, hooked noses, a very large mouth, and very long, sharp teeth, set far apart. They were not as yet wicked, but they promised well to be, for they had already bitten little children.

They had been put to bed early, all seven in one bed, with every one a crown of gold upon her head. There was in the same chamber a bed of the like size, and the Ogre's wife put the seven little boys into this bed, after which she went to bed herself.

Little Thumb, who had observed that the Ogre's daughters had crowns of gold upon their heads, and was afraid lest the Ogre should repent his not killing them that evening, got up about midnight, and, taking his brothers' bonnets and his own, went very softly and put them upon the heads of the seven little Ogresses, after having taken off their crowns of gold, which he put upon his own head and his brothers', so that the Ogre might take them for his daughters, and his daughters for the little boys whom he wanted to kill.

Things turned out just as he had thought; for the Ogre, waking about midnight, regretted that he had deferred till morning to do that which he might have done overnight, and jumped quickly out of bed, taking his great knife.

"Let us see," said he, "how our little rogues do, and not make two jobs of the matter."

He then went up, groping all the way, into his daughters' chamber; and, coming to the bed where the little boys lay, and who were all fast asleep, except Little Thumb, who was terribly afraid when he found the Ogre fumbling about his head, as he had done about his brothers', he felt the golden crowns, and said:

"I should have made a fine piece of work of it, truly; it is clear I drank too much last night."

Then he went to the bed where the girls lay, and, having found the boys' little bonnets:

"Ah!" said he, "my merry lads, are you there? Let us work boldly."

And saying these words, without more ado, he cruelly murdered all his seven daughters. Well pleased with what he had done, he went to bed again.

So soon as Little Thumb heard the Ogre snore, he waked his brothers, and bade them put on their clothes quickly and follow him. They stole softly into the garden and got over the wall. They ran about all night, trembling all the while, without knowing which way they went.

The Ogre, when he woke, said to his wife: "Go upstairs and dress those young rascals who came here last night." The Ogress was very much surprised at this goodness of her husband, not dreaming after what manner she should dress them; but, thinking that he had ordered her to go up and put on their clothes, she went, and was horrified when she perceived her seven daughters all dead.

She began by fainting away, as was only natural in such a case. The Ogre, fearing his wife was too long in doing what he had ordered, went up himself to help her. He was no less amazed than his wife at this frightful spectacle.

"Ah! what have I done?" cried he. "The wretches shall pay for it, and that instantly."

He threw a pitcher of water upon his wife's face, and having brought her to herself, "Give me quickly," cried he, "my seven-leagued boots, that I may go and catch them."

He went out into the country, and, after running in all directions, he came at last into the very road where the poor children were, and not above a hundred paces from their father's house. They espied the Ogre, who went at one step from mountain to mountain, and over rivers as easily as the narrowest brooks. Little Thumb, seeing a hollow rock near the place where they were, hid his brothers in it, and crowded into it himself, watching always what would become of the Ogre.

The Ogre, who found himself tired with his long and fruitless journey (for these boots of seven leagues greatly taxed the wearer), had a great mind to rest himself, and, by chance, went to sit down upon the rock in which the little boys had hidden themselves. As he was worn out with fatigue, he fell asleep, and, after reposing himself some time, began to snore so frightfully that the poor children were no less afraid of him than when he held up his great knife and was going to take their lives. Little Thumb was not so much frightened as his brothers, and told them that they should run away at once toward home while the Ogre was asleep so soundly, and that they need not be in any trouble about him. They took his advice, and got home quickly.

Little Thumb then went close to the Ogre, pulled off his boots gently, and put them on his own legs. The boots were very long and large, but as they were fairy boots, they had the gift of becoming big or little, according to the legs of those who wore them; so that they fitted his feet and legs as well as if they had been made for him. He went straight to the Ogre's house, where he saw his wife crying bitterly for the loss of her murdered daughters.

"Your husband," said Little Thumb, "is in very great danger, for he has been taken by a gang of thieves, who have sworn to kill him if he does not give them all his gold and silver. At the very moment they held their daggers at his throat he perceived me and begged me to come and tell you the condition he was in, and to say that you should give me all he has of value, without retaining any one thing; for otherwise they will kill him without mercy. As his case is very pressing, he desired me to make use of his seven-leagued boots, which you see I have on, so that I might make the more haste and that I might show you that I do not impose upon you."

The good woman, being greatly frightened, gave him all she had; for this Ogre was a very good husband, though he ate up little children. Little Thumb, having thus got all the Ogre's money, came home to his father's house, where he was received with abundance of joy.

There are many people who do not agree in regard to this act of Little Thumb's, and pretend that he never robbed the Ogre at all, and that he only thought he might very justly take off his seven-leagued boots because he made no other use of them but to run after little children. These folks affirm that they are very well assured of this, because they have drunk and eaten often at the woodcutter's house. They declare that when Little Thumb had taken off the Ogre's boots he went to Court, where he was informed that they were very much in trouble about a certain army, which was two hundred leagues off, and anxious as to the success of a battle. He went, they say, to the King and told him that if he desired it, he would bring him news from the army before night.

The King promised him a great sum of money if he succeeded. Little Thumb returned that very same night with the news; and, this first expedition causing him to be known, he earned as much as he wished, for the King paid him very well for carrying his orders to the army. Many ladies employed him also to carry messages, from which he made much money. After having for some time carried on the business of a messenger and gained thereby great wealth, he went home to his father, and it is impossible to express the joy of his family. He placed them all in comfortable circumstances, bought places for his father and brothers, and by that means settled them very handsomely in the world, while he successfully continued to make his own way.

Questions for Study

1. What economic conditions of European peasants are reflected in this tale? How do the people cope with difficult times?

2. What qualities does the forest represent to the various characters in the story?

3. What traits characterize Little Thumb? What do each of his adventures reveal about his abilities? In what ways is he "little"? How does he compensate for his littleness?

4. What else is "little" in this tale? What or who is "large"? How do the large things threaten the little things? What chances of surviving these threats are there?

5. How are food and eating important to the plot and themes of the story?

6. How is the ogre plot related to the famine plot (the family's hardships, recounted at the beginning)?

Katie Woodencloak

This anonymous Norwegian fairy tale was collected in 1906. Its similarity to "Cinderella" illustrates how folktales "traveled" from culture to culture and how several tales could be blended to form new tales.

*O*nce on a time there was a King who had become a widower. By his Queen he had one daughter, who was so clever and lovely, there wasn't a cleverer or lovelier

Princess in all the world. So the King went on a long time sorrowing for the Queen, whom he had loved so much, but at last he got weary of living alone, and married another Queen, who was a widow, and had, too, an only daughter; but this daughter was just as bad and ugly as the other was kind, and clever, and lovely. The stepmother and her daughter were jealous of the Princess, because she was so lovely; but so long as the King was at home, they dared n't do her any harm, he was so fond of her.

Well, after a time he fell into war with another King, and went out to battle with his host, and then the stepmother thought she might do as she pleased; and so she both starved and beat the Princess, and was after her in every hole and corner of the house. At last she thought everything too good for her, and turned her out to herd cattle. So there she went about with the cattle, and herded them in the woods and on the fells. As for food, she got little or none, and she grew thin and wan, and was always sobbing and sorrowful. Now in the herd there was a great dun° bull, which always kept himself so neat and sleek, and often and often he came up to the Princess, and let her pat him. So one day when she sat there, sad, and sobbing, and sorrowful, he came up to her and asked her outright why she was always in such grief. She answered nothing, but went on weeping.

"Ah!" said the Bull, "I know all about it quite well, though you won't tell me; you weep because the Queen is bad to you, and because she is ready to starve you to death. But food you've no need to fret about, for in my left ear lies a cloth, and when you take and spread it out, you may have as many dishes as you please."

So she did that, took the cloth and spread it out on the grass, and lo! it served up the nicest dishes one could wish to have; there was wine too, and mead, and sweet cake. Well, she soon got up her flesh again, and grew so plump, and rosy, and white, that the Queen and her scrawny chip of a daughter turned blue and yellow for spite. The Queen couldn't at all make out how her stepdaughter got to look so well on such bad fare, so she told one of her maids to go after her in the wood, and watch and see how it all was, for she thought some of the servants in the house must give her food. So the maid went after her, and watched in the wood, and then she saw how the stepdaughter took the cloth out of the Bull's ear, and spread it out, and how it served up the nicest dishes which the stepdaughter ate and made good cheer over. All this the maid told the Queen when she went home.

And now the King came home from war, and had won the fight against the other king with whom he went out to battle. So there was great joy throughout the palace, and no one was gladder than the king's daughter. But the Queen shammed sick, and took to her bed, and paid the doctor a great fee to get him to say she could never be well again unless she had some of the Dun Bull's flesh to eat. Both the king's daughter and the folk in the palace asked the doctor if nothing else would help her, and prayed hard for the Bull, for every one was fond of him, and they all said there wasn't that Bull's match in all the land. But, no; he must and should be slaughtered, nothing else would do. When the king's daughter heard that, she got very sorrowful, and went down into the byre to the Bull. There, too, he stood and hung down his head, and looked so downcast that she began to weep over him.

"What are you weeping for?" asked the Bull.

So she told him how the King had come home again, and how the Queen had

°*dun.* Grayish brown.

shammed sick and got the doctor to say she could never be well and sound again unless she got some of the Dun Bull's flesh to eat, and so now he was to be slaughtered.

"If they get me killed first," said the Bull, "they'll soon take your life too. Now, if you're of my mind, we'll just start off, and go away to-night."

Well, the Princess thought it bad, you may be sure, to go and leave her father, but she thought it still worse to be in the house with the Queen; and so she gave her word to the Bull to come to him.

At night, when all had gone to bed, the Princess stole down to the byre to the Bull, and so he took her on his back, and set off from the homestead as fast as ever he could. And when the folk got up at cockrow next morning to slaughter the Bull, why, he was gone; and when the King got up and asked for his daughter, she was gone too. He sent out messengers on all sides to hunt for them, and gave them out in all the parish churches; but there was no one who had caught a glimpse of them. Meanwhile, the Bull went through many lands with the King's daughter on his back, and so one day they came to a great copper-wood, where both the trees, and branches, and leaves, and flowers, and everything, were nothing but copper.

But before they went into the wood, the Bull said to the King's daughter:

"Now, when we get into this wood, mind you take care not to touch even a leaf of it, else it's all over both with me and you, for here dwells a Troll with three heads who owns this wood."

No, bless her, she'd be sure to take care not to touch anything. Well, she was very careful, and leant this way and that to miss the boughs, and put them gently aside with her hands; but it was such a thick wood, 'twas scarce possible to get through; and so, with all her pains, somehow or other she tore off a leaf, which she held in her hand.

"*AU! AU!* what have you done now?" said the Bull; "there's nothing for it now but to fight for life or death; but mind you keep the leaf safe."

Soon after they got to the end of the wood, and a Troll with three heads came running up:

"Who is this that touches my wood?" said the Troll.

"It's just as much mine as yours," said the Bull.

"Ah!" roared the Troll, "we'll try a fall about that."

"As you choose," said the Bull.

So they rushed at one another, and fought; and the Bull he butted, and gored, and kicked with all his might and main; but the Troll gave him as good as he brought, and it lasted the whole day before the Bull got the mastery; and then he was so full of wounds, and so worn out, he could scarce lift a leg. Then they were forced to stay there a day to rest, and then the Bull bade the King's daughter to take the horn of ointment which hung at the Troll's belt, and rub him with it. Then he came to himself again, and the day after they trudged on again. So they travelled many, many days, until, after a long, long time, they came to a silver wood, where both the trees, and branches, and leaves, and flowers, and everything, were silvern.

Before the Bull went into the wood, he said to the King's daughter:

"Now, when we get into this wood, for heaven's sake mind you take good care; you mustn't touch anything, and not pluck off so much as one leaf, else it is all over both with me and you; for here is a Troll with six heads who owns it, and him I don't think I should be able to master."

"No," said the King's daughter; "I'll take good care and not touch anything you don't wish me to touch."

But when they got into the wood, it was so close and thick, they could scarce get along. She was as careful as careful could be, and leant to this side and that to miss the boughs, and put them on one side with her hands, but every minute the branches struck her across the eyes, and in spite of all her pains, it so happened she tore off a leaf.

"*AU! AU!* what have you done now?" said the Bull. "There's nothing for it now but to fight for life and death, for this Troll has six heads, and is twice as strong as the other, but mind you keep the leaf safe, and don't lose it."

Just as he said that, up came the Troll:

"Who is this," he said, "that touches my wood?"

"It's as much mine as yours," said the Bull.

"That we'll try a fall about that," roared the Troll.

"As you choose," said the Bull, and rushed at the Troll, and gored out his eyes, and drove his horns right through his body, so that the entrails gushed out; but the Troll was almost a match for him, and it lasted three whole days before the Bull got the life gored out of him. But then he, too, was so weak and wretched, it was as much as he could do to stir a limb, and so full of wounds, that the blood streamed from him. So he said to the King's daughter she must take the horn of ointment that hung at the Troll's belt, and rub him with it. Then she did that, and he came to himself; but they were forced to stay there a week to rest before the Bull had strength enough to go on.

At last they set off again, but the Bull was still poorly, and they went rather slow at first. So, to spare time, the King's daughter said, as she was young and light of foot, she could very well walk, but she couldn't get leave to do that. No; she must seat herself up on his back again. So on they travelled through many lands a long time, and the King's daughter did not know in the least whither they went; but after a long, long time they came to a gold wood. It was so grand, the gold dropped from every twig, and all the trees, and boughs, and flowers, and leaves, were of pure gold. Here, too, the same thing happened as had happened in the silver wood and copper wood. The Bull told the King's daughter she mustn't touch it for anything, for there was a Troll with nine heads who owned it, and he was much bigger and stouter than both the others put together, and he didn't think he could get the better of him. No; she'd be sure to take heed not to touch it; that he might know very well. But when they got into the wood, it was far thicker and closer than the silver wood, and the deeper they went into it, the worse it got. The wood went on, getting thicker and thicker, and closer and closer; and at last she thought there was no way at all to get through it. She was in such an awful fright of plucking off anything, that she sat, and twisted, and turned herself this way and that, and hither and thither, to keep clear of the boughs, and she put them on one side with her hands; but every moment the branches struck her across the eyes, so that she couldn't see what she was clutching at; and lo! before she knew how it came about, she had a gold apple in her hand. Then she was so bitterly sorry, she burst into tears, and wanted to throw it away; but the Bull said, she must keep it safe and watch it well, and comforted her as well as he could; but he thought it would be a hard tussle, and he doubted how it would go.

Just then up came the Troll with the nine heads, and he was so ugly, the King's daughter scarcely dared to look at him.

"Who is this that touches my wood?" he roared.

"It's just as much mine as yours," said the Bull.

"That we'll try a fall about," roared the Troll again.

"Just as you choose," said the Bull; and so they rushed at one another, and fought, and it was such a dreadful sight, the King's daughter was ready to swoon away. The Bull gored out the Troll's eyes, and drove his horns through and through his body, till the entrails came tumbling out; but the Troll fought bravely; and when the Bull got one head gored to death, the rest breathed life into it again, and so it lasted a whole week before the Bull was able to get the life out of them all. But then he was utterly worn out and wretched. He couldn't stir a foot, and his body was all one wound. He couldn't so much as ask the King's daughter to take the horn of ointment which hung at the Troll's belt, and rub it over him. But she did it all the same, and then he came to himself by little and little; but they had to lie there and rest three weeks before he was fit to go on again.

Then they set off at a snail's pace, for the Bull said they had still a little further to go, and so they crossed over many high hills and thick woods. So after a while they got upon the fells.

"Do you see anything?" asked the Bull.

"No, I see nothing but the sky and the wild fell," said the King's daughter.

So when they clomb higher up, the fell got smoother, and they could see further off.

"Do you see anything now?" asked the Bull.

"Yes, I see a castle far, far away," said the Princess.

"That's not so little though," said the Bull.

After a long, long time, they came to a great cairn, where there was a spur of the fell that stood sheer across the way.

"Do you see anything now?" asked the Bull.

"Yes, now I see the castle close by," said the King's daughter, "and now it is much, much bigger."

"Thither you're to go," said the Bull. "Right underneath the castle is a pig-stye, where you are to dwell. When you come thither you'll find a wooden cloak, all made of strips of lath; that you must put on, and go up to the castle and say your name is 'Katie Woodencloak,' and ask for a place. But before you go, you must take your penknife and cut my head off, and then you must flay me, and roll up the hide, and lay it under the wall of rock yonder, and under the hide you must lay the copper leaf, and the silvern leaf, and the golden apple. Yonder, up against the rock, stands a stick; and when you want anything, you've only got to knock on the wall of rock with that stick."

At first she wouldn't do anything of the kind; but when the Bull said it was the only thanks he would have for what he had done for her, she couldn't help herself. So, however much it grieved her heart, she hacked and cut away with her knife at the big beast till she got both his head and his hide off, and then she laid the hide up under the wall of rock, and put the copper leaf, and the silvern leaf, and the golden apple inside it.

So when she had done that, she went over to the pig-stye, but all the while she went she sobbed and wept. There she put on the wooden cloak, and so went up to the palace. When she came into the kitchen she begged for a place, and told them her name was Katie Woodencloak. Yes, the cook said she might have a place—she might have leave to be there in the scullery, and wash up, for the lassie who did that work before had just gone away.

"But as soon as you get weary of being here, you'll go your way too, I'll be bound."

No; she was sure she wouldn't do that.

So there she was, behaving so well, and washing up so handily. The Sunday after there were to be strange guests at the palace, so Katie asked if she might have leave to carry up water for the Prince's bath; but all the rest laughed at her, and said;

"What should you do there? Do you think the Prince will care to look at you, you who are such a fright!"

But she wouldn't give it up, and kept on begging and praying; and at last she got leave. So when she went up the stairs, her wooden cloak made such a clatter, the Prince came out and asked:

"Pray who are you?"

"Oh! I was just going to bring up water for your Royal Highness's bath," said Katie.

"Do you think now," said the Prince, "I'd have anything to do with the water you bring?" and with that he threw the water over her.

So she had to put up with that, but then she asked leave to go to church; well, she got that leave too, for the church lay close by. But, first of all, she went to the rock, and knocked on its face with the stick which stood there, just as the Bull had said. And straightway out came a man, who said:

"What's your will?"

So the Princess said she had got leave to go to church and hear the priest preach, but she had no clothes to go in. So he brought out a kirtle, which was as bright as the copper wood, and she got a horse and saddle beside. Now, when she got to the church, she was so lovely and grand, all wondered who she could be, and scarce one of them listened to what the priest said, for they looked too much at her. As for the Prince, he fell so deep in love with her, he didn't take his eyes off her for a single moment.

So, as she went out of church, the Prince ran after her, and held the church door open for her; and so he got hold of one of her gloves, which was caught in the door. When she went away and mounted her horse, the Prince went up to her again, and asked whence she came.

"Oh! I'm from Bath," said Katie; and while the Prince took out the glove to give it to her, she said:

> Bright before and dark behind,
> Clouds come rolling on the wind;
> That this Prince may never see
> Where my good steed goes with me.

The Prince had never seen the like of that glove, and went about far and wide asking after the land whence the proud lady, who rode off without her glove, said she came; but there was no one who could tell where "Bath" lay.

Next Sunday some one had to go up to the Prince with a towel.

"Oh! may I have leave to go up with it?" said Katie.

"What's the good of your going?" said the others; "you saw how it fared with you last time."

But Katie wouldn't give in; she kept on begging and praying, till she got leave; and then she ran up the stairs, so that her wooden cloak made a great clatter. Out came the Prince, and when he saw it was Katie, he tore the towel out of her hand, and threw it into her face.

"Pack yourself off, you ugly Troll," he cried; "do you think I'd have a towel which you have touched with your smutty fingers?"

After that the Prince set off to church, and Katie begged for leave to go too. They all asked what business she had at church—she who had nothing to put on but that wooden cloak, which was so black and ugly. But Katie said the priest was such a brave man to preach, what he said did her so much good; and so at last she got leave. Now she went again to the rock and knocked, and so out came the man, and gave her a kirtle far finer than the first one; it was all covered with silver, and it shone like the silver wood; and she got besides a noble steed, with a saddle-cloth broidered with silver, and a silver bit.

So when the King's daughter got to the church, the folk were still standing about in the churchyard. And all wondered and wondered who she could be, and the Prince was soon on the spot, and came and wished to hold her horse for her while she got off. But she jumped down, and said there was no need, for her horse was so well broke, it stood still when she bid it, and came when she called it. So they all went into church, but there was scarce a soul that listened to what the priest said, for they looked at her a deal too much; and the Prince fell still deeper in love than the first time.

When the sermon was over, and she went out of church, and was going to mount her horse, up came the Prince again, and asked her whence she came.

"Oh! I'm from Towelland," said the King's daughter; and as she said that, she dropped her riding-whip, and when the Prince stooped to pick it up, she said:

> Bright before and dark behind,
> Clouds come rolling on the wind;
> That this Prince may never see
> Where my good steed goes with me.

So away she was again; and the Prince couldn't tell what had become of her. He went about far and wide asking after the land whence she said she came, but there was no one who could tell him where it lay; and so the Prince had to make the best he could of it.

Next Sunday some one had to go up to the Prince with a comb. Katie begged for leave to go up with it, but the others put her in mind how she had fared the last time, and scolded her for wishing to go before the Prince—such a black and ugly fright as she was in her wooden cloak. But she wouldn't leave off asking till they let her go up to the Prince with his comb. So, when she came clattering up the stairs again, out came the Prince, and took the comb, and threw it at her, and bade her be off as fast as she could. After that the Prince went to church, and Katie begged for leave to go too. They asked again what business she had there, she who was so foul and black, and who had no clothes to show herself in. Might be the Prince or some one else would

see her, and then both she and all the others would smart for it; but Katie said they had
something else to do than to look at her; and she wouldn't leave off begging and praying till they gave her leave to go.

So the same thing happened now as had happened twice before. She went to
the rock and knocked with the stick, and then the man came out and gave her a kirtle
which was far grander than either of the others. It was almost all pure gold, and studded with diamonds; and she got besides a noble steed, with a gold broidered saddle-
cloth and a golden bit.

Now when the King's daughter got to the church, there stood the priest and all
the people in the churchyard waiting for her. Up came the Prince running, and wanted
to hold her horse, but she jumped off, and said:

"No; thanks—there's no need, for my horse is so well broke, it stands still when
I bid him."

So they all hastened into church, and the priest got into the pulpit, but no one
listened to a word he said; for they all looked too much at her, and wondered whence
she came; and the Prince, he was far deeper in love than either of the former times.
He had no eyes, or ears, or sense for anything, but just to sit and stare at her.

So when the sermon was over, and the King's daughter was to go out of the
church, the Prince had got a firkin of pitch poured out in the porch, that he might
come and help her over it; but she didn't care a bit—she just put her foot right down
into the midst of the pitch, and jumped across it; but then one of her golden shoes
stuck fast in it, and as she got on her horse, up came the Prince running out of the
church, and asked whence she came.

"I'm from Combland," said Katie. But when the Prince wanted to reach her the
gold shoe, she said:

> Bright before and dark behind,
> Clouds come rolling on the wind;
> That this Prince may never see
> Where my good steed goes with me.

So the Prince couldn't tell still what had become of her, and he went about a
weary time all over the world asking for "Combland"; but when no one could tell him
where it lay, he ordered it to be given out everywhere that he would wed the woman
whose foot could fit the gold shoe.

So many came of all sorts from all sides, fair and ugly alike; but there was no one
who had so small a foot as to be able to get on the gold shoe. And after a long, long
time, who should come but Katie's wicked stepmother, and her daughter, too, and her
the gold shoe fitted; but ugly she was, and so loathly she looked, the Prince only kept
his word sore against his will. Still they got ready the wedding-feast, and she was
dressed up and decked out as a bride; but as they rode to church, a little bird sat upon
a tree and sang:

> A bit off her heel,
> And a bit off her toe;
> Katie Woodencloak's tiny shoe
> Is full of blood—that's all I know.

And sure enough, when they looked to it the bird told the truth, for blood gushed out of the shoe.

Then all the maids and women who were about the palace had to go up to try on the shoe, but there was none of them whom it would fit at all.

"But where's Katie Woodencloak?" asked the Prince, when all the rest had tried the shoe, for he understood the song of birds very well, and bore in mind what the little bird had said.

"Oh! she think of that!" said the rest; "it's no good her coming forward. Why, she's legs like a horse."

"Very true, I daresay," said the Prince; "but since all the others have tried, Katie may as well try too."

"Katie," he bawled out through the door; and Katie came trampling up stairs, and her wooden cloak clattered as if a whole regiment of dragoons were charging up.

"Now, you must try the shoe on, and be a Princess, you too," said the other maids, and laughed and made game of her.

So Katie took up the shoe, and put her foot into it like nothing, and threw off her wooden cloak; and so there she stood in her gold kirtle, and it shone so that the sunbeams glistened from her; and lo! on her other foot she had the fellow to the gold shoe.

So when the Prince knew her again, he grew so glad, he ran up to her and threw his arms around her, and gave her a kiss; and when he heard she was a King's daughter, he got gladder still, and then came the wedding-feast; and so

Snip, snip, snover,
This story's over.

Questions for Study

1. The story has three parts: the Princess at home, the Princess with the Bull, and the Princess at the Prince's castle. These parts may each have come from independent stories. Why have they been brought together here? Are the three parts related?

2. What repetitions occur in this story? How are the repeated elements different?

3. What is the Bull's relationship to the Princess? Why does he help her? How does he help her? Why does she have to kill the Bull?

4. Some folklorists speculate that European folktales often contain vestiges of pagan religions that were suppressed when Christianity became dominant. From what kind of religion might the details about the bull have come?

5. What characterizes the Prince?

6. Why does the Princess hide her true identity from the Prince?

7. Does this story have any parallel to the real-life experiences of females?

Ngomba's Balloon (Bakongo)

This folktale, from the Bakongo peoples, who live along the Congo River in central Africa, shares some of the traits of European fairy tales. It was collected in 1898.

*F*our little maidens one day started to go out fishing. One of them was suffering sadly from sores, which covered her from head to foot. Her name was Ngomba. The other three, after a little consultation, agreed that Ngomba should not accompany them; and so they told her to go back.

"Nay," said Ngomba, "I will do no such thing. I mean to catch fish for mother as well as you."

Then the three maidens beat Ngomba until she was glad to run away. But she determined to catch fish also, so she walked and walked, she hardly knew whither, until at last she came upon a large lake. Here she commenced fishing and singing:

> If my mother
> > [She catches a fish and puts it in her basket.]
> Had taken care of me,
> > [She catches another fish and puts it in her basket.]
> I should have been with them,
> > [She catches another fish and puts it in her basket.]
> And not here alone.
> > [She catches another fish and puts it in her basket.]

But a Mpunia (murderer) had been watching her for some time, and now he came up to her and accosted her:

"What are you doing here?"

"Fishing. Please, don't kill me! See, I am full of sores, but I can catch plenty of fish."

The Mpunia watched her as she fished and sang:

> Oh, I shall surely die!
> > [She catches a fish and puts it in her basket.]
> Mother, you will never see me!
> > [She catches another fish and puts it in her basket.]
> But I don't care,
> > [She catches another fish and puts it in her basket.]
> For no one cares for me.
> > [She catches another fish and puts it in her basket.]

"Come with me," said the Mpunia.

"Nay, this fish is for mother, and I must take it to her."
"If you do not come with me, I will kill you."

> Oh! Am I to die
>> [She catches a fish and puts it in her basket.]
> On the top of my fish?
>> [She catches another fish and puts it in her basket.]
> If mother had loved me,
>> [She catches another fish and puts it in her basket.]
> To live I should wish.
>> [She catches another fish and puts it in her basket.]

"Take me and cure me, dear Mpunia, and I will serve you."

The Mpunia took her to his home in the woods, and cured her. Then he placed her in the paint-house and married her.

Now the Mpunia was very fond of dancing, and Ngomba danced beautifully, so that he loved her very much, and made her mistress over all his prisoners and goods.

"When I go out for a walk," he said to her, "I will tie this string round my waist; and that you may know when I am still going away from you, or returning, the string will be stretched tight as I depart, and will hang loose as I return."

Ngomba pined for her mother, and therefore entered into a conspiracy with her people to escape. She sent them every day to cut the leaves of the mateva-palm, and ordered them to put them in the sun to dry. Then she set them to work to make a huge ntenda, or basket. And when the Mpunia returned, he remarked to her that the air was heavy with the smell of mateva.

Now she had made all her people put on clean clothes, and when they knew that he was returning, she ordered them to come to him and flatter him. So now they approached him, and some called him "father" and others "uncle"; and others told him how he was a father and a mother to them. And he was very pleased, and danced with them.

The next day when he returned he said he smelt mateva.

Then Ngomba cried, and told him that he was both father and mother to her, and that if he accused her of smelling of mateva, she would kill herself.

He could not stand this sadness, so he kissed her and danced with her until all was forgotten.

The next day Ngomba determined to try her ntenda, to see if it would float in the air. Thus four women lifted it on high, and gave it a start upwards, and it floated beautifully. Now the Mpunia happened to be up a tree, and he espied this great ntenda floating in the air; and he danced and sang for joy, and wished to call Ngomba, that she might dance with him.

That night he smelt mateva again, and his suspicions were aroused; and when he thought how easily his wife might escape him, he determined to kill her. Accordingly, he gave her to drink some palm-wine that he had drugged. She drank it, and slept as he put his sommo (the iron that the natives make red hot, and with which they burn the hole through the stem of their pipes) into the fire. He meant to kill her by pushing this red hot wire up her nose.

But as he was almost ready, Ngomba's little sister, who had changed herself into a cricket and hidden herself under her bed, began to sing. The Mpunia heard her and felt forced to join in and dance, and thus he forgot to kill his wife. But after a time she ceased singing, and then he began to heat the wire again. The cricket then sang again, and again he danced and danced, and in his excitement tried to wake Ngomba to dance also. But she refused to awake, telling him that the medicine he had given her made her feel sleepy. Then he went out and got some palm-wine, and as he went she drowsily asked him if he had made the string fast. He called all his people, dressed himself, and made them all dance.

The cock crew.

The iron wire was still in the fire. The Mpunia made his wife get up and fetch more palm-wine.

Then the cock crew again, and it was daylight.

When the Mpunia had left her for the day, Ngomba determined to escape that very day. So she called her people and made them try the ntenda again; and when she was certain that it would float, she put all her people, and all the Mpunia's ornaments, into it. Then she got in and the ntenda began to float away over the tree-tops in the direction of her mother's town.

When the Mpunia, who was up a tree, saw it coming towards him, he danced and sang for joy, and only wished that his wife had been there to see this huge ntenda flying through the air. It passed just over his head, and then he knew that the people in it were his. So that he ran after it in the tops of the trees, until he saw it drop in Ngomba's town. And he determined to go there also and claim his wife.

The ntenda floated round the house of Ngomba's mother, and astonished all the people there, and finally settled down in front of it. Ngomba cried to the people to come and let them out. But they were afraid and did not dare, so that she came out herself and presented herself to her mother.

Her relations at first did not recognise her; but after a little while they fell upon her and welcomed her as their long-lost Ngomba.

Then the Mpunia entered the town and claimed Ngomba as his wife.

"Yes," her relations said, "she is your wife, and you must be thanked for curing her of her sickness."

And while some of her relations were entertaining the Mpunia, others were preparing a place for him and his wife to be seated. They made a large fire, and boiled a great quantity of water, and dug a deep hole in the ground. This hole they covered over with sticks and a mat, and when all was ready they led the Mpunia and his wife to it, and requested them to be seated. Ngomba sat near her husband, who, as he sat down, fell into the hole. The relations then brought boiling water and fire, and threw it over him until he died.

Questions for Study

1. How is this story similar to and different from "Little Thumb" and "Katie Woodencloak"? Is it a "fairy tale"?

2. How are males and females presented in this story?

3. What characterizes Ngomba? What qualities allow her to triumph? What does she achieve?

4. What characterizes Mpunia? What is Ngomba's attitude toward him?

5. How is Ngomba's illness important?

6. Does this story have any application to real-life situations?

TRICKSTER TALES

Trickster tales feature a protagonist whose physical smallness and weakness is counterbalanced by his shrewdness and, sometimes, ruthlessness. Western cultures have trickster tales, but in non-Western societies, the trickster takes on mythological properties. He is often present at the creation of the world and is an associate of the creator. He constantly tries to outwit and outdo any force that opposes him, including the deity, and he sometimes preys upon innocent and unsuspecting creatures. He delights in the game of tricking for its own sake, and worries little about consequences. His natural form is as an animal—spider, rabbit, tortoise, crow, wolf, coyote—but he can shift to human form as well. Sometimes he shifts back and forth from animal to human form. The trickster seems indestructible. If he fails in one story, he is resurrected in succeeding stories to trick again.

Trickster protagonists appear in the folk and literary traditions of many cultures—Till Eulenspiegel in German folklore, Prometheus in Greek myth, Robin Goodfellow in English folklore (Puck in Shakespeare's *A Midsummer Night's Dream*), American outlaw figures like Billy the Kid and Jesse James, American literary characters like Rip Van Winkle and Huckleberry Finn—but tricksters are especially prominent in the tribal cultures of Africa and North America. The best-known African trickster hero is Kwaku Anansi, the spider. Among Native Americans, the best known trickster hero is crow or coyote.

Anansi Plays Dead (Ashanti)

The source of this folktale, collected in 1957, is the Ashanti peoples, who live in a region of West Africa that is now the Ivory Coast and Ghana.

*O*ne year there was a famine in the land. But Anansi and his wife Aso and his sons had a farm, and there was food enough for all of them. Still the thought of famine throughout the country made Anansi hungry. He began to plot how he could have the best part of the crops for himself. He devised a clever scheme.

One day he told his wife that he was not feeling well and that he was going to see a sorcerer. He went away and didn't return until night. Then he announced that he had received very bad news. The sorcerer had informed him, he said, that he was about to die. Also, Anansi said, the sorcerer had prescribed that he was to be buried at the far end of the farm, next to the yam patch. When they heard this news, Aso, Kweku Tsin, and Intikuma were very sad. But Anansi had more instructions. Aso was to place in his coffin a pestle and mortar, dishes, spoons, and cooking pots, so that Anansi could take care of himself in the Other World.

In a few days, Anansi lay on his sleeping mat as though he were sick, and in a short time he pretended to be dead. So Aso had him buried at the far end of the farm, next to the yam patch, and they put in his coffin all of the cooking pots and other things he had asked for.

But Anansi stayed in the grave only while the sun shone. As soon as it grew dark, he came out of the coffin and dug up some yams and cooked them. He ate until he was stuffed. Then he returned to his place in the coffin. Every night he came out to select the best part of the crops and eat them, and during the day he hid in his grave.

Aso and her sons began to observe that their best yams and corn and cassava were being stolen from the fields. So they went to Anansi's grave and held a special service there. They asked Anansi's soul to protect the farm from thieves.

That night Anansi again came out, and once more he took the best crops and ate them. When Aso and her sons found out that Anansi's soul was not protecting them, they devised a plan to catch the person who was stealing their food. They made a figure out of sticky gum. It looked like a man. They set it up in the yam patch.

That night Anansi crawled out of his coffin to eat. He saw the figure standing there in the moonlight.

"Why are you standing in my fields?" Anansi said.

The gum-man didn't answer.

"If you don't get out of my fields, I will give you a thrashing," Anansi said.

The gum-man was silent.

"If you don't go quickly, I will have to beat you," Anansi said.

There was no reply. The gum-man just stood there. Anansi lost his temper. He gave the gum-man a hard blow with his right hand. It stuck fast to the gum-man. Anansi couldn't take it away.

"Let go of my right hand," Anansi said. "You are making me angry!"

But the gum-man didn't let go.

"Perhaps you don't know my strength," Anansi said fiercely. "There is more power in my left hand than in my right. Do you want to try it?"

As there was no response from the gum-man, Anansi struck him with his left hand. Now both his hands were stuck.

"You miserable creature," Anansi said, "so you don't listen to me! Let go at once and get out of my fields or I will really give you something to remember! Have you ever heard of my right foot?"

There was no sound from the gum-man, so Anansi gave him a kick with his right foot. It, too, stuck.

"Oh, you like it, do you?" Anansi shouted. "Then try this one, too!"

He gave a tremendous kick with his left foot, and now he was stuck by both hands and both feet.

"Oh, are you the stubborn kind?" Anansi cried. "Have you ever heard of my head?"

And he butted the gum-man with his head, and that stuck as well.

"I'm giving you your last chance now," Anansi said sternly. "If you leave quietly, I won't complain to the chief. If you don't, I'll give you a squeeze you will remember!"

The gum-man was still silent. So Anansi took a deep breath and gave a mighty squeeze. Now he was completely stuck. He couldn't move this way or that. He couldn't move at all.

In the morning when Aso, Kweku Tsin, and Intikuma came out to the fields, they found Anansi stuck helplessly to the gum-man. They understood everything. They took him off the gum-man and led him toward the village to be judged by the chief. People came to the edge of the trail and saw Anansi all stuck up with gum. They laughed and jeered and sang songs about him. He was deeply shamed, and covered his face with his headcloth. And when Aso, Kweku Tsin, and Intikuma stopped at a spring to drink, Anansi broke away and fled. He ran into the nearest house, crawled into the rafters, and hid in the darkest corner he could find.

From that day until now, Anansi has not wanted to face people because of their scoffing and jeering, and that is why he is often found hiding in dark corners.

Questions for Study

1. What characterizes Anansi? What are his gifts, limitations, and values?

2. What leads to Anansi's defeat?

3. Does the tone of the narrative lead us to sympathize with Anansi?

4. What is the other people's attitude toward Anansi? How do they respond to his tricks?

Old Boss and John at the Praying Tree

Among Africans who were brought as slaves to the Americas, the trickster survived in two forms: as Brother Rabbit (Buh Rabbit or Br'er Rabbit) and as John the slave. Brother Rabbit contends with Brother Fox (another, less successful trickster) and the slow-witted Brother Bear. John is always trying to put one over on the slave-owner master. This story was collected during the 1950s among African Americans who had migrated from the South to Michigan.

*T*his also happened back in the old days too. It was one year on a plantation when crops were bad. There wasn't enough food for all the slave hands, no flour at all;

all they had to eat was fatback and cornbread. John and his buddy was the only slickers on the farm. They would have two kinds of meat in the house, all the lard they could use, plenty flour and plenty sugar, biscuits every morning for breakfast. (They was rogues.) The Boss kept a-missing meat, but they was too slick for him to catch 'em at it.

Every morning, he'd ask John, "How you getting along over there with your family?" John said, "Well, I'm doing all right, Old Marster. *(High-pitched, whiny)* I'm fair's a middling and spick as a ham, coffee in the kittle, bread on the fire, if that ain't living I hope I die."

The Old Boss checked on John. And he saw his hams and lard and biscuits all laid up in John's place. (In those days people branded their hams with their own name.) He said, "John, I can see why you're living so high. You got all my hams and things up there." "Oh, no," John told him, "those ain't none of your ham, Boss. God give me them ham. God is good, just like you, and God been looking out for me, because I pray every night."

Boss said, "I'm still going to kill you John, because I know that's my meat."

Old John was real slick. He asked his Marster, "Tonight meet me at the old 'simmon tree. I'm going to show you God is good to me. I'm going to have some of your same ham, some of your same lard, and some of your same flour."

So that night about eight o'clock (it was dark by then in the winter), John went for his partner. They get everything all set up in the tree before John goes for Old Boss. They go out to the tree. Old Boss brings along his double-barreled shotgun, and he tells John, "Now if you don't get my flour and stuff, just like you said you would, you will never leave this tree."

So John gets down on his knees and begins to pray. "Now, Lord, I never axed you for nothing that I didn't get. You know Old Marster here is about to kill me, thinking I'm stealing. Not a child of yours would steal, would he, Lord?" He says, "Now I'm going to pat on this tree three times. And I want you to rain down persimmons." John patted on the tree three times and his partner shook down all the persimmons all over Old Boss. Boss shakes himself and says, "John, Old Boss is so good to you, why don't you have God send my meat down?"

John said, "Don't get impatient; I'm going to talk to him a little while longer for you." So John prayed, "Now Lord, you know me and I know you. Throw me down one of Old Boss's hams with his same brand on it."

Just at that time the ham hit down on top of Old Boss's head. Old Boss grabbed the ham, and said, "John, I spec you better not pray no more." (Old Boss done got scared.) But John kept on praying and the flour fell. Old Boss told John, "Come on John, don't pray no more." "I just want to show you I'm a child of God," John tells him, and he prays again. "Send me down a sack of Old Boss's sugar, the same weight and the same name like on all his sacks."

"John, if you pray any more no telling what might happen to us," Boss said. "I'll give you a forty-acre farm and a team of mules if you just don't pray no more." John didn't pay no attention; he prayed some more. "Now God, I want you to do me a personal favor. That's to hop down out of the tree and horsewhip the hell out of Old Boss." So his buddy jumped out with a white sheet and laid it on Old Boss.

Boss said, "You see what you gone done, John; you got God down on me. From now on you can go free."

Questions for Study

1. What are the similarities and differences of this tale and "Anansi Plays Dead"?

2. What is John's relationship to Old Boss? How do Old Boss and John treat each other?

3. What qualities does John have that make him a successful trickster?

4. What risks does John take in order to play his tricks?

5. What does this tale suggest about the nature of slavery in the United States?

How Coyote Got His Cunning (Karock)

This tale was collected early in 1930 from among the Karock peoples, who live along the Klamath River in northern California.

Kareya was the god who in the very beginning created the world. First he made the fishes in the ocean, then he made the animals on the land, and last of all he made a man. He had, however, given all the animals the same amount of rank and power.

So he went to the man he had made and said, "Make as many bows and arrows as there are animals. I am going to call all the animals together, and you are to give the longest bow and arrow to the one that should have the most power, and the shortest to the one that should have the least.

So the man set to work to make the bows and arrows, and at the end of nine days he had made bows enough for all the animals created by Kareya. Then Kareya called all the animals together in a certain place and told them that the man would come to them on the morrow with the bows, and the one to whom he gave the longest would have the most power.

Each animal wanted to be the one to get the longest bow. Coyote schemed how he might outwit all the others. He determined to stay awake all night, while the others slept, and so go forth first in the morning to meet the man, and get the longest bow for himself. So when the animals went to sleep, Coyote lay down and pretended to sleep. But about midnight Coyote began to get sleepy. He got up and walked around, scratching his eyes to keep them open. As the time passed he grew more sleepy. He resorted to skipping and jumping to keep awake, but the noise awakened some of the other animals, so he had to stop.

About the time the morning star came up Coyote was so sleepy that he couldn't keep his eyes open any longer. So he took two little sticks and sharpened them at the ends. With these he propped open his eyes. Then he felt it was safe for him to sleep, since his eyes were open and could watch the morning star rising. He would get up before the star had completely risen, for then all the other animals would be getting up. But in a few minutes Coyote was fast asleep. The sharp sticks pierced right through his eyelids and instead of keeping them open they pinned them tightly closed. When the rest of the animals got up Coyote lay fast asleep.

The animals went to meet the man. Cougar received the longest bow; Bear received the next, and so on until the next to the last bow was given to Frog.

The man, however, still had the shortest bow left.

"What animal have I missed?" he cried out.

The animals began to look about and they soon spied Coyote, lying fast asleep. They all laughed heartily and danced around him. Then they led him to the man, for Coyote's eyes were pinned together by the sticks and he could not see. The man pulled out the sticks from Coyote's eyes and then gave him the shortest bow. All the animals laughed. This made the man pity Coyote, who was to be weakest of all animals, so he prayed to Kareya about Coyote. Kareya answered, and gave to Coyote more cunning than to all the other animals. And so that is how Coyote got his great amount of cunning.

Questions for Study

1. What details characterize Coyote? Does the tone of the narrative encourage us to sympathize with him?

2. The tale seems to establish an opposition between strength and weakness. What or who is "strong"? What or who is "weak"?

3. What does Coyote lose and gain?

LITERARY TALES

Literary tales are distinguishable from folktales by their artifice. In contrast to authors of literary tales, folktale tellers think of themselves less as authors and more as faithful repeaters of stories they have learned from others. They might change a few details here and there, but their concern is to be faithful to the tradition and render the tale accurately. Authors of literary tales try to create works of art. Even if their tale is traditional, they want to make it fresh and original. The artistic quality of literary tales is evident in their language (poetry or graceful prose), themes, symbols, figures of speech, development of setting and social context, and intricate plotting. The well plotted tale usually climaxes with an event that makes clear the connection between all the actions. Authors of literary tales are fond of climactic revelations that expose ironic relationships.

The tales included in this section come from two famous works whose stories are linked together by frame stories. The work opens with a story—the frame story—in which one or more people agree to tell stories. Next come the stories themselves. After all the stories are told, the work concludes with the ending of the frame story. An important feature of some frame collections is the social status and position of the story tellers and the interplay between the theme and the stories they tell. Sometimes, as in Chaucer, the frame story is as important as the stories and adds thematic depth to them.

The Thousand and One Nights

The origin of *The Thousand and One Nights* seems to be a Persian book of fairy tales, now lost. This work was translated into Arabic about A.D. 850. Over the years stories were added and subtracted until at the end of the eighteenth century a "standard" version was put together in Egypt by an unknown editor. The stories, many of which came from non-Islamic cultures, have been retold so as to reflect Islamic life during the Middle Ages. The frame story comes from India. The first translation in the West was by the Frenchman Antoine Gallard and appeared in twelve volumes between 1704 and 1717. Since that time, *The Thousand and One Nights* has been the best-known Arabic work in the West. The stories, like those of Aladdin and Sinbad the Sailor, are often very long, consisting of a string of episodes that have little relation to one another. Included here are the opening dedication, the beginning of the frame story, one relatively short tale, the conclusion of the frame story, and the closing benediction.

"The Young Woman and Her Five Lovers" is one of the many short tales that are sandwiched between the longer tales in *The Thousand and One Nights.* Many of these short tales are comic and, like this one, manifest an earthy sense of humor.

The Thousand and One Nights concludes with a return to the frame story. Shahrazad has kept Shahriyar enthralled by her tales for nearly three years. But now, upon completion of her final story, she makes an appeal to Shahriyar.

In the Name of Allah the Compassionate the Merciful

Praise be to Allah Lord of the Creation, and blessing and peace eternal upon the Prince of Apostles, our master Mohammed.

The annals of former generations are lessons to the living: a man may look back upon the fortunes of his predecessors and be admonished; and contemplate the history of past ages and be purged of folly. Glory to Him who has made the heritage of antiquity a guide for our own time!

From this heritage are derived the Tales of the Thousand and One Nights, together with all that is in them of fable and adventure.

The Tale of King Shahriyar and His Brother Shahzaman

*I*t is related—but Allah alone is wise and all-knowing—that long ago there lived in the lands of India and China a Sassanid king who commanded great armies and had numerous courtiers, followers, and servants. He left two sons, both renowned for their horsemanship—especially the elder, who inherited the kingdom of his father and governed it with such justice that all his subjects loved him. He was called King Shahriyar. His younger brother was named Shahzaman and was king of Samarkand.

The two brothers continued to reign happily in their kingdoms, and after a period of twenty years King Shahriyar felt a great longing to see his younger brother. He ordered his Vizier to go to Samarkand and invite him to his court.

The Vizier set out promptly on his mission and journeyed many days and nights through deserts and wildernesses until he arrived at Shahzaman's city and was admitted to his presence. He gave him King Shahriyar's greetings and informed him of his master's wish to see him. King Shahzaman was overjoyed at the prospect of visiting his brother. He made ready to leave his kingdom, and sent out his tents, camels, mules, servants, and retainers. Then he appointed his Vizier as his deputy and set out for his brother's dominions.

It so happened, however, that at midnight he remembered a present which he had left at his palace. He returned for it unheralded, and entering his private chambers found his wife lying on a couch in the arms of a black slave. At this the world darkened before his eyes; and he thought: 'If this can happen when I am scarcely out of my city, how will this foul woman act when I am far away?' He then drew his sword and killed them both as they lay on the couch. Returning at once to his retainers, he gave orders for departure, and journeyed until he reached his brother's capital.

Shahriyar rejoiced at the news of his approach and went out to meet him. He embraced his guest and welcomed him to his festive city. But while Shahriyar sat entertaining his brother, Shahzaman, haunted by the thought of his wife's perfidy, was pale and sick at heart. Shahriyar perceived his distress, but said nothing, thinking that he might be troubled over the affairs of his kingdom. After a few days, however, Shahriyar said to him: "I see that you are pale and care-worn." Shahzaman answered: "I am afflicted with a painful sore." But he kept from him the story of his wife's treachery. Then Shahriyar invited his brother to go hunting with him, hoping that the sport might dispel his gloom. Shahzaman declined, and Shahriyar went alone to the hunt.

While Shahzaman sat at one of the windows overlooking the King's garden, he saw a door open in the palace, through which came twenty slave-girls and twenty Negroes. In their midst was his brother's queen, a woman of surpassing beauty. They made their way to the fountain, where they all undressed and sat on the grass. The King's wife then called out: "Come Mass'ood!" and there promptly came to her a black slave, who mounted her after smothering her with embraces and kisses. So also did the Negroes with the slave-girls, revelling together till the approach of night.

When Shahzaman beheld this spectacle, he thought: 'By Allah, my misfortune is lighter than this!' He was dejected no longer, and ate and drank after his long abstinence.

Shahriyar, when he returned from the hunt was surprised to see his brother restored to good spirits and full health. "How is it, my brother," asked Shahriyar, "that when I last saw you, you were pale and melancholy, and now you look well and contented?"

"As for my melancholy," replied Shahzaman, "I shall now tell you the reason: but I cannot reveal the cause of my altered condition. Know then, that after I had received your invitation, I made preparations for the journey and left my city; but having forgotten the pearl which I was to present to you, I returned for it to the palace. There, on my couch, I found my wife lying in the embrace of a black slave. I killed them both and came to your kingdom, my mind oppressed with bitter thoughts."

When he heard these words, Shahriyar urged him to tell the rest of his story. And so Shahzaman related to him all that he had seen in the King's garden that day.

Alarmed, but half in doubt, Shahriyar exclaimed: "I will not believe that till I have seen it with my own eyes."

"Then let it be given out," suggested his brother, "that you intend to go to the hunt again. Conceal yourself here with me, and you shall witness what I have seen."

Upon this Shahriyar announced his intention to set forth on another expedition. The troops went out of the city with the tents, and King Shahriyar followed them. And after he had stayed a while in the camp, he gave orders to his slaves that no one was to be admitted to the King's tent. He then disguised himself and returned unnoticed to the palace, where his brother was waiting for him. They both sat at one of the windows overlooking the garden; and when they had been there a short time, the Queen and her women appeared with the black slaves, and behaved as Shahzaman had described.

Half demented at the sight, Shahriyar said to his brother: "Let us renounce our royal state and roam the world until we find out if any other king has ever met with such disgrace."

Shahzaman agreed to his proposal, and they went out in secret and travelled for many days and nights until they came to a meadow by the seashore. They refreshed themselves at a spring of water and sat down to rest under a tree.

Suddenly the waves of the sea surged and foamed before them, and there arose from the deep a black pillar which almost touched the sky. Struck with terror at the sight, they climbed into the tree. When they reached the top they were able to see that it was a jinnee of gigantic stature, carrying a chest on his head. The jinnee waded to the shore and walked towards the tree which sheltered the two brothers. Then, having seated himself beneath it, he opened the chest, and took from it a box, which he also opened; and there rose from the box a beautiful young girl, radiant as the sun.

"Chaste and honourable lady, whom I carried away on your wedding-night," said the jinnee, "I would sleep a little." Then, laying his head upon her knees, the jinnee fell fast asleep.

Suddenly the girl lifted her head and saw the two Kings high in the tree. She laid the jinnee's head on the ground, and made signs to them which seemed to say: 'Come down, and have no fear of the jinnee.'

The two Kings pleaded with her to let them hide in safety, but the girl replied: "If you do not come down, I will wake the jinnee, and he shall put you to a cruel death."

They climbed down in fear, and at once she said: "Come, pierce me with your rapiers."

Shahriyar and Shahzaman faltered. But the girl repeated angrily: "If you do not do my bidding, I will wake the jinnee."

Afraid of the consequences, they proceeded to mount her in turn.

When they had remained with her as long as she desired, she took from her pocket a large purse, from which she drew ninety-eight rings threaded on a string. "The owners of these," she laughed triumphantly, "have all enjoyed me under the very horn of this foolish jinnee. Therefore, give me your rings also."

The two men gave her their rings.

"This jinnee," she added, "carried me away on my bridal night and imprisoned me in a box which he placed inside a chest. He fastened the chest with seven locks and deposited it at the bottom of the roaring sea. But he little knew how cunning we women are."

The two Kings marvelled at her story, and said to each other: "If such a thing could happen to a mighty jinnee, then our own misfortune is light indeed." And they returned at once to the city.

As soon as they entered the palace, King Shahriyar put his wife to death, together with her women and the black slaves. Thenceforth he made it his custom to take a virgin in marriage to his bed each night, and kill her the next morning. This he continued to do for three years, until a clamor rose among the people, some of whom fled the country with their daughters.

At last came the day when the Vizier roamed the city in search of a virgin for the King, and could find none. Dreading the King's anger, he returned to his house with a heavy heart.

Now the Vizier had two daughters. The elder was called Shahrazad, and the younger Dunyazad. Shahrazad possessed many accomplishments and was versed in the wisdom of the poets and the legends of ancient kings.

That day Shahrazad noticed her father's anxiety and asked him what it was that troubled him. When the Vizier told her of his predicament, she said: "Give me in marriage to this King: either I shall die and be a ransom for the daughters of Moslems, or live and be the cause of their deliverance."

He earnestly pleaded with her against such a hazard; but Shahrazad was resolved, and would not yield to her father's entreaties.

"Beware," said the Vizier, "of the fate of the donkey in the fable:

The Fable of the Donkey, the Ox, and the Farmer

"There was once a wealthy farmer who owned many herds of cattle. He knew the languages of beasts and birds. In one of his stalls he kept an ox and a donkey. At the end of each day, the ox came to the place where the donkey was tied and found it well swept and watered; the manger filled with sifted straw and well-winnowed barley; and the donkey lying at his ease (for his master seldom rode him).

"It chanced that one day the farmer heard the ox say to the donkey: 'How fortunate you are! I am worn out with toil, while you rest here in comfort. You eat well-sifted barley and lack nothing. It is only occasionally that your master rides you. As for me, my life is perpetual drudgery at the plough and the millstone.'

"The donkey answered: 'When you go out into the field and the yoke is placed upon your neck, pretend to be ill and drop down on your belly. Do not rise even if they beat you; or if you do rise, lie down again. When they take you back and place the fodder before you, do not eat it. Abstain for a day or two; and thus shall you find a rest from toil.'

"Remember that the farmer was there and heard what passed between them.

"And so when the ploughman came to the ox with his fodder, he ate scarcely any of it. And when the ploughman came the following morning to take him out into the field, the ox appeared to be far from well. Then the farmer said to the ploughman: 'Take the donkey and use him at the plough all day!'

"The man returned, took the donkey in place of the ox, and drove him at the plough all day.

"When the day's work was done and the donkey returned to the stall, the ox thanked him for his good counsel. But the donkey made no reply and bitterly repented his rashness.

"Next day the ploughman came and took the donkey again and made him labor till evening; so that when the donkey returned with his neck flayed by the yoke, and in a pitiful state of exhaustion, the ox again expressed his gratitude to him, and praised his sagacity.

"'If only I had kept my wisdom to myself!' thought the donkey. Then, turning to the ox, he said: 'I have just heard my master say to his servant: "If the ox does not recover soon, take him to the slaughterhouse and dispose of him." My anxiety for your safety prompts me, my friend, to let you know of this before it is too late. And peace be with you!'

"When he heard the donkey's words, the ox thanked him and said: 'Tomorrow I will go to work freely and willingly.' He ate all his fodder and even licked the manger clean.

"Early next morning the farmer, accompanied by his wife, went to visit the ox in his stall. The ploughman came and led out the ox, who, at the sight of his master, broke wind and frisked about in all directions. And the farmer laughed so, he fell over on his back."

When she heard her father's story, Shahrazad said: "Nothing will shake my faith in the mission I am destined to fulfil."

So the Vizier arrayed his daughter in bridal garments and decked her with jewels and made ready to announce Shahrazad's wedding to the King.

Before saying farewell to her sister, Shahrazad gave her these instructions: "When I am received by the King, I shall send for you. Then, when the King has finished his act with me, you must say: 'Tell me, my sister, some tale of marvel to beguile the night.' Then I will tell you a tale which, if Allah wills, shall be the means of our deliverance."

The Vizier went with his daughter to the King. And when the King had taken the maiden Shahrazad to his chamber and had lain with her, she wept and said: "I have a young sister to whom I wish to bid farewell."

The King sent for Dunyazad. When she arrived, she threw her arms round her sister's neck, and seated herself by her side.

Then Dunyazad said to Shahrazad: "Tell us, my sister, a tale of marvel, so that the night may pass pleasantly."

"Gladly," she answered, "if the King permits."

And the King, who was troubled with sleeplessness, eagerly listened to the tale of Shahrazad.

The Young Woman and Her Five Lovers

Once upon a time, in a certain city, there lived a rich and beautiful young woman whose husband was a great traveller. It so chanced that he once journeyed to a distant land and was absent so long that at last his wife succumbed to the temptations of the flesh and fell in love with a handsome youth who himself loved her tenderly.

One day the youth was engaged in a savage brawl and a complaint was lodged against him with the Governor of that city, who had him thrown into prison. The young woman was deeply grieved at the news of her lover's arrest. Without losing a moment she put on her finest robes and hurried to the Governor's house.

She greeted the Governor and handed him a petition which read: "My noble master, the young man So-and-so, whom you have arrested and thrown into prison, is my brother and my sole support. He is the victim of a villainous plot, for those who testified against him were false witnesses. I hereby beseech you to consider the justice of my cause and to order his release."

When he had read the petition the Governor lifted his eyes to the young woman and was so smitten with her seductive looks that he fell in love with her at sight. "Wait in the harem of my house," he said, "whilst I write out an order for your brother's release. I will join you there presently."

The young woman, who lacked neither cunning nor knowledge of the ways of men, at once perceived the Governor's intent and answered: "You will be welcome, sir, at my own house, but custom forbids me to enter a stranger's dwelling."

"And where is your house?" asked the old man, transported with joy.

"At such-and-such a place," she replied. "I will expect you there this evening."

Taking leave of the enamored Governor, the young woman went to the Cadi's° house. "Consider, sir, I pray you, the wrong that has been done me," she began, "and Allah will reward you."

"Who has dared to wrong you?" asked the Cadi indignantly.

"Sir," she answered, "my brother, the sole pillar of my house, has on false witness been imprisoned by the Governor. I beg you to intercede on his behalf."

But as soon as the Cadi set eyes on the young woman his heart began to throb with a violent longing for her, and he said: "I shall instantly request the Governor to set your brother free. Meanwhile, wait for me in my harem. I will join you there presently."

"My pious master," she replied, "it is more fitting that I should wait for you in my own house, where there are neither slaves nor maidservants to intrude upon our privacy."

"And where is your house?" asked the Cadi eagerly.

"In such-and-such a place," she answered. "I will expect you there this evening."

Cadi. A minor magistrate.

The young woman then hastened to the Vizier's° house. She handed him her petition and implored him to release the youth from prison. Captivated by her beauty, the Vizier promised to do as she desired and pressed her to accompany him to his sleeping chamber. But the young woman put off his advances with winning grace, saying: "I shall be delighted to receive you at my own house this evening."

"And where is your house?" asked the Vizier.

"In such-and-such a place," she replied.

Then she made her way to the royal palace and sought an audience with the King. She kissed the ground before him and begged him on her knees to order the youth's release. But as soon as his eyes fell upon the young woman, the King was seized with a passionate desire to lie with her.

"I will at once send for the Governor and order him to free your brother," he said. "Meanwhile, wait for me in my private chamber."

"Your majesty," she answered, "a helpless woman cannot but obey the command of a mighty king. If this be indeed your majesty's wish, I shall regard it as a mark of high favor; but if the King will graciously consent to vouchsafe me a visit at my own house this evening, he will do me an even greater honour."

"It shall be as you wish," replied the King.

After directing him to her house, the young woman left the royal presence, and went to look for a carpenter's shop. When she had found one she said to the carpenter: "Make me a large cupboard with four compartments, one above the other. To each compartment let there be a separate door fitted with a stout lock, and have it delivered at my house, at such-and-such a place, early this evening. What will be your charge?"

"Four dinars," answered the carpenter. "But if you will consent, sweet lady, to step into the backroom of my shop, I will ask no payment at all."

"In that case," said the young woman, "you will be welcome at my own house this evening . . . But I have just remembered that I require five compartments in that cupboard and not four."

"I hear and obey," replied the carpenter, beaming with joy.

He set to work at once whilst the young woman waited in his shop. In a few hours a large cupboard with five compartments was completed, and his fair customer hired a porter and had it carried to her house.

She next took four strangely fashioned garments to a dyer, and after having them each dyed a different color, returned home and made ready for the evening. She prepared meat and drink, arranged fruit and flowers, and burned incense in the braziers. At sunset she arrayed herself in splendid robes, putting on her richest jewels and sweetest perfumes, and sat waiting for her distinguished guests.

The first to arrive was the Cadi. She bowed low before him and, taking him by the hand, led him to a couch. No sooner had they seated themselves than the Cadi began to dally with her, and it was not long before he was roused to a frenzy of passion. But when he was about to throw himself upon her, the young woman said: "First take off your clothes and turban. You will be more comfortable in this light robe and bonnet."

Burning with desire, the Cadi promptly cast aside his clothes, and had scarcely put on the curious yellow robe and bonnet which his hostess handed him, when a knocking was heard at the door.

Vizier. A minister of state.

"Who may that be?" asked the Cadi, wincing with impatience.

"By Allah, that must be my husband!" she exclaimed in great agitation.

"What is to be done? Where shall I go?" cried the Cadi.

"Have no fear," she replied. "I will hide you in this cupboard."

The young woman took the Cadi by the hand, and, after he had crouched low she pushed him into the lowest compartment of the cupboard, and locked the door upon him. Then she went to admit her next visitor.

This proved to be the Governor. The young woman kissed the ground before him and said: "Pray regard this dwelling as your own. The night is still young; take off your robes and put on this nightshirt."

Delighted at the suggestion, the Governor quickly stripped himself of his heavy robes and slipped on an ill-cut garment of red cloth, while his hostess swathed his head in an old rag of many colors.

"First," said the young woman, as the Governor made ready to begin the amorous sport, "you must write me an order for my brother's release."

The Governor instantly wrote the order, and, setting his seal upon it, handed it to her. Then they dallied with each other, but as he was on the point of mounting her, there came a knocking at the door.

"That must be my husband!" exclaimed the young woman in terror.

"What is to be done?" cried the Governor, greatly perturbed.

"Climb up into that cupboard and stay there until I get rid of him," said the young woman, as she bundled him into the second compartment and locked the door. Then she went to admit her third visitor.

This was the Vizier. She kissed the ground before him and gave him a courteous welcome. "Sir," she said, "you do me great honor by stepping into this humble house." Then she begged him to take off his clothes and turban, saying: "Pray put on this light shirt and bonnet. They are better fitted for a night of revelry and merrymaking."

When the Vizier had put off his ministerial vestments, his hostess helped him into a blue shirt and a long, red nightcap. But just as he was about to enjoy her, the King arrived. And the young woman made the worthy Vizier climb up into the third compartment of the cupboard, and locked the door upon him.

When the King entered the young woman kissed the ground before him, saying: "Your slave lacks words to thank your majesty for this honor."

Having invited him to sit down, she soon prevailed upon him to take off his costly robes and to put on a tattered old shirt scarcely worth ten dirhams. When the King was on the point of achieving his desire, however, a violent knocking at the door sent him scampering into the fourth compartment of the cupboard. Then she went to let the carpenter in.

"Pray, what kind of cupboard is this you have made me?" snapped the young woman at the carpenter as he stepped into the reception hall. "Why, the top compartment is so small that it is quite useless."

"It is a very large compartment," protested the fat carpenter. "It could hold me and three others of my size."

"Try then," she said. And when the carpenter had climbed up into the fifth compartment of the cupboard, the door was locked upon him.

The young woman took the Governor's order to the superintendent of the prison, and rejoiced to see her lover free at last. She told him all that had happened, adding: "We must now leave this city and go live in a distant land." Then they hurried back to the house, packed up all their valuables, and set out for another kingdom.

Not daring to utter a sound, the five men stayed in the cupboard without food or drink for three days; and for three days they resolutely held their water. The carpenter, however, was the first to give in; and his piss fell on the King below him. Then the King pissed on the Vizier; and the Vizier pissed on the Governor; and the Governor pissed on the Cadi.

"Filth! Filth!" shouted the Cadi. "Has not our punishment been cruel enough? Must we be made to suffer in this vile fashion also?"

The Governor and the Vizier were the next to speak, and the three recognized each other's voice.

"Allah's curse be upon this woman!" exclaimed the Vizier. "She has locked all the senior officers of the kingdom in this cupboard. Thank Allah the King has been spared!"

"Hold your tongue!" muttered the King. "I am here too. And if I am not mistaken, I must have been the first to fall into the snares of this impudent whore."

"And to think that I made her this cupboard with my own hands!" groaned the carpenter from the top compartment.

It was not long, however, before the neighbors, seeing no one enter or leave the house, began to suspect foul play. They all crowded around the door debating what action they should take.

"Let us break down the door," urged one, "and find out if there is anyone at home."

"We must investigate the matter," said another, "lest the Governor or the King himself should learn of it and have us thrown into prison for failing to do our duty."

The neighbors forced open the door, and on entering the hall what should they find but a large wooden cupboard echoing with the groans of famished men!

"There must be a jinnee in this cupboard!" exclaimed one of the neighbors.

"Let us set fire to it!" cried another.

"Good people," howled the Cadi from within, "in Allah's name do not burn us alive!"

But they gave no heed to his cries and said to each other:
"The jinn have been known to assume human shape and speak with men's voices."

Seeing that they were still in doubt, the Cadi intoned aloud some verses from the Koran and entreated them to draw closer. They came near, and in a few words he related to them all that had happened. The neighbors promptly called in a carpenter, who forced the locks, and delivered from the cupboard five men rigged out in fancy costume.

The luckless lovers burst out laughing when they saw each other and, after putting on their clothes, departed, each to his own house.

Conclusion and Benediction

Now during this time Shahrazad had borne King Shahriyar three sons. On the thousand and first night, when she had ended the tale of Ma'aruf, she rose and kissed the ground before him, saying: "Great King, for a thousand and one nights I have been recounting to you the fables of past ages and the legends of ancient kings. May I make so bold as to crave a favor of your majesty?"

The King replied: "Ask, and it shall be granted."

Shahrazad called out to the nurses, saying: "Bring me my children."

Three little boys were instantly brought in; one walking, one crawling on all fours, and the third sucking at the breast of his nurse. Shahrazad ranged the little ones before the King and, again kissing the ground before him, said: "Behold these three whom Allah has granted to us. For their sake I implore you to spare my life. For if you destroy the mother of these infants, they will find none among women to love them as I would."

The King embraced his three sons, and his eyes filled with tears as he answered: "I swear by Allah, Shahrazad, that you were already pardoned before the coming of these children. I loved you because I found you chaste and tender, wise and eloquent. May Allah bless you, and bless your father and mother, your ancestors, and all your descendants. O, Shahrazad, this thousand and first night is brighter for us than the day!"

Shahrazad rejoiced; she kissed the King's hand and called down blessings upon him.

The people were overjoyed at the news of Shahrazad's salvation. Next morning King Shahriyar summoned to his presence the great ones of the city, the chamberlains, the nabobs, and the officers of his army. When they had all assembled in the great hall of the palace, Shahriyar proclaimed his decision to spare the life of his bride. Then he called his Vizier, Shahrazad's father, and invested him with a magnificent robe of honor, saying: "Allah has raised up your daughter to be the salvation of my people. I have found her chaste, wise, and eloquent, and repentance has come to me through her."

Then the King bestowed robes of honor upon the courtiers and the captains of his army, and gave orders for the decoration of his capital.

The city was decked and lighted; and in the streets and market-squares drums rattled, trumpets blared and clarions sounded. The King lavished alms on the poor and the needy, and all the people feasted at the King's expense for thirty days and thirty nights.

Shahriyar reigned over his subjects in all justice, and lived happily with Shahrazad until they were visited by the Destroyer of all earthly pleasures, the Annihilator of men.

> Now praise and glory be to Him who sits throned in eternity above the shifts of time; who, changing all things, remains Himself unchanged; who alone is the Paragon of all perfection. And blessing and peace be upon His chosen Messenger, the Prince of Apostles, our master Mohammed, to whom we pray for an auspicious end.

Questions for Study

1. What characterizes Shahriyar? Does the narrator present him sympathetically?

2. What characterizes Shahrazad? What are her gifts? What seem to be her goals? What is admirable about her?

3. What is the Vizier trying to say to Shahrazad by telling her "The Fable of the Donkey, the Ox, and the Farmer"? What are the possible morals of the fable?

4. How is "The Young Woman and Her Five Lovers" relevant to Shahrazad's circumstances? Why might she tell this story to Shahriyar?

5. What characterizes the young woman in this tale? What qualities enable her to trick her lovers? What does she achieve?

6. What does Shahrazad achieve? Is the conclusion of her story a happy ending?

GEOFFREY CHAUCER

The Nun's Priest's Tale (The Canterbury Tales)

Geoffrey Chaucer (c. 1340-1400) was born and reared in London, England, and held numerous important positions in the service of the English kings and nobility. He was also one of the great English poets. The story reprinted here, "The Nun's Priest's Tale," is from his best-known work, *The Canterbury Tales.* He designed *The Canterbury Tales* about 1387, and it was left unfinished at his death; only twenty-four tales survive. Chaucer brought to bear on *The Canterbury Tales* enormous knowledge of European literature, philosophy, theology, and science. Most of the tales in the collection are retellings of tales from many different sources. The frame story, contained in the Prologue, is Chaucer's invention and describes twenty-nine pilgrims assembled at the Tabard Inn in Southwark, England. They are getting ready to make their pilgrimage to the shrine of St. Thomas Becket at Canterbury. The innkeeper proposes that each of the pilgrims tell four stories, two on the way to Canterbury and two on the way back. Chaucer vividly describes each of the pilgrims and thereby provides a realistic and detailed description of English life in the Middle Ages. Many of the stories reflect the characters who tell them, as well as the tellers' personalities. The teller of the story reprinted here is the nun's priest, who accompanies one of the other pilgrims, the aristocratic nun. The innkeeper (the "host") describes the priest as a big, muscular fellow with strong appetites.

Chaucer wrote in Middle English, a dialect of English current during the transition period between Old English, the language of

Beowulf, and modern English, the language of Shakespeare. Old English is like a foreign language to us, but we can read Middle English if we know something about its pronunciation and its archaic diction. For ease of reading, "The Nun's Priest's Tale," as reprinted here, is translated into modern English. Chaucer probably adapted this story from one of the episodes in the medieval French collection of beast fables called *Reynard the Fox.* The translator, Theodore Morrison, retains the verse form of Chaucer's original: rhymed couplets with iambic pentameter lines. That is, every two lines of the poem have the same end rhyme, and each line contains five iambs. An iamb is a unit of sound that has an unaccented vowel followed by an accented vowel (as in the word *bĕgín).* Lines twelve and thirteen of the prologue to the tale illustrate Chaucer's verse form:

> Aňd thís iš whát hě tŏld uš, ĕvĕry one, ⟵
>
> Thĭs précioŭs príest, thĭs goódlў mán, Sir John. ⟵

end rhyme

Because a strict adherence to any metrical pattern makes the language seem mechanical and stilted, the translator, like Chaucer himself, frequently departs from the iambic pattern. One of the great pleasures of *The Canterbury Tales* is its lively and fluent language.

Prologue to the Nun's Priest's Tale

> Then spoke our Host, with a rude voice and bold,
> And said to the Nun's Priest, "Come over here,
> You priest, come hither, you Sir John, draw near!
> Tell us a thing to make our spirits glad.
> 5 Be cheerful, though the jade you ride is bad.
> What if your horse is miserable and lean?
> If he will carry you, don't care a bean!
> Keep up a joyful heart, and look alive."
> "Yes, Host," he answered, "as I hope to thrive,
> 10 If I weren't merry, I know I'd be reproached."
> And with no more ado his tale he broached,
> And this is what he told us, every one,
> This precious priest, this goodly man, Sir John.

The Nun's Priest's Tale

> Once a poor widow, aging year by year,
> 15 Lived in a tiny cottage that stood near
> A clump of shade trees rising in a dale.

This widow, of whom I tell you in my tale,
Since the last day that she had been a wife
Had led a very patient, simple life.
20   She had but few possessions to content her.
By thrift and husbandry of what God sent her
She and two daughters found the means to dine.
She had no more than three well-fattened swine,
As many cows, and one sheep, Moll by name.
25   Her bower and hall were black from the hearth-flame
Where she had eaten many a slender meal.
No dainty morsel did her palate feel
And no sharp sauce was needed with her pottage.
Her table was in keeping with her cottage.
30   Excess had never given her disquiet.
Her only doctor was a moderate diet,
And exercise, and a heart that was contented.
If she did not dance, at least no gout prevented;
No apoplexy had destroyed her head.
35   She never drank wine, whether white or red.
She served brown bread and milk, loaves white or black,
Singed bacon, all this with no sense of lack,
And now and then an egg or two. In short,
She was a dairy woman of a sort.
40   She had a yard, on the inside fenced about
With hedges, and an empty ditch without,
In which she kept a cock, called Chanticleer.
In all the realm of crowing he had no peer.
His voice was merrier than the merry sound
45   Of the church organ grumbling out its ground
Upon a saint's day. Stouter was this cock
In crowing than the loudest abbey clock.
Of astronomy instinctively aware,
He kept the sun's hours with celestial care,
50   For when through each fifteen degrees it moved,
He crowed so that it couldn't be improved.
His comb, like a crenelated castle wall,
Red as fine coral, stood up proud and tall.
His bill was black; like polished jet it glowed,
55   And he was azure-legged and azure-toed.
As lilies were his nails, they were so white;
Like burnished gold his hue, it shone so bright.
This cock had in his princely sway and measure
Seven hens to satisfy his every pleasure,
60   Who were his sisters and his sweethearts true,
Each wonderfully like him in her hue,

Of whom the fairest-feathered throat to see
Was fair Dame Partlet. Courteous was she,
Discreet, and always acted debonairly.
65 She was sociable, and bore herself so fairly,
Since the very time that she was seven nights old,
The heart of Chanticleer was in her hold
As if she had him locked up, every limb.
He loved her so that all was well with him.
70 It was a joy, when up the sun would spring,
To hear them both together sweetly sing,
"My love has gone to the country, far away!"
For as I understand it, in that day
The animals and birds could sing and speak.
75   Now as this cock, one morning at daybreak,
With each of the seven hens that he called spouse,
Sat on his perch inside the widow's house,
And next him fair Dame Partlet, in his throat
This Chanticleer produced a hideous note
80 And groaned like a man who is having a bad dream;
And Partlet, when she heard her husband scream,
Was all aghast, and said, "Soul of my passion,
What ails you that you groan in such a fashion?
You are always a sound sleeper. Fie, for shame!"
85   And Chanticleer awoke and answered, "Dame,
Take no offense, I beg you, on this score.
I dreamt, by God, I was in a plight so sore
Just now, my heart still quivers from the fright.
Now God see that my dream turns out all right
90 And keep my flesh and body from foul seizure!
I dreamed I was strutting in our yard at leisure
When there I saw, among the weeds and vines,
A beast, he was like a hound, and had designs
Upon my person, and would have killed me dead.
95 His coat was not quite yellow, not quite red,
And both his ears and tail were tipped with black
Unlike the fur along his sides and back.
He had a small snout and a fiery eye.
His look for fear still makes me almost die.
100 This is what made me groan, I have no doubt."
   "For shame! Fie on you, faint heart!" she burst out.
"Alas," she said, "by the great God above,
Now you have lost my heart and all my love!
I cannot love a coward, as I'm blest!
105 Whatever any woman may protest,
We all want, could it be so, for our part,

Husbands who are wise and stout of heart,
No blabber, and no niggard, and no fool,
Nor afraid of every weapon or sharp tool,
110   No braggart either, by the God above!
How dare you say, for shame, to your true love
That there is anything you ever feared?
Have you no man's heart, when you have a beard?
Alas, and can a nightmare set you screaming?
115   God knows there's only vanity in dreaming!
Dreams are produced by such unseemly capers
As overeating; they come from stomach vapors
When a man's humors° aren't behaving right
From some excess. This dream you had tonight,
120   It comes straight from the superfluity
Of your red choler, certain as can be,
That causes people terror in their dreams
Of darts and arrows, and fire in red streams,
And of red beasts, for fear that they will bite,
125   Of little dogs, or of being in a fight;
As in the humor of melancholy lies
The reason why so many a sleeper cries
For fear of a black bull or a black bear
Or that black devils have him by the hair.
130   Through other humors also I could go
That visit many a sleeping man with woe,
But I will finish as quickly as I can.
    "Cato,° that has been thought so wise a man,
Didn't he tell us, 'Put no stock in dreams'?
135   Now, sir," she said, "when we fly down from our beams,
For God's sake, go and take a laxative!
On my salvation, as I hope to live,
I give you good advice, and no mere folly:
Purge both your choler and your melancholy!
140   You mustn't wait or let yourself bog down,
And since there is no druggist in this town
I shall myself prescribe for what disturbs
Your humors, and instruct you in the herbs
That will be good for you. For I shall find
145   Here in our yard herbs of the proper kind
For purging you both under and above.
Don't let this slip your mind, for God's own love!

---

[118]*humors.* The four fluids that people in the Middle Ages believed governed the body and the emotions. An excess of one or more of the humors, like red choler (l. 121) or bile, would cause mental imbalance.
[133]*Cato.* An author of a book of maxims.

Yours is a very choleric complexion.
When the sun is in the ascendant, my direction
150 Is to beware those humors that are hot.
Avoid excess of them; if you should not,
I'll bet a penny, as a true believer,
You'll die of ague, or a tertian° fever.
A day or so, if you do as I am urging,
155 You shall have worm-digestives, before purging
With fumitory° or with hellebore
Or other herbs that grow here by the score;
With caper-spurge, or with the goat-tree berry
Or the ground-ivy, found in our yard so merry.
160 Peck 'em up just as they grow, and eat 'em in!
Be cheerful, husband, by your father's kin!
Don't worry about a dream. I say no more."
     "Madame," he answered, "thanks for all your lore.
But still, to speak of Cato, though his name
165 For wisdom has enjoyed so great a fame,
And though he counseled us there was no need
To be afraid of dreams, by God, men read
Of many a man of more authority
Than this Don Cato could pretend to be
170 Who in old books declare the opposite,
And by experience they have settled it,
That dreams are omens and prefigurations
Both of good fortune and of tribulations
That life and its vicissitudes present.
175 This question leaves no room for argument.
The very upshot makes it plain, indeed.
     "One of the greatest authors that men read
Informs us that two fellow travelers went,
Once on a time, and with the best intent,
180 Upon a pilgrimage, and it fell out
They reached a town where there was such a rout
Of people, and so little lodging space,
They could not find even the smallest place
Where they could both put up. So, for that night,
185 These pilgrims had to do as best they might,
And since they must, they parted company.
Each of them went off to his hostelry
And took his lodging as his luck might fall.

---

[153]*tertian*. Daily.
[156]*fumitory*. An herb, along with hellebore (l. 156), caper-spurge (l. 158), goat-tree berry (l. 158), and ground-ivy
(l. 159), used as laxatives ("purges").

Among plow oxen in a farmyard stall
190   One of them found a place, though it was rough.
His friend and fellow was lodged well enough
As his luck would have it, or his destiny
That governs all us creatures equally.
And so it happened, long before the day,
195   He had a dream as in his bed he lay.
He dreamed that his parted friend began to call
And said, 'Alas, for in an ox's stall
This night I shall be murdered where I lie.
Come to my aid, dear brother, or I die.
200   Come to me quickly, come in haste!' he said.
He started from his sleep, this man, for dread,
But when he had wakened, he rolled back once more
And on this dream of his he set no store.
As a vain thing he dismissed it, unconcerned.
205   Twice as he slept that night the dream returned,
And still another and third time his friend
Came in a dream and said, 'I have met my end!
Look on my wounds! They are bloody, deep, and wide.
Now rise up early in the morningtide
210   And at the west gate of the town,' said he,
'A wagon with a load of dung you'll see.
Have it arrested boldly. Do as bidden,
For underneath you'll find my body hidden.
My money caused my murder, truth to tell,'
215   And told him each detail of how he fell,
With piteous face, and with a bloodless hue.
And do not doubt it, he found the dream was true,
For on the morrow, as soon as it was day,
To the place where his friend had lodged he made his way,
220   And no sooner did he reach this ox's stall
Than for his fellow he began to call.
    "Promptly the stableman replied, and said,
'Your friend is gone, sir. He got out of bed
And left the town as soon as day began.'
225   "At last suspicion overtook this man.
Remembering his dreams, he would not wait,
But quickly went and found at the west gate,
Being driven to manure a farmer's land
As it might seem, a dung cart close at hand
230   That answered the description every way,
As you yourself have heard the dead man say.
And he began to shout courageously
For law and vengeance on this felony.

'My friend was killed this very night! He lies
235   Flat in this load of dung, with staring eyes.
I call on those who should keep rule and head,
The magistrates and governors here,' he said.
'Alas! Here lies my fellow, done to death!'
    "Why on this tale should I waste further breath?
240   The people sprang and flung the cart to ground
And in the middle of the dung they found
The dead man, while his murder was still new.
    "O blessed God, thou art so just and true,
Murder, though secret, ever thou wilt betray!
245   Murder will out, we see it day by day.
Murder so loathsome and abominable
To God is, who is just and reasonable,
That he will never suffer it to be
Concealed, though it hide a year, or two, or three.
250   Murder will out; to this point it comes down.
    "Promptly the magistrates who ruled that town
Have seized the driver, and put him to such pain,
And the stableman as well, that under strain
Of torture they were both led to confess
255   And hanged by the neck-bone for their wickedness.
    "Here's proof enough that dreams are things to dread!
And in the same book I have also read,
In the very chapter that comes right after this—
I don't speak idly, by my hope of bliss—
260   Two travelers who for some reason planned
To cross the ocean to a distant land
Found that the wind, by an opposing fate,
Blew contrary, and forced them both to wait
In a fair city by a harborside.
265   But one day the wind changed, toward eventide,
And blew just as it suited them instead.
Cheerfully these travelers went to bed
And planned to sail the first thing in the morning.
But to one of them befell a strange forewarning
270   And a great marvel. While asleep he lay,
He dreamed a curious dream along toward day.
He dreamed that a man appeared at his bedside
And told him not to sail, but wait and bide.
'Tomorrow,' he told the man, 'if you set sail,
275   You shall be drowned. I have told you my whole tale.'
He woke, and of this warning he had met
He told his friend, and begged him to forget
His voyage, and to wait that day and bide.

His friend, who was lying close at his bedside,
280   Began to laugh, and told him in derision,
'I am not so flabbergasted by a vision
As to put off my business for such cause.
I do not think your dream is worth two straws!
For dreams are but a vain absurdity.
285   Of apes and owls and many a mystery
People are always dreaming, in a maze
Of things that never were seen in all their days
And never shall be. But I see it's clear
You mean to waste your time by waiting here.
290   I'm sorry for that, God knows; and so good day.'
With this he took his leave and went his way.
But not the half his course had this man sailed—
I don't know why, nor what it was that failed—
When by an accident the hull was rent
295   And ship and man under the water went
In full view of the vessels alongside
That had put out with them on the same tide.
Now then, fair Partlet, whom I love so well,
From old examples such as these I tell
300   You may see that none should give too little heed
To dreams; for I say seriously, indeed,
That many a dream is too well worth our dread.
    "Yes, in St. Kenelm's° life I have also read—
He was the son of Cynewulf, the king
305   Of Mercia—how this Kenelm dreamed a thing.
One day, as the time when he was killed drew near,
He saw his murder in a dream appear.
His nurse explained his dream in each detail,
And warned him to be wary without fail
310   Of treason; yet he was but seven years old,
And therefore any dream he could but hold
Of little weight, in heart he was so pure.
I'd give my shirt, by God, you may be sure,
If you had read his story through like me!
315   "Moreover, Partlet, I tell you truthfully,
Macrobius° writes—and by his book we know
The African vision of great Scipio—
Confirming dreams, and holds that they may be
Forewarnings of events that men shall see.

303*St. Kenelm.* A ninth century king of Mercia who was murdered by his mother.

316*Macrobius.* An author of a book about the Roman statesman and author Cicero, who described the dream of Scipio, a Roman general.

320 Again, I beg, look well at what is meant
By the Book of Daniel in the Old Testament,
Whether *he* held that dreams are vanity!
Read also about Joseph. You shall see
That dreams, or some of them—I don't say all—
325 Warn us of things that afterward befall.
Think of the king of Egypt, Don Pharaoh;
Of his butler and his baker think also,
Whether they found that dreams have no result.
Whoever will search through kingdoms and consult
330 Their histories reads many a wondrous thing
Of dreams. What about Croesus, Lydian king—
Didn't he dream he was sitting on a tree,
Which meant he would be hanged? Andromache,
The woman who was once great Hector's wife,
335 On the day that Hector was to lose his life,
The very night before his blood was spilled
She dreamed of how her husband would be killed
If he went out to battle on that day.
She warned him; but he would not heed nor stay.
340 In spite of her he rode out on the plain,
And by Achilles he was promptly slain.
But all that story is too long to tell,
And it is nearly day. I must not dwell
Upon this matter. Briefly, in conclusion,
345 I say this dream will bring me to confusion
And mischief of some sort. And furthermore,
On laxatives, I say, I set no store,
For they are poisonous, I'm sure of it.
I do not trust them! I like them not one bit!
350   "Now let's talk cheerfully, and forget all this.
My pretty Partlet, by my hope of bliss,
In one thing God has sent me ample grace,
For when I see the beauty of your face,
You are so scarlet-red about the eye,
355 It is enough to make my terrors die.
For just as true as *In principio*
Mulier est hominis confusio—
And Madame, what this Latin means is this:
'Woman is man's whole comfort and true bliss'—
360 When I feel you soft at night, and I beside you,
Although it's true, alas, I cannot ride you
Because our perch is built so narrowly,
I am then so full of pure felicity
That I defy whatever sort of dream!"

365   And day being come, he flew down from the beam,
       And with him his hens fluttered, one and all;
       And with a "cluck, cluck" he began to call
       His wives to where a kernel had been tossed.
       He was a prince, his fears entirely lost.
370   The morning had not passed the hour of prime
       When he treaded° Partlet for the twentieth time.
       Grim as a lion he strolled to and fro,
       And strutted only on his either toe.
       He would not deign to set foot on the ground.
375   "Cluck, cluck," he said, whenever he had found
       A kernel, and his wives came running all.
       Thus royal as a monarch in his hall
       I leave to his delights this Chanticleer,
       And presently the sequel you shall hear.
380   After the month in which the world began,
       The month of March, when God created man,
       Had passed, and when the season had run through
       Since March began just thirty days and two,
       It happened that Chanticleer, in all his pride,
385   While his seven hens were walking by his side,
       Lifted his eyes, beholding the bright sun,
       Which in the sign of Taurus° had then run
       Twenty and one degrees and somewhat more,
       And knew by instinct, not by learned lore,
390   It was the hour of prime. He raised his head
       And crowed with lordly voice. "The sun," he said,
       "Forty and one degrees and more in height
       Has climbed the sky. Partlet, my world's delight,
       Hear all these birds, how happily they sing,
395   And see the pretty flowers, how they spring,
       With solace and with joy my spirits dance!"
       But suddenly he met a sore mischance,
       For in the end joys ever turn to woes.
       Quickly the joys of earth are gone, God knows,
400   And could a rhetorician's art indite it,
       He would be on solid ground if he should write it,
       In a chronicle, as true notoriously!
       Now every wise man, listen well to me.
       This story is as true, I undertake,
405   As the very book of Lancelot of the Lake
       On which the women set so great a store.

---

371 *treaded.* Embraced.
387 *Taurus.* The bull, one of the signs of the zodiac.

Now to my matter I will turn once more.
   A sly iniquitous fox, with black-tipped ears,
Who had lived in the neighboring wood for some three years,
His fated fancy swollen to a height,
410   Had broken through the hedges that same night
Into the yard where in his pride sublime
Chanticleer with his seven wives passed the time.
Quietly in a bed of herbs he lay
Till it was past the middle of the day,
415   Waiting his hour on Chanticleer to fall
As gladly do these murderers, one and all,
Who lie in wait, concealed, to murder men.
O murderer, lurking traitorous in your den!
O new Iscariot,° second Ganelon,
420   False hypocrite, Greek Sinon, who brought on
The utter woe of Troy and all her sorrow!
O Chanticleer, accursed be that morrow
When to the yard you flew down from the beams!
That day, as you were well warned in your dreams,
425   Would threaten you with dire catastrophe.
But that which God foresees must come to be,
As there are certain scholars who aver.
Bear witness, any true philosopher,
That in the schools there has been great altercation
430   Upon this question, and much disputation
By a hundred thousand scholars, man for man.
I cannot sift it down to the pure bran
As can the sacred Doctor, Augustine,
Or Boëthius, or Bishop Bradwardine,°
435   Whether God's high foreknowledge so enchains me
I needs must do a thing as it constrains me—
"Needs must"—that is, by plain necessity;
Or whether a free choice is granted me
To do it or not do it, either one,
440   Though God must know all things before they are done;
Or whether his foresight nowise can constrain
Except contingently, as some explain;
I will not labor such a high concern.
My tale is of a cock, as you shall learn,
445   Who took his wife's advice, to his own sorrow,
And walked out in the yard that fatal morrow.

---

[420]*Iscariot.* Judas Iscariot betrayed Jesus. Ganelon (l. 420) betrayed Roland (in the French epic *The Song of Roland*). Sinon (l. 421) betrayed the Trojans by persuading them to accept the wooden horse.
[434]*Augustine, Boëtheus, and Bishop Bradwardine.* Medieval philosophers and theologians.

Women have many times, as wise men hold,
Offered advice that left men in the cold.
450 A woman's counsel brought us first to woe
And out of Paradise made Adam go
Where he lived a merry life and one of ease.
But since I don't know whom I may displease
By giving women's words an ill report,
455 Pass over it; I only spoke in sport.
There are books about it you can read or skim in,
And you'll discover what they say of women.
I'm telling you the cock's words, and not mine.
Harm in no woman at all can I divine.
460   Merrily bathing where the sand was dry
Lay Partlet, with her sisters all near by,
And Chanticleer, as regal as could be,
Sang merrily as the mermaid in the sea;
For the *Physiologus*° itself declares
465 that they know how to sing the merriest airs.
And so it happened that as he fixed his eye
Among the herbs upon a butterfly,
He caught sight of this fox who crouched there low.
He felt no impulse then to strut or crow,
470 But cried "cucock!" and gave a fearful start
Like a man who has been frightened to the heart.
For instinctively, if he should chance to see
His opposite, a beast desires to flee,
Even the first time that it meets his eye.
475   This Chanticleer, no sooner did he spy
The fox than promptly enough he would have fled.
But "Where are you going, kind sir?" the fox said.
"Are you afraid of me, who am your friend?
Truly, I'd be a devil from end to end
480 If I meant you any harm or villainy.
I have not come to invade your privacy.
In truth, the only reason that could bring
This visit of mine was just to hear you sing.
Beyond a doubt, you have as fine a voice
485 As any angel who makes heaven rejoice.
Also you have more feeling in your note
Than Boëthius, or any tuneful throat.
Milord your father once—and may God bless
His soul—your noble mother too, no less,
490 Have been inside my house, to my great ease.

464*Physiologus*. A treatise on zoology.

And verily sir, I should be glad to please
You also. But for singing, I declare,
As I enjoy my eyes, that precious pair,
Save you, I never heard a man so sing
495   As your father did when night was on the wing.
Straight from the heart, in truth, came all his song,
And to make his voice more resonant and strong
He would strain until he shut his either eye,
So loud and lordly would he make his cry,
500   And stand up on his tiptoes therewithal
And stretch his neck till it grew long and small.
He had such excellent discretion, too,
That whether his singing, all the region through,
Or his wisdom, there was no one to surpass.
505   I read in that old book, *Don Burnel the Ass,*°
Among his verses once about a cock
Hit on the leg by a priest who threw a rock
When he was young and foolish; and for this
He caused the priest to lose his benefice.°
510   But no comparison, in all truth, lies
Between your father, so prudent and so wise,
And this other cock, for all his subtlety.
Sing, sir! Show me, for holy charity,
Can you imitate your father, that wise man?"
515   Blind to all treachery, Chanticleer began
To beat his wings, like one who cannot see
The traitor, ravished by his flattery.
     Alas, you lords, about your court there slips
Many a flatterer with deceiving lips
520   Who can please you more abundantly, I fear,
Than he who speaks the plain truth to your ear.
Read in Ecclesiastes,° you will see
What flatterers are. Lords, heed their treachery!
     This Chanticleer stood tiptoe at full height.
525   He stretched his neck, he shut his eyelids tight,
And he began to crow a lordly note.
The fox, Don Russell, seized him by the throat
At once, and on his back bore Chanticleer
Off toward his den that in the grove stood near,
530   For no one yet had threatened to pursue.
     O destiny, that no man may eschew!

[505]*Don Burnel the Ass.* A twelfth century poem by Nigel Wireker.
[509]*benefice.* An ecclesiastical appointment with a fixed income.
[522]*Ecclesiastes.* A book in the Hebrew Bible.

Alas, that he left his safe perch on the beams!
Alas, that Partlet took no stock in dreams!
And on a Friday happened this mischance!
535   Venus, whose pleasures make the whole world dance,
Since Chanticleer was ever your true servant,
And of your rites with all his power observant
For pleasure rather than to multiply,
Would you on Friday suffer him to die?
540   Geoffrey,° dear master of the poet's art,
Who when your Richard perished by a dart
Made for your king an elegy so burning,
Why have I not your eloquence and learning
To chide, as you did, with a heart so filled,
545 Fridays? For on a Friday he was killed.
Then should I show you how I could complain
For Chanticleer in all his fright and pain!
    In truth, no lamentation ever rose,
No shriek of ladies when before its foes
550 Ilium fell, and Pyrrhus with drawn blade
Had seized King Priam by the beard and made
An end of him—the *Aeneid* tells the tale—
Such as the hens made with their piteous wail
In their enclosure, seeing the dread sight
555 Of Chanticleer. But at the shrillest height
Shrieked Partlet. She shrieked louder than the wife
Of Hasdrubal, when her husband lost his life
And the Romans burned down Carthage; for her state
Of torment and of frenzy was so great
560 She willfully chose the fire for her part,
Leaped in, and burned herself with steadfast heart.
    Unhappy hens, you shrieked as when for pity,
While the tyrant Nero put to flames the city
Of Rome, rang out the shriek of senators' wives
565 Because their husbands had all lost their lives;
This Nero put to death these innocent men.
But I will come back to my tale again.
    Now this good widow and her two daughters heard
These woeful hens shriek when the crime occurred,
570 And sprang outdoors as quickly as they could
And saw the fox, who was making for the wood
Bearing this Chanticleer across his back.
"Help, help!" they cried. They cried, "Alas! Alack!
The fox, the fox!" and after him they ran,

540*Geoffrey* of Vinsauf, author of a poem about Richard I. He berates Friday for being the day on which the king died.

575 And armed with clubs came running many a man.
Ran Coll the dog, and led a yelping band;
Ran Malkyn, with a distaff° in her hand;
Ran cow and calf, and even the very hogs,
By the yelping and the barking of the dogs

580 And men's and women's shouts so terrified
They ran till it seemed their hearts would burst inside;
They squealed like fiends in the pit, with none to still them.
The ducks quacked as if men were going to kill them.
The geese for very fear flew over the trees.

585 Out of the beehive came the swarm of bees.
Ah! Bless my soul, the noise, by all that's true,
So hideous was that Jack Straw's° retinue
Made never a hubbub that was half so shrill
Over a Fleming they were going to kill

590 As the clamor made that day over the fox.
They brought brass trumpets, and trumpets made of box,
Of horn, of bone, on which they blew and squeaked,
And those who were not blowing whooped and shrieked.
It seemed as if the very heavens would fall!

595   Now hear me, you good people, one and all!
Fortune, I say, will suddenly override
Her enemy in his very hope and pride!
This cock, as on the fox's back he lay,
Plucked up his courage to speak to him and say.

600 "God be my help, sir, but I'd tell them all,
That is, if I were you, 'Plague on you fall!
Go back, proud fools! Now that I've reached the wood,
I'll eat the cock at once, for all the good
Your noise can do. Here Chanticleer shall stay.'"

605   "Fine!" said the fox. "I'll do just what you say."
But the cock, as he was speaking, suddenly
Out of his jaws lurched expeditiously,
And flew at once high up into a tree.
And when the fox saw that the cock was free,

610 "Alas," he said, "alas, O Chanticleer!
Inasmuch as I have given you cause for fear
By seizing you and bearing you away,
I have done you wrong, I am prepared to say.
But, sir, I did it with no ill intent.

615 Come down, and I shall tell you what I meant.
So help me God, it's truth I'll offer you!"

---

[577] *distaff.* A staff used for spinning thread by hand.
[587] *Jack Straw.* A leader of the Peasants' Revolt in 1381. The rebellion attacked in part the Flemings (l. 589) who lived in London.

"No, no," said he. "We're both fools, through and through.
But curse my blood and bones for the chief dunce
If you deceive me oftener than once!
620 You shall never again by flattery persuade me
To sing and wink my eyes, by him that made me.
For he that willfully winks when he should see,
God never bless him with prosperity!"
"Ah," said the fox, "with mischief may God greet
625 The man ungoverned, rash, and indiscreet
Who babbles when to hold his tongue were needful!"
Such is it to be reckless and unheedful
And trust in flattery. But you who hold
That this is a mere trifle I have told,
630 Concerning only a fox, or a cock and hen,
Think twice, and take the moral, my good men!
For truly, of whatever is written, all
Is written for our doctrine, says St. Paul.
Then take the fruit, and let the chaff lie still.
635 Now, gracious God, if it should be your will,
As my Lord teaches, make us all good men
And bring us to your holy bliss! Amen.

Epilogue to the Nun's Priest's Tale

"Sir Chaplain," said our good Host, "by St. Paul's,
A blessing on your britches and your balls!
640 This was a merry tale of Chanticleer.
But, on my word, if you were secular,
You'd make a cock to tread the hens all right!
If your strength is equaled by your appetite
You'd need some hens, according to my view;
645 Seven times seventeen, I think, would be too few.
Look at the sinews on this gentle priest,
What a big neck, and what a span of chest!
He peers round like a sparrowhawk in eye.
His cheeks need no brazil-wood for a dye
650 Or coccus grain brought in from Portugal.
Now, sir, good luck go with you for your tale!"

Questions for Study

1. "The Nun's Priest's Tale" is rich in detail. Is Chaucer successful in using such a multiplicity of details to create a unified work of art? Does any of the detail seem unnecessary?

2. How is the information about the widow's farm relevant to the story of Chanticleer? Are there parallels between the human and the animal spheres?

3. What characterizes Partlet? What is the nature of her relationship with Chanticleer?

4. What characterizes Chanticleer? What are his weaknesses? What persuasive ploys does the fox use to trick Chanticleer? Why is Chanticleer susceptible to them?

5. What details characterize the Nun's Priest? What is the Host's attitude toward him?

6. What does the way the Nun's Priest tells the story—the kinds of information he includes, his digressions, the morals he draws from the story—reveal about him? What does Chaucer seem to think of the Nun's Priest?

7. What do we learn about the Middle Ages from this story? What beliefs and practices does the story reveal about Chaucer's world?

8. What references are made in this story to the biblical account of the Fall? (See pp. 45–47 for the complete account.) In what ways is this story a retelling of the story of the Fall?

9. "The Nun's Priest's Tale" has been called mock-heroic. In a mock-heroic narrative an author uses the conventions of epic or romance to treat something trivial. Can you find evidence in this tale to support this claim? How is this narrative different from and similar to *Beowulf* (chapter three) and *Sir Gawain and the Green Knight* (chapter five)?

FOR FURTHER READING

Appiah, Peggy. *Ananse the Spider: Tales from an Ashanti Village.* New York: Pantheon Books, 1966. Appiah collects and translates African trickster tales.

Bettleheim, Bruno. *The Uses of Enchantment: The Meaning and Importance of Fairy Tales.* New York: Knopf, 1976. Bettleheim was a psychoanalyst who provides a Freudian analysis of fairy tales and readers' responses to fairy tales. He offers a controversial defense of why children should be allowed to hear and read fairy tales.

Brunvand, Jan Harold. *The Vanishing Hitchhiker: American Urban Legends and Their Meanings.* New York: Norton, 1981. Brunvand retells and comments on fictional stories that Americans tell one another as true.

Darnton, Robert. "Peasants Tell Tales: The Meaning of Mother Goose." *The Great Cat Massacre and Other Episodes in French Cultural History.* New York: Basic Books, 1984. 9–72. Darnton rejects Bettleheim's theories, developed in *The Uses of Enchantment,* of the sources and meanings of fairy tales and offers instead a historical explanation of why and how tales were told in the Middle Ages.

Dundes, Alan. *Cinderella: A Casebook*. New York: Wildman Press, 1983. This anthology reprints versions of the world's most famous folk tale along with scholarly essays about them.

Lopes, Barry Holstun. *Giving Birth to Thunder, Sleeping with His Daughter: Coyote Builds North America*. Kansas City: Sheed Andrews and McMeel, 1977. Lopes provides a collection of raucous Native American trickster tales.

Luthi, Max. *Once Upon a Time: On the Nature of Fairy Tales*. Trans. Lee Chadeayne and Paul Gottwald. New York: Frederick Ungar, 1970. Luthi analyzes the European fairy tale.

Propp, Vladimir I. *Morphology of the Folktale*. Ed. Svatava Pirkova-Jakobson. Trans. Laurence Scott. Bloomington: U of Indiana P, 1958. Propp's study of the structure of the folktale has influenced much scholarship on narrative.

Radin, Paul. *The Trickster: A Study in American Indian Mythology*. London: Routledge and Kegan Paul, 1956. Radin's book is the standard study of the trickster tale.

Roberts, John W. *From Trickster to Badman: The Black Folk Hero in Slavery and Freedom*. Philadelphia: U of Pennsylvania P, 1989. Roberts traces the transformation of the trickster hero from Br'er Rabbit and John the slave into the outlaw hero.

Thompson, Stith. *The Folktale*. New York: The Dryden Press, 1946. Thompson, in this thorough study of the folktale, examines the nature and sources of the many kinds of folktales.

Chapter Five
The Romance

INTRODUCTION

The word *romance* comes from Old French *romanz*, which meant "the speech of the people." It was used to distinguish the spoken language—French—from the written language—Latin or "Roman." Later the word was applied to the other languages derived from Latin—"romance languages"—and to the works written in them. Since many of these works, especially those in French, were about knights and chivalry, the word during the Middle Ages came to stand for stories about this subject matter.

But the genre of narrative fiction that we call *romance* incorporates other subject matter as well and is much older than the Middle Ages. The first romances were written in Greece between the first and fourth centuries A.D. Writers of these romances abandoned or departed from traditional stories, like those used in epics, and instead invented stories about couples who fall in love, are separated by various catastrophes, but overcome them to be reunited. Romances lost favor after the fall of the Roman Empire, but regained popular favor in the twelfth century and were enormously popular throughout the Middle Ages. The most famous of the medieval romances featured stories about King Arthur and the knights of the Round Table. The first full treatment of King Arthur was Geoffrey of Monmouth's *History of the Kings of Britain* (A.D. 1136). The King Arthur stories were then reworked and augmented by French writers like Chrétien de Troyes. These stories were in turn retold in English by Thomas Malory in *Le Morte D'Arthur* (1469-70). Three other great medieval romances are Gottfried von Strassburg's *Tristan und*

Isolde (c. 1210), Wolfram von Eschenbach's *Parzival* (c. 1210), and the anonymous *Sir Gawain and the Green Knight* (c. 1370).

After a diminished popularity during the Renaissance, romance became popular again in the seventeenth century, when French writers like Paul Scarron and Magdeleine de Scudéry wrote lengthy romances about heroic noblemen and beautiful noblewomen who fall in love and display bravery, loyalty, and honor through numerous incredible adventures. **Gothic romance** developed in the eighteenth century with the publication of Horace Walpole's *The Castle of Otranto: A Gothic Story* (1764). Gothic romances featured scary settings, demented villains, threatened heroines, supernatural forces, and mysterious happenings. Other popular gothic romances of that period were Ann Radcliffe's *The Mysteries of Udolpho* (1794), Matthew Lewis's *The Monk* (1796), and Mary Shelley's *Frankenstein* (1818). Romances about King Arthur regained popularity in the nineteenth and twentieth centuries with works like Tennyson's *The Idylls of the King* (1842-85) and T. H. White's *The Once and Future King* (1939-58).

Ever since the vogue of chivalric romance in the Middle Ages, romances have, in one form or another, continued to dominate lists of popular literature. Many of the sub-genres of narrative fiction—detective, cowboy, spy, gothic, historical, science fiction, and fantasy—are forms of romance. Some modern writers, like C. S. Lewis and J. R. R. Tolkien, both scholars of medieval literature, consciously imitated medieval romances in their fantasy fiction. American westerns are in effect stories of medieval knights adapted to the Western plains. Detective fiction often presents the detective as a kind of knight who abides by a chivalric code of honor and bravely quests for truth through the mazelike streets of the urban landscape. The American writer Raymond Chandler even named his detective hero Philip Marlowe after Sir Thomas Malory; "Marlowe" is a variation on "Malory." The popular acclaim of such works has been further enhanced by film and television, which have made romance a staple form of popular entertainment today.

A general definition of romance is that **romance** is a long narrative in either poetry or prose featuring idealized characters who experience surprising and improbable events in an idealized setting. Romance includes many of the same elements as folk tales, especially legends and fairy tales, but is different from them in that it is longer than most of them and it is more consciously "literary." A romance, in other words, is created by one author who employs literary devices like figures of speech, intricate plotting, symbolism, and subtle diction more fully and obviously than folk narrators do.

Although the subject matter of romances varies according to the cultures in which they are created, romances have a number of traits in common. First, romance is meant to be entertaining. This function, entertainment, sets romance apart from epic. The primary function of epic is to depict the deeply felt concerns and values of a culture, those things that give a culture its identity. Epic is often entertaining and includes some of the same conventions as romance, but epic can also be harshly realistic. It can depict the unpleasant difficulties and predicaments of a culture, some of which may seem unsolvable. Like epic—and like all literature—romance reflects culture, but people take it less seriously than epic because they see it as a diversion, as play and fun.

Second, romance provides an escape from real life. It deemphasizes the unpleasant and glamorizes the appealing. Its protagonists are attractive, they engage in exciting activities, they live in desirable places and circumstances, and they vanquish the forces that threaten them. Unlike epic, which is nearly always based on historical people and events, romance consists of at least some fictional—that is, made up—materials. Its characters, settings, and plots, furthermore, are unashamedly implausible. We expect happy endings in romances even though in real life they would be improbable. Even when romances include characters and events that we might expect to be unappealing, like the monsters and frightening locales of gothic fiction, such conventions are so implausible that they excite rather than threaten the reader, and they are counterbalanced by glamorized characters and happy endings.

Third, romance relies heavily on formulas or conventions. All literature is based on conventions, but the conventions of romance are much less hidden than the conventions of other forms of narrative. Real life has no conventions; it simply *is.* Literary conventions, therefore, are always distortions of real life. But people who enjoy romance do not mind. They find the conventions of romance interesting in themselves. Authors of romance, therefore, are much less concerned about making the conventions conform to the logic of the real world. Their heroes and heroines fall in love instantly and for no apparent reason except that the conventions of romance require it. The hero and heroine have one fantastic adventure after another, not because the adventures follow logically one from the other, but because the conventions of romance call for many adventures.

Two of the most recognizable and repeated conventions of romance are the adventure story and the love story. In the adventure story, the hero or heroine's noble qualities are tested by a series of dangerous circumstances. On a simple level, the circumstances merely test their physical skills. On more complex levels, the circumstances challenge their intellectual dexterity and moral commitments. The love story is often blended with the adventure story. The hero and heroine fall in love. Their future together is threatened by fate or, more likely, by villains. The villains put them through harrowing events. The hero and heroine vanquish the villains and get married. The details of these formulas vary enormously from romance to romance, but the outlines of the formulas remain the same.

The literary critic Northrup Frye says that all the conventions of romance are governed by polarized opposites. The characters, settings, and actions of romance represent extremes of good and evil rather than mixtures of the two, as in real life. The hero and heroine are idealized forms of goodness; the villains and other adversaries (like dragons and monsters) are idealized forms of evil. The settings are never like the places in which real people live but are either idyllic or demonic. The idyllic world is an earthly paradise "associated with happiness, security, and peace." The demonic world is a kind of hell filled with "exciting adventures, but adventures which involve separation, loneliness, humiliation, pain, and the threat of more pain" (*The Secular Scripture: A Study of the Structure of Romance,* Cambridge: Harvard UP, 1976, 53).

The typical plot of romance, Frye says, follows the pattern of a "descent." The narrative begins with the hero and heroine in an idyllic place. Villainy or fate forces them to "descend" into a demonic world of danger and evil. As they defeat their adversaries they "ascend" again to the idyllic world (97-101). The descent, according to Frye, threatens the identity of the hero and heroine. Their integrity is placed into question. They become confused about who they are or what they believe. The turning point from descent to ascent is often a severe identity crisis that turns them toward a renewed understanding of themselves. When they finally regain the lost idyllic world, they have recovered their identity and are whole again. In adventure stories, the hero and heroine are restored to their heroic stature. In love stories, the hero and heroine find a new identity by getting married (54, 140-47).

Finally, romance expresses ideas. This quality may seem paradoxical, since the purpose of romance is to entertain and to provide an escape from real life. But because authors of romance deemphasize the ambiguities of real life, their characters, settings, and actions can easily be connected to ideas. An author may describe a character in only vague terms, but when an author becomes specific about why the hero is a hero, why the heroine is a heroine, and why the villain is a villain, then the author associates the characters and their actions with certain values. These values may belong solely to the author, but more likely they also belong to the culture from which the author comes.

The most obviously thematic romances are allegories. An **allegory** is a narrative whose characters, settings, and actions clearly symbolize ideas. Allegory functions on two levels of meaning—a literal level, in which the characters, actions, and settings are meant to be taken for their own sake, and a thematic level, in which the details of the narrative symbolize ideas. During the Middle Ages allegorical romances were popular and their symbolic meanings were often quite explicit. In "The Return of the Banished Wife," for example, a tale from the *Gesta Romanorum,* a popular collection of short allegories, a prince banishes his wife because she has committed adultery. When she repents and begs to be reinstated, the prince asks advice from his four sisters. The first sister, Justice, insists that because the wife broke the law, she should continue to be punished. The second sister, Truth, says that if the wife is allowed to return, then the truth of her adultery will be ignored. The third sister, Mercy, begs for the wife's forgiveness. Because the three sisters cannot agree, the fourth sister, Peace, flees. The prince, however, brings Peace back and has the other sisters embrace her. With the reestablishment of harmony among them, he "hastened to his erring wife. She was received with every honor and ended her days in peace." On the literal level of meaning, the sisters are simply four people who, for various reasons, do not agree. On the thematic level, they symbolize attitudes that the author feels must be brought into harmony before a humane treatment of erring people can occur.

Most authors of romance are more subtle and complex in developing ideas than this simple narrative. Perhaps the greatest and most complex allegorical romance is Edmund Spenser's *The Faerie Queene* (1589-96). In this work Spenser proposes to recount the adventures of twelve knights. These knights symbolize different virtues and undergo their adventures on the twelve days of the Faerie

Queen's annual festival. The Faerie Queen herself symbolizes Glory, but Spenser makes it clear that she also stands for the monarch of England, Queen Elizabeth I. Spenser devotes a long "book" to each knight's adventures. On the first day, for example, the Red Cross Knight, who represents Holiness, fights on behalf of Una (Truth) against Archimago (Hypocrisy) and Duessa (Falsehood). The other knights—Spenser finished only six books—symbolize Temperance, Chastity, Friendship, Justice, and Courtesy. On a literal level, *The Faerie Queene* is an enjoyable story of heroes doing battle against nasty adversaries in a land filled with wonder and magic. On a symbolic level, however, the work's themes are multilayered and intricately interwoven because of the numerous allegorical characters and references to contemporary historical events. The protagonists of each book, furthermore, are complex psychologically because they grow in their understanding and practice of the virtues they embody.

Many recent authors also use the enjoyable conventions of romance to make us feel good about the ideas implicit in their narratives. C. S. Lewis adapts the forms of medieval romance to promulgate his belief in conservative Christianity. The political journalist William F. Buckley writes spy stories to persuade us of the evils of communism. In his westerns, Louis L'Amour tries to persuade us that practical know-how, rugged individualism, and love of the land are distinctly American virtues.

Sir Gawain and the Green Knight

We do not know the name of the author of *Sir Gawain and the Green Knight,* but he apparently was a contemporary of Geoffrey Chaucer (1340–1400) and lived in the northwest Midlands of England (the general vicinity of modern-day Yorkshire). Because of his theological themes, we can hypothesize that he may have been a priest connected with a noble family, but no one knows for sure. Whatever his position, he was a learned and sophisticated person. The sole manuscript containing *Sir Gawain* dates from the late fourteenth century and contains three other poems, the first of which is a dream allegory called *Pearl.* Scholars have dubbed the author of *Sir Gawain,* then, the *Pearl* poet. He probably composed the poems about 1375.

Sir Gawain is unusual among medieval romances for its structural and thematic unity. The author avoids the episodic plotting typical of medieval romances and instead weaves together three plots found separately in folklore and earlier romances: the beheading game, the agreement to exchange winnings, and the temptation. These three strands in the work seem at first unrelated, but at the end the author ties them together in surprising and intricate ways. The structure of the work is equally subtle. The poem has four parts of roughly the same length. In the first, the Green Knight appears at Camelot and proposes the beheading game. In the second, Gawain quests for the Green

Knight's abode. In the third, he sojourns at the mysterious castle. And in the fourth, he confronts the Green Knight. Each of these parts has its own purposeful order. The third part, for example, consists of three hunts, and each of these hunts is divided into three sections. All four parts of the romance combine to create an evolving psychological portrayal of Gawain and to support the themes revealed at the end.

The themes of the work center on the author's Christian beliefs. *Sir Gawain* is typical of medieval romances in that it presents the chivalric code as worthy of imitation. Arthur's court and Gawain in particular are reputedly the greatest examplars of chivalry in the world. But perhaps because the author writes late in the tradition of chivalric romance, he takes a somewhat more critical stance toward chivalry. In looking at chivalry through the lens of Christian values, he finds it wanting. Throughout *Sir Gawain,* then, there is an undercurrent of satire. At the same time the author praises chivalry, he also exposes its weaknesses. We become fully aware of his thematic purposes only at the end, when he makes them clear. We are as surprised as Gawain, and like Gawain we are invited to reconsider the events of the story in light of Christian rather than chivalric values. But *Sir Gawain* is more than just a good-humored satire of chivalry. Gawain's experiences are not just his alone. The author wants us to see that they are ours as well.

The north Midlands dialect in which *Sir Gawain* was written is more difficult to understand than Chaucer's London dialect, which became the basis for modern English. Translations of the poem, then, are almost essential for modern readers. Margaret Williams's translation, reprinted here, maintains the verse form of the original. The structure of most of the lines is similar to that of *Beowulf* and other Old English poems. The line is divided into two parts by a pause (caesura). Each part has two stressed vowels, and three of the stresses are linked by alliteration. The first line of the translation illustrates this pattern:

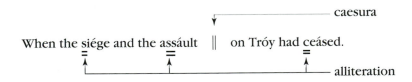

Sir Gawain is different from Old English poetry in its use of rhyme. Each stanza of the poem begins with a long unit of four-stressed lines. This unit varies in length and is unrhymed. The stanza ends with a two-stressed line (called a "bob") and four three-stressed lines (called a "wheel"). The rhyme scheme of the bob and wheel unit is *abab*. A glance at the first few pages of Williams's translation will illustrate these structural features of the stanzas.

Part One

When the siege and the assault on Troy° had ceased,
the city broken, burnt to brands and ashes,
the man who there twined the strands of treason
was tried for his treachery—it was such truly!
It was lordly Aeneas and his lofty kinsmen   5
who beat down the provinces and became possessors
of most of the wealth in the Western Isles.
At the time when great Romulus pressed on to Rome,
with boastful pride he builds up that city
and gives it his own name, as it is now called.   10
Ticius goes to Tuscany and takes on house-building,
Longobardus then founds new homes in Lombardy,
while far over the French sea Felix Brutus
settles Britain on its many broad banks
       joyfully,   15
  where war and woe and wonders
  have reigned alternately,
  and often bliss and blunders
  in quick turns come to be.

2 When Britain had been built by this mighty baron,   20
bold men were bred there; they loved battling,
and as time moved on they stirred up trouble.
Marvels have happened in this place, more often
than in any other, since then, that I have known.
But of all Britain's kings who have carried on here,   25
Arthur, I have heard, was always the courtliest.
I intend to reveal a strange event in his land
such that some men hold it an utter marvel,
a baffling adventure among the wonders of Arthur.
If you will listen to this lay° but a little while,   30
I will tell it straight off, as I heard it in town
      by tongue,
  as it is set, well-stocked,
  in a story brave and strong,
  with true letters interlocked,   35
  told in this land for long.

---

[1]*Troy.* The opening and closing stanzas of the poem place Gawain's story in a broad historical context that begins with the fall of Troy. Aeneas, the son of the king of Troy and the hero of Virgil's *Aeneid,* flees the burning city. His descendants travel westward into Europe ("the Western Isles") and give their names to the kingdoms they found. The last of these is Aeneas's great-grandson, Felix Brutus, who crosses the English Channel (the "French Sea") and founds Britain. The traitor mentioned in line three is probably Antenor, one of Aeneas's fellow warriors.

[30]*lay.* A story in verse meant to be sung.

3   This King was at Camelot at Christmas time
     with many fair lords, the best of his followers,
     all the gorgeous brotherhood of the gracious Round Table
     in right costly revelry and reckless mirth.   40
     Many a time these men tourneyed there,
     jousting gayly; these gentle knights
     then set out for the court to sing carols.
     The feasting went on fifteen full days,
     with all the meats and mirth that men could think of: 45
     such noisy glee, glorious to hear,
     such a fine din by day, such dancing by night!
     All was high-hearted happiness in those halls and chambers
     among lords and ladies, what each one liked best.
     With the world's best delights they lived together,   50
     the best-known knights, next to Christ Himself,
     and the loveliest ladies that ever lived,
     and he, comeliest of kings, who holds court there.
     For all this fair company was in its fresh age
                                   in that hall,   55
               under heaven the luckiest men,
               with a king highest of all.
               How hard to find again
               so brave a troop at call!

4   While the new year was still fresh, a new-comer,   60
     the nobility on the dais that day was served double.
     As the King and his knights came into the hall,
     the singing in the chapel softened to an end;
     a loud cry then broke out from clerics and others,
     Noel, celebrated new, its name called out often.   65
     Then the gallant lords ran forth to give largesse,
     cried New Year gifts aloud, gave them out by hand
     and debated busily about these gifts;
     the ladies laughed loudly, though they had lost,
     and the winner was not sorry—you may well believe!   70
     They kept up their mirth until meal-time;
     after washing properly they went to their seats,
     the better man placed first, as always seems best,
     Queen Gwenevere, lovely, well-gowned, in the middle,
     set out on the grand dais, adorned on all sides   75
     with fine silks around her, a canopy over her,
     treasured tapestries of Tharsia° and of Toulouse°
     embroidered and set with the best gems
     that would prove high-priced to buy with pennies

---

77 *Tharsia.* Turkey. *Toulouse.* A city in southwestern France.

any day.

She, the loveliest there,
glanced around with eyes of gray.
That he saw one more fair
no man could truly say.

80

5 But Arthur would not eat till all were served;
he was jolly in his youthfulness, and somewhat childish.
He took life lightly; little did he like
to lie down or sit still for very long,
so busy his young blood and his wild brain kept him.
Also, he was moved by another motive
that urged his noble spirit; he would never eat
on such a regal day till someone related
an unheard-of tale of some adventurous thing,
some great marvel that he might believe,
of princes, of arms, or of other adventures,
or till someone asked him for an able knight
to join with in jousting, to meet in jeopardy
and risk life for life, each leaving it to the other
to gain the advantage, as fortune might grant.
This was the King's custom when he held court
at each splendid feast with his courtly followers

85

90

95

100

in the hall.

And so, with his proud air
he stands up straight and tall
and fresh, that New Year there,
making mirth with all.

105

6 So there he stands, the strong King himself,
making graceful small-talk before the high table.
Good Gawain is placed there next to Gwenevere,
Agravain of the Hard Hand on the other side,
both sons of the King's sister, both trusty knights.
Bishop Baldwin presides at the table, above them,
and Ywain, Urien's son, eats beside him.
These were seated on the dais, honorably served,
while many true men sat at the side-tables.
Then the first course came in with a fine blare of trumpets
adorned with bright banners hanging down.
A new noise of drums and of noble pipes,
loud, wild warblings, awoke such a din
that many a heart leaped high at their strains.
Dainties were served up, delicate dishes,
plenty of fresh meat, and so many platters
that there was scarcely place in front of the people

110

115

120

to set down the silverware holding various
                                        stews on the cloth.   125
        Each man served himself
        as he pleased, nothing loath;
        each two had dishes twelve,
        good beer and bright wine both.

7   Now I will say no more of their service,   130
     for everyone knows well there was nothing wanting.
     Another noise swiftly drew near, a new one,
     that the Prince might have leave to take his life-food.
     For scarce had the festal sounds ceased for a while
     and the first course been fittingly served in court,   135
     than there flings in at the door a gruesome fellow,
     the mightiest on earth, measured by his height;
     from the neck to the waist so square-built and weighty,
     with loins and limbs so massive and long
     that I judge he must have been half-giant on this earth.   140
     A man still, I grant, one of the greatest
     and handsomest—for his size—that goes on horseback;
     for though in back and breast his body was forbidding
     yet his belly and waist were worthily slim,
     and his features fitted the form that he had,   145
                                        cut clean
        Men wondered at the hue
        that in his face was seen.
        He rode as a foe might do,
        and was, all over, bright green!   150

8   In green was this warrior decked—all his garments:
     a strait coat stretching down that stuck to his sides,
     a gay mantle over it, made fair within
     with close-cut fur showing, the lining clean
     and cheerful with bright ermine, his hood also,   155
     falling back from his locks and laid on his shoulders.
     Neat, well-gartered hose of that same green
     were fastened on his calf, with clean spurs beneath
     of bright gold upon silk strips richly barred,
     pointed shoes on his feet as he prances up.   160
     Indeed, all his vesture° was like clean verdure,°
     both the bars of his belt and other bright stones
     that were richly ranged in the clean array
     covering him and his saddle, upon worked silk.
     It would be too troublesome to name half the trifles   165

161 *vesture.* Clothing. *verdure.* Growing, very green vegetation.

embroidered on it, with birds and butterflies,
gay, gawdily green, with gold everywhere.
The pendants of his trappings, the proud cropper,°
his metal bit-studs,° were brightly enamelled;
and so were the stirrups that he stood in,   170
like his saddle-bows and his fine tail-skirts
that glimmered and gleamed all over with green stones.
The horse that he rode was just as handsome,
                     surely.
     A green horse great and thick,   175
     steed hard to rein was he
     with his fancy bridle; quick
     like his rider he seemed to be.

9   This knight was a fine sight in his green outfit,
the hair on his head matching that of his horse.   180
Fair flowing locks enfolded his shoulders,
a beard like a big bush hung over his breast;
this, with the handsome hair hanging from his head
was clipped off all around above the elbows,
hiding his upper arms, as though he had on   185
a king's hood-cape that enclosed his neck.
The mane of his horse was much like it,
well curled and combed, caught up in knots,
folded with gold thread about the fair green,
now a strand of hair, now one of gold.   190
The tail and the top-lock were twined in the same way,
both bound up with a bright green band,
set with rare stones to the end of the docked tail,
then tied with a thong in a thick knot above it
where many bright bells of burnished gold rang.   195
Such a mount on this earth, or such a man riding it,
had never been beheld by any eyes before
                  in that hall.
     His look was lightning bright—
     beholders all said so.   200
     It seemed that no man might
     stand up beneath his blow.

10   Yet he had no helmet, no hauberk° either,
no breast-shield, no plates of protecting armor,
no shaft, no shield against shoving and smiting,   205

---

[168]*cropper*. An ornamental strap that loops around a horse's tail and is attached to the saddle.
[169]*bit-studs*. Ornamental bosses on the horse's bit.
[203]*hauberk*. A coat of mail shaped like a tunic that covers the body from the neck to the knees. Mail is a flexible armor made of interlocking metal rings.

but in one hand he carried a bob° of holly
that grows the greenest when groves are bare,
an axe in the other, a huge one, monstrous,
a cruel blade to talk of, if one could find words.
Its head was as long as a whole ell-yard,°   210
the spike was fashioned from green steel and gold,
the blade burnished bright with a broad edge
as well-shaped for shearing as a sharp razor.
The stiff staff-handle that the stern man gripped
was wound with iron to the wand's end   215
and engraved with green in graceful workmanship.
A lace was twisted round it, tied at the top
and along the handle in many loops
with lots of costly tassels attached to it
by buttons of bright green; it was richly braided.   220
This hero sweeps in and enters the hall,
driving towards the high dais, fearing no danger;
he hailed no-one, but from high up looked them over.
The first words that he spoke: "Where is," said he,
"the top-man of this get-together? Gladly I would   225
set my eyes on that man; to talk sense with him
                              I'm bound."
          On the knights his look he threw;
          he swaggered all around
          then stopped, and studied who   230
          was there the most renowned.

11   All turned with a long stare to look at the fellow,
     for each man marvelled what it might mean
     that a knight and a horse could have such a hue,
     grown green as the grass—greener, it seemed,   235
     glowing more bright than green enamel on gold.
     The by-standers studied him, drawing stealthily nearer,
     all wondering what in the world he was up to.
     Many marvels they had seen, but such as this—never.
     The folk there took it for a phantom or fairy spell.   240
     So noble men were afraid to give any answer;
     all were stunned at his voice, and sat stone-still
     in a swoonlike silence through the sumptuous hall.
     As if all had slipped asleep, their jesting sank down
                              suddenly—   245
          not, I think, due to fear,
          but rather to courtesy.

206*bob.* A cluster.
210*ell-yard.* A measuring rod of forty-five inches.

> Let him whom all revere
> ask who that man may be!

12 Arthur from the high dais watched this adventure;   250
he courteously showed reverence—he could not know fear—
and said "Welcome indeed, Sir, to this place.
I am called Arthur, master of this castle.
Alight graciously; linger, I pray thee,
and later we shall ask what thou art after."   255
Said the knight: "So help me, He who sits above;
it is not my purpose to stay long in this place.
But since thy renown, Sire, has risen so high,
and thy city, thy bold men, are held to be best,
most stalwart in their steel gear as they ride on steeds,   260
the strongest and worthiest that the world shows,
proved best to sport with in noble pastimes,
and since courtesy is here shown, as I have heard tell,
all this, truly, draws me here at this time.
Be sure by this branch that I am bearing,   265
that I travel in peace and seek no trouble.
For had I come fitted out in fighting wise,
I have a hauberk at home and a helmet too,
a shield and sharp spear shining bright,
and other weapons to wield, I know well, also;   270
but I want no war, so I wear softer raiment.
But if thou art as bold as all men say,
thou wilt graciously grant me the game that I ask,
> by right."
> > Arthur answered back   275
> > and said: "Sir! Courteous knight!
> > If thou cravest a battle-crack
> > thou shalt not miss a fight!"

13 "No, I seek no fight, in faith I tell thee;
there is no-one on the benches but beardless children.   280
If I were wholly armed on my high steed,
no man here could match me, their might is so weak!
Thus I crave in this court a Christmas game,
for it is Yule and New Year, here are many brisk knights.
If any one in this house thinks himself so hardy,   285
had such bold blood and such a mad brain
as to stoutly dare strike one stroke for another,
I'll give him as a gift this rich gisarm,
this axe—it's plenty heavy—to handle at will,
and I'll take the first blow, bare as I now sit.   290
If any knight is so testy as to try out what I say,

let him run lightly to me and lay hold of this weapon.
I quit-claim it forever, let him keep it for his own,
and I shall take his stroke, standing stiff on this floor,
if thou grant me this doom: to deal him another.   295
So stay!
   And let his respite be
   a twelvemonth and a day.
   Now hurry, and let's see
   who has a word to say!"   300

14 If he had stunned them at first, stiller were they now—
all the hall-retainers, the high and the low.
The fellow on the steed turned about in his saddle;
strangely he rolled his red eyes all around,
bent his bristling brows, bright-gleaming, green,   305
and waved his beard, watching who would rise.
When no-one cared to speak he coughed loudly,
cleared his throat pompously and called out:
"What! Is this Arthur's house," said that hero,
"of which much talk runs through so many realms?   310
Where now your vain-glory, your power to vanquish,
your fierceness, your grimness, your great words?
Now the revelry and renown of the Round Table
are overcome by the words of one man speaking;
all are dazed with dread without one dint given!"   315
Then he laughed so loudly that the lord was grieved;
the blood shot for shame into his shining cheeks
and face.
   Like the wind he began to rave,
   as did all in that place.   320
   The King was always brave;
   nearer he stepped, a pace.

15 He said: "Sir, by heaven, thy request is silly;
asking for folly, thou art fit to find it!
I know of none aghast at thy great words.   325
Give me now thy gisarm, for God's sake,
and I shall grant the boon that thou hast begged."
He runs lightly to him, laying hold of his hand,
then fiercely the other man lights on his feet.
Now Arthur has his axe; he grips the handle,   330
and sternly swings it round as if to strike with it.
The strong man before him stood at full height,
above all in the house by a head or more.
With a stern look he stood there; he stroked his beard,
and with a calm countenance drew down his coat,   335

no more daunted or dismayed for those mighty strokes
than if some man on the bench had brought him a drink
of wine.

Gawain, sitting by the Queen,
to the King did incline.   340
"I beg—and it's clear-seen—
this contest must be mine!

16   "If you, glorious Lord," said Gawain to the King,
"would bid me rise from this bench and stand beside you,
that without lacking manners I may leave this table,   345
and if my liege° lady were not to dislike it,
I would give you counsel before this noble court.
For I think it untoward, if the truth may be told,
when such a thing is openly asked in your hall,
that you take it on yourself—though you may wish to—   350
while so many bold men sit about you on benches,
none under heaven, I trust, more high-spirited,
or better on the battle-field when strife breaks out.
I am the weakest, I know, the slowest witted,
and my life the least loss, if you like the truth.   355
But since you are my uncle I am worth praising
(with nothing good but your blood, I own, in my body),
since a deed so foolish should not fall to you,
and since I asked you first, let it fall to me.
If my request is unfitting, let this fine court decide,   360
without blame."

The knights talked secretly,
and they all said the same:
let the crowned King go free
and give Gawain the game.   365

17   Then the King commanded the knight to come;
he eagerly rose and turned round gracefully,
knelt before the King and caught up the weapon.
The gracious King let him have it, and with lifted hand
gave him God's blessing, and gladly bade him   370
be hardy of heart and of hand both.
"Cousin," said the King, "take care in cutting him;
by handling him right, I readily believe
thou wilt dare face the blow that he deals thee later."
With the gisarm in hand Gawain goes to the fellow   375
who boldly stands up to him, not one bit dismayed.
Then the knight in green says to Sir Gawain:

---

³⁴⁶*liege.* Someone to whom a vassal owes service and allegiance. Gawain, like all the knights of the Round Table is, according to feudal law, a vassal to King Arthur and Queen Gwenevere.

"Let us re-form our compact before we go further.
First I ask thee, Knight, what thy name is;
tell me truly so that I may trust thee."   380
"In faith," said the good knight, "Gawain I am called,
who will offer this buffet—come what may afterwards—
and a twelvemonth from now will take one from thee
with what weapon thou wilt, and let no other warrior
                                be there."   385
       This answer then he had:
       "Sir Gawain, I swear,
       that I am mighty glad
       to take thy blow. I dare!"

"Bi-gosh!" said the Green Knight. "Sir Gawain, I'm delighted   390
to take from thy hand what I asked for here.
Thou hast readily rehearsed, by true reasoning,
clearly, the whole covenant I asked of the King,
except to pledge me, Knight, by a true promise,
to seek me thyself, wherever thou thinkest   395
I may be found on earth, and fetch such wages
as thou dealest me today before this daring band!"
"Where shall I hunt?" said Gawain. "Where is thy home?
I know not where thy mansion is, by Him that made me;
I know not thee, knight, nor thy court nor thy name.   400
But teach me truly, tell me what thou art called,
and I'll use all my wits to find my way there;
I swear so, in truth, on my certain honor."
"That's enough on New Year's, no more is needed,"
said the man in green to the courteous Gawain.   405
"If I tell thee truly, when I've taken thy rap
and thou hast neatly smitten, smartly I'll let thee know
of my house and home, and mine own name;
thou shalt then test my conduct, and keep thy covenant.
If I make no speeches thou shalt speed the better,   410
lingering in thine own land and looking no further.
                             Stop, ho!
       Take thy grim tool to thee,
       and let us see thy blow."
       Said Gawain: "Sir, gladly!"   415
       He strokes his axe edge—so!

19   The Green Knight quickly gets down on the ground,
bows his head a little and lays bare the flesh.
His long luscious locks he laid over his crown
and then bared his naked neck for this business.   420
Gawain gripped his axe and swung it aloft;

setting his left foot before him on the floor
he let it fall lightly on the naked flesh,
so that the sharp edge shivered the bones,
passed through the white flesh and cut it apart   425
till the bright steel blade bit into the ground.
The fair head, off its neck, then hit the earth;
many kicked it away as it rolled around.
Blood gurgled from the body and gleamed on the green.
For all that, the fellow neither faltered nor fell,   430
but stoutly started forth on his stiff shanks
and roughly reached out to where the men stood,
caught up his lovely head and straightway lifted it.
Then he goes to his steed, snatches up the bridle,
steps into the steel bows and straddles aloft,   435
holding his head by the hair in his hands.
The man sat as sedately there in his saddle
as though nothing ailed him; yet there he was
                      with no head.
      He turned his trunk about,   440
      the ugly body bled.
      Many felt fear and doubt
      by the time his say was said.

20   Then he held his head in his hands, high up,
turning the face to the lady, the loveliest on the dais.   445
It lifted its eyelids, looked with a broad stare,
and spoke thus with its mouth, as you may now hear:
"Look, Gawain; be prompt to keep thy promise,
and loyally seek for me, Sir, till thou findest me;
thou hast pledged in this hall, in hearing of these knights.   450
To the Green Chapel go, I charge thee, to get
such a dint as thou hast dealt—thou hast deserved it—
to be duly paid back at New Year's dawn.
Knight of the Green Chapel, so many men know me;
if thou tryest to find me thou shalt not fail.   455
Therefore come, or be fit to be called a recreant."°
With a violent wrench he turned the reins
and swept out the hall door, his head in his hand,
while fire flew from the flint of his foal's hooves.
No-one knew to what region he then rode off;   460
no more could they say whence he came at first.
                      What then?
      The King and Gawain grinned there,
      at the Green Knight laughed again.

456*recreant.* A coward.

> The tale spread, to declare   465
> this marvel among men.

21   In his heart Arthur pondered, yet the polite King
let no sign be seen, but said aloud
with courteous words to the comely Queen:
"Dear Lady, today be not dismayed;   470
such tricks are becoming at Christmastide,
interludes played for laughing and singing,
between noble carols of knights and ladies.
Nonetheless, it's time now to turn to my dinner,
for I have seen a marvel; I cannot say otherwise!"   475
He glanced at Sir Gawain, and graciously said:
"Now, Sir, hang up thine axe; it has hewn enough."
It was put over the dais, to hang on the dosser°
where all men might gaze on it as a marvel,
and tell of this wonder in a true account.   480
Then they pressed to the table, these princes together,
the King and the good knight, and gallant men served them
double portions of dainties in the noblest way possible,
with all manner of meats, and minstrelsy too.
They passed that day happily till darkness came   485
                              on the land.
> Now think well, Sir Gawain,
> lest thou shouldst fail to stand,
> or this adventure gain
> that thou hast taken in hand.   490

Part Two

22   This adventure was a New Year's gift to Arthur
when, in the young year, he yearned for a brave tale.
Though words failed them when they went to their seats,
they are facing hard work, their hands cram-full of it.
Gawain was glad when games began in the hall;   495
no wonder what must come weighed heavily on him!
Though men's minds are merry when they have drunk much,
a year flies by swiftly, yielding never the same;
the beginning and end are seldom at one.
This Yule-tide went by, and the year after it,   500
and each season in order followed the other.
After Christmas comes the crabbed Lent
that tries flesh with fish and with simpler food.

---

[478]*dosser.* A cloth or tapestry hung at the back of a throne.

But then the world's weather struggles with winter,
the cold melts away, clouds are uplifted,   505
the rain shimmers down in warm showers
and falls on the fair turf; flowers appear.
The ground and groves too are clothed in green,
birds are busy building and brightly sing
in the solace of the soft summer that swiftly flows over   510
                           the land.
      Buds swell and open wide
      where the rich, thick hedges stand;
      bird-calls from every side
      are heard in the proud woodland.   515

23   Then comes the summer season with soft breezes,
when the west wind sighs on seeds and herbs;
very lovely the plants that are pushing upward,
while the dripping dew drops down from the leaves,
awaiting the blissful gleam of the bright sun.   520
But autumn draws near and hardens all,
gives warning to ripen before the winter;
it strikes with drought till the dust rises
from the face of the fields, flying high up.
Wrathful winds in the sky wrestle with the sun,   525
leaves loosen from the lime trees and light on the ground,
and gray grows the grass that was once green.
All that first arose now ripens and rots.
Thus the year runs on with many yesterdays,
and winter returns, as the world's way is,   530
                       no fear,
      until the Michaelmas° moon
      gave sign of winter near.
      Then Gawain must think soon
      of his own journey drear.   535

24   Yet till All-Hallows Day° he lingers with Arthur,
who then, for his sake, served a festal banquet
with much high revelry of the Round Table.
Courteous knights and comely ladies
were all lost in grief for love of that man;   540
nonetheless, they tried to talk mirthfully,
joylessly jesting for the gentle knight's sake.
After meal-time he talked to his uncle, mournfully;
he spoke of his journey, and said plainly:

532*Michaelmas.* The Feast of St. Michael the Archangel, 29 September.
536*All-Hallows Day.* All Saints' Day, 1 November.

"Liege Lord of my life, I now ask your leave.   545
You know how this case stands; I can keep no longer
from telling you my troubles, though they are trifling,
for I must face my blow without fail tomorrow,
and search for the knight in green, as God guides me."
The best men of the castle then came together,   550
Ywan and Eric, and many others,
Sir Dodinel de Sauvage, the Duke of Clarence,
Lancelot and Lionel, and the good Lucan,
Sir Bors and Sir Bedivere, big men both,
and many more worthies, with Mador de la Port.   555
All this courtly company came up to the King
to counsel the Knight, with care-filled hearts.
Much heavy sorrow spread through the hall
that one as worthy as Gawain should go on that errand,
bear a dread blow, then no more swing his brand   560
                         on high.
        The Knight still made good cheer,
        and said: "Why would I fly?
        Facing destiny's dark fear,
        what can a man do but try?"   565

25   All that day he lingers; at dawn he makes ready,
asking early for his arms, that were all brought in.
A Toulouse carpet first they spread on the floor,
and plenty of gold gear glinted on it.
The strong man steps onto it and handles the steel.   570
They put on him a doublet of dear silk from Tharsia,
then a well-cut cape closed tightly above it,
fashioned inside with shining white fur.
They fixed steel-toed shoes on the knight's feet;
they wrapped elegant greaves° around his legs,   575
with knee-pieces fitted on, polished clean
and tied about his knees with knots of gold.
Then came the plates that cunningly encased
his thick strong thighs, attached with thongs;
then the byrny° woven of bright steel rings   580
enfolded the knight with its fine weaving,
with a well-burnished brace on both arms,
handsome elbow pieces, plated gloves
and all the good gear that would be a gain to him
                        in that ride: 585
        a rich heraldic shirt,

---

[575]*greaves.* Pieces of armor that protect the back and front of the legs from the knee to the ankle.
[580]*byrny.* A coat of mail.

gold spurs worn with pride,
and a trusty sword, well girt°
by a silk sash to his side.

26 When he was cased in armor his harness looked costly;   590
the least lacings or loops all gleamed with gold.
So, harnessed as he was, he heard the mass
offered and celebrated at the high altar.
Then he comes to the King and his court-comrades,
taking leave graciously of the lords and ladies   595
who kissed and escorted him, trusting him to Christ.
Gryngolet was all ready, girded with a saddle
that gleamed gayly with many gold fringes,
new studs put in everywhere, prepared for the journey.
The bridle was barred and bound with bright gold;   600
the trimming on the straps and on the proud skirts,
on the crupper° and the coverlet, accorded with the saddle-bows,
and everywhere, set on red, were rich gold nails,
till all glittered and glowed like gleams of sunlight.
Then he takes his helmet and hastily kisses it;   605
it was strongly stapled and stuffed within.
It sat high on his head, held fast behind
by a light linen band over the beaver,°
embroidered and bound with the best gems
on broad silk borders, with birds on the seams,   610
such as painted parrots perching at intervals,
turtle-doves and true-love-knots twined in as thickly
as though many maidens had made it for seven winters
                              right there.
      A circlet of great price   615
      was set upon his hair.
      Of diamonds its device;
      brilliant they were, and fair.

27 They showed him the shield bearing red-shining gules,°
with the Pentangle° painted on it in pure gold hues.   620
He caught it by the baldric° and cast it round his neck;
it fitted the hero in handsome fashion.
Why the Pentangle suited that noble prince
I am set on telling you, though it slows me up.

588*girt.* Attached.
602*crupper.* (see l. 168).
608*beaver.* A movable part of the helmet that protects the mouth and chin.
619*gules.* The heraldic color red.
620*Pentangle.* A five-pointed star, drawn without lifting the hand.
621*baldric.* A belt worn over the shoulder to support a sword or shield.

It was a sign that Solomon set forth long ago   625
as a token of truth, by a title that it has:
it is a figure that holds five points,
and each line overlaps and locks in the other,
and so it is endless; the English call it
everywhere, as I hear, the Endless Knot.   630
It thus accords with this knight and his clear arms:
forever faithful in five ways, and five times each way,
Gawain's goodness was known, like gold refined,
free from all villainy, with courtly virtues
                     made clean.   635
      Thus the Pentangle new
      on his shield and coat was seen,
      for a man of speech most true
      and knight of gentlest mien.

28   First, he was found faultless in his five wits,   640
then he never failed in his five fingers,
and all his faith on earth was in the five wounds
that Christ bore on the cross, as the Creed tells us.
And wherever he found himself facing warfare,
he thought steadily of this, over all things: 645
that his strength was found in the five joys
that heaven's courteous Queen° had in her Child.
For this cause the Knight, in a comely fashion,
had her image painted on the broad part of his shield;
by a glance at her he heartened his courage.   650
The fifth set of five that I find him following
is: open free-handedness, fellowship beyond others,
cleanness and courtesy that were never corrupted,
and, best of all, pity; these perfect fives
were more deep-set in him than in other heroes.   655
Indeed, all these five traits were so fixed in this knight,
each so knit to the other, that none had an end;
and they formed into five points that never failed,
never overlapped, and were never sundered,
nowhere ending, I find, at any one place,   660
where the drawing began or drew to an end.
Therefore, on his bright shield this sign was shaped
royally, with red gold upon red gules,
the perfect Pentangle, as people called it
                     in their lore.   665
      Now he's ready, Gawain the fair;
      well-set, a lance he bore.

[647]*heaven's courteous Queen.* Mary, mother of Jesus.

He said goodbye right there,
as he thought, forevermore.

29 His spur-pricked steed sprang forth on the way   670
    so fast that stone-sparks were struck out after him.
    Those who saw that gallant one sighed from their hearts,
    and all the knights there said to each other,
    in their care for the comely man: "By Christ, it's a shame
    to lose thee, my Lord, and thy life so noble!   675
    To find such on earth, in faith, is not easy.
    It would have been wiser to go more warily,
    and have yonder daring man dubbed a duke,
    brilliant leader of men; that would be like him!
    That were better than being broken to nothing,   680
    beheaded by an elvish man through uppish pride.
    Whoever knew a king to take such counsel
    from knights' foolish goings-on in Christmas games?"
    And then warm tears welled up in their eyes
    when that handsome knight went away from home   685
                            that day.
        No time he there abode,
        but swiftly went his way.
        By winding paths he rode;
        I heard the book so say.   690

30 Now the knight goes riding through the realms of Logres,°
    Sir Gawain, for God's sake, though he thought it no game!
    Comradeless, he must linger alone at night,
    never finding before him the food that he likes,
    no companion but his horse in copses and downs,   695
    no-one to parley with, on the pathways, but God,
    till he draws very near to North Wales.
    All the isles of Anglesey are there on his left;
    he crosses the fords in the low fore-lands,
    over at Holy Head, then holds to the mainland   700
    in the wilderness of Wirral; few men were there
    who loved either God or man with a good heart.
    And ever, as he pressed on, he asked those he met
    if they knew any gossip of a Green Knight,
    or of a Green Chapel on the grounds nearby,   705
    and all tossed back "no"; never in their lives
    had they seen any man of such a color

---

691 *Logres.* Gawain travels from Logres, Arthur's kingdom in southern England, to northern Wales. Anglesey (l. 698)
is an island off the coast of North Wales. He then goes through a dense forest called the wilderness of Wirral
(l. 701) in England just above Wales and on to his final destination, the Green Chapel, located somewhere in west
central England.

as green.
The knight took roadways strange;
on many grim banks he's been.   710
His mood would often change
till that chapel he had seen.

31   He climbed over many cliffs in strange countries;
far-wandering he rides, a friendless stranger.
At each bank or water-course that the warrior passed   715
he found a foe facing him (strange if he failed to!)
so foul and fierce that he had to fight it.
The knight met so many marvels in the mountains
that it would be tiresome to tell of the tenth part.
Sometimes he wars with dragons, with wolves as well,   720
sometimes with wood-trolls that lurk in twisted crags,
with bulls and bears both, with boars at other times,
and with giants who puffed after him from high precipices.
Were he not brave and steady, serving the Lord,
he would doubtless have died, undone, more than once.   725
Though this warring was troublesome, winter was worse
as the clear cold water showered from the clouds
and froze as it fell on the faded earth.
Nearly slain by the sleet, he sleeps in his armor
more nights than enough, among naked rocks   730
where, clattering from the cliffs a cold brook runs down
and hangs high overhead in hard icicles.
Thus in peril and in pain, in a sore plight,
this knight roamed the country-side till Christmas-Eve,
alone.   735
Well did he, in that tide,
to Mary make his moan;
may she show him where to ride
and make some shelter known!

32   In the morning he rides merrily past a mountain   740
into a deep forest, fearsomely wild,
high hills on each hand with holtwood° under them,
huge hoary oaks, hundreds together.
Hazel and hawthorn were here tangled up
with rough ragged moss rampant everywhere,   745
and many birds, unhappy on the bare twigs,
were piteously piping for pain of the cold.
The knight on Gryngolet goes straight on under them
through quagmires and marshes, a lonely man,

742*holtwood.* A wood, a copse.

fearful for his duty, lest he should fail   750
to give service to the Lord who, that selfsame night,
had been born of a maid, to end our battling.
Thus, sighing, he said, "I beseech Thee, Lord,
and Mary, mildest of mothers so dear,
for some harbor where I may hear mass worthily,   755
and Thy Matins tomorrow; meekly I ask it.
And so I pray promptly my Pater and Ave
                        and Creed."
          He rode on in his prayer,
          lamenting each misdeed.   760
          He signed himself often there
          "May Christ's cross fill my need!"

33   When the knight had crossed himself three times, no more,
     he was aware of a dwelling by a moat in the woods
     above a lawn on a hill, locked under the boughs   765
     of mighty tree-trunks along the moat-side,
     a castle, the handsomest that ever knight cared for,
     placed there in a meadow, a park all around,
     with a palisade set thick with pointed spikes
     that enclosed many trees for more than two miles.   770
     From the far side the knight gazed on that stronghold
     as it gleamed and shone through the shimmering oaks.
     He lowered his helm politely, heartily thanking
     Jesus and Saint Julian who, with such gentility,
     had both shown courtesy, harkening to his cry.   775
     "Now, good hostel," said the knight, "I beseech you to grant!"
     Then he pricked Gryngolet with his gilt heels,
     and by chance made his way to the chief gate
     that straightway brought him to the bridge's end,
                       at last.   780
          The bridge was stoutly made,
          upraised, the gates locked fast.
          The walls were well arrayed;
          it feared no storm-wind's blast.

34   The knight on his horse was held back at the banks   785
     of a double ditch drawn round the place;
     the wall reached into the water wondrously deep,
     before towering up to a huge height over it,
     all of hard-cut stone up to the cornices,
     with horn-work under battlements, in the best manner,   790
     with gay turrets geared between them
     and many lovely loops, interlocking cleanly.
     Safer defence the knight had never yet seen.

Within, he beheld the high-standing hall,
towers placed around it, with horn-like pinnacles,   795
fair turrets, well-joined and fearfully high,
with carved summits, all cleverly made.
Chalk-white chimneys he picked out, plenty of them,
on the roofs of the towers that twinkled whitely.
Many painted pinnacles were powdered about   800
in the castle embrasures,° clustering so thickly
that they seemed to be pared out of paper only.
The gallant knight on his horse thought it good enough
just to manage to come within that cloister,
find harbor in that hostel while the holy-days lasted,   805
               well-spent.
     He called, and soon there came
     a porter most pleasant;
     from the wall he asked his claim
     and hailed the knight-errant.   810

35   "Good Sir," said Gawain, "wilt thou go on my errand
to the high lord of this house, and ask him to harbor me?"
"Yes, Peter!" said the porter, "and upon my word,
you are welcome to linger, Sir, while you will."
The man went off, and again hurried back   815
with many ready folk to receive the knight.
They let down the great drawbridge and graciously went out,
getting down on their knees on the cold ground
to welcome this knight in the worthiest way.
They opened the broad gate for him, pulled it back wide;   820
bidding them rise, he rode over the bridge.
Several men seized his saddle as he dismounted,
then plenty of stalwarts stabled his steed.
The knights and squires then came downstairs
to bring this man into the hall with bliss.   825
When he lifted his helmet, many hurried
to take it from his hand, to serve the handsome one;
his sword and blazoned shield were both taken.
Then he greeted graciously each of those grooms,
while proud men pressed round to honor the prince.   830
Still clad in heavy armor he was brought to the hall;
a fair fire in the grate was fiercely burning.
The lord of those people came politely from his room
to meet the man standing there with the best manners.
He said: "You are welcome to do as you will;   835

801*embrasures.* An opening in a wall or parapet with the sides slanted outward.

what is here is all yours, every wish you may now
      fulfill."
  "My thanks," said Gawain then,
  "May Christ repay you still!"
  In each other's arms these men   840
  embraced with glad good will.

36 Gawain glanced at the one who greeted him well,
and thought what a bold man managed that castle,
a huge hero, in fact, at the height of his years.
Broad and bright was his beard, all beaver-hued,   845
a firm man, stiffly striding on stalwart shanks,
with a face fierce as fire, free of his speech,
well-suited, indeed (so it seemed to the knight)
to hold lordship over his fine liegemen.
The lord led him to a room and loudly commanded 850
that a man be assigned to serve him humbly.
Swiftly at his bidding there were servants enough
who brought him to a bright bower, with fine bedding
and curtains of clean silk with clear gold hems,
curious coverlets with lovely counterpanes°   855
of bright fur on top, embroidered at the edges,
curtains running on ropes through red-gold rings,
tapestries on the walls from Toulouse and Tharsia,
underfoot on the floor carpets to fit them.
The man was disrobed amid mirthful talk,   860
freed from his byrny and his bright armor.
Readily the servants brought rich garments
to change and put on, choosing the best.
As soon as he took one and was apparelled in it,
one that fitted him well with wide-sailing skirts,   865
in his face was springtime, so it truly seemed
to each man who beheld him so many-hued;
so glowing and lovely were his limbs under it,
that a comelier knight Christ had never made,
      they thought.   870
  In the whole world, far or near,
  he seemed to have been wrought
  a prince without a peer
  in the field where fierce men fought.

37 A chair before the chimney where charcoal burned 875
was at once decked out for Sir Gawain, with drapes

855*counterpanes.* Bedspreads.

and cushions on the quilt covers cleverly made.
Then the man was covered with a cheery mantle
of brown silk fabric embroidered richly,
fair, furred within with the finest skins,   880
all adorned with ermine, his hood also.
He settled in his seat so suitably rich
and first warmed himself; then he felt more cheerful.
Soon a table was set up on handsome trestles,
covered with a clean cloth that shone clear white,   885
with top-cloth, salt cellars and silver spoons.
Willingly the knight washed and went to his meal.
Waiters served him, with seemly politeness,
several excellent stews with the best seasoning,
double portions, as was fit, many kinds of fish,   890
some baked in bread, some broiled on coals,
some boiled, some in stew savored with spice,
and all the cunning sauces that a man could crave.
The knight called it a feast, freely and often,
most courteously, till the household claimed that he was   895
                                    well-bred.
        "All this your penance is;
        soon you'll be better fed!"
        The man made mirth at this
        as the wine went to his head.   900

38   They watched him, and asked in a tactful way,
     by private questions put to the prince himself,
     to tell them courteously of the court he came from,
     the one that noble Arthur held as his own,
     the splendid royal King of the Round Table,   905
     and if Gawain himself was sitting in their home,
     come just for Christmas, by chance in this case.
     When the lord learned what a leader he had there
     he laughed loudly, so delightful he thought it,
     and all the men in the castle made it their pleasure   910
     to appear in his presence, promptly this time,
     since all worth and prowess and polished manners
     pertain to his person; he is always praise-worthy,
     and of all men on earth the most famous.
     Each servant, very softly, said to his fellow: 915
     "Now we shall see knightly conduct, surely,
     and the impeccable terms of noble talk;
     we may learn without asking how to speak effectively,
     since we find here the father of fine-breeding.
     Truly God has given grace in a goodly way   920
     in granting to us such a guest as Gawain,

when men, for His birth's sake, shall blissfully sit
and sing.

    Understanding of manners fine
    this man will surely bring;   925
    I know that those who hear
    will learn of love-talking."

39   When the dinner was over the dignitaries rose;
    it was nearing the time when night settles down.
    The chaplains then led the way to the chapel   930
    and rang the bells (as they rightly do)
    for the solemn even-song of the festal season.
    The lord goes to it, and his lady also;
    gracefully she enters her elegant pew.
    Gawain follows eagerly and goes right there;   935
    the lord catches his cloak, leads him to a seat
    as one known familiarly, calls him by name,
    saying he was more welcome than any man in the world.
    The knight thanked him earnestly, they embraced each other
    and soberly sat together throughout the service.   940
    Then the lady was pleased to look at the knight
    as she moved from her pew with many fair maidens.
    She was fairest in skin, in features and face,
    in form and in color and in fine manners;
    much lovelier than Gwenevere—so the man thought.   945
    He goes to the chancel to salute that gracious one.
    Another lady led her by the left hand,
    one older than she, very aged, it would seem,
    highly reverenced, with retainers all round.
    But the two ladies were unlike to look upon;   950
    if the one was fresh the other was yellow!
    On the one a rich red rioted everywhere;
    rough wrinkled cheeks hung in rolls on the other.
    The kerchiefs of one—set with many clear pearls
    displayed bare on her breast and her bright throat— 955
    shone brighter than snowdrifts shed on the hills;
    the other had wound up her neck in a wimple,
    and bound her black chin with chalkwhite veils.
    Her forehead was muffled in folded silk,
    adorned and tricked out with trifles all around   960
    till nothing was bare but the lady's black brows,
    the two eyes, the nose and the naked lips,
    and these were sour to see, strangely bleared.
    A grand lady indeed! Let men, before God,
decide!   965

    Her body was thick and short,

> her hips were round and wide.
> But of more lovesome sort
> was the other at her side!

40   Gawain glanced at the pretty one looking graciously at him,   970
  and went, with leave from the lord, to meet them.
  He greets the elder, bowing gracefully low;
  he takes the lovelier lightly in his arms
  and kisses her handsomely, holding forth like a knight.
  They crave his acquaintance, and at once he asks   975
  to be their true servant, if it so please them.
  They take him between them and lead him, talking,
  to a seat by the chimney-side, then promptly send
  for spices; men hurried to get them, unsparingly,
  and joy-giving wine they got also, each time.   980
  The courteous lord right often leaped up,
  urged them to merriment, time and again,
  snatched off his hood gaily, hung it on a spear
  and waved it: a prize that they might win!
  Mirth carried them away that Christmas-time.   985
  "I'm bound, by my faith, to out-play the best of you
  before I go hoodless, with the help of my friends!"
  Thus with laughing words the lord makes merry,
  to gladden Gawain with games in the hall
>   that night,   990
>   until the time befell
>   when the lord sent for a light.
>   Sir Gawain said farewell,
>   then off, with bed in sight.

41   On the morning when every man remembers the time   995
  when Our Lord (who would die for our destiny) was born,
  joy awoke in each home in the world for His sake.
  So it did there, that day, with many dainties;
  at each meal there were courses cleverly cooked
  for the strong men dressed in their best on the dais.   1000
  The ancient old lady had the place of honor,
  the gracious lord stayed by her side, I am sure.
  Gawain and the sweet lady sat together,
  right in the middle where meats were first brought;
  then through the big hall, as seemed best to them,   1005
  each, by degrees, was served by a groom.
  There was food, there was mirth, there was much joy;
  it would be too troublesome to tell all about it,
  and point out everything, even though I took pains!

Yet I know that Gawain and the graceful lady   1010
found such comfort in company together
(through delightful dalliance of dark-whispered words,
clean, courteous talk, free from all coarseness)
that their play, in truth, surpassed each prince there
                           in his game.   1015
        Trumpets, drums, loud airs,
        and the sound of piping came.
        Each minded his own affairs,
        and those two did the same.

42   Pleasure filled that day and the day after,   1020
and the third, just as pleasant, pressed hard upon them.
On Saint John's day° the joy was delicious to hear;
it was their last playtime, so the people thought.
Some guests must go in the gray morning,
so they stayed awake wonderfully, drinking their wine   1025
and dancing endlessly to delightful carols.
At last, when it grew late, they took their leave;
each strong worthy now must go on his way.
Gawain says good-bye; the good man takes hold of him,
leads him to his own chamber beside the chimney,   1030
there draws him apart and thanks him dearly
for the delicate favor that he had done for them:
to honor their house in that high season
and embellish their castle with his fair countenance.
"Be sure, Sir, while I live I shall be the better   1035
since Gawain was my guest at God's own feast."
"I am grateful," said Gawain, "in good faith, Sir, to you.
The honor goes to you; may the high King give it!
I am ready at your will, Sir, to fulfill your wishes,
as beholden to you, in high and in low,   1040
                  by right."
        The lord then did his best
        to longer keep the knight.
        Gawain, to that request
        said by no means he might.   1045

43   Then the lord, in polite words, wanted to know
what dark deed had driven him in those festal days
so rashly from the King's court, to ride off alone
before all the holidays were over in town.
"Indeed," said the knight, "you have spoken the truth;   1050

1022*Saint John's day.* 27 December.

a high errand drove me in haste from those dwellings.
For I have been summoned to seek out a place,
not knowing where to fare in the whole world to find it.
I would not miss arriving on New Year's morn
for all the land in Logres, so may Our Lord help me!   1055
For this, Sir, a request; I require of you here
to tell me, in truth, if you have heard tell
of the Green Chapel, of what ground it stands on,
of the knight that keeps it; he's colored green!
We established a covenant by statute between us,   1060
to meet that landmark, if I hope to live on.
There are but a few hours before that New Year,
and I would look on that fellow, if God lets me,
more gladly, by God's Son, than have other good things.
So, if you are willing, I must wander on.   1065
I have barely three days left now for this business,
and I had rather fall dead than fail in my errand."
The lord said, laughing: "You had better linger;
I shall guide you to your tryst before the time ends.
Stop fretting for the Green Chapel and its grounds.   1070
You shall lie in your bed, Sir, in lazy ease
for four days, then go forth on the first of the year,
reach that place at midmorn, for your pleasure in the woods
                                        so dense.
       Dwell here till New Year's day,   1075
       then rise and set off thence.
       We will put you on your way;
       it is not two miles hence."

44   Then Gawain was glad and laughed gamely.
"I heartily thank you, and for other things too.   1080
Now luck is with me; I shall, at your will
stay here, and do whatsoever you say."
Then the lord seized him, made him sit down,
had the ladies fetched to furnish more pleasure.
They had a joyous time, just they themselves;   1085
the lord talked merrily, all for love's sake,
like a man with his wits lost, not minding what he does.
He called to the knight, crying out loudly:
"You are pledged to do whatever deed I bid.
Will you keep that promise, here, on one point?"   1090
"Yes, Sir, indeed," the trusty knight said.
"While I stay in your home I am at your service."
"You've been travelling," said the lord, "on a long journey,
then staying up late. You are not well restored

by food or by sleep, I know that for certain.   1095
You must linger in your room and lie at ease
tomorrow until mass-time, then go to your meal
when ready, with my wife, who remains with you
to cheer you with company, till I'm back at court.
                   You stay.   1100
     Early, I'll rise from rest
     and to hunting take my way."
     Gawain grants this request
     and bows in his graceful way.

45 "And further," said the host, "we'll form a bargain: 1105
Whatever I win in the woods will be yours,
and what you achieve here, exchange with me.
Sweet Sir, we shall swap—swear on it truly—
whatever we win, man, for better or worse!"
"By God," said good Gawain, "I grant all this.   1110
What pleases you is a pleasure to me."
"Bring beverages! The bargain is made!"
So said the castle's lord; both of them laughed.
They drank, they dallied, they dealt in small-talk,
these lords and ladies, as long as they liked.   1115
Then with frenchified politeness and fair speeches
they stopped, stood together, and spoke in still voices,
kissed each other lightly and took their leave.
And many brisk grooms with gleaming torches
brought each man at last to his bed   1120
                  so soft.
     Yet before they went to bed
     they recalled their promise oft.
     The lord of that home-stead
     could well hold sport aloft.   1125

Part Three

46 Right early, before day, the company rises.
Guests who have to go call to their grooms
who spring up promptly to saddle the horses.
They prepare their outfits, pack up their bags,
dress up in their richest riding array,
then leap up quickly and catch their bridles,
each off on the way that he wants to go.
The liege-lord of the land was not the last
arrayed for riding, with many attendants.

He has a hasty bite after hearing mass,   1135
then hurries—bugles blowing—to the hunting field.
By the time daylight had touched the earth
he and his men were on their tall horses.
The careful dog-trainers coupled their hounds,
opened the kennel door and called them out,   1140
blowing loud on their bugles three long notes.
When the brachets° bayed and raised a bold noise,
they chastised and checked those that went chasing off,
a hundred hunters, so I heard tell—
$\qquad\qquad\qquad\qquad\qquad$ fine men.   1145
$\qquad$ To their stations keepers go,
$\qquad$ the dogs are unleashed then.
$\qquad$ For the good blasts they blow
$\qquad$ the forest rings again.

47   At the first questing cry the wild creatures quaked.   1150
Deer drove through the dales, foolish with dread;
they hurried to high places, but hastily then
they were stopped by the beaters, stoutly shouting.
These let go by the harts° with their high heads,
the proud bucks also with broad palm-antlers;   1155
for the true lord had forbidden, in the time of closed season,
that any man should attack the male deer.
Hinds° were hauled in with "Hey!" and "Look out!"
Does were driven with great din to the deep vales
where slanting arrows were seen slipping by;   1160
in each forest nook a feather whizzed through
and bit deep into brown hide with its broad head.
Ho! They bay and they bleed, they are dying on the banks,
and the rachets° still follow, rushing in a rout,
while hunters with high horns hasten after them   1165
with cries that ring out as though cliffs were crumbling.
Any wild beast who dodged the shooting bow-men
was pulled down, torn to bits at the meeting place.
They were worried on the heights and harried to the waters,
so skillful the hunters in the hidden stations,   1170
so huge the greyhounds that soon got hold of them
and fetched them down as fast as the folk could look,
$\qquad\qquad\qquad\qquad\qquad$ just right!
$\qquad$ Bliss swept the lord away;

[1142]*brachets.* Hunting dogs.
[1154]*harts.* Male deer.
[1158]*hinds.* Female deer.
[1164]*rachets.* Hunting dogs.

he would gallop, then alight.   1175
   With joy he passed that day,
   thus, until dark night.

48   So the lord is frolicking on the linden woods' fringe
   while Gawain—good man—lies in a gorgeous bed,
   lingering while the daylight dances on the walls   1180
   under a fine coverlet, curtained about.
   As he slid into slumber he heard, slily,
   a little din at the door that opened deftly;
   lifting his head from under the linen,
   he caught up the corner of the curtain a little   1185
   and looked out warily to see what it was.
   It was the lady, so lovely to look at,
   who closed the door after her secretly, quietly,
   and came towards the bed; the man, embarrassed,
   lay down slily and pretended to sleep.   1190
   And she stepped stilly, and stole towards the bed,
   drew back the curtain and crept within,
   then sat down softly on the bedside,
   and lingered strangely long to look for his waking.
   The knight lay lurking for a long time,   1195
   searching his conscience for what this case meant
   or what it amounted to; he thought it a marvel,
   but said to himself: "It would be more seemly
   to find out, by speaking on the spot, what she wants."
   So he wakened, twisted round and turned towards her,   1200
   unlocked his lids and looked as if wondering,
   and signed himself,° to honor his Savior by his words,
              aright.
      With chin and cheek most sweet,
      mingling red and white,   1205
      lovely was she to greet,
      with small lips laughing bright.

49   "Good morning, Sir Gawain," said the gracious lady.
    "You are no wary sleeper, since one can slip in;
   you are taken, right off! Unless we make truce   1210
   I shall bind you in your bed, be sure of that!"
   All in laughing, the lady made these light jests.
   "Good morning, fair one," said Gawain, delighted.
   "It shall be as you will, and I am well pleased;
   I give in heartily and cry out for grace,   1215
   and that is best, I think, for so it must be."

1202*signed himself.* Made the sign of the cross.

And thus he plays back to her, with blithe laughter.
"But if, lovely lady, you would give me leave,
set free your prisoner and pray him to rise,
I'd get out of this bed and clothe myself better;   1220
I would be more comfortable conversing with you."
"Indeed, no, fair Sir," said that sweet one.
"You shan't rise from your bed; I'll plan something better.
I shall hold you here safe, on the other side also,
then talk with my knight whom I have now caught.   1225
I guess it for a fact, you are Sir Gawain
whom all the world worships wherever he rides;
your honor, your courtly ways, are courteously praised
by lords, by ladies, by everyone living.
And now we are here, indeed, we two alone.   1230
My lord and his followers have gone afar,
other men are in bed, my maids also,
the door drawn and fastened with a firm bolt,
and since I have in this house he whom all like,
my time, while I have it, with good talking   1235
                    I'll fill.
          My body now is free
          to take at your own will;
          and I, perforce, will be
          your own servant still."   1240

50   "In good faith," said Gawain, "I seem to be gaining,
          though I am not the sort that you are speaking of;
          to deserve such reverence as you here render me
          I am unworthy, as I well know myself.
          By God, I would be glad, if you thought good,   1245
          in words or in service to set myself
          to giving you pleasure—that would be pure joy."
          "In good faith, Sir Gawain," said the gracious lady,
          "the worth and the prowess that please all others,
          if I lessened or belittled them I would lack good breeding.   1250
          There are ladies enough who would far liefer°
          have thee in their hold, fair Sir, as I have,
          (to dally pleasantly with your polite words
          and so find comfort and relieve their cares)
          than all the goods or the gold that they have.   1255
          But, praise that same Lord who rules the skies,
          I have wholly in my hands him whom all desire,
                    through grace."

1251*far liefer.* Very gladly.

She made great cheer, for sure,
she, so fair of face.   1260
The knight with speeches pure
answered in every case.

51   "Madame," said he merrily, "Mary reward you!
I have, in good faith, found your generosity noble.
Folk fashion their deeds after other folk;   1265
the fine things they say of me are foolish, unmerited.
But your worshipful self thinks well of everything."
"By Mary," said the fine lady, "I find it otherwise.
Were I worth the host of all women now living,
with all the wealth of the world in my hands,   1270
forced to bargain and choose to buy me a lord,
from the nature I've seen, Knight, here in thee
—beauty, good breeding and blithe demeanor—
and from what I have heard and hold to be true,
no champion on earth should be chosen before you."   1275
"Noble lady," the man said, "you have made a better choice.
But I am proud of the price that you put on me;
soberly, I'm your servant, my sovereign I hold you,
and your knight I become. May Christ repay you!"
So they murmured this-and-that till past mid-morning,   1280
and the lady let on that she loved him much
while the man, on his guard, behaved gracefully.
"Were I the loveliest of women," so the lady was thinking,
"there's little love in his manner"—for he must face danger
                               with speed,   1285
         a blow to lay him low;
         he could not shun that deed.
         So the lady made to go
         and he at once agreed.

52   She gave him good-day, glanced at him, laughing,   1290
then, standing there, stunned him with strong words:
"May He who prospers speech repay you this sport!
But whether you are Gawain—a doubt goes through me."
"Why?" asked the knight, and he said it anxiously,
fearful of failing in speech-formality;   1295
but the woman blessed him and answered this way:
"One as good as Gawain is granted to be,
revealing courtesy so clearly in himself,
not lightly could linger so long near a lady
without craving a kiss in his great courtesy,   1300
at some trifling hint at the tale's ending!"

Then Gawain said: "Willingly; do as you want.
I shall kiss at your command, as becomes a knight
and more, lest he displease; so plead no further."
At that she comes nearer, catches him in her arms,   1305
bends down courteously and kisses the man.
Graciously they commend one another to Christ.
She goes out the door without more ado;
he hastens to rise and soon arrays himself,
calls to his chamberlain, chooses his robe,   1310
and when he is clothed comes forth blithely to mass.
Then he went to the meal that was waiting, worthy of him,
and made merry all day till the moon arose,
                              with game.
    Better no man could do: 1315
    on each side a noble dame,
    the old, the young one too.
    Among them, much joy came.

53   The lord of the land was still lingering in sport,
hunting holt and heath for the barren hinds.   1320
The number there slain, before the sun sloped down,
of does and other deer, is too difficult to count.
Fiercely the folk flocked in for the finish,
and quickly made a quarry of the deer there killed.
The nobles hurried in with men enough;   1325
they gathered the fattest of the game there
and cut it up carefully, as is the custom;
they searched the flesh of some, to assay it,°
and in the poorest found it two fingers deep.
They slit the throat-hollow, seized the stomach,   1330
flayed it with a sharp knife, tied the white flesh,
ripped the four limbs apart and rent off the hide.
They broke the belly and took out the bowels,
throwing them away quickly, then the flesh-knot.
They gripped the throat, and thriftily divided   1335
the gullet from the wind-pipe and pulled out the guts,
then sheared off the shoulder-blades with sharp knives,
pulling them through a small hole, to leave whole the sides.
They sliced the breast and split it in two,
then they began again on the gullet   1340
and rapidly cut it right up to the fork,
threw out the waste part, and after that
fittingly slit the fillets by the ribs,

1328*assay it.* Find out about its quality.

cleared them off neatly near the backbone
as far as the haunches, till all hung together,   1345
then heaved it up whole and hewed it off;
some parts, I know, are named numbles,° and these
        they find.
   At the forking of the thigh,
   loose skin they cut behind;   1350
   to hew it in two they try,
   and the backbone they unbind.

54 They then hewed off both the head and the neck,
  swiftly sundering the sides from the spine,
  and the "raven's fee"° they flung into the bushes.   1355
  They ran a hole in each thick side through the ribs,
  and hung up both by the hocks° of the haunches;
  each fellow had for his fee what was fitting.
  On the hide of a fair beast they fed their hounds
  with the liver, the lungs, and the paunch's lining;   1360
  bread soaked with blood was blended with it.
  Boldly they blew the prize-blast; the rachets bayed.
  They took their flesh-meat and turned towards home,
  sounding right stoutly many shrill notes.
  When daylight was gone all the company gathered   1365
  in the noble castle where the knight waited,
        all still,
   with bliss and bright fires burning.
   The lord drew near, until
   Gawain and the one returning   1370
   met with right good will.

55 The lord commanded that his household be called,
  that both ladies come downstairs with their damsels.
  Before the by-standers he bade his followers
  bring all his venison before him at once.   1375
  Making a game of it, he called Gawain,
  told him the number of nimble beasts taken,
  showed him how fair the fat flesh on the ribs.
  "Are you pleased with this sport? Have I won praise?
  Have I merited thanks by this skill of mine?"   1380
  "Yes, indeed," said the other, "here are the best spoils
  I've seen for seven years in the winter season."

[1347] *numbles.* Internal organs.
[1355] *"raven's fee."* The gristle, thrown away for the ravens to eat.
[1357] *hocks.* The joints at the bottom and back of the deer's legs, corresponding to human ankles.

"I leave it to you, Gawain," the lord answered.
"According to our covenant, you may claim it as yours."
"That is true," said the knight, "and I'll tell you, too,   1385
what I've worthily won within these walls;
yes, with as much good will it is yours."
He enfolds the man's fair neck in his arms,
kissing him as nicely as he knows how.
"There, take my winnings; I've won nothing more.   1390
I would give it freely were it even greater."
"That's good," said the fine man; "I give thanks for it.
Such a gift is the best; you had better tell me
where you won this same wealth by your own wits."
"That was not in our pact," said he. "Press me no further.   1395
You have taken what's yours; trust that no more can be
                              your due."
          They laughed and acted gay
          with courtly jesting true,
          then to supper went straightway   1400
          with enough dainties new.

56   Then they sat in their chamber by the chimney side
      where the waiters kept plying them with choice wine,
      and, still making game, they agreed in the morning
      to keep the same promise they had pledged before: 1405
      whatever chance befell, to make an exchange
      of the new things gained when they met at night.
      They accepted this covenant before the whole court;
      beverages were brought in, jokes bandied about,
      then with lordly manners they took leave at last,   1410
      and each man went briskly off to his bed.
      When the cock had crowed and called only three times
      the lord leaped from his bed, his liegemen too.
      They took their meal, heard mass properly,
      and were ready for the woods before day had risen,   1415
                              for the chase.
          Huntsmen with loud horns
          in the fields' open space
          uncoupled among the thorns
          hounds ready for the race.   1420

57   They cried the quest soon by the marsh-side;
      hunters urged on the hounds that first held the scent,
      hurling wild words at them with a horrible noise;
      the hounds that heard them hurried up swiftly
      and fell fast on the trail, forty at once.   1425

Then such clamor and uproar of gathered rachets
arose, that the rocks all about rang loudly;
hunters heartened them with their horns and voices.
Then all in a swarm they swayed on together
between a forest pool and a frightful crag;   1430
on a stone-pile by the cliff, at the swamp-side,
there where the rough rocks had ruggedly fallen,
they pressed on to the lair with the people following.
They raced round the crag and the rock-pile both,
these men, for they knew well that he was in there—
the beast for whom the blood-hounds were baying.   1435
They beat in the bushes and bade him rise up;
wildly he lunged at the men in his way.
The most splendid of wild swine swung out at them
     there;
long away from the herd, he was hoary with age.   1440
He was a brave one, the biggest of boars,
mighty grim when he growled; then many grieved,
for at one thrash he thrust three men to earth,
then hurtled forth speedily, doing no more harm.
The others hallooed: "Hi!", cried loudly: "Hey! Hey!"   1445
Many merry voices of men and of horns
cried after the boar with clamor and noise:
                                        now quell!
          Often he waits at bay
          and maims the pack who fell;   1450
          he hurts the hounds, and they
          right loudly yowl and yell.

58   A band then showed up to shoot at him,
     aimed with their arrows and hit him often.
     The points failed on the skin protecting his shoulders   1455
     and the barbs would not bite into his brows;
     though the shaven shafts shivered into pieces,
     the heads hopped off wherever they hit.
     But, stunned by the blows of strong strokes
     and brain-mad for the fray, he rushes at the folk,   1460
     hurting them fiercely as he hurries on;
     many, frightened at that, drew back in fear.
     But the lord dashed after him on a light horse;
     like a bold hunter he blows his bugle,
     sounds the rally, riding through rank shrubbery,   1465
     chasing this wild swine till the sun shone high.
     Thus they passed that whole day in these same doings,
     while our lovable knight lies in his bed,

Gawain, comfortable at home, under bed-clothes rich
                              of hue.   1470
        The lady did not forget
        her greeting to renew.
        Right early she was set
        to move his mind anew.

59   She approaches the curtain and peeps at the knight.   1475
     Sir Gawain welcomes her at once, worthily,
     and she retorts, ready with her words,
     settles softly beside him, laughs heartily,
     and with loving looks speaks in low words:
     "Sir, if you are Gawain, it seems wonderful   1480
     that a man so well trained in polite ways
     should not act in company with correct manners,
     or, if you do know them, should drop them from mind.
     You have totally forgotten what I taught you yesterday
     in the plainest talk in which I could tell you."   1485
     "What is that?" said the knight. "Surely, I know nothing.
     If what you mention is true, the blame is all mine."
     "I gave a lesson in kissing," said the fair lady,
     "how to claim one quickly when the chance comes;
     that becomes a knight who tries to be courteous!"   1490
     "Stop such talk, my dear," the strong man answered.
     "That I dare not do, lest I be denied;
     if refused, I would be wrong for having requested."
     "My faith!" said the merry lady. "You will not be refused;
     you are strong and can use force, if you feel like it, 1495
     if one were so rude as to refuse you!"
     "Yes, by God," said Gawain. "What you say is good,
     but force is unlucky in the land I live in,
     so too a gift not given with good will.
     I am at your command, to kiss when you like;   1500
     you may start when you please and stop when you think well,
                              for a space."
        Then the lady bent low
        and sweetly kissed his face,
        and long they talked on so   1505
        of true love's grief and grace.

60   "I would know from you, Sir," that noble one said,
     "without rousing your anger, what is the reason
     why one young and fresh as you are at this time,
     so courteous, so knightly, as all know you to be—   1510
     for the choice parts of chivalry, the points most praised,

are love's loyal sport and the true lore of arms;
telling the struggles of these true knights,
that is the title and text of such writings:
how heroes for true love have ventured their lives,   1515
have endured for love's sake most doleful days,
then avenged all and ended their cares by valor,
bringing bliss into bowers by their bountifulness.
And you are the noblest knight of your times;
your renowned honor runs before you everywhere,   1520
yet I have sat by you here twice already
and have won from your mouth not a single word
that savors of love, either less or more!
And you, so polite, so deft with your promises,
ought to yearn to show to such a young thing   1525
some token of love's true craft, and teach her.
Why! Are you ignorant, you whom all praise?
Do you think me too dull to harken to dalliance?
       For shame!
   Alone I come and sit   1530
   to learn from you this game;
   come, teach me by your wit
   while my lord's too far to blame."

61 "In good faith," said Gawain, "may God repay you!
It brings great gladness and right good cheer   1535
that one worthy as you are should want to come
and take pains with so poor a man, playing with your knight
with favorable demeanor; it delights me.
But to take up the task of expounding true love,
to touch on such themes and tales of arms   1540
to you who, I know well, are so much wiser
in that art, by a half, than a hundred such
as I am or shall be while I live on earth,
would be manifold folly, fair one, by my faith!
I shall do as you please with all my power,   1545
as I am bound to do; I will be evermore
your very servant; so may the Lord save me!"
Thus the fair lady tried him, and attempted often
to win him to wickedness, to what she wanted.
But his defence was so gracious that no fault was seen,   1550
no evil on either side, and they knew nothing
       but bliss
   Long they laughed and played;
   at last she gave a kiss,
   with fair goodbyes, and stayed   1555
   no longer after this.

62   Then the man bestirs himself, rising for mass,
      and their dinner was dished up and duly served.
      The knight spent all day in sport with the ladies,
      but the lord was galloping through the open lands   1560
      for the unlucky boar that swung past the banks
      and bit asunder the backs of the best brachets
      while he waited at bay, till the bowmen broke in
      and made him, despite himself, move onward,
      so fierce flew the arrows where the folk gathered.   1565
      Yet he forced the stoutest to stop sometimes,
      till at last, so spent he could speed on no more,
      he came with what haste he could to a hole
      in a rise by a rock where the brook runs.
      He gets the bank at his back, begins to scrape;   1570
      the froth from his mouth's ugly corners foams out
      as he whets his white tusks. They were all too tired,
      the men so bold who were standing by,
      to hurt him from afar; in such danger, none dared
                               draw near.   1575
               He had hurt so many before
               that all were full of fear
               that his tusks would tear them more
               so frenzied did he appear.

63   Then the knight came himself, urging his horse,   1580
      seeing the boar at bay with the men beside him.
      He alights gracefully and leaves his courser,
      draws a bright brand and bravely strides on,
      hurrying through the ford where the fierce thing waited.
      The wild beast was aware of him, weapon in hand;   1585
      his hairs bristled up, hatefully he snorted
      till many feared for the man, lest the worst befall him.
      Then the swine rushed out and set full on him,
      till the knight and the boar were both in one heap
      where the water ran rough. The boar had the worst of it,   1590
      for the man aimed a blow as they first met,
      set his sharp sword in the breast-bone, surely,
      drove it up to the hilt till the heart split.
      Snarling he gave way and, crossing the water,
                               he fled.   1595
               A hundred hounds came fast,
               and their fierce bites brought dread.
               Men drove him forth at last
               and the dogs killed him dead.

64 The capture was blown on bright-sounding horns   1600
    with loud, high halooing from men lusty enough;
    brachets bayed at the beast as their masters bade,
    the leading huntsmen of that hard chase.
    A man who was wise in woodland craft
    zestfully begins the boar's dismembering.   1605
    First he hews off the head and sets it on high,
    then rends straight down the back very roughly,
    tears out the bowels, burns them on the coals,
    and with these mixed with bread rewards the brachets.
    Then he slices the brawn into broad, bright slabs,   1610
    pulls out edible entrails in the proper manner;
    yet in one whole he puts the halves together,
    then stoutly hangs them on a strong pole.
    Now with this same swine they hasten homeward,
    with the boar's head borne before the hero   1615
    who had slain it with the force of his own strong hand
                                        at the ford.
                He did not see Gawain
                for a long time in the hall,
                but, to claim rewards again,   1620
                the knight came at his call.

65 The lord called with loud words, laughing merrily
    and talking joyously when he saw Sir Gawain.
    The good ladies were called and the household gathered;
    he shows them the sliced flesh, and tells the story   1625
    of the weight and the length of the wild swine
    and of the fierce war as he fled through the woods.
    The knight courteously commended his deed
    and praised it as proof of his great prowess,
    for such brawn in a beast, the bold knight said,   1630
    and such sides on a swine he had never seen.
    Then they handled the huge head; the handsome man praised it
    and let on to feel horror, to honor the lord.
    "Now, Gawain," said the good man, "this game is your own,
    by our fast-binding promise, as you know, faithfully."   1635
    "That is true," said the man, "and just as truthfully
    I shall again give you my gains, on my honor."
    He clasps the knight's neck and delicately kisses him,
    then at once served him in the same way again.
    "Now we are even," said Gawain, "this evening-time,   1640
    by all the covenants made since I came hither,
                                so true!"

The lord said: "By Saint Gile!
No better man than you!
You'll be rich in a short while   1645
if such bargaining you do!"

66   Then they put up the tables on their trestles
and covered them with cloths; the clear light then
wakened on the walls from waxen torches;
the meal was set out and served through the hall.   1650
A happy clamor rang out from the crowd
around the hearth-fire, and in varied fashion
at supper and afterwards, many noble songs,
tunes for Christmastime, and new carols,
with all sorts of mirth that men tell of—   1655
our lovable knight always by the lady's side.
So gracious was her manner as she dealt with the man
with still, stolen glances to please that staunch one,
that he was bewildered and blamed himself.
But through good breeding he would not gainsay° her;   1660
he dealt with her delicately, however the deed might turn
                              at last.
        After playing in the hall
        as long as the wish might last,
        from his room he heard the lord call;   1665
        to the chimney side they passed.

67   There they drank and played, and promised again
to observe the same terms on New Year's eve.
But the knight asked leave to be off in the morning;
that appointment was near to which he was pledged.   1670
The lord put him off and pressed him to linger,
saying: "As a man of honor, I assure thee in truth
thou shalt be at the Green Chapel to take thy chances,
Sir, with the New Year's light, long before prime.°
So, lie in thy room and lounge at ease;   1675
I shall hunt in the woods, bring thee the winnings,
and change booty with thee when I come back,
for I have tested thee twice and found thee trustworthy.
Now, 'third throw the best!' Think of that in the morning;
make merry while we may and be mindful of joy,   1680
for sorrow is met with whenever men wish."
This was graciously granted, and Gawain lingered on;
cheering drinks were brought, then to bed they went

1660*gainsay.* Deny.   1674*prime.* Dawn.

                    with their light.
           Sir Gawain lies and sleeps   1685
           right still and soft all night;
           the lord to his purpose keeps,
           and early is clad aright.

68   After mass the lord and his men took a morsel.
     Merry was the morning; he asked for his mount;   1690
     all the hunters who were following him on horseback
     were soon high on their steeds before the hall gate.
     Very fair were the fields, for the frost clung;
     ruddy-red through cloud-banks the sun was rising,
     skirting the clouds into the clear sky.   1695
     The hunters loosened their hounds by a holt side;
     rocks rang in the covert with the cry of horns.
     Some fell on the track where the fox lurked,
     trailing back and forth with tricky wiles.
     A small hound gives the cry, hunters call after him,   1700
     the pack falls in line, panting fast,
     running in a rabble right on his trail
     while he scampers before them. They soon find him,
     and when they catch sight of him swiftly pursue,
     crying after him clearly, with a fierce clamor   1705
     as he dodges and turns through many dense groves,
     doubles back and harkens by a hedge, often.
     At last, by a little ditch, he leaps a thorn hedge,
     steals out stealthily by a skirting thicket,
     trying to slip the hounds by a trick, through the woods.   1710
     Too late he found himself near a fine hunting-station
     where three strong hounds at once harried him,
                        all gray
           Quick, he swerved again
           and staunchly ran astray;   1715
           driven by great pain
           in the wood he went away.

69   Then it was lively sport to listen to the hounds
     when the whole pack met and mingled together;
     at that sight they called down loud curses on his head,   1720
     as if clustering cliffs had clattered into heaps.
     Here he was halooed when the heroes met him,
     loudly taunted with testy shouts;
     there he was threatened, often called a thief,
     and with trail-dogs at his tail he could not tarry.   1725
     Often they ran at him when he rushed out

and as often reeled in again; so wily was Renard!°
Yes, he led till they got left, the lord and his followers,
through the hills in this manner until mid-day,
while at home the noble knight wholesomely sleeps   1730
within handsome curtains through that cold morning.
But the lady's love would not let her sleep
or fail in the purpose fixed in her heart.
She arose swiftly and came straight there
in a gorgeous mantle that reached to the ground,   1735
all finely furred with well-finished skins,
on her head no bright colors, but well-cut gems
twisted through her hair in clusters of twenty;
her fair face and neck were left naked,
her breast bare in front and behind also.   1740
She comes through the chamber door, closes it after her,
casts up a window and calls to the knight,
promptly rallying him with pleasant words
                                          and cheer.
            "Ah, man! How canst thou sleep   1745
            when the morning is so clear?"
            He was drowsing deep,
            but then he began to hear.

70   In the moody gloom of a dream the noble man muttered
     like a man mourning for many dire thoughts: 1750
     how destiny, that day, would deal him his Wyrd°
     at the Green Chapel when he meets the champion
     and waits for his buffet without more words.
     When that fair one came he recovered his wits,
     swung out of his dreams and speedily answered.   1755
     Then the lovely lady, laughing sweetly,
     bent down to his fair face and daintily kissed him.
     He welcomes her worthily, with well-bred manners;
     seeing her so glorious, so gayly attired,
     so faultless in feature, with such fine coloring,   1760
     joy ardently welled up, warming his heart.
     With sly, gentle smiles they broke into merry speech;
     all was blissful happiness between them, with joy
                                          alight.
            They bantered words so good   1765
            with much gladness bright;

1727 *Renard.* The wily fox hero of a series of beast fables popular in the Middle Ages.
1751 *Wyrd.* Fate.

> great peril between them stood,
> had not Mary watched her knight!

71 For that precious princess pressed him so strongly,
   urged him so near the edge that he needs must   1770
   either return her love or rudely refuse her.
   He was careful of courtesy, lest he prove craven,
   more careful of the mischief if she made him sin
   and be traitor to the man who ruled that mansion.
   "God shield us," said the knight, "that shall never be!"   1775
   With a little love-laughter he lightly turned off
   all the fond speeches that fell from her mouth.
   Said the lady to the brave knight: "You are to blame
   if you love not the person near whom you are lying,
   who's more wounded in heart than anyone in the world,   1780
   unless you have a sweetheart who suits you better,
   and are pledged to some fair one by so fast a bond
   that you don't want to break it; that I now believe.
   Tell me so now, truly, I pray you;
   by all the loves there are, let not the truth hide   1785
>   under guile!"
>   The knight said: "By Saint John!"
>   And with a gracious smile:
>   "In faith, I yet have none,
>   nor will have, for a while."   1790

72 "That word," said the lady, "is the worst of all,
   but it's a true answer, and troubles me sorely.
   Now kiss me graciously and I'll go away;
   I can but mourn on earth, as a maiden who loves much."
   Sighing, she leaned down and kissed him sweetly,   1795
   then, before starting off, stood still, saying:
   "Now dear, at this parting, do me this favor:
   give me some gift, thy glove perhaps,
   to remember thee by, Sir, and so lessen my mourning."
   "Indeed," said the knight, "I wish now I had here   1800
   the best thing, for thy love, that I have in the land.
   For you have earned, in truth, and most excellently,
   more reward, by right, than I can reckon.
   But to give you a love-token would avail little;
   it would not honor you to own just now   1805
   a glove for a keepsake, of Gawain's giving,
   and I am here on an errand to an unknown land,
   with no servants with trunks full of treasured things.
   That troubles me, Lady, for love's sake, at this time.

Each man does his best; take it not amiss,   1810
                            nor repine."
            "No, knight of honor true,"
            said that beauty, clad so fine,
            "though I have no gift from you,
            you shall have one of mine."   1815

73   She gave him a rich ring of red gold-work,
     with a gleaming stone standing out on it
     that shot blazing beams like the bright sun;
     be sure it was worth a vast deal of wealth!
     But the knight refused it, and firmly said: 1820
     "No gifts for good and all, just now, gracious one.
     I have none to offer, and none will I take."
     She begged him earnestly; he refused her bidding
     and swore hard, by his truth, that he would not touch it.
     Sorry that he spurned it, she said at once: 1825
     "If you refuse my ring for seeming too rich,
     and you do not want to be so indebted,
     I shall give you my girdle, a less gain to you!"
     Lightly, she took a lace that lay round her waist,
     fastened to her skirts under her fair mantle;   1830
     it was made of green silk all set with gold,
     bordered with nothing less, embroidered by hand.
     She pressed it on the knight, light-heartedly pleading
     that he would take it, though it was worthless.
     And he swore that he would not, in any way, touch   1835
     either gold or treasure, till God send him grace
     to achieve the adventure he had undertaken.
     "And therefore, I pray you, be not displeased;
     give up your urging, for to grant this I'll never
                            agree.   1840
            I am dearly in your debt
            for your gracious ways to me.
            Come heat or cold, ever yet
            your servant true I'll be."

74   "Do you refuse this silk," said the fair lady then,   1845
     "because it is so simple? So it seems indeed.
     Look! it's so little, worth less than nothing!
     But one who knew what qualities are knitted into it
     would perhaps appraise it at a higher price.
     If a man is girded with this green lace,   1850
     while he has it fairly fastened about him
     no hero under heaven can hew him down;

he cannot be slain by any sleights° on earth."
The knight hesitated; it came into his heart
that this would be a jewel in the jeopardy ahead   1855
when he found himself at the Chapel to face his blow;
it would be a good way to get through alive!
So he listened to her pleading, letting her speak
as she pressed the belt on him and bade him take it,
until he agreed. She gave it with good will,   1860
asking him, for her sake, not to let it be seen,
but conceal it from her lord; the knight consented
that no-one, truly, save they two should know it
                                by right.
    He thanked her heartily,   1865
    and thought with all his might.
    By that time, kisses three
    she had given her brave knight.

75   Then she takes her leave and lets him be;
she could get no more pleasure out of that man.   1870
When she has gone, Sir Gawain soon gets ready,
rises and robes himself in noble array,
lays by the love-lace that the lady gave him,
hiding it carefully where he could find it.
His chief idea was to get to the chapel.   1875
He approached a priest privately, and there prayed him
to purify his life, and plainly teach him
how to save his soul when his end was in sight.
He confessed fully, declared his faults,
great and small, and sought for mercy,   1880
then implored absolution from the priest
who absolved him well and made him as clean
as if doomsday were due the next morning.
Then he makes merrier among the fair ladies
with lovely carols and all kinds of joy   1885
than ever before that day, till the dark night,
                                blissfully.
    Each man was well treated there
    by him, and said: "Just see!
    He has shown no merrier air   1890
    since he came, till now—surely!"

76   Let him linger in that shelter; may love come his way!
The lord is abroad, still leading his men.

1853*sleights.* Cunning tricks.

He has outstripped the fox that he followed so long,
springing over a thorn-hedge to spy out the rascal.   1895
When he heard the hounds pressing hard after him
Renard came racing through a rugged grove
with the whole rabble rushing right at his heels.
The man watched for the wild thing, waiting warily,
then drew out his bright brand and thrust at the beast   1900
who swerved from its sharp edge and tried to shunt.
A hound hurried up to him as he hastened off,
and right at the horses' feet they all fell on him
and worried that wily one with a wild noise.
The lord alights quickly and soon catches him,   1905
snatches him hastily from the mouths of the hounds,
holds him high over head, halooing loudly;
many bold hounds were baying up at him.
Hunters hurried in with their many horns,
sounding high the recall, till they saw the knight.   1910
When the gallant company had all gathered,
those who carried bugles blew them together
and the others halooed, those who had no horns.
It was the merriest hound-baying that ever men heard,
a mighty noise raised there for Renard's soul,   1915
                          a din!
          Men pat and rub each head
          of the hounds who praises win;
          then they take Renard, dead,
          and strip him of his skin.   1920

77   Then they turn towards home, for night-time is near,
     blowing right stoutly on their sturdy horns.
     The lord alights at last at his loved home,
     finds a fire on the hearth with the hero beside it,
     good Sir Gawain, who was glad to be there   1925
     among the ladies, enjoying their love-making.
     He wore a blue robe that reached to the floor,
     his softly furred surcoat fitted him well
     and a hood to match it hung on his shoulders,
     both adorned with white fur all around them.   1930
     He met the good man in the middle of the hall
     greeting him jokingly in just the right way:
     "I shall now be the first to fulfill our pledge
     that we luckily spoke of as we drank unsparingly."
     He took hold of the knight and kissed him three times   1935
     with relish, as soundly as he rightly could.
     "By Christ," said that other, "you made a lucky catch
     in getting these wares, if the bargain was good!"

"Yes, ask not the cost," said the other quickly,
"since plainly I have paid the price that I owe." 1940
"Mary!" said the other man. "My gift is much less,
for all day I have hunted, and I have nothing
but this foul fox's skin; the fiend take such goods!
That's a poor price to pay for such precious things
as you've heartily thrust on me, these three kisses 1945
              so good."
        "Enough," said Sir Gawain,
        "I thank you, by the Rood."°
        And how the fox was slain
        he was told, there where he stood. 1950

78   With mirth, with minstrelsy, with the meats they wanted,
they made as merry as any men might
while the ladies were laughing with light jests.
Both Gawain and the good man were glad as could be—
short of all going silly or getting drunk! 1955
Lord and retainers both bandied their jokes
till the time came when the two must part;
the knights were bound for their beds at last.
Then he humbly took leave of the lord first;
the well-bred knight thanked him warmly: 1960
"For the happy sojourn I have had here,
and your honor at this festival, the High King repay you!
I give myself over as your man, if you like,
for I must, as you know, move on tomorrow.
Give me someone, as you promised, to guide my way 1965
to the Green Chapel, that God may allow me
to do on the New Year what my Wyrd dooms for me."
"By my faith," said the good man, "with good will
I shall promptly do all that I promised you."
He assigned him a servant to set him on the way 1970
leading over the downs, that nothing might daunt him
riding in the woods by a path through the groves
              most nigh.
        And now Gawain must thank
        for favors heaped so high. 1975
        To the ladies of proud rank
        the knight then said goodbye.

79   He kissed them sorrowfully and spoke to all,
beseeching them to accept his earnest thanks,

1948 *Rood.* Cross.

and they promptly said the same thing to him.   1980
They commended him to Christ with cold sighing.
He parted courteously from the household company,
telling every man that he met of his thanks
for the service, the kindness, the care each had taken
to be always busy about serving him;   1985
and the men were as pained to part from him there
as though they had dwelt with that dauntless knight always.
Then with servants and lights he was led to his chamber
and brought cheerfully to bed, to be at rest.
If he slept soundly, I dare not say so;   1990
he had much to be mindful of about the next morning
                              in thought.
         So let him lie there still
         nearer to what he sought.
         If you, for a while, keep still,   1995
         I shall tell you what day brought.

Part Four

80   The New Year draws close now, the night passes,
     day breaks through the dark as the Lord bids it;
     but the world's wildest weather wakened outside,
     clouds cast their coldness to earth, keenly,   2000
     with sting enough from the north to pain the naked.
     Snow shivered down sharply, snapping at the wild things;
     the whistling winds whipped out of the sky
     and drove each dale full of deep drifts.
     The knight listened while he lay in his bed;   2005
     though he locks his eye-lids, little can he sleep!
     By each cock that crew he knew too well what called him.
     He got up early before the dawn glimmered,
     for light shone from a lamp lit in his chamber.
     Calling to his chamberlain who quickly answered   2010
     he said to bring his byrny and saddle his horse.
     The other got up and fetched his garments,
     then made Gawain ready in a great fashion.
     First he put clothes on him to ward off the cold,
     then his other harness that was handsomely kept,   2015
     all the pieces of plate-armor polished clean,
     rings rubbed clear of rust in his rich mail-shirt.
     All was fresh as at first; he found words of thanks
                              at need.
         He then put on each piece,   2020

well shined up, fine indeed.
The most sprightly from here to Greece,
the man bade bring his steed.

81 He then garbed himself in his richest garments—
his coat with blazonry of the best needle-work   2025
stitched upon velvet, stones of high value
set in it, well-made with embroidered seams,
finely furred inside with a fair lining.
Yet the lace was not left out, the lady's gift;
Gawain could not forget it, for his own good!   2030
After belting his sword on his broad thighs
he twisted the love-token twice about him.
The knight folded it well round his neck with delight;
the girdle of green silk suited that fine man,
on the royal red cloth so rich to look at.   2035
Not for its great worth he wore this girdle,
nor for pride in its pendants, though they were polished
and glittering gold gleamed at their ends,
but to save himself when he needs must suffer,
waiting death with no struggle, with no sword or   2040
                                knife for defence.
        When the bold man was dressed
        quickly he parted thence.
        To that famed court he expressed
        his thanks in recompense.   2045

82 Then Gryngolet was made ready, a great, huge horse
comfortably stabled in secure fashion;
the proud steed was fit and eager to prance.
The knight comes up to look at his coat,   2050
and says soberly to himself, swearing by his honor:
"The servants in this castle are mindful of courtesy,
their lord well maintains them; may they have joy!
And the dear lady living here, may love come her way!
If for charity they so cherish a guest
with such perfect manners, may He repay them   2055
who owns heaven above—and all of you also!
If my life goes on a while longer in this world,
I shall somehow reward you, willingly, if I may."
He steps into the stirrups and springs aloft.
A man gives him his shield; he lays it on his shoulder   2060
and strikes spurs into Gryngolet with his gilt heels.
The steed kicks the stones; waiting no more, he starts
                                to prance.

On horseback the knight sits, fit
to bear his spear and lance.   2065
"This castle to Christ I commit!"
He wishes it good chance.

83   The bridge was drawn down, and the broad gates
      unbarred and borne open on both sides.
      The man blessed himself quickly and crossed the boarding;   2070
      he praised the porter kneeling before the prince
      wishing good-day and God-speed—may He save Gawain!
      He went on his way with only one waiting-man
      to tell him where to turn off for that terrible place
      where he has to meet a hideous onslaught.   2075
      They go on by banks where the boughs are bare;
      they climb along cliffs where the cold clings.
      Clouds hung high overhead; underneath it was ugly,
      mist drizzling on the moor and melting on the mountains.
      Each hill had a hat on, a huge mist-cloak;   2080
      brooks boiled and broke against their banks,
      brightly spattering the shores as they shot down.
      Very wandering was the way they must take through the woods,
      until soon came the hour for the sun to rise
                              that day.   2085
          They were on a hill-top high,
          around the white snow lay.
          The man that rode so nigh
          then bade his master stay.

84   "I have led you here, my Lord, at this time,   2090
      and you are not far from that famous place
      that you've searched for and sought so earnestly.
      I speak the truth now, since I know you,
      and you are the living man whom I love most:
      if you follow my thought you will fare better.   2095
      The place that you press toward is held to be perilous;
      a being dwells in that waste, the worst on earth,
      for he is staunch and stern and loves to strike out,
      huger than any man on this middle-earth,
      with a body bigger than the best four   2100
      who are in Arthur's house, Hector° or any other.
      He offers this chance at the Green Chapel:
      if one passes that place, even though proudly armed,

2101 *Hector.* The greatest Trojan warrior, killed by Achilles at the siege of Troy.

he dings° him to death with one dash of the hand.
He is a violent man who shows no mercy,   2105
for whether churl or chaplain rides by that chapel,
monk or mass-priest, or any man else,
he's as pleased to slay them as to still live himself!
So I say, as sure as you sit in that saddle,
if you get there you'll die—if that knight deals with you!   2110
Trust me truly in this, though you had twenty lives
                                        to spend.
       He dwelt here long of yore,
       battling without end.
       Against his buffets sore   2115
       your life you can't defend.

85   "And so, good Sir Gawain, let him get on alone;
go by another way, for God's own sake!
Ride to some other country where Christ will help you.
I shall hurry home, and I hereupon promise   2120
to swear by God and all His good saints
—so help me God, holy relics, and other good oaths—
truly to keep your secret, and tell no tales
of you trying to make off, for any man I know."
"Many thanks," said Gawain, and added grudgingly: 2125
"Good luck to you, Sir, for wishing my good;
I am certain you would loyally keep my secret.
But though you hid it faithfully, if I passed on,
taking flight through fear in the fashion you speak of,
I would be a coward knight, never to be excused.   2130
I will go to the chapel and take what chance comes;
I will talk to that fellow and tell him what I like,
come well-being or woe, whatever Wyrd wills me
                                        to brave.
       Though he stands there fierce to fight   2135
       with his big stick—the knave!
       the Lord can shape things right;
       His servants He will save."

86   "Marry!" said the other, "if thou dost insist
on bringing thine own doom down on thyself,   2140
and on losing thy life, I will no longer hinder.
Here: put helmet on head and take spear in hand,
and ride down this road by yonder rock's side
till thou get to the bottom of that grim valley.

²¹⁰⁴*dings.* Beats.

Look a little beyond the field on thy left hand   2145
and see in that valley the very chapel,
and on the ground the stout man who there keeps guard.
Now farewell, in God's name, Gawain the noble!
For all the gold in the world I would not go
through this forest in thy company one foot further."   2150
And there in the woods the man wields his bridle,
hits his horse with his heels as hard as he can,
leaps over the fields and leaves the knight
                                              alone.
     "By God Himself," said Gawain,   2155
     "I will not grieve nor groan.
     To God's will I bow again;
     I give Him all I own."

87   Then he spurs Gryngolet, sets out on the path,
     goes in by a ridge at a grove's side   2160
     and rides by the rough bank right into the dale.
     Then he looks around and all appears wild to him,
     seeing no sign of refuge on any side,
     only banks high and steep in both directions
     with rough gnarled rocks and rugged stones;   2165
     the clouds seemed grazed by the jagged cliffs.
     Then he halted a moment, holding in his horse,
     and turned his face everywhere to find the chapel.
     He saw no such anywhere—he thought it strange—
     save a little off in a field what looked like a mound,   2170
     a bare barrow° by the bank of a brimming stream
     near the falls of brook that was flowing there.
     The brook bubbled as though it were boiling.
     The knight urges his horse and comes to the hill,
     alights gracefully and fastens to a linden tree   2175
     the reins of his fine steed on a rough branch.
     Then he went to the mound and walked all around it,
     debating within himself what it might be.
     It had a hole in the end and on either side,
     overgrown with patches of grass everywhere,   2180
     and all was hollow within, only an old cave
     or a crevice of an old crag; which he could not guess
                                              or say well.
          "Ah, Lord!" said the gentle knight,
          "is this the Green Chapel?   2185

2171*barrow.* Hill.

Here, at about midnight
might the devil his Matins° tell!

88   "Now indeed," said Gawain, "it is gruesome here;
this oratory° is ugly, overgrown with weeds.
Well it suits that creature clothed all in green   2190
to do his devotions in the devil's way!
Now I feel it is the fiend, in my five wits,
who has arranged this meeting to undo me here.
It's a chapel of mischance; bad luck check-mate it!
It's the cursedest church that I ever came into."   2195
With helmet on head and lance in hand
he made for the rocks of that rough dwelling.
Then he heard from the high hill, on a hard rock
beyond the stream, on a bank, a strangely loud noise.
Ho! It clattered on the cliff as though to cleave it,   2200
like a scythe being ground upon a grind-stone.
Ho! It whirred and whirled like water at a mill.
Ho! It rushed and rang, nerve-wracking to hear!
"By God!" said Gawain. "That devise, I guess,
is meant to honor me, to meet me fitly   2205
                                        on the spot.
        "Let God work, Ah, lo!
        Sighing will help me not.
        Though my life I forgo,
        noise scares me not a jot!"   2210

89   Then the knight called out, high and clear:
"Who is master of this place, to keep his promise?
For Gawain the Good has now got right here.
If anyone wants something, let him come at once
—now or never—to do what he needs to!"   2215
"Wait!" came from the bank above his head.
"Thou shalt soon have all I once promised thee."
Yet the noise went on rushing rapidly a while
as he kept on with his whetting before coming down.
He makes his way by a crag and comes through a hole,   2220
whirling out of the nook with a nasty weapon,
a Danish axe new-sharpened for dealing the blow,
with a huge head bending towards the handle,
filed on a grind-stone, four feet broad
—no smaller for the lace girdle that gleamed brightly!   2225
And the man in green, all geared as at first,

2187*Matins*. Morning prayers.   2189*oratory*. A small chapel.

the face and the legs, the locks and the beard
(save that flat on the ground he walked on his feet),
set the handle on the stones and stalked nearer.
When he came to the water he would not wade,   2230
but hopped over on his axe and haughtily strode
over the broad field, fiercely angry,
                              through snow.
       Sir Gawain went to meet
       the knight, not bowing low.   2235
       The other said: "Now, Sir Sweet,
       thou wilt keep thy word, I know!"

90   "Gawain," said the green man, "God must look after thee!
Thou art welcome indeed, Sir, to my estate;
thou hast timed thy travel as a true man should,   2240
knowing the covenant we came to between us:
this time a twelvemonth didst thou take what fell to thee,
and I, this New Year, will eagerly repay thee.
We are in this valley by ourselves, verily;
there are none to part us, struggle as we please!   2245
Take the helmet from thy head, and have here thy payment;
make no more resistance than I made then
when you whipped my head off at one whop."
"No," said Gawain. "By God who gave me a soul,
I begrudge not one grain of any grief that comes.   2250
Only stop after one stroke, and I shall stand still
and show no reluctance to doing what you like—
                              nowhere."
       He bent his neck down low
       till the white flesh lay bare,   2255
       as if no fear could show.
       He flinched for no dread there!

91   The man dressed in green quickly drew himself up,
lifting his grim tool as if to smite Gawain;
With all the strength in his body he swung it aloft   2260
and aimed as desperately as though to destroy him.
Had it fallen down with the force he displayed
the ever-brave man would have died of that blow.
But Gawain glanced sidewise at that gisarm°
as it glided down to kill him on the ground;   2265
his shoulders shrank a little from the sharp iron.
The other with a swerve swept the bright blade aside,

2264gisarm. An ax.

then reproved the prince with puffed-up words,
"Thou art not Gawain," said he, "who is held so good,
who never flinched from a host on hill or in vale;   2270
now thou shrinkest for fear before feeling harm!
Such cowardice in that knight I could not hear of.
I swerved not, nor fled, Sir, when thou didst swing at me;
I offered no cavilling in King Arthur's house.
My head flew to my feet, yet I never fled,   2275
and thou, before harm falls, shrinkest in heart.
The better man it behooves me to be now called,
                              therefore!"
    "I shrank once," Gawain said,
    "and so I will no more.   2280
    But once on the stones, my head
    I never can restore!

92   "Be quick, man, by my faith, and come to the point!
Deal my destiny to me, and do it out of hand.
I'll stand up to thy stroke and stagger no more   2285
till thine axe has hit me; here is my word for it!"
"Have at thee!" said the other, and heaved it aloft,
glaring as crossly as if he were crazy.
He swung mightily, but never cut the man,
withholding his hand hastily before it could do hurt.   2290
Gawain faithfully waited and flinched in no limb,
but stood as still as a stone, or else a stump
that grapples the rocky ground with a hundred roots.
Then the man in green called out merrily:
"So, now thou art whole-hearted, I must really hit.   2295
Turn up that grand hood that Arthur gave thee,
keep thy neck from this cut—if it can survive!"
Then Gawain, in mighty anger, said grimly:
"Why, thrash on, fierce man; thou threatenest too long;
I think my heart is afraid of thine own self."   2300
"Indeed," said the fellow, "for talking so fiercely
I will dally no longer, nor delay thine errand
                              right now."
    Then he stands firm for the blow
    and puckers both lip and brow.   2305
    Not strange if the other feared so
    that he hoped for no rescue now!

93   Lightly lifting his blade he let it fall square
with the barbed edge right on the bare neck;
though he hammered hard he hurt him not at all,   2310

but nicked him on one side and severed the skin.
The sharp edge reached the flesh through the fair fat,
till bright blood shot over his shoulders to the ground.
When the knight saw blood gleaming on the snow,
he sprang forth, feet together, more than a spear's length,   2315
firmly seized his helmet, set it on his head,
swung his fair shield around before his shoulders,
drew out his bright sword and spoke boldly.
Never since that man had been born of his mother
had he ever been half so happy in this world!   2320
"Cease thy blows, man, ask no more of me!
I have taken one stroke in this place without struggling.
If you give me more I shall gladly requite,
and toss them back readily—trust me for that—
                as a foe!   2325
        But one stroke was to fall;
        the compact was made so,
        formed in Arthur's hall.
        Therefore, good Sir, now ho!"

94   The man turned away, resting on his axe,   2330
set the shaft on the brook-shore and leaned on the sharp edge,
looking at the knight who had come to his land.
He saw him stand firm, fearless, undreading,
armed and dauntless; it did his heart good!
Then he speaks merrily in a mighty voice,   2335
telling the knight in roaring tones:
"Bold Sir, in these fields be not so fierce;
no man has mistreated thee with bad manners here,
nor acted but by contract made at the King's court.
I pledged one stroke—thou hast it; think thee well-paid.   2340
I release thee from the rest of all other rights.
Had I been brisker I could have dealt a buffet
more wrathfully, perhaps, and done thee real harm.
I threatened thee first with a feigned one, merrily,
not rending with a sore gash; I treated thee rightly,   2345
for the bargain that we framed on that first night.
For truly thou wert faithful and found trustworthy,
giving me all thy gains, as a good man should.
The second feint I made, Sir, for the morning
thou didst kiss my fair wife; those kisses thou gavest me.   2350
For these I tried thee with but two bare feints,
                no blow!
        A true man takes his due
        and then needs dread no woe.

The third time thou wast not true;   2355
   one tap thou must take—so!

95 "That's my garment thou art wearing, that same woven girdle;
my own wife wove it, as indeed I know well!
I know well, too, thy kisses, and all thy ways,
and my wife's wooing—I worked that myself!   2360
I sent her to try thee; thou art, I think truly,
the most faultless man who walks on his feet!
As a pearl is more precious than a white pea,
so is Gawain, in good faith, than other fine knights.
But you were a little lacking, Sir, wanting in loyalty,   2365
not for underhand doings or for wooing, either,
but for love of your life—the less I blame you!"
The strong knight stood a long while in a study,
so grievously ashamed that he groaned within;
all his heart's blood burned in his face   2370
and he shrank while the man talked on, for shame.
Then the first word that the knight uttered was:
"Cursed be cowardice and covetousness, both!
In you is villainy, and vice that spoils virtue."
He caught at the knot, loosening the clasp,   2375
and fiercely flung his belt at the bold man himself.
"See! There goes falseness; may evil go with it!
For fear of thy blow, cowardice forced me
to accord with covetousness, to forsake what becomes me:
liberality and loyalty that belong to knights.   2380
Now I am faulty and false, who have always feared
treachery and untruth—may trouble take them,
                         and care!
   I acknowledge, Knight, here still
   faultily did I fare;   2385
   let me now do thy will
   and after I shall beware."

96 Then the other man laughed, and said amiably:
"I hold it all healed, the harm that I met with.
Thou hast confessed so clean, declaring thy faults,   2390
openly doing penance at the point of my axe-edge,
I hold thee purged of offence, purified as clean
as if thou hadst not failed since thou was first born.
And I give thee, Sir, this gold-hemmed girdle;
it's as green as my gown. Sir Gawain, may you ever   2395
remember this contest as thou ridest out
among famous princes; it is a fair token

of the Green Chapel's adventure between chivalrous knights.
And you must come again, this New Year, to my castle,
to revel for the rest of this regal feast,   2400
                              pleasantly."
                 He pressed him hard, the lord:
                 "With my wife you will be
                 again in good accord,
                 though she was your enemy."   2405

97   "No, indeed!" said the knight; he seized his helmet,
     lifted it gracefully and thanked the lord.
     "I have sojourned long enough. May joy be with you;
     may He who rewards courtesy repay you freely!
     Commend me to that courtly one, your comely wife,   2410
     to both one and the other of mine honored ladies
     who contrived to beguile their knight by a trick.
     But it is no marvel if a fool go mad,
     and through woman's wiles be won, to his sorrow!
     So Adam in the garden was beguiled by one,   2415
     and Solomon by several, and Samson after him—
     Delilah dealt him his doom—and then David
     was deluded by Bathsheba and bore much misery.
     Since guile ruined such, it would be a gain
     to love women and not trust them, if a knight only would!   2420
     These were noblest in former times, favored by fortune
     more happily than other men who have been, under heaven,
                              bemused.
                 All these by wiles were caught
                 by women whom they used.   2425
                 Though now beguiled, I ought
                 to hold myself excused.

98   "But your girdle," added Gawain, "may God reward you!
     That I'll wear with good will, not for the fair gold,
     for the sash or the silk or the side-pendants,   2430
     not for wealth or honor or the proud workmanship,
     but in sign of my ill-doing; I shall see it often
     when I ride about, famous, and feel remorseful
     for the faultiness and weakness of perverse flesh—
     how fit it is to incur the stain of filth!   2435
     Thus when pride pricks me for prowess in arms,
     a look at this love-lace will bring my heart low.
     But one thing, I pray you—be not displeased—
     since you're lord of the land yonder where I lived
     with you so worshipfully—may He reward you   2440
     who upholds the heavens and reigns on high—

by what name you are rightly called, then no more?"
"That I shall tell thee," retorted the other.
"Bercilak de Hautdesert I am here called,
by the might of Morgan le Faye,° who dwells in my mansion,   2445
by her skillful lore and well-learned tricks.
Many magic arts she once took from Merlin,
for she had pleasant love-affairs in times long past
with that notable wizard, as your knights at home
                                all know.   2450
        Morgan the goddess, she;
        that's her name—just so!
        There is none of high degree
        that she cannot lay low.

99   "She sent me in this garb to your glorious hall   2455
to test its pride, and so prove true
what is rumored, the renown of the Round Table.
She worked this wonder on me to shake your wits,
to so daunt Gwenevere as to make her die
of dismay at that fellow who spoke like a phantom   2460
with his head in his hands before the high table.
She's the one now at home, that ancient lady;
she is thy very aunt, Arthur's half-sister,
daughter of Tintagel's Duchess, on whom trusty Uther
begot Arthur, now so nobly renowned.   2465
Therefore I urge thee, Knight, come to thine aunt,
make merry in my house. My menials love thee,
and Sir, I wish thee as well, by my faith,
as any one under God, for thy great loyalty."
He answered: No! He would not by any means.   2470
They embrace and kiss, and commend one another
to the Prince of paradise, and part right there
                                in the snow.
        Gawain on his horse is keen
        to be off to the King's court so.   2475
        And then the knight, bright green,
        goes where he wants to go.

2445 *Morgan le Faye.* Morgan le Faye was King Arthur's half-sister, daughter of Igraine, the Duchess of Tintagle
(l. 2464), and Uther, Arthur's father (l. 2464). Morgan possessed magical powers and was thus called a *fé* (Faye), the
French word for *fairy.* Gawain is the son of Arthur's half-sister Morgause. He is, therefore, nephew to both Morgan
(l. 2463) and Arthur. Merlin (l. 2447) is the wizard who helped Arthur become king. The poet's references to these
family relationships may be his way of alluding to the doom that will ultimately fall on Arthur's kingdom. Merlin
tricked Uther and Igraine into an adulterous relationship. They conceived Arthur against whom Morgan conspired.
Arthur's incest with Morgause conceived Mordred, who threw Arthur's kingdom into civil war and brought about
its ruin

100 Gawain rides through the world by wild ways now
on Gryngolet, his life given back by grace.
He lodged often in houses, and often outdoors,　　　　　　2480
met adventures in the valleys and always vanquished;
I cannot tell everything in my tale at this time.
The hurt that he had in his neck was healing,
and around it he bore the glittering belt,
aslant like a baldric bound to his side,　　　　　　　　2485
the lace in a knot tied under his left arm
as a token that he had been caught in a fault.
Thus the knight came back, safe and sound, to court.
Joy woke in that castle when the great King knew
that good Gawain had come; good news to him!　　　　　2490
The King kissed the knight, the Queen also,
then many goodly knights sought to greet him;
they asked how he fared, and he told them—fantastic!
He made known the grim troubles he had gone through:
what happened at the chapel, the knight's behavior,　　　2495
the love of the lady, and the lace at last.
He showed them the nick in his bare neck
that he got for disloyalty at the lord's hands,
　　　　　　　　　　　　in blame.
　　　He grieved at his disgrace,　　　　　　　　　　　2500
　　　he groaned and took the blame;
　　　the blood rushed to his face
　　　when he told it, to his shame.

101 "See, Lord," said the knight as he handled the lace,
"I bear this band round my neck, to blame me　　　　　2505
for the injury and the loss that I underwent,
for the cowardice and covetousness in which I was caught.
It's a token of the untruth in which I was taken;
I must wear it as long as my life lasts.
No one may hide a wrong, or ever remove it,　　　　　2510
for once fixed on him it cannot be unfastened."
The King comforted the knight, and the court also
laughed loudly at all this; they courteously agreed
—those lords and ladies who belonged to the Table—
that each of the brotherhood should have a baldric　　　2515
of bright green bound obliquely about him,
and for that knight's sake should wear the same.
That was agreed on, for the good of the Round Table,
and anyone wearing it was honored ever after,
as written in the best of the books of romance.　　　　2520
Thus in Arthur's times this adventure took place,

and all the Brut books° bear witness to it.
Since the bold Brutus first abode here
after the seige and the assault had ceased at Troy,
                I know   2525
        such adventures here-to-fore
        have befallen, long ago.
        May He who a thorn-crown wore
        to His own bliss bring us so!

Amen

Questions for Study

1. The author opens and closes *Sir Gawain* with references to the fall of Troy and the founding of European kingdoms, including England. Why does he place the story in this historical context?

2. Scholars speculate that the beheading game had its origin in pagan agricultural religions. The Green Knight was probably once a vegetation god and the beheading game a ritual "death" performed in winter to appease the god and ensure that the crops would grow in the spring. The beheading game is one of several ways in which the author weaves a death-and-resurrection motif into the narrative. What are other ways? How are they related to the work's themes?

3. The Green Knight has a sense of humor. Do any of the other characters? How is comedy or humor important in the poem?

4. The physical world of the poem is varied. It includes Arthur's court, the landscape through which Gawain travels, the mysterious castle, and the Green Chapel. The author uses much detail to bring this physical world to life. What characterizes each of these places? What makes them attractive or unattractive? In what ways are they symbolic or thematically important?

5. How does the passage of the seasons structure the poem? What is the importance of the Christmas and New Years' holidays?

6. Part III of the poem features three hunts, each of which takes place on a different day. The author interrupts the story of each hunt to tell what happens in Gawain's bedchamber between Gawain and the host's wife. He then finishes the story of the hunt. Why does the author structure the hunt stories in this way? What is the relationship between the action in the bedchamber and the hunts?

2522*Brut books*. Books about the history of Britain, founded by Felix Brutus.

7. How is each of these hunts and bedchamber scenes different? Is the change meaningful?

8. According to the laws of chivalry, Gawain must turn down the lady's proposal but not hurt her feelings. How do these constraints govern the dialogue between the two? In what ways are their dialogues like sparring matches? What does the lady want? What persuasive ploys does she use to attain her ends?

9. What are the temptations Gawain faces? How successful is he in resisting them? What is his failure? What is his punishment?

10. Once the Green Knight reveals his identity and passes judgment on Gawain, how is his attitude toward Gawain different from Gawain's attitude toward himself? How is the attitude of Arthur and his court different from Gawain's attitude toward himself? What do you think is the author's attitude toward Gawain? How does the Christian concept of human nature conflict with the chivalric concept in the poem?

11. What is Morgan le Faye's role in the poem? When does she first appear? What does her physical appearance reveal about her? How are the family relationships revealed at the end relevant to the rest of the narrative?

12. In what ways does *Sir Gawain* parallel the biblical myth of the Fall? (See pp. 45–47 for biblical accounts of the Fall.)

13. What oppositions and contrasts does the poet establish?

14. How well do Northrup Frye's theories about the patterns of romance (briefly summarized on p. 237) apply to *Sir Gawain and the Green Knight?*

15. *Sir Gawain* includes numerous references to "courtesy." Given what the narrator and the characters say about courtesy and the ways in which the characters attempt to practice it, how would you define it?

FOR FURTHER READING

Beer, Gillian. *The Romance.* London: Methuen, 1970. This short book provides a survey of the history and conventions of romance. It discusses definitions and compares romance to realistic literature like the novel.

Cawelti, John G. *Adventure, Mystery, and Romance: Formula Stories as Art and Popular Culture.* Chicago: U of Chicago P, 1976. Cawelti analyzes the cultural context and forms of popular romance today.

Fox, Denton, ed. *Twentieth Century Interpretations of Sir Gawain and the Green Knight: A Collection of Critical Essays.* Englewood Cliffs: Prentice-Hall, 1968. These essays represent diverse and sometimes conflicting approaches to the work.

Frye, Northrup. *The Secular Scripture: A Study of the Structure of Romance.* Cambridge: Harvard UP, 1976. Frye draws upon his knowledge of numerous romances from many cultures and periods to discuss the conventions of romance. He makes interesting comparisons between myth and romance and sees both as continuing to the present. This is a readable and stimulating book.

Goodman, Jennifer R. *The Legend of Arthur in British and American Literature.* Boston: Twayne, 1988. Goodman provides an overview of Arthurian material from its origins to the present.

Ker, William P. *Epic and Romance: Essays on Medieval Literature.* New York: Dover, 1957. In this study of epic and romance in medieval literature, Ker makes valuable definitions of epic and romance and traces their history from Homer to the Middle Ages.

Reeve, Clara. *The Progress of Romance through Times, Countries, and Manners.* New York: Garland Publishing, 1970. Reeve published her history of romance in 1785 when the novel was a new genre. She makes penetrating observations about how the romance is different from the novel. She was herself the author of gothic romances, including *The Old English Baron.*

Sir Gawain and the Green Knight. Ed. J. R. R. Tolkien, E. V. Gordon, and Norman Davis. 2nd ed. Oxford: Clarendon Press, 1967. Tolkien's introduction to this scholarly edition of *Sir Gawain* is excellent.

Vinaver, Eugene. *The Rise of Romance.* Oxford: Oxford UP, 1971. Vinaver discusses the evolution of romance and its relationship to the novel. He focuses largely on medieval romance.

Chapter Six
Narrative Poetry

INTRODUCTION

The medium of most stories is language. Although it is possible to have stories without language, such stories are limited in their complexity. Stained glass windows in medieval churches were meant to tell religious stories to illiterate people. But unless church officials explained the pictures, the pictures made little sense, just as they make little sense to us unless we know the stories. Language, therefore, seems inescapable for all but the simplest stories.

The language of most modern narrative is prose. But before the twentieth century, many authors wrote narratives in poetry. Why? What benefits does poetry bring to narrative? In the ancient world, certain narratives, especially myths, were composed in poetry because of their association with rituals. The narratives were chanted or sung, and poetry molds language to that purpose. The ancients also saw poetic language as magical. The language itself, accompanied by the myth, had supernatural power. Other ancient narratives, like epics, were composed in poetry, partly because poetry is easier to memorize than prose and partly because of the prestige of poetic language. The quasi-mystical properties of poetry were considered appropriate for the grandeur of epic narratives.

In more recent times poetry confers other benefits: To begin with, poetry calls into being a narrator's voice. More fully than prose, poetry can give a sense of someone speaking the narrative out loud. Prose is a medium for speedy and clear communication. We can breeze through much prose without hearing it or thinking about its language, but poetry slows us down. It forces us to pay attention to the language itself, to *hear* the language rather than just skim over it silently. Poetry almost demands to be read out loud. When we hear poetry, whether in our minds or out loud, we collaborate with the author to create a narrative voice.

To cite a second benefit, poetry enlivens the narrative with beautiful language. All human speech has appealing sound qualities, but the difference between normal speech—prose—and poetry lies in poetry's capacity to regularize and organize those sound qualities in much the same way that a composer of music organizes sound pitches into harmonies and melodies. Perhaps the most obvious sound qualities of poetry are rhythm and rhyme. Human beings respond with pleasure to both. Such qualities are enjoyable in themselves, and thus fix our attention on the narrative simply by being part of it; but they also provide means of developing the narrative. They slow the action down or speed it up, call attention to certain events and ideas, provide structuring devices like line length and stanza.

A third benefit of poetry is the increase in subtlety and intensity of the narrative it offers. Poetry communicates more subtly than prose because it relies more heavily on implication than on direct statement. And it is more intense because it concentrates its content into the fewest words possible. Poets achieve this concentration through careful selection of details, through indirect methods of communication, like symbolism and metaphor, and through sound devices that underscore ideas and call attention to parallel concepts. (A poet might rhyme two words, for example, not simply to create pretty sounds but to make us aware of connections between the concepts the words represent.) This concentration may result in "gaps" in the narrative, which readers can usually fill in by noticing the implications in the poem's language. Robert Browning's "Porphyria's Lover" (p. 337) is short, but its implications allow us to construct a much longer prose version of the story the poem tells. The same statement is true of medieval ballads (pp. 308–309), whose stories are fragmentary but whose implications lead us to connect the fragments and enlarge them into more complete stories.

Apart from its poetic qualities, narrative poetry is similar to any other kind of narrative. The same questions apply: What are the main conflicts in the plot? What are the characters like? What motivates them? When does the action occur? How is the physical landscape related to characters, action, and theme? What ideas does the narrative represent? Who is narrating? Why? What is the speaker's attitude toward the characters, events, and setting of the narrative?

In addition to the narrative elements in the poem, we need also to understand its poetic elements. The musical quality of poetry comes from its rhythm and word sounds. Poets achieve rhythm by regularizing the natural rhythms of human speech into metrical patterns. A **metrical pattern** is the repetition of a rhythmical unit, called a **meter. Scansion** is a method of marking the meter of a poem. We *scan* a poem by indicating the unaccented and accented syllables of one or more lines. The most common meter in English poetry is the **iamb,** which consists of an unaccented syllable followed by an accented syllable: *ălóne.* A single rhythmical unit is called a **foot.** A frequently used line of English poetry is iambic pentameter (five iambic feet per line): ălóne Ĭ rówed ŭpón thĕ místŷ séa. Other meters are the **trochee** (an accented syllable followed by an unaccented syllable, as in *lónelŷ),* the **anapest** (two unaccented syllables followed by one accented syllable, as in *ŏvĕrwhélm*), the **dactyl** (an accented syllable followed by two unaccented sylla-bles, as in *róyăltў*), and the **spondee** (two accented syllables, as in *drúmbéat*). A poet usually establishes a regular rhythm for a poem and then departs from the rhythm at crucial points. These departures often emphasize the meaning of certain words, signal shifts in the action, and make the language seem more natural. A poem may be obviously rhythmical, like Wordsworth's "Strange Fits of Passion Have I Known" (p. 316) and Tennyson's "The Lady of Shalott" (p. 331), or subtly rhythmical, like Browning's "Porphyria's Lover" (p. 337). Whatever the case, poets choose the rhythm carefully to match the content of the poem.

Another way that poets create musical effects is to arrange words into pat-terns of sound. **Rhyme** is the repetition of accented vowels and the sounds that follow: mine/wine, expression/repression, soul/control, sound/confound. Rhyme links both vowel and consonant sounds. We usually think of rhyme as occurring at the end of lines, but rhyme can occur within lines as well. Similar to rhyme is **asso-nance,** which links only like vowel sounds: own/mow/slope/soul, wide/con-fined/dime/style. **Alliteration** links like consonant sounds at the beginnings of words: bitter/bite/bog/betray, screech/scream/scratch/scram. In contrast to allit-eration, **consonance** links consonant sounds at the end of words:: stretch/match/itch/teach. **Onomatopoeia** is the use of words that sound like what they mean: fizz, splash, smash, buzz, boom, hiss. The word sounds of poetry can be pretty and even fun, but poets also use them to establish moods and to call atten-tion to relationships among words and what they represent.

Diction is the poet's choice of words, not just for their sound qualities but for their meaning. Poets are sensitive to subtle shades of meanings, to double mean-ings, and to denotative and connotative meanings of words. **Denotation** is the object or idea—the referent—that the word represents. The denotative meaning of a word is usually equivalent to the definition in a dictionary. **Connotation** is the subjective, emotional association a word has for one person or a group of people. The denotation of the word *mother,* for example, is "female parent," but the con-notations include such associations as warmth, protection, mercy, and home. By using the connotative meanings of words, poets increase the implications of the poem without increasing the number of words.

Imagery may call to mind the visual sense, but imagery in literature appeals to all the senses—sight, sound, taste, touch, smell. Imagery establishes the physi-cal world of the poem—the landscape, animals, buildings, clothing, utensils, food, colors, times of day, seasons—that help make up the setting. Imagery also com-municates *atmosphere*—how we feel about the narrative. If the physical world is grey and foggy, we are likely to feel somber; if it is colorful and bright, we are likely to feel cheery.

Metaphor has both a general and a specific meaning. Generally, it means any analogy (an **analogy** is a comparison between things that may seem dissimilar at first glance but that have underlying similarities). "Love" and "the north star" would seem unrelated, but Shakespeare links them metaphorically in one of his best-known sonnets, Sonnet 116. Specifically, metaphor means a particular kind of analogy and is contrasted with the simile. A **simile** is a comparison that is signaled by the use of *like* or *as:* "Her tears were like falling rain." A **metaphor** is also a comparison, but it eliminates the words *like* and *as* and directly equates the compared items: "Her tears were the sweet rain that fell on his parched soul." Poets use metaphors to clarify abstract concepts, to present familiar concepts in a fresh way, and to influence our attitude toward something. When Robert Burns says his love is like "a red red rose," we think of her as beautiful, delicate, fragrant, and soft, the qualities of a red rose.

A structuring device used in much narrative poetry is the stanza. A **stanza** is a repeated grouping of two or more lines of poetry. Stanzas are separated from one another by spaces.

Poets may structure stanzas in whatever way they want, but they may also choose to work within already established stanzaic structures. These are called **fixed forms.** An example of a fixed stanzaic form is **Spenserian stanza,** named after its creator, Edmund Spenser, who used it for *The Faerie Queen.* The Spenserian stanza has nine lines. The first eight are iambic pentameter; the ninth is iambic hexameter (six iambic feet). The rhyme scheme is *ababbcbcc.* The **rhyme scheme** of a stanza or entire poem is the pattern established by end rhymes. Rhyme scheme is usually marked by letters of the alphabet. The following stanza from John Keats's "The Eve of St. Agnes" (p. 318) is an example of Spenserian stanza:

They told her how, upon St. Agnes' Eve,	a
Young virgins might have visions of delight,	b
And soft adorings from their loves receive	a
Upon the honeyed middle of the night,	b
If ceremonies due they did aright;	b
As, supperless to bed they must retire,	c
And couch supine their beauties, lilly white;	b
Nor look behind, nor sideways, but require	c
Of Heaven with upward eyes for all that they desire.	c

Stanzas allow poets to accomplish several purposes. Since a stanza usually contains a single action or a single thought, poets can divide the poem into definite units, each of which focuses attention on one thing—an action, a place, a feeling, an idea. Stanzas, therefore, are similar to paragraphs in prose. Stanzas also create a narrative rhythm. They are like waves, all of the same size, that come one after the other in regular intervals. This repetition of standard units, in conjunction with elements of sound like meter and rhyme, has a mesmerizing effect, like the ticking of a clock, and is part of the charm of stories narrated in poetry. Finally, stanzas allow the poet to move the story forward in clear increments. Because the stanzas take the same form, the reader more readily sees changes in content that occur from one stanza to the next, or from one part of a stanza to another part. Sometimes, of course, the changes are dramatic and therefore obvious, but other times they are subtle—a change of just a few words.

Two metrical patterns that poets often use to deemphasize the musical qualities of poetical language and make it seem more like everyday speech are blank verse and free verse. **Blank verse** is iambic pentameter with no end rhyme. Many poets writing in English, including Shakespeare, Milton, and Wordsworth, have relied heavily on blank verse. An example of blank verse in this chapter is Robert Frost's "Home Burial" (p. 354). **Free verse** contains no end rhyme, no regular metrical patterns, and no lines of fixed lengths. Poets create musical effects within free verse lines by means of assonance, alliteration, rhyme, and onomatopoeia. They establish rhythm by repeating phrases of the same syntactical structure:

> Grabbing his satchel,
> flinging open the door,
> running past the cemetery,
> splashing through the puddles,
> he reached the bus in time.

The poems by Zora Neale Hurston and Alice Walker in this chapter as well as those by most twentieth century poets who write in English are free verse poems.

There are potentially as many kinds of narrative poems as there are poets who write them. Two kinds of long narrative poem, epic and romance, are discussed in chapters two (epic) and four (romance). The poems in this chapter are relatively short and range from medieval ballads to recent poems. All of these poems were written originally in the English language by authors from Great Britain and the United States.

The Demon Lover and Edward, Edward

"The Demon Lover" and "Edward, Edward" belong to a large body of poems that come from England and Scotland and especially from the border region of the two countries. These poems, often called **medieval ballads** or **Scottish border ballads,** were first written down in the eighteenth century, but their origins are much older, many of them going back at least to the Middle Ages. They are anonymous compositions passed on from generation to generation by folk artists.

Medieval ballads share many traits in common. Because they were meant to be sung, their stanzas are short and relatively simple. The typical ballad stanza consists of four lines. The first and third lines have four stressed syllables; the second and fourth have three. The lines may or may not conform to a metrical pattern. The rhyme scheme is usually *abcb.*

Medieval ballads often include a convention called **incremental repetition,** the repetition of a phrase or stanza with slight but meaningful changes of phrasing. In "Edward, Edward" (p. 312) the changes ("increments") include new information that moves the plot slowly but inexorably toward a climax. Ballads usually focus on a climactic, tense, often sensational moment in a story. Details of the story are highly selective, leaving much to the hearer's or reader's imagination.

Characterization is minimal, transitions are abrupt, and narrative tone is objective, unemotional, and nonjudgmental. The plots of "The Demon Lover" (a person who loves or marries a supernatural being) and "Edward, Edward" (a son or daughter who murders a family member) have received countless treatments in the ballad tradition. "The Demon Lover" was collected by Sir Walter Scott in *Minstrelsy of the Scottish Border* (1802-03) and "Edward, Edward" by Francis James Child in *English and Scottish Ballads* (1857). The spellings in both of these poems represent the sounds of the Scots dialect of English in which the poems were originally composed.

THE DÆMON LOVER

"O where have you been, my long, long love,
    This long seven years and more?"—
"O I'm come to seek my former vows
    Ye granted me before."—

5   "O hold your tongue of your former vows,
    For they will breed sad strife;
O hold your tongue of your former vows,
    For I am become a wife."

He turn'd him right and round about,
10   And the tear blinded his ee;°
"I wad never hae trodden on Irish ground,
    If it had not been for thee.

"I might hae had a king's daughter,
    Far, far beyond the sea;
15   I might have had a king's daughter,
    Had it not been for love o' thee."—

"If ye might have had a king's daughter,
    Yer sell ye had to blame;
Ye might have taken the king's daughter,
20   For ye kend° that I was nane."°—

"O faulse are the vows of womankind,
    But fair is their faulse bodie;
I never wad hae trodden on Irish ground,
    Had it not been for love o' thee."—

[10]*ee.* Eye.
[20]*kend.* Knew. *nane.* None.

25   "If I was to leave my husband dear,
     And my two babes also,
  O what have you to take me to,
     If with you I should go?"—

  "I hae seven ships upon the sea,
30   The eighth brought me to land;
  With four-and-twenty bold mariners,
     And music on every hand."

  She has taken up her two little babes,
     Kiss'd them baith cheek and chin;
35   "O fair ye weel, my ain two babes,
     For I'll never see you again."

  She set her foot upon the ship,
     No mariners could she behold;
  But the sails were o' the taffetie,
40   And the masts o' the beaten gold.

  She had not sail'd a league, a league,
     A league but barely three,
  When dismal grew his countenance,
     And drumlie° grew his ee.

45   The masts that were like the beaten gold,
     Bent not on the heaving seas;
  But the sails, that were o' the taffetie,
     Fill'd not in the east land breeze.—

  They had not sailed a league, a league,
50   A league but barely three,
  Until she espied his cloven foot,
     And she wept right bitterlie.

  "O hold your tongue of your weeping," says he,
     "Of your weeping now let me be;
55   I will show you how the lilies grow
     On the banks of Italy."—

  "O what hills are yon, yon pleasant hills,
     That the sun shines sweetly on?"—
  "O yon are the hills of heaven," he said,
60   "Where you will never win."—

---

[44]*drumlie.* Troubled.

"O whaten a mountain is yon," she said,
  "All so dreary wi' frost and snow?"—
"O yon is the mountain of hell," he cried,
  "Where you and I will go."

65 And aye when she turn'd her round about,
    Aye taller he seem'd for to be;
Until that the tops o' that gallant ship
    Nae taller were than he.

The clouds grew dark, and the wind grew loud,
70   And the levin° fill'd her ee;
And waesome° wail'd the snaw-white sprites
    Upon the gurlie° sea.

He strack the tap-mast wi' his hand,
    The fore-mast wi' his knee;
75 And he brake that gallant ship in twain,
    And sank her in the sea.

Questions for Study

1. What is the rhythm and rhyme scheme of this poem? How do these complement narrative elements, like characterization and plot? What phrases and repetitions of phrases seem especially important to the narrative?

2. What line of reasoning does the demon lover use to persuade the woman to go with him?

3. Why does she go with him?

4. What are the gaps in the narratives? (What information has been omitted?) Where do the gaps occur? Does the poem give clues about how we might reconstruct the missing parts of the story?

5. At what point do we begin to think that the lover may be false? At what point does the woman become aware that he is false?

6. How are images of turning important? Are they meaningful?

7. How does the physical setting change to reflect the demonic qualities of the lover?

70*levin.* A flash of bright light, like lightning.
71*waesome.* Woeful.
72*gurlie.* Grim, growling.

EDWARD, EDWARD

"Why does your brand° sae drap wi' bluid,°
    Edward, Edward?
Why does your brand sae drap wi' bluid,
    And why sae sad gang ye° O?"
5   "O I ha'e killed my hawk sae guid,
    Mither, mither:
O I ha'e killed my hawk sae guid,
    And I had nae mair bot he O."

"Your hawkes bluid was never sae red,
10   Edward, Edward:
Your hawkes bluid was never sae red,
    My dear son I tell thee O."
"O I ha'e killed my red-roan steed,
    Mither, mither:
15   O I ha'e killed my red-roan steed,
    That erst° was sae fair and free O."

"Your steed was auld, and ye ha'e gat mair,
    Edward, Edward:
Your steed was auld, and ye ha'e gat mair,
20   Some other dule° ye drie° O."
"O I ha'e killed my fadir dear,
    Mither, mither:
O I ha'e killed my fadir deir,
    Alas! and wae is me O!"

25   "And whatten penance wul you drie, for that,
    Edward, Edward?
And whatten penance will ye drie for that?
    My dear son, now tell me O."
"I'll set my feet in yonder boat,
30   Mither, mither:
I'll set my feet in yonder boat,
    And I'll fare over the sea O."

"And what wul ye do wi' your towers and your hall,
    Edward, Edward?
35   And what wul ye do wi' your towers and your hall,

---

¹*brand.* Sword.   *bluid.* Blood.
⁴*gang ye.* Do you go.   ¹⁶*erst.* Once.
²⁰*dule.* Woe.   *drie.* Suffer.

That were sae fair to see O?"
"I'll let them stand til they doun fall,
    Mither, mither:
I'll let them stand til they doun fall,
40   For here never mair maun I be O."

"And what wul ye leave to your bairns° and your wife,
    Edward, Edward?
And what wul ye leave to your bairns and your wife,
    When ye gang over the sea O?"
45   "The world's room, let them beg through life,
    Mither, mither:
The world's room, let them beg through life,
    For them never mair wul I see O."

"And what wul ye leave to your ain mither dear,
50   Edward, Edward?
And what wul ye leave to your ain mither dear?
    My dear son, now tell me O."
"The curse of hell frae me shall ye bear,
    Mither, mither:
55   The curse of hell frae me shall ye bear,
    Sic counsils ye gave to me O."

Questions for Study

1. What is the rhythm and rhyme scheme of this poem? How do these complement narrative elements, like characterization and plot? What phrases and repetitions of phrases seem especially important to the narrative?

2. What are the gaps in the narrative? (What information has been omitted?) From
   the details in the poem, can you reconstruct the story that leads up to this family tragedy?

3. Why does the son not tell his mother what happened right away? Why does he
   lie to her at first?

4. What is the nature of the son's relationship with his mother? What details in the
   poem help establish this relationship?

5. What is the nature of the son's relationship with his wife and children?

6. What new information do we learn in each stanza? Are there reasons for arranging the information in this order?

[41] *bairns.* Children.

7. How does the incremental repetition from stanza to stanza affect our reaction to the story as it unfolds? How would we respond to the story if it were narrated in a different way?

SIR WALTER SCOTT

Lochinvar

Although Sir Walter Scott (1771-1832) was born and educated in Edinburgh, Scotland, he spent most of his life in the Border country between England and Scotland, emersing himself in its history and folkways. His first major work was a three-volume anthology of Border ballads, *Minstrelsy of the Scottish Border* (1802-03), which included ballads that he had collected as well as ballads of his own composition. He began his writing career with a series of long narratives in poetry, like *Marmion* (1808) and *The Lady of the Lake* (1810). These were enormously popular, but in 1814, with the publication of *Waverley,* Scott turned to writing novels, which were even more popular than his poems. Like his poems, these novels explore the past, especially the medieval past. Scott, like many people in the Western world during the nineteenth century, was fascinated with the architecture, artifacts, values, customs, and literary forms of medieval chivalry. "Lochinvar" is a song sung by one of the characters in *Marmion,* whose main character, a misguided nobleman, serves Henry VIII of England. Like many of Scott's poems in the early part of his career, "Lochinvar" has affinities with Border ballads as well as medieval romances.

> Oh! young Lochinvar is come out of the west,
> Through all the wide Border his steed was the best;
> And save his good broadsword he weapons had none,
> He rode all unarmed and he rode all alone.
> 5   So faithful in love and so dauntless in war,
> There never was knight like the young Lochinvar.
>
> He stayed not for brake and he stopped not for stone,
> He swam the Eske river where ford there was none;
> But ere he alighted at Netherby gate
> 10   The bride had consented, the gallant came late:

For a laggard in love and a dastard in war
Was to wed the fair Ellen of brave Lochinvar.

So boldly he entered the Netherby Hall,
Among bridesmen, and kinsmen, and brothers, and all:
15   Then spoke the bride's father, his hand on his sword,—
For the poor craven bridegroom said never a word,—
"Oh! come ye in peace here, or come ye in war,
Or to dance at our bridal, young Lord Lochinvar?"—

"I long wooed your daughter, my suit you denied;
20   Love swells like the Solway, but ebbs like its tide—
And now am I come, with this lost love of mine,
To lead but one measure, drink one cup of wine.
There are maidens in Scotland more lovely by far,
That would gladly be bride to the young Lochinvar."

25   The bride kissed the goblet; the knight took it up,
He quaffed off the wine, and he threw down the cup.
She looked down to blush, and she looked up to sigh,
With a smile on her lips and a tear in her eye.
He took her soft hand ere her mother could bar,—
30   "Now tread we a measure!" said young Lochinvar.

So stately his form, and so lovely her face,
That never a hall such a galliard did grace;
While her mother did fret, and her father did fume,
And the bridegroom stood dangling his bonnet and plume;
35   And the bride-maidens whispered, "'T were better by far
To have matched our fair cousin with young Lochinvar."

One touch to her hand and one word in her ear,
When they reached the hall-door, and the charger stood near;
So light to the croupe the fair lady he swung,
40   So light to the saddle before her he sprung!
"She is won! we are gone, over bank, bush, and scaur;°
They'll have fleet steeds that follow," quoth young Lochinvar.

There was mounting 'mong Græmes of the Netherby clan;
Forsters, Fenwicks, and Musgraves, they rode and they ran:
45   There was racing and chasing on Cannobie Lee,
But the lost bride of Netherby ne'er did they see.
So daring in love and so dauntless in war,
Have ye e'er heard of gallant like young Lochinvar?

---

[41] *scaur.* The ridge of a hill.

Questions for Study

1. What is the metrical pattern of "Lochinvar"? What is the rhyme scheme? Why did Scott choose them for this story?

2. Scott was a collector of medieval folk ballads. How is this poem similar to and different from medieval ballads (pp. 308–309)?

3. What actions and qualities characterize Lochinvar? How is he contrasted with the bridegroom?

4. What ploys does Lochinvar use to spirit the bride away?

WILLIAM WORDSWORTH

Strange Fits of Passion
Have I Known

William Wordsworth (1770–1850) was born and reared in the Lake District of northern England, a beautiful, sparsely settled countryside of clear lakes and low mountains. After going away to college and living briefly in France and southern England, he returned home and settled there permanently. Wordsworth's affinity for nature and especially his home countryside informs much of his poetry. Along with Sir Walter Scott, William Blake, and his friend Samuel Taylor Coleridge, he was one of the first of the English Romantic poets. His joint publication with Coleridge of *Lyrical Ballads* in 1798 is often cited as the beginning of the Romantic movement in England. Romanticism is a complex phenomenon, but some of its traits were an emphasis on emotion and mystery as opposed to intellect and rationality; a fascination with the past, especially the Middle Ages; an imitation of medieval literary forms, like the ballad and chivalric romance; a focus on the poet's sensibility and aspirations rather than on societal restraints; a use of dreamlike situations and images; a celebration of romantic love; and a presentation of nature as a source of spiritual inspiration and guidance. The ballad-like "Strange Fits of Passion Have I Known" appeared in the second edition of *Lyrical Ballads* (1800). This poem is usually grouped with four other poems called the "Lucy" poems, which describe a young woman whom the speaker loves but who dies before they can fulfill their love.

Strange fits of passion° have I known:
And I will dare to tell,
But in the Lover's ear alone,
What once to me befell.

5   When she I loved looked every day
Fresh as a rose in June,
I to her cottage bent my way,
Beneath an evening-moon.

Upon the moon I fixed my eye,
10   All over the wide lea;
With quickening pace my horse drew nigh
Those paths so dear to me.

And now we reached the orchard-plot;
And, as we climbed the hill,
15   The sinking moon to Lucy's cot°
Came near, and nearer still.

In one of those sweet dreams I slept,
Kind Nature's gentlest boon!
And all the while my eyes I kept
20   On the descending moon.

My horse moved on; hoof after hoof
He raised, and never stopped:
When down behind the cottage roof,
At once, the bright moon dropped.

25   What fond and wayward thoughts will slide
Into a Lover's head!
"O mercy!" to myself I cried,
"If Lucy should be dead!"

Questions for Study

1. How is this poem dreamlike? What is the "sweet dream" (l. 17)?

2. What is the significance of the moon?

3. What contrasts does the poem establish?

4. What concepts do the end rhymes emphasize and link?

[1]*passion.* Grief.   [15]*cot.* Cottage.

JOHN KEATS

The Eve of St. Agnes

John Keats (1795–1821) was born in London to tradespeople. Because he was orphaned at age fourteen, he was taken out of school and apprenticed to a surgeon and apothecary. But Keats was a high-spirited youth who loved reading, music, and theater. Much to the consternation of his family, he gave up his medical studies to become a poet. He was beset by problems nearly all of his short life. A favorite brother died of tuberculosis. He fell deeply in love with Fanny Brawne, but they could not marry because of Keats's poverty and ill health. Filled with the inspiration and gift to write great poetry, he felt himself in a race with death to get his poems written down. At age twenty-six, he died of tuberculosis. Despite the shortness of his career, Keats was one of the great Romantic poets. His poetry is sensuous, intensely emotional, but also controlled and profoundly thoughtful. He wrote his most brilliant poetry in one year—1819. One of the poems from this year is The Eve of St. Agnes (published in 1820). The stanzaic form of this poem is Spenserian stanza (see p. 307 for an explanation and illustration of the Spenserian stanza). Typical of many poems from the Romantic period, this poem is set during the Middle Ages and incorporates conventions of medieval romance. The action of the poem centers on a popular belief associated with St. Agnes—who was martyred at age thirteen, about A.D. 303, and became the patron saint of virgins—that a girl, if she performed the appropriate rituals, would have a vision of her future husband on St. Agnes's Eve, 20 January.

1

> St. Agnes' Eve—Ah, bitter chill it was!
> The owl, for all his feathers, was a-cold;
> The hare limped trembling through the frozen grass,
> And silent was the flock in woolly fold:
> 5   Numb were the Beadsman's° fingers, while he told
> His rosary, and while his frosted breath,
> Like pious incense from a censer old,
> Seemed taking flight for heaven, without a death,
> Past the sweet Virgin's picture, while his prayer he saith.

---

[5] *Beadsman*. A holy man, paid to pray for people. He "tells" the beads of his rosary by counting them as he prays.

2

10   His prayer he saith, this patient, holy man;
Then takes his lamp, and riseth from his knees,
And back returneth, meagre, barefoot, wan,
Along the chapel aisle by slow degrees:
The sculptured dead, on each side, seem to freeze,
15   Imprisoned in black, purgatorial rails:
Knights, ladies, praying in dumb orat'ries,°
He passeth by; and his weak spirit fails
To think how they may ache in icy hoods and mails.

3

Northward he turneth through a little door,
20   And scarce three steps, ere Music's golden tongue
Flattered to tears this aged man and poor;
But no—already had his deathbell rung:
The joys of all his life were said and sung:
His was harsh penance on St. Agnes' Eve:
25   Another way he went, and soon among
Rough ashes sat he for his soul's reprieve,
And all night kept awake, for sinners' sake to grieve.

4

That ancient Beadsman heard the prelude soft;
And so it chanced, for many a door was wide,
30   From hurry to and fro. Soon, up aloft,
The silver, snarling trumpets 'gan to chide:
The level chambers, ready with their pride,
Were glowing to receive a thousand guests:
The carvèd angels, ever eager-eyed,
35   Stared, where upon their heads the cornice rests,
With hair blown back, and wings put cross-wise on their breasts.

5

At length burst in the argent° revelry,
With plume, tiara, and all rich array,
Numerous as shadows haunting faerily
40   The brain, new stuffed, in youth, with triumphs gay

16*orat'ries.* Chapels.
37*argent.* The heraldic color silver.

Of old romance. These let us wish away,
And turn, sole-thoughted, to one Lady there,
Whose heart had brooded, all that wintry day,
On love, and winged St. Agnes' saintly care,
45   As she had heard old dames full many times declare.

6

They told her how, upon St. Agnes' Eve,
Young virgins might have visions of delight,
And soft adorings from their loves receive
Upon the honeyed middle of the night,
50   If ceremonies due they did aright;
As, supperless to bed they must retire,
And couch supine their beauties, lilly white;
Nor look behind, nor sideways, but require
Of Heaven with upward eyes for all that they desire.

7

55   Full of this whim was thoughtful Madeline:
The music, yearning like a God in pain,
She scarcely heard: her maiden eyes divine,
Fixed on the floor, saw many a sweeping train
Pass by—she heeded not at all: in vain
60   Came many a tiptoe, amorous cavalier,
And back retired; not cooled by high disdain,
But she saw not: her heart was otherwhere:
She sighed for Agnes' dreams, the sweetest of the year.

8

She danced along with vague, regardless eyes,
65   Anxious her lips, her breathing quick and short:
The hallowed hour was near at hand: she sighs
Amid the timbrels,° and the thronged resort
Of whisperers in anger, or in sport;
'Mid looks of love, defiance, hate, and scorn,
70   Hoodwinked with faery fancy; all amort,°
Save to St. Agnes and her lambs unshorn,°
And all the bliss to be before tomorrow morn.

---

[67]*timbrels.* Small hand drums.

[70]*amort.* As if dead.

[71]*lambs unshorn.* Two lambs, brought to the altar at mass on St. Agnes's Day. Nuns would later spin and weave the wool from the lambs.

9

So, purposing each moment to retire,
She lingered still. Meantime, across the moors,
75   Had come young Porphyro, with heart on fire
For Madeline. Beside the portal doors,
Buttressed from moonlight, stands he, and implores
All saints to give him sight of Madeline,
But for one moment in the tedious hours,
80   That he might gaze and worship all unseen;
Perchance speak, kneel, touch, kiss—in sooth such things have been.

10

He ventures in: let no buzzed whisper tell:
All eyes be muffled, or a hundred swords
Will storm his heart, Love's feverous citadel:
85   For him, those chambers held barbarian hordes,
Hyena foemen, and hot-blooded lords,
Whose very dogs would execrations howl
Against his lineage: not one breast affords
Him any mercy, in that mansion foul,
90   Save one old beldame,° weak in body and in soul.

11

Ah, happy chance! the aged creature came,
Shuffling along with ivory-headed wand,
To where he stood, hid from the torch's flame,
Behind a broad hall-pillar, far beyond
95   The sound of merriment and chorus bland:
He startled her; but soon she knew his face,
And grasped his fingers in her palsied hand,
Saying, "Mercy, Porphyro! hie thee from this place:
They are all here tonight, the whole blood-thirsty race!

12

100   "Get hence! get hence! there's dwarfish Hildebrand;
He had a fever late, and in the fit
He cursed thee and thine, both house and land:
Then there's that old Lord Maurice, not a whit
More tame for his grey hairs—Alas me! flit!

90*beldame.* An old woman.

105 Flit like a ghost away."—"Ah, Gossip° dear,
    We're safe enough; here in this arm-chair sit,
    And tell me how"—"Good Saints! not here, not here;
  Follow me, child, or else these stones will be thy bier."

13

    He followed through a lowly archèd way,
110 Brushing the cobwebs with his lofty plume,
    And as she muttered "Well-a—well-a-day!"
    He found him in a little moonlight room,
    Pale, latticed, chill, and silent as a tomb.
    "Now tell me where is Madeline," said he,
115 "O tell me, Angela, by the holy loom
    Which none but secret sisterhood may see,
  When they St. Agnes' wool are weaving piously."

14

    "St. Agnes! Ah! it is St. Agnes' Eve—
    Yet men will murder upon holy days:
120 Thou must hold water in a witch's sieve,°
    And be liege-lord of all the Elves and Fays,
    To venture so: it fills me with amaze
    To see thee, Porphyro!—St. Agnes' Eve!
    God's help! my lady fair the conjuror plays
125 This very night: good angels her deceive!
  But let me laugh awhile, I've mickle° time to grieve."

15

    Feebly she laugheth in the languid moon,
    While Porphyro upon her face doth look,
    Like puzzled urchin on an aged crone
130 Who keepeth closed a wondrous riddle-book,
    As spectacled she sits in chimney nook.
    But soon his eyes grew brilliant, when she told
    His lady's purpose; and he scarce could brook
    Tears, at the thought of those enchantments cold,
135 And Madeline asleep in lap of legends old.

---

[105]*Gossip.* Godmother; friend.
[120]*witch's sieve.* A sieve that will hold water.
[126]*mickle.* Much.

16

Sudden a thought came like a full-blown rose,
Flushing his brow, and in his pained heart
Made purple riot: then doth he propose
A strategem, that makes the beldame start:
140   "A cruel man and impious thou art:
Sweet lady, let her pray, and sleep, and dream
Alone with her good angels, far apart
From wicked men like thee. Go, go!—I deem
Thou canst not surely be the same that thou didst seem."

17

145   "I will not harm her, by all saints I swear,"
Quoth Porphyro: "O may I ne'er find grace
When my weak voice shall whisper its last prayer,
If one of her soft ringlets I displace,
Or look with ruffian passion in her face:
150   Good Angela, believe me by these tears;
Or I will, even in a moment's space,
Awake, with horrid shout, my foemen's ears,
And beard them, though they be more fanged than wolves and bears."

18

"Ah! why wilt thou affright a feeble soul?
155   A poor, weak, palsy-stricken, churchyard thing,
Whose passing-bell may ere the midnight toll;
Whose prayers for thee, each morn and evening,
Were never missed."—Thus plaining,° doth she bring
A gentler speech from burning Porphyro;
160   So woeful, and of such deep sorrowing,
That Angela gives promise she will do
Whatever he shall wish, betide her weal or woe.

19

Which was, to lead him, in close secrecy,
Even to Madeline's chamber, and there hide
165   Him in a closet, of such privacy
That he might see her beauty unespied,
And win perhaps that night a peerless bride,

158*plaining.* Complaining.

       While legioned faeries paced the coverlet,
       And pale enchantment held her sleepy-eyed.
170   Never on such a night have lovers met,
    Since Merlin paid his Demon° all the monstrous debt.

20

       "It shall be as thou wishest," said the Dame:
       "All cates° and dainties shall be stored there
       Quickly on this feast-night: by the tambour frame°
175   Her own lute thou wilt see: no time to spare,
       For I am slow and feeble, and scarce dare
       On such a catering trust my dizzy head.
       Wait here, my child, with patience; kneel in prayer
       The while: Ah! thou must needs the lady wed,
180 Or may I never leave my grave among the dead."—

21

       So saying, she hobbled off with busy fear.
       The lover's endless minutes slowly passed;
       The dame returned, and whispered in his ear
       To follow her; with aged eyes aghast
185   From fright of dim espial. Safe at last,
       Through many a dusky gallery, they gain
       The maiden's chamber, silken, hushed, and chaste;
       Where Porphyro took covert, pleased amain.°
His poor guide hurried back with agues in her brain.

22

190   Her faltering hand upon the balustrade,
       Old Angela was feeling for the stair,
       When Madeline, St. Agnes' charmèd maid,
       Rose, like a missioned spirit, unaware:
       With silver taper's light, and pious care,
195   She turned, and down the aged gossip led
       To a safe level matting. Now prepare,
       Young Porphyro, for gazing on that bed;
She comes, she comes again, like ring-dove frayed° and fled.

---

[171]*Demon.* Vivien, who turned one of Merlin's tricks against him and killed him.
[173]*cates.* Delicacies.
[174]*tambour frame.* A frame for embroidery work.
[188]*pleased amain.* Very pleased.
[198]*frayed.* Frightened.

23

Out went the taper as she hurried in;
200   Its little smoke, in pallid moonshine, died:
        She closed the door, she panted, all akin
        To spirits of the air, and visions wide:
        No uttered syllable, or, woe betide!
        But to her heart, her heart was voluble,
205   Paining with eloquence her balmy side;
        As though a tongueless nightingale should swell
Her throat in vain, and die, heart-stifled, in her dell.

24

A casement high and triple-arched there was,
All garlanded with carven imag'ries
210   Of fruits, and flowers, and bunches of knot-grass,
        And diamonded with panes of quaint device,
        Innumerable of stains and splendid dyes,
        As are the tiger-moth's deep-damasked wings;
        And in the midst, 'mong thousand heraldries,
215   And twilight saints, and dim emblazonings,
A shielded scutcheon blushed with blood of queens and kings.

25

Full on this casement shone the wintry moon,
And threw warm gules° on Madeline's fair breast,
As down she knelt for heaven's grace and boon;
220   Rose-bloom fell on her hands, together pressed,
        And on her silver cross soft amethyst,
        And on her hair a glory, like a saint:
        She seemed a splendid angel, newly dressed,
        Save wings, for heaven:—Porphyro grew faint:
225   She knelt, so pure a thing, so free from mortal taint.

26

Anon his heart revives: her vespers done,
Of all its wreathèd pearls her hair she frees;
Unclasps her warmèd jewels one by one;
Loosens her fragrant bodice; by degrees
230   Her rich attire creeps rustling to her knees:
        Half-hidden, like a mermaid in sea-weed,

[218]*gules.* The heraldic color red.

Pensive awhile she dreams awake, and sees,
   In fancy, fair St. Agnes in her bed,
But dares not look behind, or all the charm is fled.

27

235   Soon, trembling in her soft and chilly nest,
   In sort of wakeful swoon, perplexed she lay,
   Until the poppied warmth of sleep oppressed
   Her soothèd limbs, and soul fatigued away;
   Flown, like a thought, until the morrow-day;
240   Blissfully havened both from joy and pain;
   Clasped like a missal° where swart Paynims pray;
   Blinded alike from sunshine and from rain,
As though a rose should shut, and be a bud again.

28

   Stol'n to this paradise, and so entranced,
245   Porphyro gazed upon her empty dress,
   And listened to her breathing, if it chanced
   To wake into a slumberous tenderness;
   Which when he heard, that minute did he bless,
   And breathed himself: then from the closet crept,
250   Noiseless as fear in a wide wilderness,
   And over the hushed carpet, silent, stepped,
And 'tween the curtains peeped, where, lo!—how fast she slept.

29

   Then by the bed-side, where the faded moon
   Made a dim, silver twilight, soft he set
255   A table, and, half anguished, threw thereon
   A cloth of woven crimson, gold, and jet:—
   O for some drowsy Morphean° amulet!
   The boisterous, midnight, festive clarion,
   The kettle-drum, and far-heard clarinet,
260   Affray his ears, though but in dying tone:—
The hall door shuts again, and all the noise is gone.

30

And still she slept an azure-lidded sleep,

241*Clasped like a missal.* A prayer book held tightly in a place where pagans worship.
257*Morphean.* Sleep-inducing.

In blanchèd linen, smooth, and lavendered,
While he from forth the closet brought a heap
265   Of candied apple, quince, and plum, and gourd;
With jellies soother° than the creamy curd,
And lucent syrups, tinct° with cinnamon;
Manna and dates, in argosy transferred
From Fez;° and spiced dainties, every one,
270   From silken Samarcand° to cedared Lebanon.

31

These delicates he heaped with glowing hand
On golden dishes and in baskets bright
Of wreathed silver: sumptuous they stand
In the retired quiet of the night,
275   Filling the chilly room with perfume light.—
"And now, my love, my seraph fair, awake!
Thou art my heaven, and I thine eremite:°
Open thine eyes, for meek St. Agnes' sake,
Or I shall drowse beside thee, so my soul doth ache."

32

280   Thus whispering, his warm, unnervèd arm
Sank in her pillow. Shaded was her dream
By the dusk curtains:—'twas a midnight charm
Impossible to melt as icèd stream:
The lustrous salvers in the moonlight gleam;
285   Broad golden fringe upon the carpet lies:
It seemed he never, never could redeem
From such a stedfast spell his lady's eyes;
So mused awhile, entoiled in woofèd° phantasies.

33

Awakening up, he took her hollow lute,—
290   Tumultuous,—and, in chords that tenderest be,
He played an ancient ditty, long since mute,

266 *soother.* Smoother.
267 *tinct.* Tinctured.
269 *Fez.* A city in Morocco.
270 *Samarcand.* A Russian city famous for silk manufacture.
277 *eremite.* Religious hermit.
288 *woofèd.* Woven.

In Provence called, "La belle dame sans merci:"°
Close to her ear touching the melody;—
Wherewith disturbed, she uttered a soft moan:
295   He ceased—she panted quick—and suddenly
Her blue affrayèd eyes wide open shone:
Upon his knees he sank, pale as smooth-sculptured stone.

34

Her eyes were open, but she still beheld,
Now wide awake, the vision of her sleep:
300   There was a painful change, that nigh expelled
The blisses of her dream so pure and deep
At which fair Madeline began to weep,
And moan forth witless words with many a sigh;
While still her gaze on Porphyro would keep;
305   Who knelt, with joinèd hands and piteous eye,
Fearing to move or speak, she looked so dreamingly.

35

"Ah, Porphyro!" said she, "but even now
Thy voice was at sweet tremble in mine ear,
Made tuneable with every sweetest vow;
310   And those sad eyes were spiritual and clear:
How changed thou art! how pallid, chill, and drear!
Give me that voice again, my Porphyro,
Those looks immortal, those complainings dear!
Oh leave me not in this eternal woe,
315   For if thou diest, my Love, I know not where to go."

36

Beyond a mortal man impassioned far
At these voluptuous accents, he arose,
Ethereal, flushed, and like a throbbing star
Seen mid the sapphire heaven's deep repose;
320   Into her dream he melted, as the rose
Blendeth its odor with the violet,—
Solution sweet: meantime the frost-wind blows
Like Love's alarum pattering the sharp sleet
Against the window-panes; St. Agnes' moon hath set.

---

29 *La belle dame sans merci.* The beautiful woman without pity, the title of a poem by the medieval French poet Alain Chartier and of a ballad-like poem by Keats.

37

325   'Tis dark: quick pattereth the flaw-blown° sleet:
          "This is no dream, my bride, my Madeline!"
          'Tis dark: the icèd gusts still rave and beat:
          "No dream, alas! alas! and woe is mine!
          Porphyro will leave me here to fade and pine.—
330   Cruel! what traitor could thee hither bring?
          I curse not, for my heart is lost in thine,
          Though thou forsakest a deceivèd thing;—
      A dove forlorn and lost with sick unprunèd wing."

38

          "My Madeline! sweet dreamer! lovely bride!
335   Say, may I be for aye thy vassal blest?
          Thy beauty's shield, heart-shaped and vermeil dyed?
          Ah, silver shrine, here will I take my rest
          After so many hours of toil and quest,
          A famished pilgrim,—saved by miracle.
340   Though I have found, I will not rob thy nest
          Saving of thy sweet self; if thou thinkest well
      To trust, fair Madeline, to no rude infidel.

39

          "Hark! 'tis an elfin-storm from faery land,
          Of haggard° seeming, but a boon indeed:
345   Arise—arise! the morning is at hand;—
          The bloated wassaillers will never heed:—
          Let us away, my love, with happy speed;
          There are no ears to hear, or eyes to see,—
          Drowned all in Rhenish° and the sleepy mead:°
350   Awake! arise! my love, and fearless be,
      For o'er the southern moors I have a home for thee."

40

          She hurried at his words, beset with fears,
          For there were sleeping dragons all around,

325*flaw-blown.* Gust-blown.
344*haggard.* Wild.
349*Rhenish.* Wine from the Rhine River valley.   *mead.* An alcoholic drink made from honey.

At glaring watch, perhaps, with ready spears—
355   Down the wide stairs a darkling way° they found.—
In all the house was heard no human sound.
A chain-drooped lamp was flickering by each door;
The arras, rich with horseman, hawk, and hound,
Fluttered in the besieging wind's uproar;
360   And the long carpets rose along the gusty floor.

41

They glide, like phantoms, into the wide hall;
Like phantoms, to the iron porch, they glide;
Where lay the Porter, in uneasy sprawl,
With a huge empty flagon by his side:
365   The wakeful bloodhound rose, and shook his hide,
But his sagacious eye an inmate owns:
By one, and one, the bolts full easy slide:—
The chains lie silent on the footworn stones;—
The key turns, and the door upon its hinges groans.

42

370   And they are gone: aye, ages long ago
These lovers fled away into the storm.
That night the Baron dreamt of many a woe,
And all his warrior-guests, with shade and form
Of witch, and demon, and large coffin-worm,
375   Were long be-nightmared. Angela the old
Died palsy-twitched, with meagre face deform;
The Beadsman, after thousand aves° told,
For aye unsought for slept among his ashes cold.

Questions for Study

1. How does Keats establish the impression of coldness in the first stanza? What other stanzas are particularly noticeable for their imagery? How does Keats's imagery in these stanzas relate to the sense of the lines?

2. The stanzaic form of this poem is Spenserian (see p. 307 for a description). What effect on the narrative does this stanzaic form have? How, for example,

---

355*darkling way*. A dark passageway.
377*aves*. Prayers that begin with *Ave Maria*, Hail Mary.

does Keats use the longer final line? Do the end rhymes link concepts in meaningful ways?

3. How do the beadsman and Angela contrast with the revellers inside the hall and with Porphyro and Madeline? What other contrasts does Keats establish?

4. What happens in stanzas 33-37?

5. What characterizes each of the main characters—Porphyro, Madeline, the beadsman, Angela, Madeline's kinfolk?

6. Why does Keats end the poem with a storm and with the beadsman and Angela?

ALFRED, LORD TENNYSON

The Lady of Shalott

Alfred, Lord Tennyson (1809–92) was, along with the American poet Henry Wadsworth Longfellow, the most popular poet writing in the English language during the nineteenth century. Their poetry was accessible to people of many educational backgrounds, including even children. Tennyson was born and reared in the central part of England. His father was a country parson from a socially prominent family. After graduating from Cambridge University, Tennyson embarked upon a career as a poet with the publication in the early 1830s of several books of poetry. But his career suffered a setback because of the cool critical reception of his books and because of the death of his closest university friend, Arthur Hallam. During a ten-year period, Tennyson revised his poems, wrote new poems, and worked on *In Memoriam,* a long poetic tribute to Hallam that he published finally in 1850. With the publication of *In Memoriam,* Tennyson's reputation and financial security were assured. In that same year he became poet laureate of England, and in 1884 he was made a lord of the realm by the queen. "The Lady of Shalott" appeared in Tennyson's second volume of poems, *Poems* (1832), but he rewrote it for the reissue of that volume in 1842. "The Lady of Shalott" is his first treatment of King Arthur and anticipates his epic-like narrative of the rise and fall of Arthur's kingdom, the *Idylls of the King* (1859–88). "The Lady of Shalott," like nearly all of Tennyson's early poetry, was written under the influence of the English Romantic poets, especially John Keats.

Part I

On either side the river lie
Long fields of barley and of rye,
That clothe the wold° and meet the sky;
And thro' the field the road runs by
5   To many-tower'd Camelot;
And up and down the people go,
Gazing where the lilies blow°
Round an island there below,
     The island of Shalott.

10 Willows whiten, aspens quiver,
Little breezes dusk and shiver
Thro' the wave that runs for ever
By the island in the river
     Flowing down to Camelot.
15 Four gray walls, and four gray towers,
Overlook a space of flowers,
And the silent isle imbowers
     The Lady of Shalott.

By the margin, willow-veil'd,
20 Slide the heavy barges trail'd
By slow horses; and unhail'd
The shallop° flitteth silken-sail'd
     Skimming down to Camelot:
But who hath seen her wave her hand?
25 Or at the casement seen her stand?
Or is she known in all the land,
     The Lady of Shalott?

Only reapers, reaping early
In among the bearded barley,
30 Hear a song that echoes cheerly
From the river winding clearly,
     Down to tower'd Camelot:
And by the moon the reaper weary,
Piling sheaves in uplands airy,
35 Listening, whispers, "'T is the fairy
     Lady of Shalott."

[3]*wold.* Hilly, open country.
[7]*blow.* Bloom.
[22]*shallop.* A small boat.

Part II

There she weaves by night and day
A magic web with colors gay.
She has heard a whisper say,
40   A curse is on her if she stay
        To look down to Camelot.
She knows not what the curse may be,
And so she weaveth steadily,
And little other care hath she,
45   The Lady of Shalott.

And moving thro' a mirror clear
That hangs before her all the year,
Shadows of the world appear.
There she sees the highway near
50   Winding down to Camelot:
There the river eddy whirls,
And there the surly village-churls,
And the red cloaks of market girls,
        Pass onward from Shalott.

55   Sometimes a troop of damsels glad,
An abbot on an ambling pad,°
Sometimes a curly shepherd-lad,
Or long-hair'd page in crimson clad,
        Goes by to tower'd Camelot;
60   And sometimes thro' the mirror blue
The knights come riding two and two:
She hath no loyal knight and true,
        The Lady of Shalott.

But in her web she still delights
65   To weave the mirror's magic sights,
For often thro' the silent nights
A funeral, with plumes and lights,
        And music, went to Camelot:
Or when the moon was overhead,
70   Came two young lovers lately wed;
"I am half-sick of shadows," said
        The Lady of Shalott.

56 *pad.* A horse.

Part III

A bow-shot from her bower-eaves,
He rode between the barley sheaves,
75   The sun came dazzling thro' the leaves,
And flamed upon the brazen greaves°
    Of bold Sir Lancelot.
A redcross knight for ever kneel'd
To a lady in his shield,
80   That sparkled on the yellow field,
    Beside remote Shalott.

The gemmy bridle glitter'd free,
Like to some branch of stars we see
Hung in the golden Galaxy.
85   The bridle bells rang merrily
    As he rode down to Camelot:
And from his blazon'd baldric° slung
A mighty silver bugle hung,
And as he rode his armor rung,
90   Beside remote Shalott.

All in the blue unclouded weather
Thick-jewell'd shone the saddle-leather,
The helmet and the helmet-feather
Burn'd like one burning flame together,
95   As he rode down to Camelot.
As often thro' the purple night,
Below the starry clusters bright,
Some bearded meteor, trailing light,
    Moves over still Shalott.

100   His broad clear brow in sunlight glow'd;
On burnish'd hooves his war-horse trode;
From underneath his helmet flow'd
His coal-black curls as on he rode,
    As he rode down to Camelot.
105   From the bank and from the river
He flash'd into the crystal mirror,
"Tirra lirra," by the river
    Sang Sir Lancelot.

---

[76]*greaves.* Armor to protect the lower legs.
[87]*baldric.* An ornamented belt worn diagonally across the chest to support a sword or bugle.

She left the web, she left the loom,
110   She made three paces thro' the room,
She saw the water-lily bloom,
She saw the helmet and the plume,
    She look'd down to Camelot.
Out flew the web and floated wide;
115   The mirror crack'd from side to side;
"The curse is come upon me," cried
    The Lady of Shalott.

Part IV

In the stormy east-wind straining,
The pale yellow woods were waning,
120   The broad stream in his banks complaining,
Heavily the low sky raining
    Over tower'd Camelot;
Down she came and found a boat
Beneath a willow left afloat,
125   And round about the prow she wrote
    The Lady of Shalott.

And down the river's dim expanse—
Like some bold seër in a trance,
Seeing all his own mischance—
130   With a glassy countenance
    Did she look to Camelot.
And at the closing of the day
She loosed the chain, and down she lay;
The broad stream bore her far away,
135   The Lady of Shalott.

Lying, robed in snowy white
That loosely flew to left and right—
The leaves upon her falling light—
Thro' the noises of the night
140   She floated down to Camelot:
And as the boat-head wound along
The willowy hills and fields among,
They heard her singing her last song,
    The Lady of Shalott.

145   Heard a carol, mournful, holy,
Chanted loudly, chanted lowly,

Till her blood was frozen slowly,
And her eyes were darken'd wholly,
    Turn'd to tower'd Camelot;
150 For ere she reach'd upon the tide
The first house by the water-side,
Singing in her song she died,
    The Lady of Shalott.

Under tower and balcony,
155 By garden-wall and gallery,
A gleaming shape she floated by,
A corse between the houses high,
    Silent into Camelot.
Out upon the wharfs they came,
160 Knight and burgher, lord and dame,
And round the prow they read her name,
    The Lady of Shalott.

Who is this? and what is here?
And in the lighted palace near
165 Died the sound of royal cheer;
And they cross'd themselves for fear,
    All the knights at Camelot:
But Lancelot mused a little space;
He said, "She has a lovely face;
170 God in his mercy lend her grace,
    The Lady of Shalott."

Questions for Study

1. What is the metrical pattern of the poem? What is the stanzaic pattern (rhyme scheme, line lengths)? What word sounds does Tennyson use? How are they related to the sense of the lines? What effect does Tennyson seem to strive for through the musical qualities of the poem? How well do they fit the story?

2. How does Tennyson describe the setting? What is the atmosphere of the poem? How does he want us to feel about the setting? What images does he use to present the setting?

3. The poem has four parts. What is the focus of attention in each part? What changes from part to part?

4. Does the poem have symbolic meaning? What might the mirror symbolize? The web? The window? The tower where the Lady lives? Camelot? Sir Lancelot?

5. What choice does the Lady make when she looks directly at Camelot? What does she give up? What does she gain?

6. How is this poem similar to and different from Keats's "Eve of St. Agnes"?

ROBERT BROWNING

Porphyria's Lover

Robert Browning (1812-89) was born and reared on the outskirts of London. His father, who was a well-to-do bank clerk, had a very large library. And it was from this library, from private tutors, from two years at the University of London, and from reading on his own that Browning received his education. Like Tennyson, he was a revered poet during the later half of the nineteenth century. But unlike Tennyson, he was willing to use dissonant, difficult, and even harsh poetic language to explore complex moral and psychological topics. During his marriage to the poet Elizabeth Barrett (1846 until her death in 1861), he lived in Italy, where he absorbed the rich artistic and historical heritage that informed much of his finest poetry. He is best known today for his dramatic monologues and dialogues, of which "Porphyria's Lover" (1836) is one of the first. These poems feature a speaker or speakers who recount one or more incidents in their lives. Like the realistic novelists who were Browning's contemporaries, Browning attempted to probe the psychology of his characters. He was especially interested in disturbed and criminal speakers who reveal more about themselves than they are aware. His most ambitious exercise in the dramatic monologue is a long novel-like poem, *The Ring and the Book* (1868), in which a variety of characters reflect on a murder that occurred during the seventeenth century in Rome. He published "Porphyria's Lover" and another dramatic monologue under the title *Madhouse Cells.*

> The rain set early in to-night,
>   The sullen wind was soon awake,
> It tore the elm-tops down for spite,
>   And did its worst to vex the lake:
> 5   I listened with heart fit to break.

When glided in Porphyria; straight
    She shut the cold out and the storm,
And kneeled and made the cheerless grate
    Blaze up, and all the cottage warm;
10   Which done, she rose, and from her form
Withdrew the dripping cloak and shawl,
    And laid her soiled gloves by, untied
Her hat and let the damp hair fall,
    And, last, she sat down by my side
15   And called me. When no voice replied,
She put my arm about her waist,
    And made her smooth white shoulder bare,
And all her yellow hair displaced,
    And, stooping, made my cheek lie there,
20   And spread, o'er all, her yellow hair,
Murmuring how she loved me—she
    Too weak, for all her heart's endeavor,
To set its struggling passion free
    From pride, and vainer ties dissever,
25   And give herself to me for ever.
But passion sometimes would prevail,
    Nor could to-night's gay feast restrain
A sudden thought of one so pale
    For love of her, and all in vain:
30   So, she was come through wind and rain.
Be sure I looked up at her eyes
    Happy and proud; at last I knew
Porphyria worshipped me; surprise
    Made my heart swell, and still it grew
35   While I debated what to do.
That moment she was mine, mine, fair,
    Perfectly pure and good: I found
A thing to do, and all her hair
    In one long yellow string I wound
40   Three times her little throat around,
And strangled her. No pain felt she;
    I am quite sure she felt no pain.
As a shut bud that holds a bee,
    I warily oped her lids: again
45   Laughed the blue eyes without a stain.
And I untightened next the tress
    About her neck; her cheek once more
Blushed bright beneath my burning kiss:
    I propped her head up as before,
50   Only, this time my shoulder bore

Her head, which droops upon it still:
　　The smiling rosy little head,
So glad it has its utmost will,
　　That all it scorned at once is fled,
55　　And I, its love, am gained instead!
Porphyria's love: she guessed not how
　　Her darling one wish would be heard.
And thus we sit together now,
　　And all night long we have not stirred,
60　　And yet God has not said a word!

Questions for Study

1. What is the relationship between Porphyria and her lover? What is the social and economic status of each?

2. What has Porphyria decided to do? What reasons has she given for her decision?

3. How does she treat the speaker? What does she mean to communicate to him by her actions? What does she seem to intend for him in the future?

4. Where does the action occur? What is the occasion for Porphyria's visit? How is the weather important?

5. What does the speaker do? Why? What does he think he has achieved?

6. What does the speaker reveal about himself that he does not fully understand or recognize? What do we understand about him that he does not?

CHRISTINA ROSSETTI

Goblin Market

Christina Rossetti (1830-94) and her equally famous brother Dante Gabriel Rossetti grew up in the rich artistic and political environment established by her father, an exiled Italian patriot, and her Anglo-Italian mother. Their London home was a meeting place of poets, musicians, and political activists. In the early part of her career she was closely associated with her brother's circle of artist friends, the Pre-Raphaelite Brotherhood, who aspired to return English literature and art to the forms and subject matter of Italian literature and art before Raphael. It was during this period that she published her first book of poetry,

Goblin Market and Other Poems (1862). These poems reflect interests that governed her poetry throughout her career. She was a devout Christian. She studied and felt an intense sympathy with the natural world. She identified with and spoke for the problems and concerns of females. In addition to "Goblin Market," one of her best known poems today is the Christmas carol "In the Bleak Mid-Winter."

Morning and evening
Maids heard the goblins cry:
"Come buy our orchard fruits,
Come buy, come buy:
5   Apples and quinces,
Lemons and oranges,
Plump unpecked cherries,
Melons and raspberries,
Bloom-down-cheeked peaches,
10   Swart-headed mulberries,
Wild free-born cranberries,
Crab-apples, dewberries,
Pine-apples, blackberries,
Apricots, strawberries;—
15   All ripe together
In summer weather,—
Morns that pass by,
Fair eves that fly;
Come buy, come buy:
20   Our grapes fresh from the vine,
Pomegranates full and fine,
Dates and sharp bullaces,°
Rare pears and greengages,°
Damsons° and bilberries,°
25   Taste them and try:
Currants and gooseberries,
Bright-fire-like barberries,
Figs to fill your mouth,
Citrons from the South,
30   Sweet to tongue and sound to eye;
Come buy, come buy."

---

[22]*bullaces,* [23]*greengages,* and [24]*damsons.* Varieties of plums.
[24]*bilberries.* Berries that are similar to blueberries.

Evening by evening
Among the brookside rushes,
Laura bowed her head to hear,
35   Lizzie veiled her blushes:
Crouching close together
In the cooling weather,
With clasping arms and cautioning lips,
With tingling cheeks and finger-tips.
40   "Lie close," Laura said,
Pricking up her golden head:
"We must not look at goblin men,
We must not buy their fruits:
Who knows upon what soil they fed
45   Their hungry thirsty roots?"
"Come buy," call the goblins
Hobbling down the glen.
"O," cried Lizzie, "Laura, Laura,
You should not peep at goblin men."
50   Lizzie covered up her eyes,
Covered close lest they should look;
Laura reared her glossy head,
And whispered like the restless brook:
"Look, Lizzie, look, Lizzie,
55   Down the glen tramp little men.
One hauls a basket,
One bears a plate,
One lugs a golden dish
Of many pounds' weight.
60   How fair the vine must grow
Whose grapes are so luscious;
How warm the wind must blow
Through those fruit bushes."
"No," said Lizzie, "no, no, no;
65   Their offers should not charm us,
Their evil gifts would harm us."
She thrust a dimpled finger
In each ear, shut eyes and ran:
Curious Laura chose to linger
70   Wondering at each merchant man.
One had a cat's face,
One whisked a tail,
One tramped at a rat's pace,
One crawled like a snail,
75   One like a wombat prowled obtuse and furry,

One like a ratel° tumbled hurry-scurry.
She heard a voice like voice of doves
Cooing all together:
They sounded kind and full of loves
80   In the pleasant weather.

Laura stretched her gleaming neck
Like a rush-imbedded swan,
Like a lily from the beck,°
Like a moonlit poplar branch,
85   Like a vessel at the launch
When its last restraint is gone.

Backwards up the mossy glen
Turned and trooped the goblin men,
With their shrill repeated cry,
90   "Come buy, come buy."
When they reached where Laura was
They stood stock still upon the moss,
Leering at each other,
Brother with queer brother;
95   Signalling each other,
Brother with sly brother.
One set his basket down,
One reared his plate;
One began to weave a crown
100   Of tendrils, leaves, and rough nuts brown
(Men sell not such in any town);
One heaved the golden weight
Of dish and fruit to offer her:
"Come buy, come buy," was still their cry.
105   Laura stared but did not stir,
Longed but had no money:
The whisk-tailed merchant bade her taste
In tones as smooth as honey,
The cat-faced purr'd,
110   The rat-paced spoke a word
Of welcome, and the snail-paced even was heard;
One parrot-voiced and jolly
Cried "Pretty Goblin" still for "Pretty Polly";—
One whistled like a bird.

---

⁷⁶*ratel.* A badger-like mammal (pronounced *ray-tell*).
⁸³*beck.* A creek.

115 But sweet-tooth Laura spoke in haste:
  "Good folk, I have no coin;
  To take were to purloin:
  I have no copper in my purse,
  I have no silver either,
120 And all my gold is on the furze
  That shakes in windy weather
  Above the rusty heather."
  "You have much gold upon your head,"
  They answered altogether:
125 "Buy from us with a golden curl."
  She clipped a precious golden lock,
  She dropped a tear more rare than pearl,
  Then sucked their fruit globes fair or red:
  Sweeter than honey from the rock,
130 Stronger than man-rejoicing wine,
  Clearer than water flowed that juice;
  She never tasted such before,
  How should it cloy with length of use?
  She sucked and sucked and sucked the more
135 Fruits which that unknown orchard bore;
  She sucked until her lips were sore;
  Then flung the emptied rinds away,
  But gathered up one kernel stone,
  And knew not was it night or day
140 As she turned home alone.

  Lizzie met her at the gate
  Full of wise upbraidings:
  "Dear, you should not stay so late,
  Twilight is not good for maidens;
145 Should not loiter in the glen
  In the haunts of goblin men.
  Do you not remember Jeanie,
  How she met them in the moonlight,
  Took their gifts both choice and many,
150 Ate their fruits and wore their flowers
  Plucked from bowers
  Where summer ripens at all hours?
  But ever in the noonlight
  She pined and pined away;
155 Sought them by night and day,
  Found them no more, but dwindled and grew gray;
  Then fell with the first snow,
  While to this day no grass will grow

Where she lies low:
160   I planted daisies there a year ago
That never blow.°
You should not loiter so."
"Nay, hush," said Laura:
"Nay, hush, my sister:
165   I ate and ate my fill,
Yet my mouth waters still;
To-morrow night I will
Buy more,"—and kissed her.
"Have done with sorrow;
170   I'll bring you plums to-morrow
Fresh on their mother twigs,
Cherries worth getting;
You cannot think what figs
My teeth have met in,
175   What melons icy-cold
Piled on a dish of gold
Too huge for me to hold,
What peaches with a velvet nap,
Pellucid grapes without one seed:
180   Odorous indeed must be the mead
Whereon they grow, and pure the wave they drink,
With lilies at the brink,
And sugar-sweet their sap."

Golden head by golden head,
185   Like two pigeons in one nest
Folded in each other's wings,
They lay down in their curtained bed:
Like two blossoms on one stem,
Like two flakes of new-fallen snow,
190   Like two wands of ivory
Tipped with gold for awful kings.
Moon and stars gazed in at them,
Wind sang to them lullaby,
Lumbering owls forbore to fly,
195   Not a bat flapped to and fro
Round their rest:
Cheek to cheek and breast to breast
Locked together in one nest.

Early in the morning
200   When the first cock crowed his warning,

161*blow*. Bloom.

Neat like bees, as sweet and busy,
Laura rose with Lizzie:
Fetched in honey, milked the cows,
Aired and set to rights the house,
205   Kneaded cakes of whitest wheat,
Cakes for dainty mouths to eat,
Next churned butter, whipped up cream,
Fed their poultry, sat and sewed;
Talked as modest maidens should:
210   Lizzie with an open heart,
Laura in an absent dream,
One content, one sick in part;
One warbling for the mere bright day's delight,
One longing for the night.

215   At length slow evening came:
They went with pitchers to the reedy brook;
Lizzie most placid in her look,
Laura most like a leaping flame.
They drew the gurgling water from its deep;
220   Lizzie plucked purple and rich golden flags,
Then turning homeward said: "The sunset flushes
Those furthest loftiest crags;
Come, Laura, not another maiden lags,
No wilful squirrel wags,
225   The beasts and birds are fast asleep."
But Laura loitered still among the rushes
And said the bank was steep.

    And said the hour was early still,
The dew not fallen, the wind not chill:
230   Listening ever, but not catching
The customary cry,
"Come buy, come buy,"
With its iterated jingle
Of sugar-baited words:
235   Not for all her watching
Once discerning even one goblin
Racing, whisking, tumbling, hobbling;
Let alone the herds
That used to tramp along the glen,
240   In groups or single,
Of brisk fruit-merchant men.

    Till Lizzie urged: "O Laura, come;
I hear the fruit-call, but I dare not look:

You should not loiter longer at this brook:
245   Come with me home.
The stars rise, the moon bends her arc,
Each glow-worm winks her spark,
Let us get home before the night grows dark;
For clouds may gather
250   Though this is summer weather,
Put out the lights and drench us through;
Then if we lost our way what should we do?"

Laura turned cold as stone
To find her sister heard that cry alone,
255   That goblin cry,
"Come buy our fruits, come buy."
Must she then buy no more such dainty fruit?
Must she no more such succous pasture find,
Gone deaf and blind?
260   Her tree of life drooped from the root:
She said not one word in her heart's sore ache;
But peering thro' the dimness, naught discerning,
Trudged home, her pitcher dripping all the way;
So crept to bed, and lay
265   Silent till Lizzie slept;
Then sat up in a passionate yearning,
And gnashed her teeth for balked desire, and wept
As if her heart would break.

Day after day, night after night,
270   Laura kept watch in vain,
In sullen silence of exceeding pain.
She never caught again the goblin cry:
"Come buy, come buy";—
She never spied the goblin men
275   Hawking their fruits along the glen:
But when the noon waxed bright
Her hair grew thin and gray;
She dwindled, as the fair full moon doth turn
To swift decay, and burn
280   Her fire away.

One day remembering her kernel-stone
She set it by a wall that faced the south;
Dewed it with tears, hoped for a root,
Watched for a waxing shoot,
285   But there came none;

It never saw the sun,
It never felt the trickling moisture run:
While with sunk eyes and faded mouth
She dreamed of melons, as a traveller sees
290   False waves in desert drouth
With shade of leaf-crowned trees,
And burns the thirstier in the sandful breeze.

She no more swept the house,
Tended the fowls or cows,
295   Fetched honey, kneaded cakes of wheat,
Brought water from the brook:
But sat down listless in the chimney-nook
And would not eat.

Tender Lizzie could not bear
300   To watch her sister's cankerous care,
Yet not to share.
She night and morning
Caught the goblins' cry:
"Come buy our orchard fruits,
305   Come buy, come buy."
Beside the brook, along the glen,
She heard the tramp of goblin men,
The voice and stir
Poor Laura could not hear;
310   Longed to buy fruit to comfort her,
But feared to pay too dear.
She thought of Jeanie in her grave,
Who should have been a bride;
But who for joys brides hope to have
315   Fell sick and died
In her gay prime,
In earliest winter-time,
With the first glazing rime,
With the first snow-fall of crisp winter-time.

320   Till Laura, dwindling,
Seemed knocking at Death's door:
Then Lizzie weighed no more
Better and worse,
But put a silver penny in her purse,
325   Kissed Laura, crossed the heath with clumps of furze
At twilight, halted by the brook;
And for the first time in her life

Began to listen and look.

Laughed every goblin
330 When they spied her peeping:
Came towards her hobbling,
Flying, running, leaping,
Puffing and blowing,
Chuckling, clapping, crowing,
335 Clucking and gobbling,
Mopping and mowing,
Full of airs and graces,
Pulling wry faces,
Demure grimaces,
340 Cat-like and rat-like,
Ratel and wombat-like,
Snail-paced in a hurry,
Parrot-voiced and whistler,
Helter-skelter, hurry-skurry,
345 Chattering like magpies,
Fluttering like pigeons,
Gliding like fishes,—
Hugged her and kissed her;
Squeezed and caressed her;
350 Stretched up their dishes,
Panniers and plates:
"Look at our apples
Russet and dun,
Bob at our cherries,
355 Bite at our peaches,
Citrons and dates,
Grapes for the asking,
Pears red with basking
Out in the sun,
360 Plums on their twigs;
Pluck them and suck them,
Pomegranates, figs."

"Good folk," said Lizzie,
Mindful of Jeanie,
365 "Give me much and many";—
Held out her apron,
Tossed them her penny.
"Nay, take a seat with us,
Honor and eat with us,"
370 They answered grinning:

"Our feast is but beginning.
Night yet is early,
Warm and dew-pearly,
Wakeful and starry:
375 Such fruits as these
No man can carry;
Half their bloom would fly,
Half their dew would dry,
Half their flavor would pass by.
380 Sit down and feast with us,
Be welcome guest with us,
Cheer you and rest with us."
"Thank you," said Lizzie; "but one waits
At home alone for me:
385 So, without further parleying,
If you will not sell me any
Of your fruits though much and many,
Give me back my silver penny
I tossed you for a fee."
390 They began to scratch their pates,
No longer wagging, purring,
But visibly demurring,
Grunting and snarling.
One called her proud,
395 Cross-grained, uncivil;
Their tones waxed loud,
Their looks were evil.
Lashing their tails
They trod and hustled her,
400 Elbowed and jostled her,
Clawed with their nails,
Barking, mewing, hissing, mocking,
Tore her gown and soiled her stocking,
Twitched her hair out by the roots,
405 Stamped upon her tender feet,
Held her hands and squeezed their fruits
Against her mouth to make her eat.

    White and golden Lizzie stood,
Like a lily in a flood,—
410 Like a rock of blue-veined stone
Lashed by tides obstreperously,—
Like a beacon left alone
In a hoary roaring sea,
Sending up a golden fire,—

415 Like a fruit-crowned orange-tree
White with blossoms honey-sweet
Sore beset by wasp and bee,—
Like a royal virgin town
Topped with gilded dome and spire
420 Close beleaguered by a fleet
Mad to tug her standard down.

One may lead a horse to water,
Twenty cannot make him drink.
Though the goblins cuffed and caught her,
425 Coaxed and fought her,
Bullied and besought her,
Scratched her, pinched her black as ink,
Kicked and knocked her,
Mauled and mocked her,
430 Lizzie uttered not a word;
Would not open lip from lip
Lest they should cram a mouthful in;
But laughed in heart to feel the drip
Of juice that syrupped all her face,
435 And lodged in dimples of her chin,
And streaked her neck which quaked like curd.
At last the evil people,
Worn out by her resistance,
Flung back her penny, kicked their fruit
440 Along whichever road they took,
Not leaving root or stone or shoot.
Some writhed into the ground,
Some dived into the brook
With ring and ripple,
445 Some scudded on the gale without a sound,
Some vanished in the distance.

In a smart, ache, tingle,
Lizzie went her way;
Knew not was it night or day;
450 Sprang up the bank, tore through the furze,
Threaded copse and dingle,
And heard her penny jingle
Bouncing in her purse,—
Its bounce was music to her ear.
455 She ran and ran
As if she feared some goblin man
Dogged her with gibe or curse

Or something worse:
But not one goblin skurried after,
460 Nor was she pricked by fear;
The kind heart made her windy-paced
That urged her home quite out of breath with haste
And inward laughter.

She cried "Laura," up the garden,
465 "Did you miss me?
Come and kiss me.
Never mind my bruises,
Hug me, kiss me, suck my juices
Squeezed from goblin fruits for you,
470 Goblin pulp and goblin dew.
Eat me, drink me, love me;
Laura, make much of me:
For your sake I have braved the glen
And had to do with goblin merchant men."

475 Laura started from her chair,
Flung her arms up in the air,
Clutched her hair:
"Lizzie, Lizzie, have you tasted
For my sake the fruit forbidden?
480 Must your light like mine be hidden,
Your young life like mine be wasted,
Undone in mine undoing
And ruined in my ruin,
Thirsty, cankered, goblin-ridden?"
485 She clung about her sister,
Kissed and kissed and kissed her:
Tears once again
Refreshed her shrunken eyes,
Dropping like rain
490 After long sultry drouth;
Shaking with aguish fear, and pain,
She kissed and kissed her with a hungry mouth.

Her lips began to scorch,
That juice was wormwood to her tongue,
495 She loathed the feast:
Writhing as one possessed she leaped and sung,
Rent all her robe, and wrung
Her hands in lamentable haste,
And beat her breast.

500 Her locks streamed like the torch
     Borne by a racer at full speed,
     Or like the mane of horses in their flight,
     Or like an eagle when she stems° the light
     Straight toward the sun,
505 Or like a caged thing freed,
     Or like a flying flag when armies run.

        Swift fire spread through her veins, knocked at her heart,
     Met the fire smouldering there
     And overbore its lesser flame;
510 She gorged on bitterness without a name:
     Ah! fool, to choose such part
     Of soul-consuming care!
     Sense failed in the mortal strife:
     Like the watch-tower of a town
515 Which an earthquake shatters down,
     Like a lightning-stricken mast,
     Like a wind-uprooted tree
     Spun about,
     Like a foam-topped water-spout
520 Cast down headlong in the sea,
     She fell at last;
     Pleasure past and anguish past,
     Is it death or is it life?

        Life out of death.
525 That night long Lizzie watched by her,
     Counted her pulse's flagging stir,
     Felt for her breath,
     Held water to her lips, and cooled her face
     With tears and fanning leaves:
530 But when the first birds chirped about their eaves,
     And early reapers plodded to the place
     Of golden sheaves,
     And dew-wet grass
     Bowed in the morning winds so brisk to pass,
535 And new buds with new day
     Opened of cup-like lilies on the stream,
     Laura awoke as from a dream,
     Laughed in the innocent old way,

503*stems*. Flies against.

Hugged Lizzie but not twice or thrice;
540 Her gleaming locks showed not one thread of gray,
Her breath was sweet as May,
And light danced in her eyes.

Days, weeks, months, years
Afterwards, when both were wives
545 With children of their own;
Their mother-hearts beset with fears,
Their lives bound up in tender lives;
Laura would call the little ones
And tell them of her early prime,
550 Those pleasant days long gone
Of not-returning time:
Would talk about the haunted glen,
The wicked, quaint fruit-merchant men,
Their fruits like honey to the throat,
555 But poison in the blood;
(Men sell not such in any town):
Would tell them how her sister stood
In deadly peril to do her good,
And win the fiery antidote:
560 Then joining hands to little hands
Would bid them cling together,
"For there is no friend like a sister,
In calm or stormy weather,
To cheer one on the tedious way,
565 To fetch one if one goes astray,
To lift one if one totters down,
To strengthen whilst one stands."

Questions for Study

1. What is the importance of food in this poem? How is it described? To what tastes does goblin food appeal?

2. How does Laura change? How does she become different from Lizzie? What values does each girl represent?

3. What are the metaphors and similes of the poem? Where do they appear? What do they mean?

4. What images and sounds does the poet associate with Laura, Lizzie, and the goblins? Why?

5. Where does the poet change the length of the lines? Why? Where does she alter the regular metrical pattern? How does she use end rhyme to emphasize and link concepts? What other word sounds are important?

6. What do the goblins and their food symbolize?

7. How is this poem similar to and different from prose fairy tales, like those in chapter four (p. 181)?

ROBERT FROST

Home Burial

Although Robert Frost (1874-1963) was born and spent his early childhood in California, he is most associated with New England, where his family moved when he was eleven and which provided the subject matter of nearly all his poetry. He graduated from high school in 1891 and several years later married his co-valedictorian, Elinor White. After an unsuccessful attempt at farming in New Hampshire, he and his family moved to London so that he could make a start as a poet. He published his first book, *A Boy's Will* (1913), while he was in England, and followed it soon with a second, *North of Boston* (1914). Both of these books were well-received enough for Frost to move back to New England. He achieved financial stability from the increasing popularity of his poetry, from teaching, and from nationwide lecture tours. Toward the end of his life, he was the best-known poet in the United States. Unlike many twentieth century poets, Frost wrote in conformity to traditional poetic forms, like blank verse and the sonnet. Frost's poetry reflects his deep affinity with the New England countryside and with those folk, like farmers, woodcutters, and tramps, who live close to the earth. "Home Burial," which appeared for the first time in *North of Boston,* is one of the many blank verse dramatic monologues and dialogues that Frost wrote throughout his career.

> He saw her from the bottom of the stairs
> Before she saw him. She was starting down,
> Looking back over her shoulder at some fear.
> She took a doubtful step and then undid it
> 5   To raise herself and look again. He spoke

Advancing toward her: "What is it you see
From up there always—for I want to know."
She turned and sank upon her skirts at that,
And her face changed from terrified to dull.

10 He said to gain time: "What is it you see,"
Mounting until she cowered under him.
"I will find out now—you must tell me, dear."
She, in her place, refused him any help
With the least stiffening of her neck and silence.

15 She let him look, sure that he wouldn't see,
Blind creature; and a while he didn't see.
But at last he murmured, "Oh," and again, "Oh."

"What is it—what?" she said.

   "Just that I see."

"You don't," she challenged. "Tell me what it is."

20 "The wonder is I didn't see at once.
I never noticed it from here before.
I must be wonted to it—that's the reason.
The little graveyard where my people are!
So small the window frames the whole of it.

25 Not so much larger than a bedroom, is it?
There are three stones of slate and one of marble,
Broad-shouldered little slabs there in the sunlight
On the sidehill. We haven't to mind *those*.
But I understand: it is not the stones,

30 But the child's mound—"

   "Don't, don't, don't, don't," she cried.

She withdrew shrinking from beneath his arm
That rested on the banister, and slid downstairs;
And turned on him with such a daunting look,
He said twice over before he knew himself:

35 "Can't a man speak of his own child he's lost?"

"Not you! Oh, where's my hat? Oh, I don't need it!
I must get out of here. I must get air.
I don't know rightly whether any man can."

"Amy! Don't go to someone else this time.

40 Listen to me. I won't come down the stairs."

He sat and fixed his chin between his fists.
"There's something I should like to ask you, dear."

"You don't know how to ask it."

  "Help me, then."
Her fingers moved the latch for all reply.

45 "My words are nearly always an offence.
I don't know how to speak of anything
So as to please you. But I might be taught
I should suppose. I can't say I see how.
A man must partly give up being a man
50 With women-folk. We could have some arrangement
By which I'd bind myself to keep hands off
Anything special you're a-mind to name.
Though I don't like such things 'twixt those that love.
Two that don't love can't live together without them.
55 But two that do can't live together with them."
She moved the latch a little. "Don't—don't go.
Don't carry it to someone else this time.
Tell me about it if it's something human.
Let me into your grief. I'm not so much
60 Unlike other folks as your standing there
Apart would make me out. Give me my chance.
I do think, though, you overdo it a little.
What was it brought you up to think it the thing
To take your mother-loss of a first child
65 So inconsolably—in the face of love.
You'd think his memory might be satisfied—"

"There you go sneering now!"
    "I'm not, I'm not!
You make me angry. I'll come down to you.
God, what a woman! And it's come to this,
70 A man can't speak of his own child that's dead."

"You can't because you don't know how.
If you had any feelings, you that dug
With your own hand—how could you?—his little grave;
I saw you from that very window there,
75 Making the gravel leap and leap in air,
Leap up, like that, like that, and land so lightly
And roll back down the mound beside the hole.
I thought, Who is that man? I didn't know you.

And I crept down the stairs and up the stairs
80   To look again, and still your spade kept lifting.
Then you came in. I heard your rumbling voice
Out in the kitchen, and I don't know why,
But I went near to see with my own eyes.
You could sit there with the stains on your shoes
85   Of the fresh earth from your own baby's grave
And talk about your everyday concerns.
You had stood the spade up against the wall
Outside there in the entry, for I saw it."

"I shall laugh the worst laugh I ever laughed.
90   I'm cursed. God, if I don't believe I'm cursed."

"I can repeat the very words you were saying.
'Three foggy mornings and one rainy day
Will rot the best birch fence a man can build.'
Think of it, talk like that at such a time!
95   What had how long it takes a birch to rot
To do with what was in the darkened parlour.
You *couldn't* care! The nearest friends can go
With anyone to death, comes so far short
They might as well not try to go at all.
100   No, from the time when one is sick to death,
One is alone, and he dies more alone.
Friends make pretence of following to the grave,
But before one is in it, their minds are turned
And making the best of their way back to life
105   And living people, and things they understand.
But the world's evil. I won't have grief so
If I can change it. Oh, I won't, I won't!"

"There, you have said it all and you feel better.
You won't go now. You're crying. Close the door.
110   The heart's gone out of it: why keep it up.
Amy! There's someone coming down the road!"

"*You*—oh, you think the talk is all. I must go—
Somewhere out of this house. How can I make you—"

"If—you—do!" She was opening the door wider.
"Where do you mean to go? First tell me that.
115   I'll follow and bring you back by force. I *will!*—"

Questions for Study

1. The verse form of this poem is "blank verse." (See p. 307 for a description of blank verse.) What, if anything, does Frost lose by using this form? What does he gain? Since there is no end rhyme, does he give up musical devices altogether? Are his departures from the iambic metrical pattern meaningful?

2. What is the conflict between Amy and her husband? What does she accuse him of? What does he offer her? How has she been coping with her pain up to now? How has he coped with his pain?

3. How are Amy and her husband different? Which character does Frost seem to sympathize with the most?

4. What is the future of their marriage?

5. How is nature important to the characterization and themes of this poem? What attitudes toward nature do the two characters have?

ZORA NEALE HURSTON

Sermon

Zora Neale Hurston (1891–1960) was born and reared in an all-African-American town, Eatonville, Florida, which provided the material for some of her finest writing. Her father was a Baptist preacher whose oratory gave her a strong sense of the poetic quality of African-American speech. She attended college at Howard University in Washington, D.C., and then at Barnard College in New York City. While she was in New York, she was a vibrant participant in the Harlem Renaissance, a cultural movement in which African-American writers, musicians, and artists expressed the history and conditions of African Americans to a receptive audience of both whites and African Americans. After she graduated from Barnard, she returned to Eatonville to record the oral artistic traditions of the African-American community in Florida. She incorporated the fruits of this fieldwork in her best novel, *Their Eyes Were Watching God* (1937), and in her autobiography, *Dust Tracks on a Road* (1942). But her most direct representation of it is in her nonfiction book *Mules and Men* (1935), which takes the reader on a cultural tour of the Eatonville area. The free verse poem "Sermon" is an excerpt from that book. The setting is a sawmill camp in a swamp near Eatonville. The "quarters" is where the workers and their families live.

*T*he men were still coming into the quarters from various parts of the "job." The children played "Shoo-round," and "Chick-mah-Chick" until Mrs. Williams called her four year old Frankie and put her to sleep by rocking her and singing "Mister Frog."

It wasn't black dark, but night was peeping around the corner. The quarters were getting alive. Woofing, threats and brags up and down the line.

Three figures in the dusk-dark detached themselves from the railroad track and came walking into the quarters. A tall black grim-faced man with a rusty black reticule, followed by two women.

Everybody thought he was a bootlegger and yelled orders to him to that effect. He paid no attention, but set down his bag slowly, opened it still slower and took out a dog-eared Bible and opened it. The crowd quieted down. They knew he was a travelling preacher, a "stump-knocker" in the language of the "job."

Some fell silent to listen. Others sucked their teeth and either went back into their houses or went on to the jook.

When he had a reasonable amount of attention he nodded to the woman at his left and she raised "Death comes a Creepin'" and the crowd helped out. At the end the preacher began:

You all done been over in Pentecost (got to feeling spiritual by singing) and now we going to talk about de woman that was taken from man. I take my text from Genesis two and twenty-one (Gen. 2:21)

> Behold de Rib!
> Now, my beloved,
> Behold means to look and see.
> Look at dis woman God done made,
> 5   But first thing, ah hah!
> Ah wants you to gaze upon God's previous works.
> Almighty and arisen God, hah!
> Peace-giving and prayer-hearing God,
> High-riding and strong armded God
> 10   Walking acrost his globe creation, hah!
> Wid de blue elements for a helmet
> And a wall of fire round his feet
> He wakes de sun every morning from his fiery bed
> Wid de breath of his smile
> 15   And commands de moon wid his eyes.
> And Oh—
> Wid de eye of Faith
> I can see him
> Standing out on de eaves of ether
> 20   Breathing clouds from out his nostrils,
> Blowing storms from 'tween his lips
> I can see!!

Him seize de mighty axe of his proving power
And smite the stubborn-standing space,
25   And laid it wide open in a mighty gash—
Making a place to hold de world
I can see him—
Molding de world out of thought and power
And whirling it out on its eternal track,
30   Ah hah, my strong armded God!
He set de blood red eye of de sun in de sky
And told it,
Wait, wait! Wait there till Shiloh come
I can see!
35   Him mold de mighty mountains
And melting de skies into seas.
Oh, Behold, and look and see! hah
We see in de beginning
He made de bestes every one after its kind,
40   De birds that fly de trackless air,
De fishes dat swim de mighty deep—
Male and fee-male, hah!
Then he took of de dust of de earth
And made man in his own image.
45   And man was alone,
Even de lion had a mate
So God shook his head
And a thousand million diamonds
Flew out from his glittering crown
50   And studded de evening sky and made de stars.
So God put Adam into a deep sleep
And took out a bone, ah hah!
And it is said that it was a rib.
Behold de rib!
55   A bone out of a man's side.
He put de man to sleep and made wo-man,
And men and women been sleeping together ever since.
Behold de rib!
Brothers, if God
60   Had taken dat bone out of man's head
He would have meant for woman to rule, hah
If he had taken a bone out of his foot,
He would have meant for us to dominize and rule.
He could have made her out of back-bone
65   And then she would have been behind us.
But, no, God Amighty, he took de bone out of his side
So dat places de woman beside us;

Hah! God knowed his own mind.
Behold de rib!
70   And now I leave dis thought wid you,
Let us all go marchin' up to de gates of Glory.
Tramp! tramp! tramp!
In step wid de host dat John saw.
Male and female like God made us
75   Side by side.
Oh, behold de rib!
And less all set down in Glory together
Right round his glorified throne
And praise his name forever.
80   Amen.

At the end of the sermon the woman on the preacher's left raised, "Been a Listenin' All de Night Long," and the preacher descended from his fiery cloud and lifted the collection in his hat. The singers switched to, "You Can't Hide, Sinners, You Can't Hide." The sparse contribution taken, the trio drifted back into the darkness of the railroad, walking towards Kissimmee.

Questions for Study

1. What musical devices does Hurston use in the preacher's sermon? How and why does she vary the lengths of the lines? Does the sermon have a metrical pattern? How are word sounds related to the sense of the lines?

2. What images, metaphors, and similes does Hurston use? Why?

3. How does the preacher characterize God?

4. What ideas does the preacher present in his account of the creation of Adam and Eve?

5. How is the preacher's account of creation similar to and different from the biblical account (p. 30). What characterizes the language in both accounts?

ALICE WALKER

Early Losses: A Requiem

Alice Walker's (1944–) parents were African-American sharecroppers who lived in rural Georgia. She attended Spelman College and Sarah

Lawrence College. While she was in college, she visited Africa. After her graduation from Sarah Lawrence, she worked as a caseworker in the New York City welfare department and as a volunteer in the drive to register African-American voters in Mississippi in 1966. She published her first collection of poems, *Once,* in 1968, and her first collection of short stories, *In Love and Trouble,* in 1973. Her best-known work, the novel *The Color Purple* (1982), focuses on topics that characterize nearly all of her work: African history and culture, African-American history and culture, and the status of women. She was influenced by the writings of Zora Neale Hurston and was instrumental in bringing Hurston's work to public acclaim. In "Looking for Zora," included in *In Search of Our Mother's Gardens* (1983), a collection of essays and reminiscences, she describes her successful quest to find Hurston's grave in Florida. "Early Losses: A Requiem" first appeared in 1974 in a literary magazine and then in her collection of poems *Good Night, Willie Lee, I'll See You in the Morning* (1979).

Part I

Nyanu was appointed
as my Lord. The husband chosen
by the elders
before my birth.
5   He sipped wine with
my father
and when I was born
brought a parrot as
his gift
10   to play with me.
Paid baskets of grain
and sweet berries
to make me fat
for his pleasure.

15   Omunu was my playmate
who helped consume
Nyanu's gifts.
Our fat selves grew
together
20   knee and knee.
It was Omunu I wished

to share my tiny
playing house.

Him I loved as the sun
25   must seek and chase
its own reflection
across the sky.
My brothers, before you
turn away—

30   The day the savages came
to ambush our village
it was Nyanu who struggled
bravely
Omunu ran and hid
35   behind his parent's house.
He was a coward but
only nine
as was I; who trembled
beside him as we two
40   were stolen away
Nyanu's dead body
begging remembrance
of his tiny morsel
taken from his mouth.
45   Nor was I joyful that he was dead
only glad that now I would not have
to marry him.

Omunu clasped my hands
within the barkcloth pouch
50   and I his head
a battered flower
bent low
upon its stalk
Our cries pounded back
55   into our throats
by thudding blows
we could not see
our mothers' cries
at such a distance
60   we could not hear
and over the miles
we feasted on homesickness

our mothers' tears and
the dew
65   all we consumed of homeland
before we left.

At the great water Omunu fought
to stay with me
at such a tender age
70   our hearts we set
upon each other
as the retreating wave
brings its closest friend
upon its back.
75   We cried out in words
that met an echo
and Omunu vanished
down a hole that
smelled of blood and
80   excrement and death
and I was "saved"
for sport among
the sailors of the crew.
Only nine, upon a ship. My mouth
85   my body a mystery
that opened with each tearing
lunge. Crying for Omunu
who was not seen
again
90   by these eyes.

Listen to your sister, singing
in the field.
My body forced to receive
grain and wild berries
95   and milk so I could seem
a likely wench
—my mother's child
sold for a price. My father's
child again for sale.
100   I prayed to all our Gods
"Come down to me"
Hoist the burden no child
was meant to bear
and decipher the prayer

105   from within each song
       —the song despised—
       my belly become a stronghold
       for a stranger
       who will not recall
110   when he is two
       the contours of
       his mother's face.
       See the savages turn back
       my lips
115   and with hot irons
       brand me neck and thigh.

       I could not see the horizon
       for the sky
       a burning eye
120   the sun, beloved in the shade,
       became an enemy
       a pestle pounding long
       upon my head.
       You walked with me.
125   And when day sagged into night
       some one of you of my own choice
       shared my rest. Omunu
       risen from the ocean
130   out of the stomachs of whales
       the teeth of sharks
       lying beside me sleeping
       knee and knee.
       We could not speak always
135   of hearts
       for in the morning if they
       sold you
       how could I flatten
       a wrinkled face?
140   The stupor of dread
       made smooth the look
       that to my tormentors
       was born erased.
       I mourned for you. And if you died
145   took out my heart upon my lap
       and rested it.

       See me old at thirty

my sack of cotton weighted
to the ground. My hair
150   enough to cover a marble
my teeth like rattles
made of chalk
my breath a whisper
of decay.
155   The slack of my belly
falling to my knees.
I shrink to become a tiny size
a delicate morsel
upon my mother's knee
160   prepared like bread. The shimmering
of the sun a noise
upon my head.

To the child that's left
I offer a sound
165   without a promise
a clue
of what it means.

The sound itself is all.

Part II: The Child

A sound like a small wind
170   finding the door of a
hollow reed
my mother's farewell
glocked up from the back
of her throat

175   *the sound itself is all*

all I have
to remember a mother
I scarcely knew.
"Omunu" to me; who never knew
180   what "Omunu" meant. Whether home
or man or trusted God. "Omunu."
Her only treasure,
and never spent.

Questions for Study

1. Who is the speaker in Part I? To whom is she speaking? Why is she speaking? What is her relationship with her hearers?

2. What is the focus of each section of Part I?

3. In this free verse poem, how are the varied line lengths important to the sense of the lines? Why are some lines shorter than others?

4. Why does Walker allow phrases to run into one another? Why does she sometimes omit punctuation that would mark the end of phrases?

5. What happens to the speaker and Omunu? What does Omunu mean to her? Why does the speaker begin her account with Nyanu?

6. Who is the speaker in Part II? What does the speaker mean by the last two lines?

FOR FURTHER READING

Child, Francis James, ed. *English and Scottish Ballads.* 8 vols. Boston: Little, Brown, 1857. Child's great collection of medieval ballads is arranged in roughly chronological order of composition.

Fussell, Paul, Jr. *Poetic Meter and Poetic Form.* New York: Random House, 1967. Fussell provides a lucid, entertaining explanation of metrical patterns and poetic structures and how one uses them to analyze poetry.

Holman, C. Hugh, and William Harmon. *A Handbook to Literature.* 5th ed. New York: Macmillan, 1986. Holman and Harmon's encyclopedia of literary terms lucidly describes the elements of poetry.

Kroeber, Karl. *Romantic Narrative Art.* Madison: U of Wisconsin P, 1960. Kroeber analysizes the narrative poetry of Wordsworth, Byron, Keats, Scott, Coleridge and other Romantic poets. In the introduction he discusses narrative poetry in general.

Lupack, Alan, ed. *"Arthur the Greatest King": An Anthology of Modern Arthurian Poems.* New York: Garland Publishing, Inc., 1988. This collection reprints nineteenth and twentieth century poems on Arthurian characters and events.

Mieder, Wolfgang, ed. *Disenchantments: An Anthology of Modern Fairy Tale Poetry.* Hanover: U of Vermont P, 1985. The poems in this collection are responses to and retellings of famous fairy tales.

Opie, Iona and Peter, eds. *The Oxford Book of Narrative Verse.* New York: Oxford UP, 1983. In this anthology the Opies collect a wide variety of narrative poetry in English.

Scholes, Robert. *Elements of Poetry.* New York: Oxford UP, 1969. Scholes provides a brief introduction to the elements of poetry. He makes an interesting distinction between "dramatic" and "narrative" poetry.

Turco, Lewis. *The New Book of Forms: A Handbook of Poetics.* Hanover: University Press of New England, 1986. In this encyclopedia of the elements and forms of poetry, the author illustrates his definition of each form with at least one poem.

Wheeler, Charles B. *The Design of Poetry.* New York: Norton, 1966. Wheeler briefly defines the elements of poetry.

Williams, Miller. *Patterns of Poetry: An Encyclopedia of Forms.* Baton Rouge: Louisiana State UP, 1986. Miller gives a thorough description of the elements and forms of poetry.

Chapter Seven
The Short Story

INTRODUCTION

Historically, the short story is a recent form of literature. Whereas some narrative forms, like myth, epic, fable, and the tale are thousands of years old and thrive in preliterate societies, the short story is less than 200 years old and seems to take its substance from a literate, democratic, and scientific culture. The short story emerged as an identifiable form in the first four decades of the nineteenth century. Among the first short story writers were Nicolai Gogol in Russia; Prosper Merimée in France; E. T. A. Hoffmann, Ludwig Tieck, and Heinrich von Kleist in Germany; and Washington Irving, Edgar Allan Poe, and Nathaniel Hawthorne in the United States.

Poe was probably the first critic to state a theory of the short story. His 1842 review of Hawthorne's *Twice-Told Tales* and his expansion of that review in 1847 are famous explanations of what he thought the new form should be. Poe made three main points. He said, first of all, that the short prose narrative is superior to long narrative because brevity allows the work to create a "totality" of effect. Readers should be able to read the story in one sitting, without interruption, so the story should take no more than about one hour to read. Second, the story should create a single, preconceived effect. Everything in the story—every word, every sentence—should help establish this effect: "If his [the writer's] very initial sentence tend not to the outbringing of this effect, then he has failed in his first step. In the whole composition there should be no word written, of which the tendency, direct or indirect, is not to the one preestablished design. And by such means, with such care and skill, a picture is at length painted which leaves in the mind of him who contemplates it with a kindred art, a sense of the fullest satisfaction. The idea of the tale has been presented unblemished, because undisturbed." Poe's third point is that the short story may deal with "Truth." The difference, he says, between the poem and the short story is that the poem presents the "Beautiful," whereas the short story presents "Truth." Poe does not specify what he means by "Truth," but he seems to mean themes or ideas about real life.

Poe's analysis of the short story was perceptive and influential. Many short stories, including his own, have the qualities Poe said they should have. But his analysis raises questions that he does not answer. What kind of "effect" was he talking about? What did he mean by "Truth"? What about stories that have more than one effect or that are long? Are they not short stories? What about tales by artists like Boccaccio and Chaucer, tales that are as carefully crafted as Poe's short stories, as coherent and unified, and often create a single effect? Are they short stories?

Since Poe and his contemporaries were virtually inventing the short story from scratch, they lacked the vantage point that we have. We can look back over the entire history of the short story and draw upon many examples to try to answer some of the questions that Poe left unanswered. We can see that the short story, like all great literary genres, is complex, overlaps with other forms, and continues to evolve. Defining it with precision is probably impossible, but we can nonetheless identify some of its typical traits.

Perhaps the most important characteristic of the short story is the way the author handles characterization. Characters in a short story are generally like people in real life. They are not divine beings, as in myths; they are not mere stand-ins for ideas, as they are in parables; they are not animals or other strange creatures, as in animal fables; they do not have supernatural powers or receive supernatural aid, as in fairy tales. Rather, they are people like those we meet in everyday life—people like us. They have many of the same experiences that we have. They face dilemmas that we face. They inhabit places that we recognize. They have something like the complexity of real people. They have the range of abilities and limitations that people in real life have.

The point of view that authors adopt in short stories helps establish this realistic presentation of characters. In general, authors of short stories put us *inside* characters' minds and thus give us access to characters' inner lives. In contrast, authors of tales tell us a great deal about what happens to characters but very little about what goes on inside the characters' minds. At the beginning of the Grimm version of the fairy tale "Cinderella," for example, we learn that Cinderella falls into disfavor and discomfort. But we learn next to nothing about how she feels—about the loss of her mother, about the strange withdrawal of protection by her father, about the unfairness of her stepmother, about the nastiness of her stepsisters. We know only that she "weeps" a lot. Again, when she experiences her miraculous transformation at the end, we get no hint of how she feels. Is she startled by the supernatural aid? Is she apprehensive about dancing with the prince? Is she afraid that she might be recognized? Does she love the prince? Is she glad that her stepsisters are so cruelly punished? The tale is stone silent on these matters.

Other tales may provide more information about characters' inner lives than "Cinderella," but only in a generalized way. Characters may be "grieved," "greatly surprised," "terrified," "pleased," "very sad," "impatient," "passionately in love." They may do things that reveal their inner states, such as tremble, blush, burst into tears, wring their hands, faint. But information in tales rarely goes beyond such general indications of emotional states. The result is that characters in tales fail to have the variety and subtlety of emotions and thoughts that real people have. Characters in tales lack the individuality of real people.

Short stories, on the other hand, put us in constant contact with characters' minds. The most prevalent points of view in short stories are first-person and limited omniscient. In the first-person point of view, a character in the story narrates the story. The narrator uses "I" and tells about his or her involvement in the action. In the limited omniscient point of view, the narrator stands outside the story but represents the consciousness of one character. Both points of view focus attention on the thoughts and feelings of the characters. They push the short story away from an emphasis on action and toward an emphasis on characterization.

As a result, characterization is more complex in short stories than in tales. Characters are not limited to just one or two emotional states but are likely to have many. They shift from attitude to attitude. They have contradictory thoughts. They develop feelings that they do not understand. They are influenced by the network of factors that affect real people: family history, intimate relationships, work, cultural values, physical health, talents, social and physical environment, money.

Finally, perhaps the most important observation we can make about characters in short stories is that they usually change. Characters in tales can change. Their outward circumstances may change—from poverty to wealth, exclusion to acceptance, singleness to marriage. Their outlook may also change—from foolish to wise, cruel to kind, careless to careful. But whereas authors of tales merely report such changes, authors of short stories make us experience them by filtering them through the inner lives of the characters. We experience the speed— slow, gradual, sudden—with which characters recognize different circumstances or attitudes. We share the characters' emotions—delight, fear, anguish, surprise— in response to change. We share the characters' recognition of the differences the changes will make in their lives. We experience the degree to which characters understand change; sometimes we understand the changes more fully than they do. In "Young Goodman Brown," for example, Hawthorne uses a limited omniscient point of view to place us inside the mind of Goodman Brown. We experience along with him the mental process, at first gradual but increasingly rapid, that leads to his radical transformation at the end of the story.

The plot of the short story usually springs from the desires and actions of the characters. We may think that in some short stories "nothing seems to happen." But in fact the "action" in short stories consists largely of the mental conflicts of characters. The outward events of short stories, then, are frequently undramatic in themselves. They are often the daily, ordinary activities of real people. But the outward events of short stories are highly dramatic in the context of the protagonists' mental lives. The scope of the plot accounts for the shortness of the short story.

Short stories are in a sense fragmentary. They typically focus on one key event or at most several events in a character's life. The form of the plot is typically a movement toward an epiphany. An **epiphany** is a moment of discovery in which a character achieves a new understanding about the nature of reality. The epiphany in a short story is often the climax of the plot and usually triggers a change in the protagonist. After the epiphany, the protagonist sees the world in a new way and will act accordingly.

The language of the short story corresponds to the realistic portrayal of characters. It is prose, the language of everyday speech, but it is not merely simple, as it sometimes is in the tale. Like the language of poetry, the language of the short story is characterized by indirect methods of communication—subtle word choice, metaphor, symbolism, syntactical structures that suggest the ways in which characters are thinking. This sophisticated quality of language points to one of the characteristics of the short story that Poe insisted on—the careful crafting of the short story. Some short stories may seem to be indifferently thrown together, but most have the kind of controlled craftsmanship that we associate with poetry. Every word, every image, every event is usually there for a purpose. They often all fit together to create a unified whole. The result is a compression and conciseness that demand more concentration and alertness from the reader than many earlier forms of short narrative.

Almost all of the short stories printed in this chapter are well-known masterpieces from the English, European, and American tradition. The earliest stories, like those of Irving, Poe, and Hawthorne, represent a transition from tale to short story. But many of the other stories have affinities with earlier short fiction forms. Jewett's "A White Heron," Bowen's "The Demon Lover," Malamud's "The Magic Barrel," and Oates's "Where Are You Going, Where Have You Been?" incorporate elements of the fairy tale. Kafka's "A Country Doctor," Lawrence's "The Rocking-Horse Winner," Jackson's "The Lottery," and Prager's "A Visit from the Footbinder" have qualities of the fable. Hawthorne's "Young Goodman Brown" and Boyle's "Greasy Lake" seem to harken back to myth. The arrangement of the stories is chronological by date of publication.

WASHINGTON IRVING

Rip Van Winkle

Washington Irving (1783–1859) was one of the first, if not the first, persons to write short stories. He, Edgar Allan Poe, and Nathaniel Hawthorne were among those writers in the early part of the nineteenth century who made the transition from the tale to the short story. Their stories, then, have some of the qualities of both tale and short story. This blend of qualities is especially apparent in Irving's two most famous stories, "Rip Van Winkle" and "The Legend of Sleepy Hollow," which are based in part on German fairy tales that Irving had read at the urging of Sir Walter Scott. The episode of "Rip Van Winkle" in which Rip meets the ghosts playing nine pins comes from a German fairy tale called "Peter Klaus." But although there are obvious fairy tale elements in "Rip Van Winkle," Irving grants Rip a believable psychological depth that makes Rip more than the one-dimensional character typical of the tale.

Irving was born in New York City into a large and literary family. He began writing at an early age and was publishing essays in one of his brother's newspapers before he was twenty. After traveling in Europe for several years, he returned home to study law. But his real interest was in writing. In 1808 he published *A History of New York,* a satirical and funny narrative supposedly by an eccentric but dimwitted antiquarian named Diedrich Knickerbocker. After serving in the War of 1812, Irving went abroad again, this time to work in a brother's import business at Liverpool, England. When the business failed, Irving turned to writing as a means of self-support. In 1819, he published his best-known book, *The Sketch Book,* which includes both "Rip Van Winkle" and "The Legend of Sleepy Hollow." Irving never equalled the excellence of *The Sketch Book,* but after its publication he had a long and distinguished career as diplomat and author of stories, biographies, and histories.

Irving's handling of point of view is a notable feature of *The Sketch Book.* The supposed author of *The Sketch Book* is Geoffrey Crayon, an American who has lived in England for a number of years and is now printing "sketches"—personal essays—and stories that he has collected. Included in this collection are "Rip Van Winkle" and "The Legend of Sleepy Hollow," which are not by Geoffrey Crayon but are by Diedrich Knickerbocker. But even Knickerbocker disclaims responsibility for these stories; he says he has heard them from other sources and is only writing them down. In short, we have multiple layers of authors: Irving (the real author), Geoffrey Crayon (the "false" author of *The Sketch Book*), Diedrich Knickerbocker (author or "recorder" of "Rip" and "Legend"), and the sources from which Knickerbocker got the stories. Irving's play with point of view is part of the fun of "Rip" and "Legend"; it also opens up opportunities for interpretation.

[*T*he following Tale was found among the papers of the late Diedrich Knickerbocker, an old gentleman of New-York, who was very curious in the Dutch History of the province, and the manners of the descendants from its primitive settlers. His historical researches, however, did not lie so much among books as among men;

for the former are lamentably scanty on his favorite topics; whereas he found the old burghers, and still more, their wives, rich in that legendary lore, so invaluable to true history. Whenever, therefore, he happened upon a genuine Dutch family, snugly shut up in its low-roofed farmhouse, under a spreading sycamore, he looked upon it as a little clasped volume of black-letter, and studied it with the zeal of a bookworm.

The result of all these researches was a history of the province, during the reign of the Dutch governors, which he published some years since. There have been various opinions as to the literary character of his work, and, to tell the truth, it is not a whit better than it should be. Its chief merit is its scrupulous accuracy, which, indeed, was a little questioned, on its first appearance, but has since been completely established; and it is now admitted into all historical collections, as a book of unquestionable authority.

The old gentleman died shortly after the publication of his work, and now, that he is dead and gone, it cannot do much harm to his memory, to say, that his time might have been much better employed in weightier labors. He, however, was apt to ride his hobby his own way; and though it did now and then kick up the dust a little in the eyes of his neighbors, and grieve the spirit of some friends for whom he felt the truest deference and affection, yet his errors and follies are remembered "more in sorrow than in anger," and it begins to be suspected, that he never intended to injure or offend. But however his memory may be appreciated by critics, it is still held dear by many folk, whose good opinion is well worth having; particularly by certain biscuit-bakers, who have gone so far as to imprint his likeness on their new-year cakes, and have thus given him a chance for immortality, almost equal to the being stamped on a Waterloo medal, or a Queen Anne's farthing.]

Rip Van Winkle

A Posthumous Writing of Diedrich Knickerbocker

> By Woden, God of Saxons,
> From whence comes Wensday, that is Wodensday,
> Truth is a thing that ever I will keep
> Unto thylke day in which I creep into
> My sepulchre.—CARTWRIGHT°

Whoever has made a voyage up the Hudson, must remember the Kaatskill mountains. They are a dismembered branch of the great Appalachian family, and are seen away to the west of the river, swelling up to a noble height, and lording it over the surrounding country. Every change of season, every change of weather, indeed every hour of the day, produces some change in the magical hues and shapes of these mountains; and they are regarded by all the good wives, far and near, as perfect barometers. When the weather is fair and settled, they are clothed in blue and purple, and print their bold outlines on the clear evening sky; but sometimes, when the rest of the

---

Cartwright. A quotation from a play by the English dramatist William Cartwright (1611-1643).

landscape is cloudless, they will gather a hood of gray vapors about their summits, which, in the last rays of the setting sun, will glow and light up like a crown of glory.

At the foot of these fairy mountains, the voyager may have descried the light smoke curling up from a village, whose shingle roofs gleam among the trees, just where the blue tints of the upland melt away into the fresh green of the nearer landscape. It is a little village of great antiquity, having been founded by some of the Dutch colonists, in the early times of the province, just about the beginning of the government of the good Peter Stuyvesant° (may he rest in peace!) and there were some of the houses of the original settlers standing within a few years, built of small yellow bricks brought from Holland, having latticed windows and gable fronts, surmounted with weathercocks.

In that same village, and in one of these very houses (which to tell the precise truth, was sadly time-worn and weatherbeaten), there lived many years since, while the country was yet a province of Great Britain, a simple, good-natured fellow, of the name of Rip Van Winkle. He was a descendant of the Van Winkles who figured so gallantly in the chivalrous days of Peter Stuyvesant, and accompanied him to the siege of Fort Christina. He inherited, however, but little of the martial character of his ancestors. I have observed that he was a simple good-natured man; he was moreover a kind neighbor, and an obedient henpecked husband. Indeed, to the latter circumstance might be owing that meekness of spirit which gained him such universal popularity; for those men are most apt to be obsequious and conciliating abroad, who are under the discipline of shrews at home. Their tempers, doubtless, are rendered pliant and malleable in the fiery furnace of domestic tribulation, and a curtain lecture is worth all the sermons in the world for teaching the virtues of patience and long-suffering. A termagant wife may, therefore, in some respects, be considered a tolerable blessing; and if so, Rip Van Winkle was thrice blessed.

Certain it is, that he was a great favorite among all the good wives of the village, who, as usual with the amiable sex, took his part in all family squabbles, and never failed, whenever they talked those matters over in their evening gossipings, to lay all the blame on Dame Van Winkle. The children of the village, too, would shout with joy whenever he approached. He assisted at their sports, made their playthings, taught them to fly kites and shoot marbles, and told them long stories of ghosts, witches, and Indians. Whenever he went dodging about the village, he was surrounded by a troop of them hanging on his skirts, clambering on his back, and playing a thousand tricks on him with impunity; and not a dog would bark at him throughout the neighborhood.

The great error in Rip's composition was an insuperable aversion to all kinds of profitable labor. It could not be from the want of assiduity or perseverance; for he would sit on a wet rock, with a rod as long and heavy as a Tartar's lance, and fish all day without a murmur, even though he should not be encouraged by a single nibble. He would carry a fowling-piece on his shoulder for hours together, trudging through woods and swamps, and up hill and down dale, to shoot a few squirrels or wild pigeons. He would never refuse to assist a neighbor, even in the roughest toil, and was a foremost man at all country frolics for husking Indian corn or building stone fences.

Peter Stuyvesant. Last governor of New Netherlands (1647-1664), which later became the English colony New York.

The women of the village, too, used to employ him to run their errands, and to do such little odd jobs as their less obliging husbands would not do for them;—in a word, Rip was ready to attend to anybody's business but his own; but as to doing family duty, and keeping his farm in order, he found it impossible.

In fact, he declared it was of no use to work on his farm; it was the most pestilent little piece of ground in the whole country; every thing about it went wrong, and would go wrong in spite of him. His fences were continually falling to pieces; his cow would either go astray, or get among the cabbages; weeds were sure to grow quicker in his fields than anywhere else; the rain always made a point of setting in just as he had some out-door work to do; so that though his patrimonial estate had dwindled away under his management, acre by acre, until there was little more left than a mere patch of Indian corn and potatoes, yet it was the worst conditioned farm in the neighborhood.

His children, too, were as ragged and wild as if they belonged to nobody. His son Rip, an urchin begotten in his own likeness, promised to inherit the habits, with the old clothes of his father. He was generally seen trooping like a colt at his mother's heels, equipped in a pair of his father's cast-off galligaskins, which he had much ado to hold up with one hand, as a fine lady does her train in bad weather.

Rip Van Winkle, however, was one of those happy mortals, of foolish, well-oiled dispositions, who take the world easy, eat white bread or brown, whichever can be got with least thought or trouble, and would rather starve on a penny than work for a pound. If left to himself, he would have whistled life away in perfect contentment; but his wife kept continually dinning in his ears about his idleness, his carelessness, and the ruin he was bringing on his family.

Morning, noon, and night, her tongue was incessantly going, and every thing he said or did was sure to produce a torrent of household eloquence. Rip had but one way of replying to all lectures of the kind, and that, by frequent use, had grown into a habit. He shrugged his shoulders, shook his head, cast up his eyes, but said nothing. This, however, always provoked a fresh volley from his wife, so that he was fain to draw off his forces, and take to the outside of the house—the only side which, in truth, belongs to a henpecked husband.

Rip's sole domestic adherent was his dog Wolf, who was as much henpecked as his master; for Dame Van Winkle regarded them as companions in idleness, and even looked upon Wolf with an evil eye as the cause of his master's going so often astray. True it is, in all points of spirit befitting an honorable dog, he was as courageous an animal as ever scoured the woods—but what courage can withstand the ever-during and all-besetting terrors of a woman's tongue? The moment Wolf entered the house, his crest fell, his tail drooped to the ground, or curled between his legs, he sneaked about with a gallows air, casting many a sidelong glance at Dame Van Winkle, and at the least flourish of a broomstick or ladle, he would fly to the door with yelping precipitation.

Times grew worse and worse with Rip Van Winkle, as years of matrimony rolled on: a tart temper never mellows with age, and a sharp tongue is the only edge tool that grows keener with constant use. For a long while he used to console himself, when driven from home, by frequenting a kind of perpetual club of the sages, philosophers, and other idle personages of the village, which held its sessions on a bench before a small inn, designated by a rubicund portrait of his majesty George the Third. Here they used to sit in the shade, of a long lazy summer's day, talking listlessly over village gossip, or telling endless sleepy stories about nothing. But it would have been worth any statesman's money to have heard the profound discussions that sometimes took place, when by chance an old newspaper fell into their hands, from some passing traveller. How solemnly they would listen to the contents, as drawled out by Derrick Van Bummel, the schoolmaster, a dapper learned little man, who was not to be daunted by the most gigantic word in the dictionary; and how sagely they would deliberate upon public events some months after they had taken place.

The opinions of this junto were completely controlled by Nicholas Vedder, a patriarch of the village, and landlord of the inn, at the door of which he took his seat from morning till night, just moving sufficiently to avoid the sun, and keep in the shade of a large tree; so that the neighbors could tell the hour by his movements as accurately as by a sun-dial. It is true, he was rarely heard to speak, but smoked his pipe incessantly. His adherents, however (for every great man has his adherents), perfectly understood him, and knew how to gather his opinions. When any thing that was read or related displeased him, he was observed to smoke his pipe vehemently, and to send forth short, frequent, and angry puffs; but when pleased, he would inhale the smoke slowly and tranquilly, and emit it in light and placid clouds, and sometimes taking the pipe from his mouth, and letting the fragrant vapor curl about his nose, would gravely nod his head in token of perfect approbation.

From even this strong hold the unlucky Rip was at length routed by his termagant wife, who would suddenly break in upon the tranquillity of the assemblage, and call the members all to nought; nor was that august personage, Nicholas Vedder himself, sacred from the daring tongue of this terrible virago, who charged him outright with encouraging her husband in habits of idleness.

Poor Rip was at last reduced almost to despair, and his only alternative to escape from the labor of the farm and clamor of his wife, was to take gun in hand, and stroll away into the woods. Here he would sometimes seat himself at the foot of a tree, and share the contents of his wallet with Wolf, with whom he sympathized as a fellow-sufferer in persecution. "Poor Wolf," he would say, "thy mistress leads thee a dog's life of it; but never mind, my lad, whilst I live thou shalt never want a friend to stand by thee!" Wolf would wag his tail, look wistfully in his master's face, and if dogs can feel pity, I verily believe he reciprocated the sentiment with all his heart.

In a long ramble of the kind, on a fine autumnal day, Rip had unconsciously scrambled to one of the highest parts of the Kaatskill mountains. He was after his favorite sport of squirrel-shooting, and the still solitudes had echoed and reechoed with the reports of his gun. Panting and fatigued, he threw himself, late in the afternoon, on a green knoll covered with mountain herbage, that crowned the brow of a precipice. From an opening between the trees, he could overlook all the lower country for many a mile of rich woodland. He saw at a distance the lordly Hudson, far, far below him, moving on its silent but majestic course, with the reflection of a purple cloud, or the sail of a lagging bark, here and there sleeping on its glassy bosom, and at last losing itself in the blue highlands.

On the other side he looked down into a deep mountain glen, wild, lonely, and shagged, the bottom filled with fragments from the impending cliffs, and scarcely lighted by the reflected rays of the setting sun. For some time Rip lay musing on this scene; evening was gradually advancing; the mountains began to throw their long blue shadows over the valleys; he saw that it would be dark long before he could reach the village; and he heaved a heavy sigh when he thought of encountering the terrors of Dame Van Winkle.

As he was about to descend he heard a voice from a distance hallooing, "Rip Van Winkle! Rip Van Winkle!" He looked round, but could see nothing but a crow winging its solitary flight across the mountain. He thought his fancy must have deceived him, and turned again to descend, when he heard the same cry ring through the still evening air, "Rip Van Winkle! Rip Van Winkle!"—at the same time Wolf bristled up his back, and giving a low growl, skulked to his master's side, looking fearfully down into the glen. Rip now felt a vague apprehension stealing over him: he looked anxiously in the same direction, and perceived a strange figure slowly toiling up the rocks, and bending under the weight of something he carried on his back. He was surprised to see any human being in this lonely and unfrequented place, but supposing it to be some one of the neighborhood in need of his assistance, he hastened down to yield it.

On nearer approach, he was still more surprised at the singularity of the stranger's appearance. He was a short square-built old fellow, with thick bushy hair, and a grizzled beard. His dress was of the antique Dutch fashion—a cloth jerkin strapped round the waist—several pair of breeches, the outer one of ample volume, decorated with rows of buttons down the sides, and bunches at the knees. He bore on his shoulder a stout keg, that seemed full of liquor, and made signs for Rip to approach and assist him with the load. Though rather shy and distrustful of this new acquaintance, Rip complied with his usual alacrity, and mutually relieving one another, they clambered up a narrow gully, apparently the dry bed of a mountain torrent. As they ascended, Rip every now and then heard long rolling peals, like distant thunder, that seemed to issue out of a deep ravine or rather cleft between lofty rocks, toward which their rugged path conducted. He paused for an instant, but supposing it to be the muttering of one of those transient thunder-showers which often take place in mountain heights, he proceeded. Passing through the ravine, they came to a hollow, like a small amphitheatre, surrounded by perpendicular precipices, over the brinks of which, impending trees shot their branches, so that you only caught glimpses of the azure sky, and the bright evening cloud. During the whole time, Rip and his companion had labored on in silence; for though the former marvelled greatly what could be the object of carrying a keg of liquor up this wild mountain, yet there was something strange and incomprehensible about the unknown, that inspired awe, and checked familiarity.

On entering the amphitheatre, new objects of wonder presented themselves. On a level spot in the center was a company of odd-looking personages playing at ninepins. They were dressed in a quaint outlandish fashion: some wore short doublets, others jerkins, with long knives in their belts, and most of them had enormous breeches, of similar style with that of the guide's. Their visages, too, were peculiar; one had a large beard, broad face, and small piggish eyes; the face of another seemed to consist entirely of nose, and was surmounted by a white sugar-loaf hat, set off with a little red cock's tail. They all had beards of various shapes and colors. There was one who seemed to be the commander. He was a stout old gentleman, with a weather-beaten countenance; he wore a laced doublet, broad belt and hanger,° high-crowned hat and feather, red stockings, and high-heeled shoes, with roses in them. The whole group

---

hanger. A short sword.

reminded Rip of the figures in an old Flemish painting, in the parlor of Dominie Van Shaick, the village parson, and which had been brought over from Holland at the time of the settlement.

What seemed particularly odd to Rip, was, that though these folks were evidently amusing themselves, yet they maintained the gravest faces, the most mysterious silence, and were, withal, the most melancholy party of pleasure he had ever witnessed. Nothing interrupted the stillness of the scene but the noise of the balls, which, whenever they were rolled, echoed along the mountains like rumbling peals of thunder.

As Rip and his companion approached them, they suddenly desisted from their play, and stared at him with such fixed statue-like gaze, and such strange, uncouth, lack-luster countenances, that his heart turned within him, and his knees smote together. His companion now emptied the contents of the keg into large flagons, and made signs to him to wait upon the company. He obeyed with fear and trembling; they quaffed the liquor in profound silence, and then returned to their game.

By degrees, Rip's awe and apprehension subsided. He even ventured, when no eye was fixed upon him, to taste the beverage, which he found had much of the flavor of excellent Hollands. He was naturally a thirsty soul, and was soon tempted to repeat the draught. One taste provoked another, and he reiterated his visits to the flagon so often, that at length his senses were overpowered, his eyes swam in his head, his head gradually declined, and he fell into a deep sleep.

On waking, he found himself on the green knoll whence he had first seen the old man of the glen. He rubbed his eyes—it was a bright sunny morning. The birds were hopping and twittering among the bushes, and the eagle was wheeling aloft, and breasting the pure mountain breeze. "Surely," thought Rip, "I have not slept here all night." He recalled the occurrences before he fell asleep. The strange man with the keg of liquor—the mountain ravine—the wild retreat among the rocks—the wobegone party at nine-pins—the flagon—"Oh! that flagon! that wicked flagon!" thought Rip—"what excuse shall I make to Dame Van Winkle?"

He looked round for his gun, but in place of the clean well-oiled fowling-piece, he found an old fire-lock lying by him, the barrel encrusted with rust, the lock falling off, and the stock worm-eaten. He now suspected that the grave roysters of the mountain had put a trick upon him, and having dosed him with liquor, had robbed him of his gun. Wolf, too, had disappeared, but he might have strayed away after a squirrel or partridge. He whistled after him, and shouted his name, but all in vain; the echoes repeated his whistle and shout, but no dog was to be seen.

He determined to revisit the scene of the last evening's gambol, and if he met with any of the party, to demand his dog and gun. As he rose to walk, he found himself stiff in the joints, and wanting in his usual activity. "These mountain beds do not agree with me," thought Rip, "and if this frolic should lay me up with a fit of the rheumatism, I shall have a blessed time with Dame Van Winkle." With some difficulty he got down into the glen; he found the gully up which he and his companion had ascended the preceding evening; but to his astonishment a mountain stream was now foaming down it, leaping from rock to rock, and filling the glen with babbling murmurs. He, however, made shift to scramble up its sides, working his toilsome way through thickets of birch, sassafras, and witch-hazel; and sometimes tripped up or entangled by the wild grape vines that twisted their coils or tendrils from tree to tree, and spread a kind of network in his path.

At length he reached to where the ravine had opened through the cliffs to the amphitheatre; but no traces of such opening remained. The rocks presented a high impenetrable wall, over which the torrent came tumbling in a sheet of feathery foam, and fell into a broad deep basin, black from the shadows of the surrounding forest. Here, then, poor Rip was brought to a stand. He again called and whistled after his dog; he was only answered by the cawing of a flock of idle crows, sporting high in air about a dry tree that overhung a sunny precipice; and who, secure in their elevation, seemed to look down and scoff at the poor man's perplexities. What was to be done? The morning was passing away, and Rip felt famished for want of his breakfast. He grieved to give up his dog and gun; he dreaded to meet his wife; but it would not do to starve among the mountains. He shook his head, shouldered the rusty firelock, and with a heart full of trouble and anxiety, turned his steps homeward.

As he approached the village, he met a number of people, but none whom he knew, which somewhat surprised him, for he had thought himself acquainted with every one in the country round. Their dress, too, was of a different fashion from that to which he was accustomed. They all stared at him with equal marks of surprise, and whenever they cast their eyes upon him, invariably stroked their chins. The constant recurrence of this gesture, induced Rip, involuntarily, to do the same, when, to his astonishment, he found his beard had grown a foot long!

He had now entered the skirts of the village. A troop of strange children ran at his heels, hooting after him, and pointing at his gray beard. The dogs, too, not one of which he recognized for an old acquaintance, barked at him as he passed. The very village was altered: it was larger and more populous. There were rows of houses which he had never seen before, and those which had been his familiar haunts had disappeared. Strange names were over the doors—strange faces at the windows—every thing was strange. His mind now misgave him; he began to doubt whether both he and the world around him were not bewitched. Surely this was his native village, which he had left but the day before. There stood the Kaatskill mountains—there ran the silver Hudson at a distance—there was every hill and dale precisely as it had always been—Rip was sorely perplexed—"That flagon last night," thought he, "has addled my poor head sadly!"

It was with some difficulty that he found the way to his own house, which he approached with silent awe, expecting every moment to hear the shrill voice of Dame Van Winkle. He found the house gone to decay—the roof fallen in, the windows shattered, and the doors off the hinges. A half-starved dog, that looked like Wolf, was skulking about it. Rip called him by name, but the cur snarled, showed his teeth, and passed on. This was an unkind cut indeed.—"My very dog," sighed poor Rip, "has forgotten me!"

He entered the house, which, to tell the truth, Dame Van Winkle had always kept in neat order. It was empty, forlorn, and apparently abandoned. This desolateness overcame all his connubial fears—he called loudly for his wife and children—the lonely chambers rang for a moment with his voice, and then all again was silence.

He now hurried forth, and hastened to his old resort, the village inn—but it too was gone. A large rickety wooden building stood in its place, with great gaping windows, some of them broken, and mended with old hats and petticoats, and over the door was painted, "The Union Hotel, by Jonathan Doolittle." Instead of the great tree that used to shelter the quiet little Dutch inn of yore, there now was reared a tall naked pole, with something on the top that looked like a red night-cap, and from it was fluttering a flag, on which was a singular assemblage of stars and stripes—all this was strange and incomprehensible. He recognized on the sign, however, the ruby face of King George, under which he had smoked so many a peaceful pipe, but even this was singularly metamorphosed. The red coat was changed for one of blue and buff, a sword was held in the hand instead of a scepter, the head was decorated with a cocked hat, and underneath was painted in large characters, GENERAL WASHINGTON.

There was, as usual, a crowd of folk about the door, but none that Rip recollected. The very character of the people seemed changed. There was a busy, bustling, disputatious tone about it, instead of the accustomed phlegm and drowsy tranquillity. He looked in vain for the sage Nicholas Vedder, with his broad face, double chin, and fair long pipe, uttering clouds of tobacco smoke, instead of idle speeches; or Van Bummel, the schoolmaster, doling forth the contents of an ancient newspaper. In place of these, a lean bilious-looking fellow, with his pockets full of handbills, was haranguing vehemently about rights of citizens—election—members of Congress—liberty—Bunker's hill—heroes of seventy-six—and other words which were a perfect Babylonish jargon to the bewildered Van Winkle.

The appearance of Rip, with his long, grizzled beard, his rusty fowling-piece, his uncouth dress, and an army of women and children at his heels, soon attracted the attention of the tavern politicians. They crowded round him, eyeing him from head to foot, with great curiosity. The orator bustled up to him, and drawing him partly aside, inquired, "on which side he voted?" Rip stared in vacant stupidity. Another short but busy little fellow pulled him by the arm, and rising on tiptoe, inquired in his ear, "whether he was Federal or Democrat." Rip was equally at a loss to comprehend the question; when a knowing, self-important old gentleman, in a sharp cocked hat, made his way through the crowd, putting them to the right and left with his elbows as he passed, and planting himself before Van Winkle, with one arm a-kimbo, the other resting on his cane, his keen eyes and sharp hat penetrating, as it were, into his very soul, demanded in an austere tone, "what brought him to the election with a gun on his shoulder, and a mob at his heels, and whether he meant to breed a riot in the village?"

"Alas! gentlemen," cried Rip, somewhat dismayed, "I am a poor, quiet man, a native of the place, and a loyal subject of the King, God bless him!"

Here a general shout burst from the bystanders—"a tory! a tory! a spy! a refugee! hustle him! away with him!"

It was with great difficulty that the self-important man in the cocked hat restored order; and having assumed a tenfold austerity of brow, demanded again of the unknown culprit, what he came there for, and whom he was seeking. The poor man humbly assured him that he meant no harm, but merely came there in search of some of his neighbors, who used to keep about the tavern.

"Well—who are they?—name them."

Rip bethought himself a moment, and inquired, "Where's Nicholas Vedder?"

There was a silence for a little while, when an old man replied, in a thin, piping voice, "Nicholas Vedder? why, he is dead and gone these eighteen years! There was a wooden tomb-stone in the church-yard that used to tell all about him, but that's rotten and gone too."

"Where's Brom Dutcher?"

"Oh, he went off to the army in the beginning of the war; some say he was killed at the storming of Stony-Point—others say he was drowned in the squall, at the foot of Antony's Nose. I don't know—he never came back again."

"Where's Van Bummel, the schoolmaster?"

"He went off to the wars, too; was a great militia general, and is now in Congress."

Rip's heart died away, at hearing of these sad changes in his home and friends, and finding himself thus alone in the world. Every answer puzzled him, too, by treating of such enormous lapses of time, and of matters which he could not understand: war—Congress—Stony-Point!—he had no courage to ask after any more friends, but cried out in despair, "Does nobody here know Rip Van Winkle?"

"Oh, Rip Van Winkle!" exclaimed two or three. "Oh to be sure! that's Rip Van Winkle yonder, leaning against the tree."

Rip looked, and beheld a precise counterpart of himself as he went up the mountain; apparently as lazy and certainly as ragged. The poor fellow was now completely confounded. He doubted his own identity, and whether he was himself or another man. In the midst of his bewilderment, the man in the cocked hat demanded who he was, and what was his name?

"God knows," exclaimed he at his wit's end; "I'm not myself—I'm somebody else—that's me yonder—no—that's somebody else, got into my shoes—I was myself last night, but I fell asleep on the mountain, and they've changed my gun, and every thing's changed, and I'm changed, and I can't tell what's my name, or who I am!"

The by-standers began now to look at each other, nod, wink significantly, and tap their fingers against their foreheads. There was a whisper, also, about securing the gun, and keeping the old fellow from doing mischief; at the very suggestion of which, the self-important man with the cocked hat retired with some precipitation. At this critical moment a fresh comely woman pressed through the throng to get a peep at the gray-bearded man. She had a chubby child in her arms, which, frightened at his looks, began to cry. "Hush, Rip," cried she, "hush, you little fool; the old man won't hurt you." The name of the child, the air of the mother, the tone of her voice, all awakened a train of recollections in his mind.

"What is your name, my good woman?" asked he.

"Judith Gardenier."

"And your father's name?"

"Ah, poor man. Rip Van Winkle was his name; but it's twenty years since he went away from home with his gun, and never has been heard of since—his dog came home without him; but whether he shot himself, or was carried away by the Indians, nobody can tell. I was then but a little girl."

Rip had but one question more to ask; but he put it with a faltering voice:

"Where's your mother?"

Oh, she too had died but a short time since: she broke a blood-vessel in a fit of passion at a New-England peddler.

There was a drop of comfort, at least, in this intelligence. The honest man could contain himself no longer. He caught his daughter and her child in his arms. "I am your father!" cried he—"Young Rip Van Winkle once—old Rip Van Winkle now!—Does nobody know poor Rip Van Winkle?"

All stood amazed, until an old woman, tottering out from among the crowd, put her hand to her brow, and peering under it in his face for a moment, exclaimed, "Sure enough! it is Rip Van Winkle—it is himself. Welcome home again, old neighbor— Why, where have you been these twenty long years?"

Rip's story was soon told, for the whole twenty years had been to him but as one night. The neighbors stared when they heard it; some were seen to wink at each other, and put their tongues in their cheeks; and the self-important man in the cocked hat, who, when the alarm was over, had returned to the field, screwed down the corners of his mouth, and shook his head—upon which there was a general shaking of the head throughout the assemblage.

It was determined, however, to take the opinion of old Peter Vanderdonk, who was seen slowly advancing up the road. He was a descendant of the historian of that name, who wrote one of the earliest accounts of the province. Peter was the most ancient inhabitant of the village, and well versed in all the wonderful events and traditions of the neighborhood. He recollected Rip at once, and corroborated his story in the most satisfactory manner. He assured the company that it was a fact, handed down from his ancestor the historian, that the Kaatskill mountains had always been haunted by strange beings. That it was affirmed that the great Hendrick Hudson, the first discoverer of the river and country, kept a kind of vigil there every twenty years, with his crew of the Half-moon, being permitted in this way to revisit the scenes of his enterprise, and keep a guardian eye upon the river and the great city called by his name. That his father had once seen them in their old Dutch dresses playing at nine-pins in a hollow of the mountain; and that he himself had heard, one summer afternoon, the sound of their balls, like distant peals of thunder.

To make a long story short, the company broke up, and returned to the more important concerns of the election. Rip's daughter took him home to live with her; she had a snug, well-furnished house, and a stout cheery farmer for a husband, whom Rip recollected for one of the urchins that used to climb upon his back. As to Rip's son and heir, who was the ditto of himself, seen leaning against the tree, he was employed to work on the farm, but evinced an hereditary disposition to attend to any thing else but his business.

Rip now resumed his old walks and habits; he soon found many of his former cronies, though all rather the worse for the wear and tear of time; and preferred making friends among the rising generation, with whom he soon grew into great favor.

Having nothing to do at home, and being arrived at that happy age when a man can be idle with impunity, he took his place once more on the bench, at the inn door, and was reverenced as one of the patriarchs of the village, and a chronicle of the old times "before the war." It was some time before he could get into the regular track of gossip, or could be made to comprehend the strange events that had taken place during his torpor. How that there had been a revolutionary war—that the country had thrown off the yoke of old England—and that, instead of being a subject of his majesty George the Third, he was now a free citizen of the United States. Rip, in fact, was no politician; the changes of states and empires made but little impression on him; but there was one species of despotism under which he had long groaned, and that was— petticoat government. Happily, that was at an end; he had got his neck out of the yoke of matrimony, and could go in and out whenever he pleased, without dreading the tyranny of Dame Van Winkle. Whenever her name was mentioned, however, he shook his head, shrugged his shoulders, and cast up his eyes; which might pass either for an expression of resignation to his fate, or joy at his deliverance.

He used to tell his story to every stranger that arrived at Mr. Doolittle's hotel. He was observed, at first, to vary on some points every time he told it, which was doubt-less owing to his having so recently awaked. It at last settled down precisely to the tale I have related, and not a man, woman, or child in the neighborhood, but knew it by heart. Some always pretended to doubt the reality of it, and insisted that Rip had been out of his head, and that this was one point on which he always remained flighty. The old Dutch inhabitants, however, almost universally gave it full credit. Even to this day, they never hear a thunder-storm of a summer afternoon about the Kaatskill, but they say Hendrick Hudson and his crew are at their game of nine-pins: and it is a common wish of all henpecked husbands in the neighborhood, when life hangs heavy on their hands, that they might have a quieting draught out of Rip Van Winkle's flagon.

Note. The foregoing tale, one would suspect, had been suggested to Mr. Knickerbocker by a little German superstition about the Emperor Frederick der Rothbart and the Kypphaüser mountain: the subjoined note, however, which he had appended to the tale, shows that it is an absolute fact, narrated with his usual fidelity.

"The story of Rip Van Winkle may seem incredible to many, but nevertheless I give it my full belief, for I know the vicinity of our old Dutch settlements to have been very subject to marvellous events and appearances. Indeed, I have heard many stranger stories than this, in the villages along the Hudson, all of which were too well authenticated to admit of a doubt. I have even talked with Rip Van Winkle myself, who, when last I saw him, was a very venerable old man, and so perfectly rational and consistent on every other point, that I think no conscientious person could refuse to take this into the bargain; nay, I have seen a certificate on the subject taken before a country justice, and signed with a cross, in the justice's own handwriting. The story, therefore, is beyond the possibility of doubt.   D.K."

Questions for Study

1. The narrator of the story is supposedly Diedrich Knickerbocker. What are his character traits? Is he a reliable narrator? What is his source for the story?

2. Some critics have suggested that Rip made up the story of the nine pins. Is there any evidence in the story to support this view? Why would Rip have done such a thing?

3. Irving relies upon character stereotypes in this story. What are they? At what point does Rip cease to be a stereotype and become more like a real person?

4. Why does Irving place the story in the context of the American Revolution? What would the story be like if Irving had left that context out?

5. Who and what changes in this story?

6. What do you think are the themes of the story?

NATHANIEL HAWTHORNE

Young Goodman Brown

Nathaniel Hawthorne (1804–64) was born in Salem, Massachusetts. His father, a sea captain, died when Hawthorne was four years old. With the help of his mother's family, he was able to attend Bowdoin College in Maine, where he formed lasting friendships with several people, including Franklin Pierce, who became the fourteenth president of the United States (1852–56). After graduating from college, Hawthorne led a somewhat reclusive life, during which time he honed his skills as a writer and produced some of his finest stories, including "Young Goodman Brown." His engagement to Sophia Peabody in 1838 and marriage in 1842 brought Hawthorne out of seclusion. He worked in the Boston Custom House and later the Salem Custom House to help support his family. With the loss of his job at the Salem Custom House (because of a change of political administration), and with the help of a small inheritance received by his wife, he found time to write *The Scarlet Letter*. Its publication in 1850 caused a sensation and gave Hawthorne a measure of financial security. He published three more novels during his lifetime: *The House of the Seven Gables* (1851), *The Blithedale Romance* (1852), and *The Marble Faun* (1860). His finest stories were collected in two volumes, *Twice-Told Tales* (1837) and *Mosses from an Old Manse* (1846).

As a writer, Hawthorne was haunted by the Puritan history of New England. One of his ancestors was a judge in the Salem witch trials of 1692, who condemned nineteen innocent people to be executed. Another ancestor carried out harsh penalties, including whipping, for Quakers, who dissented from Puritan dogma. "Young Goodman Brown," like *The Scarlet Letter, The House of the Seven Gables,* and many of his most penetrating stories, is a return to the Puritan past, a dramatization of the psychological tensions created by Puritanism. Hawthorne published "Young Goodman Brown" in a literary magazine in 1835 and collected it in *Mosses from an Old Manse.*

Young Goodman° Brown came forth at sunset into the street at Salem village; but put his head back, after crossing the threshold, to exchange a parting kiss with his young wife. And Faith, as the wife was aptly named, thrust her own pretty head into the street, letting the wind play with the pink ribbons of her cap while she called to Goodman Brown.

Goodman. A polite title of address for someone of humble birth.

"Dearest heart," whispered she, softly and rather sadly, when her lips were close to his ear, "prithee put off your journey until sunrise and sleep in your own bed to-night. A lone woman is troubled with such dreams and such thoughts that she's afeard of herself sometimes. Pray tarry with me this night, dear husband, of all nights in the year."

"My love and my Faith," replied young Goodman Brown, "of all nights in the year, this one night must I tarry away from thee. My journey, as thou callest it, forth and back again, must needs be done 'twixt now and sunrise. What, my sweet, pretty wife, dost thou doubt me already, and we but three months married?"

"Then God bless you!" said Faith, with the pink ribbons; "and may you find all well when you come back."

"Amen!" cried Goodman Brown. "Say thy prayers, dear Faith, and go to bed at dusk, and no harm will come to thee."

So they parted; and the young man pursued his way until, being about to turn the corner by the meeting-house, he looked back and saw the head of Faith still peeping after him with a melancholy air, in spite of her pink ribbons.

"Poor little Faith!" thought he, for his heart smote him. "What a wretch am I to leave her on such an errand! She talks of dreams, too. Methought as she spoke there was trouble in her face, as if a dream had warned her what work is to be done tonight. But no, no; 't would kill her to think it. Well, she's a blessed angel on earth; and after this one night I'll cling to her skirts and follow her to heaven."

With this excellent resolve for the future, Goodman Brown felt himself justified in making more haste on his present evil purpose. He had taken a dreary road, darkened by all the gloomiest trees of the forest, which barely stood aside to let the narrow path creep through, and closed immediately behind. It was all as lonely as could be; and there is this peculiarity in such a solitude, that the traveller knows not who may be concealed by the innumerable trunks and the thick boughs overhead; so that with lonely footsteps he may yet be passing through an unseen multitude.

"There may be a devilish Indian behind every tree," said Goodman Brown to himself; and he glanced fearfully behind him as he added, "What if the devil himself should be at my very elbow!"

His head being turned back, he passed a crook of the road, and, looking forward again, beheld the figure of a man, in grave and decent attire, seated at the foot of an old tree. He arose at Goodman Brown's approach and walked onward side by side with him.

"You are late, Goodman Brown," said he. "The clock of the Old South was striking as I came through Boston, and that is full fifteen minutes agone."

"Faith kept me back a while," replied the young man, with a tremor in his voice, caused by the sudden appearance of his companion, though not wholly unexpected.

It was now deep dusk in the forest, and deepest in that part of it where these two were journeying. As nearly as could be discerned, the second traveller was about fifty years old, apparently in the same rank of life as Goodman Brown, and bearing a considerable resemblance to him, though perhaps more in expression than features. Still they might have been taken for father and son. And yet, though the elder person was as simply clad as the younger, and as simple in manner too, he had an indescribable air of one who knew the world, and who would not have felt abashed at the governor's dinner table or in King William's court, were it possible that his affairs should call him thither. But the only thing about him that could be fixed upon as remarkable was his staff, which bore the likeness of a great black snake, so curiously wrought that it might almost be seen to twist and wriggle itself like a living serpent. This, of course, must have been an ocular deception, assisted by the uncertain light.

"Come, Goodman Brown," cried his fellow-traveller, "this is a dull pace for the beginning of a journey. Take my staff, if you are so soon weary."

"Friend," said the other, exchanging his slow pace for a full stop, "having kept covenant by meeting thee here, it is my purpose now to return whence I came. I have scruples touching the matter thou wot'st° of."

"Sayest thou so?" replied he of the serpent, smiling apart. "Let us walk on, nevertheless, reasoning as we go; and if I convince thee not thou shalt turn back. We are but a little way in the forest yet."

"Too far! too far!" exclaimed the goodman, unconsciously resuming his walk. "My father never went into the woods on such an errand, nor his father before him. We have been a race of honest men and good Christians since the days of the martyrs; and shall I be the first of the name of Brown that ever took this path and kept"—

"Such company, thou wouldst say," observed the elder person, interpreting his pause. "Well said, Goodman Brown! I have been as well acquainted with your family as with ever a one among the Puritans; and that's no trifle to say. I helped your grandfather, the constable, when he lashed the Quaker woman so smartly through the streets of Salem; and it was I that brought your father a pitch-pine knot, kindled at my own hearth, to set fire to an Indian village, in King Philip's war.° They were my good friends, both; and many a pleasant walk have we had along this path, and returned merrily after midnight. I would fain be friends with you for their sake."

"If it be as thou sayest," replied Goodman Brown, "I marvel they never spoke of these matters; or, verily, I marvel not, seeing that the least rumor of the sort would have driven them from New England. We are a people of prayer, and good works to boot, and abide no such wickedness."

"Wickedness or not," said the traveller with the twisted staff, "I have a very general acquaintance here in New England. The deacons of many a church have drunk the communion wine with me; the selectmen of divers towns make me their chairman; and a majority of the Great and General Court are firm supporters of my interest. The governor and I, too—But these are state secrets."

"Can this be so?" cried Goodman Brown, with a stare of amazement at his undisturbed companion. "Howbeit, I have nothing to do with the governor and council; they have their own ways, and are no rule for a simple husbandman like me. But, were I to go on with thee, how should I meet the eye of that good old man, our minister, at Salem village? Oh, his voice would make me tremble both Sabbath day and lecture day."

Thus far the elder traveller had listened with due gravity; but now burst into a fit of irrepressible mirth, shaking himself so violently that his snake-like staff actually seemed to wriggle in sympathy.

"Ha! ha! ha!" shouted he again and again; then composing himself, "Well, go on, Goodman Brown, go on; but, prithee, don't kill me with laughing."

---

wot'st. Knowest.

King Philip's war. A war fought by the English colonists 1675-1676 against the Wampanoog Indians, led by Metacom, also known as "King Philip."

"Well, then, to end the matter at once," said Goodman Brown, considerably net-tled, "there is my wife, Faith. It would break her dear little heart; and I'd rather break my own."

"Nay, if that be the case," answered the other, "e'en go thy ways, Goodman Brown. I would not for twenty old women like the one hobbling before us that Faith should come to any harm."

As he spoke he pointed his staff at a female figure on the path, in whom Goodman Brown recognized a very pious and exemplary dame, who had taught him his catechism in youth, and was still his moral and spiritual adviser, jointly with the minister and Deacon Gookin.

"A marvel, truly, that Goody° Cloyse should be so far in the wilderness at night-fall," said he. "But with your leave, friend, I shall take a cut through the woods until we have left this Christian woman behind. Being a stranger to you, she might ask whom I was consorting with and whither I was going."

"Be it so," said his fellow-traveller. "Betake you to the woods, and let me keep the path."

Accordingly the young man turned aside, but took care to watch his companion, who advanced softly along the road until he had come within a staff's length of the old dame. She, meanwhile, was making the best of her way, with singular speed for so aged a woman, and mumbling some indistinct words—a prayer, doubtless—as she went. The traveller put forth his staff and touched her withered neck with what seemed the serpent's tail.

"The devil!" screamed the pious old lady.

"Then Goody Cloyse knows her old friend?" observed the traveller, confronting her and leaning on his writhing stick.

"Ah, forsooth, and is it your worship indeed?" cried the good dame. "Yea, truly is it, and in the very image of my old gossip, Goodman Brown, the grandfather of the silly fellow that now is. But—would your worship believe it?—my broomstick hath strangely disappeared, stolen, as I suspect, by that unhanged witch, Goody Cory, and that, too, when I was all anointed with the juice of smallage, and cinquefoil, and wolf's bane"—

"Mingled with fine wheat and the fat of a new-born babe," said the shape of old Goodman Brown.

"Ah, your worship knows the recipe," cried the old lady, cackling aloud. "So, as I was saying, being all ready for the meeting, and no horse to ride on, I made up my mind to foot it; for they tell me there is a nice young man to be taken into communion to-night. But now your good worship will lend me your arm, and we shall be there in a twinkling."

"That can hardly be," answered her friend. "I may not spare you my arm, Goody Cloyse; but here is my staff, if you will."

So saying, he threw it down at her feet, where, perhaps, it assumed life, being one of the rods which its owner had formerly lent to the Egyptian magi. Of this fact, however, Goodman Brown could not take cognizance. He had cast up his eyes in

---

Goody. A contraction of "Goodwife," a polite title of address for a married woman of humble birth.

astonishment, and, looking down again, beheld neither Goody Cloyse nor the serpen-
tine staff, but his fellow-traveller alone, who waited for him as calmly as if nothing had
happened.

"That old woman taught me my catechism," said the young man; and there was
a world of meaning in this simple comment.

They continued to walk onward, while the elder traveller exhorted his companion to make good speed and persevere in the path, discoursing so aptly that his
arguments seemed rather to spring up in the bosom of his auditor than to be suggested
by himself. As they went, he plucked a branch of maple to serve for a walking stick,
and began to strip it of the twigs and little boughs, which were wet with evening dew.
The moment his fingers touched them they became strangely withered and dried up
as with a week's sunshine. Thus the pair proceeded, at a good free pace, until suddenly, in a gloomy hollow of the road, Goodman Brown sat himself down on the
stump of a tree and refused to go any farther.

"Friend," said he, stubbornly, "my mind is made up. Not another step will I
budge on this errand. What if a wretched old woman do choose to go to the devil
when I thought she was going to heaven: is that any reason why I should quit my dear
Faith and go after her?"

"You will think better of this by and by," said his acquaintance, composedly. "Sit
here and rest yourself a while; and when you feel like moving again, there is my staff
to help you along."

Without more words, he threw his companion the maple stick, and was as
speedily out of sight as if he had vanished into the deepening gloom. The young man
sat a few moments by the roadside, applauding himself greatly, and thinking with how
clear a conscience he should meet the minister in his morning walk, nor shrink from
the eye of good old Deacon Gookin. And what calm sleep would be his that very night,
which was to have been spent so wickedly, but so purely and sweetly now, in the arms
of Faith! Amidst these pleasant and praiseworthy meditations, Goodman Brown heard
the tramp of horses along the road, and deemed it advisable to conceal himself within
the verge of the forest, conscious of the guilty purpose that had brought him thither,
though now so happily turned from it.

On came the hoof tramps and the voices of the riders, two grave old voices, conversing soberly as they drew near. These mingled sounds appeared to pass along the
road, within a few yards of the young man's hiding-place; but, owing doubtless to the
depth of the gloom at that particular spot, neither the travellers nor their steeds were
visible. Though their figures brushed the small boughs by the wayside, it could not be
seen that they intercepted, even for a moment, the faint gleam from the strip of bright
sky athwart which they must have passed. Goodman Brown alternately crouched and
stood on tiptoe, pulling aside the branches and thrusting forth his head as far as he
durst without discerning so much as a shadow. It vexed him the more, because he
could have sworn, were such a thing possible, that he recognized the voices of the
minister and Deacon Gookin, jogging along quietly, as they were wont to do, when
bound to some ordination or ecclesiastical council. While yet within hearing, one of
the riders stopped to pluck a switch.

"Of the two, reverend sir," said the voice like the deacon's, "I had rather miss an
ordination dinner than to-night's meeting. They tell me that some of our community

are to be here from Falmouth and beyond, and others from Connecticut and Rhode Island, besides several of the Indian powwows, who, after their fashion, know almost as much deviltry as the best of us. Moreover, there is a goodly young woman to be taken into communion."

"Mighty well, Deacon Gookin!" replied the solemn old tones of the minister. "Spur up, or we shall be late. Nothing can be done, you know, until I get on the ground."

The hoofs clattered again; and the voices, talking so strangely in the empty air, passed on through the forest, where no church had ever been gathered or solitary Christian prayed. Whither, then, could these holy men be journeying so deep into the heathen wilderness? Young Goodman Brown caught hold of a tree for support, being ready to sink down on the ground, faint and overburdened with the heavy sickness of his heart. He looked up to the sky, doubting whether there really was a heaven above him. Yet there was the blue arch, and the stars brightening in it.

"With heaven above and Faith below, I will yet stand firm against the devil!" cried Goodman Brown.

While he still gazed upward into the deep arch of the firmament and had lifted his hands to pray, a cloud, though no wind was stirring, hurried across the zenith and hid the brightening stars. The blue sky was still visible, except directly overhead, where this black mass of cloud was sweeping swiftly northward. Aloft in the air, as if from the depths of the cloud, came a confused and doubtful sound of voices. Once the listener fancied that he could distinguish the accents of towns-people of his own, men and women, both pious and ungodly, many of whom he had met at the communion table, and had seen others rioting at the tavern. The next moment, so indistinct were the sounds, he doubted whether he had heard aught but the murmur of the old forest, whispering without a wind. Then came a stronger swell of those familiar tones, heard daily in the sunshine at Salem village, but never until now from a cloud of night. There was one voice, of a young woman, uttering lamentations, yet with an uncertain sorrow, and entreating for some favor, which, perhaps, it would grieve her to obtain; and all the unseen multitude, both saints and sinners, seemed to encourage her onward.

"Faith!" shouted Goodman Brown, in a voice of agony and desperation; and the echoes of the forest mocked him, crying, "Faith! Faith!" as if bewildered wretches were seeking her all through the wilderness.

The cry of grief, rage, and terror was yet piercing the night, when the unhappy husband held his breath for a response. There was a scream, drowned immediately in a louder murmur of voices, fading into far-off laughter, as the dark cloud swept away, leaving the clear and silent sky above Goodman Brown. But something fluttered lightly down through the air and caught on the branch of a tree. The young man seized it, and beheld a pink ribbon.

"My Faith is gone!" cried he, after one stupefied moment. "There is no good on earth; and sin is but a name. Come, devil; for to thee is this world given."

And, maddened with despair, so that he laughed loud and long, did Goodman Brown grasp his staff and set forth again, at such a rate that he seemed to fly along the forest path rather than to walk or run. The road grew wilder and drearier and more faintly traced, and vanished at length, leaving him in the heart of the dark wilderness, still rushing onward with the instinct that guides mortal man to evil. The whole forest was peopled with frightful sounds—the creaking of the trees, the howling of wild beasts, and the yell of Indians; while sometimes the wind tolled like a distant church bell, and sometimes gave a broad roar around the traveller, as if all Nature were laughing him to scorn. But he was himself the chief horror of the scene, and shrank not from its other horrors.

"Ha! ha! ha!" roared Goodman Brown when the wind laughed at him. "Let us hear which will laugh loudest. Think not to frighten me with your deviltry. Come witch, come wizard, come Indian powwow, come devil himself, and here comes Goodman Brown. You may as well fear him as he fear you."

In truth, all through the haunted forest there could be nothing more frightful than the figure of Goodman Brown. On he flew among the black pines, brandishing his staff with frenzied gestures, now giving vent to an inspiration of horrid blasphemy, and now shouting forth such laughter as set all the echoes of the forest laughing like demons around him. The fiend in his own shape is less hideous than when he rages in the breast of man. Thus sped the demoniac on his course, until, quivering among the trees, he saw a red light before him, as when the felled trunks and branches of a clearing have been set on fire, and throw up their lurid blaze against the sky, at the hour of midnight. He paused, in a lull of the tempest that had driven him onward, and heard the swell of what seemed a hymn, rolling solemnly from a distance with the weight of many voices. He knew the tune; it was a familiar one in the choir of the village meeting-house. The verse died heavily away, and was lengthened by a chorus, not of human voices, but of all the sounds of the benighted wilderness pealing in awful harmony together. Goodman Brown cried out, and his cry was lost to his own ear by its unison with the cry of the desert.

In the interval of silence he stole forward until the light glared full upon his eyes. At one extremity of an open space, hemmed in by the dark wall of the forest, arose a rock, bearing some rude, natural resemblance either to an altar or a pulpit, and surrounded by four blazing pines, their tops aflame, their stems untouched, like candles at an evening meeting. The mass of foliage that had overgrown the summit of the rock was all on fire, blazing high into the night and fitfully illuminating the whole field. Each pendent twig and leafy festoon was in a blaze. As the red light arose and fell, a numerous congregation alternately shone forth, then disappeared in shadow, and again grew, as it were, out of the darkness, peopling the heart of the solitary woods at once.

"A grave and dark-clad company," quoth Goodman Brown.

In truth they were such. Among them, quivering to and fro between gloom and splendor, appeared faces that would be seen next day at the council board of the province, and others which, Sabbath after Sabbath, looked devoutly heavenward, and benignantly over the crowded pews, from the holiest pulpits in the land. Some affirm that the lady of the governor was there. At least there were high dames well known to her, and wives of honored husbands, and widows, a great multitude, and ancient maidens, all of excellent repute, and fair young girls, who trembled lest their mothers should espy them. Either the sudden gleams of light flashing over the obscure field bedazzled Goodman Brown, or he recognized a score of the church members of Salem village famous for their especial sanctity. Good old Deacon Gookin had arrived, and waited at the skirts of that venerable saint, his revered pastor. But, irreverently consorting with these grave, reputable, and pious people, these elders of the church, these chaste dames and dewy virgins, there were men of dissolute lives and women of spotted fame, wretches given over to all mean and filthy vice, and suspected even of horrid crimes. It was strange to see that the good shrank not from the wicked, nor were the sinners abashed by the saints. Scattered also among their pale-faced enemies were the Indian priests, or powwows, who had often scared their native forest with more hideous incantations than any known to English witchcraft.

"But where is Faith?" thought Goodman Brown, and, as hope came into his heart, he trembled.

Another verse of the hymn arose, a slow and mournful strain, such as the pious love, but joined to words which expressed all that our nature can conceive of sin, and darkly hinted at far more. Unfathomable to mere mortals is the lore of fiends. Verse after verse was sung; and still the chorus of the desert swelled between like the deepest tone of a mighty organ; and with the final peal of that dreadful anthem there came a sound, as if the roaring wind, the rushing streams, the howling beasts, and every other voice of the unconcerted wilderness were mingling and according with the voice of guilty man in homage to the prince of all. The four blazing pines threw up a loftier flame, and obscurely discovered shapes and visages of horror on the smoke wreaths above the impious assembly. At the same moment the fire on the rock shot redly forth and formed a glowing arch above its base, where now appeared a figure. With reverence be it spoken, the figure bore no slight similitude, both in garb and manner, to some grave divine of the New England churches.

"Bring forth the converts!" cried a voice that echoed through the field and rolled into the forest.

At the word, Goodman Brown stepped forth from the shadow of the trees and approached the congregation, with whom he felt a loathful brotherhood by the sympathy of all that was wicked in his heart. He could have well-nigh sworn that the shape of his own dead father beckoned him to advance, looking downward from a smoke wreath, while a woman, with dim features of despair, threw out her hand to warn him back. Was it his mother? But he had no power to retreat one step, nor to resist, even in thought, when the minister and good old Deacon Gookin seized his arms and led him to the blazing rock. Thither came also the slender form of a veiled female, led between Goody Cloyse, that pious teacher of the catechism, and Martha Carrier, who had received the devil's promise to be queen of hell. A rampant hag was she. And there stood the proselytes beneath the canopy of fire.

"Welcome, my children," said the dark figure, "to the communion of your race. Ye have found thus young your nature and your destiny. My children, look behind you!"

They turned; and flashing forth, as it were, in a sheet of flame, the fiend worshippers were seen; the smile of welcome gleamed darkly on every visage.

"There," resumed the sable form, "are all whom ye have reverenced from youth. Ye deemed them holier than yourselves, and shrank from your own sin, contrasting it with their lives of righteousness and prayerful aspirations heavenward. Yet here are they all in my worshipping assembly. This night it shall be granted you to know their secret deeds: how hoary-bearded elders of the church have whispered wanton words to the young maids of their households; how many a woman, eager for widows' weeds, has given her husband a drink at bedtime and let him sleep his last sleep in her bosom; how beardless youths have made haste to inherit their fathers' wealth; and how fair damsels—blush not, sweet ones—have dug little graves in the garden, and bidden me, the sole guest, to an infant's funeral. By the sympathy of your human hearts for sin ye shall scent out all the places—whether in church, bed-chamber, street, field, or forest—where crime has been committed, and shall exult to behold the whole earth one stain of guilt, one mighty blood spot. Far more than this. It shall be yours to penetrate, in every bosom, the deep mystery of sin, the fountain of all wicked arts, and which inexhaustibly supplies more evil impulses than human power—than my power at its utmost—can make manifest in deeds. And now, my children, look upon each other."

They did so; and, by the blaze of the hell-kindled torches, the wretched man beheld his Faith, and the wife her husband, trembling before that unhallowed altar.

"Lo, there ye stand, my children," said the figure, in a deep and solemn tone, almost sad with its despairing awfulness, as if his once angelic nature could yet mourn for our miserable race. "Depending upon one another's hearts, ye had still hoped that virtue were not all a dream. Now are ye undeceived. Evil is the nature of mankind. Evil must be your only happiness. Welcome again, my children, to the communion of your race."

"Welcome," repeated the fiend worshippers, in one cry of despair and triumph.

And there they stood, the only pair, as it seemed, who were yet hesitating on the verge of wickedness in this dark world. A basin was hollowed, naturally, in the rock. Did it contain water, reddened by the lurid light? or was it blood? or, perchance, a liquid flame? Herein did the shape of evil dip his hand and prepare to lay the mark of baptism upon their foreheads, that they might be partakers of the mystery of sin, more conscious of the secret guilt of others, both in deed and thought, than they could now be of their own. The husband cast one look at his pale wife, and Faith at him. What polluted wretches would the next glance show them to each other, shuddering alike at what they disclosed and what they saw!

"Faith! Faith!" cried the husband, "look up to heaven, and resist the wicked one."

Whether Faith obeyed he knew not. Hardly had he spoken when he found himself amid calm night and solitude, listening to a roar of the wind which died heavily away through the forest. He staggered against the rock, and felt it chill and damp; while a hanging twig, that had been all on fire, besprinkled his cheek with the coldest dew.

The next morning young Goodman Brown came slowly into the street of Salem village, staring around him like a bewildered man. The good old minister was taking a walk along the graveyard to get an appetite for breakfast and meditate his sermon, and bestowed a blessing, as he passed, on Goodman Brown. He shrank from the venerable saint as if to avoid an anathema. Old Deacon Gookin was at domestic worship, and the holy words of his prayer were heard through the open window. "What God doth the wizard pray to?" quoth Goodman Brown. Goody Cloyse, that excellent old Christian, stood in the early sunshine at her own lattice, catechizing a little girl who had brought her a pint of morning's milk. Goodman Brown snatched away the child as from the grasp of the fiend himself. Turning the corner by the meeting-house, he spied the head of Faith, with the pink ribbons, gazing anxiously forth, and bursting into such joy at sight of him that she skipped along the street and almost kissed her husband before the whole village. But Goodman Brown looked sternly and sadly into her face, and passed on without a greeting.

Had Goodman Brown fallen asleep in the forest and only dreamed a wild dream of a witch-meeting?

Be it so if you will; but, alas! it was a dream of evil omen for young Goodman Brown. A stern, a sad, a darkly meditative, a distrustful, if not a desperate man did he become from the night of that fearful dream. On the Sabbath day, when the congregation were singing a holy psalm, he could not listen because an anthem of sin rushed loudly upon his ear and drowned all the blessed strain. When the minister spoke from the pulpit with power and fervid eloquence, and, with his hand on the open Bible, of the sacred truths of our religion, and of saint-like lives and triumphant deaths, and of future bliss or misery unutterable, then did Goodman Brown turn pale, dreading lest the roof should thunder down upon the gray blasphemer and his hearers. Often, awaking suddenly at midnight, he shrank from the bosom of Faith; and at morning or eventide, when the family knelt down at prayer, he scowled and muttered to himself, and gazed sternly at his wife, and turned away. And when he had lived long, and was borne to his grave a hoary corpse, followed by Faith, an aged woman, and children and grandchildren, a goodly procession, besides neighbors not a few, they carved no hopeful verse upon his tombstone, for his dying hour was gloom.

Questions for Study

1. Why does Brown go into the forest? Once he is in the forest, he refuses several times to go farther. Why does he change his mind?

2. Who or what is the stranger? What do he and the forest symbolize?

3. Where does Hawthorne establish a contrast between what Brown sees and what he thinks he sees? Why does Hawthorne do this?

4. In each stage of Brown's journey, how does the setting correspond to his state of mind?

5. Is Brown wise or foolish to believe what the stranger tells him? What choices does Brown have after listening to the stranger? Does he make the right choices?

6. How does this story follow the pattern of the myth of the Fall? (See p. 45 for biblical accounts of the myth.)

EDGAR ALLAN POE

The Cask of Amontillado

During his troubled and relatively brief life, Edgar Allan Poe (1809–49) achieved excellence in a number of literary fields. He was a savvy editor, almost always increasing the circulation of the journals he edited. He wrote innovative poetry. He was one of the first writers of the short story. He was a feisty and penetrating critic of poetry and fiction. He virtually invented the detective story. And although his work was not well-known during his lifetime, it has become among the most popular and influential in the English language.

Poe was born to traveling actors who died when he was very young. Although John Allan, a well-to-do Richmond merchant, took Poe into his household, Poe and Allan were constantly at odds. Poe had to look elsewhere for financial support. He attended the University of Virginia and West Point briefly, and then turned to editing and writing to make a living. Shortly after dropping out of West Point, he published his third collection of poems, *Poems* (1831). He married his thirteen-year-old cousin, Virginia Clemm, in 1832, and began publishing stories in newspapers. His success as an editor of magazines and newspapers in Richmond, New York, and Philadelphia was undermined by heavy bouts of drinking. The publications of his fiction—the science fiction novel *The Narrative of Arthur Gordon Pym* (1838) and a collection of stories *Tales of the Grotesque and Arabesque* (1839)— sold poorly. His sadness over the death of his wife in 1847 was mitigated by increasing success as a lecturer and writer, by an engagement to an old friend in Richmond, and by his attempt to stop drinking. But in October, 1849, on a trip to Baltimore, Poe died, under mysterious circumstances, from heavy drinking, illness, and overexposure.

"The Cask of Amontillado" is one of Poe's finest stories. It reflects his fascination with the gothic tradition of fiction that emerged in the later eighteenth century and had become a prominent feature of European Romanticism by the time Poe began his career. As he says in reviews of Hawthorne's *Twice-Told Tales*, he attempts in his gothic stories to create a mood of horror or fright. But he is also intrigued by the psychology of his protagonists, almost all of whom are deeply troubled, if not criminally insane. As first-person narrators, they reveal more about themselves than they realize.

*T*he thousand injuries of Fortunato I had borne as I best could, but when he ventured upon insult I vowed revenge. You, who so well know the nature of my soul, will not suppose, however, that I gave utterance to a threat. *At length* I would be avenged; this was a point definitely settled—but the very definitiveness with which it was resolved precluded the idea of risk. I must not only punish but punish with impunity. A wrong is unredressed when retribution overtakes its redresser. It is equally unredressed when the avenger fails to make himself felt as such to him who has done the wrong.

It must be understood that neither by word nor deed had I given Fortunato cause to doubt my good will. I continued, as was my wont, to smile in his face, and he did not perceive that my smile *now* was at the thought of his immolation.

He had a weak point—this Fortunato—although in other regards he was a man to be respected and even feared. He prided himself on his connoisseurship in wine. Few Italians have the true virtuoso spirit. For the most part their enthusiasm is adopted to suit the time and opportunity, to practise imposture upon the British and Austrian *millionaires.* In painting and gemmary, Fortunato, like his countrymen, was a quack, but in the matter of old wines he was sincere. In this respect I did not differ from him materially;—I was skilful in the Italian vintages myself, and bought largely whenever I could.

It was about dusk, one evening during the supreme madness of the carnival season, that I encountered my friend. He accosted me with excessive warmth, for he had been drinking much. The man wore motley.° He had on a tight-fitting parti-striped dress, and his head was surmounted by the conical cap and bells. I was so pleased to see him that I thought I should never have done wringing his hand.

I said to him—"My dear Fortunato, you are luckily met. How remarkably well you are looking to-day. But I have received a pipe° of what passes for Amontillado,° and I have my doubts."

"How?" said he. "Amontillado? A pipe? Impossible! And in the middle of the carnival!"

"I have my doubts," I replied; "and I was silly enough to pay the full Amontillado price without consulting you in the matter. You were not to be found, and I was fearful of losing a bargain."

"Amontillado!"

"I have my doubts."

"Amontillado!"

"And I must satisfy them."

"Amontillado!"

"As you are engaged, I am on my way to Luchresi. If any one has a critical turn it is he. He will tell me——"

"Luchresi cannot tell Amontillado from Sherry."

"And yet some fools will have it that his taste is a match for your own."

"Come, let us go."

"Whither?"

"To your vaults."

"My friend, no; I will not impose upon your good nature. I perceive you have an engagement. Luchresi——"

"I have no engagement:—come."

"My friend, no. It is not the engagement, but the severe cold with which I perceive you are afflicted. The vaults are insufferably damp. They are encrusted with niter."

"Let us go, nevertheless. The cold is merely nothing. Amontillado! You have

---

motley. The traditional multicolored dress of a court jester. The cap is conical in shape and is topped by bells.
pipe. A large wine cask.
Amontillado. A Spanish wine.

been imposed upon. And as for Luchresi, he cannot distinguish Sherry from Amontillado."

Thus speaking, Fortunato possessed himself of my arm; and putting on a mask of black silk and drawing a *roquelaire*° closely about my person, I suffered him to hurry me to my palazzo.

There were no attendants at home; they had absconded to make merry in honor of the time. I had told them that I should not return until the morning, and had given them explicit orders not to stir from the house. These orders were sufficient, I well knew, to insure their immediate disappearance, one and all, as soon as my back was turned.

I took from their sconces two flambeaux, and giving one to Fortunato, bowed him through several suites of rooms to the archway that led into the vaults. I passed down a long and winding staircase, requesting him to be cautious as he followed. We came at length to the foot of the descent, and stood together upon the damp ground of the catacombs of the Montresors.

The gait of my friend was unsteady, and the bells upon his cap jingled as he strode.

"The pipe," he said.

"It is farther on," said I; "but observe the white web-work which gleams from these cavern walls."

He turned towards me, and looked into my eyes with two filmy orbs that distilled the rheum of intoxication.

"Niter?" he asked, at length.

"Niter," I replied. "How long have you had that cough?"

"Ugh! ugh! ugh!—ugh! ugh! ugh!—ugh! ugh! ugh!—ugh! ugh! ugh!—ugh! ugh! ugh!"

My poor friend found it impossible to reply for many minutes.

"It is nothing," he said, at last.

"Come," I said, with decision, "we will go back; your health is precious. You are rich, respected, admired, beloved; you are happy, as once I was. You are a man to be missed. For me it is no matter. We will go back; you will be ill, and I cannot be responsible. Besides, there is Luchresi——"

"Enough," he said; "the cough is a mere nothing; it will not kill me. I shall not die of a cough."

"True—true," I replied; "and, indeed, I had no intention of alarming you unnecessarily—but you should use all proper caution. A draught of this Medoc will defend us from the damps."

Here I knocked off the neck of a bottle which I drew from a long row of its fellows that lay upon the mould.

"Drink," I said, presenting him the wine.

He raised it to his lips with a leer. He paused and nodded to me familiarly, while his bells jingled.

"I drink," he said, "to the buried that repose around us."

"And I to your long life."

He again took my arm, and we proceeded.

---

roquelaire. A knee-length cloak.

"These vaults," he said, "are extensive."

"The Montresors," I replied, "were a great and numerous family."

"I forget your arms."

"A huge human foot d'or, in a field azure; the foot crushes a serpent rampant whose fangs are imbedded in the heel."

"And the motto?"

"Nemo me impune lacessit."°

"Good!" he said.

The wine sparkled in his eyes and the bells jingled. My own fancy grew warm with the Medoc. We had passed through long walls of piled skeletons, with casks and puncheons intermingling, into the inmost recesses of the catacombs. I paused again, and this time I made bold to seize Fortunato by an arm above the elbow.

"The niter!" I said; "see, it increases. It hangs like moss upon the vaults. We are below the river's bed. The drops of moisture trickle among the bones. Come, we will go back ere it is too late. Your cough——"

"It is nothing," he said; "let us go on. But first, another draught of the Medoc."

I broke and reached him a flagon of De Grâve. He emptied it at a breath. His eyes flashed with a fierce light. He laughed and threw the bottle upwards with a gesticulation I did not understand.

I looked at him in surprise. He repeated the movement—a grotesque one.

"You do not comprehend?" he said.

"Not I," I replied.

"Then you are not of the brotherhood."

"How?"

"You are not of the masons."

"Yes, yes," I said; "yes, yes."

"You? Impossible! A mason?"

"A mason," I replied.

"A sign," he said, "a sign."

"It is this," I answered, producing from beneath the folds of my *roquelaire* a trowel.

"You jest," he exclaimed, recoiling a few paces. "But let us proceed to the Amontillado."

"Be it so," I said, replacing the tool beneath the cloak and again offering him my arm. He leaned upon it heavily. We continued our route in search of the Amontillado. We passed through a range of low arches, descended, passed on, and descending again, arrived at a deep crypt, in which the foulness of the air caused our flambeaux rather to glow than flame.

At the most remote end of the crypt there appeared another less spacious. Its walls had been lined with human remains, piled to the vault overhead, in the fashion of the great catacombs of Paris. Three sides of this interior crypt were still ornamented in this manner. From the fourth side the bones had been thrown down, and lay promiscuously upon the earth, forming at one point a mound of some size. Within the wall thus exposed by the displacing of the bones, we perceived a still interior crypt or

---

Nemo me impune lacessit. No one dare attack me with impunity.

recess, in depth about four feet, in width three, in height six or seven. It seemed to have been constructed for no especial use within itself, but formed merely the interval between two of the colossal supports of the roof of the catacombs, and was backed by one of their circumscribing walls of solid granite.

It was in vain that Fortunato, uplifting his dull torch, endeavoured to pry into the depth of the recess. Its termination the feeble light did not enable us to see.

"Proceed," I said; "herein is the Amontillado. As for Luchresi——"

"He is an ignoramus," interrupted my friend, as he stepped unsteadily forward, while I followed immediately at his heels. In an instant he had reached the extremity of the niche, and finding his progress arrested by the rock, stood stupidly bewildered. A moment more and I had fettered him to the granite. In its surface were two iron staples, distant from each other about two feet, horizontally. From one of these depended a short chain, from the other a padlock. Throwing the links about his waist, it was but the work of a few seconds to secure it. He was too much astounded to resist. Withdrawing the key I stepped back from the recess.

"Pass your hand," I said, "over the wall; you cannot help feeling the niter. Indeed, it is *very* damp. Once more let me *implore* you to return. No? Then I must positively leave you. But I must first render you all the little attentions in my power."

"The Amontillado!" ejaculated my friend, not yet recovered from his astonishment.

"True," I replied; "the Amontillado."

As I said these words I busied myself among the pile of bones of which I have before spoken. Throwing them aside, I soon uncovered a quantity of building stone and mortar. With these materials and with the aid of my trowel, I began vigorously to wall up the entrance of the niche.

I had scarcely laid the first tier of the masonry when I discovered that the intoxication of Fortunato had in a great measure worn off. The earliest indication I had of this was a low moaning cry from the depth of the recess. It was *not* the cry of a drunken man. There was then a long and obstinate silence. I laid the second tier, and the third, and the fourth; and then I heard the furious vibrations of the chain. The noise lasted for several minutes, during which, that I might hearken to it with the more satisfaction, I ceased my labors and sat down upon the bones. When at last the clanking subsided, I resumed the trowel, and finished without interruption the fifth, the sixth, and the seventh tier. The wall was now nearly upon a level with my breast. I again paused, and holding the flambeaux over the mason-work, threw a few feeble rays upon the figure within.

A succession of loud and shrill screams, bursting suddenly from the throat of the chained form, seemed to thrust me violently back. For a brief moment I hesitated, I trembled. Unsheathing my rapier, I began to grope with it about the recess; but the thought of an instant reassured me. I placed my hand upon the solid fabric of the catacombs, and felt satisfied. I reapproached the wall; I replied to the yells of him who clamored. I re-echoed, I aided, I surpassed them in volume and in strength. I did this, and the clamorer grew still.

It was now midnight, and my task was drawing to a close. I had completed the eighth, the ninth and the tenth tier. I had finished a portion of the last and the eleventh; there remained but a single stone to be fitted and plastered in. I struggled with its weight; I placed it partially in its destined position. But now there came from out the niche a low laugh that erected the hairs upon my head. It was succeeded by a sad voice, which I had difficulty in recognizing as that of the noble Fortunato. The voice said—

"Ha! ha! ha!—he! he! he!—a very good joke, indeed—an excellent jest. We will have many a rich laugh about it at the palazzo—he! he! he!—over our wine—he! he! he!"

"The Amontillado!" I said.

"He! he! he!—he! he! he!—yes, the Amontillado. But is it not getting late? Will not they be awaiting us at the palazzo, the Lady Fortunato and the rest? Let us be gone."

"Yes," I said, "let us be gone."

"For the love of God, Montresor!"

"Yes," I said, "for the love of God!"

But to these words I hearkened in vain for a reply. I grew impatient. I called aloud—

"Fortunato!"

No answer. I called again—

"Fortunato!"

No answer still. I thrust a torch through the remaining aperture and let it fall within. There came forth in return only a jingling of the bells. My heart grew sick; it was the dampness of the catacombs that made it so. I hastened to make an end of my labor. I forced the last stone into its position; I plastered it up. Against the new masonry I re-erected the old rampart of bones. For the half of a century no mortal has disturbed them. *In pace requiescat!°*

Questions for Study

1. Montresor does not specify the "injuries" that Fortunato has done to him. Can you guess what they might be? How serious are they? What should one do about such "injuries"?

2. Critics have called this story a masterpiece of irony. What are some of the ironies in the story?

3. What characterizes Fortunato? Are we sympathetic to him?

4. On several occasions, Montresor suggests that they return to the carnival rather than continue into the catacombs. Why does Fortunato continue? How does Montresor manipulate him to continue?

5. To whom might Montresor be telling this story? Why?

6. What is Montresor's attitude toward his crime? Does he reveal more about himself than he realizes?

In pace requiescat! May he rest in peace!

7. How is this story similar to Browning's "Porphyria's Lover" (see p. 337)?

8. What is the setting of this story? How is the setting important? Are any aspects of the setting symbolic?

SARAH ORNE JEWETT

A White Heron

Nearly all of Sarah Orne Jewett's (1849-1909) fiction is set in the coastal region of Maine, where she lived all of her life. She was born in South Berwick, Maine, an inland port that before the Civil War had been a bustling center for shipbuilding and logging but that after the war became less prosperous as the shipping industry shifted from sailing ships to steam-driven and metal-clad ships. Jewett's father had a strong influence on her career. He was a medical doctor who encouraged Jewett to read widely and who took her with him on his medical visits into the rural areas around South Berwick. She planned to become a doctor but because of delicate health decided instead to become a writer. She began publishing short fiction in her teens and continued with a succession of well-received novels and short stories for the rest of her life. Her fiction exhibits a love and scientific knowledge of nature, an awareness of the hardships caused by the economic decline of her region, and a sympathy with the problems and status of women. Because of the economic difficulties experienced in Maine after the war, many men sought job opportunities outside the region, leaving the women behind. Jewett's female characters often have to live without men. Sometimes they choose to do so. In her autobiographical novel *The Country Doctor* (1884), the protagonist, Nan Prince, rejects marriage in order to become a country doctor. Jewett's finest novel *The Country of the Pointed Firs* features a protagonist, Mrs. Todd, who is a strong, unifying force in her community. "A White Heron" was published in *A White Heron and Other Stories* (1886).

I

*T*he woods were already filled with shadows one June evening, just before eight o'clock, though a bright sunset still glimmered faintly among the trunks of the trees. A little girl was driving home her cow, a plodding, dilatory, provoking creature in her behavior, but a valued companion for all that. They were going away from the western light, and striking deep into the dark woods, but their feet were familiar with the path, and it was no matter whether their eyes could see it or not.

There was hardly a night the summer through when the old cow could be found waiting at the pasture bars; on the contrary, it was her greatest pleasure to hide herself away among the high huckleberry bushes, and though she wore a loud bell she had made the discovery that if one stood perfectly still it would not ring. So Sylvia had to hunt for her until she found her, and call Co'! Co'! with never an answering Moo, until her childish patience was quite spent. If the creature had not given good milk and plenty of it, the case would have seemed very different to her owners. Besides, Sylvia had all the time there was, and very little use to make of it. Sometimes in pleasant weather it was a consolation to look upon the cow's pranks as an intelligent attempt to play hide and seek, and as the child had no playmates she lent herself to this amusement with a good deal of zest. Though this chase had been so long that the wary animal herself had given an unusual signal of her whereabouts, Sylvia had only laughed when she came upon Mistress Moolly at the swamp-side, and urged her affectionately homeward with a twig of birch leaves. The old cow was not inclined to wander farther, she even turned in the right direction for once as they left the pasture, and stepped along the road at a good pace. She was quite ready to be milked now, and seldom stopped to browse. Sylvia wondered what her grandmother would say because they were so late. It was a great while since she had left home at half past five o'clock, but everybody knew the difficulty of making this errand a short one. Mrs. Tilley had chased the hornéd torment too many summer evenings herself to blame any one else for lingering, and was only thankful as she waited that she had Sylvia, nowadays, to give such valuable assistance. The good woman suspected that Sylvia loitered occasionally on her own account; there never was such a child for straying about out-of-doors since the world was made! Everybody said that it was a good change for a little maid who had tried to grow for eight years in a crowded manufacturing town, but, as for Sylvia herself, it seemed as if she never had been alive at all before she came to live at the farm. She thought often with wistful compassion of a wretched dry geranium that belonged to a town neighbor.

"'Afraid of folks,'" old Mrs. Tilley said to herself, with a smile, after she had made the unlikely choice of Sylvia from her daughter's houseful of children, and was returning to the farm. "'Afraid of folks,' they said! I guess she won't be troubled no great with 'em up to the old place!" When they reached the door of the lonely house and stopped to unlock it, and the cat came to purr loudly, and rub against them, a deserted pussy, indeed, but fat with young robins, Sylvia whispered that this was a beautiful place to live in, and she never should wish to go home.

The companions followed the shady wood-road, the cow taking slow steps, and the child very fast ones. The cow stopped long at the brook to drink, as if the pasture were not half a swamp, and Sylvia stood still and waited, letting her bare feet cool themselves in the shoal water, while the great twilight moths struck softly against her. She waded on through the brook as the cow moved away, and listened to the thrushes with a heart that beat fast with pleasure. There was a stirring in the great boughs overhead. They were full of little birds and beasts that seemed to be wide-awake, and going about their world, or else saying good-night to each other in sleepy twitters. Sylvia herself felt sleepy as she walked along. However, it was not much farther to the house, and the air was soft and sweet. She was not often in the woods so late as this, and it made her feel as if she were a part of the gray shadows and the moving leaves. She was just thinking how long it seemed since she first came to the farm a year ago, and wondering if everything went on in the noisy town just the same as when she was there; the thought of the great red-faced boy who used to chase and frighten her made her hurry along the path to escape from the shadow of the trees.

Suddenly this little woods-girl is horror-stricken to hear a clear whistle not very far away. Not a bird's whistle, which would have a sort of friendliness, but a boy's whistle, determined, and somewhat aggressive. Sylvia left the cow to whatever sad fate might await her, and stepped discreetly aside into the bushes, but she was just too late. The enemy had discovered her, and called out in a very cheerful and persuasive tone, "Halloa, little girl, how far is it to the road?" and trembling Sylvia answered almost inaudibly, "A good ways."

She did not dare to look boldly at the tall young man, who carried a gun over his shoulder, but she came out of her bush and again followed the cow, while he walked alongside.

"I have been hunting for some birds," the stranger said kindly, "and I have lost my way, and need a friend very much. Don't be afraid," he added gallantly. "Speak up and tell me what your name is, and whether you think I can spend the night at your house, and go out gunning early in the morning."

Sylvia was more alarmed than before. Would not her grandmother consider her much to blame? But who could have foreseen such an accident as this? It did not appear to be her fault, and she hung her head as if the stem of it were broken, but managed to answer "Sylvy," with much effort when her companion again asked her name.

Mrs. Tilley was standing in the doorway when the trio came into view. The cow gave a loud moo by way of explanation.

"Yes, you'd better speak up for yourself, you old trial! Where'd she tucked herself away this time, Sylvy?" Sylvia kept an awed silence; she knew by instinct that her grandmother did not comprehend the gravity of the situation. She must be mistaking the stranger for one of the farmer-lads of the region.

The young man stood his gun beside the door, and dropped a heavy game-bag beside it; then he bade Mrs. Tilley good-evening, and repeated his wayfarer's story, and asked if he could have a night's lodging.

"Put me anywhere you like," he said. "I must be off early in the morning, before day; but I am very hungry, indeed. You can give me some milk at any rate, that's plain."

"Dear sakes, yes," responded the hostess, whose long slumbering hospitality seemed to be easily awakened. "You might fare better if you went out on the main road a mile or so, but you're welcome to what we've got. I'll milk right off, and you make yourself at home. You can sleep on husks or feathers," she proffered graciously. "I raised them all myself. There's good pasturing for geese just below here towards the ma'sh. Now step round and set a plate for the gentleman, Sylvy!" And Sylvia promptly stepped. She was glad to have something to do, and she was hungry herself.

It was a surprise to find so clean and comfortable a little dwelling in this New England wilderness. The young man had known the horrors of its most primitive housekeeping, and the dreary squalor of that level of society which does not rebel at the companionship of hens. This was the best thrift of an old-fashioned farmstead, though on such a small scale that it seemed like a hermitage. He listened eagerly to the old woman's quaint talk, he watched Sylvia's pale face and shining gray eyes with ever growing enthusiasm, and insisted that this was the best supper he had eaten for a month; then, afterward, the new-made friends sat down in the doorway together while the moon came up.

Soon it would be berry-time, and Sylvia was a great help at picking. The cow was a good milker, though a plaguy thing to keep track of, the hostess gossiped frankly, adding presently that she had buried four children, so that Sylvia's mother, and a son (who might be dead) in California were all the children she had left. "Dan, my boy, was a great hand to go gunning," she explained sadly. "I never wanted for pa'tridges or gray squer'ls while he was to home. He's been a great wand'rer, I expect, and he's no hand to write letters. There, I don't blame him, I'd ha' seen the world myself if it had been so I could.

"Sylvia takes after him," the grandmother continued affectionately, after a minute's pause. "There ain't a foot o' ground she don't know her way over, and the wild creatur's counts her one o' themselves. Squer'ls she'll tame to come an' feed right out o' her hands, and all sorts o' birds. Last winter she got the jay-birds to bangeing here, and I believe she'd 'a' scanted herself of her own meals to have plenty to throw out amongst 'em, if I had n't kep' watch. Anything but crows, I tell her, I'm willin' to help support,—though Dan he went an' tamed one o' them that did seem to have reason same as folks. It was round here a good spell after he went away. Dan an' his father they did n't hitch,—but he never held up his head ag'in after Dan had dared him an' gone off."

The guest did not notice this hint of family sorrows in his eager interest in something else.

"So Sylvy knows all about birds, does she?" he exclaimed, as he looked round at the little girl who sat, very demure but increasingly sleepy, in the moonlight. "I am making a collection of birds myself. I have been at it ever since I was a boy." (Mrs. Tilley smiled.) "There are two or three very rare ones I have been hunting for these five years. I mean to get them on my own ground if they can be found."

"Do you cage 'em up?" asked Mrs. Tilley doubtfully, in response to this enthusiastic announcement.

"Oh, no, they're stuffed and preserved, dozens and dozens of them," said the ornithologist, "and I have shot or snared every one myself. I caught a glimpse of a white heron three miles from here on Saturday, and I have followed it in this direction. They have never been found in this district at all. The little white heron, it is," and he turned again to look at Sylvia with the hope of discovering that the rare bird was one of her acquaintances.

But Sylvia was watching a hop-toad in the narrow footpath.

"You would know the heron if you saw it," the stranger continued eagerly. "A queer tall white bird with soft feathers and long thin legs. And it would have a nest perhaps in the top of a high tree, made of sticks, something like a hawk's nest."

Sylvia's heart gave a wild beat; she knew that strange white bird, and had once stolen softly near where it stood in some bright green swamp grass, away over at the other side of the woods. There was an open place where the sunshine always seemed strangely yellow and hot, where tall, nodding rushes grew, and her grandmother had warned her that she might sink in the soft black mud underneath and never be heard of more. Not far beyond were the salt marshes and beyond those was the sea, the sea which Sylvia wondered and dreamed about, but never had looked upon, though its great voice could often be heard above the noise of the woods on stormy nights.

"I can't think of anything I should like so much as to find that heron's nest," the handsome stranger was saying. "I would give ten dollars to anybody who could show it to me," he added desperately, "and I mean to spend my whole vacation hunting for it if need be. Perhaps it was only migrating, or had been chased out of its own region by some bird of prey."

Mrs. Tilley gave amazed attention to all this, but Sylvia still watched the toad, not divining, as she might have done at some calmer time, that the creature wished to get to its hole under the doorstep, and was much hindered by the unusual spectators at that hour of the evening. No amount of thought, that night, could decide how many wished-for treasures the ten dollars, so lightly spoken of, would buy.

The next day the young sportsman hovered about the woods, and Sylvia kept him company, having lost her first fear of the friendly lad, who proved to be most kind and sympathetic. He told her many things about the birds and what they knew and where they lived and what they did with themselves. And he gave her a jack-knife, which she thought as great a treasure as if she were a desert-islander. All day long he did not once make her troubled or afraid except when he brought down some unsus-pecting singing creature from its bough. Sylvia would have liked him vastly better without his gun; she could not understand why he killed the very birds he seemed to like so much. But as the day waned, Sylvia still watched the young man with loving admiration. She had never seen anybody so charming and delightful; the woman's heart, asleep in the child, was vaguely thrilled by a dream of love. Some premonition of that great power stirred and swayed these young foresters who traversed the solemn woodlands with soft-footed silent care. They stopped to listen to a bird's song; they pressed forward again eagerly, parting the branches,—speaking to each other rarely and in whispers; the young man going first and Sylvia following, fascinated, a few steps behind, with her gray eyes dark with excitement.

She grieved because the longed-for white heron was elusive, but she did not lead the guest, she only followed, and there was no such thing as speaking first. The sound of her own unquestioned voice would have terrified her,—it was hard enough to answer yes or no when there was need of that. At last evening began to fall, and they drove the cow home together, and Sylvia smiled with pleasure when they came to the place where she heard the whistle and was afraid only the night before.

II

Half a mile from home, at the farther edge of the woods, where the land was highest, a great pine-tree stood, the last of its generation. Whether it was left for a boundary mark, or for what reason, no one could say; the woodchoppers who had felled its mates were dead and gone long ago, and a whole forest of sturdy trees, pines and oaks and maples, had grown again. But the stately head of this old pine towered above them all and made a landmark for sea and shore miles and miles away. Sylvia knew it well. She had always believed that whoever climbed to the top of it could see the ocean; and the little girl had often laid her hand on the great rough trunk and looked up wistfully at those dark boughs that the wind always stirred, no matter how hot and still the air might be below. Now she thought of the tree with a new excitement, for why, if one climbed it at break of day, could not one see all the world, and easily discover whence the white heron flew, and mark the place, and find the hidden nest?

What a spirit of adventure, what wild ambition! What fancied triumph and delight and glory for the later morning when she could make known the secret! It was almost too real and too great for the childish heart to bear.

All night the door of the little house stood open, and the whippoorwills came and sang upon the very step. The young sportsman and his old hostess were sound asleep, but Sylvia's great design kept her broad awake and watching. She forgot to think of sleep. The short summer night seemed as long as the winter darkness, and at last when the whippoorwills ceased, and she was afraid the morning would after all come too soon, she stole out of the house and followed the pasture path through the woods, hastening toward the open ground beyond, listening with a sense of comfort and companionship to the drowsy twitter of a half-awakened bird, whose perch she had jarred in passing. Alas, if the great wave of human interest which flooded for the first time this dull little life should sweep away the satisfactions of an existence heart to heart with nature and the dumb life of the forest!

There was the huge tree asleep yet in the paling moonlight, and small and hopeful Sylvia began with utmost bravery to mount to the top of it, with tingling, eager blood coursing the channels of her whole frame, with her bare feet and fingers, that pinched and held like bird's claws to the monstrous ladder reaching up, up, almost to the sky itself. First she must mount the white oak tree that grew alongside, where she was almost lost among the dark branches and the green leaves heavy and wet with dew; a bird fluttered off its nest, and a red squirrel ran to and fro and scolded pettishly at the harmless housebreaker. Sylvia felt her way easily. She had often climbed there, and knew that higher still one of the oak's upper branches chafed against the pine trunk, just where its lower boughs were set close together. There, when she made the dangerous pass from one tree to the other, the great enterprise would really begin.

She crept out along the swaying oak limb at last, and took the daring step across into the old pine-tree. The way was harder than she thought; she must reach far and hold fast, the sharp dry twigs caught and held her and scratched her like angry talons, the pitch made her thin little fingers clumsy and stiff as she went round and round the tree's great stem, higher and higher upward. The sparrows and robins in the woods below were beginning to wake and twitter to the dawn, yet it seemed much lighter there aloft in the pine-tree, and the child knew that she must hurry if her project were to be of any use.

The tree seemed to lengthen itself out as she went up, and to reach farther and farther upward. It was like a great main-mast to the voyaging earth; it must truly have been amazed that morning through all its ponderous frame as it felt this determined spark of human spirit creeping and climbing from higher branch to branch. Who knows how steadily the least twigs held themselves to advantage this light, weak creature on her way! The old pine must have loved his new dependent. More than all the hawks, and bats, and moths, and even the sweet-voiced thrushes, was the brave, beating heart of the solitary gray-eyed child. And the tree stood still and held away the winds that June morning while the dawn grew bright in the east.

Sylvia's face was like a pale star, if one had seen it from the ground, when the last thorny bough was past, and she stood trembling and tired but wholly triumphant, high in the tree-top. Yes, there was the sea with the dawning sun making a golden dazzle over it, and toward that glorious east flew two hawks with slow-moving pinions. How low they looked in the air from that height when before one had only seen them far up, and dark against the blue sky. Their gray feathers were as soft as moths; they seemed only a little way from the tree, and Sylvia felt as if she too could go flying away among the clouds. Westward, the woodlands and farms reached miles and miles into the distance; here and there were church steeples, and white villages; truly it was a vast and awesome world.

The birds sang louder and louder. At last the sun came up bewilderingly bright. Sylvia could see the white sails of ships out at sea, and the clouds that were purple and rose-colored and yellow at first began to fade away. Where was the white heron's nest in the sea of green branches, and was this wonderful sight and pageant of the world the only reward for having climbed to such a giddy height? Now look down again, Sylvia, where the green marsh is set among the shining birches and dark hemlocks; there where you saw the white heron once you will see him again; look, look! a white spot of him like a single floating feather comes up from the dead hemlock and grows larger, and rises, and comes close at last, and goes by the landmark pine with steady sweep of wing and outstretched slender neck and crested head. And wait! wait! do not move a foot or a finger, little girl, do not send an arrow of light and consciousness from your two eager eyes, for the heron has perched on a pine bough not far beyond yours, and cries back to his mate on the nest, and plumes his feathers for the new day!

The child gives a long sigh a minute later when a company of shouting cat-birds comes also to the tree, and vexed by their fluttering and lawlessness the solemn heron goes away. She knows his secret now, the wild, light, slender bird that floats and wavers, and goes back like an arrow presently to his home in the green world beneath. Then Sylvia, well satisfied, makes her perilous way down again, not daring to look far below the branch she stands on, ready to cry sometimes because her fingers ache and her lamed feet slip. Wondering over and over again what the stranger would say to her, and what he would think when she told him how to find his way straight to the heron's nest.

"Sylvy, Sylvy!" called the busy old grandmother again and again, but nobody answered, and the small husk bed was empty, and Sylvia had disappeared.

The guest waked from a dream, and remembering his day's pleasure hurried to dress himself that it might sooner begin. He was sure from the way the shy little girl looked once or twice yesterday that she had at least seen the white heron, and now she must really be persuaded to tell. Here she comes now, paler than ever, and her worn old frock is torn and tattered, and smeared with pine pitch. The grandmother and the sportsman stand in the door together and question her, and the splendid moment has come to speak of the dead hemlock-tree by the green marsh.

But Sylvia does not speak after all, though the old grandmother fretfully rebukes her, and the young man's kind appealing eyes are looking straight in her own. He can make them rich with money; he has promised it, and they are poor now. He is so well worth making happy, and he waits to hear the story she can tell.

No, she must keep silence! What is it that suddenly forbids her and makes her dumb? Has she been nine years growing, and now, when the great world for the first time puts out a hand to her, must she thrust it aside for a bird's sake? The murmur of the pine's green branches is in her ears, she remembers how the white heron came flying through the golden air and how they watched the sea and the morning together, and Sylvia cannot speak; she cannot tell the heron's secret and give its life away.

Dear loyalty, that suffered a sharp pang as the guest went away disappointed later in the day, that could have served and followed him and loved him as a dog loves! Many a night Sylvia heard the echo of his whistle haunting the pasture path as she came home with the loitering cow. She forgot even her sorrow at the sharp report of his gun and the piteous sight of thrushes and sparrows dropping silent to the ground, their songs hushed and their pretty feathers stained and wet with blood. Were the birds better friends than their hunter might have been,—who can tell? Whatever treasures were lost to her, woodlands and summer-time, remember! Bring your gifts and graces and tell your secrets to this lonely country child!

Questions for Study

1. How has Sylvia's life changed since she came to live with her grandmother? What characterizes Sylvia?

2. Some critics have argued that "A White Heron" is similar in form to fairy tales. What qualities of the fairy tale does it have? How is Sylvia similar to a fairy tale heroine?

3. Why is Sylvia drawn to the hunter? Why does she finally refuse his request? What does she lose by refusing him?

4. What might the white heron symbolize?

5. When does Sylvia's epiphany occur? What does she learn?

6. In the final paragraph the narrator (Jewett?) addresses Sylvia. Why does she do this? What does she tell Sylvia?

7. What are the themes of this story?

ANTON CHEKHOV

The Lady with the Pet Dog

Anton Chekhov (1860–1904) was a great writer of both short stories and plays. He was born in a small provincial town in Russia. His family moved to Moscow in 1876 when his father's grocery business went bankrupt. Chekhov remained behind to finish high school, then joined his family two years later to enter medical school at the University of Moscow. While in medical school, he published humorous stories in newspapers and magazines and thereby helped alleviate his family's poverty. Although he graduated from medical school in 1884 and practiced medicine intermittently, his first love was writing. He soon published a collection of his humorous stories (1884) and wrote his first play, *Ivanov*, performed in 1887. The tone of Chekhov's work became more somber as his tuberculosis, contracted in 1884, worsened and after he made an eye-opening trip to Siberia and the Russian penal colony on the island of Sakhalin, where he witnessed the brutal treatment of prisoners. His stories took on an increasingly realistic and pessimistic quality as he dealt with social problems such as the harshness of peasant life in the provinces and the hypocrisy of the upperclasses. In many of these stories, Chekhov brought to the surface an intense feeling of isolation and alienation felt by his characters. Chekhov's plays, like *The Sea Gull* (1896), *Uncle Vanya* (1897), *The Three Sisters* (1901), and *The Cherry Orchard* (1903), depict Russia in a state of increasing social turmoil, poised for some kind of final upheaval. Although Chekhov died before the Russian revolutions of 1905 and 1917, some of his works seem almost to predict them. His marriage in 1901 to an actress in the Moscow Art Theater, the company that performed his plays to great acclaim, was happy, but his health was in serious decline. He died of tuberculosis only a few years later.

"The Lady with the Pet Dog" is one of his later stories, published in 1899. In it Chekhov maintains an objective, almost scientific attitude toward his characters that was typical of his mature fiction, but in this story he seems to extend a sympathy toward them as well. In this treatment of adulterous love, he establishes many parallels to Tolstoy's novel *Anna Karenina,* including the heroine's first name, but unlike Tolstoy he avoids a tragic ending.

I

*T*hey were saying a new face had been seen on the esplanade: a lady with a pet dog. Dmitry Dmitrich Gurov, who had already spent two weeks in Yalta° and regarded himself as an old hand, was beginning to show an interest in new faces. He was sitting in Vernet's coffeehouse when he saw a young lady, blonde and fairly tall, wearing a beret and walking along the esplanade. A white Pomeranian was trotting behind her.

Later he encountered her several times a day in the public gardens or in the

Yalta. A resort town in southern Russia on the Black Sea.

square. She walked alone, always wearing the same beret, and always accompanied by the Pomeranian. No one knew who she was, and people called her simply "the lady with the pet dog."

"If she is here alone without a husband or any friends," thought Gurov, "then it wouldn't be a bad idea to make her acquaintance."

He was under forty, but he already had a twelve-year-old daughter and two boys at school. He had married young, when still a second-year student at college, and by now his wife looked nearly twice as old as he did. She was a tall, erect woman with dark eyebrows, dignified and imposing, who called herself a thinking person. She read a good deal, used simplified spelling in her letters, and called her husband Dimitry instead of Dmitry. Though he secretly regarded her as a woman of limited intelligence, narrow-minded and rather dowdy, he stood in awe of her and disliked being at home. Long ago he had begun being unfaithful to her, and he was now constantly unfaithful, and perhaps that was why he nearly always spoke ill of women, and whenever they were discussed in his presence he would call them "the lower race."

It seemed to him that he had been so schooled by bitter experience that he was entitled to call them anything he liked, but he was unable to live for even two days without "the lower race." In the company of men he was bored, cold, ill at ease, and uncommunicative, but felt at home among women, and knew what to say to them and how to behave; and even when he was silent in their presence he felt at ease. In his appearance, in his character, in his whole nature, there was something charming and elusive, which made him attractive to women and cast a spell over them. He knew this, and was himself attracted to them by some mysterious power.

Repeated and bitter experience had taught him that every fresh intimacy, which at first seems to give the spice of variety to life and a sense of delightful and easy conquest, inevitably ends by introducing excessively complicated problems, and creating intolerable situations—this is particularly true of the well-intentioned Moscow people, who are irresolute and slow to embark on adventures. But with every new encounter with an interesting woman he forgot all about his former experiences, and the desire to live surged in him, and everything suddenly seemed simple and amusing.

One evening when he was dining in the public gardens, the lady in the beret came strolling up and sat down at the next table. Her expression, her clothes, her way of walking, the way she did her hair, suggested that she belonged to the upper classes, that she was married, that she was paying her first visit to Yalta, and that she was alone and bored. . . . Stories told about immorality in Yalta are largely untrue, and for his part Gurov despised them, knowing they were mostly invented by people who were only too ready to sin, if they had the chance. . . . But when the lady sat down at the next table a few yards away from him, he remembered all those stories of easy conquests and trips to the mountains, and he was suddenly possessed with the tempting thought of a quick and temporary liaison, a romance with an unknown woman of whose very name he was ignorant.

He beckoned invitingly at the Pomeranian, and when the little dog came up to him, he shook his finger at it. The Pomeranian began to bark. Then Gurov wagged his finger again.

The lady glanced up at him and immediately lowered her eyes.

"He doesn't bite!" she said, and blushed.

"May I give him a bone?" Gurov said, and when she nodded, he asked politely: "Have you been long in Yalta?"

"Five days."

"And I am dragging through my second week."

There was silence for a while.

"Time passes so quickly, and it is so dull here," she said without looking at him.

"It's quite the fashion to say it is boring here," he replied. "People who live out their lives in places like Belevo or Zhizdro are not bored, but when they come here they say: 'How dull! All this dust!' One would think they live in Granada!"

She laughed. Then they both went on eating in silence, like complete strangers, but after dinner they walked off together and began to converse lightly and playfully like people who are completely at their ease and contented with themselves, and it is all the same to them where they go or what they talk about. They walked and talked about the strange light of the sea, the soft warm lilac color of the water, and the golden pathway made by the moonlight. They talked of how sultry it was after a hot day. Gurov told her he came from Moscow, that he had been trained as a philologist, though he now worked in a bank, that at one time he had trained to be an opera singer, but had given it up, and he told her about the two houses he owned in Moscow. From her he learned that she grew up in St. Petersburg and had been married in the town of S——, where she had been living for the past two years, that she would stay another month in Yalta, and perhaps her husband, who also needed a rest, would come to join her. She was not sure whether her husband was a member of a government board or on the zemstvo° council, and this amused her. Gurov learned that her name was Anna Sergeyevna.

Afterwards in his room at the hotel he thought about her, and how they would surely meet on the following day. It was inevitable. Getting into bed, he recalled that only a little while ago she was a schoolgirl, doing lessons like his own daughter, and he remembered how awkward and timid she was in her laughter and in her manner of talking with a stranger—it was probably the first time in her life that she had found herself alone, in a situation where men followed her, gazed at her, and talked with her, always with a secret purpose she could not fail to guess. He thought of her slender and delicate throat and her lovely gray eyes.

"There's something pathetic about her," he thought, as he fell asleep.

II

A week had passed since they met. It was a holiday. Indoors it was oppressively hot, but the dust rose in clouds out of doors, and the people's hats whirled away. All day long Gurov was plagued with thirst, and kept going to the soft-drink stand to offer Anna Sergeyevna a soft drink or an ice cream. There was no refuge from the heat.

In the evening when the wind dropped they walked to the pier to watch the steamer come in. There were a great many people strolling along the pier: they had come to welcome friends, and they carried bunches of flowers. Two peculiarities of a

zemstvo. County.

festive Yalta crowd stood out distinctly: the elderly ladies were dressed like young women, and there were innumerable generals.

Because there was a heavy sea, the steamer was late, and already the sun was going down. The steamer had to maneuver for a long time before it could take its place beside the jetty. Anna Sergeyevna scanned the steamer and the passengers through her lorgnette, as though searching for someone she knew, and when she turned to Gurov her eyes were shining. She talked a good deal, with sudden abrupt questions, and quickly forgot what she had been saying; and then she lost her lorgnette in the crush.

The smartly dressed people went away, and it was now too dark to recognize faces. The wind had dropped, but Gurov and Anna Sergeyevna still stood there as though waiting for someone to come off the steamer. Anna Sergeyevna had fallen silent, and every now and then she would smell her flowers. She did not look at Gurov.

"The weather is better this evening," he said. "Where shall we go now? We might go for a drive."

He gazed at her intently and suddenly embraced her and kissed her on the lips, overwhelmed by the perfume and moisture of the flowers. And then, frightened, he looked around—had anyone observed them?

"Let us go to your . . . " he said softly.

They walked away quickly.

Her room was oppressively hot, and there was the scent of the perfume she had bought at a Japanese shop. Gurov gazed at her, and all the while he was thinking: "How strange are our meetings!" Out of the past there came to him the memory of other careless, good-natured women, happy in their love-making, grateful for the joy he gave them, however short, and then he remembered other women, like his wife, whose caresses were insincere and who talked endlessly in an affected and hysterical manner, with an expression which said this was not love or passion but something far more meaningful; and then he thought of the few very beautiful cold women on whose faces there would suddenly appear the glow of a fierce flame, a stubborn desire to take, to wring from life more than it can give: women who were no longer in their first youth, capricious, imprudent, unreflecting, and domineering, and when Gurov grew cold to them, their beauty aroused his hatred, and the lace trimming of their lingerie reminded him of fish scales.

But here there was all the shyness and awkwardness of inexperienced youth: a feeling of embarrassment, as though someone had suddenly knocked on the door. Anna Sergeyevna, "the lady with the pet dog," accepted what had happened in her own special way, gravely and seriously, as though she had accomplished her own downfall, an attitude which he found odd and disconcerting. Her features faded and drooped away, and on both sides of her face the long hair hung mournfully down, while she sat musing disconsolately like an adulteress in an antique painting.

"It's not right," she said. "You're the first person not to respect me."

There was a watermelon on the table. Gurov cut off a slice and began eating it slowly. For at least half an hour they were silent.

There was something touching about Anna Sergeyevna, revealing the purity of a simple and naïve woman who knew very little about life. The single candle burning on the table barely illuminated her face, but it was clear that she was deeply unhappy.

"Why should I not respect you?" Gurov said. "You don't know what you are saying."

"God forgive me!" she said, and her eyes filled with tears. "It's terrible!"

"You don't have to justify yourself."

"How can I justify myself? No, I am a wicked, fallen woman! I despise myself, and have no desire to justify myself! It isn't my husband I have deceived, but myself! And not only now, I have been deceiving myself for a long time. My husband may be a good, honest man, but he is also a flunky! I don't know what work he does, but I know he is a flunky! When I married him I was twenty. I was devoured with curiosity. I longed for something better! Surely, I told myself, there is another kind of life! I wanted to live! To live, only to live! I was burning with curiosity. You won't understand, but I swear by God I was no longer in control of myself! Something strange was going on in me. I could not hold back. I told my husband I was ill, and I came here. . . . And now I have been walking about as though in a daze, like someone who has gone out of his senses. . . . And now I am nothing else but a low, common woman, and anyone may despise me!"

Gurov listened to her, bored to death. He was irritated with her naïve tone, and with her remorse, so unexpected and so out of place. But for the tears in her eyes, he would have thought she was joking or playing a part.

"I don't understand," he said gently. "What do you want?"

She laid her face against his chest and pressed close to him.

"Believe me, believe me, I beg you," she said. "I love all that is honest and pure in life, and sin is hateful to me. I don't know what I am doing. There are simple people who say: 'The Evil One led her astray,' and now I can say of myself that the Evil One has led me astray."

"Don't say such things," he murmured.

Then he gazed into her frightened, staring eyes, kissed her, spoke softly and affectionately, and gradually he was able to quieten her, and she was happy again; and then they both began to laugh.

Afterwards when they went out, there was not a soul on the esplanade. The town with its cypresses looked like a city of the dead, but the sea still roared and hurled itself against the shore. A single boat was rocking on the waves, and the lantern on it shone with a sleepy light.

They found a cab and drove to Oreanda.

"I discovered your name in the foyer just now," he said. "It was written up on the board—von Diederichs. Is your husband German?"

"No, I believe his grandfather was German, but he himself is an Orthodox Russian."

At Oreanda they sat on a bench not far from the church and gazed below at the sea and were lost in silence. Yalta was scarcely visible through the morning mist. Motionless white clouds covered the mountaintops. No leaves rustled, but the cicadas sang, and the monotonous muffled thunder of the sea, coming up from below, spoke of the peace, the eternal sleep awaiting us. This muffled thunder rose from the sea when neither Yalta nor Oreanda existed, and so it roars and will roar, dully, indifferently, after we have passed away. In this constancy of the sea, in her perfect indifference to our living and dying, there lies perhaps the promise of our eternal salvation, the unbroken stream of life on earth, and its unceasing movement toward perfection. Sitting beside the young woman, who looked so beautiful in the dawn, Gurov was soothed and enchanted by the fairylike scene—the sea and the mountains, the clouds and the broad sky. He pondered how everything in the universe, if properly understood, would be entirely beautiful, but for our own thoughts and actions when we lose sight of the higher purposes of life and our human dignity.

Someone came up to them—probably a coast guard—looked at them and then walked away. His coming seemed full of mystery and beauty. Then in the glow of the early dawn they saw the steamer coming from Feodossia, its lights already doused.

"There is dew on the grass," said Anna Sergeyevna after a silence.

"Yes, it's time to go home."

They went back to the town.

Thereafter they met every day at noon on the esplanade, lunched and dined together, went out on excursions, and admired the sea. She complained of sleeping badly and of the violent beating of her heart, and she kept asking the same questions over and over again, alternately surrendering to jealousy and the fear that he did not really respect her. And often in the square or in the public gardens, when there was no one near, he would suddenly draw her to him and kiss her passionately. Their perfect idleness, those kisses in the full light of day, exchanged circumspectly and furtively for fear that anyone should see them, the heat, the smell of the sea, the continual glittering procession of idle, fashionable, well-fed people—all this seemed to give him a new lease of life. He kept telling Anna Sergeyevna how beautiful and seductive she was; he was impatient and passionate for her; and he never left her side, while she brooded continually, always trying to make him confess that he had no respect for her, did not love her at all, and saw in her nothing but a loose woman. Almost every evening at a late hour they would leave the town and drive out to Oreanda or to the waterfall, and these excursions were invariably a success, while the sensations they enjoyed were invariably beautiful and sublime.

All this time they were waiting for her husband to come, but he sent a letter saying he was having trouble with his eyes and imploring her to come home as soon as possible. Anna Sergeyevna made haste to obey.

"It's a good thing I am going away," she told Gurov. "It is fate."

She took a carriage to the railroad station, and he went with her. The drive took nearly a whole day. When she had taken her seat in the express train, and when the second bell had rung, she said: "Let me have one more look at you! Just one more! Like that!"

She did not cry, but looked sad and ill, and her face trembled.

"I shall always think of you and remember you," she said. "God be with you! Think kindly of me! We shall never meet again—that's all for the good, for we should never have met. God bless you!"

The train moved off rapidly, and soon its lights vanished, and in a few moments the sound of the engine grew silent, as though everything were conspiring to put an end to this sweet oblivion, this madness. Alone on the platform, gazing into the dark distance, Gurov listened to the crying of the cicadas and the humming of the telegraph wires with the feeling that he had only just this moment woken up. And he told himself that this was just one more of the many adventures in his life, and it was now over, and there remained only a memory. . . . He was confused, sad, and filled with a faint sensation of remorse. After all, this young woman whom he would never meet again, had not been happy with him. He had been affectionate and sincere, but in his manner, his tone, his caresses, there had always been a suggestion of irony, the insulting arrogance of a successful male who was almost twice her age. And always she had called him kind, exceptional, noble: obviously he had seemed to her different from what he really was, and unintentionally he had deceived her. . . .

Here at the railroad station there was the scent of autumn in the air; and the evening was cold.

"It's time for me to go north, too," Gurov thought as he left the platform. "High time!"

III

At home in Moscow winter was already at hand. The stoves were heated, and it was still dark when the children got up to go to school, and the nurse would light the lamp for a short while. Already there was frost. When the first snow falls, and people go out for the first time on sleighs, it is good to see the white ground, the white roofs: one breathes easily and lightly, and one remembers the days of one's youth. The old lime trees and birches have a kindly look about them: they lie closer to one's heart than cypresses and palms; and below their branches one has no desire to dream of mountains and the sea.

Gurov, a native of Moscow, arrived there on a fine, frosty day, and when he put on his fur coat and warm gloves and went for a stroll along the Petrovka, and when on Saturday evening he heard the church bells ringing, then his recent travels and all the places he had visited lost their charm for him. Little by little he became immersed in Moscow life, eagerly read three newspapers a day, and declared that on principle he never read Moscow newspapers. Once more he was caught up in a whirl of restaurants, clubs, banquets, and celebrations, and it was flattering to have famous lawyers and actors visiting his house, and flattering to play cards with a professor at the doctors' club. He could eat a whole portion of *selyanka*, a cabbage stew, straight off the frying pan. . . .

So a month would pass, and the image of Anna Sergeyevna, he thought, would vanish into the mists of memory, and only rarely would she visit his dreams with her touching smile, like the other women who appeared in his dreams. But more than a month went by, soon it was the dead of winter, and the memory of Anna Sergeyevna remained as vivid as if he had parted from her only the day before. And these memories kept glowing with an even stronger flame. Whether it was in the silence of the evening when he was in his study and heard the voices of his children preparing their lessons, or listening to a song or the music in a restaurant or a storm howling in the chimney, suddenly all his memories would spring to life again: what happened on the pier, the misty mountains in the early morning, the steamer coming in from Feodossia, their kisses. He would pace up and down the room for a long while, remembering it all and smiling to himself, and later these memories would fill his dreams, and in his imagination the past would mingle with the future. When he closed his eyes, he saw her as though she were standing before him in the flesh, younger, lovelier, tenderer than she had really been; and he imagined himself a finer person than he had been in Yalta. In the evenings she peered at him from the bookshelves, the fireplace, a corner of the room; he heard her breathing and the soft rustle of her skirts. In the street he followed the women with his eyes, looking for someone who resembled her.

He began to feel an overwhelming desire to share his memories with someone. But in his home it was impossible for him to talk of his love, and away from home—there was no one. The tenants who lived in his house and his colleagues at the bank were equally useless. And what could he tell them? Had he really been in love? Was there anything beautiful, poetic, edifying, or even interesting, in his relations with Anna Sergeyevna? He found himself talking about women and love in vague generalities, and nobody guessed what he meant, and only his wife twitched her dark eyebrows and said: "Really, Dimitry, the role of a coxcomb does not suit you at all!"

One evening he was coming out of the doctors' club with one of his card partners, a government official, and he could not prevent himself from saying: "If you only knew what a fascinating woman I met in Yalta!"

The official sat down in the sleigh, and was driving away when he suddenly turned round and shouted: "Dmitry Dmitrich!"

"What?"

"You were quite right just now! The sturgeon wasn't fresh!"

These words, in themselves so commonplace, for some reason aroused Gurov's indignation: they seemed somehow dirty and degrading. What savage manners, what awful faces! What wasted nights, what dull days devoid of interest! Frenzied card playing, gluttony, drunkenness, endless conversations about the same thing. Futile pursuits and conversations about the same topics taking up the greater part of the day and the greater part of a man's strength, so that he was left to live out a curtailed, bobtailed life with his wings clipped—an idiotic mess—impossible to run away or escape—one might as well be in a madhouse or a convict settlement.

Gurov, boiling with indignation, did not sleep a wink that night, and all the next day he suffered from a headache. On the following nights, too, he slept badly, sitting up in bed, thinking, or pacing the floor of his room. He was fed up with his children, fed up with the bank, and had not the slightest desire to go anywhere or talk about anything.

During the December holidays he decided to go on a journey and told his wife he had to go to St. Petersburg on some business connected with a certain young friend of his. Instead he went to the town of S——. Why? He hardly knew himself. He wanted to see Anna Sergeyevna and talk with her and if possible arrange a rendezvous.

He arrived at S—— during the morning and took the best room in the hotel, where the floor was covered with gray army cloth and on the table there was an inkstand, gray with dust, topped by a headless rider holding a hat in his raised hand. The porter gave him the necessary information: von Diederichs lived on Old Goncharnaya Street in a house of his own not far from the hotel; lived on a grand scale, luxuriously, and kept his own horses; the whole town knew him. The porter pronounced the name "Driderits."

He was in no hurry. He walked along Old Goncharnaya Street and found the house. In front of the house stretched a long gray fence studded with nails.

"You'd run away from a fence like that," Gurov thought, glancing now at the windows of the house, now at the fence.

He thought: "Today is a holiday, and her husband is probably at home. In any case it would be tactless to go up to the house and upset her. And if I sent her a note it might fall into her husband's hands and bring about a catastrophe! The best thing is to trust to chance." So he kept walking up and down the street by the fence, waiting for the chance. He saw a beggar entering the gates, only to be attacked by dogs, and about an hour later he heard someone playing on a piano, but the sounds were very faint and indistinct. Probably Anna Sergeyevna was playing. Suddenly the front door opened, and an old woman came out, followed by the familiar white Pomeranian. Gurov thought of calling out to the dog, but his heart suddenly began to beat violently and he was so excited he could not remember the dog's name.

As he walked on, he came to hate the gray fence more and more, and it occurred to him with a sense of irritation that Anna Sergeyevna had forgotten him and was perhaps amusing herself with another man, and that was very natural in a young woman who had nothing to look at from morning to night but that damned fence. He went back to his hotel room and for a long while sat on the sofa, not knowing what to do. Then he ordered dinner and took a long nap.

"How absurd and tiresome it is!" he thought when he woke and looked at the dark windows, for evening had fallen. "Well, I've had some sleep, and what is there to do tonight?"

He sat up in the bed, which was covered with a cheap gray blanket of the kind seen in hospitals, and he taunted himself with anger and vexation.

"You and your lady with the pet dog. . . . There's a fine adventure for you! You're in a nice fix now!"

However, at the railroad station that morning his eye had been caught by a playbill advertising in enormous letters the first performance of *The Geisha*. He remembered this, and drove to the theater.

"It's very likely that she goes to first nights," he told himself.

The theater was full. There, as so often in provincial theaters, a thick haze hung above the chandeliers, and the crowds in the gallery were fidgeting noisily. In the first row of the orchestra the local dandies were standing with their hands behind their backs, waiting for the curtain to rise, while in the governor's box the governor's daughter, wearing a boa, sat in front, the governor himself sitting modestly behind the drapes, with only his hands visible. The curtain was swaying; the orchestra spent a long time tuning up. While the audience was coming in and taking their seats, Gurov was looking impatiently around him.

And then Anna Sergeyevna came in. She sat in the third row, and when Gurov looked at her his heart seemed to stop, and he understood clearly that the whole world contained no one nearer, dearer, and more important than Anna. This slight woman, lost amid a provincial rabble, in no way remarkable, with her silly lorgnette in her hands, filled his whole life: she was his sorrow and his joy, the only happiness he desired for himself; and to the sounds of the wretched orchestra, with its feeble provincial violins, he thought how beautiful she was. He thought and dreamed.

There came with Anna Sergeyevna a young man with small side whiskers, very tall and stooped, who inclined his head at every step and seemed to be continually bowing. Probably this was the husband she once described as a flunky one day in Yalta when she was in a bitter mood. And indeed in his lanky figure, his side whiskers, his small bald patch, there was something of a flunky's servility. He smiled sweetly, and in his buttonhole there was an academic badge like the number worn by a waiter.

During the first intermission the husband went away to smoke, and she remained in her seat. Gurov, who was also sitting in the orchestra, went up to her and said in a trembling voice, with a forced smile: "How are you?"

She looked up at him and turned pale, then glanced at him again in horror, unable to believe her eyes, tightly gripping the fan and the lorgnette, evidently fighting to overcome a feeling of faintness. Both were silent. She sat, he stood, and he was frightened by her distress, and did not dare sit beside her. The violins and flutes sang out as they were tuned. Suddenly he was afraid, as it occurred to him that all the people in the boxes were staring down at them. She stood up and walked quickly to the exit; he followed her, and both of them walked aimlessly up and down the corridors, while crowds of lawyers, teachers, and civil servants, all wearing the appropriate uniforms and badges, flashed past; and the ladies, and the fur coats hanging from pegs, also flashed past; and the draft blew through the place, bringing with it the odor of cigar stubs. Gurov, whose heart was beating wildly, thought: "Oh Lord, why are these people here and this orchestra?"

At that moment he recalled how, when he saw Anna Sergeyevna off at the station in the evening, he had told himself it was all over and they would never meet again. But how far away the end seemed to be now!

Anna paused on a narrow dark stairway which bore the inscription: "This way to the upper balcony."

"How you frightened me!" she said, breathing heavily, pale and stunned. "How you frightened me! I am half dead! Why did you come? Why?"

"Do try to understand, Anna—please understand . . ." he said in a hurried whisper. "I implore you, please understand . . . "

She looked at him with dread, with entreaty, with love, intently, to retain his features all the more firmly in her memory.

"I've been so unhappy," she went on, not listening to him. "All this time I've thought only of you, I've lived on thoughts of you. I tried to forget, to forget—why, why have you come?"

A pair of schoolboys were standing on the landing above them, smoking and peering down, but Gurov did not care, and drawing Anna to him, he began kissing her face, her cheeks, her hands.

"What are you doing? What are you doing?" she said in terror, pushing him away from her. "We have both lost our senses! Go away now—tonight! . . . I implore you by everything you hold sacred. . . . Someone is coming!"

Someone was climbing up the stairs.

"You must go away . . . " Anna Sergeyevna went on in a whisper. "Do you hear, Dmitry Dmitrich? I'll come and visit you in Moscow. I have never been happy. I am miserable now, and I shall never be happy again, never! Don't make me suffer any more! I swear I'll come to Moscow! We must separate now. My dear precious darling, we have to separate!"

She pressed his hand and went quickly down the stairs, all the while gazing back at him, and it was clear from the expression in her eyes that she was miserable. For a while Gurov stood there, listening to her footsteps, and then all sounds faded away, and he went to look for his coat and left the theater.

IV

And Anna Sergeyevna began coming to see him in Moscow. Every two or three months she would leave the town of S——, telling her husband she was going to consult a specialist in women's disorders, and her husband neither believed her nor disbelieved her. In Moscow she always stayed at the Slavyansky Bazaar Hotel, and the moment she arrived she would send a redcapped hotel messenger to Gurov. He would visit her, and no one in Moscow ever knew about their meetings.

One winter morning he was going to visit her as usual. (The messenger from the hotel had come the evening before, but he was out.) His daughter accompanied him. He was taking her to school, and the school lay on the way to the hotel. Great wet flakes of snow were falling.

"Three degrees above freezing, and it's still snowing," he told his daughter. "That's only the surface temperature of the earth—the other layers of the atmosphere have other temperatures."

"Yes, Papa. But why are there no thunderstorms in winter?"

He explained that, too. He talked, and all the while he was thinking about his meeting with the beloved, and not a living soul knew of it, and probably no one would ever know. He was living a double life: an open and public life visible to all who had any need to know, full of conventional truth and conventional lies, exactly like the lives of his friends and acquaintances, and another which followed a secret course. And by one of those strange and perhaps accidental circumstances everything that was to him meaningful, urgent, and important, everything about which he felt sincerely and did not deceive himself, everything that went to shape the very core of his existence, was concealed from others, while everything that was false and the shell where he hid in order to hide the truth about himself—his work at the bank, discussions at the club, conversations about women as "an inferior race," and attending anniversary celebrations with his wife—all this was on the surface. Judging others by himself, he refused to believe the evidence of his eyes, and therefore he imagined that all men led their real and meaningful lives under a veil of mystery and under cover of darkness. Every man's intimate existence revolved around mysterious secrets, and it was perhaps partly for this reason that all civilized men were so nervously anxious to protect their privacy.

Leaving his daughter at the school, Gurov went on to the Slavyansky Bazaar Hotel. He removed his fur coat in the lobby, and then went upstairs and knocked softly on the door. Anna Sergeyevna had been exhausted by the journey and the suspense of waiting for his arrival—she had in fact expected him the previous evening. She was wearing her favorite gray dress. She was pale, and she looked at him without smiling, and he had scarcely entered the room when she threw herself in his arms. Their kisses were lingering and prolonged, as though two years had passed since they had seen each other.

"How were things down there?" he said. "Anything new?"

"Please wait. . . . I'll tell you in a moment. . . . I can't speak yet!"

She could not speak because she was crying. She turned away from him, pressing a handkerchief to her eyes.

"Let her have her cry," he thought. "I'll sit down and wait." And he sat down in an armchair.

Then he rang and ordered tea, and while he drank the tea she remained standing with her face turned to the window. . . . She was crying from the depth of her emotions, in the bitter knowledge that their life together was so weighed down with sadness, because they could only meet in secret and were always hiding from people like thieves. And that meant surely that their lives were shattered!

"Oh, do stop crying!" he said.

It was evident to him that their love affair would not soon be over, and there was no end in sight. Anna Sergeyevna was growing more and more passionately fond of him, and it was beyond belief that he would ever tell her it must one day end; and if he had told her, she would not have believed him.

He went up to her and put his hands on her shoulders, intending to console her with some meaningless words and to fondle her; and then he saw himself in the mirror.

His hair was turning gray. It struck him as strange that he should have aged so much in these last years, and lost his good looks. Her shoulders were warm and trembling at his touch. He felt pity for her, who was so warm and beautiful, though probably it would not be long before she would begin to fade and wither, as he had done. Why did she love him so much? Women had always believed him to be other than what he was, and they loved in him not himself but the creature who came to life in their imagination, the man they had been seeking eagerly all their lives, and when they had discovered their mistake, they went on loving him. And not one of them was ever happy with him. Time passed, he met other women, became intimate with them, parted from them, never having loved them. It was anything you please, but it was not love.

And now at last, when his hair was turning gray, he had fallen in love—real love—for the first time in his life.

Anna Sergeyevna and he loved one another as people who are very close and dear love one another: they were like deeply devoted friends, like husband and wife. It seemed to them that Fate had intended them for one another, and it was beyond understanding that one had a wife, the other a husband. It was as though they were two birds of passage, one male, one female, who had been trapped and were now compelled to live in different cages. They had forgiven one another for all they were ashamed of in the past, they forgave everything in the present, and felt that this love of theirs changed them both.

Formerly in moments of depression he had consoled himself with the first argument that came into his head, but now all such arguments were foreign to him. He felt a deep compassion for her, and desired to be tender and sincere. . . .

"Don't cry, my darling," he said. "You've cried enough. Now let us talk, and we'll think of something. . . . "

Then they talked it over for a long time, trying to discover some way of avoiding secrecy and deception, and living in different towns, and being separated for long periods. How could they free themselves from their intolerable chains?

"How? How?" he asked, holding his head in his hands. "How?"

And it seemed as though in a little while the solution would be found and a lovely new life would begin for them; and to both of them it was clear that the end was still very far away, and the hardest and most difficult part was only beginning.

Questions for Study

1. What is Gurov like before he meets Anna? What characterizes his relationship with his wife and children? What is his attitude toward women?

2. What is Anna like? How does she differ from Gurov's expectations about women?

3. What do Gurov and Anna expect from their affair? What do they think will happen when they say goodbye in Yalta? What, in fact, does happen?

4. How are Yalta (a resort town on the Black Sea) and Moscow different? How does each place complement or influence Gurov's attitudes and choices? How are the seasons and weather important?

5. Gurov has several epiphanies. When do they occur? What do they reveal to him?

6. How do Gurov and Anna change? Do they change for the better or for the worse? Are they to be blamed for what they do? What will become of them?

7. What does Chekhov seem to be saying about the nature of love? What different kinds of love do we see in this story? What does Chekhov seem to be saying about the nature of "true" love?

FRANZ KAFKA

A Country Doctor

Franz Kafka (1883–1924) was born into a German-speaking Jewish family in Prague, the capital of the Kingdom of Bohemia (now the capital of Czechoslovakia). His father was a robust, energetic man who had pulled himself out of poverty to become a successful businessman. For nearly all of his life Kafka compared himself unfavorably with his father and felt guilty that he could not be as strong physically or as effective in business as his father. He took a law degree in 1906, but rather than practice law he became a bureaucrat for a state insurance bureau from 1908 until he had to retire for health reasons in 1922. Kafka was a hard-working and effective civil servant, but he felt that his real mission in life was to be a writer. Although he was shy, he formed many friendships that helped further his literary ambitions. One of his friends, the writer Max Brod, recognized Kafka's talent, prodded him to write, and secured a publisher for his works. His first book, *Meditation* (1913), was a collection of short reflections on a variety of philosophical issues. His eerie story about a civil servant who turns into a dung beetle, *The Metamorphosis,* appeared in 1915. *A Country Doctor* (1919) and *A Hunger Artist* (1924) were collections of short stories. Most of Kafka's works, however, appeared after his death, including the novels *The Trial* (1925), *The Castle* (1926), and *Amerika* (1927), and various stories, parables, and reflections. Brod published Kafka's complete works in 1935–1937.

As a writer, Kafka was influenced by his reading in Jewish mystical literature, in theology and philosophy, and in Jewish legends and tales. His fiction has a strange, dreamlike quality that seems to point to moral and philosophical themes, but these themes are often difficult to grasp. Kafka wrote the stories in *A Country Doctor* in the winter and spring of 1916–17. He was depressed by the fierceness of World War I, by the recent discovery that he had contracted tuberculosis, and by his alienation from his father. He dedicated the book to his father, hoping that it would bring about a reconciliation between them. Critics disagree about the meaning of the title story of this book. Some critics insist that it reflects the circumstances of Kafka's life. In a letter, for example, Kafka referred to his tuberculosis as "my lung-wound" and identified himself with the boy in the story. Other critics see the story as reflecting theological themes about guilt and redemption.

I was in great perplexity; I had to start on an urgent journey; a seriously ill patient was waiting for me in a village ten miles off; a thick blizzard of snow filled all the wide spaces between him and me; I had a gig, a light gig with big wheels, exactly right for our country roads; muffled in furs, my bag of instruments in my hand, I was in the courtyard all ready for the journey; but there was no horse to be had, no horse. My own horse had died in the night, worn out by the fatigues of this icy winter; my servant girl was now running round the village trying to borrow a horse; but it was hopeless, I knew it, and I stood there forlornly, with the snow gathering more and more thickly upon me, more and more unable to move. In the gateway the girl appeared, alone, and waved the lantern; of course, who would lend a horse at this time for such a journey? I strode through the courtyard once more; I could see no way out; in my confused distress I kicked at the dilapidated door of the yearlong uninhabited pigsty. It flew open and flapped to and fro on its hinges. A steam and smell as of horses came out from it. A dim stable lantern was swinging inside from a rope. A man, crouching on his hams in that low space, showed an open blue-eyed face. "Shall I yoke up?" he asked, crawling out on all fours. I did not know what to say and merely stooped down to see what else was in the sty. The servant girl was standing beside me. "You never know what you're going to find in your own house," she said, and we both laughed. "Hey there, Brother, hey there, Sister!" called the groom, and two horses, enormous creatures with powerful flanks, one after the other, their legs tucked close to their bodies, each well-shaped head lowered like a camel's, by sheer strength of buttocking squeezed out through the door hole which they filled entirely. But at once they were standing up, their legs long and their bodies steaming thickly. "Give him a hand," I said, and the willing girl hurried to help the groom with the harnessing. Yet hardly was she beside him when the groom clipped hold of her and pushed his face against hers. She screamed and fled back to me; on her cheek stood out in red the marks of two rows of teeth. "You brute," I yelled in fury, "do you want a whipping?" but in the same moment reflected that the man was a stranger; that I did not know where he came from, and that of his own free will he was helping me out when everyone else had failed me. As if he knew my thoughts he took no offense at my threat but, still busied with the horses, only turned round once towards me. "Get in," he said then, and indeed: everything was ready. A magnificent pair of horses, I observed, such as I had never sat behind, and I climbed in happily. "But I'll drive, you don't know the way," I said. "Of course," said he, "I'm not coming with you anyway, I'm staying with Rose." "No," shrieked Rose, fleeing into the house with a justified presentiment that her fate was inescapable; I heard the door chain rattle as she put it up; I heard the key turn in the lock; I could see, moreover, how she put out the lights in the entrance hall and in further flight all through the rooms to keep herself from being discovered. "You're coming with me," I said to the groom, "or I won't go, urgent as my journey is. I'm not thinking of paying for it by handing the girl over to you." "Gee up!" he said; clapped his hands; the gig whirled off like a log in a freshet; I could just hear the door of my house splitting and bursting as the groom charged at it and then I was deafened and blinded by a storming rush that steadily buffeted all my senses. But this only for a moment, since, as if my patient's farmyard had opened out just before my courtyard gate, I was already there; the horses had come quietly to a standstill; the blizzard had stopped; moonlight all around; my patient's parents hurried out of the house, his sister behind them; I was almost lifted out of the gig; from their confused ejaculations I gathered not a word; in the sickroom the air was almost unbreathable; the neglected stove was smoking; I wanted to push open a window; but first I had to look at my patient. Gaunt, without any fever, not cold, not warm, with vacant eyes, without a shirt, the youngster heaved himself up from under the feather bedding, threw his arms round my neck, and whispered in my ear: "Doctor, let me die." I glanced round the room; no one had heard it; the parents were leaning forward in silence waiting for my verdict; the sister had set a chair for my handbag; I opened the bag and hunted among my instruments; the boy kept clutching at me from his bed to remind me of his entreaty; I picked up a pair of tweezers, examined them in the candlelight and laid them down again. "Yes," I thought blasphemously, "in cases like this the gods are helpful, send the missing horse, add to it a second because of the urgency, and to crown everything bestow even a groom—" And only now did I remember Rose again; what was I to do, how could I rescue her, how could I pull her away from under that groom at ten miles' distance, with a team of horses I couldn't control. These horses, now, they had somehow slipped the reins loose, pushed the windows open from outside, I did not know how; each of them had stuck a head in at a window and, quite unmoved by the startled cries of the family, stood eyeing the patient. "Better go back at once," I thought, as if the horses were summoning me to the return journey, yet I permitted the patient's sister, who fancied that I was dazed by the heat, to take my fur coat from me. A glass of rum was poured out for me, the old man clapped me on the shoulder, a familiarity justified by this offer of his treasure. I shook my head; in the narrow confines of the old man's thoughts I felt ill; that was my only reason for refusing the drink.

The mother stood by the bedside and cajoled me towards it; I yielded, and, while one of the horses whinnied loudly to the ceiling, laid my head to the boy's breast, which shivered under my wet beard. I confirmed what I already knew; the boy was quite sound, something a little wrong with his circulation, saturated with coffee by his solicitous mother, but sound and best turned out of bed with one shove. I am no world reformer and so I let him lie. I was the district doctor and did my duty to the uttermost, to the point where it became almost too much. I was badly paid and yet generous and helpful to the poor. I had still to see that Rose was all right, and then the boy might have his way and I wanted to die too. What was I doing there in that endless winter! My horse was dead, and not a single person in the village would lend me another. I had to get my team out of the pigsty; if they hadn't chanced to be horses I should have had to travel with swine. That was how it was. And I nodded to the family. They knew nothing about it, and, had they known, would not have believed it. To write prescriptions is easy, but to come to an understanding with people is hard. Well, this should be the end of my visit, I had once more been called out needlessly, I was used to that, the whole district made my life a torment with my night bell, but that I should have to sacrifice Rose this time as well, the pretty girl who had lived in my house for years almost without my noticing her—that sacrifice was too much to ask, and I had somehow to get it reasoned out in my head with the help of what craft I could muster, in order not to let fly at this family, which with the best will in the world could not restore Rose to me. But as I shut my bag and put an arm out for my fur coat, the family meanwhile standing together, the father sniffing at the glass of rum in his hand, the mother, apparently disappointed in me—why, what do people expect?—biting her lips with tears in her eyes, the sister fluttering a blood-soaked towel, I was somehow ready to admit conditionally that the boy might be ill after all. I went towards him, he welcomed me smiling as if I were bringing him the most nourishing invalid broth—ah, now both horses were whinnying together; the noise, I suppose, was ordained by heaven to assist my examination of the patient—and this time I discovered that the boy was indeed ill. In his right side, near the hip, was an open wound as big as the palm of my hand. Rose-red, in many variations of shade, dark in the hollows, lighter at the edges, softly granulated, with irregular clots of blood, open as a surface mine to the daylight. That was how it looked from a distance. But on a closer inspection there was another complication. I could not help a low whistle of surprise. Worms, as thick and as long as my little finger, themselves rose-red and blood-spotted as well, were wriggling from their fastness in the interior of the wound towards the light, with small white heads and many little legs. Poor boy, you were past helping. I had discovered your great wound; this blossom in your side was destroying you. The family was pleased; they saw me busying myself; the sister told the mother, the mother the father, the father told several guests who were coming in, through the moonlight at the open door, walking on tiptoe, keeping their balance with outstretched arms. "Will you save me?" whispered the boy with a sob, quite blinded by the life within his wound. That is what people are like in my district. Always expecting the impossible from the doctor. They have lost their ancient beliefs; the parson sits at home and unravels his vestments, one after another; but the doctor is supposed to be omnipotent with his merciful surgeon's hand. Well, as it pleases them; I have not thrust my services on them; if they misuse me for sacred ends, I let that happen to me too; what better do I want, old country doctor that I am, bereft of my servant girl! And so they came, the family and the village elders, and stripped my clothes off me; a school choir with the teacher at the head of it stood before the house and sang these words to an utterly simple tune:

> Strip his clothes off, then he'll heal us,
> If he doesn't, kill him dead!
> Only a doctor, only a doctor.

Then my clothes were off and I looked at the people quietly, my fingers in my beard and my head cocked to one side. I was altogether composed and equal to the situation and remained so, although it was no help to me, since they now took me by the head and feet and carried me to the bed. They laid me down in it next to the wall, on the side of the wound. Then they all left the room; the door was shut; the singing stopped; clouds covered the moon; the bedding was warm around me; the horses' heads in the open windows wavered like shadows. "Do you know," said a voice in my ear, "I have very little confidence in you. Why, you were only blown in here, you didn't come on your own feet. Instead of helping me, you're cramping me on my deathbed. What I'd like best is to scratch your eyes out." "Right," I said, "it is a shame. And yet I am a doctor. What am I to do? Believe me, it is not too easy for me either." "Am I supposed to be content with this apology? Oh, I must be, I can't help it. I always have to put up with things. A fine wound is all I brought into the world; that was my sole endowment." "My young friend," said I, "your mistake is: you have not a wide enough view. I have been in all the sickrooms, far and wide, and I tell you: your wound is not so bad. Done in a tight corner with two strokes of the ax. Many a one proffers his side and can hardly hear the ax in the forest, far less that it is coming nearer to him." "Is that really so, or are you deluding me in my fever?" "It is really so, take the word of honor of an official doctor." And he took it and lay still. But now it was time for me to think of escaping. The horses were still standing faithfully in their places. My clothes, my fur coat, my bag were quickly collected; I didn't want to waste time dressing; if the horses raced home as they had come, I should only be springing, as it were, out of this bed into my own. Obediently a horse backed away from the window; I threw my bundle into the gig; the fur coat missed its mark and was caught on a hook only by the sleeve. Good enough. I swung myself on to the horse. With the reins loosely trailing, one horse barely fastened to the other, the gig swaying behind, my fur coat last of all in the snow. "Gee up!" I said, but there was no galloping; slowly, like old men, we crawled through the snowy wastes; a long time echoed behind us the new but faulty song of the children:

> O be joyful, all you patients,
> The doctor's laid in bed beside you!

Never shall I reach home at this rate; my flourishing practice is done for; my successor is robbing me, but in vain, for he cannot take my place; in my house the disgusting groom is raging; Rose is his victim; I do not want to think about it any more. Naked, exposed to the frost of this most unhappy of ages, with an earthly vehicle, unearthly horses, old man that I am, I wander astray. My fur coat is hanging from the back of the gig, but I cannot reach it, and none of my limber pack of patients lifts a finger. Betrayed! Betrayed! A false alarm on the night bell once answered—it cannot be made good, not ever.

Questions for Study

1. What details of the story make it dreamlike?

2. Dreams are notoriously difficult to interpret. What aspects of "A Country Doctor" seem contradictory or difficult to understand?

3. What are possible symbolic meanings of the pigsty, the horses, the groom, the blizzard, the patient's wound, the doctor's nakedness?

4. The wound contains opposite qualities; for example, a rose (something beautiful) vs. the worms (something repulsive). What other oppositions does the story include? Do any of these oppositions suggest themes?

5. What does the doctor tell us about the kind of life he lives? What, for example, is his attitude toward his patients? What is their attitude toward him? Do these details suggest why he would have this dream?

6. In what ways is fatalism (a belief that we cannot control events) manifested in this story?

7. Why does the doctor feel betrayed?

JAMES JOYCE

Araby

James Joyce (1882–1941) made the geography, social patterns, and people of Dublin, Ireland, the subject matter of all his fiction. He was born, reared, and educated in Dublin. In the Catholic schools he attended through high school, he seemed destined for the priesthood, but gradually he became alienated from Catholicism and replaced it with a powerful devotion to the goal of becoming a great artist. Toward the end of his college career, he decided that he had to leave Ireland in order to write about it. He went to Paris in 1902, then taught English in Switzerland, and finally settled in Paris, where he lived until forced to leave by the onset of World War II. He died shortly thereafter in Switzerland.

Although Joyce wrote essays, poetry, and one play, *The Exiles*

(1918), his most important work, consists of four books. *Dubliners* (1914) is a collection of fifteen stories about various people who live in Dublin. Joyce arranged the stories to suggest interrelationships among certain stories and to lead the reader in a progressive discovery of Dublin. The collection climaxes with "The Dead," a lyrical, extended story about patriotism, intellectual pursuits, family life, the passage of time, and the life of the artist. *A Portrait of the Artist as a Young Man* (1916) is an autobiographical novel about the coming of age of an artist. The family and experiences of the protagonist, Stephen Dedalus, are strikingly like Joyce's own. Joyce continued Stephen Dedalus's story in his second novel, *Ulysses* (1922), in which he employs the experimental device of stream-of-consciousness. The main character of *Ulysses* is the exuberant Irish Jew, Leopold Bloom, whom Joyce parallels to Odysseus, the hero of Homer's *Odyssey*. His final novel, *Finnegans Wake* (1939), consists entirely of the dream of the protagonist, Humphrey Chimpden Earwicker. The "dream" language that Joyce devised for this novel makes it an extreme challenge to understand. "Araby" is the third story in *Dubliners*.

*N*orth Richmond Street, being blind, was a quiet street except at the hour when the Christian Brothers' School set the boys free. An uninhabited house of two storeys stood at the blind end, detached from its neighbors in a square ground. The other houses of the street, conscious of decent lives within them, gazed at one another with brown imperturbable faces.

The former tenant of our house, a priest, had died in the back drawing-room. Air, musty from having been long enclosed, hung in all the rooms, and the waste room behind the kitchen was littered with old useless papers. Among these I found a few paper-covered books, the pages of which were curled and damp: *The Abbot,* by Walter Scott, *The Devout Communicant* and *The Memoirs of Vidocq.* I liked the last best because its leaves were yellow. The wild garden behind the house contained a central apple-tree and a few straggling bushes under one of which I found the late tenant's rusty bicycle-pump. He had been a very charitable priest; in his will he had left all his money to institutions and the furniture of his house to his sister.

When the short days of winter came dusk fell before we had well eaten our dinners. When we met in the street the houses had grown sombre. The space of sky above us was the color of ever-changing violet and towards it the lamps of the street lifted their feeble lanterns. The cold air stung us and we played till our bodies glowed. Our shouts echoed in the silent street. The career of our play brought us through the dark muddy lanes behind the houses where we ran the gantlet of the rough tribes from the cottages, to the back doors of the dark dripping gardens where odors arose from the ashpits, to the dark odorous stables where a coachman smoothed and combed the horse or shook music from the buckled harness. When we returned to the street light from the kitchen windows had filled the areas. If my uncle was seen turning the

corner we hid in the shadow until we had seen him safely housed. Or if Mangan's sister came out on the doorstep to call her brother in to his tea we watched her from our
shadow peer up and down the street. We waited to see whether she would remain or
go in and, if she remained, we left our shadow and walked up to Mangan's steps
resignedly. She was waiting for us, her figure defined by the light from the half-opened
door. Her brother always teased her before he obeyed and I stood by the railings looking at her. Her dress swung as she moved her body and the soft rope of her hair tossed
from side to side.

Every morning I lay on the floor in the front parlor watching her door. The blind
was pulled down to within an inch of the sash so that I could not be seen. When she
came out on the doorstep my heart leaped. I ran to the hall, seized my books and followed her. I kept her brown figure always in my eye and, when we came near the
point at which our ways diverged, I quickened my pace and passed her. This happened morning after morning. I had never spoken to her, except for a few casual
words, and yet her name was like a summons to all my foolish blood.

Her image accompanied me even in places the most hostile to romance. On
Saturday evenings when my aunt went marketing I had to go to carry some of the
parcels. We walked through the flaring streets, jostled by drunken men and bargaining women, amid the curses of laborers, the shrill litanies of shop-boys who stood on
guard by the barrels of pigs' cheeks, the nasal chanting of street-singers, who sang a
come-all-you about O'Donovan Rossa, or a ballad about the troubles in our native land.
These noises converged in a single sensation of life for me: I imagined that I bore my
chalice safely through a throng of foes. Her name sprang to my lips at moments in
strange prayers and praises which I myself did not understand. My eyes were often full
of tears (I could not tell why) and at times a flood from my heart seemed to pour itself
out into my bosom. I thought little of the future. I did not know whether I would ever
speak to her or not or, if I spoke to her, how I could tell her of my confused adoration.
But my body was like a harp and her words and gestures were like fingers running
upon the wires.

One evening I went into the back drawing-room in which the priest had died. It
was a dark rainy evening and there was no sound in the house. Through one of the
broken panes I heard the rain impinge upon the earth, the fine incessant needles of
water playing in the sodden beds. Some distant lamp or lighted window gleamed
below me. I was thankful that I could see so little. All my senses seemed to desire to
veil themselves and, feeling that I was about to slip from them, I pressed the palms of
my hands together until they trembled, murmuring: *O love! O love!* many times.

At last she spoke to me. When she addressed the first words to me I was so confused that I did not know what to answer. She asked me was I going to *Araby*. I forget
whether I answered yes or no. It would be a splendid bazaar, she said; she would love
to go.

—And why can't you? I asked.

While she spoke she turned a silver bracelet round and round her wrist. She
could not go, she said, because there would be a retreat that week in her convent. Her
brother and two other boys were fighting for their caps and I was alone at the railings.
She held one of the spikes, bowing her head towards me. The light from the lamp
opposite our door caught the white curve of her neck, lit up her hair that rested there
and, falling, lit up the hand upon the railing. It fell over one side of her dress and
caught the white border of a petticoat, just visible as she stood at ease.

—It's well for you, she said.

—If I go, I said, I will bring you something.

What innumerable follies laid waste my waking and sleeping thoughts after that evening! I wished to annihilate the tedious intervening days. I chafed against the work of school. At night in my bedroom and by day in the classroom her image came between me and the page I strove to read. The syllables of the word *Araby* were called to me through the silence in which my soul luxuriated and cast an Eastern enchantment over me. I asked for leave to go to the bazaar on Saturday night. My aunt was surprised and hoped it was not some Freemason affair. I answered few questions in class. I watched my master's face pass from amiability to sternness; he hoped I was not beginning to idle. I could not call my wandering thoughts together. I had hardly any patience with the serious work of life which, now that it stood between me and my desire, seemed to me child's play, ugly monotonous child's play.

On Saturday morning I reminded my uncle that I wished to go to the bazaar in the evening. He was fussing at the hallstand, looking for the hat-brush, and answered me curtly:

—Yes, boy, I know.

As he was in the hall I could not go into the front parlor and lie at the window. I left the house in bad humor and walked slowly towards the school. The air was pitilessly raw and already my heart misgave me.

When I came home to dinner my uncle had not yet been home. Still it was early. I sat staring at the clock for some time and, when its ticking began to irritate me, I left the room. I mounted the staircase and gained the upper part of the house. The high cold empty gloomy rooms liberated me and I went from room to room singing. From the front window I saw my companions playing below in the street. Their cries reached me weakened and indistinct and, leaning my forehead against the cool glass, I looked over at the dark house where she lived. I may have stood there for an hour, seeing nothing but the brown-clad figure cast by my imagination, touched discreetly by the lamplight at the curved neck, at the hand upon the railings and at the border below the dress.

When I came downstairs again I found Mrs Mercer sitting at the fire. She was an old garrulous woman, a pawnbroker's widow, who collected used stamps for some pious purpose. I had to endure the gossip of the tea-table. The meal was prolonged beyond an hour and still my uncle did not come. Mrs Mercer stood up to go: she was sorry she couldn't wait any longer, but it was after eight o'clock and she did not like to be out late, as the night air was bad for her. When she had gone I began to walk up and down the room, clenching my fists. My aunt said:

—I'm afraid you may put off your bazaar for this night of Our Lord.

At nine o'clock I heard my uncle's latchkey in the halldoor. I heard him talking to himself and heard the hallstand rocking when it had received the weight of his overcoat. I could interpret these signs. When he was midway through his dinner I asked him to give me the money to go to the bazaar. He had forgotten.

—The people are in bed and after their first sleep now, he said.

I did not smile. My aunt said to him energetically:

—Can't you give him the money and let him go? You've kept him late enough as it is.

My uncle said he was very sorry he had forgotten. He said he believed in the old saying: *All work and no play makes Jack a dull boy.* He asked me where I was going and, when I had told him a second time he asked me did I know *The Arab's Farewell to his Steed.* When I left the kitchen he was about to recite the opening lines of the piece to my aunt.

I held a florin tightly in my hand as I strode down Buckingham Street towards the station. The sight of the streets thronged with buyers and glaring with gas recalled to me the purpose of my journey. I took my seat in a third-class carriage of a deserted train. After an intolerable delay the train moved out of the station slowly. It crept onward among ruinous houses and over the twinkling river. At Westland Row Station a crowd of people pressed to the carriage doors; but the porters moved them back, saying that it was a special train for the bazaar. I remained alone in the bare carriage. In a few minutes the train drew up beside an improvised wooden platform. I passed out on to the road and saw by the lighted dial of a clock that it was ten minutes to ten. In front of me was a large building which displayed the magical name.

I could not find any sixpenny entrance and, fearing that the bazaar would be closed, I passed in quickly through a turnstile, handing a shilling to a weary-looking man. I found myself in a big hall girdled at half its height by a gallery. Nearly all the stalls were closed and the greater part of the hall was in darkness. I recognised a silence like that which pervades a church after a service. I walked into the center of the bazaar timidly. A few people were gathered about the stalls which were still open. Before a curtain, over which the words *Café Chantant* were written in colored lamps, two men were counting money on a salver. I listened to the fall of the coins.

Remembering with difficulty why I had come I went over to one of the stalls and examined porcelain vases and flowered tea-sets. At the door of the stall a young lady was talking and laughing with two young gentlemen. I remarked their English accents and listened vaguely to their conversation.

—O, I never said such a thing!

—O, but you did!

—O, but I didn't!

—Didn't she say that?

—Yes, I heard her.

—O, there's a . . . fib!

Observing me the young lady came over and asked me did I wish to buy anything. The tone of her voice was not encouraging; she seemed to have spoken to me out of a sense of duty. I looked humbly at the great jars that stood like eastern guards at either side of the dark entrance to the stall and murmured:

—No, thank you.

The young lady changed the position of one of the vases and went back to the two young men. They began to talk of the same subject. Once or twice the young lady glanced at me over her shoulder.

I lingered before her stall, though I knew my stay was useless, to make my interest in her wares seem the more real. Then I turned away slowly and walked down the middle of the bazaar. I allowed the two pennies to fall against the sixpence in my pocket. I heard a voice call from one end of the gallery that the light was out. The upper part of the hall was now completely dark.

Gazing up into the darkness I saw myself as a creature driven and derided by vanity; and my eyes burned with anguish and anger.

Questions for Study

1. How is the narrator's journey to the bazaar, "Araby" (a word for Arabia), like a medieval chivalric romance? (See p. 235 for a discussion of romance. *Sir Gawain and the Green Knight*, p. 239, is a medieval romance.)

2. What is the narrator's image of Mangan's sister? How does it contrast with his image of the young lady at the end of the story?

3. How do characters and details of setting clash with the narrator's illusions?

4. The last paragraph is the narrator's epiphany? What does it reveal to him? What is the cause of his epiphany?

5. How are images of light and dark important in the story?

D. H. LAWRENCE

The Rocking-Horse Winner

D. H. Lawrence (1885–1930) was born and reared in a coal-mining town in Nottinghamshire, England. His father was a coal miner and his mother was an ex-school teacher who was determined that Lawrence, by going to school, would escape having to work in the mines. Although he had to drop out of school briefly when he was fifteen, Lawrence graduated from Nottingham University College with a teaching certificate in 1906. He taught elementary school for two years and launched his writing career with three novels in rapid succession. The third of these, *Sons and Lovers* (1913), is an autobiographical novel about his childhood, his parents' stormy relationship, his intimate relationship with two female friends, his passionate attachment to his mother, and his mother's death in 1910. In 1912 he eloped to Germany with Frieda Weekley, the wife of his French professor at Nottingham University, and for the rest of his life moved fitfully from locale to locale in Europe, Mexico, and the United States. He died of tuberculosis in Venice.

His fiction was often controversial because of his willingness to deal explicitly with sexuality and to use taboo language. His novel *The Rainbow* (1915) was seized by the police and declared obscene. As a result, no publisher would at first publish the sequel to *The Rainbow*, *Women in Love* (1920), perhaps his best novel. And the complete version of his final novel *Lady Chatterley's Lover* (1928) was banned in

Great Britain and the United States until 1959. But despite Lawrence's sensational treatment of sexuality, he was really a moralist who felt that modern society had strayed from the path of health and right conduct. His essays, short stories, and novels are attacks upon the greed, mechanization, and hypocrisy of modern society. They are also celebrations of generosity, unrepressed love, and honesty of expression, all of which Lawrence felt were exemplified in the natural world. "The Rocking-Horse Winner," one of his many short stories, was published in 1926.

*T*here was a woman who was beautiful, who started with all the advantages, yet she had no luck. She married for love, and the love turned to dust. She had bonny children, yet she felt they had been thrust upon her, and she could not love them. They looked at her coldly, as if they were finding fault with her. And hurriedly she felt that she must cover up some fault in herself. Yet what it was that she must cover up she never knew. Nevertheless, when her children were present, she always felt the center of her heart go hard. This troubled her, and in her manner she was all the more gentle and anxious for her children, as if she loved them very much. Only she herself knew that at the center of her heart was a hard little place that could not feel love, no, not for anybody. Everybody else said of her: "She is such a good mother. She adores her children." Only she herself, and her children themselves, knew it was not so. They read it in each other's eyes.

There were a boy and two little girls. They lived in a pleasant house, with a garden, and they had discreet servants, and felt themselves superior to anyone in the neighborhood.

Although they lived in style, they felt always an anxiety in the house. There was never enough money. The mother had a small income, and the father had a small income, but not nearly enough for the social position which they had to keep up. The father went into town to some office. But though he had good prospects, these prospects never materialized. There was always the grinding sense of the shortage of money, though the style was always kept up.

At last the mother said: "I will see if *I* can't make something." But she did not know where to begin. She racked her brains, and tried this thing and the other, but could not find anything successful. The failure made deep lines come into her face. Her children were growing up, they would have to go to school. There must be more money, there must be more money. The father, who was always very handsome and expensive in his tastes, seemed as if he never *would* be able to do anything worth doing. And the mother, who had a great belief in herself, did not succeed any better, and her tastes were just as expensive.

And so the house came to be haunted by the unspoken phrase: *There must be more money! There must be more money!* The children could hear it all the time, though nobody said it aloud. They heard it at Christmas, when the expensive and splendid toys filled the nursery. Behind the shining modern rocking-horse, behind the smart doll's house, a voice would start whispering: "There *must* be more money! There *must* be more money!" And the children would stop playing, to listen for a moment. They would look into each other's eyes, to see if they had all heard. And each one saw in the eyes of the other two that they too had heard. "There *must* be more money! There *must* be more money!"

It came whispering from the springs of the still-swaying rocking-horse, and even the horse, bending his wooden, champing head, heard it. The big doll, sitting so pink and smirking in her new pram, could hear it quite plainly, and seemed to be smirking all the more self-consciously because of it. The foolish puppy, too, that took the place of the teddy-bear, he was looking so extraordinarily foolish for no other reason but that he heard the secret whisper all over the house: "There *must* be more money!"

Yet nobody ever said it aloud. The whisper was everywhere, and therefore no one spoke it. Just as no one ever says: "We are breathing!" in spite of the fact that breath is coming and going all the time.

"Mother," said the boy Paul one day, "why don't we keep a car of our own? Why do we always use uncle's, or else a taxi?"

"Because we're the poor members of the family," said the mother.

"But why *are* we, mother?"

"Well—I suppose," she said slowly and bitterly, "it's because your father has no luck."

The boy was silent for some time.

"Is luck money, mother?" he asked, rather timidly.

"No, Paul. Not quite. It's what causes you to have money."

"Oh!" said Paul vaguely. "I thought when Uncle Oscar said *filthy lucker,* it meant money."

"*Filthy lucre* does mean money," said the mother. "But it's lucre, not luck."

"Oh!" said the boy. "Then what *is* luck, mother?"

"It's what causes you to have money. If you're lucky you have money. That's why it's better to be born lucky than rich. If you're rich, you may lose your money. But if you're lucky, you will always get more money."

"Oh! Will you? And is father not lucky?"

"Very unlucky, I should say," she said bitterly.

The boy watched her with unsure eyes.

"Why?" he asked.

"I don't know. Nobody ever knows why one person is lucky and another unlucky."

"Don't they? Nobody at all? Does *nobody* know?"

"Perhaps God. But He never tells."

"He ought to, then. And aren't you lucky either, mother?"

"I can't be, if I married an unlucky husband."

"But by yourself, aren't you?"

"I used to think I was, before I married. Now I think I am very unlucky indeed."

"Why?"

"Well—never mind! Perhaps I'm not really," she said.

The child looked at her to see if she meant it. But he saw, by the lines of her mouth, that she was only trying to hide something from him.

"Well, anyhow," he said stoutly, "I'm a lucky person."

"Why?" said his mother, with a sudden laugh.

He stared at her. He didn't even know why he had said it.

"God told me," he asserted, brazening it out.

"I hope He did, dear!" she said, again with a laugh, but rather bitter.

"He did, mother!"

"Excellent!" said the mother, using one of her husband's exclamations.

The boy saw she did not believe him; or rather, that she paid no attention to his assertion. This angered him somewhere, and made him want to compel her attention.

He went off by himself, vaguely, in a childish way, seeking for the clue to 'luck'. Absorbed, taking no heed of other people, he went about with a sort of stealth, seeking inwardly for luck. He wanted luck, he wanted it, he wanted it. When the two girls were playing dolls in the nursery, he would sit on his big rocking-horse, charging madly into space, with a frenzy that made the little girls peer at him uneasily. Wildly the horse careered, the waving dark hair of the boy tossed, his eyes had a strange glare in them. The little girls dared not speak to him.

When he had ridden to the end of his mad little journey, he climbed down and stood in front of his rocking-horse, staring fixedly into its lowered face. Its red mouth was slightly open, its big eye was wide and glassy-bright.

"Now!" he would silently command the snorting steed. "Now, take me to where there is luck! Now take me!"

And he would slash the horse on the neck with the little whip he had asked Uncle Oscar for. He *knew* the horse could take him to where there was luck, if only he forced it. So he would mount again and start on his furious ride, hoping at last to get there. He knew he could get there.

"You'll break your horse, Paul!" said the nurse.

"He's always riding like that! I wish he'd leave off!" said his elder sister Joan.

But he only glared down on them in silence. Nurse gave him up. She could make nothing of him. Anyhow, he was growing beyond her.

One day his mother and his Uncle Oscar came in when he was on one of his furious rides. He did not speak to them.

"Hallo, you young jockey! Riding a winner?" said his uncle.

"Aren't you growing too big for a rocking-horse? You're not a very little boy any longer, you know," said his mother.

But Paul only gave a blue glare from his big, rather close-set eyes. He would speak to nobody when he was in full tilt. His mother watched him with an anxious expression on her face.

At last he suddenly stopped forcing his horse into the mechanical gallop and slid down.

"Well, I got there!" he announced fiercely, his blue eyes still flaring, and his sturdy long legs straddling apart.

"Where did you get to?" asked his mother.

"Where I wanted to go," he flared back at her.

"That's right, son!" said Uncle Oscar. "Don't you stop till you get there. What's the horse's name?"

"He doesn't have a name," said the boy.

"Gets on without all right?" asked the uncle.

"Well, he has different names. He was called Sansovino last week."

"Sansovino, eh? Won the Ascot. How did you know this name?"

"He always talks about horse-races with Bassett," said Joan.

The uncle was delighted to find that his small nephew was posted with all the racing news. Bassett, the young gardener, who had been wounded in the left foot in the war and had got his present job through Oscar Cresswell, whose batman he had been, was a perfect blade of the 'turf'. He lived in the racing events, and the small boy lived with him.

Oscar Cresswell got it all from Bassett.

"Master Paul comes and asks me, so I can't do more than tell him, sir," said Bassett, his face terribly serious, as if he were speaking of religious matters.

"And does he ever put anything on a horse he fancies?"

"Well—I don't want to give him away—he's a young sport, a fine sport, sir. Would you mind asking him himself? He sort of takes a pleasure in it, and perhaps he'd feel I was giving him away, sir, if you don't mind."

Bassett was serious as a church.

The uncle went back to his nephew and took him off for a ride in the car.

"Say, Paul, old man, do you ever put anything on a horse?" the uncle asked.

The boy watched the handsome man closely.

"Why, do you think I oughtn't to?" he parried.

"Not a bit of it! I thought perhaps you might give me a tip for the Lincoln."

The car sped on into the country, going down to Uncle Oscar's place in Hampshire.

"Honor bright?" said the nephew.

"Honor bright, son!" said the uncle.

"Well, then, Daffodil."

"Daffodil! I doubt it, sonny. What about Mirza?"

"I only know the winner," said the boy. "That's Daffodil."

"Daffodil, eh?"

There was a pause. Daffodil was an obscure horse comparatively.

"Uncle!"

"Yes, son?"

"You won't let it go any further, will you? I promised Bassett."

"Bassett be damned, old man! What's he got to do with it?"

"We're partners. We've been partners from the first. Uncle, he lent me my first five shillings, which I lost. I promised him, honor bright, it was only between me and him; only you gave me that ten-shilling note I started winning with, so I thought you were lucky. You won't let it go any further, will you?"

The boy gazed at his uncle from those big, hot, blue eyes, set rather close together. The uncle stirred and laughed uneasily.

"Right you are, son! I'll keep your tip private. Daffodil, eh? How much are you putting on him?"

"All except twenty pounds," said the boy. "I keep that in reserve."

The uncle thought it a good joke.

"You keep twenty pounds in reserve, do you, you young romancer? What are you betting, then?"

"I'm betting three hundred," said the boy gravely. "But it's between you and me, Uncle Oscar! Honor bright?"

The uncle burst into a roar of laughter.

"It's between you and me all right, you young Nat Gould," he said, laughing. "But where's your three hundred?"

"Bassett keeps it for me. We're partners."

"You are, are you! And what is Bassett putting on Daffodil?"

"He won't go quite as high as I do, I expect. Perhaps he'll go a hundred and fifty."

"What, pennies?" laughed the uncle.

"Pounds," said the child, with a surprised look at his uncle. "Bassett keeps a bigger reserve than I do."

Between wonder and amusement Uncle Oscar was silent. He pursued the matter no further, but he determined to take his nephew with him to the Lincoln races.

"Now, son," he said, "I'm putting twenty on Mirza, and I'll put five on for you on any horse you fancy. What's your pick?"

"Daffodil, uncle."

"No, not the fiver on Daffodil!"

"I should if it was my own fiver," said the child.

"Good! Good! Right you are! A fiver for me and a fiver for you on Daffodil."

The child had never been to a race-meeting before, and his eyes were blue fire. He pursed his mouth tight and watched. A Frenchman just in front had put his money on Lancelot. Wild with excitement, he flayed his arms up and down, yelling *Lancelot! Lancelot!* in his French accent.

Daffodil came in first, Lancelot second, Mirza third. The child, flushed and with eyes blazing, was curiously serene. His uncle brought him four five-pound notes, four to one.

"What am I to do with these?" he cried, waving them before the boy's eyes.

"I suppose we'll talk to Bassett," said the boy. "I expect I have fifteen hundred now; and twenty in reserve; and this twenty."

His uncle studied him for some moments.

"Look here, son!" he said. "You're not serious about Bassett and that fifteen hundred, are you?"

"Yes, I am. But it's between you and me, uncle. Honor bright?"

"Honor bright all right, son! But I must talk to Bassett."

"If you'd like to be a partner, uncle, with Bassett and me, we could all be partners. Only, you'd have to promise, honor bright, uncle, not to let it go beyond us three. Bassett and I are lucky, and you must be lucky, because it was your ten shillings I started winning with. . . . "

Uncle Oscar took both Bassett and Paul into Richmond Park for an afternoon, and there they talked.

"It's like this, you see, sir," Bassett said. "Master Paul would get me talking about racing events, spinning yarns, you know, sir. And he was always keen on knowing if I'd made or if I'd lost. It's about a year since, now, that I put five shillings on Blush of Dawn for him: and we lost. Then the luck turned, with that ten shillings he had from you: that we put on Singhalese. And since that time, it's been pretty steady, all things considering. What do you say, Master Paul?"

"We're all right when we're sure," said Paul. "It's when we're not quite sure that we go down."

"Oh, but we're careful then," said Bassett.

"But when are you *sure?*" smiled Uncle Oscar.

"It's Master Paul, sir," said Bassett in a secret, religious voice. "It's as if he had it from heaven. Like Daffodil, now, for the Lincoln. That was as sure as eggs."

"Did you put anything on Daffodil?" asked Oscar Cresswell.

"Yes, sir. I made my bit."

"And my nephew?"

Bassett was obstinately silent, looking at Paul.

"I made twelve hundred, didn't I, Bassett? I told uncle I was putting three hundred on Daffodil."

"That's right," said Bassett, nodding.

"But where's the money?" asked the uncle.

"I keep it safe locked up, sir. Master Paul he can have it any minute he likes to ask for it."

"What, fifteen hundred pounds?"

"And twenty! And *forty,* that is, with the twenty he made on the course."

"It's amazing!" said the uncle.

"If Master Paul offers you to be partners, sir, I would, if I were you: if you'll excuse me," said Bassett.

Oscar Cresswell thought about it.

"I'll see the money," he said.

They drove home again, and, sure enough, Bassett came round to the garden-house with fifteen hundred pounds in notes. The twenty pounds reserve was left with Joe Glee, in the Turf Commission deposit.

"You see, it's all right, uncle, when I'm *sure!* Then we go strong, for all we're worth. Don't we, Bassett?"

"We do that, Master Paul."

"And when are you sure?" said the uncle, laughing.

"Oh, well, sometimes I'm *absolutely* sure, like about Daffodil," said the boy; "and sometimes I have an idea; and sometimes I haven't even an idea, have I, Bassett? Then we're careful, because we mostly go down."

"You do, do you! And when you're sure, like about Daffodil, what makes you sure, sonny?"

"Oh, well, I don't know," said the boy uneasily. "I'm sure, you know, uncle; that's all."

"It's as if he had it from heaven, sir," Bassett reiterated.

"I should say so!" said the uncle.

But he became a partner. And when the Leger was coming on Paul was 'sure' about Lively Spark, which was a quite inconsiderable horse. The boy insisted on putting a thousand on the horse, Bassett went for five hundred, and Oscar Cresswell two hundred. Lively Spark came in first, and the betting had been ten to one against him. Paul had made ten thousand.

"You see," he said, "I was absolutely sure of him."

Even Oscar Cresswell had cleared two thousand.

"Look here, son," he said, "this sort of thing makes me nervous."

"It needn't, uncle! Perhaps I shan't be sure again for a long time."

"But what are you going to do with your money?" asked the uncle.

"Of course," said the boy, "I started it for mother. She said she had no luck, because father is unlucky, so I thought if *I* was lucky, it might stop whispering."

"What might stop whispering?"

"Our house. I *hate* our house for whispering."

"What does it whisper?"

"Why—why"—the boy fidgeted—"why, I don't know. But it's always short of money, you know, uncle."

"I know it, son, I know it."

"You know people send mother writs, don't you, uncle?"

"I'm afraid I do," said the uncle.

"And then the house whispers, like people laughing at you behind your back. It's awful, that is! I thought if I was lucky——"

"You might stop it," added the uncle.

The boy watched him with big blue eyes, that had an uncanny cold fire in them, and he said never a word.

"Well, then!" said the uncle. "What are we doing?"

"I shouldn't like mother to know I was lucky," said the boy.

"Why not, son?"

"She'd stop me."

"I don't think she would."

"Oh!"—and the boy writhed in an odd way—"I *don't* want her to know, uncle."

"All right, son! We'll manage it without her knowing."

They managed it very easily. Paul, at the other's suggestion, handed over five thousand pounds to his uncle, who deposited it with the family lawyer, who was then to inform Paul's mother that a relative had put five thousand pounds into his hands, which sum was to be paid out a thousand pounds at a time, on the mother's birthday, for the next five years.

"So she'll have a birthday present of a thousand pounds for five successive years," said Uncle Oscar. "I hope it won't make it all the harder for her later."

Paul's mother had her birthday in November. The house had been 'whispering' worse than ever lately, and, even in spite of his luck, Paul could not bear up against it. He was very anxious to see the effect of the birthday letter, telling his mother about the thousand pounds.

When there were no visitors, Paul now took his meals with his parents, as he was beyond the nursery control. His mother went into town nearly every day. She had discovered that she had an odd knack of sketching furs and dress materials, so she worked secretly in the studio of a friend who was the chief 'artist' for the leading drapers. She drew the figures of ladies in furs and ladies in silk and sequins for the newspaper advertisements. This young woman artist earned several thousand pounds a year, but Paul's mother only made several hundreds, and she was again dissatisfied. She so wanted to be first in something, and she did not succeed, even in making sketches for drapery advertisements.

She was down to breakfast on the morning of her birthday. Paul watched her face as she read her letters. He knew the lawyer's letter. As his mother read it, her face hardened and became more expressionless. Then a cold, determined look came on her mouth. She hid the letter under the pile of others, and said not a word about it.

"Didn't you have anything nice in the post for your birthday, mother?" said Paul.

"Quite moderately nice," she said, her voice cold and absent.

She went away to town without saying more.

But in the afternoon Uncle Oscar appeared. He said Paul's mother had had a long interview with the lawyer, asking if the whole five thousand could not be advanced at once, as she was in debt.

"What do you think, uncle?" said the boy.

"I leave it to you, son."

"Oh, let her have it, then! We can get some more with the other," said the boy.

"A bird in the hand is worth two in the bush, laddie!" said Uncle Oscar.

"But I'm sure to *know* for the Grand National; or the Lincolnshire; or else the Derby. I'm sure to know for *one* of them," said Paul.

So Uncle Oscar signed the agreement, and Paul's mother touched the whole five thousand. Then something very curious happened. The voices in the house suddenly went mad, like a chorus of frogs on a spring evening. There were certain new furnishings, and Paul had a tutor. He was *really* going to Eton, his father's school, in the following autumn. There were flowers in the winter, and a blossoming of the luxury Paul's mother had been used to. And yet the voices in the house, behind the sprays of mimosa and almond-blossom, and from under the piles of iridescent cushions, simply trilled and screamed in a sort of ecstasy: "There must be more money! Oh-h-h; there *must* be more money. Oh, now, now-w! Now-w-w—there *must* be more money!— more than ever! More than ever!"

It frightened Paul terribly. He studied away at his Latin and Greek with his tutor. But his intense hours were spent with Bassett. The Grand National had gone by: he had not 'known', and he lost a hundred pounds. Summer was at hand. He was in agony for the Lincoln. But even for the Lincoln he didn't 'know', and he lost fifty pounds. He became wild-eyed and strange, as if something were going to explode in him.

"Let it alone, son! Don't you bother about it!" urged Uncle Oscar. But it was as if the boy couldn't really hear what his uncle was saying.

"I've got to know for the Derby! I've got to know for the Derby!" the child reiterated, his big blue eyes blazing with a sort of madness.

His mother noticed how overwrought he was.

"You'd better go to the seaside. Wouldn't you like to go now to the seaside, instead of waiting? I think you'd better," she said, looking down at him anxiously, her heart curiously heavy because of him.

But the child lifted his uncanny blue eyes.

"I couldn't possibly go before the Derby, mother!" he said. "I couldn't possibly!"

"Why not?" she said, her voice becoming heavy when she was opposed. "Why not? You can still go from the seaside to see the Derby with your Uncle Oscar, if that's what you wish. No need for you to wait here. Besides, I think you care too much about these races. It's a bad sign. My family has been a gambling family, and you won't know till you grow up how much damage it has done. But it has done damage. I shall have to send Bassett away, and ask Uncle Oscar not to talk racing to you, unless you promise to be reasonable about it: go away to the seaside and forget it. You're all nerves!"

"I'll do what you like, mother, so long as you don't send me away till after the Derby," the boy said.

"Send you away from where? Just from this house?"

"Yes," he said, gazing at her.

"Why, you curious child, what makes you care about this house so much, suddenly? I never knew you loved it."

He gazed at her without speaking. He had a secret within a secret, something he had not divulged, even to Bassett or to his Uncle Oscar.

But his mother, after standing undecided and a little bit sullen for some moments, said:

"Very well, then! Don't go to the seaside till after the Derby, if you don't wish it. But promise me you won't let your nerves go to pieces. Promise you won't think so much about horse-racing and *events,* as you call them!"

"Oh, no," said the boy casually. "I won't think much about them, mother. You needn't worry. I wouldn't worry, mother, if I were you."

"If you were me and I were you," said his mother, "I wonder what we *should* do!"

"But you know you needn't worry, mother, don't you?" the boy repeated.

"I should be awfully glad to know it," she said wearily.

"Oh, well, you *can,* you know. I mean, you *ought* to know you needn't worry," he insisted.

"Ought I? Then I'll see about it," she said.

Paul's secret of secrets was his wooden horse, that which had no name. Since he was emancipated from a nurse and a nursery-governess, he had had his rocking-horse removed to his own bedroom at the top of the house.

"Surely you're too big for a rocking-horse!" his mother had remonstrated.

"Well, you see, mother, till I can have a *real* horse, I like to have *some* sort of animal about," had been his quaint answer.

"Do you feel he keeps you company?" she laughed.

"Oh yes! He's very good, he always keeps me company, when I'm there," said Paul.

So the horse, rather shabby, stood in an arrested prance in the boy's bedroom.

The Derby was drawing near, and the boy grew more and more tense. He hardly heard what was spoken to him, he was very frail, and his eyes were really uncanny. His mother had sudden strange seizures of uneasiness about him. Sometimes, for half an hour, she would feel a sudden anxiety about him that was almost anguish. She wanted to rush to him at once, and know he was safe.

Two nights before the Derby, she was at a big party in town, when one of her rushes of anxiety about her boy, her first-born, gripped her heart till she could hardly speak. She fought with the feeling, might and main, for she believed in common sense. But it was too strong. She had to leave the dance and go downstairs to telephone to the country. The children's nursery-governess was terribly surprised and startled at being rung up in the night.

"Are the children all right, Miss Wilmot?"

"Oh yes, they are quite all right."

"Master Paul? Is he all right?"

"He went to bed as right as a trivet. Shall I run up and look at him?"

"No," said Paul's mother reluctantly. "No! Don't trouble. It's all right. Don't sit up. We shall be home fairly soon." She did not want her son's privacy intruded upon.

"Very good," said the governess.

It was about one o'clock when Paul's mother and father drove up to their house. All was still. Paul's mother went to her room and slipped off her white fur cloak. She had told her maid not to wait up for her. She heard her husband downstairs, mixing a whisky and soda.

And then, because of the strange anxiety at her heart, she stole upstairs to her son's room. Noiselessly she went along the upper corridor. Was there a faint noise? What was it?

She stood, with arrested muscles, outside his door, listening. There was a strange, heavy, and yet not loud noise. Her heart stood still. It was a soundless noise, yet rushing and powerful. Something huge, in violent, hushed motion. What was it? What in God's name was it? She ought to know. She felt that she knew the noise. She knew what it was.

Yet she could not place it. She couldn't say what it was. And on and on it went, like a madness.

Softly, frozen with anxiety and fear, she turned the door-handle.

The room was dark. Yet in the space near the window, she heard and saw something plunging to and fro. She gazed in fear and amazement.

Then suddenly she switched on the light, and saw her son, in his green pajamas, madly surging on the rocking-horse. The blaze of light suddenly lit him up, as he urged the wooden horse, and lit her up, as she stood, blonde, in her dress of pale green and crystal, in the doorway.

"Paul!" she cried. "Whatever are you doing?"

"It's Malabar!" he screamed in a powerful, strange voice. "It's Malabar!"

His eyes blazed at her for one strange and senseless second, as he ceased urging his wooden horse. Then he fell with a crash to the ground, and she, all her tormented motherhood flooding upon her, rushed to gather him up.

But he was unconscious, and unconscious he remained, with some brain-fever. He talked and tossed, and his mother sat stonily by his side.

"Malabar! It's Malabar! Bassett, Bassett, I *know*! It's Malabar!"

So the child cried, trying to get up and urge the rocking-horse that gave him his inspiration.

"What does he mean by Malabar?" asked the heart-frozen mother.

"I don't know," said the father stonily.

"What does he mean by Malabar?" she asked her brother Oscar.

"It's one of the horses running for the Derby," was the answer.

And, in spite of himself, Oscar Cresswell spoke to Bassett, and himself put a thousand on Malabar: at fourteen to one.

The third day of the illness was critical: they were waiting for a change. The boy, with his rather long, curly hair, was tossing ceaselessly on the pillow. He neither slept nor regained consciousness, and his eyes were like blue stones. His mother sat, feeling her heart had gone, turned actually into a stone.

In the evening, Oscar Cresswell did not come, but Bassett sent a message, saying could he come up for one moment, just one moment? Paul's mother was very angry at the intrusion, but on second thoughts she agreed. The boy was the same. Perhaps Bassett might bring him to consciousness.

The gardener, a shortish fellow with a little brown moustache and sharp little brown eyes, tiptoed into the room, touched his imaginary cap to Paul's mother, and stole to the bedside, staring with glittering, smallish eyes at the tossing, dying child.

"Master Paul!" he whispered. "Master Paul! Malabar came in first all right, a clean win. I did as you told me. You've made over seventy thousand pounds, you have; you've got over eighty thousand. Malabar came in all right, Master Paul."

"Malabar! Malabar! Did I say Malabar, mother? Did I say Malabar? Do you think I'm lucky, mother? I knew Malabar, didn't I? Over eighty thousand pounds! I call that lucky, don't you, mother? Over eighty thousand pounds! I knew, didn't I know I knew? Malabar came in all right. If I ride my horse till I'm sure, then I tell you, Bassett, you can go as high as you like. Did you go for all you were worth, Bassett?"

"I went a thousand on it, Master Paul."

"I never told you, mother, that if I can ride my horse, and *get there,* then I'm absolutely sure—oh, absolutely! Mother, did I ever tell you? I *am* lucky!"

"No, you never did," said his mother.

But the boy died in the night.

And even as he lay dead, his mother heard her brother's voice saying to her: "My God, Hester, you're eighty-odd thousand to the good, and a poor devil of a son to the bad. But, poor devil, poor devil, he's best gone out of a life where he rides his rocking-horse to find a winner."

Questions for Study

1. What does Paul lack? What does he want?

2. How well-to-do are Paul's parents?

3. How do Paul's mother's obsessions and values influence him? What is his mother's attitude toward him?

4. What does the rocking horse symbolize?

5. Why does Paul take comfort in his relationship with his uncle and Bassett? What do they understand that his mother does not? What is his uncle's attitude toward his mother? What does his uncle's final comment mean?

6. How is this story similar to fables and fairy tales? Does the story have a moral?

WILLIAM FAULKNER

A Rose for Emily

William Faulkner (1897–1962) made Oxford, Mississippi, and its surrounding countryside, the center of his fictional universe. He was born near Oxford, and after his family moved there when he was five, he lived in Oxford off and on for the remainder of his life. His great-grand-father was famous in the region as a colonel in the Civil War, a builder of a railroad, an author of a Southern romance, and an influential busi-nessman and politician who was murdered by a political rival. Faulkner used his great-grandfather as a model for the strong and will-ful aristocratic patriarchs who dominated the region before the war. Like Hawthorne, with whom Faulkner felt an artistic kinship, he saw his family and region as having declined since the frontier days when the settlers first came to the region.

After attending the University of Mississippi for one year and serving briefly in the Canadian Air Force, Faulkner decided to become a writer. With the encouragement of the novelist Sherwood Anderson, whom he met while working in New Orleans, Faulkner published his first novel, *Soldier's Pay* (1926), and made a tour of Europe. Upon his return he published a second novel, *Mosquitos* (1927), but he found his richest material in *Sartoris* (1929), the first of the novels set in the fictional Yoknapatawpha County. Faulkner followed *Sartoris* with a series of brilliant novels that incorporated some of the experi-ments with form initiated by the British authors Virginia Woolf and James Joyce. These novels include *The Sound and the Fury* (1929), *As I Lay Dying* (1930), *Sanctuary* (1931), *Light in August* (1932), *Absalom, Absalom* (1936), and *The Hamlet* (1940). Faulkner is best known as a novelist, but he wrote many stories. "A Rose for Emily" was the first of his stories to be published in a national magazine (the *Forum,* 1930).

I

When Miss Emily Grierson died, our whole town went to her funeral: the men through a sort of respectful affection for a fallen monument, the women mostly out of curiosity to see the inside of her house, which no one save an old manservant—a combined gardener and cook—had seen in at least ten years.

It was a big, squarish frame house that had once been white, decorated with cupolas and spires and scrolled balconies in the heavily lightsome style of the seven-ties, set on what had once been our most select street. But garages and cotton gins had encroached and obliterated even the august names of that neighborhood; only Miss Emily's house was left, lifting its stubborn and coquettish decay above the cotton wag-ons and the gasoline pumps—an eyesore among eyesores. And now Miss Emily had gone to join the representatives of those august names where they lay in the cedar-bemused cemetery among the ranked and anonymous graves of Union and Confederate soldiers who fell at the battle of Jefferson.

Alive, Miss Emily had been a tradition, a duty, and a care; a sort of hereditary obligation upon the town, dating from that day in 1894 when Colonel Sartoris, the mayor—he who fathered the edict that no Negro woman should appear on the streets without an apron—remitted her taxes, the dispensation dating from the death of her father on into perpetuity. Not that Miss Emily would have accepted charity. Colonel Sartoris invented an involved tale to the effect that Miss Emily's father had loaned money to the town, which the town, as a matter of business, preferred this way of repaying. Only a man of Colonel Sartoris' generation and thought could have invented it, and only a woman could have believed it.

When the next generation, with its more modern ideas, became mayors and aldermen, this arrangement created some little dissatisfaction. On the first of the year they mailed her a tax notice. February came, and there was no reply. They wrote her a formal letter, asking her to call at the sheriff's office at her convenience. A week later the mayor wrote her himself, offering to call or to send his car for her, and received in reply a note on paper of an archaic shape, in a thin, flowing calligraphy in faded ink, to the effect that she no longer went out at all. The tax notice was also enclosed, without comment.

They called a special meeting of the Board of Aldermen. A deputation waited upon her, knocked at the door through which no visitor had passed since she ceased giving china-painting lessons eight or ten years earlier. They were admitted by the old Negro into a dim hall from which a stairway mounted into still more shadow. It smelled of dust and disuse—a close, dank smell. The Negro led them into the parlor. It was furnished in heavy, leather-covered furniture. When the Negro opened the blinds of one window, they could see that the leather was cracked; and when they sat down, a faint dust rose sluggishly about their thighs, spinning with slow motes in the single sun-ray. On a tarnished gilt easel before the fireplace stood a crayon portrait of Miss Emily's father.

They rose when she entered—a small, fat woman in black, with a thin gold chain descending to her waist and vanishing into her belt, leaning on an ebony cane with a tarnished gold head. Her skeleton was small and spare; perhaps that was why what would have been merely plumpness in another was obesity in her. She looked bloated, like a body long submerged in motionless water, and of that pallid hue. Her eyes, lost in the fatty ridges of her face, looked like two small pieces of coal pressed into a lump of dough as they moved from one face to another while the visitors stated their errand.

She did not ask them to sit. She just stood in the door and listened quietly until the spokesman came to a stumbling halt. Then they could hear the invisible watch ticking at the end of the gold chain.

Her voice was dry and cold. "I have no taxes in Jefferson. Colonel Sartoris explained it to me. Perhaps one of you can gain access to the city records and satisfy yourselves."

"But we have. We are the city authorities, Miss Emily. Didn't you get a notice from the sheriff, signed by him?"

"I received a paper, yes," Miss Emily said. "Perhaps he considers himself the sheriff . . . I have no taxes in Jefferson."

"But there is nothing on the books to show that, you see. We must go by the—"

"See Colonel Sartoris. I have no taxes in Jefferson."

"But, Miss Emily—"

"See Colonel Sartoris." (Colonel Sartoris had been dead almost ten years.) "I have no taxes in Jefferson. Tobe!" The Negro appeared. "Show these gentlemen out."

II

So she vanquished them, horse and foot, just as she had vanquished their fathers thirty years before about the smell. That was two years after her father's death and a short time after her sweetheart—the one we believed would marry her—had deserted her. After her father's death she went out very little; after her sweetheart went away, people hardly saw her at all. A few of the ladies had the temerity to call, but were not received, and the only sign of life about the place was the Negro man—a young man then—going in and out with a market basket.

"Just as if a man—any man—could keep a kitchen properly," the ladies said; so they were not surprised when the smell developed. It was another link between the gross, teeming world and the high and mighty Griersons.

A neighbor, a woman, complained to the mayor, Judge Stevens, eighty years old.

"But what will you have me do about it, madam?" he said.

"Why, send her word to stop it," the woman said. "Isn't there a law?"

"I'm sure that won't be necessary," Judge Stevens said. "It's probably just a snake or a rat that nigger of hers killed in the yard. I'll speak to him about it."

The next day he received two more complaints, one from a man who came in diffident deprecation. "We really must do something about it, Judge. I'd be the last one in the world to bother Miss Emily, but we've got to do something." That night the Board of Aldermen met—three graybeards and one younger man, a member of the rising generation.

"It's simple enough," he said. "Send her word to have her place cleaned up. Give her a certain time to do it in, and if she don't . . . "

"Dammit, sir," Judge Stevens said, "will you accuse a lady to her face of smelling bad?"

So the next night, after midnight, four men crossed Miss Emily's lawn and slunk about the house like burglars, sniffing along the base of the brickwork and at the cellar openings while one of them performed a regular sowing motion with his hand out of a sack slung from his shoulder. They broke open the cellar door and sprinkled lime there, and in all the outbuildings. As they recrossed the lawn, a window that had been dark was lighted and Miss Emily sat in it, the light behind her, and her upright torso motionless as that of an idol. They crept quietly across the lawn and into the shadow of the locusts that lined the street. After a week or two the smell went away.

That was when people had begun to feel really sorry for her. People in our town, remembering how old lady Wyatt, her great-aunt, had gone completely crazy at last, believed that the Griersons held themselves a little too high for what they really were. None of the young men were quite good enough for Miss Emily and such. We had long thought of them as a tableau, Miss Emily a slender figure in white in the background, her father a spraddled silhouette in the foreground, his back to her and clutching a horsewhip, the two of them framed by the back-flung front door. So when she got to be thirty and was still single, we were not pleased exactly, but vindicated; even with insanity in the family she wouldn't have turned down all of her chances if they had really materialized.

When her father died, it got about that the house was all that was left to her; and in a way, people were glad. At last they could pity Miss Emily. Being left alone, and a pauper, she had become humanized. Now she too would know the old thrill and the old despair of a penny more or less.

The day after his death all the ladies prepared to call at the house and offer condolence and aid, as is our custom. Miss Emily met them at the door, dressed as usual and with no trace of grief on her face. She told them that her father was not dead. She did that for three days, with the ministers calling on her, and the doctors, trying to persuade her to let them dispose of the body. Just as they were about to resort to law and force, she broke down, and they buried her father quickly.

We did not say she was crazy then. We believed she had to do that. We remembered all the young men her father had driven away, and we knew that with nothing left, she would have to cling to that which had robbed her, as people will.

III

She was sick for a long time. When we saw her again, her hair was cut short, making her look like a girl, with a vague resemblance to those angels in colored church windows—sort of tragic and serene.

The town had just let the contracts for paving the sidewalks, and in the summer after her father's death they began the work. The construction company came with niggers and mules and machinery, and a foreman named Homer Barron, a Yankee—a big, dark, ready man, with a big voice and eyes lighter than his face. The little boys would follow in groups to hear him cuss the niggers, and the niggers singing in time to the rise and fall of picks. Pretty soon he knew everybody in town. Whenever you heard a lot of laughing anywhere about the square, Homer Barron would be in the center of the group. Presently we began to see him and Miss Emily on Sunday afternoons driving in the yellow-wheeled buggy and the matched team of bays from the livery stable.

At first we were glad that Miss Emily would have an interest, because the ladies all said, "Of course a Grierson would not think seriously of a Northerner, a day laborer." But there were still others, older people, who said that even grief could not cause a real lady to forget *noblesse oblige*—without calling it *noblesse oblige.* They just said, "Poor Emily. Her kinsfolk should come to her." She had some kin in Alabama; but years ago her father had fallen out with them over the estate of old lady Wyatt, the crazy woman, and there was no communication between the two families. They had not even been represented at the funeral.

And as soon as the old people said, "Poor Emily," the whispering began. "Do you suppose it's really so?" they said to one another. "Of course it is. What else could . . ." This behind their hands; rustling of craned silk and satin behind jalousies closed upon the sun of Sunday afternoon as the thin, swift clop-clop-clop of the matched team passed: "Poor Emily."

She carried her head high enough—even when we believed that she was fallen. It was as if she demanded more than ever the recognition of her dignity as the last Grierson; as if it had wanted that touch of earthiness to reaffirm her imperviousness. Like when she bought the rat poison, the arsenic. That was over a year after they had begun to say "Poor Emily," and while the two female cousins were visiting her.

"I want some poison," she said to the druggist. She was over thirty then, still a slight woman, though thinner than usual, with cold, haughty black eyes in a face the flesh of which was strained across the temples and about the eye-sockets as you imagine a lighthouse-keeper's face ought to look. "I want some poison," she said.

"Yes, Miss Emily. What kind? For rats and such? I'd recom—"

"I want the best you have. I don't care what kind."

The druggist named several. "They'll kill anything up to an elephant. But what you want is—"

"Arsenic," Miss Emily said. "Is that a good one?"

"Is . . . arsenic? Yes, ma'am. But what you want—"

"I want arsenic."

The druggist looked down at her. She looked back at him, erect, her face like a strained flag. "Why, of course," the druggist said. "If that's what you want. But the law requires you to tell what you are going to use it for."

Miss Emily just stared at him, her head tilted back in order to look him eye for eye, until he looked away and went and got the arsenic and wrapped it up. The Negro delivery boy brought her the package; the druggist didn't come back. When she opened the package at home there was written on the box, under the skull and bones: "For rats."

IV

So the next day we all said, "She will kill herself"; and we said it would be the best thing. When she had first begun to be seen with Homer Barron, we had said, "She will marry him." Then we said, "She will persuade him yet," because Homer himself had remarked—he liked men, and it was known that he drank with the younger men in the Elks' Club—that he was not a marrying man. Later we said, "Poor Emily" behind the jalousies as they passed on Sunday afternoon in the glittering buggy, Miss Emily with her head high and Homer Barron with his hat cocked and a cigar in his teeth, reins and whip in a yellow glove.

Then some of the ladies began to say that it was a disgrace to the town and a bad example to the young people. The men did not want to interfere, but at last the ladies forced the Baptist minister—Miss Emily's people were Episcopal—to call upon her. He would never divulge what happened during that interview, but he refused to go back again. The next Sunday they again drove about the streets, and the following day the minister's wife wrote to Miss Emily's relations in Alabama.

So she had blood-kin under her roof again and we sat back to watch developments. At first nothing happened. Then we were sure that they were to be married. We learned that Miss Emily had been to the jeweler's and ordered a man's toilet set in silver, with the letters H.B. on each piece. Two days later we learned that she had bought a complete outfit of men's clothing, including a nightshirt, and we said, "They are married." We were really glad. We were glad because the two female cousins were even more Grierson than Miss Emily had ever been.

So we were not surprised when Homer Barron—the streets had been finished some time since—was gone. We were a little disappointed that there was not a public blowing-off, but we believed that he had gone on to prepare for Miss Emily's coming, or to give her a chance to get rid of the cousins. (By that time it was a cabal, and we were all Miss Emily's allies to help circumvent the cousins.) Sure enough, after another week they departed. And, as we had expected all along, within three days Homer Barron was back in town. A neighbor saw the Negro man admit him at the kitchen door at dusk one evening.

And that was the last we saw of Homer Barron. And of Miss Emily for some time. The Negro man went in and out with the market basket, but the front door remained closed. Now and then we would see her at a window for a moment, as the men did that night when they sprinkled the lime, but for almost six months she did not appear on the streets. Then we knew that this was to be expected too; as if that quality of her father which had thwarted her woman's life so many times had been too virulent and too furious to die.

When we next saw Miss Emily, she had grown fat and her hair was turning gray. During the next few years it grew grayer and grayer until it attained an even pepper-and-salt iron-gray, when it ceased turning. Up to the day of her death at seventy-four it was still that vigorous iron-gray, like the hair of an active man.

From that time on her front door remained closed, save for a period of six or seven years, when she was about forty, during which she gave lessons in china-painting. She fitted up a studio in one of the downstairs rooms, where the daughters and granddaughters of Colonel Sartoris' contemporaries were sent to her with the same regularity and in the same spirit that they were sent to church on Sundays with a twenty-five-cent piece for the collection plate. Meanwhile her taxes had been remitted.

Then the newer generation became the backbone and the spirit of the town, and the painting pupils grew up and fell away and did not send their children to her with boxes of color and tedious brushes and pictures cut from the ladies' magazines. The front door closed upon the last one and remained closed for good. When the town got free postal delivery, Miss Emily alone refused to let them fasten the metal numbers above her door and attach a mailbox to it. She would not listen to them.

Daily, monthly, yearly we watched the Negro grow grayer and more stooped, going in and out with the market basket. Each December we sent her a tax notice, which would be returned by the post office a week later, unclaimed. Now and then we would see her in one of the downstairs windows—she had evidently shut up the top floor of the house—like the carven torso of an idol in a niche, looking or not looking at us, we could never tell which. Thus she passed from generation to generation—dear, inescapable, impervious, tranquil, and perverse.

And so she died. Fell ill in the house filled with dust and shadows, with only a doddering Negro man to wait on her. We did not even know she was sick; we had long since given up trying to get any information from the Negro. He talked to no one, probably not even to her, for his voice had grown harsh and rusty, as if from disuse.

She died in one of the downstairs rooms, in a heavy walnut bed with a curtain, her gray head propped on a pillow yellow and moldy with age and lack of sunlight.

V

The Negro met the first of the ladies at the front door and let them in, with their hushed, sibilant voices and their quick, curious glances, and then he disappeared. He walked right through the house and out the back and was not seen again.

The two female cousins came at once. They held the funeral on the second day, with the town coming to look at Miss Emily beneath a mass of bought flowers, with the crayon face of her father musing profoundly above the bier and the ladies sibilant and macabre; and the very old men—some in their brushed Confederate uniforms—on the porch and the lawn, talking of Miss Emily as if she had been a contemporary of theirs, believing that they had danced with her and courted her perhaps, confusing time with its mathematical progression, as the old do, to whom all the past is not a diminishing road but, instead, a huge meadow which no winter ever quite touches, divided from them now by the narrow bottle-neck of the most recent decade of years.

Already we knew that there was one room in that region above stairs which no one had seen in forty years, and which would have to be forced. They waited until Miss Emily was decently in the ground before they opened it.

The violence of breaking down the door seemed to fill this room with pervading dust. A thin, acrid pall as of the tomb seemed to lie everywhere upon this room decked and furnished as for a bridal: upon the valance curtains of faded rose color, upon the rose-shaded lights, upon the dressing table, upon the delicate array of crystal and the man's toilet things backed with tarnished silver, silver so tarnished that the monogram was obscured. Among them lay a collar and tie, as if they had just been removed, which, lifted, left upon the surface a pale crescent in the dust. Upon a chair hung the suit, carefully folded; beneath it the two mute shoes and the discarded socks.

The man himself lay in the bed.

For a long while we just stood there, looking down at the profound and fleshless grin. The body had apparently once lain in the attitude of an embrace, but now the long sleep that outlasts love, that conquers even the grimace of love, had cuckolded him. What was left of him, rotted beneath what was left of the nightshirt, had become inextricable from the bed in which he lay; and upon him and upon the pillow beside him lay that even coating of the patient and biding dust.

Then we noticed that in the second pillow was the indentation of a head. One of us lifted something from it, and leaning forward, that faint and invisible dust dry and acrid in the nostrils, we saw a long strand of iron-gray hair.

Questions for Study

1. Faulkner has the narrator tell Emily's story out of chronological sequence. Why?

2. What are the major conflicts in Emily's life? What is their proper chronological order? How does one conflict lead to another?

3. How do Emily's father and his generation of Southerners influence her? Who in the story belongs to this older generation? What are their beliefs and values?

4. What's wrong with Emily? Why does she take up with Homer Barron? Why does she deal with him the way she does?

5. How does Faulkner use the house to establish the atmosphere of the story? What images characterize the house? To what senses does Faulkner appeal?

6. What do the narrator and the other townspeople think of Emily?

7. How is this story similar to Hawthorne's "Young Goodman Brown" (p. 385) and Poe's "The Cask of Amontillado" (p. 394)?

ZORA NEALE HURSTON

Sweat

Zora Neale Hurston (1901–60) was born and reared in Eatonville, Florida, the first incorporated black town in the United States. Her father, a Baptist preacher, deserted the family when Hurston was young, and her mother died when Hurston was nine. She was passed from relative to relative and as a result had little formal schooling. Nonetheless, she attended Morgan College in Baltimore for two years, then Howard University in Washington, D.C., and finally Barnard College in New York City. While she was in New York she was a vibrant participant in the Harlem Renaissance, a cultural and artistic movement in which African-American artists expressed the dimensions of African-American culture. While at Barnard Hurston studied with the anthropologist Franz Boas, and after her graduation in 1928 she did fieldwork in the Eatonville area and then the Caribbean islands. The products of this work were two collections of folklore, *Mules and Men* (1935), which focuses on Florida, and *Tell My Horse* (1938), which focuses on Haiti and other islands in the Caribbean.

Almost all of her fiction features strong women who struggle against the restrictions of a male-dominated society and who quest for their own identify and fulfillment. In her finest novel, *Their Eyes Were Watching God* (1937), the heroine, Janie Mae, suffers through two bad marriages until at last she finds love and independence. Hurston also incorporates into her fiction a lyrical treatment of African-American folkways and language. *Dust Tracks on a Dirt Road* (1942) is her autobiography. By the time of her death in 1960, she had become poor and her work had been virtually forgotten. But in the 1970s a number of young black writers, most notably Alice Walker, publicized and celebrated her work. Today she has gained a large following. "Sweat" (1926) is one of a handful of stories she published in journals during the 1920s.

*I*t was eleven o'clock of a Spring night in Florida. It was Sunday. Any other night, Delia Jones would have been in bed for two hours by this time. But she was a washwoman, and Monday morning meant a great deal to her. So she collected the soiled clothes on Saturday when she returned the clean things. Sunday night after church, she sorted and put the white things to soak. It saved her almost a half-day's start. A great hamper in the bedroom held the clothes that she brought home. It was so much neater than a number of bundles lying around.

She squatted on the kitchen floor beside the great pile of clothes, sorting them into small heaps according to color, and humming a song in a mournful key, but wondering through it all where Sykes, her husband, had gone with her horse and buckboard.

Just then something long, round, limp and black fell upon her shoulders and slithered to the floor beside her. A great terror took hold of her. It softened her knees and dried her mouth so that it was a full minute before she could cry out or move. Then she saw that it was the big bull whip her husband liked to carry when he drove.

She lifted her eyes to the door and saw him standing there bent over with laughter at her fright. She screamed at him.

"Sykes, what you throw dat whip on me like dat? You know it would skeer me—looks just like a snake, an' you knows how skeered Ah is of snakes."

"Course Ah knowed it! That's how come Ah done it." He slapped his leg with his hand and almost rolled on the ground in his mirth. "If you such a big fool dat you got to have a fit over a earth worm or a string, Ah don't keer how bad Ah skeer you."

"You ain't got no business doing it. Gawd knows it's a sin. Some day Ah'm goin-tuh drop dead from some of yo' foolishness. 'Nother thing, where you been wid mah rig? Ah feeds dat pony. He ain't fuh you to be drivin' wid no bull whip."

"You sho' is one aggravatin' nigger woman!" he declared and stepped into the room. She resumed her work and did not answer him at once. "Ah done tole you time and again to keep them white folks' clothes outa dis house."

He picked up the whip and glared at her. Delia went on with her work. She went out into the yard and returned with a galvanized tub and set it on the washbench. She saw that Sykes had kicked all of the clothes together again, and now stood in her way truculently, his whole manner hoping, *praying,* for an argument. But she walked calmly around him and commenced to re-sort the things.

"Next time, Ah'm gointer kick 'em outdoors," he threatened as he struck a match along the leg of his corduroy breeches.

Delia never looked up from her work, and her thin, stooped shoulders sagged further.

"Ah ain't for no fuss t'night Sykes. Ah just come from taking sacrament at the church house."

He snorted scornfully. "Yeah, you just come from de church house on a Sunday night, but heah you is gone to work on them clothes. You ain't nothing but a hypocrite. One of them amen-corner Christians—sing, whoop, and shout, then come home and wash white folks' clothes on the Sabbath."

He stepped roughly upon the whitest pile of things, kicking them helter-skelter as he crossed the room. His wife gave a little scream of dismay, and quickly gathered them together again.

"Sykes, you quit grindin' dirt into these clothes! How can Ah git through by Sat'day if Ah don't start on Sunday?"

Ah don't keer if you never git through. Anyhow, Ah done promised Gawd and a couple of other men, Ah ain't gointer have it in mah house. Don't gimme no lip neither, else Ah'll throw 'em out and put mah fist up side yo' head to boot."

Delia's habitual meekness seemed to slip from her shoulders like a blown scarf. She was on her feet; her poor little body, her bare knuckly hands bravely defying the strapping hulk before her.

"Looka heah, Sykes, you done gone too fur. Ah been married to you fur fifteen years, and Ah been takin' in washin' fur fifteen years. Sweat, sweat, sweat! Work and sweat, cry and sweat, pray and sweat!"

"What's that got to do with me?" he asked brutally.

"What's it got to do with you, Sykes? Mah tub of suds is filled yo' belly with vittles more times than yo' hands is filled it. Mah sweat is done paid for this house and Ah reckon Ah kin keep on sweatin' in it."

She seized the iron skillet from the stove and struck a defensive pose, which act surprised him greatly, coming from her. It cowed him and he did not strike her as he usually did.

"Naw you won't," she panted, "that ole snaggle-toothed black woman you runnin' with ain't comin' heah to pile up on *mah* sweat and blood. You ain't paid for nothin' on this place, and Ah'm gointer stay right heah till Ah'm toted out foot foremost."

"Well, you better quit gittin' me riled up, else they'll be totin' you out sooner than you expect. Ah'm so tired of you Ah don't know whut to do. Gawd! How Ah hates skinny wimmen!"

A little awed by this new Delia, he sidled out of the door and slammed the back gate after him. He did not say where he had gone, but she knew too well. She knew very well that he would not return until nearly daybreak also. Her work over, she went on to bed but not to sleep at once. Things had come to a pretty pass!

She lay awake, gazing upon the debris that cluttered their matrimonial trail. Not an image left standing along the way. Anything like flowers had long ago been drowned in the salty stream that had been pressed from her heart. Her tears, her sweat, her blood. She had brought love to the union and he had brought a longing after the flesh. Two months after the wedding, he had given her the first brutal beating. She had the memory of his numerous trips to Orlando with all of his wages when he had returned to her penniless, even before the first year had passed. She was young and soft then, but now she thought of her knotty, muscled limbs, her harsh knuckly hands, and drew herself up into an unhappy little ball in the middle of the big feather bed. Too late now to hope for love, even if it were not Bertha it would be someone else. This case differed from the others only in that she was bolder than the others. Too late for everything except her little home. She had built it for her old days, and planted one by one the trees and flowers there. It was lovely to her, lovely.

Somehow, before sleep came, she found herself saying aloud: "Oh well, whatever goes over the Devil's back, is got to come under his belly. Sometime or ruther, Sykes, like everybody else, is gointer reap his sowing." After that she was able to build a spiritual earthworks against her husband. His shells could no longer reach her. AMEN. She went to sleep and slept until he announced his presence in bed by kicking her feet and rudely snatching the covers away.

"Gimme some kivah heah, an' git yo' damn foots over on yo' own side! Ah oughter mash you in yo' mouf fuh drawing dat skillet on me."

Delia went clear to the rail without answering him. A triumphant indifference to all that he was or did.

II

The week was as full of work for Delia as all other weeks, and Saturday found her behind her little pony, collecting and delivering clothes.

It was a hot, hot day near the end of July. The village men on Joe Clarke's porch even chewed cane listlessly. They did not hurl the cane-knots as usual. They let them dribble over the edge of the porch. Even conversation had collapsed under the heat.

"Heah come Delia Jones," Jim Merchant said, as the shaggy pony came 'round the bend of the road toward them. The rusty buckboard was heaped with baskets of crisp, clean laundry.

"Yep," Joe Lindsay agreed. "Hot or col', rain or shine, jes'ez reg'lar ez de weeks roll roun' Delia carries 'em an' fetches 'em on Sat'day."

"She better if she wanter eat," said Moss. "Sykes Jones ain't wuth de shot an' powder hit would tek tuh kill 'em. Not to huh he ain't."

"He sho' ain't," Walter Thomas chimed in. "It's too bad, too, cause she wuz a right pretty li'l trick when he got huh. Ah'd uh mah'ied huh mahself if he hadnter beat me to it."

Delia nodded briefly at the men as she drove past.

"Too much knockin' will ruin *any* 'oman. He done beat huh 'nough tuh kill three women, let 'lone change they looks," said Elijah Moseley. "How Syke kin stommuck dat big black greasy Mogul he's layin' roun' wid, gits me. Ah swear dat eight-rock couldn't kiss a sardine can Ah done thowed out de back do' 'way las' yeah."

"Aw, she's fat, thass how come. He's allus been crazy 'bout fat women," put in Merchant. "He'd a' been tied up wid one long time ago if he could a' found one tuh have him. Did Ah tell yuh 'bout him come sidlin' roun' *mah* wife—bringin' her a basket uh pecans outa his yard fuh a present? Yessir, mah wife! She tol' him tuh take 'em right straight back home, 'cause Delia works so hard ovah dat washtub she reckon everything on de place taste lak sweat an' soapsuds. Ah jus' wisht Ah'd a' caught 'im 'roun' dere! Ah'd a' made his hips ketch on fiah down dat shell road."

"Ah know he done it, too. Ah sees 'im grinnin' at every 'oman dat passes," Walter Thomas said. "But even so, he useter eat some mighty big hunks uh humble pie tuh git dat li'l 'oman he got. She wuz ez pritty ez a speckled pup! Dat wuz fifteen years ago. He useter be so skeered uh losin' huh, she could make him do some parts of a husband's duty. Dey never wuz de same in de mind."

"There oughter be a law about him," said Lindsay. "He ain't fit tuh carry guts tuh a bear."

Clarke spoke for the first time. "Tain't no law on earth dat kin make a man be decent if it ain't in 'im. There's plenty men dat takes a wife lak dey do a joint uh sugarcane. It's round, juicy an' sweet when dey gits it. But dey squeeze an' grind, squeeze an' grind an' wring tell dey wring every drop uh pleasure dat's in 'em out. When dey's satisfied dat dey is wrung dry, dey treats 'em jes' lak dey do a cane-chew. Dey thows 'em away. Dey knows whut dey is doin' while dey is at it, an' hates theirselves fuh it but they keeps on hangin' after huh tell she's empty. Den dey hates huh fuh bein' a cane-chew an' in de way."

"We oughter take Syke an' dat stray 'oman uh his'n down in Lake Howell swamp an' lay on de rawhide till they cain't say Lawd a' mussy. He allus wuz uh ovahbearin niggah, but since dat white 'oman from up north done teached 'im how to run a automobile, he done got too beggety to live—an' we oughter kill 'im," Old Man Anderson advised.

A grunt of approval went around the porch. But the heat was melting their civic virtue and Elijah Moseley began to bait Joe Clarke.

"Come on, Joe, git a melon outa dere an' slice it up for yo' customers. We'se all sufferin' wid de heat. De bear's done got *me!*"

"Thass right, Joe, a watermelon is jes' whut Ah needs tuh cure de eppizudicks," Walter Thomas joined forces with Moseley. "Come on dere, Joe. We all is steady customers an' you ain't set us up in a long time. Ah chooses dat long, bowlegged Floridy favorite."

"A god, an' be dough. You all gimme twenty cents and slice away," Clarke retorted. "Ah needs a col' slice m'self. Heah, everybody chip in. Ah'll lend y'all mah meat knife."

The money was all quickly subscribed and the huge melon brought forth. At that moment, Sykes and Bertha arrived. A determined silence fell on the porch and the melon was put away again.

Merchant snapped down the blade of his jackknife and moved toward the store door.

"Come on in, Joe, an' gimme a slab uh sow belly an' uh pound uh coffee—almost fuhgot 'twas Sat'day. Got to git on home." Most of the men left also.

Just then Delia drove past on her way home, as Sykes was ordering magnificently for Bertha. It pleased him for Delia to see.

"Git whutsoever yo' heart desires, Honey. Wait a minute, Joe. Give huh two bottles uh strawberry soda-water, uh quart parched ground-peas, an' a block uh chewin' gum."

With all this they left the store, with Sykes reminding Bertha that this was his town and she could have it if she wanted it.

The men returned soon after they left, and held their watermelon feast.

"Where did Syke Jones git da 'oman from nohow?" Lindsay asked.

"Ovah Apopka. Guess dey musta been cleanin' out de town when she lef'. She don't look lak a thing but a hunk uh liver wid hair on it."

"Well, she sho' kin squall," Dave Carter contributed. "When she gits ready tuh laff, she jes' opens huh mouf an' latches it back tuh de las' notch. No ole granpa alligator down in Lake Bell ain't got nothin' on huh."

III

Bertha had been in town three months now. Sykes was still paying her room-rent at Della Lewis'—the only house in town that would have taken her in. Sykes took her frequently to Winter Park to 'stomps'. He still assured her that he was the swellest man in the state.

"Sho' you kin have dat li'l ole house soon's Ah git dat 'oman outa dere. Everything b'longs tuh me an' you sho' kin have it. Ah sho' 'bominates uh skinny 'oman. Lawdy, you sho' is got one portly shape on you! You kin git anything you wants. Dis is mah town an' you sho' kin have it."

Delia's work-worn knees crawled over the earth in Gethsemane and up the rocks of Calvary many, many times during these months. She avoided the villagers and meeting places in her efforts to be blind and deaf. But Bertha nullified this to a degree, by coming to Delia's house to call Sykes out to her at the gate.

Delia and Sykes fought all the time now with no peaceful interludes. They slept and ate in silence. Two or three times Delia had attempted a timid friendliness, but she was repulsed each time. It was plain that the breaches must remain agape.

The sun had burned July to August. The heat streamed down like a million hot arrows, smiting all things living upon the earth. Grass withered, leaves browned, snakes went blind in shedding and men and dogs went mad. Dog days!

Delia came home one day and found Sykes there before her. She wondered, but started to go on into the house without speaking, even though he was standing in the kitchen door and she must either stoop under his arm or ask him to move. He made no room for her. She noticed a soap box beside the steps, but paid no particular attention to it, knowing that he must have brought it there. As she was stooping to pass under his outstretched arm, he suddenly pushed her backward, laughingly.

"Look in de box dere Delia, Ah done brung yuh somethin'!"

She nearly fell upon the box in her stumbling, and when she saw what it held, she all but fainted outright.

"Syke! Syke, mah Gawd! You take dat rattlesnake 'way from heah! You *gottuh*. Oh, Jesus, have mussy!"

"Ah ain't got tuh do nuthin' uh de kin'—fact is Ah ain't got tuh do nothin' but die. Tain't no use uh you puttin' on airs makin' out lak you skeered uh dat snake—he's gointer stay right heah tell he die. He wouldn't bite me cause Ah knows how tuh handle 'im. Nohow he wouldn't risk breakin' out his fangs 'gin *yo* skinny laigs."

"Naw, now Syke, don't keep dat thing 'round tryin' tuh skeer me tuh death. You knows Ah'm even feared uh earth worms. Thass de biggest snake Ah evah did see. Kill 'im Syke, please."

"Doan ast me tuh do nothin' fuh yuh. Goin' 'round tryin' tuh be so damn asterperious. Naw, Ah ain't gonna kill it. Ah think uh damn sight mo' uh him dan you! Dat's a nice snake an' anybody doan lak 'im kin jes' hit de grit."

The village soon heard that Sykes had the snake, and came to see and ask questions.

"How de hen-fire did you ketch dat six-foot rattler, Syke?" Thomas asked.

"He's full uh frogs so he cain't hardly move, thass how Ah eased up on 'm. But

Ah'm a snake charmer an' knows how tuh handle 'em. Shux, dat ain't nothin'. Ah could ketch one eve'y day if Ah so wanted tuh."

"Whut he needs is a heavy hick'ry club leaned real heavy on his head. Dat's de bes' way tuh charm a rattlesnake."

"Naw, Walt, y'all jes' don't understand dese diamon' backs lak Ah do," said Sykes in a superior tone of voice.

The village agreed with Walter, but the snake stayed on. His box remained by the kitchen door with its screen wire covering. Two or three days later it had digested its meal of frogs and literally came to life. It rattled at every movement in the kitchen or the yard. One day as Delia came down the kitchen steps she saw his chalky-white fangs curved like scimitars hung in the wire meshes. This time she did not run away with averted eyes as usual. She stood for a long time in the doorway in a red fury that grew bloodier for every second that she regarded the creature that was her torment.

That night she broached the subject as soon as Sykes sat down to the table.

"Syke, Ah wants you tuh take dat snake 'way fum heah. You done starved me an' Ah put up widcher, you done beat me an Ah took dat, but you done kilt all mah insides bringin' dat varmint heah."

Sykes poured out a saucer full of coffee and drank it deliberately before he answered her.

"A whole lot Ah keer 'bout how you feels inside uh out. Dat snake ain't goin' no damn wheah till Ah gits ready fuh 'im tuh go. So fur as beatin' is concerned, yuh ain't took near all dat you gointer take ef yuh stay 'round *me.*"

Delia pushed back her plate and got up from the table. "Ah hates you, Sykes," she said calmly. "Ah hates you tuh de same degree dat Ah useter love yuh. Ah done took an' took till mah belly is full up tuh mah neck. Dat's de reason Ah got mah letteɪ fum de church an' moved mah membership tuh Woodbridge—so Ah don't haftuh take no sacrament wid yuh. Ah don't wantuh see yuh 'round me atall. Lay 'round wid dat 'oman all yuh wants tuh, but gwan 'way fum me an' mah house. Ah hates yuh lak uh suck-egg dog."

Sykes almost let the huge wad of corn bread and collard greens he was chewing fall out of his mouth in amazement. He had a hard time whipping himself up to the proper fury to try to answer Delia.

"Well, Ah'm glad you does hate me. Ah'm sho' tiahed uh you hangin' ontuh me. Ah don't want yuh. Look at yuh stringey ole neck! Yo' rawbony laigs an' arms is enough tuh cut uh man tuh death. You looks jes' lak de devvul's doll-baby tuh *me.* You cain't hate me no worse dan Ah hates you. Ah been hatin' *you* fuh years."

"Yo' ole black hide don't look lak nothin' tuh me, but uh passle uh wrinkled up rubber, wid yo' big ole yeahs flappin' on each side lak uh paih uh buzzard wings. Don't think Ah'm gointuh be run 'way fum mah house neither. Ah'm goin' tuh de white folks 'bout *you,* mah young man, de very nex' time you lay yo' han's on me. Mah cup is done run ovah." Delia said this with no signs of fear and Sykes departed from the house, threatening her, but made not the slightest move to carry out any of them.

That night he did not return at all, and the next day being Sunday, Delia was glad she did not have to quarrel before she hitched up her pony and drove the four miles to Woodbridge.

She stayed to the night service—'love feast'—which was very warm and full of spirit. In the emotional winds her domestic trials were borne far and wide so that she sang as she drove homeward,

Jurden water, black an' col
Chills de body, not de soul
An' Ah wantah cross Jurden in uh calm time.

She came from the barn to the kitchen door and stopped.

"Whut's de mattah, ol' Satan, you ain't kickin' up yo' racket?" She addressed the snake's box. Complete silence. She went on into the house with a new hope in its birth struggles. Perhaps her threat to go to the white folks had frightened Sykes! Perhaps he was sorry! Fifteen years of misery and suppression had brought Delia to the place where she would hope *anything* that looked towards a way over or through her wall of inhibitions.

She felt in the match-safe behind the stove at once for a match. There was only one there.

"Dat niggah wouldn't fetch nothin' heah tuh save his rotten neck, but he kin run thew whut Ah brings quick enough. Now he done toted off nigh on tuh haff uh box uh matches. He done had dat 'oman heah in mah house, too."

Nobody but a woman could tell how she knew this even before she struck the match. But she did and it put her into a new fury.

Presently she brought in the tubs to put the white things to soak. This time she decided she need not bring the hamper out of the bedroom; she would go in there and do the sorting. She picked up the pot-bellied lamp and went in. The room was small and the hamper stood hard by the foot of the white iron bed. She could sit and reach through the bedposts—resting as she worked.

"*Ah wantah cross Jurden in uh calm time.*" She was singing again. The mood of the 'love feast' had returned. She threw back the lid of the basket almost gaily. Then, moved by both horror and terror, she sprang back toward the door. *There lay the snake in the basket!* He moved sluggishly at first, but even as she turned round and round, jumped up and down in an insanity of fear, he began to stir vigorously. She saw him pouring his awful beauty from the basket upon the bed, then she seized the lamp and ran as fast as she could to the kitchen. The wind from the open door blew out the light and the darkness added to her terror. She sped to the darkness of the yard, slamming the door after her before she thought to set down the lamp. She did not feel safe even on the ground, so she climbed up in the hay barn.

There for an hour or more she lay sprawled upon the hay a gibbering wreck.

Finally she grew quiet, and after that came coherent thought. With this stalked through her a cold, bloody rage. Hours of this. A period of introspection, a space of retrospection, then a mixture of both. Out of this an awful calm.

"Well, Ah done de bes' Ah could. If things ain't right, Gawd knows tain't mah fault."

She went to sleep—a twitch sleep—and woke up to a faint gray sky. There was a loud hollow sound below. She peered out. Sykes was at the wood-pile, demolishing a wire-covered box.

He hurried to the kitchen door, but hung outside there some minutes before he entered, and stood some minutes more inside before he closed it after him.

The gray in the sky was spreading. Delia descended without fear now, and crouched beneath the low bedroom window. The drawn shade shut out the dawn, shut in the night. But the thin walls held back no sound.

"Dat ol' scratch is woke up now!" She mused at the tremendous whirr inside, which every woodsman knows, is one of the sound illusions. The rattler is a ventriloquist. His whirr sounds to the right, to the left, straight ahead, behind, close under foot—everywhere but where it is. Woe to him who guesses wrong unless he is prepared to hold up his end of the argument! Sometimes he strikes without rattling at all.

Inside, Sykes heard nothing until he knocked a pot lid off the stove while trying to reach the match-safe in the dark. He had emptied his pockets at Bertha's.

The snake seemed to wake up under the stove and Sykes made a quick leap into the bedroom. In spite of the gin he had had, his head was clearing now.

"Mah Gawd!" he chattered, "ef Ah could on'y strack uh light!"

The rattling ceased for a moment as he stood paralyzed. He waited. It seemed that the snake waited also.

"Oh, fuh de light! Ah thought he'd be too sick"—Sykes was muttering to himself when the whirr began again, closer, right underfoot this time. Long before this, Sykes' ability to think had been flattened down to primitive instinct and he leaped—onto the bed.

Outside Delia heard a cry that might have come from a maddened chimpanzee, a stricken gorilla. All the terror, all the horror, all the rage that man possibly could express, without a recognizable human sound.

A tremendous stir inside there, another series of animal screams, the intermittent whirr of the reptile. The shade torn violently down from the window, letting in the red dawn, a huge brown hand seizing the window stick, great dull blows upon the wooden floor punctuating the gibberish of sound long after the rattle of the snake had abruptly subsided. All this Delia could see and hear from her place beneath the window, and it made her ill. She crept over to the four-o'clocks and stretched herself on the cool earth to recover.

She lay there. "Delia, Delia!" She could hear Sykes calling in a most despairing tone as one who expected no answer. The sun crept on up, and he called. Delia could not move—her legs had gone flabby. She never moved, he called, and the sun kept rising.

"Mah Gawd!" She heard him moan, "Mah Gawd fum Heben!" She heard him stumbling about and got up from her flower-bed. The sun was growing warm. As she approached the door she heard him call out hopefully, "Delia, is dat you Ah heah?"

She saw him on his hands and knees as soon as she reached the door. He crept an inch or two toward her—all that he was able, and she saw his horribly swollen neck and his one open eye shining with hope. A surge of pity too strong to support bore her away from that eye that must, could not, fail to see the tubs. He would see the lamp. Orlando with its doctors was too far. She could scarcely reach the chinaberry tree, where she waited in the growing heat while inside she knew the cold river was creeping up and up to extinguish that eye which must know by now that she knew.

Questions for Study

1. What stages has Delia and Sykes's marriage gone through? What are the points of disagreement between them?

2. What do the porch sitters contribute to our understanding of Sykes and Delia? Since they restate what the narrator tells us, are their comments revealing?

3. What does Sykes hope to gain by using the snake? What does the snake mean to him? What does it mean to Delia? What does it symbolize?

4. Why does Delia not try to help Sykes at the end? Should she have?

5. What is the meaning of the title?

RICHARD WRIGHT

The Man Who Was Almost a Man

Richard Wright (1908–60) was born on a farm near Natchez, Mississippi. His father, a sharecropper, deserted the family when Wright was five. His mother tried to make ends meet by doing domestic work but suffered paralytic strokes when Wright was about eleven. Because she was unable to work, she and her family moved in with her mother, a strict Seventh Day Adventist, who imposed a religious regimen on Wright that he resented and rebelled against. As Wright grew into adolescence, he rebelled also against the extreme limitations that white racism imposed on his freedom of expression and opportunity. At sixteen, he finished his formal education when he graduated from the ninth grade. No longer able to stand the constraints of home, he ran away to Memphis, where he read H. L. Mencken, Sinclair Lewis, Theodore Dreiser, and other social critics. Their use of language and fiction to attack the narrowmindedness and hypocrisy of the American middle class inspired Wright to become a writer. He left Memphis for Chicago in 1927 and was joined soon after by his family. He did odd jobs, including a stint as a writer for the Federal Writers' Project. During a period when he was unemployed, a relief worker introduced him to her husband, a professor of sociology at the University of Chicago, who provided Wright a program of reading in history, sociology, philosophy, and literature. He joined the Communist party in 1932, believing that the Communist movement could liberate African Americans. He moved to New York in 1937 to become the Harlem editor of the Communist party newspaper, the *Daily Worker.* Disillusioned with the party's own brand of intellectual tyranny, he left the party in 1944.

His first book, *Uncle Tom's Children* (1938), was a collection of short stories. His next two books were blockbuster bestsellers that brought him fame and financial security and that graphically publicized the plight of African Americans. The novel *Native Son* (1940) recounts the story of Bigger Thomas, a restless youth living in the South Side ghetto, who accidentally kills a wealthy white woman. *Black Boy* (1945), Wright's autobiography, covers his life up to the point when he escapes from Memphis to go to Chicago. After the success of these two books, Wright felt compelled to leave the United States. He went to Paris in 1946 and remained there the rest of his life. The novels he wrote in Europe, notably *The Outsider* (1953), reflect his interest in European existentialist philosophy. In *Black Power* (1954) and other nonfiction books, he wrote about his travels to Africa and Indonesia where he witnessed revolutions against colonial rule. "The Man Who Was Almost a Man," originally published in 1940, was collected after Wright's death in *Eight Men* (1961).

*D*ave struck out across the fields, looking homeward through paling light. Whut's the use talkin wid em niggers in the field? Anyhow, his mother was putting supper on the table. Them niggers can't understan nothing. One of these days he was going to get a gun and practice shooting, then they couldn't talk to him as though he were a little boy. He slowed, looking at the ground. Shucks, Ah ain scareda them even ef they are biggern me! Aw, Ah know whut Ahma do. Ahm going by ol Joe's sto n git that Sears Roebuck catlog n look at them guns. Mebbe Ma will lemme buy one when she gits mah pay from ol man Hawkins. Ahma beg her t gimme some money. Ahm ol ernough to hava gun. Ahm seventeen. Almost a man. He strode, feeling his long loose-jointed limbs. Shucks, a man oughta hava little gun aftah he done worked hard all day.

He came in sight of Joe's store. A yellow lantern glowed on the front porch. He mounted steps and went through the screen door, hearing it bang behind him. There was a strong smell of coal oil and mackerel fish. He felt very confident until he saw fat Joe walk in through the rear door, then his courage began to ooze.

"Howdy, Dave! Whutcha want?"

"How yuh, Mistah Joe? Aw, Ah don wanna buy nothing. Ah jus wanted t see ef yuhd lemme look at tha catlog erwhile."

"Sure! You wanna see it here?"

"Nawsuh. Ah wans t take it home wid me. Ah'll bring it back termorrow when Ah come in from the fiels."

"You plannin on buying something?"

"Yessuh."

"Your ma lettin you have your own money now?"

"Shucks. Mistah Joe, Ahm gittin t be a man like anybody else!"

Joe laughed and wiped his greasy white face with a red bandanna.

"Whut you plannin on buyin?"

Dave looked at the floor, scratched his head, scratched his thigh, and smiled. Then he looked up shyly.

"Ah'll tell yuh, Mistah Joe, ef yuh promise yuh won't tell."

"I promise."

"Waal, Ahma buy a gun."

"A gun? Whut you want with a gun?"

"Ah wanna keep it."

"You ain't nothing but a boy. You don't need a gun."

"Aw, lemme have the catlog, Mistah Joe. Ah'll bring it back."

Joe walked through the rear door. Dave was elated. He looked around at barrels of sugar and flour. He heard Joe coming back. He craned his neck to see if he were bringing the book. Yeah, he's got it. Gawddog, he's got it!

"Here, but be sure you bring it back. It's the only one I got."

"Sho, Mistah Joe."

"Say, if you wanna buy a gun, why don't you buy one from me? I gotta gun to sell."

"Will it shoot?"

"Sure it'll shoot."

"Whut kind is it?"

"Oh, it's kinda old . . . a left-hand Wheeler. A pistol. A big one."

"Is it got bullets in it?"

"It's loaded."

"Kin Ah see it?"

"Where's your money?"

"Whut yuh wan fer it?"

"I'll let you have it for two dollars."

"Just two dollahs? Shucks, Ah could buy tha when Ah git mah pay."

"I'll have it here when you want it."

"Awright, suh. Ah be in fer it."

He went through the door, hearing it slam again behind him. Ahma git some money from Ma n buy me a gun! Only two dollahs! He tucked the thick catalogue under his arm and hurried.

"Where yuh been, boy?" His mother held a steaming dish of black-eyed peas.

"Aw, Ma, Ah jus stopped down the road t talk wid the boys."

"Yuh know bettah t keep suppah waitin."

He sat down, resting the catalogue on the edge of the table.

"Yuh git up from there and git to the well n wash yosef! Ah ain feedin no hogs in mah house!"

She grabbed his shoulder and pushed him. He stumbled out of the room, then came back to get the catalogue.

"Whut this?"

"Aw, Ma, it's jusa catlog."

"Who yuh git it from?"

"From Joe, down at the sto."

"Waal, thas good. We kin use it in the out house."

"Naw, Ma." He grabbed for it. "Gimme ma catlog, Ma."

She held onto it and glared at him.

"Quit hollerin at me! Whut's wrong wid yuh? Yuh crazy?"

"But Ma, please. It ain mine! It's Joe's! He tol me t bring it back t im termorrow."

She gave up the book. He stumbled down the back steps, hugging the thick book under his arm. When he had splashed water on his face and hands, he groped back to the kitchen and fumbled in a corner for the towel. He bumped into a chair; it clattered to the floor. The catalogue sprawled at his feet. When he had dried his eyes he snatched up the book and held it again under his arm. His mother stood watching him.

"Now, ef yuh gonna act a fool over that ol book, Ah'll take it n burn it up."

"Naw, Ma, please."

"Waal, set down n be still!"

He sat down and drew the oil lamp close. He thumbed page after page, unaware of the food his mother set on the table. His father came in. Then his small brother.

"Whutcha got there, Dave?" his father asked.

"Jusa catlog," he answered, not looking up.

"Yeah, here they is!" His eyes glowed at blue-and-black revolvers. He glanced up, feeling sudden guilt. His father was watching him. He eased the book under the table and rested it on his knees. After the blessing was asked, he ate. He scooped up peas and swallowed fat meat without chewing. Buttermilk helped to wash it down. He did not want to mention money before his father. He would do much better by cornering his mother when she was alone. He looked at his father uneasily out of the edge of his eye.

"Boy, how come yuh don quit foolin wid tha book n eat yo suppah?"

"Yessuh."

"How you n ol man Hawkins gittin erlong?"

"Suh?"

"Can't yuh hear? Why don yuh lissen? Ah ast yu how wuz yuh n ol man Hawkins gittin erlong?"

"Oh, swell, Pa. Ah plows mo lan than anybody over there."

"Waal, yuh oughta keep yo mind on whut yuh doin."

"Yessuh."

He poured his plate full of molasses and sopped it up slowly with a chunk of cornbread. When his father and brother had left the kitchen, he still sat and looked again at the guns in the catalogue, longing to muster courage enough to present his case to his mother. Lawd, ef Ah only had tha pretty one! He could almost feel the slickness of the weapon with his fingers. If he had a gun like that he would polish it and keep it shining so it would never rust. N Ah'd keep it loaded, by Gawd!

"Ma?" His voice was hesitant.

"Hunh?"

"Ol man Hawkins give yuh mah money yit?"

"Yeah, but ain no usa yuh thinking bout throwin nona it erway. Ahm keepin tha money sos yuh kin have cloes t go to school this winter."

He rose and went to her side with the open catalogue in his palms. She was washing dishes, her head bent low over a pan. Shyly he raised the book. When he spoke, his voice was husky, faint.

"Ma, Gawd knows Ah wans one of these."

"One of whut?" she asked, not raising her eyes.

"One of these," he said again, not daring even to point. She glanced up at the page, then at him with wide eyes.

"Nigger, is yuh gone plumb crazy?"

"Aw, Ma—"

"Git outta here! Don yuh talk t me bout no gun! Yuh a fool!"

"Ma, Ah kin buy one fer two dollahs."

"Not ef Ah knows it, yuh ain!"

"But yuh promised me one—"

"Ah don care whut Ah promised! Yuh ain nothing but a boy yit!"

"Ma, ef yuh lemme buy one Ah'll never ast yuh fer nothing no mo."

"Ah tol yuh t git outta here! Yuh ain gonna toucha penny of tha money fer no gun! Thas ow come Ah has Mistah Hawkins t pay yo wages t me, cause Ah knows yuh ain got no sense."

"But, Ma, we needa gun. Pa ain got no gun. We needa gun in the house. Yuh kin never tell whut might happen."

"Now don yuh try to maka fool outta me, boy! Ef we did hava gun, yuh wouldn't have it!"

He laid the catalogue down and slipped his arm around her waist.

"Aw, Ma, Ah done worked hard alla summer n ain ast yuh fer nothin, is Ah, now?"

"Thas whut yuh spose t do!"

"But Ma, Ah wans a gun. Yuh kin lemme have two dollahs outta mah money. Please, Ma. I kin give it to Pa . . . Please, Ma! Ah loves yuh, Ma."

When she spoke her voice came soft and low.

"Whut yu wan wida gun, Dave? Yuh don need no gun. Yuh'll git in trouble. N ef yo pa jus thought Ah let yuh have money to buy a gun he'd hava fit."

"Ah'll hide it, Ma. It ain but two dollahs."

"Lawd, chil, whut's wrong wid yuh?"

"Ain nothin wrong, Ma. Ahm almos a man now. Ah wans a gun."

"Who gonna sell yuh a gun?"

"Ol Joe at the sto."

"N it don cos but two dollahs?"

"Thas all, Ma. Jus two dollahs. Please, Ma."

She was stacking the plates away; her hands moved slowly, reflectively. Dave kept an anxious silence. Finally, she turned to him.

"Ah'll let yuh git tha gun ef yuh promise me one thing."

"Whut's tha, Ma?"

"Yuh bring it straight back t me, yuh hear? It be fer Pa."

"Yessum! Lemme go now, Ma."

She stooped, turned slightly to one side, raised the hem of her dress, rolled down the top of her stocking, and came up with a slender wad of bills.

"Here," she said. "Lawd knows yuh don need no gun. But yer pa does. Yuh bring it right back t me, yuh hear? Ahma put it up. Now ef yuh don, Ahma have yuh pa lick yuh so hard yuh won fergit it."

"Yessum."

He took the money, ran down the steps, and across the yard.

"Dave! Yuuuuuh Daaaaave!"

He heard, but he was not going to stop now. "Naw, Lawd!"

The first movement he made the following morning was to reach under his pillow for the gun. In the gray light of dawn he held it loosely, feeling a sense of power. Could kill a man with a gun like this. Kill anybody, black or white. And if he were holding his gun in his hand, nobody could run over him; they would have to respect him. It was a big gun, with a long barrel and a heavy handle. He raised and lowered it in his hand, marveling at its weight.

He had not come straight home with it as his mother had asked; instead he had stayed out in the fields, holding the weapon in his hand, aiming it now and then at some imaginary foe. But he had not fired it; he had been afraid that his father might hear. Also he was not sure he knew how to fire it.

To avoid surrendering the pistol he had not come into the house until he knew that they were all asleep. When his mother had tiptoed to his bedside late that night and demanded the gun, he had first played possum; then he had told her that the gun was hidden outdoors, that he would bring it to her in the morning. Now he lay turning it slowly in his hands. He broke it, took out the cartridges, felt them, and then put them back.

He slid out of bed, got a long strip of old flannel from a trunk, wrapped the gun in it, and tied it to his naked thigh while it was still loaded. He did not go in to breakfast. Even though it was not yet daylight, he started for Jim Hawkins' plantation. Just as the sun was rising he reached the barns where the mules and plows were kept.

"Hey! That you, Dave?"

He turned. Jim Hawkins stood eying him suspiciously.

"What're yuh doing here so early?"

"Ah didn't know Ah wuz gittin up so early, Mistah Hawkins. Ah wuz fixin t hitch up ol Jenny n take her t the fiels."

"Good. Since you're so early, how about plowing that stretch down by the woods?"

"Suits me, Mistah Hawkins."

"O.K. Go to it!"

He hitched Jenny to a plow and started across the fields. Hot dog! This was just what he wanted. If he could get down by the woods, he could shoot his gun and nobody would hear. He walked behind the plow, hearing the traces creaking, feeling the gun tied tight to his thigh.

When he reached the woods, he plowed two whole rows before he decided to take out the gun. Finally, he stopped, looked in all directions, then untied the gun and held it in his hand. He turned to the mule and smiled.

"Know whut this is, Jenny? Naw, yuh wouldn know! Yuhs jusa ol mule! Anyhow, this is a gun, n it kin shoot, by Gawd!"

He held the gun at arm's length. Whut t hell, Ahma shoot this thing! He looked at Jenny again.

"Lissen here, Jenny! When Ah pull this ol trigger, Ah don wan yuh t run n acka fool now!"

Jenny stood with head down, her short ears pricked straight. Dave walked off about twenty feet, held the gun far out from him at arm's length, and turned his head. Hell, he told himself, Ah ain afraid. The gun felt loose in his fingers; he waved it wildly for a moment. Then he shut his eyes and tightened his forefinger. Bloom! A report half deafened him and he thought his right hand was torn from his arm. He heard Jenny whinnying and galloping over the field, and he found himself on his knees, squeezing his fingers hard between his legs. His hand was numb; he jammed it into his mouth, trying to warm it, trying to stop the pain. The gun lay at his feet. He did not quite know what had happened. He stood up and stared at the gun as though it were a living thing. He gritted his teeth and kicked the gun. Yuh almos broke mah arm! He turned to look for Jenny; she was far over the fields, tossing her head and kicking wildly.

"Hol on there, ol mule!"

When he caught up with her she stood trembling, walling her big white eyes at him. The plow was far away; the traces had broken. Then Dave stopped short, looking, not believing. Jenny was bleeding. Her left side was red and wet with blood. He went closer. Lawd, have mercy! Wondah did Ah shoot this mule? He grabbed for Jenny's mane. She flinched, snorted, whirled, tossing her head.

"Hol on now! Hol on."

Then he saw the hole in Jenny's side, right between the ribs. It was round, wet, red. A crimson stream streaked down the front leg, flowing fast. Good Gawd! Ah wuzn't shootin at tha mule. He felt panic. He knew he had to stop that blood, or Jenny would bleed to death. He had never seen so much blood in all his life. He chased the mule for half a mile, trying to catch her. Finally she stopped, breathing hard, stumpy tail half arched. He caught her mane and led her back to where the plow and gun lay. Then he stooped and grabbed handfuls of damp black earth and tried to plug the bullet hole. Jenny shuddered, whinnied, and broke from him.

"Hol on! Hol on now!"

He tried to plug it again, but blood came anyhow. His fingers were hot and sticky. He rubbed dirt into his palms, trying to dry them. Then again he attempted to plug the bullet hole, but Jenny shied away, kicking her heels high. He stood helpless. He had to do something. He ran at Jenny; she dodged him. He watched a red stream of blood flow down Jenny's leg and form a bright pool at her feet.

"Jenny . . . Jenny," he called weakly.

His lips trembled. She's bleeding t death! He looked in the direction of home, wanting to go back, wanting to get help. But he saw the pistol lying in the damp black clay. He had a queer feeling that if he only did something, this would not be; Jenny would not be there bleeding to death.

When he went to her this time, she did not move. She stood with sleepy, dreamy eyes; and when he touched her she gave a low-pitched whinny and knelt to the ground, her front knees slopping in blood.

"Jenny . . . Jenny . . . " he whispered.

For a long time she held her neck erect; then her head sank, slowly. Her ribs swelled with a mighty heave and she went over.

Dave's stomach felt empty, very empty. He picked up the gun and held it gingerly between his thumb and forefinger. He buried it at the foot of a tree. He took a stick and tried to cover the pool of blood with dirt—but what was the use? There was Jenny lying with her mouth open and her eyes walled and glassy. He could not tell Jim Hawkins he had shot his mule. But he had to tell something. Yeah, Ah'll tell em Jenny started gittin wil n fell on the joint of the plow. . . . But that would hardly happen to a mule. He walked across the field slowly, head down.

It was sunset. Two of Jim Hawkins' men were over near the edge of the woods digging a hole in which to bury Jenny. Dave was surrounded by a knot of people, all of whom were looking down at the dead mule.

"I don't see how in the world it happened," said Jim Hawkins for the tenth time.

The crowd parted and Dave's mother, father, and small brother pushed into the center.

"Where Dave?" his mother called.

"There he is," said Jim Hawkins.

His mother grabbed him.

"Whut happened, Dave? Whut yuh done?"

"Nothin."

"C mon, boy, talk," his father said.

Dave took a deep breath and told the story he knew nobody believed.

"Waal," he drawled. "Ah brung ol Jenny down here sos Ah could do mah plowin. Ah plowed bout two rows, just like yuh see." He stopped and pointed at the long rows of upturned earth. "Then somethin musta been wrong wid ol Jenny. She wouldn ack right a-tall. She started snortin n kickin her heels. Ah tried t hol her, but she pulled erway, rearin n goin in. Then when the point of the plow was stickin up in the air, she swung erroun n twisted herself back on it . . . She stuck herself n started t bleed. N fo Ah could do anything, she wuz dead."

"Did you ever hear of anything like that in all your life?" asked Jim Hawkins.

There were white and black standing in the crowd. They murmured. Dave's mother came close to him and looked hard into his face. "Tell the truth, Dave," she said.

"Looks like a bullet hole to me," said one man.

"Dave, whut yuh do wid the gun?" his mother asked.

The crowd surged in, looking at him. He jammed his hands into his pockets, shook his head slowly from left to right, and backed away. His eyes were wide and painful.

"Did he hava gun?" asked Jim Hawkins.

"By Gawd, Ah tol yuh tha wuz a gun wound," said a man, slapping his thigh.

His father caught his shoulders and shook him till his teeth rattled.

"Tell whut happened, yuh rascal! Tell whut . . . "

Dave looked at Jenny's stiff legs and began to cry.

"Whut yuh do wid tha gun?" his mother asked.

"Whut wuz he doin wida gun?" his father asked.

"Come on and tell the truth," said Hawkins. "Ain't nobody going to hurt you . . . "

His mother crowded close to him.

"Did yuh shoot tha mule, Dave?"

Dave cried, seeing blurred white and black faces.

"Ahh ddinn gggo tt sshooot hher . . . Ah ssswear ffo Gawd Ah ddin. . . . Ah wuz a-tryin t sssee ef the old gggun would sshoot—"

"Where yuh git the gun from?" his father asked.

"Ah got it from Joe, at the sto."

"Where yuh git the money?"

"Ma give it t me."

"He kept worryin me, Bob. Ah had t. Ah tol im t bring the gun right back t me . . . It was fer yuh, the gun."

"But how yuh happen to shoot that mule?" asked Jim Hawkins.

"Ah wuzn shootin at the mule, Mistah Hawkins. The gun jumped when Ah pulled the trigger . . . N fo Ah knowed anythin Jenny was there a-bleedin."

Somebody in the crowd laughed. Jim Hawkins walked close to Dave and looked into his face.

"Well, looks like you have bought you a mule, Dave."

"Ah swear fo Gawd, Ah didn go t kill the mule, Mistah Hawkins!"

"But you killed her!"

All the crowd was laughing now. They stood on tiptoe and poked heads over one another's shoulders.

"Well, boy, looks like yuh done bought a dead mule! Hahaha!"

"Ain tha ershame."

"Hohohohoho."

Dave stood, head down, twisting his feet in the dirt.

"Well, you needn't worry about it, Bob," said Jim Hawkins to Dave's father. "Just let the boy keep on working and pay me two dollars a month."

"Whut yuh wan fer yo mule, Mistah Hawkins?"

Jim Hawkins screwed up his eyes.

"Fifty dollars."

"Whut yuh do wid tha gun?" Dave's father demanded.

Dave said nothing.

"Yuh wan me t take a tree n beat yuh till yuh talk!"

"Nawsuh!"

"Whut yuh do wid it?"

"Ah throwed it erway."

"Where?"

"Ah . . . Ah throwed it in the creek."

"Waal, c mon home. N firs thing in the mawnin git to tha creek n fin tha gun."

"Yessuh."

"Whut yuh pay fer it?"

"Two dollahs."

"Take tha gun n git yo money back n carry it t Mistah Hawkins, yuh hear? N don fergit Ahma lam you black bottom good fer this! Now march yosef on home, suh!"

Dave turned and walked slowly. He heard people laughing. Dave glared, his eyes welling with tears. Hot anger bubbled in him. Then he swallowed and stumbled on.

That night Dave did not sleep. He was glad that he had gotten out of killing the mule so easily, but he was hurt. Something hot seemed to turn over inside him each time he remembered how they had laughed. He tossed on his bed, feeling his hard pillow. N Pa says he's gonna beat me . . . He remembered other beatings, and his back quivered. Naw, naw, Ah sho don wan im t beat me tha way no mo. Dam em all! Nobody ever gave him anything. All he did was work. They treat me like a mule, n then they beat me. He gritted his teeth. N Ma had t tell on me.

Well, if he had to, he would take old man Hawkins that two dollars. But that meant selling the gun. And he wanted to keep that gun. Fifty dollars for a dead mule.

He turned over, thinking how he had fired the gun. He had an itch to fire it again. Ef other men kin shoota gun, by Gawd, Ah kin! He was still, listening. Mebbe they all sleepin now. The house was still. He heard the soft breathing of his brother. Yes, now! He would go down and get that gun and see if he could fire it! He eased out of bed and slipped into overalls.

The moon was bright. He ran almost all the way to the edge of the woods. He stumbled over the ground, looking for the spot where he had buried the gun. Yeah, here it is. Like a hungry dog scratching for a bone, he pawed it up. He puffed his black cheeks and blew dirt from the trigger and barrel. He broke it and found four cartridges unshot. He looked around; the fields were filled with silence and moonlight. He clutched the gun stiff and hard in his fingers. But, as soon as he wanted to pull the trigger, he shut his eyes and turned his head. Naw, Ah can't shoot wid mah eyes closed n mah head turned. With effort he held his eyes open; then he squeezed. Blooooom! He was stiff, not breathing. The gun was still in his hands. Dammit, he'd done it! He fired again. Blooooom! He smiled. *Blooooom! Blooooom!* Click, click. There! It was empty. If anybody could shoot a gun, he could. He put the gun into his hip pocket and started across the fields.

When he reached the top of a ridge he stood straight and proud in the moonlight, looking at Jim Hawkins' big white house, feeling the gun sagging in his pocket. Lawd, ef Ah had just one mo bullet Ah'd taka shot at tha house. Ah'd like t scare ol man Hawkins jusa little . . . Jusa enough t let im know Dave Saunders is a man.

To his left the road curved, running to the tracks of the Illinois Central. He jerked his head, listening. From far off came a faint *boooof-boooof; boooof-boooof; boooof-boooof.* . . . He stood rigid. Two dollahs a mont. Les see now . . . Tha means it'll take bout two years. Shucks! Ah'll be dam!

He started down the road, toward the tracks. Yeah, here she comes! He stood beside the track and held himself stiffly. Here she comes, erroun the ben . . . C mon, yuh slow poke! C mon! He had his hand on his gun; something quivered in his stomach. Then the train thundered past, the gray and brown box cars rumbling and clinking. He gripped the gun tightly; then he jerked his hand out of his pocket. Ah betcha Bill wouldn't do it! Ah betcha . . . The cars slid past, steel grinding upon steel. Ahm ridin yuh ternight, so hep me Gawd! He was hot all over. He hesitated just a moment; then he grabbed, pulled atop of a car, and lay flat. He felt his pocket; the gun was still there. Ahead the long rails were glinting in the moonlight, stretching away, away to somewhere, somewhere where he could be a man . . .

Questions for Study

1. In the first paragraph and throughout the story, Wright moves back and forth between dialect and standard English. Why? What does he mean for these different levels of English usage to represent?

2. What does the gun mean to Dave? What does it mean to Dave's mother? What does it mean to Dave's father?

3. How responsible is Dave for Jenny's death? Is the payment scheme that Mr. Hawkins proposes fair? Is Dave wrong to run away?

4. Does Dave become a "man"? Does he change at all? What is likely to happen to him in the future? What does Wright seem to think "manhood" is?

5. Does the story reflect the racial injustice that Wright scathingly attacks in most of his other writings?

KATHERINE ANNE PORTER

The Grave

During her lifetime, Katherine Anne Porter (1890–1980) was reticent about the details of her life, but much of her fiction is autobiographical and serves as a source of information about her. This is especially true of the Miranda stories. Taken together, these stories follow Miranda, whose experiences are very similar to Porter's, from childhood to young adulthood. Like Miranda, Porter was born in Texas. Like Miranda, her mother died when she was a child, leaving her to be brought up by her father and her father's mother, a forceful and independent woman. Like Miranda, she eloped against her family's wishes when she was sixteen. And like Miranda, she worked as a reporter in Denver where she almost died of influenza during the epidemic of 1918. Porter traveled extensively in Europe, Mexico, and the United States. She was married three times. Her first collection of stories was *Flowering Judas, and Other Stories,* published first in 1930 and expanded in 1935. In addition to writing fiction, she served as a reporter, writer of screenplays, translator, essayist, and lecturer. *The Collected Stories of Katherine Anne Porter* (1965) is a gathering of all her short fiction. She wrote one novel, *Ship of Fools,* a bestseller upon its appearance in 1962.

Much of Porter's fiction, and notably the Miranda stories, focuses on the sacrifices women have to make in order to gain autonomy. Related to this theme is Porter's fascination with the pleasures and limitations of intimate relationships, especially as they occur in families. *Pale Horse, Pale Rider* (1939) includes two long Miranda stories: "Old Mortality" traces Miranda's reactions to her family's romantic legends, and "Pale Horse, Pale Rider" recounts her engagement to a soldier and her brush with death. "The Grave" is one of the four Miranda stories collected in *The Leaning Tower and Other Stories* (1944).

*T*he grandfather, dead for more than thirty years, had been twice disturbed in his long repose by the constancy and possessiveness of his widow. She removed his bones first to Louisiana and then to Texas as if she had set out to find her own burial place, knowing well she would never return to the places she had left. In Texas she set up a small cemetery in a corner of her first farm, and as the family connection grew, and oddments of relations came over from Kentucky to settle, it contained at last about twenty graves. After the grandmother's death, part of her land was to be sold for the benefit of certain of her children, and the cemetery happened to lie in the part set aside for sale. It was necessary to take up the bodies and bury them again in the family plot in the big new public cemetery, where the grandmother had been buried. At last her husband was to lie beside her for eternity, as she had planned.

The family cemetery had been a pleasant small neglected garden of tangled rose bushes and ragged cedar trees and cypress, the simple flat stones rising out of uncropped sweet-smelling wild grass. The graves were lying open and empty one burning day when Miranda and her brother Paul, who often went together to hunt rabbits and doves, propped their twenty-two Winchester rifles carefully against the rail fence, climbed over and explored among the graves. She was nine years old and he was twelve.

They peered into the pits all shaped alike with such purposeful accuracy, and looking at each other with pleased adventurous eyes, they said in solemn tones: "These were graves!" trying by words to shape a special, suitable emotion in their minds, but they felt nothing except an agreeable thrill of wonder: they were seeing a new sight, doing something they had not done before. In them both there was also a small disappointment at the entire commonplaceness of the actual spectacle. Even if it had once contained a coffin for years upon years, when the coffin was gone a grave was just a hole in the ground. Miranda leaped into the pit that had held her grandfather's bones. Scratching around aimlessly and pleasurably as any young animal, she scooped up a lump of earth and weighed it in her palm. It had a pleasantly sweet, corrupt smell, being mixed with cedar needles and small leaves, and as the crumbs fell apart, she saw a silver dove no larger than a hazel nut, with spread wings and a neat fan-shaped tail. The breast had a deep round hollow in it. Turning it up to the fierce sunlight, she saw that the inside of the hollow was cut in little whorls. She scrambled out, over the pile of loose earth that had fallen back into one end of the grave, calling to Paul that she had found something, he must guess what . . . His head appeared smiling over the rim of another grave. He waved a closed hand at her. "I've got something too!" They ran to compare treasures, making a game of it, so many guesses each, all wrong, and a final showdown with opened palms. Paul had found a thin wide gold ring carved with intricate flowers and leaves. Miranda was smitten at sight of the ring and wished to have it. Paul seemed more impressed by the dove. They made a trade, with some little bickering. After he had got the dove in his hand, Paul said, "Don't you know what this is? This is a screw head for a *coffin!* . . . I'll bet nobody else in the world has one like this!"

Miranda glanced at it without covetousness. She had the gold ring on her thumb; it fitted perfectly. "Maybe we ought to go now," she said, "Maybe one of the niggers 'll see us and tell somebody." They knew the land had been sold, the cemetery was no longer theirs, and they felt like trespassers. They climbed back over the fence, slung their rifles loosely under their arms—they had been shooting at targets with various kinds of firearms since they were seven years old—and set out to look for the rabbits and doves or whatever small game might happen along. On these expeditions Miranda always followed at Paul's heels along the path, obeying instructions about handling her gun when going through fences; learning how to stand it up properly so it would not slip and fire unexpectedly; how to wait her time for a shot and not just bang away in the air without looking, spoiling shots for Paul, who really could hit things if given a chance. Now and then, in her excitement at seeing birds whizz up suddenly before her face, or a rabbit leap across her very toes, she lost her head, and almost without sighting she flung her rifle up and pulled the trigger. She hardly ever hit any sort of mark. She had no proper sense of hunting at all. Her brother would be often completely disgusted with her. "You don't care whether you get your bird or not," he said. "That's no way to hunt." Miranda could not understand his indignation. She had seen him smash his hat and yell with fury when he had missed his aim. "What I like about shooting," said Miranda, with exasperating inconsequence, "is pulling the trigger and hearing the noise."

"Then, by golly," said Paul, "whyn't you go back to the range and shoot at bulls-eyes?"

"I'd just as soon," said Miranda, "only like this, we walk around more."

"Well, you just stay behind and stop spoiling my shots," said Paul, who, when he made a kill, wanted to be certain he had made it. Miranda, who alone brought down a bird once in twenty rounds, always claimed as her own any game they got when they fired at the same moment. It was tiresome and unfair and her brother was sick of it.

"Now, the first dove we see, or the first rabbit, is mine," he told her. "And the next will be yours. Remember that and don't get smarty."

"What about snakes?" asked Miranda idly. "Can I have the first snake?"

Waving her thumb gently and watching her gold ring glitter, Miranda lost interest in shooting. She was wearing her summer roughing outfit: dark blue overalls, a light blue shirt, a hired-man's straw hat, and thick brown sandals. Her brother had the same outfit except his was a sober hickory-nut color. Ordinarily Miranda preferred her overalls to any other dress, though it was making rather a scandal in the countryside, for the year was 1903, and in the back country the law of female decorum had teeth in it. Her father had been criticized for letting his girls dress like boys and go careering around astride barebacked horses. Big sister Maria, the really independent and fearless one, in spite of her rather affected ways, rode at a dead run with only a rope knotted around her horse's nose. It was said the motherless family was running down, with the Grandmother no longer there to hold it together. It was known that she had discriminated against her son Harry in her will, and that he was in straits about money. Some of his old neighbors reflected with vicious satisfaction that now he would probably not be so stiffnecked, nor have any more high-stepping horses either. Miranda knew this, though she could not say how. She had met along the road old women of the kind who smoked corn-cob pipes, who had treated her grandmother with most sincere respect. They slanted their gummy old eyes side-ways at the granddaughter and said, "Ain't you ashamed of yoself, Missy? It's aginst the Scriptures to dress like that. Whut yo Pappy thinkin about?" Miranda, with her powerful social sense, which was like a fine set of antennae radiating from every pore of her skin, would feel ashamed because she knew well it was rude and ill-bred to shock anybody, even bad-tempered old crones, though she had faith in her father's judgment and was perfectly comfortable in the clothes. Her father had said, "They're just what you need, and they'll save your dresses for school . . . " This sounded quite simple and natural to her. She had been brought up in rigorous economy. Wastefulness was vulgar. It was also a sin. These were truths; she had heard them repeated many times and never once disputed.

Now the ring, shining with the serene purity of fine gold on her rather grubby thumb, turned her feelings against her overalls and sockless feet, toes sticking through the thick brown leather straps. She wanted to go back to the farmhouse, take a good cold bath, dust herself with plenty of Maria's violet talcum powder—provided Maria was not present to object, of course—put on the thinnest, most becoming dress she owned, with a big sash, and sit in a wicker chair under the trees . . . These things were not all she wanted, of course; she had vague stirrings of desire for luxury and a grand way of living which could not take precise form in her imagination but were founded on family legend of past wealth and leisure. These immediate comforts were what she could have, and she wanted them at once. She lagged rather far behind Paul, and once she thought of just turning back without a word and going home. She stopped, thinking that Paul would never do that to her, and so she would have to tell him. When a rabbit leaped, she let Paul have it without dispute. He killed it with one shot.

When she came up with him, he was already kneeling, examining the wound, the rabbit trailing from his hands. "Right through the head," he said complacently, as if he had aimed for it. He took out his sharp, competent bowie knife and started to skin the body. He did it very cleanly and quickly. Uncle Jimbilly knew how to prepare the skins so that Miranda always had fur coats for her dolls, for though she never cared much for her dolls she liked seeing them in fur coats. The children knelt facing each other over the dead animal. Miranda watched admiringly while her brother stripped the skin away as if he were taking off a glove. The flayed flesh emerged dark scarlet, sleek, firm; Miranda with thumb and finger felt the long fine muscles with the silvery flat strips binding them to the joints. Brother lifted the oddly bloated belly. "Look," he said, in a low amazed voice. "It was going to have young ones."

Very carefully he slit the thin flesh from the center ribs to the flanks, and a scarlet bag appeared. He slit again and pulled the bag open, and there lay a bundle of tiny rabbits, each wrapped in a thin scarlet veil. The brother pulled these off and there they were, dark gray, their sleek wet down lying in minute even ripples, like a baby's head just washed, their unbelievably small delicate ears folded close, their little blind faces almost featureless.

Miranda said, "Oh, I want to *see*," under her breath. She looked and looked—excited but not frightened, for she was accustomed to the sight of animals killed in hunting—filled with pity and astonishment and a kind of shocked delight in the wonderful little creatures for their own sakes, they were so pretty. She touched one of them ever so carefully, "Ah, there's blood running over them," she said and began to tremble without knowing why. Yet she wanted most deeply to see and to know. Having seen, she felt at once as if she had known all along. The very memory of her former ignorance faded, she had always known just this. No one had ever told her anything outright, she had been rather unobservant of the animal life around her because she was so accustomed to animals. They seemed simply disorderly and unaccountably rude in their habits, but altogether natural and not very interesting. Her brother had spoken as if he had known about everything all along. He may have seen all this before. He had never said a word to her, but she knew now a part at least of what he knew. She understood a little of the secret, formless intuitions in her own mind and body, which had been clearing up, taking form, so gradually and so steadily she had not realized that she was learning what she had to know. Paul said cautiously, as if he were talking about something forbidden: "They were just about ready to be born." His voice dropped on the last word. "I know," said Miranda, "like kittens. I know, like babies." She was quietly and terribly agitated, standing again with her rifle under her arm, looking down at the bloody heap. "I don't want the skin," she said, "I won't have it." Paul buried the young rabbits again in their mother's body, wrapped the skin around her, carried her to a clump of sage bushes, and hid her away. He came out again at once and said to Miranda, with an eager friendliness, a confidential tone quite unusual in him, as if he were taking her into an important secret on equal terms: "Listen now. Now you listen to me, and don't ever forget. Don't you ever tell a living soul that you saw this. Don't tell a soul. Don't tell Dad because I'll get into trouble. He'll say I'm leading you into things you ought not to do. He's always saying that. So now don't you go and forget and blab out sometime the way you're always doing . . . Now, that's a secret. Don't you tell."

Miranda never told, she did not even wish to tell anybody. She thought about the whole worrisome affair with confused unhappiness for a few days. Then it sank quietly into her mind and was heaped over by accumulated thousands of impressions, for nearly twenty years. One day she was picking her path among the puddles and crushed refuse of a market street in a strange city of a strange country, when without warning, plain and clear in its true colors as if she looked through a frame upon a scene that had not stirred nor changed since the moment it happened, the episode of that far-off day leaped from its burial place before her mind's eye. She was so reasonlessly horrified she halted suddenly staring, the scene before her eyes dimmed by the vision back of them. An Indian vendor had held up before her a tray of dyed sugar sweets, in the shapes of all kinds of small creatures: birds, baby chicks, baby rabbits, lambs, baby pigs. They were in gay colors and smelled of vanilla, maybe. . . . It was a very hot day and the smell in the market, with its piles of raw flesh and wilting flowers, was like the mingled sweetness and corruption she had smelled that other day in the empty cemetery at home: the day she had remembered always until now vaguely as the time she and her brother had found treasure in the opened graves. Instantly upon this thought the dreadful vision faded, and she saw clearly her brother, whose childhood face she had forgotten, standing again in the blazing sunshine, again twelve years old, a pleased sober smile in his eyes, turning the silver dove over and over in his hands.

Questions for Study

1. How old is Miranda? At what stage in life is she? What are her family circumstances? What is her relationship with her brother?

2. What are the "graves" in the story? What do they seem to symbolize? What do the dove and ring possibly symbolize?

3. What is Miranda's epiphany? What change does it seem to signal in her?

4. Why doesn't Paul want Miranda to tell anyone about the rabbits?

5. Why does Porter add the episode about Miranda as an adult?

6. What oppositions does Porter establish? Why?

7. How is this story similar to Wright's "The Man Who Was Almost a Man" (p. 459)?

ELIZABETH BOWEN

The Demon Lover

Elizabeth Bowen (1899–1973) was born in Dublin, Ireland, and spent her childhood in England and on her family's estate in Ireland. She received her education at a private school, graduating in 1916. During World War I she worked at a hospital in Dublin for shell-shocked soldiers. She married Alan Cameron, an executive at Oxford University and then the British Broadcasting Corporation, in 1923. She and her husband settled in London, which became the locale of many of her stories and novels. Her stories, which she began publishing in 1923, and her novels, beginning with *The Hotel* (1927), were increasingly well-received by the critics and public until, by the time of her death in 1973, she had become a distinguished literary figure. In addition to writing fiction, she wrote autobiographical books and incisive essays about literature.

The world of her fiction is the world she grew up in, the middle and upper classes of English society. In the rendering of the physical, moral, and social aspects of this world, her fiction shares qualities with that of Henry James, Edith Wharton, and her friend Virginia Woolf. She often satirizes social snobbery. She portrays strong and complex females. She has a powerful sense of the physical environment and its relationship to the inner lives of her characters. She shows how the mysterious and nonrational can suddenly and unexpectedly disrupt outwardly stable and calm lives. Her best known novel, *The Death of the Heart* (1938), is about a perspicacious teenage girl who devastates the lives of three people. "The Demon Lover" (1946), like a number of her other works, is set in London during World War II.

*T*owards the end of her day in London Mrs. Drover went round to her shut-up house to look for several things she wanted to take away. Some belonged to herself, some to her family, who were by now used to their country life. It was late August; it had been a steamy, showery day: at the moment the trees down the pavement glittered in an escape of humid yellow afternoon sun. Against the next batch of clouds, already piling up ink-dark, broken chimneys and parapets stood out. In her once familiar street, as in any unused channel, an unfamiliar queerness had silted up; a cat wove itself in and out of railings, but no human eye watched Mrs. Drover's return. Shifting some parcels under her arm, she slowly forced round her latchkey in an unwilling lock, then gave the door, which had warped, a push with her knee. Dead air came out to meet her as she went in.

The staircase window having been boarded up, no light came down into the hall. But one door, she could just see, stood ajar, so she went quickly through into the room and unshuttered the big window in there. Now the prosaic woman, looking about her, was more perplexed than she knew by everything that she saw, by traces of her long former habit of life—the yellow smoke-stain up the white marble mantel-piece, the ring left by a vase on the top of the escritoire; the bruise in the wallpaper where, on the door being thrown open widely, the china handle had always hit the wall. The piano, having gone away to be stored, had left what looked like claw-marks on its part of the parquet. Though not much dust had seeped in, each object wore a film of another kind; and, the only ventilation being the chimney, the whole drawing-room smelled of the cold hearth. Mrs. Drover put down her parcels on the escritoire and left the room to proceed upstairs; the things she wanted were in a bedroom chest.

She had been anxious to see how the house was—the part-time caretaker she shared with some neighbors was away this week on his holiday, known to be not yet back. At the best of times he did not look in often, and she was never sure that she trusted him. There were some cracks in the structure, left by the last bombing, on which she was anxious to keep an eye. Not that one could do anything—

A shaft of refracted daylight now lay across the hall. She stopped dead and stared at the hall table—on this lay a letter addressed to her.

She thought first—then the caretaker *must* be back. All the same, who, seeing the house shuttered, would have dropped a letter in at the box? It was not a circular, it was not a bill. And the post office redirected, to the address in the country, every-thing for her that came through the post. The caretaker (even if he *were* back) did not know she was due in London today—her call here had been planned to be a surprise—so his negligence in the manner of this letter, leaving it to wait in the dusk and the dust, annoyed her. Annoyed, she picked up the letter, which bore no stamp. But it can-not be important, or they would know . . . She took the letter rapidly upstairs with her, without a stop to look at the writing till she reached what had been her bedroom, where she let in light. The room looked over the garden and other gardens: the sun had gone in; as the clouds sharpened and lowered, the trees and rank lawns seemed already to smoke with dark. Her reluctance to look again at the letter came from the fact that she felt intruded upon—and by someone contemptuous of her ways. However, in the tenseness preceding the fall of rain she read it: it was a few lines.

> Dear Kathleen: You will not have forgotten that today is our anniversary, and the day we said. The years have gone by at once slowly and fast. In view of the fact that nothing has changed, I shall rely upon you to keep your promise. I was sorry to see you leave London, but was satisfied that you would be back in time. You may expect me, therefore, at the hour arranged. Until then . . .
> K.

Mrs. Drover looked for the date: it was today's. She dropped the letter on to the bedsprings, then picked it up to see the writing again—her lips, beneath the remains of lipstick, beginning to go white. She felt so much the change in her own face that she went to the mirror, polished a clear patch in it and looked at once urgently and stealthily in. She was confronted by a woman of forty-four, with eyes starting out under a hatbrim that had been rather carelessly pulled down. She had not put on any more powder since she left the shop where she ate her solitary tea. The pearls her husband had given her on their marriage hung loose round her now rather thinner throat, slipping in the V of the pink wool jumper her sister knitted last autumn as they sat round the fire. Mrs. Drover's most normal expression was one of controlled worry, but of assent. Since the birth of the third of her little boys, attended by a quite serious illness, she had had an intermittent muscular flicker to the left of her mouth, but in spite of this she could always sustain a manner that was at once energetic and calm.

Turning from her own face as precipitately as she had gone to meet it, she went to the chest where the things were, unlocked it, threw up the lid and knelt to search. But as rain began to come crashing down she could not keep from looking over her shoulder at the stripped bed on which the letter lay. Behind the blanket of rain the clock of the church that still stood struck six—with rapidly heightening apprehension she counted each of the slow strokes. "The hour arranged . . . My God," she said, "*what* hour? How should I . . . ? After twenty-five years . . . "

The young girl talking to the soldier in the garden had not ever completely seen his face. It was dark; they were saying goodbye under a tree. Now and then—for it felt, from not seeing him at this intense moment, as though she had never seen him at all—she verified his presence for these few moments longer by putting out a hand, which he each time pressed, without very much kindness, and painfully, on to one of the breast buttons of his uniform. That cut of the button on the palm of her hand was, principally what she was to carry away. This was so near the end of a leave from France that she could only wish him already gone. It was August 1916. Being not kissed, being drawn away from and looked at intimidated Kathleen till she imagined spectral glitters in the place of his eyes. Turning away and looking back up the lawn she saw, through branches of trees, the drawing-room window alight: she caught a breath for the moment when she could go running back there into the safe arms of her mother and sister, and cry: "What shall I do, what shall I do? He has gone."

Hearing her catch her breath, her fiancé said, without feeling: "Cold?"

"You're going away such a long way."

"Not so far as you think."

"I don't understand?"

"You don't have to," he said. "You will. You know what we said."

"But that was—suppose you—I mean, suppose."

"I shall be with you," he said, "sooner or later. You won't forget that. You need do nothing but wait."

Only a little more than a minute later she was free to run up the silent lawn. Looking in through the window at her mother and sister, who did not for the moment perceive her, she already felt that unnatural promise drive down between her and the rest of all human kind. No other way of having given herself could have made her feel so apart, lost and foresworn. She could not have plighted a more sinister troth.

Kathleen behaved well when, some months later, her fiancé was reported missing, presumed killed. Her family not only supported her but were able to praise her courage without stint because they could not regret, as a husband for her, the man they knew almost nothing about. They hoped she would, in a year or two, console herself—and had it been only a question of consolation things might have gone much straighter ahead. But her trouble, behind just a little grief, was a complete dislocation from everything. She did not reject other lovers, for these failed to appear: for years she failed to attract men—and with the approach of her 'thirties she became natural enough to share her family's anxiousness on this score. She began to put herself out, to wonder; and at thirty-two she was very greatly relieved to find herself being courted by William Drover. She married him, and the two of them settled down in this quiet, arboreal part of Kensington: in this house the years piled up, her children were born and they all lived till they were driven out by the bombs of the next war. Her movements as Mrs. Drover were circumscribed, and she dismissed any idea that they were still watched.

As things were—dead or living the letter-writer sent her only a threat. Unable, for some minutes, to go on kneeling with her back exposed to the empty room, Mrs. Drover rose from the chest to sit on an upright chair whose back was firmly against the wall. The desuetude of her former bedroom, her married London home's whole air of being a cracked cup from which memory, with its reassuring power, had either evaporated or leaked away, made a crisis—and at just this crisis the letter-writer had, knowledgeably, struck. The hollowness of the house this evening cancelled years on years of voices, habits and steps. Through the shut windows she only heard rain fall on the roofs around. To rally herself, she said she was in a mood—and for two or three seconds shutting her eyes, told herself that she had imagined the letter. But she opened them—there it lay on the bed.

On the supernatural side of the letter's entrance she was not permitting her mind to dwell. Who, in London, knew she meant to call at the house today? Evidently, however, this had been known. The caretaker, *had* he come back, had had no cause to expect her: he would have taken the letter in his pocket, to forward it, at his own time, through the post. There was no other sign that the caretaker had been in—but, if not? Letters dropped in at doors of deserted houses do not fly or walk to tables in halls. They do not sit on the dust of empty tables with the air of certainty that they will be found. There is needed some human hand—but nobody but the caretaker had a key. Under circumstances she did not care to consider, a house can be entered without a key. It was possible that she was not alone now. She might be being waited for, downstairs. Waited for—until when? Until "the hour arranged." At least that was not six o'clock: six has struck.

She rose from the chair and went over and locked the door.

The thing was, to get out. To fly? No, not that: she had to catch her train. As a woman whose utter dependability was the keystone of her family life she was not willing to return to the country, to her husband, her little boys and her sister, without the objects she had come up to fetch. Resuming work at the chest she set about making up a number of parcels in a rapid, fumbling-decisive way. These, with her shopping parcels, would be too much to carry; these meant a taxi—at the thought of the taxi her heart went up and her normal breathing resumed. I will ring up the taxi now; the taxi cannot come too soon: I shall hear the taxi out there running its engine, till I walk calmly down to it through the hall. I'll ring up—But no: the telephone is cut off . . . She tugged at a knot she had tied wrong.

The idea of flight . . . He was never kind to me, not really. I don't remember him kind at all. Mother said he never considered me. He was set on me, that was what it was—not love. Not love, not meaning a person well. What did he do, to make me promise like that? I can't remember—But she found that she could.

She remembered with such dreadful acuteness that the twenty-five years since then dissolved like smoke and she instinctively looked for the weal left by the button on the palm of her hand. She remembered not only all that he said and did but the complete suspension of *her* existence during that August week. I was not myself—they all told me so at the time. She remembered—but with one white burning blank as where acid has dropped on a photograph: *under no conditions* could she remember his face.

So, wherever he may be waiting, I shall not know him. You have no time to run from a face you do not expect.

The thing was to get to the taxi before any clock struck what could be the hour. She would slip down the street and round the side of the square to where the square gave on the main road. She would return in the taxi, safe, to her own door, and bring the solid driver into the house with her to pick up the parcels from room to room. The idea of the taxi driver made her decisive, bold: she unlocked her door, went to the top of the staircase and listened down.

She heard nothing—but while she was hearing nothing the *passé* air of the staircase was disturbed by a draught that travelled up to her face. It emanated from the basement: down there a door or window was being opened by someone who chose this moment to leave the house.

The rain had stopped; the pavements steamily shone as Mrs. Drover let herself out by inches from her own front door into the empty street. The unoccupied houses opposite continued to meet her look with their damaged stare. Making towards the thoroughfare and the taxi, she tried not to keep looking behind. Indeed, the silence was so intense—one of those creeks of London silence exaggerated this summer by the damage of war—that no tread could have gained on hers unheard. Where her street debouched on the square where people went on living, she grew conscious of, and checked, her unnatural pace. Across the open end of the square two buses impassively passed each other: women, a perambulator, cyclists, a man wheeling a barrow signalized, once again, the ordinary flow of life. At the square's most populous corner should be—and was—the short taxi rank. This evening, only one taxi—but this, although it presented its blank rump, appeared already to be alertly waiting for her. Indeed, without looking round the driver started his engine as she panted up from behind and put her hand on the door. As she did so, the clock struck seven. The taxi faced the main road: to make the trip back to her house it would have to turn—she had settled back on the seat and the taxi had turned before she, surprised by its knowing movement, recollected that she had not "said where." She leaned forward to scratch at the glass panel that divided the driver's head from her own.

The driver braked to what was almost a stop, turned round and slid the glass panel back: the jolt of this flung Mrs. Drover forward till her face was almost into the glass. Through the aperture driver and passenger, not six inches between them, remained for an eternity eye to eye. Mrs. Drover's mouth hung open for some seconds before she could issue her first scream. After that she continued to scream freely and to beat with her gloved hands on the glass all round as the taxi, accelerating without mercy, made off with her into the hinterland of deserted streets.

Questions for Study

1. In what historical periods is this story set? How do the events of those periods affect the characters and the action?

2. What is the atmosphere of the story? What details help create the atmosphere?

3. What kind of person is Mrs. Drover? What do we learn about her emotional state from her behavior in the past and the present? Why did she marry Mr. Drover? Has their marriage been successful?

4. What characterizes the relationship between Mrs. Drover and her fiancé?

5. One critic has suggested that Mrs. Drover hallucinates some of the events. Is there any evidence to support this interpretation?

6. The title of the story comes from the medieval ballad "The Demon Lover." (See p. 309 for the text of the poem.) What parallels are there between the story and the poem?

SHIRLEY JACKSON

The Lottery

Shirley Jackson (1919–65) was born and spent her early childhood in California. Her family moved to Rochester, New York, when she was fourteen. Throughout her life she suffered from a sense of inferiority. She dropped out of the University of Rochester after her freshman year because of depression. She entered Syracuse University in 1937, where she met her future husband, Stanley Edgar Hyman, and was active with him in literary pursuits. After her graduation and marriage in 1940, they had four children and both had highly successful careers, Hyman as a literary critic and Jackson as a writer of nonfiction, short stories, and novels. Two of Jackson's nonfiction books, *Life Among the Savages* (1953) and *Raising Demons* (1957), are humorous accounts of her experiences as mother and wife. Jackson is best known for her gothic stories and novels, especially "The Lottery," which appeared in *The New Yorker* in 1948. *The New Yorker* received more mail in response to "The Lottery" than to anything published in the magazine before. Most of the mail expressed anger and outrage about the story. As in "The Lottery," Jackson wove into her gothic fiction social commentary and psychological analysis. In *The Haunting of Hill House* (1959), the main character escapes from her limited life as a spinster into the "family" of tortured ghosts who haunt the house. The novel *We Have Always Lived in the Castle* (1962) is a psychological study of a child who murders most of the members of her family.

*T*he morning of June 27th was clear and sunny, with the fresh warmth of a full-summer day; the flowers were blossoming profusely and the grass was richly green. The people of the village began to gather in the square, between the post office and the bank, around ten o'clock; in some towns there were so many people that the lottery took two days and had to be started on June 26th, but in this village, where there were only about three hundred people, the whole lottery took less than two hours, so it could begin at ten o'clock in the morning and still be through in time to allow the villagers to get home for noon dinner.

The children assembled first, of course. School was recently over for the summer, and the feeling of liberty sat uneasily on most of them; they tended to gather together quietly for a while before they broke into boisterous play, and their talk was still of the classroom and the teacher, of books and reprimands. Bobby Martin had already stuffed his pockets full of stones, and the other boys soon followed his example, selecting the smoothest and roundest stones; Bobby and Harry Jones and Dickie Delacroix—the villagers pronounced his name "Dellacroy"—eventually made a great pile of stones in one corner of the square and guarded it against the raids of the other boys. The girls stood aside, talking among themselves, looking over their shoulders at the boys, and the very small children rolled in the dust or clung to the hands of their older brothers or sisters.

Soon the men began to gather, surveying their own children, speaking of planting and rain, tractors and taxes. They stood together, away from the pile of stones in the corner, and their jokes were quiet and they smiled rather than laughed. The women, wearing faded house dresses and sweaters, came shortly after their menfolk. They greeted one another and exchanged bits of gossip as they went to join their husbands. Soon the women, standing by their husbands, began to call to their children, and the children came reluctantly, having to be called four or five times. Bobby Martin ducked under his mother's grasping hand and ran, laughing, back to the pile of stones. His father spoke up sharply, and Bobby came quickly and took his place between his father and his oldest brother.

The lottery was conducted—as were the square dances, the teenage club, the Halloween program—by Mr. Summers, who had time and energy to devote to civic activities. He was a round-faced, jovial man and he ran the coal business, and people were sorry for him, because he had no children and his wife was a scold. When he arrived in the square, carrying the black wooden box, there was a murmur of conversation among the villagers, and he waved and called, "Little late today, folks." The postmaster, Mr. Graves, followed him, carrying a three-legged stool, and the stool was put in the center of the square and Mr. Summers set the black box down on it. The villagers kept their distance, leaving a space between themselves and the stool, and when Mr. Summers said, "Some of you fellows want to give me a hand?" there was a hesitation before two men, Mr. Martin and his oldest son, Baxter, came forward to hold the box steady on the stool while Mr. Summers stirred up the papers inside it.

The original paraphernalia for the lottery had been lost long ago, and the black box now resting on the stool had been put into use even before Old Man Warner, the oldest man in town, was born. Mr. Summers spoke frequently to the villagers about making a new box, but no one liked to upset even as much tradition as was represented by the black box. There was a story that the present box had been made with some pieces of the box that had preceded it, the one that had been constructed when the first people settled down to make a village here. Every year, after the lottery, Mr. Summers began talking again about a new box, but every year the subject was allowed to fade off without anything's being done. The black box grew shabbier each year; by now it was no longer completely black but splintered badly along one side to show the original wood color, and in some places faded or stained.

Mr. Martin and his oldest son, Baxter, held the black box securely on the stool until Mr. Summers had stirred the papers thoroughly with his hand. Because so much of the ritual had been forgotten or discarded, Mr. Summers had been successful in having slips of paper substituted for the chips of wood that had been used for generations. Chips of wood, Mr. Summers had argued, had been all very well when the village was tiny, but now that the population was more than three hundred and likely to keep on growing, it was necessary to use something that would fit more easily into the black box. The night before the lottery, Mr. Summers and Mr. Graves made up the slips of paper and put them in the box, and it was then taken to the safe of Mr. Summers's coal company and locked up until Mr. Summers was ready to take it to the square next morning. The rest of the year, the box was put away, sometimes one place, sometimes another; it had spent one year in Mr. Graves's barn and another year underfoot in the post office, and sometimes it was set on a shelf in the Martin grocery and left there.

There was a great deal of fussing to be done before Mr. Summers declared the lottery open. There were the lists to make up—of heads of families, heads of households in each family, members of each household in each family. There was the proper swearing-in of Mr. Summers by the postmaster, as the official of the lottery; at one time some people remembered, there had been a recital of some sort, performed by the official of the lottery, a perfunctory, tuneless chant that had been rattled off duly each year; some people believed that the official of the lottery used to stand just so when he said or sang it, others believed that he was supposed to walk among the people, but years and years ago this part of the ritual had been allowed to lapse. There had been, also, a ritual salute, which the official of the lottery had had to use in addressing each person who came up to draw from the box, but this also had changed with time, until now it was felt necessary only for the official to speak to each person approaching. Mr. Summers was very good at all this; in his clean white shirt and blue jeans, with one hand resting carelessly on the black box, he seemed very proper and important as he talked interminably to Mr. Graves and the Martins.

Just as Mr. Summers finally left off talking and turned to the assembled villagers, Mrs. Hutchinson came hurriedly along the path to the square, her sweater thrown over her shoulders, and slid into place in the back of the crowd. "Clean forgot what day it was," she said to Mrs. Delacroix, who stood next to her, and they both laughed softly. "Thought my old man was out back stacking wood," Mrs. Hutchinson went on, "and then I looked out the window and the kids was gone, and then I remembered it was the twenty-seventh and came a-running." She dried her hands on her apron, and Mrs. Delacroix said, "You're in time, though. They're still talking away up there."

Mrs. Hutchinson craned her neck to see through the crowd and found her husband and children standing near the front. She tapped Mrs. Delacroix on the arm as a farewell and began to make her way through the crowd. The people separated good-humoredly to let her through; two or three people said, in voices just loud enough to be heard across the crowd, "Here comes your Missus, Hutchinson," and "Bill, she made it after all." Mrs. Hutchinson reached her husband, and Mr. Summers, who had been waiting, said cheerfully, "Thought we were going to have to get on without you, Tessie." Mrs. Hutchinson said, grinning, "Wouldn't have me leave m'dishes in the sink, now, would you Joe?" and soft laughter ran through the crowd as the people stirred back into position after Mrs. Hutchinson's arrival.

"Well, now," Mr. Summers said soberly, "guess we better get started, get this over with, so's we can go back to work. Anybody ain't here?"

"Dunbar," several people said. "Dunbar, Dunbar."

Mr. Summers consulted his list. "Clyde Dunbar," he said. "That's right. He's broke his leg, hasn't he? Who's drawing for him?"

"Me, I guess," a woman said, and Mr. Summers turned to look at her. "Wife draws for her husband," Mr. Summers said. "Don't you have a grown boy to do it for you, Janey?" Although Mr. Summers and everyone else in the village knew the answer perfectly well, it was the business of the official of the lottery to ask such questions formally. Mr. Summers waited with an expression of polite interest while Mrs. Dunbar answered.

"Horace's not but sixteen yet," Mrs. Dunbar said regretfully. "Guess I gotta fill in for the old man this year."

"Right," Mr. Summers said. He made a note on the list he was holding. Then he asked, "Watson boy drawing this year?"

A tall boy in the crowd raised his hand. "Here," he said. "I'm drawing for m'mother and me." He blinked his eyes nervously and ducked his head as several voices in the crowd said things like "Good fellow, Jack," and "Glad to see your mother's got a man to do it."

"Well," Mr. Summers said, "guess that's everyone. Old Man Warner make it?"

"Here," a voice said, and Mr. Summers nodded.

A sudden hush fell on the crowd as Mr. Summers cleared his throat and looked at the list. "All ready?" he called. "Now, I'll read the names—heads of families first—and the men come up and take a paper out of the box. Keep the paper folded in your hand without looking at it until everyone has had a turn. Everything clear?"

The people had done it so many times that they only half listened to the directions; most of them were quiet, wetting their lips, not looking around. Then Mr. Summers raised one hand high and said, "Adams." A man disengaged himself from the crowd and came forward. "Hi, Steve," Mr. Summers said, and Mr. Adams said, "Hi, Joe." They grinned at one another humorlessly and nervously. Then Mr. Adams reached into the black box and took out a folded paper. He held it firmly by one corner as he turned and went hastily back to his place in the crowd, where he stood a little apart from his family, not looking down at his hand.

"Allen," Mr. Summers said. "Anderson. . . . Bentham."

"Seems like there's no time at all between lotteries any more," Mrs. Delacroix said to Mrs. Graves in the back row. "Seems like we got through with the last one only last week."

"Time sure goes fast," Mrs. Graves said.

"Clark. . . . Delacroix."

"There goes my old man," Mrs. Delacroix said. She held her breath while her husband went forward.

"Dunbar," Mr. Summers said, and Mrs. Dunbar went steadily to the box while one of the women said, "Go on, Janey," and another said, "There she goes."

"We're next," Mrs. Graves said. She watched while Mr. Graves came around from the side of the box, greeted Mr. Summers gravely, and selected a slip of paper from the box. By now, all through the crowd there were men holding the small folded papers in their large hands, turning them over and over nervously. Mrs. Dunbar and her two sons stood together, Mrs. Dunbar holding the slip of paper.

"Harburt. . . . Hutchinson."

"Get up there, Bill," Mrs. Hutchinson said, and the people near her laughed.

"Jones."

"They do say," Mr. Adams said to Old Man Warner, who stood next to him, "that over in the north village they're talking of giving up the lottery."

Old Man Warner snorted. "Pack of crazy fools," he said. "Listening to the young folks, nothing's good enough for *them*. Next thing you know, they'll be wanting to go back to living in caves, nobody work any more, live *that* way for a while. Used to be a saying about 'Lottery in June, corn be heavy soon.' First thing you know, we'd all be eating stewed chickweed and acorns. There's *always* been a lottery," he added petulantly. "Bad enough to see young Joe Summers up there joking with everybody."

"Some places have already quit lotteries," Mrs. Adams said.

"Nothing but trouble in *that*," Old Man Warner said stoutly. "Pack of young fools."

"Martin." And Bobby Martin watched his father go forward. "Overdyke. . . . Percy."

"I wish they'd hurry," Mrs. Dunbar said to her older son. "I wish they'd hurry."

"They're almost through," her son said.

"You get ready to run tell Dad," Mrs. Dunbar said.

Mr. Summers called his own name and then stepped forward precisely and selected a slip from the box. Then he called, "Warner."

"Seventy-seventh year I been in the lottery," Old Man Warner said as he went through the crowd. "Seventy-seventh time."

"Watson." The tall boy came awkwardly through the crowd. Someone said, "Don't be nervous, Jack," and Mr. Summers said, "Take your time, son."

"Zanini."

After that, there was a long pause, a breathless pause, until Mr. Summers, holding his slip of paper in the air, said, "All right, fellows." For a minute, no one moved, and then all the slips of paper were opened. Suddenly, all the women began to speak at once, saying, "Who is it?," "Who's got it?," "Is it the Dunbars?," "Is it the Watsons?" Then the voices began to say, "It's Hutchinson. It's Bill," "Bill Hutchinson's got it."

"Go tell your father," Mrs. Dunbar said to her older son.

People began to look around to see the Hutchinsons. Bill Hutchinson was standing quiet, staring down at the paper in his hand. Suddenly, Tessie Hutchinson shouted to Mr. Summers, "You didn't give him time enough to take any paper he wanted. I saw you. It wasn't fair!"

"Be a good sport, Tessie," Mrs. Delacroix called, and Mrs. Graves said, "All of us took the same chance."

"Shut up, Tessie," Bill Hutchinson said.

"Well, everyone," Mr. Summers said, "that was done pretty fast, and now we've got to be hurrying a little more to get done in time." He consulted his next list. "Bill," he said, "you draw for the Hutchinson family. You got any other households in the Hutchinsons?"

"There's Don and Eva," Mrs. Hutchinson yelled. "Make *them* take their chance!"

"Daughters draw with their husbands' families, Tessie," Mr. Summers said gently. "You know that as well as anyone else."

"It wasn't *fair*," Tessie said.

"I guess not, Joe," Bill Hutchinson said regretfully. "My daughter draws with her husband's family, that's only fair. And I've got no other family except the kids."

"Then, as far as drawing for families is concerned, it's you," Mr. Summers said in explanation, "and as far as drawing for households is concerned, that's you, too. Right?"

"Right," Bill Hutchinson said.

"How many kids, Bill?" Mr. Summers asked formally.

"Three," Bill Hutchinson said. "There's Bill, Jr., and Nancy, and little Dave. And Tessie and me."

"All right, then," Mr. Summers said. "Harry, you got their tickets back?"

Mr. Graves nodded and held up the slips of paper. "Put them in the box, then," Mr. Summers directed. "Take Bill's and put it in."

"I think we ought to start over," Mrs. Hutchinson said, as quietly as she could. "I tell you it wasn't *fair.* You didn't give him time enough to choose. *Every*body saw that."

Mr. Graves had selected the five slips and put them in the box, and he dropped all the papers but those onto the ground, where the breeze caught them and lifted them off.

"Listen, everybody," Mrs. Hutchinson was saying to the people around her.

"Ready, Bill?" Mr. Summers asked, and Bill Hutchinson, with one quick glance around at his wife and children, nodded.

"Remember," Mr. Summers said, "take the slips and keep them folded until each person has taken one. Harry, you help little Dave." Mr. Graves took the hand of the little boy, who came willingly with him up to the box. "Take a paper out of the box, Davy," Mr. Summers said. Davy put his hand into the box and laughed. "Take just *one* paper," Mr. Summers said. "Harry, you hold it for him." Mr. Graves took the child's hand and removed the folded paper from the tight fist and held it while little Dave stood next to him and looked up at him wonderingly.

"Nancy next," Mr. Summers said. Nancy was twelve, and her school friends breathed heavily as she went forward, switching her skirt, and took a slip daintily from the box. "Bill, Jr.," Mr. Summers said, and Billy, his face red and his feet overlarge, nearly knocked the box over as he got a paper out. "Tessie," Mr. Summers said. She hesitated for a minute, looking around defiantly, and then set her lips and went up to the box. She snatched a paper out and held it behind her.

"Bill," Mr. Summers said, and Bill Hutchinson reached into the box and felt around, bringing his hand out at last with the slip of paper in it.

The crowd was quiet. A girl whispered, "I hope it's not Nancy," and the sound of the whisper reached the edges of the crowd.

"It's not the way it used to be," Old Man Warner said clearly. "People ain't the way they used to be."

"All right," Mr. Summers said. "Open the papers. Harry, you open little Dave's."

Mr. Graves opened the slip of paper and there was a general sigh through the crowd as he held it up and everyone could see that it was blank. Nancy and Bill, Jr., opened theirs at the same time, and both beamed and laughed, turning around to the crowd and holding their slips of paper above their heads.

"Tessie," Mr. Summers said. There was a pause, and then Mr. Summers looked at Bill Hutchinson, and Bill unfolded his paper and showed it. It was blank.

"It's Tessie," Mr. Summers said, and his voice was hushed. "Show us her paper, Bill."

Bill Hutchinson went over to his wife and forced the slip of paper out of her hand. It had a black spot on it, the black spot Mr. Summers had made the night before with the heavy pencil in the coal-company office. Bill Hutchinson held it up, and there was a stir in the crowd.

"All right, folks," Mr. Summers said. "Let's finish quickly."

Although the villagers had forgotten the ritual and lost the original black box, they still remembered to use stones. The pile of stones the boys had made earlier was ready; there were stones on the ground with the blowing scraps of paper that had come out of the box. Mrs. Delacroix selected a stone so large she had to pick it up with both hands and turned to Mrs. Dunbar. "Come on," she said. "Hurry up."

Mrs. Dunbar had small stones in both hands, and she said, gasping for breath, "I can't run at all. You'll have to go ahead and I'll catch up with you."

The children had stones already, and someone gave little Davy Hutchinson a few pebbles.

Tessie Hutchinson was in the center of a cleared space by now, and she held her hands out desperately as the villagers moved in on her. "It isn't fair," she said. A stone hit her on the side of the head.

Old Man Warner was saying, "Come on, come on, everyone." Steve Adams was in the front of the crowd of villagers, with Mrs. Graves beside him.

"It isn't fair, it isn't right," Mrs. Hutchinson screamed, and then they were upon her.

Questions for Study

1. What details at the beginning establish the ordinariness of this village? At what point do you realize that things are far from ordinary?

2. What seems to be the origin of lotteries? Why do the villagers pay so much attention to the forms and rituals of the lottery? Why does Old Man Warner support having lotteries?

3. The villagers risk their lives in order to have lotteries. Why? What is so valuable to them about lotteries?

4. Does this story have any connection to actual practices in twentieth century life?

5. What is the irony of Mrs. Hutchinson's final statement? What does it reveal about her and about human nature in general?

6. Why do you think so many readers were outraged by the story when it appeared in *The New Yorker* in 1948?

BERNARD MALAMUD

The Magic Barrel

Bernard Malamud (1914–86) was born into a Jewish family in Brooklyn, New York, and lived there for the early part of his life. Like Morris Bober in his second novel *The Assistant,* his father was a grocer who had a difficult time making a go of his business. Malamud earned a B.A. from City College, New York, in 1936 and an M.A. from

Columbia University in 1942. He taught English for twelve years at Oregon State University. During that time he published his first collection of stories, *The Magic Barrel* (1958), and his first two novels. *The Natural* (1952) is about the rise and fall of a gifted baseball player, and *The Assistant* (1957) is about the redemption of an anti-Semitic Italian youth who becomes involved with a family similar to Malamud's own. Malamud left Oregon State in 1961 to teach at Bennington College. His third novel, *A New Life* (1961), is a satirical account of his experiences at Oregon State.

Much of Malamud's fiction deals with the Jewish experience in New York and other urban areas. He was influenced by the Yiddish fiction of Eastern Europe, which contains elements of magic and the supernatural and has a folkloric quality. Malamud's world is often bleak and lonely. His characters are impoverished materially and spiritually. They desperately need redemption. Some of them, like Roy Hobbs, the superstar baseball hero of *The Natural,* have redemption in their grasp only to let it slip away. For a few characters, however, redemption comes unexpectedly and mysteriously. Toward the end of his career, Malamud turned to another kind of redemption, social reform. His novel *The Fixer* (1966), although set in Russia at the turn of the century, parallels the social problems of the 1960s and concludes with a call for social change. *The Tenants* (1971), one of his last novels, probes the causes of racial hatred and violence.

N ot long ago there lived in uptown New York, in a small, almost meager room, though crowded with books, Leo Finkle, a rabbinical student in the Yeshivah University. Finkle, after six years of study, was to be ordained in June and had been advised by an acquaintance that he might find it easier to win himself a congregation if he were married. Since he had no present prospects of marriage, after two tormented days of turning it over in his mind, he called in Pinye Salzman, a marriage broker whose two-line advertisement he had read in the *Forward.*°

The matchmaker appeared one night out of the dark fourth-floor hallway of the graystone rooming house where Finkle lived, grasping a black, strapped portfolio that had been worn thin with use. Salzman, who had been long in the business, was of slight but dignified build, wearing an old hat, and an overcoat too short and tight for him. He smelled frankly of fish, which he loved to eat, and although he was missing a few teeth, his presence was not displeasing, because of an amiable manner curiously contrasted with mournful eyes. His voice, his lips, his wisp of beard, his bony fingers were animated, but give him a moment of repose and his mild blue eyes revealed a depth of sadness, a characteristic that put Leo a little at ease although the situation, for him, was inherently tense.

Forward. The *Jewish Daily Forward,* a Yiddish language newspaper, published in New York City.

He at once informed Salzman why he had asked him to come, explaining that his home was in Cleveland, and that but for his parents, who had married comparatively late in life, he was alone in the world. He had for six years devoted himself almost entirely to his studies, as a result of which, understandably, he had found himself without time for a social life and the company of young women. Therefore he thought it the better part of trial and error—of embarrassing fumbling—to call in an experienced person to advise him on these matters. He remarked in passing that the function of the marriage broker was ancient and honorable, highly approved in the Jewish community, because it made practical the necessary without hindering joy. Moreover, his own parents had been brought together by a matchmaker. They had made, if not a financially profitable marriage—since neither had possessed any worldly goods to speak of—at least a successful one in the sense of their everlasting devotion to each other. Salzman listened in embarrassed surprise, sensing a sort of apology. Later, however, he experienced a glow of pride in his work, an emotion that had left him years ago, and he heartily approved of Finkle.

The two went to their business. Leo had led Salzman to the only clear place in the room, a table near a window that overlooked the lamp-lit city. He seated himself at the matchmaker's side but facing him, attempting by an act of will to suppress the unpleasant tickle in his throat. Salzman eagerly unstrapped his portfolio and removed a loose rubber band from a thin packet of much-handled cards. As he flipped through them, a gesture and sound that physically hurt Leo, the student pretended not to see and gazed steadfastly out the window. Although it was still February, winter was on its last legs, signs of which he had for the first time in years begun to notice. He now observed the round white moon, moving high in the sky through a cloud menagerie, and watched with half-open mouth as it penetrated a huge hen, and dropped out of her like an egg laying itself. Salzman, though pretending through eyeglasses he had just slipped on, to be engaged in scanning the writing on the cards, stole occasional glances at the young man's distinguished face, noting with pleasure the long, severe scholar's nose, brown eyes heavy with learning, sensitive yet ascetic lips, and a certain, almost hollow quality of the dark cheeks. He gazed around at shelves upon shelves of books and let out a soft, contented sigh.

When Leo's eyes fell upon the cards, he counted six spread out in Salzman's hand.

"So few?" he asked in disappointment.

"You wouldn't believe me how much cards I got in my office," Salzman replied. "The drawers are already filled to the top, so I keep them now in a barrel, but is every girl good for a new rabbi?"

Leo blushed at this, regretting all he had revealed of himself in a curriculum vitae he had sent to Salzman. He had thought it best to acquaint him with his strict standards and specifications, but in having done so, felt he had told the marriage broker more than was absolutely necessary.

He hesitantly inquired, "Do you keep photographs of your clients on file?"

"First comes family, amount of dowry, also what kind promises," Salzman replied, unbuttoning his tight coat and settling himself in the chair. "After comes pictures, rabbi."

"Call me Mr. Finkle. I'm not yet a rabbi."

Salzman said he would, but instead called him doctor, which he changed to rabbi when Leo was not listening too attentively.

Salzman adjusted his horn-rimmed spectacles, gently cleared his throat and read in an eager voice the contents of the top card:

"Sophie P. Twenty four years. Widow one year. No children. Educated high school and two years college. Father promises eight thousand dollars. Has wonderful wholesale business. Also real estate. On the mother's side comes teachers, also one actor. Well known on Second Avenue."

Leo gazed up in surprise. "Did you say a widow?"

"A widow don't mean spoiled, rabbi. She lived with her husband maybe four months. He was a sick boy she made a mistake to marry him."

"Marrying a widow has never entered my mind."

"This is because you have no experience. A widow, especially if she is young and healthy like this girl, is a wonderful person to marry. She will be thankful to you the rest of her life. Believe me, if I was looking now for a bride, I would marry a widow."

Leo reflected, then shook his head.

Salzman hunched his shoulders in an almost imperceptible gesture of disappointment. He placed the card down on the wooden table and began to read another:

"Lily H. High school teacher. Regular. Not a substitute. Has savings and new Dodge car. Lived in Paris one year. Father is successful dentist thirty-five years. Interested in professional man. Well Americanized family. Wonderful opportunity."

"I knew her personally," said Salzman. "I wish you could see this girl. She is a doll. Also very intelligent. All day you could talk to her about books and theyater and what not. She also knows current events."

"I don't believe you mentioned her age?"

"Her age?" Salzman said, raising his brows. "Her age is thirty-two years."

Leo said after a while, "I'm afraid that seems a little too old."

Salzman let out a laugh. "So how old are you, rabbi?"

"Twenty-seven."

"So what is the difference, tell me, between twenty-seven and thirty-two? My own wife is seven years older than me. So what did I suffer?—Nothing. If Rothschild's a daughter wants to marry you, would you say on account her age, no?"

"Yes," Leo said dryly.

Salzman shook off the no in the yes. "Five years don't mean a thing. I give you my word that when you will live with her for one week you will forget her age. What does it mean five years—that she lived more and knows more than somebody who is younger? On this girl, God bless her, years are not wasted. Each one that it comes makes better the bargain."

"What subject does she teach in high school?"

"Languages. If you heard the way she speaks French, you will think it is music. I am in the business twenty-five years, and I recommend her with my whole heart. Believe me, I know what I'm talking, rabbi."

"What's on the next card?" Leo said abruptly.

Salzman reluctantly turned up the third card:

"Ruth K. Nineteen years. Honor student. Father offers thirteen thousand cash to the right bridegroom. He is a medical doctor. Stomach specialist with marvelous practice. Brother in law owns own garment business. Particular people."

Salzman looked as if he had read his trump card.

"Did you say nineteen?" Leo asked with interest.

"On the dot."

"Is she attractive?" He blushed. "Pretty?"

Salzman kissed his finger tips. "A little doll. On this I give you my word. Let me call the father tonight and you will see what means pretty."

But Leo was troubled. "You're sure she's that young?"

"This I am positive. The father will show you the birth certificate."

"Are you positive there isn't something wrong with her?" Leo insisted.

"Who says there is wrong?"

"I don't understand why an American girl her age should go to a marriage broker."

A smile spread over Salzman's face.

"So for the same reason you went, she comes."

Leo flushed. "I am pressed for time."

Salzman, realizing he had been tactless, quickly explained. "The father came, not her. He wants she should have the best, so he looks around himself. When we will locate the right boy he will introduce him and encourage. This makes a better marriage than if a young girl without experience takes for herself. I don't have to tell you this."

"But don't you think this young girl believes in love?" Leo spoke uneasily.

Salzman was about to guffaw but caught himself and said soberly, "Love comes with the right person, not before."

Leo parted dry lips but did not speak. Noticing that Salzman had snatched a glance at the next card, he cleverly asked, "How is her health?"

"Perfect," Salzman said, breathing with difficulty. "Of course, she is a little lame on her right foot from an auto accident that it happened to her when she was twelve years, but nobody notices on account she is so brilliant and also beautiful."

Leo got up heavily and went to the window. He felt curiously bitter and upbraided himself for having called in the marriage broker. Finally, he shook his head.

"Why not?" Salzman persisted, the pitch of his voice rising.

"Because I detest stomach specialists."

"So what do you care what is his business? After you marry her do you need him? Who says he must come every Friday night in your house?"

Ashamed of the way the talk was going, Leo dismissed Salzman, who went home with heavy, melancholy eyes.

Though he had felt only relief at the marriage broker's departure, Leo was in low spirits the next day. He explained it as arising from Salzman's failure to produce a suitable bride for him. He did not care for his type of clientele. But when Leo found himself hesitating whether to seek out another matchmaker, one more polished than Pinye, he wondered if it could be—his protestations to the contrary, and although he honored his father and mother—that he did not, in essence, care for the matchmaking institution? This thought he quickly put out of mind yet found himself still upset. All day he ran around in the woods—missed an important appointment, forgot to give out his laundry, walked out of a Broadway cafeteria without paying and had to run back with the ticket in his hand; had even not recognized his landlady in the street when she passed with a friend and courteously called out, "A good evening to you, Doctor Finkle." By nightfall, however, he had regained sufficient calm to sink his nose into a book and there found peace from his thoughts.

Almost at once there came a knock on the door. Before Leo could say enter, Salzman, commercial cupid, was standing in the room. His face was gray and meager, his expression hungry, and he looked as if he would expire on his feet. Yet the marriage broker managed, by some trick of the muscles, to display a broad smile.

"So good evening. I am invited?"

Leo nodded, disturbed to see him again, yet unwilling to ask the man to leave.

Beaming still, Salzman laid his portfolio on the table. "Rabbi, I got for you tonight good news."

"I've asked you not to call me rabbi. I'm still a student."

"Your worries are finished. I have for you a first-class bride."

"Leave me in peace concerning this subject." Leo pretended lack of interest.

"The world will dance at your wedding."

"Please, Mr. Salzman, no more."

"But first must come back my strength," Salzman said weakly. He fumbled with the portfolio straps and took out of the leather case an oily paper bag, from which he extracted a hard, seeded roll and a small, smoked white fish. With a quick motion of his hand he stripped the fish out of its skin and began ravenously to chew. "All day in a rush," he muttered.

Leo watched him eat.

"A sliced tomato you have maybe?" Salzman hesitantly inquired.

"No."

The marriage broker shut his eyes and ate. When he had finished he carefully cleaned up the crumbs and rolled up the remains of the fish, in the paper bag. His spectacled eyes roamed the room until he discovered, amid some piles of books, a one-burner gas stove. Lifting his hat he humbly asked, "A glass tea you got, rabbi?"

Conscience-stricken, Leo rose and brewed the tea. He served it with a chunk of lemon and two cubes of lump sugar, delighting Salzman.

After he had drunk his tea, Salzman's strength and good spirits were restored.

"So tell me, rabbi," he said amiably, "you considered some more the three clients I mentioned yesterday?"

"There was no need to consider."

"Why not?"

"None of them suits me."

"What then suits you?"

Leo let it pass because he could give only a confused answer.

Without waiting for a reply, Salzman asked, "You remember this girl I talked to you—the high school teacher?"

"Age thirty-two?"

But, surprisingly, Salzman's face lit in a smile. "Age twenty-nine."

Leo shot him a look. "Reduced from thirty-two?"

"A mistake," Salzman avowed. "I talked today with the dentist. He took me to his safety deposit box and showed me the birth certificate. She was twenty-nine years last August. They made her a party in the mountains where she went for her vacation.

When her father spoke to me the first time I forgot to write the age and I told you thirty-two, but now I remember this was a different client, a widow."

"The same one you told me about? I thought she was twenty-four?"

"A different. Am I responsible that the world is filled with widows?"

"No, but I'm not interested in them, nor for that matter, in school teachers."

Salzman pulled his clasped hands to his breast. Looking at the ceiling he devoutly exclaimed, "Yiddishe kinder, what can I say to somebody that he is not interested in high school teachers? So what then you are interested?"

Leo flushed but controlled himself.

"In what else will you be interested," Salzman went on, "if you not interested in this fine girl that she speaks four languages and has personally in the bank ten thousand dollars? Also her father guarantees further twelve thousand. Also she has a new car, wonderful clothes, talks on all subjects, and she will give you a first-class home and children. How near do we come in our life to paradise?"

"If she's so wonderful, why wasn't she married ten years ago?"

"Why?" said Salzman with a heavy laugh. "—Why? Because she is *partikiler*. This is why. She wants the *best*."

Leo was silent, amused at how he had entangled himself. But Salzman had aroused his interest in Lily H., and he began seriously to consider calling on her. When the marriage broker observed how intently Leo's mind was at work on the facts he had supplied, he felt certain they would soon come to an agreement.

Late Saturday afternoon, conscious of Salzman, Leo Finkle walked with Lily Hirschorn along Riverside Drive. He walked briskly and erectly, wearing with distinction the black fedora he had that morning taken with trepidation out of the dusty hat box on his closet shelf, and the heavy black Saturday coat he had thoroughly whisked clean. Leo also owned a walking stick, a present from a distant relative, but quickly put temptation aside and did not use it. Lily, petite and not unpretty, had on something signifying the approach of spring. She was au courant, animatedly, with all sorts of subjects, and he weighed her words and found her surprisingly sound—score another for Salzman, whom he uneasily sensed to be somewhere around, hiding perhaps high in a tree along the street, flashing the lady signals with a pocket mirror; or perhaps a cloven-hoofed Pan, piping nuptial ditties as he danced his invisible way before them, strewing wild buds on the walk and purple grapes in their path, symbolizing fruit of a union, though there was of course still none.

Lily startled Leo by remarking, "I was thinking of Mr. Salzman, a curious figure, wouldn't you say?"

Not certain what to answer, he nodded.

She bravely went on, blushing, "I for one am grateful for his introducing us. Aren't you?"

He courteously replied, "I am."

"I mean," she said with a little laugh—and it was all in good taste, or at least gave the effect of being not in bad—"do you mind that we came together so?"

He was not displeased with her honesty, recognizing that she meant to set the relationship aright, and understanding that it took a certain amount of experience in life, and courage, to want to do it quite that way. One had to have some sort of past to make that kind of beginning.

He said that he did not mind. Salzman's function was traditional and honorable—valuable for what it might achieve, which, he pointed out, was frequently nothing.

Lily agreed with a sigh. They walked on for a while and she said after a long silence, again with a nervous laugh, "Would you mind if I asked you something a little bit personal? Frankly, I find the subject fascinating." Although Leo shrugged, she went on half embarrassedly, "How was it that you came to your calling? I mean was it a sudden passionate inspiration?"

Leo, after a time, slowly replied, "I was always interested in the Law."

"You saw revealed in it the presence of the Highest?"

He nodded and changed the subject. "I understand that you spent a little time in Paris, Miss Hirschorn?"

"Oh, did Mr. Salzman tell you, Rabbi Finkle?" Leo winced but she went on, "It was ages ago and almost forgotten. I remember I had to return for my sister's wedding."

And Lily would not be put off. "When," she asked in a trembly voice, "did you become enamored of God?"

He stared at her. Then it came to him that she was talking not about Leo Finkle, but of a total stranger, some mystical figure, perhaps even passionate prophet that Salzman had dreamed up for her—no relation to the living or dead. Leo trembled with rage and weakness. The trickster had obviously sold her a bill of goods, just as he had him, who'd expected to become acquainted with a young lady of twenty-nine, only to behold, the moment he laid eyes upon her strained and anxious face, a woman past thirty-five and aging rapidly. Only his self control had kept him this long in her presence.

"I am not," he said gravely, "a talented religious person," and in seeking words to go on, found himself possessed by shame and fear. "I think," he said in a strained manner, "that I came to God not because I loved Him, but because I did not."

This confession he spoke harshly because its unexpectedness shook him.

Lily wilted. Leo saw a profusion of loaves of bread go flying like ducks high over his head, not unlike the winged loaves by which he had counted himself to sleep last night. Mercifully, then, it snowed, which he would not put past Salzman's machinations.

He was infuriated with the marriage broker and swore he would throw him out of the room the minute he reappeared. But Salzman did not come that night, and when Leo's anger had subsided, an unaccountable despair grew in its place. At first he thought this was caused by his disappointment in Lily, but before long it became evident that he had involved himself with Salzman without a true knowledge of his own intent. He gradually realized—with an emptiness that seized him with six hands—that he had called in the broker to find him a bride because he was incapable of doing it himself. This terrifying insight he had derived as a result of his meeting and conversation with Lily Hirschorn. Her probing questions had somehow irritated him into revealing—to himself more than her—the true nature of his relationship to God, and from that it had come upon him, with shocking force, that apart from his parents, he had never loved anyone. Or perhaps it went the other way, that he did not love God so well as he might, because he had not loved man. It seemed to Leo that his whole life stood starkly revealed and he saw himself for the first time as he truly was—

unloved and loveless. This bitter but somehow not fully unexpected revelation brought him to a point of panic, controlled only by extraordinary effort. He covered his face with his hands and cried.

The week that followed was the worst of his life. He did not eat and lost weight. His beard darkened and grew ragged. He stopped attending seminars and almost never opened a book. He seriously considered leaving the Yeshivah, although he was deeply troubled at the thought of the loss of all his years of study—saw them like pages torn from a book, strewn over the city—and at the devastating effect of this decision upon his parents. But he had lived without knowledge of himself, and never in the Five Books° and all the Commentaries—mea culpa° —had the truth been revealed to him. He did not know where to turn, and in all this desolating loneliness there was no *to whom,* although he often thought of Lily but not once could bring himself to go downstairs and make the call. He became touchy and irritable, especially with his landlady, who asked him all manner of personal questions; on the other hand, sensing his own disagreeableness, he waylaid her on the stairs and apologized abjectly, until mortified, she ran from him. Out of this, however, he drew the consolation that he was a Jew and that a Jew suffered. But gradually, as the long and terrible week drew to a close, he regained his composure and some idea of purpose in life: to go on as planned. Although he was imperfect, the ideal was not. As for his quest of a bride, the thought of continuing afflicted him with anxiety and heartburn, yet perhaps with this new knowledge of himself he would be more successful than in the past. Perhaps love would now come to him and a bride to that love. And for this sanctified seeking who needed a Salzman?

The marriage broker, a skeleton with haunted eyes, returned that very night. He looked, withal, the picture of frustrated expectancy—as if he had steadfastly waited the week at Miss Lily Hirschorn's side for a telephone call that never came.

Casually coughing, Salzman came immediately to the point: "So how did you like her?"

Leo's anger rose and he could not refrain from chiding the matchmaker: "Why did you lie to me, Salzman?"

Salzman's pale face went dead white, the world had snowed on him.

"Did you not state that she was twenty-nine?" Leo insisted.

"I give you my word—"

"She was thirty-five, if a day. *At least* thirty-five."

"Of this don't be too sure. Her father told me—"

"Never mind. The worst of it was that you lied to her."

"How did I lie to her, tell me?"

"You told her things about me that weren't true. You made me out to be more, consequently less than I am. She had in mind a totally different person, a sort of semi-mystical Wonder Rabbi."

"All I said, you was a religious man."

"I can imagine."

Salzman sighed. "This is my weakness that I have," he confessed. "My wife says

---

Five Books. The Torah (the first five books of the Hebrew-Bible). The Commentaries are analyses and interpretations of the Torah done by Jewish scholars.

mea culpa. I have sinned.

to me I shouldn't be a salesman, but when I have two fine people that they would be wonderful to be married, I am so happy that I talk too much." He smiled wanly. "This is why Salzman is a poor man."

Leo's anger left him. "Well, Salzman, I'm afraid that's all."

The marriage broker fastened hungry eyes on him.

"You don't want any more a bride?"

"I do," said Leo, "but I have decided to seek her in a different way. I am no longer interested in an arranged marriage. To be frank, I now admit the necessity of premarital love. That is, I want to be in love with the one I marry."

"Love?" said Salzman, astounded. After a moment he remarked, "For us, our love is our life, not for the ladies. In the ghetto they—"

"I know, I know," said Leo. "I've thought of it often. Love, I have said to myself, should be a by-product of living and worship rather than its own end. Yet for myself I find it necessary to establish the level of my need and fulfill it."

Salzman shrugged but answered, "Listen, rabbi, if you want love, this I can find for you also. I have such beautiful clients that you will love them the minute your eyes will see them."

Leo smiled unhappily. "I'm afraid you don't understand."

But Salzman hastily unstrapped his portfolio and withdrew a manila packet from it.

"Pictures," he said, quickly laying the envelope on the table.

Leo called after him to take the pictures away, but as if on the wings of the wind, Salzman had disappeared.

March came. Leo had returned to his regular routine. Although he felt not quite himself yet—lacked energy—he was making plans for a more active social life. Of course it would cost something, but he was an expert in cutting corners; and when there were no corners left he would make circles rounder. All the while Salzman's pictures had lain on the table, gathering dust. Occasionally as Leo sat studying, or enjoying a cup of tea, his eyes fell on the manila envelope, but he never opened it.

The days went by and no social life to speak of developed with a member of the opposite sex—it was difficult, given the circumstances of his situation. One morning Leo toiled up the stairs to his room and stared out the window at the city. Although the day was bright his view of it was dark. For some time he watched the people in the street below hurrying along and then turned with a heavy heart to his little room. On the table was the packet. With a sudden relentless gesture he tore it open. For a half-hour he stood by the table in a state of excitement, examining the photographs of the ladies Salzman had included. Finally, with a deep sigh he put them down. There were six, of varying degrees of attractiveness, but look at them long enough and they all became Lily Hirschorn: all past their prime, all starved behind bright smiles, not a true personality in the lot. Life, despite their frantic yoohooings, had passed them by; they were pictures in a briefcase that stank of fish. After a while, however, as Leo attempted to return the photographs into the envelope, he found in it another, a snapshot of the type taken by a machine for a quarter. He gazed at it a moment and let out a cry.

Her face deeply moved him. Why, he could at first not say. It gave him the impression of youth—spring flowers, yet age—a sense of having been used to the bone, wasted; this came from the eyes, which were hauntingly familiar, yet absolutely strange. He had a vivid impression that he had met her before, but try as he might he could not place her although he could almost recall her name, as if he had read it in her own handwriting. No, this couldn't be; he would have remembered her. It was not, he affirmed, that she had an extraordinary beauty—no, though her face was attractive enough; it was that *something* about her moved him. Feature for feature, even some of the ladies of the photographs could do better; but she leaped forth to his heart—had *lived,* or wanted to—more than just wanted, perhaps regretted how she had lived—had somehow deeply suffered: it could be seen in the depths of those reluctant eyes, and from the way the light enclosed and shone from her, and within her, opening realms of possibility: this was her own. Her he desired. His head ached and eyes narrowed with the intensity of his gazing, then as if an obscure fog had blown up in the mind, he experienced fear of her and was aware that he had received an impression, somehow, of evil. He shuddered, saying softly, it is thus with us all. Leo brewed some tea in a small pot and sat sipping it without sugar, to calm himself. But before he had finished drinking, again with excitement he examined the face and found it good: good for Leo Finkle. Only such a one could understand him and help him seek whatever he was seeking. She might, perhaps, love him. How she had happened to be among the discards in Salzman's barrel he could never guess, but he knew he must urgently go find her.

Leo rushed downstairs, grabbed up the Bronx telephone book, and searched for Salzman's home address. He was not listed, nor was his office. Neither was he in the Manhattan book. But Leo remembered having written down the address on a slip of paper after he had read Salzman's advertisement in the "personals" column of the *Forward.* He ran up to his room and tore through his papers, without luck. It was exasperating. Just when he needed the matchmaker he was nowhere to be found. Fortunately Leo remembered to look in his wallet. There on a card he found his name written and a Bronx address. No phone number was listed, the reason—Leo now recalled—he had originally communicated with Salzman by letter. He got on his coat, put a hat on over his skull cap and hurried to the subway station. All the way to the far end of the Bronx he sat on the edge of his seat. He was more than once tempted to take out the picture and see if the girl's face was as he remembered it, but he refrained, allowing the snapshot to remain in his inside coat pocket, content to have her so close. When the train pulled into the station he was waiting at the door and bolted out. He quickly located the street Salzman had advertised.

The building he sought was less than a block from the subway, but it was not an office building, nor even a loft, nor a store in which one could rent office space. It was a very old tenement house. Leo found Salzman's name in pencil on a soiled tag under the bell and climbed three dark flights to his apartment. When he knocked, the door was opened by a thin, asthmatic, gray-haired woman, in felt slippers.

"Yes?" she said, expecting nothing. She listened without listening. He could have sworn he had seen her, too, before but knew it was an illusion.

"Salzman—does he live here? Pinye Salzman," he said, "the matchmaker?"

She stared at him a long minute. "Of course."

He felt embarrassed. "Is he in?"

"No." Her mouth, though left open, offered nothing more.

"The matter is urgent. Can you tell me where his office is?"

"In the air." She pointed upward.

"You mean he has no office?" Leo asked.

"In his socks."

He peered into the apartment. It was sunless and dingy, one large room divided by a half-open curtain, beyond which he could see a sagging metal bed. The near side of a room was crowded with rickety chairs, old bureaus, a three-legged table, racks of cooking utensils, and all the apparatus of a kitchen. But there was no sign of Salzman or his magic barrel, probably also a figment of the imagination. An odor of frying fish made Leo weak to the knees.

"Where is he?" he insisted. "I've got to see your husband."

At length she answered, "So who knows where he is? Every time he thinks a new thought he runs to a different place. Go home, he will find you."

"Tell him Leo Finkle."

She gave no sign she had heard.

He walked downstairs, depressed.

But Salzman, breathless, stood waiting at his door.

Leo was astounded and overjoyed. "How did you get here before me?"

"I rushed."

"Come inside."

They entered. Leo fixed tea, and a sardine sandwich for Salzman. As they were drinking he reached behind him for the packet of pictures and handed them to the marriage broker.

Salzman put down his glass and said expectantly, "You found somebody you like?"

"Not among these."

The marriage broker turned away.

"Here is the one I want." Leo held forth the snapshot.

Salzman slipped on his glasses and took the picture into his trembling hand. He turned ghastly and let out a groan.

"What's the matter?" cried Leo.

"Excuse me. Was an accident this picture. She isn't for you."

Salzman frantically shoved the manila packet into his portfolio. He thrust the snapshot into his pocket and fled down the stairs.

Leo, after momentary paralysis, gave chase and cornered the marriage broker in the vestibule. The landlady made hysterical outcries but neither of them listened.

"Give me back the picture, Salzman."

"No." The pain in his eyes was terrible.

"Tell me who she is then."

"This I can't tell you. Excuse me."

He made to depart, but Leo, forgetting himself, seized the matchmaker by his tight coat and shook him frenziedly.

"Please," sighed Salzman. "*Please.*"

Leo ashamedly let him go. "Tell me who she is," he begged. "It's very important for me to know."

"She is not for you. She is a wild one—wild, without shame. This is not a bride for a rabbi."

"What do you mean wild?"

"Like an animal. Like a dog. For her to be poor was a sin. This is why to me she is dead now."

"In God's name, what do you mean?"

"Her I can't introduce to you," Salzman cried.

"Why are you so excited?"

"Why, he asks," Salzman said, bursting into tears. "This is my baby, my Stella, she should burn in hell."

Leo hurried up to bed and hid under the covers. Under the covers he thought his life through. Although he soon fell asleep he could not sleep her out of his mind. He woke, beating his breast. Though he prayed to be rid of her, his prayers went unanswered. Through days of torment he endlessly struggled not to love her; fearing success, he escaped it. He then concluded to convert her to goodness, himself to God. The idea alternately nauseated and exalted him.

He perhaps did not know that he had come to a final decision until he encountered Salzman in a Broadway cafeteria. He was sitting alone at a rear table, sucking the bony remains of a fish. The marriage broker appeared haggard, and transparent to the point of vanishing.

Salzman looked up at first without recognizing him. Leo had grown a pointed beard and his eyes were weighted with wisdom.

"Salzman," he said, "love has at last come to my heart."

"Who can love from a picture?" mocked the marriage broker.

"It is not impossible."

"If you can love her, then you can love anybody. Let me show you some new clients that they just sent me their photographs. One is a little doll."

"Just her I want," Leo murmured.

"Don't be a fool, doctor. Don't bother with her."

"Put me in touch with her, Salzman," Leo said humbly. "Perhaps I can be of service."

Salzman had stopped eating and Leo understood with emotion that it was now arranged.

Leaving the cafeteria, he was, however, afflicted by a tormenting suspicion that Salzman had planned it all to happen this way.

Leo was informed by letter that she would meet him on a certain corner, and she was there one spring night, waiting under a street lamp. He appeared, carrying a small bouquet of violets and rosebuds. Stella stood by the lamp post, smoking. She wore white with red shoes, which fitted his expectations, although in a troubled moment he had imagined the dress red, and only the shoes white. She waited uneasily and shyly. From afar he saw that her eyes—clearly her father's—were filled with desperate innocence. He pictured, in her, his own redemption. Violins and lit candles revolved in the sky. Leo ran forward with flowers outthrust.

Around the corner, Salzman, leaning against a wall, chanted prayers for the dead.

Questions for Study

1. Why does Finkle consult a marriage broker? What is his attitude toward Salzman's candidates? What is Salzman's attitude toward them?

2. Finkle and Salzman meet on six occasions. How is each occasion different?

3. How does Finkle get along with Lily Hirschorn? What does she expect him to be like?

4. When does Finkle's epiphany occur? What causes it? What does he realize about himself?

5. Why does Finkle respond so powerfully to the photograph of Stella? What does Stella's appearance at the end suggest about the kind of life she has lived? What characterizes her? Why does Finkle see her as his "redemption"?

6. Are there clues to suggest that Salzman schemed to bring Finkle and Stella together? What does the last sentence of the story mean?

7. What fairy tale elements does Malamud incorporate into the story? Why does he do so?

JOYCE CAROL OATES

Where Are You Going, Where Have You Been?

Joyce Carol Oates (1938–) has had an amazingly prolific career as a poet, short story writer, novelist, and critic. Ever since the publication of her first book, *By the North Gate* (1963), a collection of stories, she has produced almost a book every year. She was born and reared in Millerport, New York, an area of upstate New York that she has used for the setting of much of her fiction. She majored in English at Syracuse University and the University of Wisconsin. She has taught English at the University of Detroit and the University of Windsor, Ontario. She now teaches at Princeton University. Her fiction deals with a wide range of subject matter and takes many forms. An early novel *them* (1969) is a realistic study of urban lower-class life and racial violence. *Son of the Morning* (1978) is a psychological study of a fundamentalist preacher. *Bellefleur* (1980) is a gothic thriller. *Mysteries of Winterthurn* (1984) is a historical romance that probes the dynamics of racism, sexism, and anti-Semitism in nineteenth-century America. Oates is both a social critic and a student of human nature. She examines the effect that American social obsessions have on individuals. A frequent topic in her work is the interplay between violence and sexual attraction. "Where Are You Going, Where Have You

Been?" was originally published in 1966 and collected in *The Wheel of Love and Other Stories* (1970).

For Bob Dylan°

*H*er name was Connie. She was fifteen and she had a quick, nervous giggling habit of craning her neck to glance into mirrors or checking other people's faces to make sure her own was all right. Her mother, who noticed everything and knew everything and who hadn't much reason any longer to look at her own face, always scolded Connie about it. "Stop gawking at yourself. Who are you? You think you're so pretty?" she would say. Connie would raise her eyebrows at these familiar old complaints and look right through her mother, into a shadowy vision of herself as she was right at that moment: she knew she was pretty and that was everything. Her mother had been pretty once too, if you could believe those old snapshots in the album, but now her looks were gone and that was why she was always after Connie.

"Why don't you keep your room clean like your sister? How've you got your hair fixed—what the hell stinks? Hair spray? You don't see your sister using that junk."

Her sister June was twenty-four and still lived at home. She was a secretary in the high school Connie attended, and if that wasn't bad enough—with her in the same building—she was so plain and chunky and steady that Connie had to hear her praised all the time by her mother and her mother's sisters. June did this, June did that, she saved money and helped clean the house and cooked and Connie couldn't do a thing, her mind was all filled with trashy daydreams. Their father was away at work most of the time and when he came home he wanted supper and he read the newspaper at supper and after supper he went to bed. He didn't bother talking much to them, but around his bent head Connie's mother kept picking at her until Connie wished her mother was dead and she herself was dead, and it was all over. "She makes me want to throw up sometimes," she complained to her friends. She had a high, breathless, amused voice that made everything she said sound a little forced, whether it was sincere or not.

There was one good thing: June went places with girl friends of hers, girls who were just as plain and steady as she, and so when Connie wanted to do that her mother had no objections. The father of Connie's best girl friend drove the girls the three miles to town and left them at a shopping plaza so they could walk through the stores or go to a movie, and when he came to pick them up again at eleven he never bothered to ask what they had done.

They must have been familiar sights, walking around the shopping plaza in their shorts and flat ballerina slippers that always scuffed the sidewalk, with charm bracelets jingling on their thin wrists; they would lean together to whisper and laugh secretly if someone passed who amused or interested them. Connie had long dark blond hair that drew anyone's eye to it, and she wore part of it pulled up on her head and puffed out

Bob Dylan. Composer and musician, born 1941, who helped popularize folk and protest songs in the 1960s and 1970s.

and the rest of it she let fall down her back. She wore a pull-over jersey blouse that looked one way when she was at home and another way when she was away from home. Everything about her had two sides to it, one for home and one for anywhere that was not home; her walk, which could be childlike and bobbing, or languid enough to make anyone think she was hearing music in her head; her mouth, which was pale and smirking most of the time, but bright and pink on these evenings out; her laugh, which was cynical and drawling at home—"Ha, ha, very funny,"—but high-pitched and nervous anywhere else, like the jingling of the charms on her bracelet.

Sometimes they did go shopping or to a movie, but sometimes they went across the highway, ducking fast across the busy road, to a drive-in restaurant where older kids hung out. The restaurant was shaped like a big bottle, though squatter than a real bottle, and on its cap was a revolving figure of a grinning boy holding a hamburger aloft. One night in midsummer they ran across, breathless with daring, and right away someone leaned out a car window and invited them over, but it was just a boy from high school they didn't like. It made them feel good to be able to ignore him. They went up through the maze of parked and cruising cars to the bright-lit, fly-infested restaurant, their faces pleased and expectant as if they were entering a sacred building that loomed up out of the night to give them what haven and blessing they yearned for. They sat at the counter and crossed their legs at the ankles, their thin shoulders rigid with excitement, and listened to the music that made everything so good: the music was always in the background, like music at a church service; it was something to depend upon.

A boy named Eddie came in to talk with them. He sat backwards on his stool, turning himself jerkily around in semicircles and then stopping and turning back again, and after a while he asked Connie if she would like something to eat. She said she would and so she tapped her friend's arm on her way out—her friend pulled her face up into a brave, droll look—and Connie said she would meet her at eleven, across the way. "I just hate to leave her like that," Connie said earnestly, but the boy said that she wouldn't be alone for long. So they went out to his car, and on the way Connie couldn't help but let her eyes wander over the windshields and faces all around her, her face gleaming with a joy that had nothing to do with Eddie or even this place; it might have been the music. She drew her shoulders up and sucked in her breath with the pure pleasure of being alive, and just at that moment she happened to glance at a face just a few feet from hers. It was a boy with shaggy black hair, in a convertible jalopy painted gold. He stared at her and then his lips widened into a grin. Connie slit her eyes at him and turned away, but she couldn't help glancing back and there he was, still watching her. He wagged a finger and laughed and said, "Gonna get you, baby," and Connie turned away again without Eddie noticing anything.

She spent three hours with him, at the restaurant where they ate hamburgers and drank Cokes in wax cups that were always sweating, and then down an alley a mile or so away, and when he left her off at five to eleven only the movie house was still open at the plaza. Her girl friend was there, talking with a boy. When Connie came up, the two girls smiled at each other and Connie said, "How was the movie?" and the girl said, "*You* should know." They rode off with the girl's father, sleepy and pleased, and Connie couldn't help but look back at the darkened shopping plaza with its big empty parking lot and its signs that were faded and ghostly now, and over at the drive-in restaurant where cars were still circling tirelessly. She couldn't hear the music at this distance.

Next morning June asked her how the movie was and Connie said, "So-so."

She and that girl and occasionally another girl went out several times a week, and the rest of the time Connie spent around the house—it was summer vacation—getting in her mother's way and thinking, dreaming about the boys she met. But all the boys fell back and dissolved into a single face that was not even a face but an idea, a feeling, mixed up with the urgent insistent pounding of the music and the humid night air of July. Connie's mother kept dragging her back to the daylight by finding things for her to do or saying suddenly, "What's this about the Pettinger girl?"

And Connie would say nervously, "Oh, her. That dope." She always drew thick clear lines between herself and such girls, and her mother was simple and kind enough to believe it. Her mother was so simple, Connie thought, that it was maybe cruel to fool her so much. Her mother went scuffling around the house in old bedroom slippers and complained over the telephone to one sister about the other, then the other called up and the two of them complained about the third one. If June's name was mentioned her mother's tone was approving, and if Connie's name was mentioned it was disapproving. This did not really mean she disliked Connie, and actually Connie thought that her mother preferred her to June just because she was prettier, but the two of them kept up a pretense of exasperation, a sense that they were tugging and struggling over something of little value to either of them. Sometimes, over coffee, they were almost friends, but something would come up—some vexation that was like a fly buzzing suddenly around their heads—and their faces went hard with contempt.

One Sunday Connie got up at eleven—none of them bothered with church— and washed her hair so that it could dry all day long in the sun. Her parents and sister were going to a barbecue at an aunt's house and Connie said no, she wasn't interested, rolling her eyes to let her mother know just what she thought of it. "Stay home alone then," her mother said sharply. Connie sat out back in a lawn chair and watched them drive away, her father quiet and bald, hunched around so that he could back the car out, her mother with a look that was still angry and not at all softened through the windshield, and in the back seat poor old June, all dressed up as if she didn't know what a barbecue was, with all the running yelling kids and the flies. Connie sat with her eyes closed in the sun, dreaming and dazed with the warmth about her as if this were a kind of love, the caresses of love, and her mind slipped over onto thoughts of the boy she had been with the night before and how nice he had been, how sweet it always was, not the way someone like June would suppose but sweet, gentle, the way it was in movies and promised in songs; and when she opened her eyes she hardly knew where she was, the back yard ran off into weeds and a fence-like line of trees and behind it the sky was perfectly blue and still. The asbestos "ranch house" that was now three years old startled her—it looked small. She shook her head as if to get awake.

It was too hot. She went inside the house and turned on the radio to drown out the quiet. She sat on the edge of her bed, barefoot, and listened for an hour and a half to a program called XYZ Sunday Jamboree, record after record of hard, fast, shrieking songs she sang along with, interspersed by exclamations from "Bobby King": "An' look here, you girls at Napoleon's—Son and Charley want you to pay real close attention to this song coming up!"

And Connie paid close attention herself, bathed in a glow of slow-pulsed joy that seemed to rise mysteriously out of the music itself and lay languidly about the airless little room, breathed in and breathed out with each gentle rise and fall of her chest.

After a while she heard a car coming up the drive. She sat up at once, startled, because it couldn't be her father so soon. The gravel kept crunching all the way in from the road—the driveway was long—and Connie ran to the window. It was a car she didn't know. It was an open jalopy, painted a bright gold that caught the sunlight opaquely. Her heart began to pound and her fingers snatched at her hair, checking it, and she whispered, "Christ. Christ," wondering how bad she looked. The car came to a stop at the side door and the horn sounded four short taps, as if this were a signal Connie knew.

She went into the kitchen and approached the door slowly, then hung out the screen door, her bare toes curling down off the step. There were two boys in the car and now she recognized the driver: he had shaggy, shabby black hair that looked crazy as a wig and he was grinning at her.

"I ain't late, am I?" he said.

"Who the hell do you think you are?" Connie said.

"Toldja I'd be out, didn't I?"

"I don't even know who you are."

She spoke sullenly, careful to show no interest or pleasure, and he spoke in a fast, bright monotone. Connie looked past him to the other boy, taking her time. He had fair brown hair, with a lock that fell onto his forehead. His sideburns gave him a fierce, embarrassed look, but so far he hadn't even bothered to glance at her. Both boys wore sunglasses. The driver's glasses were metallic and mirrored everything in miniature.

"You wanta come for a ride?" he said.

Connie smirked and let her hair fall loose over one shoulder.

"Don'tcha like my car? New paint job," he said. "Hey."

"What?"

"You're cute."

She pretended to fidget, chasing flies away from the door.

"Don'tcha believe me, or what?" he said.

"Look, I don't even know who you are," Connie said in disgust.

"Hey, Ellie's got a radio, see. Mine broke down." He lifted his friend's arm and showed her the little transistor radio the boy was holding, and now Connie began to hear the music. It was the same program that was playing inside the house.

"Bobby King?" she said.

"I listen to him all the time. I think he's great."

"He's kind of great," Connie said reluctantly.

"Listen, that guy's *great*. He knows where the action is."

Connie blushed a little, because the glasses made it impossible for her to see just what this boy was looking at. She couldn't decide if she liked him or if he was just a jerk, and so she dawdled in the doorway and wouldn't come down or go back inside. She said, "What's all that stuff painted on your car?"

"Can'tcha read it?" He opened the door very carefully, as if he were afraid it might fall off. He slid out just as carefully, planting his feet firmly on the ground, the tiny metallic world in his glasses slowing down like gelatine hardening, and in the midst of it Connie's bright green blouse. "This here is my name, to begin with," he said. ARNOLD FRIEND was written in tarlike black letters on the side, with a drawing of a round, grinning face that reminded Connie of a pumpkin, except it wore sunglasses. "I wanta introduce myself, I'm Arnold Friend and that's my real name and I'm gonna be your friend, honey, and inside the car's Ellie Oscar, he's kinda shy." Ellie brought his transistor radio up to his shoulder and balanced it there. "Now, these numbers are a secret code, honey," Arnold Friend explained. He read off the numbers 33, 19, 17 and raised his eyebrows at her to see what she thought of that, but she didn't think much of it. The left rear fender had been smashed and around it was written, on the gleaming gold background: DONE BY CRAZY WOMAN DRIVER. Connie had to laugh at that. Arnold Friend was pleased at her laughter and looked up at her. "Around the other side's a lot more—you wanta come and see them?"

"No."

"Why not?"

"Why should I?"

"Don'tcha wanta see what's on the car? Don'tcha wanta go for a ride?"

"I don't know."

"Why not?"

"I got things to do."

"Like what?"

"Things."

He laughed as if she had said something funny. He slapped his thighs. He was standing in a strange way, leaning back against the car as if he were balancing himself. He wasn't tall, only an inch or so taller than she would be if she came down to him. Connie liked the way he was dressed, which was the way all of them dressed: tight faded jeans stuffed into black, scuffed boots, a belt that pulled his waist in and showed how lean he was, and a white pull-over shirt that was a little soiled and showed the hard small muscles of his arms and shoulders. He looked as if he probably did hard work, lifting and carrying things. Even his neck looked muscular. And his face was a familiar face, somehow: the jaw and chin and cheeks slightly darkened because he hadn't shaved for a day or two, and the nose long and hawklike, sniffing as if she were a treat he was going to gobble up and it was all a joke.

"Connie, you ain't telling the truth. This is your day set aside for a ride with me and you know it," he said, still laughing. The way he straightened and recovered from his fit of laughing showed that it had been all fake.

"How do you know what my name is?" she said suspiciously.

"It's Connie."

"Maybe and maybe not."

"I know my Connie," he said, wagging his finger. Now she remembered him even better, back at the restaurant, and her cheeks warmed at the thought of how she had sucked in her breath just at the moment she passed him—how she must have looked to him. And he had remembered her. "Ellie and I come out here especially for you," he said. "Ellie can sit in back. How about it?"

"Where?"

"Where what?"

"Where're we going?"

He looked at her. He took off the sunglasses and she saw how pale the skin around his eyes was, like holes that were not in shadow but instead in light. His eyes were like chips of broken glass that catch the light in an amiable way. He smiled. It was as if the idea of going for a ride somewhere, to someplace, was a new idea to him.

"Just for a ride, Connie sweetheart."

"I never said my name was Connie," she said.

"But I know what it is. I know your name and all about you, lots of things," Arnold Friend said. He had not moved yet but stood still leaning back against the side of his jalopy. "I took a special interest in you, such a pretty girl, and found out all about you—like I know your parents and sister are gone somewheres and I know where and how long they're going to be gone, and I know who you were with last night, and your best girl friend's name is Betty. Right?"

He spoke in a simple lilting voice, exactly as if he were reciting the words to a song. His smile assured her that everything was fine. In the car Ellie turned up the volume on his radio and did not bother to look around at them.

"Ellie can sit in the back seat," Arnold Friend said. He indicated his friend with a casual jerk of his chin, as if Ellie did not count and she should not bother with him.

"How'd you find out all that stuff?" Connie said.

"Listen: Betty Schultz and Tony Fitch and Jimmy Pettinger and Nancy Pettinger," he said in a chant. "Raymond Stanley and Bob Hutter—"

"Do you know all those kids?"

"I know everybody."

"Look, you're kidding. You're not from around here."

"Sure."

"But—how come we never saw you before?"

"Sure you saw me before," he said. He looked down at his boots, as if he were a little offended. "You just don't remember."

"I guess I'd remember you," Connie said.

"Yeah?" He looked up at this, beaming. He was pleased. He began to mark time with the music from Ellie's radio, tapping his fists lightly together. Connie looked away from his smile to the car, which was painted so bright it almost hurt her eyes to look at it. She looked at that name, ARNOLD FRIEND. And up at the front fender was an expression that was familiar—MAN THE FLYING SAUCERS. It was an expression kids had used the year before but didn't use this year. She looked at it for a while as if the words meant something to her that she did not yet know.

"What're you thinking about? Huh?" Arnold Friend demanded. "Not worried about your hair blowing around in the car, are you?"

"No."

"Think I maybe can't drive good?"

"How do I know?"

"You're a hard girl to handle. How come?" he said. "Don't you know I'm your friend? Didn't you see me put my sign in the air when you walked by?"

"What sign?"

"My sign." And he drew an X in the air, leaning out toward her. They were maybe ten feet apart. After his hand fell back to his side the X was still in the air, almost visible. Connie let the screen door close and stood perfectly still inside it, listening to the music from her radio and the boy's blend together. She stared at Arnold Friend. He stood there so stiffly relaxed, pretending to be relaxed, with one hand idly on the door handle as if he were keeping himself up that way and had no intention of ever moving again. She recognized most things about him, the tight jeans that showed his thighs and buttocks and the greasy leather boots and the tight shirt, and even that slippery friendly smile of his, that sleepy dreamy smile that all the boys used to get across ideas they didn't want to put into words. She recognized all this and also the singsong way he talked, slightly mocking, kidding, but serious and a little melancholy, and she recognized the way he tapped one fist against the other in homage to the perpetual music behind him. But all these things did not come together.

She said suddenly, "Hey, how old are you?"

His smile faded. She could see then that he wasn't a kid, he was much older—thirty, maybe more. At this knowledge her heart began to pound faster.

"That's a crazy thing to ask. Can'tcha see I'm your own age?"

"Like hell you are."

"Or maybe a coupla years older. I'm eighteen."

"Eighteen?" she said doubtfully.

He grinned to reassure her and lines appeared at the corners of his mouth. His teeth were big and white. He grinned so broadly his eyes became slits and she saw how thick the lashes were, thick and black as if painted with a black tarlike material. Then, abruptly, he seemed to become embarrassed and looked over his shoulder at Ellie. "Him, he's crazy," he said. "Ain't he a riot? He's a nut, a real character." Ellie was still listening to the music. His sunglasses told nothing about what he was thinking. He wore a bright orange shirt unbuttoned halfway to show his chest, which was a pale, bluish chest and not muscular like Arnold Friend's. His shirt collar was turned up all around and the very tips of the collar pointed out past his chin as if they were protecting him. He was pressing the transistor radio up against his ear and sat there in a kind of daze, right in the sun.

"He's kinda strange," Connie said.

"Hey, she says you're kinda strange! Kinda strange!" Arnold Friend cried. He pounded on the car to get Ellie's attention. Ellie turned for the first time and Connie saw with shock that he wasn't a kid either—he had a fair, hairless face, cheeks reddened slightly as if the veins grew too close to the surface of his skin, the face of a forty-year-old baby. Connie felt a wave of dizziness rise in her at this sight and she stared at him as if waiting for something to change the shock of the moment, make it all right again. Ellie's lips kept shaping words, mumbling along with the words blasting in his ear.

"Maybe you two better go away," Connie said faintly.

"What? How come?" Arnold Friend cried. "We come out here to take you for a ride. It's Sunday." He had the voice of the man on the radio now. It was the same voice, Connie thought. "Don'tcha know it's Sunday all day? And honey, no matter who you were with last night, today you're with Arnold Friend and don't you forget it! Maybe you better step out here," he said, and this last was in a different voice. It was a little flatter, as if the heat was finally getting to him.

"No. I got things to do."

"Hey."

"You two better leave."

"We ain't leaving until you come with us."

"Like hell I am—"

"Connie, don't fool around with me. I mean—I mean, don't fool around," he said, shaking his head. He laughed incredulously. He placed his sunglasses on top of his head, carefully, as if he were indeed wearing a wig, and brought the stems down behind his ears. Connie stared at him, another wave of dizziness and fear rising in her so that for a moment he wasn't even in focus but was just a blur standing there against his gold car, and she had the idea that he had driven up the driveway all right but had come from nowhere before that and belonged nowhere and that everything about him and even about the music that was so familiar to her was only half real.

"If my father comes and sees you—"

"He ain't coming. He's at a barbecue."

"How do you know that?"

"Aunt Tillie's. Right now they're—uh—they're drinking. Sitting around," he said vaguely, squinting as if he were staring all the way to town and over to Aunt Tillie's back yard. Then the vision seemed to get clear and he nodded energetically. "Yeah. Sitting around. There's your sister in a blue dress, huh? And high heels, the poor sad bitch—nothing like you, sweetheart! And your mother's helping some fat woman with the corn, they're cleaning the corn—husking the corn—"

"What fat woman?" Connie cried.

"How do I know what fat woman, I don't know every goddamn fat woman in the world!" Arnold Friend laughed.

"Oh, that's Mrs. Hornsby. . . . Who invited her?" Connie said. She felt a little light-headed. Her breath was coming quickly.

"She's too fat. I don't like them fat. I like them the way you are, honey," he said, smiling sleepily at her. They stared at each other for a while through the screen door. He said softly, "Now, what you're going to do is this: you're going to come out that door. You're going to sit up front with me and Ellie's going to sit in the back, the hell with Ellie, right? This isn't Ellie's date. You're my date. I'm your lover, honey."

"What? You're crazy—"

"Yes, I'm your lover. You don't know what that is but you will," he said. "I know that too. I know all about you. But look: it's real nice and you couldn't ask for nobody better than me, or more polite. I always keep my word. I'll tell you how it is, I'm always nice at first, the first time. I'll hold you so tight you won't think you have to try to get away or pretend anything because you'll know you can't. And I'll come inside you where it's all secret and you'll give in to me and you'll love me—"

"Shut up! You're crazy!" Connie said. She backed away from the door. She put her hands up against her ears as if she'd heard something terrible, something not meant for her. "People don't talk like that, you're crazy," she muttered. Her heart was almost too big now for her chest and its pumping made sweat break out all over her. She looked out to see Arnold Friend pause and then take a step toward the porch, lurching. He almost fell. But, like a clever drunken man, he managed to catch his balance. He wobbled in his high boots and grabbed hold of one of the porch posts.

"Honey?" he said. "You still listening?"

"Get the hell out of here!"

"Be nice, honey. Listen."

"I'm going to call the police—"

He wobbled again and out of the side of his mouth came a fast spat curse, an aside not meant for her to hear. But even this "Christ!" sounded forced. Then he began to smile again. She watched this smile come, awkward as if he were smiling from inside a mask. His whole face was a mask, she thought wildly, tanned down to his throat but then running out as if he had plastered make-up on his face but had forgotten about his throat.

"Honey—? Listen, here's how it is. I always tell the truth and I promise you this: I ain't coming in that house after you."

"You better not! I'm going to call the police if you—if you don't—"

"Honey," he said, talking right through her voice, "honey, I'm not coming in there but you are coming out here. You know why?"

She was panting. The kitchen looked like a place she had never seen before, some room she had run inside but that wasn't good enough, wasn't going to help her. The kitchen window had never had a curtain, after three years, and there were dishes in the sink for her to do—probably—and if you ran your hand across the table you'd probably feel something sticky there.

"You listening, honey? Hey?"

"—going to call the police—"

"Soon as you touch the phone I don't need to keep my promise and can come inside. You won't want that."

She rushed forward and tried to lock the door. Her fingers were shaking. "But why lock it," Arnold Friend said gently, talking right into her face. "It's just a screen door. It's just nothing." One of his boots was at a strange angle, as if his foot wasn't in it. It pointed out to the left, bent at the ankle. "I mean, anybody can break through a screen door and glass and wood and iron or anything else if he needs to, anybody at all, and specially Arnold Friend. If the place got lit up with a fire, honey, you'd come runnin' out into my arms, right into my arms an' safe at home—like you knew I was your lover and'd stopped fooling around. I don't mind a nice shy girl but I don't like no fooling around." Part of those words were spoken with a slight rhythmic lilt, and Connie somehow recognized them—the echo of a song from last year, about a girl rushing into her boy friend's arms and coming home again—

Connie stood barefoot on the linoleum floor, staring at him. "What do you want?" she whispered.

"I want you," he said.

"What?"

"Seen you that night and thought, that's the one, yes sir. I never needed to look anymore."

"But my father's coming back. He's coming to get me. I had to wash my hair first—" She spoke in a dry, rapid voice, hardly raising it for him to hear.

"No, your daddy is not coming and yes, you had to wash your hair and you washed it for me. It's nice and shining and all for me. I thank you sweetheart," he said with a mock bow, but again he almost lost his balance. He had to bend and adjust his boots. Evidently his feet did not go all the way down; the boots must have been stuffed with something so that he would seem taller. Connie stared out at him and behind him at Ellie in the car, who seemed to be looking off toward Connie's right, into nothing.

This Ellie said, pulling the words out of the air one after another as if he were just discovering them, "You want me to pull out the phone?"

"Shut your mouth and keep it shut," Arnold Friend said, his face red from bending over or maybe from embarrassment because Connie had seen his boots. "This ain't none of your business."

"What—what are you doing? What do you want?" Connie said. "If I call the police they'll get you, they'll arrest you—"

"Promise was not to come in unless you touch that phone, and I'll keep that promise," he said. He resumed his erect position and tried to force his shoulders back. He sounded like a hero in a movie, declaring something important. But he spoke too loudly and it was as if he were speaking to someone behind Connie. "I ain't made plans for coming in that house where I don't belong but just for you to come out to me, the way you should. Don't you know who I am?"

"You're crazy," she whispered. She backed away from the door but did not want to go into another part of the house, as if this would give him permission to come through the door. "What do you . . . you're crazy, you. . . . "

"Huh? What're you saying, honey?"

Her eyes darted everywhere in the kitchen. She could not remember what it was, this room.

"This is how it is, honey: you come out and we'll drive away, have a nice ride. But if you don't come out we're gonna wait till your people come home and then they're all going to get it."

"You want that telephone pulled out?" Ellie said. He held the radio away from his ear and grimaced, as if without the radio the air was too much for him.

"I toldja shut up, Ellie," Arnold Friend said, "you're deaf, get a hearing aid, right? Fix yourself up. This little girl's no trouble and's gonna be nice to me, so Ellie keep to yourself, this ain't your date—right? Don't hem in on me, don't hog, don't crush, don't bird dog, don't trail me," he said in a rapid, meaningless voice, as if he were running through all the expressions he'd learned but was no longer sure which of them was in style, then rushing on to new ones, making them up with his eyes closed. "Don't crawl under my fence, don't squeeze in my chipmunk hole, don't sniff my glue, suck my popsicle, keep your own greasy fingers on yourself!" He shaded his eyes and peered in at Connie, who was backed against the kitchen table. "Don't mind him, honey, he's just a creep. He's a dope. Right? I'm the boy for you and like I said, you come out here nice like a lady and give me your hand, and nobody else gets hurt, I mean, your nice old baldheaded daddy and your mummy and your sister in her high heels. Because listen: why bring them in this?"

"Leave me alone," Connie whispered.

"Hey, you know that old woman down the road, the one with the chickens and stuff—you know her?"

"She's dead!"

"Dead? What? You know her?" Arnold Friend said.

"She's dead—"

"Don't you like her?"

"She's dead—she's—she isn't here any more—"

"But don't you like her, I mean, you got something against her? Some grudge or something?" Then his voice dipped as if he were conscious of a rudeness. He touched the sunglasses perched up on top of his head as if to make sure they were still there. "Now, you be a good girl."

"What are you going to do?"

"Just two things, or maybe three," Arnold Friend said. "But I promise it won't last long and you'll like me the way you get to like people you're close to. You will. It's all over for you here, so come on out. You don't want your people in any trouble, do you?"

She turned and bumped against a chair or something, hurting her leg, but she ran into the back room and picked up the telephone. Something roared in her ear, a tiny roaring, and she was so sick with fear that she could do nothing but listen to it—the telephone was clammy and very heavy and her fingers groped down to the dial but were too weak to touch it. She began to scream into the phone, into the roaring. She cried out, she cried for her mother, she felt her breath start jerking back and forth in her lungs as if it were something Arnold Friend was stabbing her with again and again with no tenderness. A noisy sorrowful wailing rose all about her and she was locked inside it the way she was locked inside the house.

After a while she could hear again. She was sitting on the floor with her wet back against the wall.

Arnold Friend was saying from the door, "That's a good girl. Put the phone back."

She kicked the phone away from her.

"No, honey. Pick it up. Put it back right."

She picked it up and put it back. The dial tone stopped.

"That's a good girl. Now, you come outside."

She was hollow with what had been fear but what was now just an emptiness. All that screaming had blasted it out of her. She sat, one leg cramped under her, and deep inside her brain was something like a pinpoint of light that kept going and would not let her relax. She thought, I'm not going to see my mother again. She thought, I'm not going to sleep in my bed again. Her bright green blouse was all wet.

Arnold Friend said, in a gentle-loud voice that was like a stage voice, "The place where you came from ain't there any more, and where you had in mind to go is cancelled out. This place you are now—inside your daddy's house—is nothing but a cardboard box I can knock down any time. You know that and always did know it. You hear me?"

She thought, I have got to think. I have got to know what to do.

"We'll go out to a nice field, out in the country here where it smells so nice and it's sunny," Arnold Friend said. "I'll have my arms tight around you so you won't need to try to get away and I'll show you what love is like, what it does. The hell with this house! It looks solid all right," he said. He ran a fingernail down the screen and the noise did not make Connie shiver, as it would have the day before. "Now, put your hand on your heart, honey. Feel that? That feels solid too but we know better. Be nice to me, be sweet like you can because what else is there for a girl like you but to be sweet and pretty and give in?—and get away before her people come back?"

She felt her pounding heart. Her hand seemed to enclose it. She thought for the first time in her life that it was nothing that was hers, that belonged to her, but just a pounding, living thing inside this body that wasn't really hers either.

"You don't want them to get hurt," Arnold Friend went on. "Now, get up, honey. Get up all by yourself."

She stood.

"Now, turn this way. That's right. Come over here to me.—Ellie, put that away, didn't I tell you? You dope. You miserable creepy dope," Arnold Friend said. His words were not angry but only part of an incantation. The incantation was kindly. "Now, come out through the kitchen to me, honey, and let's see a smile, try it, you're a brave, sweet little girl and now they're eating corn and hot dogs cooked to bursting over an outdoor fire, and they don't know one thing about you and never did and honey, you're better than them because not a one of them would have done this for you."

Connie felt the linoleum under her feet; it was cool. She brushed her hair back out of her eyes. Arnold Friend let go of the post tentatively and opened his arms for her, his elbows pointing in toward each other and his wrists limp, to show that this was an embarrassed embrace and a little mocking, he didn't want to make her self-conscious.

She put out her hand against the screen. She watched herself push the door slowly open as if she were back safe somewhere in the other doorway, watching this body and this head of long hair moving out into the sunlight where Arnold Friend waited.

"My sweet little blue-eyed girl," he said in a half-sung sigh that had nothing to do with her brown eyes but was taken up just the same by the vast sunlit reaches of the land behind him and on all sides of him—so much land that Connie had never seen before and did not recognize except to know that she was going to it.

Questions for Study

1. In the first paragraph (and throughout the story), where does the narrator state her opinions? How are the narrator's opinions different from Connie's? What does the narrator know that Connie does not?

2. What characterizes Connie's relationship with her family? What is each member of the family like? Do they treat Connie well? Does she treat them well?

3. How is music important in the story? What does it mean to Connie? How does it shape her fantasy life? When is music played? How is Arnold Friend related to the music? Why does Oates dedicate the story to Bob Dylan?

4. What does Arnold Friend want from Connie? What does he promise her?

5. How does Connie's attitude toward Arnold Friend change? Why does she make the choice she does at the end? What will happen to her?

6. Oates has said that "Arnold Friend is a fantastic figure: He is Death, he is the 'elf-knight' of the ballads, he is the Imagination, he is a Dream, he is a Lover, a Demon, and all that." What does he symbolize?

7. How is this story similar to Bowen's "The Demon Lover" (p. 474)? How does it parallel the ballad "The Demon Lover" (p. 309).

TONI CADE BAMBARA

The Lesson

Toni Cade Bambara (1939–) was born and educated in New York City. She earned a B.A. at Queens College in 1959 and an M.A. at the City College of New York in 1964. She studied acting in Florence, Italy, and mime in Paris, France. She did graduate work in linguistics, and studied dance with several companies. She has worked as a social worker, college teacher, and consultant for a television station. During the 1960s she was active in the civil rights movement and continues to be involved with African-American communities in New York and other cities. She has taken part in many writing workshops and is a promoter and teacher of African-American literature. Two anthologies edited by her are *The Black Woman* (1970) and *Tales and Stories for Black Folks* (1971). Her fiction reflects a strong concern for the status of women. Her novels are *The Salt Eaters* (1980), about a friendship between two women, and *If Blessing Comes* (1987). "The Lesson" is from her first collection of stories, *Gorilla, My Love* (1972). A second collection of stories is *The Sea Birds Are Still Alive* (1977). She has been praised for her lyrical rendering of African-American language and her sympathetic handling of characters.

Back in the days when everyone was old and stupid or young and foolish and me and Sugar were the only ones just right, this lady moved on our block with nappy hair and proper speech and no makeup. And quite naturally we laughed at her, laughed the way we did at the junk man who went about his business like he was some big-time president and his sorry-ass horse his secretary. And we kinda hated her too, hated the way we did the winos who cluttered up our parks and pissed on our handball walls and stank up our hallways and stairs so you couldn't halfway play hide-and-seek without a goddamn gas mask. Miss Moore was her name. The only woman on the block with no first name. And she was black as hell, cept for her feet, which were fish-white and spooky. And she was always planning these boring-ass things for us to do, us being my cousin, mostly, who lived on the block cause we all moved North the same time and to the same apartment then spread out gradual to breathe. And our parents would yank our heads into some kinda shape and crisp up our clothes so we'd be presentable for travel with Miss Moore, who always looked like she was going to church, though she never did. Which is just one of things the grown-ups talked about when they talked behind her back like a dog. But when she came calling with some sachet she'd sewed up or some gingerbread she'd made or some book, why then they'd all be too embarrassed to turn her down and we'd get handed over all spruced up. She'd been to college and said it was only right that she should take responsibility for the young ones' education, and she not even related by marriage or blood. So they'd go for it. Specially Aunt Gretchen. She was the main gofer in the family. You got some ole dumb shit foolishness you want somebody to go for, you send for Aunt Gretchen. She been screwed into the go-along for so long, it's a blood-deep natural thing with her. Which is how she got saddled with me and Sugar and Junior in the first place while our mothers were in a la-de-da apartment up the block having a good ole time.

So this one day Miss Moore rounds us all up at the mailbox and it's puredee hot and she's knockin herself out about arithmetic. And school suppose to let up in summer I heard, but she don't never let up. And the starch in my pinafore scratching the shit outta me and I'm really hating this nappy-head bitch and her goddamn college degree. I'd much rather go to the pool or to the show where it's cool. So me and Sugar leaning on the mailbox being surly, which is a Miss Moore word. And Flyboy checking out what everybody brought for lunch. And Fat Butt already wasting his peanut-butter-and-jelly sandwich like the pig he is. And Junebug punchin on Q.T.'s arm for potato chips. And Rosie Giraffe shifting from one hip to the other waiting for somebody to step on her foot or ask her if she from Georgia so she can kick ass, preferably Mercedes'. And Miss Moore asking us do we know what money is, like we a bunch of retards. I mean real money, she say, like it's only poker chips or monopoly papers we lay on the grocer. So right away I'm tired of this and say so. And would much rather snatch Sugar and go to the Sunset and terrorize the West Indian kids and take their hair ribbons and their money too. And Miss Moore files that remark away for next week's lesson on brotherhood, I can tell. And finally I say we oughta get to the subway cause it's cooler and besides we might meet some cute boys. Sugar done swiped her mama's lipstick, so we ready.

So we heading down the street and she's boring us silly about what things cost and what our parents make and how much goes for rent and how money ain't divided up right in this country. And then she gets to the part about we all poor and live in the slums, which I don't feature. And I'm ready to speak on that, but she steps out in the street and hails two cabs just like that. Then she hustles half the crew in with her and hands me a five-dollar bill and tells me to calculate 10 percent tip for the driver. And we're off. Me and Sugar and Junebug and Flyboy hangin out the window and hollering to everybody, putting lipstick on each other cause Flyboy a faggot anyway, and making farts with our sweaty armpits. But I'm mostly trying to figure how to spend this money. But they all fascinated with the meter ticking and Junebug starts laying bets as to how much it'll read when Flyboy can't hold his breath no more. Then Sugar lays bets as to how much it'll be when we get there. So I'm stuck. Don't nobody want to go for my plan, which is to jump out at the next light and run off to the first bar-b-que we can find. Then the driver tells us to get the hell out cause we there already. And the meter reads eighty-five cents. And I'm stalling to figure out the tip and Sugar say give him a dime. And I decide he don't need it bad as I do, so later for him. But then he tries to take off with Junebug foot still in the door so we talk about his mama something ferocious. Then we check out that we on Fifth Avenue and everybody dressed up in stockings. One lady in a fur coat, hot as it is. White folks crazy.

"This is the place," Miss Moore say, presenting it to us in the voice she uses at the museum. "Let's look in the windows before we go in."

"Can we steal?" Sugar asks very serious like she's getting the ground rules squared away before she plays. "I beg your pardon," say Miss Moore, and we fall out. So she leads us around the windows of the toy store and me and Sugar screamin, "This is mine, that's mine, I gotta have that, that was made for me, I was born for that," till Big Butt drowns us out.

"Hey, I'm goin to buy that there."

"That there? You don't even know what it is, stupid."

"I do so," he say punchin on Rosie Giraffe. "It's a microscope."

"Whatcha gonna do with a microscope, fool?"

"Look at things."

"Like what, Ronald?" ask Miss Moore. And Big Butt ain't got the first notion. So here go Miss Moore gabbing about the thousands of bacteria in a drop of water and the somethinorother in a speck of blood and the million and one living things in the air around us is invisible to the naked eye. And what she say that for? Junebug go to town on that "naked" and we rolling. Then Miss Moore ask what it cost. So we all jam into the window smudgin it up and the price tag say $300. So then she ask how long'd take for Big Butt and Junebug to save up their allowances. "Too long," I say. "Yeh," adds Sugar, "outgrown it by that time." And Miss Moore say no, you never outgrow learning instruments. "Why, even medical students and interns and," blah, blah, blah. And we ready to choke Big Butt for bringing it up in the first damn place.

"This here costs four hundred eighty dollars," say Rosie Giraffe. So we pile up all over her to see what she pointin out. My eyes tell me it's a chunk of glass cracked with something heavy, and different-color inks dripped into the splits, then the whole thing put into a oven or something. But for $480 it don't make sense.

"That's a paperweight made of semi-precious stones fused together under tremendous pressure," she explains slowly, with her hands doing the mining and all the factory work.

"So what's a paperweight?" asks Rosie Giraffe.

"To weigh paper with, dumbbell," say Flyboy, the wise man from the East.

"Not exactly," say Miss Moore, which is what she say when you warm or way off too. "It's to weigh paper down so it won't scatter and make your desk untidy." So right away me and Sugar curtsy to each other and then to Mercedes who is more the tidy type.

"We don't keep paper on top of the desk in my class," say Junebug, figuring Miss Moore crazy or lyin one.

"At home, then," she say. "Don't you have a calendar and a pencil case and a blotter and a letter-opener on your desk at home where you do your homework?" And she know damn well what our homes look like cause she nosys around in them every chance she gets.

"I don't even have a desk," say Junebug. "Do we?"

"No. And I don't get no homework neither," say Big Butt.

"And I don't even have a home," say Flyboy like he do at school to keep the white folks off his back and sorry for him. Send this poor kid to camp posters, is his specialty.

"I do," says Mercedes. "I have a box of stationery on my desk and a picture of my cat. My godmother bought the stationery and the desk. There's a big rose on each sheet and the envelopes smell like roses."

"Who wants to know about your smelly-ass stationery," say Rosie Giraffe fore I can get my two cents in.

"It's important to have a work area all your own so that . . ."

"Will you look at this sailboat, please," say Flyboy, cuttin her off and pointin to the thing like it was his. So once again we tumble all over each other to gaze at this magnificent thing in the toy store which is just big enough to maybe sail two kittens across the pond if you strap them to the posts tight. We all start reciting the price tag like we in assembly. "Handcrafted sailboat of fiberglass at one thousand one hundred ninety-five dollars."

"Unbelievable," I hear myself say and am really stunned. I read it again for myself just in case the group recitation put me in a trance. Same thing. For some reason this pisses me off. We look at Miss Moore and she lookin at us, waiting for I dunno what.

"Who'd pay all that when you can buy a sailboat set for a quarter at Pop's, a tube of glue for a dime, and a ball of string for eight cents?" "It must have a motor and a whole lot else besides," I say. "My sailboat cost me about fifty cents."

"But will it take water?" say Mercedes with her smart ass.

"Took mine to Alley Pond Park once," say Flyboy. "String broke, Lost it. Pity."

"Sailed mine in Central Park and it keeled over and sank. Had to ask my father for another dollar."

"And you got the strap," laugh Big Butt. "The jerk didn't even have a string on it. My old man wailed on his behind."

Little Q.T. was staring hard at the sailboat and you could see he wanted it bad. But he too little and somebody'd just take it from him. So what the hell. "This boat for kids, Miss Moore?"

"Parents silly to buy something like that just to get all broke up," say Rosie Giraffe.

"That much money it should last forever," I figure.

"My father'd buy it for me if I wanted it."

"Your father, my ass," say Rosie Giraffe getting a chance to finally push Mercedes.

"Must be rich people shop here," say Q.T.

"You are a very bright boy," say Flyboy. "What was your first clue?" And he rap him on the head with the back of his knuckles, since Q.T. the only one he could get away with. Though Q.T. liable to come up behind you years later and get his licks in when you half expect it.

"What I want to know is," I says to Miss Moore though I never talk to her, I wouldn't give the bitch that satisfaction, "is how much a real boat costs? I figure a thousand'd get you a yacht any day."

"Why don't you check that out," she says, "and report back to the group?" Which really pains my ass. If you gonna mess up a perfectly good swim day least you could do is have some answers. "Let's go in," she say like she got something up her sleeve. Only she don't lead the way. So me and Sugar turn the corner to where the entrance is, but when we get there I kinda hang back. Not that I'm scared, what's there to be afraid of, just a toy store. But I feel funny, shame. But what I got to be shamed about? Got as much right to go in as anybody. But somehow I can't seem to get hold of the door, so I step away for Sugar to lead. But she hangs back too. And I look at her and she looks at me and this is ridiculous. I mean, damn, I have never ever been shy about doing nothing or going nowhere. But then Mercedes steps up and then Rosie Giraffe and Big Butt crowd in behind and shove, and next thing we all stuffed into the doorway with only Mercedes squeezing past us, smoothing out her jumper and walking right down the aisle. Then the rest of us tumble in like a glued-together jigsaw done all wrong. And people lookin at us. And it's like the time me and Sugar crashed into the Catholic church on a dare. But once we got in there and everything so hushed and holy and the candles and the bowin and the handkerchiefs on all the drooping heads, I just couldn't go through with the plan. Which was for me to run up to the altar and do a tap dance while Sugar played the nose flute and messed around in the holy water. And Sugar kept givin me the elbow. Then later teased me so bad I tied her up in the shower and turned it on and locked her in. And she'd be there till this day if Aunt Gretchen hadn't finally figured I was lyin about the boarder takin a shower.

Same thing in the store. We all walkin on tiptoe and hardly touchin the games and puzzles and things. And I watched Miss Moore who is steady watchin us like she waitin for a sign. Like Mama Drewery watches the sky and sniffs the air and takes note of just how much slant is in the bird formation. Then me and Sugar bump smack into each other, so busy gazing at the toys, 'specially the sailboat. But we don't laugh and go into our fat-lady bump-stomach routine. We just stare at that price tag. Then Sugar run a finger over the whole boat. And I'm jealous and want to hit her. Maybe not her, but I sure want to punch somebody in the mouth.

"Watcha bring us here for, Miss Moore?"

"You sound angry, Sylvia. Are you mad about something?" Givin me one of them grins like she tellin a grown-up joke that never turns out to be funny. And she's lookin very closely at me like maybe she plannin to do my portrait from memory. I'm mad, but I won't give her that satisfaction. So I slouch around the store bein very bored and say, "Let's go."

Me and Sugar at the back of the train watchin the tracks whizzin by large then small then gettin gobbled up in the dark. I'm thinkin about this tricky toy I saw in the store. A clown that somersaults on a bar then does chin-ups just cause you yank lightly at his leg. Cost $35. I could see me askin my mother for a $35 birthday clown. "You wanna who that costs what?" she'd say, cocking her head to the side to get a better view of the hole in my head. Thirty-five dollars could buy new bunk beds for Junior and Gretchen's boy. Thirty-five dollars and the whole household could go visit Granddaddy Nelson in the country. Thirty-five dollars would pay for the rent and the piano bill too. Who are these people that spend that much for performing clowns and $1,000 for toy sailboats? What kinda work they do and how they live and how come we ain't in on it? Where we are is who we are, Miss Moore always pointin out. But it don't necessarily have to be that way, she always adds then waits for somebody to say that poor people have to wake up and demand their share of the pie and don't none of us know what kind of pie she talkin about in the first damn place. But she ain't so smart cause I still got her four dollars from the taxi and she sure ain't gettin it. Messin up my day with this shit. Sugar nudges me in my pocket and winks.

Miss Moore lines us up in front of the mailbox where we started from, seem like years ago, and I got a headache for thinkin so hard. And we lean all over each other so we can hold up under the draggy-ass lecture she always finishes us off with at the end before we thank her for borin us to tears. But she just looks at us like she readin tea leaves. Finally she say, "Well, what did you think of F.A.O. Schwartz?"

Rosie Giraffe mumbles, "White folks crazy."

"I'd like to go there again when I get my birthday money," says Mercedes, and we shove her out the pack so she has to lean on the mailbox by herself.

"I'd like a shower. Tiring day," say Flyboy.

Then Sugar surprises me by sayin, "You know, Miss Moore, I don't think all of us here put together eat in a year what that sailboat costs." And Miss Moore lights up like somebody goosed her. "And?" she say, urging Sugar on. Only I'm standin on her foot so she don't continue.

"Imagine for a minute what kind of society it is in which some people can spend on a toy what it would cost to feed a family of six or seven. What do you think?"

"I think," say Sugar pushing me off her feet like she never done before, cause I whip her ass in a minute, "that this is not much of a democracy if you ask me. Equal chance to pursue happiness means an equal crack at the dough, don't it?" Miss Moore is besides herself and I am disgusted with Sugar's treachery. So I stand on her foot one more time to see if she'll shove me. She shuts up, and Miss Moore looks at me, sorrowfully I'm thinkin. And somethin weird is goin on, I can feel it in my chest.

"Anybody else learn anything today?" lookin dead at me. I walk away and Sugar has to run to catch up and don't even seem to notice when I shrug her arm off my shoulder.

"Well, we got four dollars anyway," she says.

"Uh hunh."

"We could go to Hascombs and get half a chocolate layer and then go to the Sunset and still have plenty money for potato chips and ice-cream sodas."

"Uh hunh."

"Race you to Hascombs," she say.

We start down the block and she gets ahead which is O.K. by me cause I'm goin to the West End and then over to the Drive to think this day through. She can run if she want to and even run faster. But ain't nobody gonna beat me at nuthin.

Questions for Study

1. What does Miss Moore want to teach Sylvia and her friends? How does she teach?

2. What kind of person is Sylvia? What is her attitude toward herself? What does she know? What does she not know?

3. What is Sylvia's attitude toward Miss Moore? What constitutes the conflict between them?

4. How does each of the places the group visits play a part in Miss Moore's lesson? How is the world Sylvia lives in different from the world represented by F. A. O. Schwartz?

5. What is Sylvia's epiphany? What does she mean by her final comments? What will become of her?

6. What is the "lesson"—to Sylvia, to us?

7. One critic has said that in Bambara's fiction there is "an undercurrent of caring for one's neighbors that sustains black Americans." Is this theme apparent in "The Lesson"?

EMILY PRAGER

A Visit from the Footbinder

Born in 1952, Emily Prager has dealt in her journalism and fiction with the destructive effects of sexism, racism, and environmental careless-ness. Her first novel, *Clea and Zeus Divorce* (1987) focuses on the ten-sions in the ten-year marriage of internationally famous performance artists. In her second novel, *Eve's Tattoo* (1991), the protagonist, a jour-nalist living in New York City, becomes obsessed with a photograph, taken in 1944 at Auschwitz, of a woman who looks strikingly like her. She identifies so completely with the woman that she tattoos her wrist with the same numbers as the woman's and invents a series of stories about who this woman was and how she ended up at Auschwitz. Through this device of multiple stories, Prager examines the dynamics of ethnic hatred as well as the roles women played in Nazi Germany. The stories in her first book, *A Visit from the Footbinder and Other Stories* (1982), satirize the social customs, often centuries old, that sub-jugate women.

"*I* shall have the finest burial tomb in China if it's the last thing I do," Lady Guo Guo muttered triumphantly to herself. It was midafternoon at the height of the sum-mer, and the Pavilion of Coolness was dark and still. She tottered over to the scrolls of snow scenes which lined the walls and meditated on them for a moment to relieve her-self from the heat.

"Sixteen summers in the making, sixteen memorable summers and finally ready for decor. Oh, how I've waited for this moment. I think blue for the burial chamber overall, or should it be green? Ah, Pleasure Mouse, do you think blue for Mummy's bur-ial chamber or green?"

Pleasure Mouse, aged six, second and youngest daughter of Lady Guo Guo, pon-dered this as she danced a series of jigs around her mother. "Blue would be lovely on you, Mummy, especially in death. Green, a bit sad and unflattering, I think."

"You are so right, Pleasure Mouse. Green reeks of decay. Such an unerring sense of taste in one so young—I see a fabulous marriage in your future. In two or three seasons, after Tiger Mouse has been wed," Lady Guo Guo looked away. "Revered Mummy," Pleasure Mouse was leaping up and down and tugging at her mother's very long sleeves, "At what hour will the footbinder come tomorrow? How long does it take? Can I wear the little shoes right away? Will I be all grown up then like Tiger Mouse?"

Lady Guo Guo shuffled quickly toward the teakwood table on which lay the blueprints of the pavilions erected to date. Pleasure Mouse ran in front of her and darted and pounced at her playfully like a performing mongoose at his colleague the performing snake.

As a result of this frolicking, Lady Guo Guo lost her balance and, grabbing on to the edge of the table to steady herself, she snapped angrily, "No answers, Pleasure Mouse! Because of your immodest behavior I will give no answers to your indelicate questions. Go now. I am very displeased."

"Yes, Mummy. I am sorry, Mummy," said Pleasure Mouse, much chastened, and, after a solemn but ladylike bow, she fled from the Pavilion of Coolness.

Pleasure Mouse raced across the white-hot courtyard, past the evaporating Felicitous Rebirth Fishpond, and into the Red Dust Pavilion, which contained the apartments of her thirteen-year-old sister, Tiger Mouse. Inside, all was light or shadow. There were no shades of gray. The pungent aroma of jasmine sachet hung on the hot, dry air like an insecure woman on the arm of her lover. As usual, Tiger Mouse was kneeling on the gaily tiled floor, dozens of open lacquer boxes spread around her, counting her shoes.

As Pleasure Mouse burst into the chamber, Tiger Mouse glanced up at her and said haughtily, "I have one thousand pairs of tiny satin shoes. If you don't believe me, you can count them for yourself. Go ahead," she said with a sweeping gesture, "count them. Go on!" Wavering slightly, hair ornaments askew, she got to her feet. Then she went on: "I have the tiniest feet in the prefecture, no longer than newborn kittens. Look. Look!"

Tiger Mouse toddled intently to a corner of the chamber in which stood the char-coal brazier used for heating in winter. Now, of course, it lay unused, iron-cold in the stifling heat. For a moment, she encircled it with her arms and rested her cheek and breast against the cool metal. Then she reached beneath it and amid a chorus of protesting squeaks brought out two newborn kittens, one in each hand, which she then placed beside each of her pointy little feet.

"Come," she cried. "Look," and she raised her skirt. Pleasure Mouse ran and squatted down before her. It was true. The newborn kittens, eyes glued shut, ears pasted to the sides of their heads, swam helplessly on the tiled floor, peeping piteously for milk. They were far more lively than Tiger Mouse's feet but certainly no bigger. Pleasure Mouse was terribly impressed.

"It is true what you say, Older Sister, and wonderful. No bigger than newborn kittens—"

"No *longer* than newborn kittens," Tiger Mouse barked.

"Indeed," Pleasure Mouse responded in a conciliatory tone and then, by way of a jest to lighten the moment, added, "Take care the mother cat does not retrieve your feet." Pleasure Mouse laughed sweetly and ran trippingly alongside Tiger Mouse as the latter, smiling faintly, wavered back to her many shoes and knelt before them.

"Tiger Mouse," Pleasure Mouse twirled around in embarrassment as she spoke, unsure of the consequences her questions might elicit, "The footbinder comes tomorrow to bind my feet. Will it hurt? What will they look like afterwards? Please tell me."

"Toads."

"What?"

"My feet are like the perfect Golden Lotus. But yours, horned toads. Big, fat ones."

"Oh, Tiger Mouse—"

"And it didn't hurt me in the least. It only hurts if you're a liar and a cheat or a sorcerer. Unworthy. Spoiled. Discourteous. And don't think that you can try on my shoes after, because you can't. They are mine. All one thousand pairs."

"Yes, Tiger Mouse." Pleasure Mouse dashed behind her and snatched up one pair of the tiny shoes and concealed them in the long sleeve of her tunic. "I must go for my music lesson now, Older Sister," she said as she hurried toward the chamber door. She stopped just short of exiting and turned and bowed. "Please excuse me."

"But perhaps," said Tiger Mouse, ignoring her request, "the pain is so great that one's sentiments are smashed like egg shells. Perhaps for many seasons, one cries out for death and cries unheeded, pines for it and yearns for it. Why should I tell you what no one told me?"

"Because I'd tell you?" answered Pleasure Mouse. But Tiger Mouse went back to counting her shoes. The audience was over.

Pleasure Mouse scampered out of the Red Dust Pavilion, past the evaporating Felicitous Rebirth Fishpond, and through the gate into the recently completed Perfect Afterlife Garden. When she reached the Bridge of Piquant Memory, she stopped to catch her breath and watch as her mother's maids watered the ubiquitous jasmine with the liquid of fermented fish in hopes that this might make it last the summer. The stench was overpowering, threatening to sicken, and Pleasure Mouse sped away along the Stream of No Regrets, through the Heavenly Thicket and into the Meadow of One Hundred Orchids, where her friends, the One Hundred Orchid Painters, sat capturing the glory of the blossom for all time.

Aged Fen Wen, the master painter, looked up from his silken scroll and smiled. For sixteen years, he had labored on Lady Guo Guo's burial tomb, at first in charge of screens and calligraphic scrolls, and now, since they were done, of wall hangings, paintings, window mats, and ivory sculpture. He had watched as Pleasure Mouse grew from a single brushstroke to an intricate design, and though he was but an artisan, he considered himself an uncle to her.

For her part, Pleasure Mouse adored Fen Wen. No matter where the old man was at work on the great estate, no matter how many leagues away, as soon as she awoke in the morning she would run and find him. During the winter when her family returned to the city, she missed him terribly, for although she loved her father, she rarely saw him. With Fen Wen there was no need to observe formalities.

Fen Wen was sitting, as was each of the ninety-nine other Orchid Painters, on an intricately carved three-legged stool before an ebony table on which lay a scroll and brushes. There were one hundred such tables, and in front of each grew a single tree, each one supporting an orchid vine, each vine bearing one perfect blossom. The trees grew in twenty rows of five across, and aged Fen Wen was giving leaf corrections at the southwestern corner of the meadow, where Pleasure Mouse now found him and, without further ado, leapt into his lap.

"Venerable Fen Wen," she said as she snuggled into his chest and looked deep into his eyes, "guess what."

Fen Wen wrinkled his Buddha-like brow and thought. "The emperor has opened an acting school in his pear garden?" he said finally.

"No."

"You have fallen in love with an imitator of animal noises?"

"No, no," Pleasure Mouse giggled happily.

"I give up," said Fen Wen, and Pleasure Mouse wiggled out of his lap and skipped in place as she related her news.

"The footbinder is coming tomorrow to bind my feet. And afterwards I shall wear tiny shoes just like these," she produced the pair she had stolen from Tiger Mouse, waved them before Fen Wen, then concealed them again, "and I will be all grown up—"

Pleasure Mouse halted abruptly. Fen Wen's great droopy eyes had filled with tears, and the Orchid Painters around him modestly looked away.

"Ah," he sighed softly. "Then we won't see you anymore."

"No. What do you mean? Why do you say that?" Pleasure Mouse grabbed on to Fen Wen's tunic and searched deeply into his eyes.

"At first, of course, you will not be able to walk at all, and then later when you have healed, you may make it as far as the front Moon Gate, but, alas, Pleasure Mouse, no farther. Never as far as this Meadow. Never as far. They won't want you to. Once your—"

"Won't be able to walk?" said Pleasure Mouse quizzically. "What do you mean? Lady Guo Guo walks. Tiger Mouse walks . . . "

Now began a silence as aged Fen Wen and the ninety-nine other Orchid Painters turned glumly toward the east, leaving Pleasure Mouse, age six, second and youngest daughter of Lady Guo Guo, alone and possessed of her first conceptual thought. Past experience joined with present and decocted future. Nuggets of comprehension, like grains of rice in a high wind, swirled behind her eyes, knocked together and blew apart. Only this softly spoken phrase was heard on earth.

"They cannot run," she said, "but I can." And she ran, through the Meadow of One Hundred Orchids, down the Path of Granted Wishes, and out the Sun Gate into the surrounding countryside.

Just outside the market town of Catchow, a mile or so down the Dragon Way near the vast estate of the prefect Lord Guo Guo, lay situated the prosperous Five Enjoyments Teahouse. On this spot one afternoon in the tenth century, three hundred years before the teahouse was built and our story began, a Taoist priest and a Buddhist nun were strolling together and came upon a beggar. Filthy and poor, he lay by the side of the road and called out to them, "Come over here. I am dying. I have only this legacy to leave." The beggar was waving something and the Taoist priest and the Buddhist nun moved closer to see what it was.

"Look," said the beggar, "it is a piece of the very silk with which the emperor bade a dancing girl swaddle her feet that they might look like points of the moon sickle. She then danced in the center of a six-foot lotus fashioned out of gold and decorated with jewels." The beggar fell backward, exhausted by his tale, and gasped for breath. The Taoist priest and the Buddhist nun examined the dirty, bloody, ragged scrap of cloth and glanced at each other with great skepticism.

"Ah yes. It is an interesting way to step from Existence into Nonexistence, is it not?" said the Buddhist nun.

"Indeed," replied the Taoist priest. "So much easier to escape Desire and sidle closer to Immortality when one can follow only a very few paths. But alas, in time, this too will pass."

There was a rattle in the beggar's throat then, and his eyes rolled upward and grasping the scrap of silk, he died.

The Taoist priest and the Buddhist nun murmured some words of prayer over the beggar's body, linked arms and continued their travels. The ragged scrap of bloody cloth fluttered to the ground and was transformed by the Goddess of Resignation into a precious stone that lay at that very spot until the year 1266, when it was discovered and made into a ring by the famous courtesan Honey Tongue, star attraction of The Five Enjoyments Tea House, which had been built nearby some years before.

Pleasure Mouse, taking extreme care not to be seen, scrambled up the back stairs of The Five Enjoyments Tea House and sneaked into the luxurious apartments of her father's good friend, the famous courtesan, Honey Tongue. She startled the beauteous lady as she sat before her mirror tinting her nails with pink balsam leaves crushed in alum. "Oh!" exclaimed Honey Tongue. "Why, it's Pleasure Mouse, isn't it? Sit down, little one, you're out of breath. What brings you here?"

Pleasure Mouse collapsed on a brocade cushion and burst into tears. The beauteous lady floated to her side and hugged her warmly to her perfumed breast. "Oh dear," crooned Honey Tongue, rocking back and forth, "oh dear oh dear oh dear," until finally Pleasure Mouse was able to speak: "Tomorrow, the footbinder comes to bind my feet and—"

Honey Tongue brought her hands to her mouth and laughed behind them. She rose from Pleasure Mouse's cushion and, still laughing, wafted back to her seat before her mirror. She fiddled for a moment with her hair ornaments and began to apply the stark white Buddha adornment to her face and afterward the deep-rose blush.

As all this seemed to contain great meaning, Pleasure Mouse ceased speaking and ran to her side, watching in the mirror everything the lovely lady did. When she was done plucking her eyebrows and smoothing on the final drop of hair oil, she smiled the loveliest of sunny smiles and said, "It's a bargain, Pleasure Mouse. The pain goes away after two years, and then you have a weapon you never dreamed of. Now, run along home before someone sees you here."

Pleasure Mouse did as she was told, but as she was speeding along the Dragon Way, trying to reach the eastern Sun Gate of the estate before she was seen, she had the bad fortune to run smack into the sedan chair procession of her father's older sister, Lao Bing. Her old auntie had come all the way from the city for the footbinding, and when she peered out the window of her sedan chair and saw Pleasure Mouse, she bellowed in an imperious tone, "Halt!"

The bearers halted abruptly and set the sedan chair down in the middle of the

Dragon Way. An enormous donkey cart, that of the night-soil collector, which had been following a few lengths behind the procession, now was forced to halt also, and a vicious verbal battle ensued between the chair bearers and the night-soil collector and his men as to who had the right of way. Lao Bing paid no attention to this melee. She opened the door of the sedan chair and cried out, "All right, Pleasure Mouse, I see you. Come over here this minute."

Pleasure Mouse ran to the sedan chair and scampered inside. As she closed the door, Lao Bing bellowed, "Drive on!" and the bearers stopped quarreling with the collector, hoisted the sedan chair poles onto their knobby-muscled shoulders, and continued in a silent run to the estate.

The sedan chair rocked like a rowboat on a storm-tossed sea. Pleasure Mouse began to feel queasy inside the dark box. The odor of Lao Bing's hair oil permeated the heavy brocades, and the atmosphere was cloying. The old one's hair ornaments jiggled in emphasis as she spoke.

"Really, Pleasure Mouse, young maidens of good family are not allowed outdoors much less outside the estate grounds. Oh, if your father knew I had found you on the Dragon Way . . . "

"Dearest Auntie," entreated Pleasure Mouse, "please don't tell. I only thought since the footbinder is coming tomorrow and I'll no longer be able to—"

"Footbinder?" Lao Bing seemed perturbed. "What footbinder? You don't mean to tell me your mother has *hired* a footbinder for tomorrow?" Pleasure Mouse nodded.

"Really, that woman spends like a spoiled concubine!" Lao Bing peeked through the curtain on the window and sighed in resignation. "All right, Pleasure Mouse, we are inside the Sun Gate now. You may get down. Halt!" The bearers halted and Lao Bing opened the door.

"Auntie?" Pleasure Mouse hesitated before the door. "What is it like?"

Lao Bing mulled the question over for a moment and then replied briskly, "It is something a woman must endure in order to make a good marriage. No more. No less, Pleasure Mouse. If you wish to live at court, you must have tiny feet. Logic, indubitable logic."

"And does it hurt, Lao Bing?" Pleasure Mouse gazed stoically into her aunt's eyes and prepared herself for the reply. The old lady never minced words.

"Beauty is the stillbirth of suffering, every woman knows that. Now scamper away, little mouse, and dream your girlish dreams, for tomorrow you will learn some secret things that will make you feel old."

Lao Bing closed the door of the sedan chair and gave the order: "Drive on!" Pleasure Mouse circled the Meadow of One Hundred Orchids, traversed The Heavenly Thicket, and made her way to the recently constructed Avenue of Lifelong Misconceptions, where she passed the afternoon contemplating her future footsize.

Lady Guo Guo was receiving in her burial chamber. It was bleak in the dense stone edifice, dim, musty and airless, but it was cool and the flaming torches affixed to the walls gave off a flickering, dangerous light. A party of silk weavers from Shantung milled nervously in one corner while their agent haggled with Lady Guo Guo over a quantity of mouse-vein-blue silk. In another corner, the head caterer waited to discuss the banquet of the dead and dodged attempts by a group of nosy flower arrangers to guess the menu. There were poetry chanters, trainers of performing insects, literary men—throngs of humanity of every occupation crammed into the burial chamber and its anteroom, hoping to be hired for a day's labor. And many had been. And many were. One local glue maker had quite literally made his fortune off Lady Guo Guo in the last sixteen years. He had retired early, well fed and happy. And he was but one among many.

It was through this teeming mass of gilders, cutlers, jugglers, sack makers, pork butchers and pawnshop owners, that Lao Bing now made her way preceded by three servants who, rather noisily and brutishly, made a path. Lady Guo Guo, distracted by the commotion, looked up from her bargaining, recognized her sister-in-law, and hurried to greet her.

"Welcome, venerable, husband's sister, to my recently completed burial chamber. Majestic, is it not? I shall enter the afterlife like a princess wearing a gown of," Lady Guo Guo snapped the bolt of silk and it unrolled like a snake across the cold stone floor, "this blue silk. My color, I think you'll admit. Thank goodness you have come with all your years of wisdom behind you," Lao Bing sniffed audibly, "for I need your advice, Lao Bing. Do we do the wall hangings in the blue with a border in a green of new apples or a green of old lizards who have recently sluffed their skin? Question two: Who shall do my death mask and who my ancestor portrait? Should the same man do both?"

"Old lizards and different men," said Lao Bing decisively, and tottered over to a sandalwood stool and sat on it. "Little Sister," she began, a note of warning in her voice, "these days the lord, your husband, reminds me of a thunderclap in clothes. Day and night the creditors camp outside the door of the prefecture. He asks why you do not use the rents from the rooming houses you inherited from your father to pay these merchants?"

"What? And deplete my family's coffers? The lord, my husband, is as tight with cash as the strings on a courtesan's purse, Lao Bing, and no tighter. Do not deceive yourself."

"Well, really," said Lao Bing, her sensibilities offended, and her message delivered, abruptly changed the subject. "They say that the fallow deer sold in the market is actually donkey flesh. It's a dreadful scandal. The city is buzzing with it. And as if that weren't enough—" Lao Bing lowered her voice, rose from her seat, and ushered Lady Guo Guo away from the throngs and down into the depression in the vast stone floor where her coffin would eventually lie. "As if that weren't enough," Lao Bing continued, sotto voce, "the emperor is using his concubines to hunt rabbits."

Lady Guo Guo was horror-struck. "What? Instead of dogs?"

Lao Bing nodded solemnly.

"But they cannot run."

"Ah, well, that's the amusement in it, don't you see? They cannot possibly keep up with the horses. They stumble and fall—"

Lady Guo Guo swayed from side to side. "No more please. I feel faint."

"You are too delicate, younger brother's wife."

"For this world but not for the next." Lady Guo Guo patted the lip of the depression to emphasize her point.

"Hmm, yes," said Lao Bing, "if it is up to you. All of which brings me to the subject of tomorrow's footbinding. Pleasure Mouse tells me you've *hired* a footbinder."

"Really, Lao Bing, expense is no object where my daughter's feet—"

"I have no concern with the expense, Little Sister. It is simply that the Guo Guo women have been binding their daughters' feet themselves for centuries. To pay an outsider to perform such an intimate, such a traditional, such an honorable and serious act is an outrage, a travesty, a shirking of responsibility, unlucky, too arrogant and a dreadful loss of face."

"Lao Bing." Lady Guo Guo climbed out of the depression with the help of a sack maker who hurried over to ingratiate himself. "You are like an old donkey on the Dragon Way, unable to forge a new path, stubbornly treading the muddy ruts of the previous donkey and cart. This footbinder is a specialist, an artist, renowned throughout the district. And what is most important in this mortal world, I'm sure you'll agree, is not who does or does not do the binding, but the size of Pleasure Mouse's feet once it's done."

Lao Bing clapped her hands, and her servants appeared by her side, hoisted her out of the depression and set her down once again on the cold stone floor. Her hair ornaments spun with the impact. "Very well," she said after some moments of icy reflection. "But let us hope that with your modern ways you have not offended any household spirits."

A breeze of fear gusted across Lady Guo Guo's features. "I am not a fool, Lao Bing," she said quietly. "In the last few days I have burned enough incense to propitiate the entire netherworld. I have begged the blessing of ancestors so long departed they failed to recognize our family name and had to be reminded. The geomancer claimed he had never seen anything like it—before he collapsed from exhaustion."

"And he is sure about tomorrow?" Lao Bing asked, and then regretted it.

"Really, Lao Bing." Lady Guo Guo turned on a tiny heel and scurried back to her bargaining table. With a snap of her fingers, she summoned two maids and instructed them to show Lao Bing to her apartments in the Red Dust Pavilion. The old lady, suddenly fatigued by her journey, waddled slowly over to her sister-in-law's side and said gently, "Forgive me, Little Sister. It is a festival fraught with sentiments, worse this time perhaps because it is my perky Pleasure Mouse."

But Lady Guo Guo had returned to her business. "I'll take the green of old lizards," she was saying to the silk weavers' agent, "at three cash per yard and not a penny more." Haggling began anew and echoed off the great stone walls. Lao Bing departed, preceded by her servants, who elbowed her way into the crowd, which parted for a moment to admit her and then closed behind her again. Just like, thought Lady Guo Guo, a python who swallows whole its prey.

In the hot, dry center of the oven-baked night, Pleasure Mouse tossed and turned and glowed with tiny drops of baby sweat. Ordinarily, the nightly strumming of the zither players out in the courtyard would have long since lulled her to sleep, but not this night. She was far too excited.

She sat up on her lacquered bed, crossed her legs, and removed from beneath her pillow, the tiny pair of shoes she had stolen from her sister. She stroked them for a moment, deep red satin with sky-blue birds and lime-green buds embroidered over all, and then placed them on the coverlet in the strongest of rays of blue moonlight.

"How sweet," she murmured to herself, "how beauteous. Soon I will embroider some for myself and I will choose . . . cats and owls. So tiny, I do not see how—"

And she glanced around to make sure she was alone and unseen, and stealthily picked up one shoe and tried to slip it on her foot. But it would not fit, in any way whatsoever. Most of her toes, her heel and half of her foot spilled over the sides. She was very disappointed. "Perhaps my feet are already too big," she sighed aloud, and might have tried once more like panicked birds who fly into the window mat and though they've gained no exit, fly again, but just then the jagged sound of breaking glass shattered her reverie, and up she sprang and hid the tiny shoes beneath her pillow.

"Who goes there?" she cried, and ran to the door of her chamber.

"Oh, great heavens, Pleasure Mouse, it's I," came the whispered reply, and Pleasure Mouse sighed with relief and slipped into the corridor. There, crisscrossed by moonlight, on her knees before a broken vial, her father's concubine, Warm Milk, age nineteen and great with child for lo these six long moons, looked up at her and wept. "Oh, Pleasure Mouse," she managed through her tears, "I've ruined the decoction. I'll never get more dog flies now in time, or earthworms, for that matter. It took weeks to collect the ingredients and I've dropped them. It's my legs. They're swollen like dead horses in the mud. And as for my feet, well, they're no longer of this earth, Pleasure Mouse," Warm Milk rolled off her knees and sat squarely on the floor, her eyes tightly shut and soft moans of agony escaping her lips as she stretched her legs out in front of her. Pleasure Mouse stared at her opulent stomach, which looked like a giant peach protruding through Warm Milk's bedclothes and wondered what creature was inside. Warm Milk bent over and began to massage her legs. Her tiny white-bandaged feet stuck out beyond the hem of her nightgown like standards of surrender at a miniature battle. "They cannot bear the weight of two, Pleasure Mouse, but never say I said so. Promise?"

Pleasure Mouse nodded solemnly. "Promise," she replied, and examined Warm Milk's feet out of the corner of her eyes.

"They stink, Pleasure Mouse, that's the worst of it, like a pork butcher's hands at the end of a market day. It frightens me, Pleasure Mouse, but never say I said so. Promise?"

Pleasure Mouse nodded furiously. She would have liked to speak but when she tried, no voice was forthcoming. Her little girl's body had begun to contract with a terrible heat and in the pit of her stomach, feelings cavorted like the boxers she had heard of at the pleasure grounds.

Warm Milk leaned back on her hands and was silent for a moment. Her waist-length blue-black hair fell about her swollen little body and gleamed in the moonlight. Her flat, round face was blue-white, as pale and ghostlike as pure white jade. So too her hands.

"I was going to the shrine of the Moon Goddess to beg her for a boy. The decoction," she sat up and gestured at the oozy pink puddle that was beginning to travel along the corridor floor, "was to drink during the supplication. They say it always works, a male child is assured. Perhaps—" Warm Milk cupped her hands in the pink slime and brought it to her lips.

"No," cried Pleasure Mouse, horrified at such intimacy with dirt. "Please don't. You will be sick. Tomorrow I will run and find you many spiders and new dog flies too!" Warm Milk smiled gratefully at the little girl. "Will you, Pleasure Mouse?" she asked. And Pleasure Mouse remembered.

"Oh, no, I can't," she cried, blushing deeply. Her slanted eyes welled up with tears like tiny diamonds in the blue moonlight. "Tomorrow, the footbinder comes to bind my feet and—"

"You shan't be running anywhere." Warm Milk sighed resignedly and sucked the liquid from the palms of her hands. "What bad fortune, Pleasure Mouse, for us both, as it turns out. For us both. But never say I said so."

"Where are your toes?" Pleasure Mouse asked suddenly and without advance thought. It was just that she had glanced at Warm Milk's feet and finally realized what was different about them.

"My what?" asked Warm Milk nervously.

"Your toes." Pleasure Mouse squatted down before the bandaged feet and pointed a tiny finger at them. "I have five toes. You have one. Did they cut the others off?" Her eyes were wide with terror.

"No." Warm Milk pulled her nightgown over her feet. "No, of course not."

"Well, what happened to them?" Pleasure Mouse looked directly into Warm Milk's kind black eyes and awaited an answer.

Warm Milk dropped her head and basked for a moment in the blue moonlight. Out in the courtyard, the zither players were at their height, their instruments warm and responsive, their male hearts carried away by the loveliness of the tune. At length, Warm Milk spoke.

"When I was but five seasons old, the elegance of my carriage and the delicacy of my stature were already known far and wide. And so my mother, on the counsel of my father, bound my feet, which was an unusual occurrence for a maid of my then lowly peasant status. I could not run. I could not play. The other girls made mockery of my condition. But when I was ten, your father spied my little shrew-nosed feet and bought me from my father for his honorable concubine. Beneath your venerable father's wing I have nestled healthfully and prosperously for many seasons but never so happily as when I see, from the heights of my sedan chair, my big-footed playmates now turned flower-drum girls hawking their wanton wares by the river's edge."

Warm Milk laughed modestly. "Do you understand me, Pleasure Mouse?" Pleasure Mouse nodded, but she wasn't sure. "Yes, Honorable Concubine, but about your toes, where—" She began again but was interrupted by the appearance of six horrified maids who should have been on duty throughout the pavilion but who, because of the closeness of the evening, had ventured into the courtyard to watch the zither players, and had quite forgotten their charges in the romance of the moonlight and song.

The corridor rang with noises of reproach and then, like ants with a cake crumb, four of the maids quickly lifted up the concubine Warm Milk and bore her away to her apartments. The remaining two hurried Pleasure Mouse into her chamber and into her bed.

"I want my dolly," said Pleasure Mouse mournfully, and the maid brought it to her. The big rag doll, fashioned for her by aged Fen Wen, with the lovely hand-painted face of the Moon Goddess, black hair of spun silk, and masterfully embroidered robes, came to her anxious mistress with open arms. Pleasure Mouse hugged her close and sniffed deeply at her silken hair. Then she slid her hand under the pillow, pulled out the tiny shoes and slipped them on the dolly's rag feet. After a bit of stuffing and pushing, the shoes fitted perfectly. And Spring Rain, for that was the dolly's name, looked so ladylike and harmonious of spirit in the tiny shoes that Pleasure Mouse forgot her fears and soon was sound asleep.

The footbinder was late. Already it was two hours past cockcrow, and the courtyard outside the Temple of Two Thousand Ancestors was buzzing with anticipation and excitement. The man with the performing fish had arrived early and so was understandably perturbed about the wait. So too the tellers of obscene stories and the kite flyer. Had it been another season, they might have chatted away the time, but it was midsummer and as the hours dragged by, the day grew hotter and the energy for physical performance ebbed slowly away. The zither players were doing their best to keep up spirits, strumming at first soothingly and then rousingly in celebration of the occasion. Hands holding fans wafted back and forth in tempo to the music, pausing only to pluck cloying hair and clothing from damp and heated skin.

Inside the dark, hot temple, Lady Guo Guo stamped her tiny foot. The din from the courtyard resounded through the walls, and she was dreadfully embarrassed before her ancestors. The geomancer, a thin, effeminate young man, shook his head and wrists.

"The propitious hour is upon us, Lady. After it passes, I cannot be responsible for the consequences."

Lao Bing, suffering mightily from the heat and certainly tired of waiting, concurred, "Really, Little Sister, we must get on with it. This is exactly what happens when you pay an outsider—oh!" Lao Bing, frustrated beyond words, ceased speaking and fanned herself wildly.

Before the altar, Pleasure Mouse sat on a stool with her feet soaking in a broth of monkey bones. She stared up at the portraits of her most recently departed ancestors, solemn in the yellow light of the prayer candles. Occasionally, her eyes traveled about the walls of the great chamber and met those of hundreds of other ancestors whom she had never known in life and of whom she had never heard.

Just after cockcrow, she had entered the temple and with the female members of her family, she had prayed to the Little-Footed Miss for the plumpest and softest and finest of Lotus Hooks. You could, Lao Bing informed her, end up with either Long Hairpins, Buddha's Heads or Red Cocoons. It all depended on the expertise of the binding, the favor of the ancestral and household spirits, and the propitiousness of the hour at which the feet were bound. The broth of monkey bones was to soften her feet, to make them malleable enough to fit into the tiny pair of red satin boots that her mother had made for her and which now sat upon the altar like an offering to the gods.

"I have paid for a footbinder, and I shall have one!" snarled Lady Guo Guo, and followed by her maids, she lurched angrily from the temple.

The sunlight caught her unawares. It struck her like the projectile of a crossbow, and she was momentarily blinded and confused. She and her small procession immediately snapped open their fans, shielded their eyes from above and held this pose, unmoving, like an operatic tableau. Those in the courtyard pushed forward and back, chattering among themselves, eagerly awaiting instructions. The zither players struck up Lady Guo Guo's favorite tune, and as her eyes adjusted to the light, she dimly perceived members of the crowd being shoved to and fro and finally propelled to one side to permit the entrance of, she focused her eyes sharply to make sure, her husband and master, the prefect, Lord Guo Guo.

Lady Guo Guo bowed as did the entire crowd and said, "Welcome, my lord, an unexpected pleasure. I had no idea you were in the neighborhood. You are stopping at The Five Enjoyments Tea House, I presume?"

"Ah, if only I could afford to," he replied pointedly. "But alas, I'm just passing through on a visit to the sub-prefect."

"Let us climb the belvedere," began Lady Guo Guo nervously, "for there we can speak in private." She hurried toward the turret, which was hard by the temple. "I call it Hereafter-View, for its beauty is quite suffocating." Lord Guo Guo followed and then stopped, carefully examining the stones at the belvedere's base.

"What stone is this?" he asked. His copyist followed, taking notes.

"Marble," Lady Guo Guo answered nonchalantly as if he ought to know.

"From?"

"From . . ." Lady Guo Guo concentrated intently. "From, from, from—forgive me, husband, I have forgotten the name. I am overwrought. Your arrival has coincided with Pleasure Mouse's footbinding. The propitious hour is upon us; I cannot—"

"Perhaps I can help you remember. It is a Chinese name?"

"No," snapped the Lady, and fled into the belvedere and up the winding marble steps. The Lord followed.

"No? Not a Chinese name, then presumably not from China. Imported then. Let me think. Annam? Champa?"

Lady Guo Guo disappeared beyond the next turn in the stairs. The Lord stayed behind.

"What?" he cried out. "Not even from the East? How luxurious! From the West, then. Ah, I know! Egypt!" Lord Guo Guo removed a knife from his sash and proceeded to carve a message into the marble wall. The knife scraped unpleasantly against the stone, and curious as to the noise, Lady Guo Guo reappeared around the bend. The message read: "Paid for by the prefect, Lord Guo Guo," and the date, "1260." The Lady gasped. "How dare you deface my belvedere?" she demanded.

"How dare you use my wealth to make the merchants rich? Pretty soon there will be no aristocracy left. At the rate you are spending, I shall be the first to go." Lord Guo Guo put away his knife.

"If you are so fearful, why do you not impose excessive taxes or put a ceiling on prices as you did last year when you bought yourself your title? As it is, I must purchase everything from the shops you own under a fraudulent name, and shoddy merchandise it is too! This marble was my one extravagance—"

"No more credit," Lord Guo Guo said simply, and Lady Guo Guo sank to her knees and sobbed.

"You men are so cruel," she cried, her tears dropping to the marble step. "Building this tomb is my one last pleasure, and you will take it from me just as you took from me my ability to walk. Well, let me tell you, you may cripple me in this endeavor, but you will never stop me."

"Men took from you your ability to walk?" the Lord said incredulously. "Is it the man who pulls the binding cloth to cripple a daughter's feet? No man could do a thing like that. No man could bear it."

"No man would marry a natural-footed woman. There is more to binding feet than just the binding!"

"If all women were natural-footed, a man would have no choice," Lord Guo Guo concluded and began descending the stairs.

Lady Guo Guo shook with fury and called after him. "Shall I leave your daughter natural-footed then? Yes. Yes. You are quite right and logical. Let our family be the one to begin the new fashion, and we shall begin it with the perky Pleasure Mouse!" In her anger, the Lady called out theatrically to her maid, "Wild Mint! Tell the footbinder to go away; we shall not need her."

"The footbinder?" asked Lord Guo Guo quietly. "Then you will not do the binding yourself?"

"Shall the prefect Lord Guo Guo's daughter be natural-footed? Your choice, my lord."

"So." The Lord grinned. "You've hired another to do the job for you? An interesting twist."

"Natural feet or lotus hooks? Be quick, my husband, the propitious hour is passing and will not come again for a full twelve seasons of growth."

Lord Guo Guo grew impatient at this last and turned his back. "These are women's things, your affairs, wife, not mine," he muttered sullenly.

Lady Guo Guo tapped her tiny foot. "What if I were to fall ill, creating a disturbance, right this moment and allow the propitious hour to pass?"

"I wouldn't let you," Lord Guo Guo snarled.

"You could not prevent me. It is a women's ritual, my husband, and as such, depends on the good omen. A mother's falling ill during a ceremony at which no man can show his face, even a father, especially a father—"

"Would you harm your daughter to harm me? What is it you seek, wife?"

"Unlimited credit, sir. Decide quickly; there is little time left."

Lord Guo Guo's nostrils flared. "You have it, ma'am" were the words that he spat out as, robes flying, he hurtled through the belvedere door. Lady Guo Guo smiled to herself and followed quickly behind.

"Here, wife." The Lord spoke through gritted teeth and thrust a walking stick into the Lady's arms. "An ebony cane. Also imported like your marble from Africa. For the Pleasure Mouse, for after."

"Thank you, my lord," said Lady Guo Guo, bowing low, "and a good journey, sir. Please come again." And with that she was off, hobbling swiftly toward the temple courtyard before Wild Mint could send the footbinder away.

Pleasure Mouse looked around nervously at Lao Bing and the geomancer, who were whispering together.

"Well," sniffed Lao Bing, "if it comes to it, I'll do it myself then. I bound three daughters of my own with perfect success. Autumn Surprise won the Emperor's commendation for the most beauteous hooks at the Hu Street small foot contest. Now she's his concubine-in-waiting, if you don't mind."

"Exquisite," said the geomancer in his whiny voice. "But did you hear about the Sung sisters?"

"What?"

"Rivals for the same young man, Black Mist cut up all of Blue Jade's tiny shoes and heaped them in the courtyard for all to see!"

"No!"

"Yes. And speaking of concubines-in-waiting, I hear the Emperor often keeps them waiting for years, and in the harems with only each other for company, I hear they use each other's hooks for—"

"The footbinder has arrived," announced Lady Guo Guo as she entered the chamber. "Let us begin."

Lao Bing sent the geomancer a parting glance of daggers. "Leave us," she hissed and then turned to inspect the famous footbinder.

"Forgive me, everyone," the footbinder waved heartily at those assembled as she strode into the temple. "The youngest daughter of the Wang family persists in unbinding on the sly. Each time she does this I tell her I shall only have to pull the bindings tighter. After all, we have two reputations to think of, hers and mine. But you can't tell a child about Lotus Boats, as you all know. They never believe it can happen to them."

Lao Bing, Lady Guo Guo, and the various maidservants in the chamber nodded in understanding.

"Children think we are born with small feet," began Lao Bing.

"Oh, if only we were," sighed Lady Guo Guo, interrupting.

Lao Bing continued. "But once in Shensi Province, I saw a natural-footed peasant girl, well, you talk of Lotus Boats, but really Fox Paws would be more accurate. Feet as large as a catapult repairman's."

Pleasure Mouse twisted around and stared at the footbinder. Barely four feet high and as round as a carved ivory ball, the tiny woman removed her pointy-hooded homespun cloak and revealed herself to be a Buddhist nun. Shaved head and eyebrows, saffron robes, face unadorned by powder or blush, the little fat turnip of a woman bent down and picked up her basket and hurried toward the altar.

Lao Bing gasped in horror and took Lady Guo Guo roughly to one side. "What is the meaning of this? She's not wearing shoes! She's barefooted and natural-footed. I've never been so embarrassed, and what about Pleasure Mouse? I—"

"Shh!" Lady Guo Guo took Lao Bing's hands and tried to explain. "Not having bound feet herself, she is better able to make a really good job of binding others. It is an esthetic act to her, objective, don't you see? For us it is so much more, so clouded. Our sympathy overcomes our good judgment. Pleasure Mouse's feet will be as hummingbirds, you'll see."

"All right," sniffed Lao Bing. "I suppose it makes some sense. But my aunt did my bindings, and merciless she was." Lao Bing's voice had risen as she remembered. "I have always felt that had it been my own mama, some sympathy might have been shown for my agony."

"Perhaps," called the footbinder from across the room. "Perhaps not."

"At any rate," Lao Bing, outraged at the interruption, went on, "I blame such newfangled notions on the barbarians from the North, the Mongol hordes. I pray such contaminate influences do not sully my perky Pleasure Mouse. But if they do, I personally—"

"Silence, please," boomed the footbinder. And then, "Send away the throngs outside the temple!"

"No kiteflyer?" asked Lady Guo Guo timidly. "But we have always had a kiteflyer for before. It is the last time—"

"No. No. The feet swell from the running and it is far too difficult. As for the teller of obscene stories, he was present when I bound the Wang girls and, sadly, he is simply neither obscene nor funny."

"He seemed amply disgusting to me," mused Lady Guo Guo as she padded toward the chamber door.

"Yes, foul," agreed Lao Bing.

"Wild Mint." Lady Guo Guo's number one maidservant rushed forward and curtsied. "Clear the courtyard."

"But the man with the performing fish?"

"Keep him on retainer. Perhaps for the inaugural ceremonies."

Wild Mint nodded and rushed out. Some angry murmurs rose and fell, but soon there was bright, hot quiet outside, disturbed now and then only by the buzz of insects. Wild Mint re-entered the chamber and took up her post behind a red-lacquered pillar.

"Where is Tiger Mouse?" Lao Bing was whispering to Lady Guo Guo.

"I am afraid she is still too delicate to attend the ritual. She cannot as yet see the humor in it." Lady Guo Guo placed her finger across her lips to command silence then and turned her attention to what the footbinder was doing.

"What are you doing?" Pleasure Mouse was asking.

The footbinder trained her beady eyes on the child and answered directly, "I am tying you to the chair with leather thongs." She finished securing the last arm and leg and paused to examine her handiwork.

"Why?" asked Pleasure Mouse, pulling a bit against the bonds.

"It hurts, Pleasure Mouse, and if you writhe all over the place you will interfere with perfection of the binding. Now here, grasp these water chestnuts in each hand and when it hurts, squeeze them with all your might and if you are lucky, your feet will turn out no bigger than they are."

Pleasure Mouse took the water chestnuts and squeezed them in her palms. The footbinder scurried around in front of the altar, head bent to her task and mumbling to herself.

"Here's a handkerchief to wipe the tears. Here's my knife. The binding cloth. Alum. Red jasmine powder. All right. I think we are all ready. Is it the propitious hour?" The footbinder glanced at Lady Guo Guo, who nodded and came forward to one side of Pleasure Mouse's chair. She patted the little girl on the shoulder and smiled weakly. Lao Bing came forward as well and stood on the opposite side. "If we begin just at the propitious hour, it won't hurt," the old lady said without much conviction.

Warm Milk entered at this moment by the side door of the temple and sat without comment next to Lao Bing on a stool carried in by her maidservants. Warm Milk did not look well, so swollen was she with womanly waters pressurized by the heat. But she smiled at Pleasure Mouse and waved one of her long, long sleeves.

The footbinder took up the knife and knelt down in front of the chair and concentrated on the broth of monkey bones and Pleasure Mouse's feet. She draped a towel over her knees and picked up one foot and dried it. She then took the knife and brought it toward Pleasure Mouse's toes. The little girl shrieked with terror and fought against her bonds. Her mother and her aunt held her down and tried to placate her. Warm Milk stood up hurriedly and cried out,

"Do not be afraid, Pleasure Mouse. She means only to cut your toenails. Truly, little one, truly."

Pleasure Mouse relaxed and tears ran down her face and onto the new silk robe that her mother had embroidered just for this occasion. The footbinder grabbed Pleasure Mouse's handkerchief, dabbed her cheeks and proceeded to cut her toenails.

"Now, what are the rules that all ladies must obey? Let me hear them while I cut."

Pleasure Mouse recited in a clear, sad voice:

> Do not walk with toes pointed upwards.
> Do not stand with heels in midair.
> Do not move skirt when sitting.
> Do not move feet when lying down.
> Do not remove the binding for there is
> nothing esthetic beneath it.

"And because, once bound, a foot does not feel well unbound. Excellent, Pleasure Mouse," said the footbinder setting down her knife and rubbing the child's feet with alum. "I can see that once your hooks are formed, you will be quite a little temptress." The footbinder winked lewdly at Lao Bing and Lady Guo Guo. "I predict buttocks like giant pitted plums, thighs like sacks of uncombed wool, a vagina with more folds than a go-between's message, and a nature as subdued as a eunuch's desire."

The women in the temple tittered modestly, and Pleasure Mouse blushed and squirmed beneath the bonds.

Suddenly, Pleasure Mouse became mesmerized by a beauteous ring on the right index finger of the footbinder's dimpled hand. It flashed in the light of the prayer candles, and as the footbinder laid out the silk binding cloths, it created, in midair, a miniature fireworks display.

"What a splendid ring," murmured Pleasure Mouse.

"What ring, dear?" asked Lady Guo Guo.

"That one, there—" Pleasure Mouse indicated the footbinder's right hand with a bob of her head, but the ring had gone, vanished.

"Never mind," said Pleasure Mouse, and squeezed the chestnuts in her tiny hands.

The footbinder took hold of the child's right foot and, leaving the big toe free, bent the other toes beneath the foot and bound them down with the long, silk cloth. The women gathered around the chair and watched the process intently. She then took a second cloth and bound, as tightly as she could, around the heel of the foot and down, again over and around the now bent toes, with the result that the heel and the toes were brought as close together as they could go, and the arch of the foot was forced upward in the knowledge that eventually it would break, restructure itself and foreshorten the foot. The last binding was applied beneath the big toe and around the heel, pushing the appendage up and inward like the point of a moon sickle. When the right foot was done, the footbinder bound the left foot in the same manner, removed the basin of monkey bone broth and retrieved the tiny shoes from the altar. She knelt before the Pleasure Mouse and, as she forced her bound feet into the shoes, Lady Guo Guo intoned a prayer: "Oh, venerable ancestors, smile favorably upon my perky Pleasure Mouse, that she may marry well and one day see her own daughter's entry into womanhood. Take the first step, my child. Take the first step."

Lady Guo Guo, Lao Bing and the footbinder untied the leather thongs and released Pleasure Mouse's arms and legs. Pleasure Mouse was silent and rigid in the chair.

"Up, dear," said Lao Bing, taking the child's elbow. "Up, you must walk."

"Take the first step," said Lady Guo Guo, grasping the other elbow.

"Up, child," said the footbinder, and she stood Pleasure Mouse on her newly fashioned feet.

Pleasure Mouse screamed. She looked down at the tiny shoes on her now strangely shaped feet and she screamed again. She jerked toward her mother and screamed a third time and tried to throw herself to the ground. The women held her up. "Walk," they chanted all together, "you must walk or you will sicken. The pain goes away in time."

"In about two years' time," crooned the courtesan, Honey Tongue. She had suddenly appeared in place of the footbinder who seemed to have vanished.

"Walk, little one, no matter how painful," Lao Bing grabbed the flailing child and shook her by the shoulders. "We have all been through it, can't you see that? You must trust us. Now walk!"

The women stepped back, and Pleasure Mouse hobbled two or three steps. Waves of agony as sharp as stiletto blades traversed the six-year-old's legs and thighs, her spine and head. She bent over like an aged crone and staggered around, not fully comprehending why she was being forced to crush her own toes with her own body weight.

Pleasure Mouse lunged toward the apparition and fell on the altar, sobbing and coughing. Honey Tongue enveloped her in a warm and perfumed aura.

"Do you wish to stay on earth, or do you wish to come with me?" Honey Tongue waved her long, long sleeve, and for a moment all was still. The women froze in their positions. Time was suspended in the temple.

"You can be a constellation, a profusion of stars in the summer sky, a High Lama in the great mountains to the East—a man, but holy. Or an orchid in the Perfect Afterlife Garden. Or you may stay as you are. It is your choice, Pleasure Mouse."

The little girl thought for a long while and then answered, "The only way to escape one's destiny is to enjoy it. I will stay here."

Honey Tongue vanished, and in her place reappeared the small, fat cabbage of a footbinder. The women wept and chattered, Pleasure Mouse moaned and bellowed in agony, and Time, its feet unbound, bounded on.

"Come, Pleasure Mouse. Sit," said the footbinder, and with her strong, muscled arms, she lifted the little girl and set her in the chair before the altar. The child sighed with relief and hung her head. The tiny shoes were stained with blood, as were her dreams of ladyhood. She whimpered softly. Warm Milk lurched painfully to her side, bent down and began to massage Pleasure Mouse's small burning legs. The women gathered around the altar, and the footbinder lit two prayer strips and recited:

Oh, Little Footed Miss, Goddess of our female fate, keep the Pleasure Mouse healthy and safe. Let her hooks be as round, white dumplings. Let them not turn to dead, brown shreds at the end of her legs. Let her blood not be poisoned or her spirit. Let her learn to walk daintily without pain, and let her not envy those who can run for they are lowly and abused. Ay, let her never forget: for them, running is not luxury but necessity. Let her marry a relative of the Emperor, if not the Emperor himself. And let her have many sons that, when the season comes, she might enter the afterlife like a princess.

Lady Guo Guo snapped her fingers. "Wild Mint, escort our new lady back to her chambers, if you please. I will come later, Pleasure Mouse, when the sun goes down, and I will bring with me an ebony cane sent by your father from the city. Look, little one, here is Spring Rain. Wild Mint sent for her that she might see you in your ladylike mantle."

"My word," gasped Lao Bing, "the doll wears the tiny shoes!"

Lady Guo Guo laughed. "So she does. How odd. Perhaps Tiger Mouse—"

Pleasure Mouse grabbed Spring Rain and ripped the shoes off her feet. She clasped the rag doll to her chest and stumbled from the temple.

Lady Guo Guo took the footbinder aside and paid her. The women wandered aimlessly from the temple into the sunlight.

"Oh dear," sighed Lao Bing. "I hurt all over again. As if fifty years ago were yesterday." She shielded her eyes from the sun with her fan.

"Must it always be so violent?" murmured Warm Milk.

"I don't know if it must be, but it always is," said the footbinder as she and Lady Guo Guo emerged from the temple.

"Have many young girls . . . died?" asked Lady Guo Guo.

"Some prefer death, Lady Gee, it is the way of the world." The footbinder climbed into her sedan chair. "I must be off," she said. "Keep the child on her hooks. I shall return in one week to wash and rebind. Please have the next smallest pair of shoes ready for my return. Goodbye."

Warm Milk curtsied to Lao Bing and Lady Guo Guo and with the aid of her maids, tottered past the departing procession toward her apartments.

Lao Bing and Lady Guo Guo watched the footbinder's sedan chair disappear through the Sun Gate, and when it was gone, Lao Bing clucked and said, "A footbinder. A footbinder. Ah, the seasons do change. I feel old, Little Sister. My toes are flattened out like cat tongues. The soles of my feet rise and fall like mountain peaks. How much did you pay her?"

"Thirty cash."

"Thirty cash!"

"It was worth it not to be the cause of pain," Lady Guo Guo said simply.

"Ah, yes, I see," sighed Lao Bing. "Well then, perhaps she won't blame you although—"

"After Tiger Mouse, I could not bear—you understand?"

"Of course." Lao Bing patted her brother's wife on the shoulder and, with a nod of her head, summoned her sedan chair.

"Farewell, Little Sister. We shall meet again in the city. I shall regale the Lord, your husband, with tales of the magnificence of your burial tomb, but be frugal, child, his patience falters."

"Thank you for your counsel, Lao Bing. It is well taken."

Lady Guo Guo closed the door of the sedan chair and waited until the pole bearers hoisted up the old lady and trotted away down the temple path.

The sun was iron-hot and glaring. Lady Guo Guo swept into a shadow of the temple eaves and stood there by herself, staring into nothingness, occasionally and absentmindedly waving her fan. After a time she ventured out into the sunlight, determined to make her way to the Pavilion of Coolness, where, she had decided, today she would take her rest. She padded past the Hereafter-View belvedere, across the Courtyard of a Thousand Fools, and right in front of the Zither Players' Wing, where the zither players caught sight of her and at once struck up her favorite tune. "China Nights" was the name of the song, and she waited politely in the white-hot sunlight until the final pings had died away. After bowing in thanks, she continued on, slower now, as she was losing strength. By the time she reached the Pavilion of Coolness, her hooks were puffy and throbbing like beating hearts.

Questions for Study

1. What image of medieval China (the time period of the setting) do the names of people and places convey? Why does the story begin with a discussion of burial chambers?

2. How is Pleasure Mouse described before the arrival of the footbinder? What do we see her doing most of the time? What is her attitude toward footbinding? What does she lose by the footbinding?

3. Who are the key female characters in the story? How does each one contribute to our understanding of the nature of this society? How is their attitude toward footbinding different from the men's attitude? What do the people think they gain by footbinding?

4. Why does the author describe the footbinding process in such detail?

5. The original cover for the book in which this story appeared—*A Visit from the Footbinder and Other Stories*—pictured a modern woman's foot crammed painfully into a high-heeled shoe. Is this an appropriate image for this story?

6. What does the story seem to be saying about the nature of human beauty? Who (or what) determines the criteria for beauty? What should the criteria be?

7. How is this story similar to Jewett's "A White Heron" (p. 401) and Jackson's "The Lottery" (p. 479)?

T. CORAGHESSAN BOYLE

Greasy Lake

T. Coraghessan Boyle (1948–) was born in Peekskill, New York. He was a music major in college and claims to have never read a book until he was eighteen. He taught high school in Garrison, New York, and then entered the Iowa Writer's Workshop in 1972. He received a Ph.D. in English from Iowa in 1977. He began publishing stories in national magazines in 1975. He has published three collections of stories: *The Descent of Man* (1979), *Greasy Lake and Other Stories* (1985), and *If the River Was Whiskey* (1989). His novels are *Water Music* (1981), *Budding Prospects: A Pastoral* (1984), *World's End* (1987), and *East Is East* (1990). His trademarks as a writer of fiction are exuberant and inventive prose, extravagant comic invention, and humorous representation of modern patterns of behavior. In *East Is East,* for example, Boyle uses the escapades of a young Japanese man, who jumps ship off the coast of Georgia and runs from the police, as a means to satirize both American and Japanese society.

> *It's about a mile down on the dark side of Route 88.*
> —*Bruce Springsteen*

*T*here was a time when courtesy and winning ways went out of style, when it was good to be bad, when you cultivated decadence like a taste. We were all dangerous characters then. We wore torn-up leather jackets, slouched around with toothpicks in our mouths, sniffed glue and ether and what somebody claimed was cocaine. When we wheeled our parents' whining station wagons out into the street we left a patch of rubber half a block long. We drank gin and grape juice, Tango, Thunderbird, and Bali Hai. We were nineteen. We were bad. We read André Gide and struck elaborate poses to show that we didn't give a shit about anything. At night, we went up to Greasy Lake.

Through the center of town, up the strip, past the housing developments and shopping malls, street lights giving way to the thin streaming illumination of the headlights, trees crowding the asphalt in a black unbroken wall: that was the way out to Greasy Lake. The Indians had called it Wakan, a reference to the clarity of its waters. Now it was fetid and murky, the mud banks glittering with broken glass and strewn with beer cans and the charred remains of bonfires. There was a single ravaged island a hundred yards from shore, so stripped of vegetation it looked as if the air force had strafed it. We went up to the lake because everyone went there, because we wanted to snuff the rich scent of possibility on the breeze, watch a girl take off her clothes and plunge into the festering murk, drink beer, smoke pot, howl at the stars, savor the incongruous full-throated roar of rock and roll against the primeval susurrus of frogs and crickets. This was nature.

I was there one night, late, in the company of two dangerous characters. Digby wore a gold star in his right ear and allowed his father to pay his tuition at Cornell; Jeff was thinking of quitting school to become a painter/musician/head-shop proprietor. They were both expert in the social graces, quick with a sneer, able to manage a Ford with lousy shocks over a rutted and gutted blacktop road at eighty-five while rolling a joint as compact as a Tootsie Roll Pop stick. They could lounge against a bank of booming speakers and trade "man"s with the best of them or roll out across the dance floor as if their joints worked on bearings. They were slick and quick and they wore their mirror shades at breakfast and dinner, in the shower, in closets and caves. In short, they were bad.

I drove. Digby pounded the dashboard and shouted along with Toots & the Maytals while Jeff hung his head out the window and streaked the side of my mother's Bel Air with vomit. It was early June, the air soft as a hand on your cheek, the third night of summer vacation. The first two nights we'd been out till dawn, looking for something we never found. On this, the third night, we'd cruised the strip sixty-seven times, been in and out of every bar and club we could think of in a twenty-mile radius, stopped twice for bucket chicken and forty-cent hamburgers, debated going to a party at the house of a girl Jeff's sister knew, and chucked two dozen raw eggs at mailboxes and hitchhikers. It was 2:00 A.M.; the bars were closing. There was nothing to do but take a bottle of lemon-flavored gin up to Greasy Lake.

The taillights of a single car winked at us as we swung into the dirt lot with its tufts of weed and washboard corrugations; '57 Chevy, mint, metallic blue. On the far side of the lot, like the exoskeleton of some gaunt chrome insect, a chopper leaned against its kickstand. And that was it for excitement: some junkie half-wit biker and a car freak pumping his girlfriend. Whatever it was we were looking for, we weren't about to find it at Greasy Lake. Not that night.

But then all of a sudden Digby was fighting for the wheel. "Hey, that's Tony Lovett's car! Hey!" he shouted, while I stabbed at the brake pedal and the Bel Air nosed up to the gleaming bumper of the parked Chevy. Digby leaned on the horn, laughing, and instructed me to put my brights on. I flicked on the brights. This was hilarious. A joke. Tony would experience premature withdrawal and expect to be confronted by grim-looking state troopers with flashlights. We hit the horn, strobed the lights, and then jumped out of the car to press our witty faces to Tony's windows; for all we knew we might even catch a glimpse of some little fox's tit, and then we could slap backs with red-faced Tony, roughhouse a little, and go on to new heights of adventure and daring.

The first mistake, the one that opened the whole floodgate, was losing my grip on the keys. In the excitement, leaping from the car with the gin in one hand and a roach clip in the other, I spilled them in the grass—in the dark, rank, mysterious night-time grass of Greasy Lake. This was a tactical error, as damaging and irreversible in its way as Westmoreland's decision to dig in at Khe Sanh. I felt it like a jab of intuition, and I stopped there by the open door, peering vaguely into the night that puddled up round my feet.

The second mistake—and this was inextricably bound up with the first—was identifying the car as Tony Lovett's. Even before the very bad character in greasy jeans and engineer boots ripped out of the driver's door, I began to realize that this chrome blue was much lighter than the robin's-egg of Tony's car, and that Tony's car didn't have rear-mounted speakers. Judging from their expressions, Digby and Jeff were privately groping toward the same inevitable and unsettling conclusion as I was.

In any case, there was no reasoning with this bad greasy character—clearly he was a man of action. The first lusty Rockette kick of his steel-toed boot caught me under the chin, chipped my favorite tooth, and left me sprawled in the dirt. Like a fool, I'd gone down on one knee to comb the stiff hacked grass for the keys, my mind making connections in the most dragged-out, testudineous way, knowing that things had gone wrong, that I was in a lot of trouble, and that the lost ignition key was my grail and my salvation. The three or four succeeding blows were mainly absorbed by my right buttock and the tough piece of bone at the base of my spine.

Meanwhile, Digby vaulted the kissing bumpers and delivered a savage kung-fu blow to the greasy character's collarbone. Digby had just finished a course in martial arts for phys-ed credit and had spent the better part of the past two nights telling us apocryphal tales of Bruce Lee types and of the raw power invested in lightning blows shot from coiled wrists, ankles, and elbows. The greasy character was unimpressed. He merely backed off a step, his face like a Toltec mask, and laid Digby out with a single whistling roundhouse blow . . . but by now Jeff had got into the act, and I was beginning to extricate myself from the dirt, a tinny compound of shock, rage, and impotence wadded in my throat.

Jeff was on the guy's back, biting at his ear. Digby was on the ground, cursing. I went for the tire iron I kept under the driver's seat. I kept it there because bad characters always keep tire irons under the driver's seat, for just such an occasion as this. Never mind that I hadn't been involved in a fight since sixth grade, when a kid with a sleepy eye and two streams of mucus depending from his nostrils hit me in the knee with a Louisville slugger; never mind that I'd touched the tire iron exactly twice before, to change tires: it was there. And I went for it.

I was terrified. Blood was beating in my ears, my hands were shaking, my heart turning over like a dirtbike in the wrong gear. My antagonist was shirtless, and a single cord of muscle flashed across his chest as he bent forward to peel Jeff from his back like a wet overcoat. "Motherfucker," he spat, over and over, and I was aware in that instant that all four of us—Digby, Jeff, and myself included—were chanting "motherfucker, motherfucker," as if it were a battle cry. (What happened next? the detective asks the murderer from beneath the turned-down brim of his porkpie hat. I don't know, the murderer says, something came over me. Exactly.)

Digby poked the flat of his hand in the bad character's face and I came at him like a kamikaze, mindless, raging, stung with humiliation—the whole thing, from the initial boot in the chin to this murderous primal instant involving no more than sixty hyperventilating, gland-flooding seconds—I came at him and brought the tire iron down across his ear. The effect was instantaneous, astonishing. He was a stunt man and this was Hollywood, he was a big grimacing toothy balloon and I was a man with a straight pin. He collapsed. Wet his pants. Went loose in his boots.

A single second, big as a zeppelin, floated by. We were standing over him in a circle, gritting our teeth, jerking our necks, our limbs and hands and feet twitching with glandular discharges. No one said anything. We just stared down at the guy, the car freak, the lover, the bad greasy character laid low. Digby looked at me; so did Jeff. I was still holding the tire iron, a tuft of hair clinging to the crook like dandelion fluff, like down. Rattled, I dropped it in the dirt, already envisioning the headlines, the pitted faces of the police inquisitors, the gleam of handcuffs, clank of bars, the big black shadows rising from the back of the cell . . . when suddenly a raw torn shriek cut through me like all the juice in all the electric chairs in the country.

It was the fox. She was short, barefoot, dressed in panties and a man's shirt. "Animals!" she screamed, running at us with her fists clenched and wisps of blow-dried hair in her face. There was a silver chain round her ankle, and her toenails flashed in the glare of the headlights. I think it was the toenails that did it. Sure, the gin and the cannabis and even the Kentucky Fried may have had a hand in it, but it was the sight of those flaming toes that set us off—the toad emerging from the loaf in *Virgin Spring,* lipstick smeared on a child: she was already tainted. We were on her like Bergman's deranged brothers—see no evil, hear none, speak none—panting, wheezing, tearing at her clothes, grabbing for flesh. We were bad characters, and we were scared and hot and three steps over the line—anything could have happened.

It didn't.

Before we could pin her to the hood of the car, our eyes masked with lust and greed and the purest primal badness, a pair of headlights swung into the lot. There we were, dirty, bloody, guilty, dissociated from humanity and civilization, the first of the Urcrimes behind us, the second in progress, shreds of nylon panty and spandex brassiere dangling from our fingers, our flies open, lips licked—there we were, caught in the spotlight. Nailed.

We bolted. First for the car, and then, realizing we had no way of starting it, for the woods. I thought nothing. I thought escape. The headlights came at me like accusing fingers. I was gone.

Ram-bam-bam, across the parking lot, past the chopper and into the feculent undergrowth at the lake's edge, insects flying up in my face, weeds whipping, frogs and snakes and red-eyed turtles splashing off into the night: I was already ankle-deep in muck and tepid water and still going strong. Behind me, the girl's screams rose in intensity, disconsolate, incriminating, the screams of the Sabine women, the Christian martyrs, Anne Frank dragged from the garret. I kept going, pursued by those cries, imagining cops and bloodhounds. The water was up to my knees when I realized what I was doing: I was going to swim for it. Swim the breadth of Greasy Lake and hide myself in the thick clot of woods on the far side. They'd never find me there.

I was breathing in sobs, in gasps. The water lapped at my waist as I looked out over the moon-burnished ripples, the mats of algae that clung to the surface like scabs. Digby and Jeff had vanished. I paused. Listened. The girl was quieter now, screams tapering to sobs, but there were male voices, angry, excited, and the high-pitched ticking of the second car's engine. I waded deeper, stealthy, hunted, the ooze sucking at my sneakers. As I was about to take the plunge—at the very instant I dropped my shoulder for the first slashing stroke—I blundered into something. Something unspeakable, obscene, something soft, wet, moss-grown. A patch of weed? A log? When I reached out to touch it, it gave like a rubber duck, it gave like flesh.

In one of those nasty little epiphanies for which we are prepared by films and TV and childhood visits to the funeral home to ponder the shrunken painted forms of dead grandparents, I understood what it was that bobbed there so inadmissibly in the dark.

Understood, and stumbled back in horror and revulsion, my mind yanked in six different directions (I was nineteen, a mere child, an infant, and here in the space of five minutes I'd struck down one greasy character and blundered into the waterlogged carcass
of a second), thinking. The keys, the keys, why did I have to go and lose the keys? I
stumbled back, but the muck took hold of my feet—a sneaker snagged, balance lost—
and suddenly I was pitching face forward into the buoyant black mass, throwing out
my hands in desperation while simultaneously conjuring the image of reeking frogs and
muskrats revolving in slicks of their own deliquescing juices. AAAAArrrgh! I shot from
the water like a torpedo, the dead man rotating to expose a mossy beard and eyes cold
as the moon. I must have shouted out, thrashing around in the weeds, because the
voices behind me suddenly became animated.

"What was that?"

"It's them, it's them: they tried to, tried to . . . *rape* me!" Sobs.

A man's voice, flat Midwestern accent. "You sons a bitches, we'll kill you!"

Frogs, crickets.

Then another voice, harsh, *r*-less, Lower East Side: "Mother-fucker!" I recognized
the verbal virtuosity of the bad greasy character in the engineer boots. Tooth chipped,
sneakers gone, coated in mud and slime and worse, crouching breathless in the weeds
waiting to have my ass thoroughly and definitively kicked and fresh from the hideous
stinking embrace of a three-days-dead-corpse, I suddenly felt a rush of joy and vindica-
tion: the son of a bitch was alive! Just as quickly, my bowels turned to ice. "Come on
out of there, you pansy motherfuckers!" the bad greasy character was screaming. He
shouted curses till he was out of breath.

The crickets started up again, then the frogs. I held my breath. All at once there
was a sound in the reeds, a swishing, a splash: thunk-a-thunk. They were throwing
rocks. The frogs fell silent. I cradled my head. Swish, swish, thunk-a-thunk. A wedge of
feldspar the size of a cue ball glanced off my knee. I bit my finger.

It was then that they turned to the car. I heard a door slam, a curse, and then the
sound of the headlights shattering—almost a good-natured sound, celebratory, like
corks popping from the necks of bottles. This was succeeded by the dull booming of
the fenders, metal on metal, and then the icy crash of the windshield. I inched forward,
elbows and knees, my belly pressed to the muck, thinking of guerrillas and comman-
dos and *The Naked and the Dead*. I parted the weeds and squinted the length of the
parking lot.

The second car—it was a Trans-Am—was still running, its high beams washing
the scene in a lurid stagy light. Tire iron flailing, the greasy bad character was laying
into the side of my mother's Bel Air like an avenging demon, his shadow riding up the
trunks of the trees. Whomp. Whomp. Whomp-whomp. The other two guys—blond
types, in fraternity jackets—were helping out with tree branches and skull-sized boulders. One of them was gathering up bottles, rocks, muck, candy wrappers, used con-
doms, pop-tops, and other refuse and pitching it through the window on the driver's
side. I could see the fox, a white bulb behind the windshield of the '57 Chevy.
"Bobbie," she whined over the thumping, "come *on*." The greasy character paused a
moment, took one good swipe at the left taillight, and then heaved the tire iron halfway
across the lake. Then he fired up the '57 and was gone.

Blond head nodded at blond head. One said something to the other, too low for me to catch. They were no doubt thinking that in helping to annihilate my mother's car they'd committed a fairly rash act, and thinking too that there were three bad characters connected with that very car watching them from the woods. Perhaps other possibilities occurred to them as well—police, jail cells, justices of the peace, reparations, lawyers, irate parents, fraternal censure. Whatever they were thinking, they suddenly dropped branches, bottles, and rocks and sprang for their car in unison, as if they'd choreographed it. Five seconds. That's all it took. The engine shrieked, the tires squealed, a cloud of dust rose from the rutted lot and then settled back on darkness.

I don't know how long I lay there, the bad breath of decay all around me, my jacket heavy as a bear, the primordial ooze subtly reconstituting itself to accommodate my upper thighs and testicles. My jaws ached, my knee throbbed, my coccyx was on fire. I contemplated suicide, wondered if I'd need bridgework, scraped the recesses of my brain for some sort of excuse to give my parents—a tree had fallen on the car, I was blindsided by a bread truck, hit and run, vandals had got to it while we were playing chess at Digby's. Then I thought of the dead man. He was probably the only person on the planet worse off than I was. I thought about him, fog on the lake, insects chirring eerily, and felt the tug of fear, felt the darkness opening up inside me like a set of jaws. Who was he, I wondered, this victim of time and circumstance bobbing sorrowfully in the lake at my back. The owner of the chopper, no doubt, a bad older character come to this. Shot during a murky drug deal, drowned while drunkenly frolicking in the lake. Another headline. My car was wrecked; he was dead.

When the eastern half of the sky went from black to cobalt and the trees began to separate themselves from the shadows, I pushed myself up from the mud and stepped out into the open. By now the birds had begun to take over for the crickets, and dew lay slick on the leaves. There was a smell in the air, raw and sweet at the same time, the smell of the sun firing buds and opening blossoms. I contemplated the car. It lay there like a wreck along the highway, like a steel sculpture left over from a vanished civilization. Everything was still. This was nature.

I was circling the car, as dazed and bedraggled as the sole survivor of an air blitz, when Digby and Jeff emerged from the trees behind me. Digby's face was crosshatched with smears of dirt; Jeff's jacket was gone and his shirt was torn across the shoulder. They slouched across the lot, looking sheepish, and silently came up beside me to gape at the ravaged automobile. No one said a word. After a while Jeff swung open the driver's door and began to scoop the broken glass and garbage off the seat. I looked at Digby. He shrugged. "At least they didn't slash the tires," he said.

It was true: the tires were intact. There was no windshield, the headlights were staved in, and the body looked as if it had been sledge-hammered for a quarter a shot at the county fair, but the tires were inflated to regulation pressure. The car was drivable. In silence, all three of us bent to scrape the mud and shattered glass from the interior. I said nothing about the biker. When we were finished, I reached in my pocket for the keys, experienced a nasty stab of recollection, cursed myself, and turned to search the grass. I spotted them almost immediately, no more than five feet from the open door, glinting like jewels in the first tapering shaft of sunlight. There was no reason to get philosophical about it: I eased into the seat and turned the engine over.

It was at that precise moment that the silver Mustang with the flame decals rumbled into the lot. All three of us froze; then Digby and Jeff slid into the car and slammed the door. We watched as the Mustang rocked and bobbed across the ruts and finally jerked to a halt beside the forlorn chopper at the far end of the lot. "Let's go," Digby said. I hesitated, the Bel Air wheezing beneath me.

Two girls emerged from the Mustang. Tight jeans, stiletto heels, hair like frozen fur. They bent over the motorcycle, paced back and forth aimlessly, glanced once or twice at us, and then ambled over to where the reeds sprang up in a green fence round the perimeter of the lake. One of them cupped her hands to her mouth. "Al," she called. "Hey, Al!"

"Come on," Digby hissed. "Let's get out of here."

But it was too late. The second girl was picking her way across the lot, unsteady on her heels, looking up at us and then away. She was older—twenty-five or -six—and as she came closer we could see there was something wrong with her: she was stoned or drunk, lurching now and waving her arms for balance. I gripped the steering wheel as if it were the ejection lever of a flaming jet, and Digby spat out my name, twice, terse and impatient.

"Hi," the girl said.

We looked at her like zombies, like war veterans, like deaf-and-dumb pencil peddlers.

She smiled, her lips cracked and dry. "Listen," she said, bending from the waist to look in the window, "you guys seen Al?" Her pupils were pinpoints, her eyes glass. She jerked her neck. "That's his bike over there—Al's. You seen him?"

Al. I didn't know what to say. I wanted to get out of the car and retch, I wanted to go home to my parents' house and crawl into bed. Digby poked me in the ribs. "We haven't seen anybody," I said.

The girl seemed to consider this, reaching out a slim veiny arm to brace herself against the car. "No matter," she said, slurring the *t*'s, "he'll turn up." And then, as if she'd just taken stock of the whole scene—the ravaged car and our battered faces, the desolation of the place—she said: "Hey, you guys look like some pretty bad characters—been fightin', huh?" We stared straight ahead, rigid as catatonics. She was fumbling in her pocket and muttering something. Finally she held out a handful of tablets in glassine wrappers: "Hey, you want to party, you want to do some of these with me and Sarah?"

I just looked at her. I thought I was going to cry. Digby broke the silence. "No, thanks," he said, leaning over me. "Some other time."

I put the car in gear and it inched forward with a groan, shaking off pellets of glass like an old dog shedding water after a bath, heaving over the ruts on its worn springs, creeping toward the highway. There was a sheen of sun on the lake. I looked back. The girl was still standing there, watching us, her shoulders slumped, hand outstretched.

Questions for Study

1. What is the economic and social background of the narrator and his friends? How do they see themselves at the beginning of the story? What do they think they know? What don't they know?

2. How is Greasy Lake described? To what senses does Boyle appeal? What do the details of the description suggest about the kind of place it is? What does it represent to the people who go there?

3. To what are the boys initiated at Greasy Lake? What experiences constitute their initiation?

4. Are the keys symbolic? The lake? The corpse?

5. What light does the quotation from Bruce Springsteen throw on the themes of the story?

6. How does this story resemble the myth of the Fall? (See p. 45 for a discussion of the myth.)

7. How do the girls at the end complete the boys' initiation?

8. How is this story similar to Hawthorne's "Young Goodman Brown"?

FOR FURTHER READING

Allen, Walter. *The Short Story in English.* New York: Oxford UP, 1981. Allen begins this historical survey of the short story with a brief discussion of the nature of the short story as distinct from earlier forms of short fiction.

Hanson, Clare, ed. *Re-reading the Short Story.* New York: St. Martin's Press, 1989. This anthology is a collection of essays presented at a symposium on the short story held in 1986.

Lohafer, Susan. *Coming to Terms with the Short Story.* Baton Rouge: Louisiana State UP, 1983. Lohafer's book is an excellent study of the short story in light of recent theories of literary criticism. It includes a useful bibliography.

Lohafer, Susan, and Jo Ellyn Clarey, eds. *Short Story Theory at a Crossroads.* Baton Rouge: Louisiana State UP, 1989. The topics of this collection of essays on the short story include definitions of the short story, new theoretical approaches, audience response, and endings.

Magill, Frank N., ed. *Critical Survey of Short Fiction.* Seven volumes. Englewood Cliffs: Salem Press, 1981. Volumes 1–2 include essays about short fiction; volumes 3–7 include discussions of well-known short story writers and their work. The essays in the first two volumes discuss definitions, elements, history, the traditions in different countries, and genres.

May, Charles E., ed. *Short Story Theories.* Columbus: Ohio UP, 1976. May collects here essays by critics and writers of the short story.

O'Connor, Frank. *The Lonely Voice: A Study of the Short Story.* Cleveland: World Publishing Co., 1963. O'Connor is one of the finest modern practitioners of the short story. This book-length study is thoughtful and beautifully written.

Poe, Edgar Allan. Review of Hawthorne's *Twice-Told Tales* (*Graham's Magazine,* 1842); review of Hawthorne's *Twice-Told Tales* and *Mosses from an Old Manse* (*Godey's Lady's Book,* 1847). *Essays and Reviews.* New York: Library of America. 569-88. Poe's reviews are among the first critical discussions of the short story.

Reid, Ian. *The Short Story.* New York: Methuen, 1977. This introduction to short fiction discusses the short story as one of many kinds of short fiction.

Short Story Criticism. Detroit: Gale Research Co., 1988-. This ongoing series features excerpts from criticism of short stories.

Twentieth-Century Short Story Explication. Hamden, Conn.: Shoe String Press, 1977-. This ongoing series lists works of criticism on short fiction written since 1800.

Chapter Eight
The Novel

INTRODUCTION

In its broadest sense, the term **novel** is used today for any relatively long fictional narrative written in prose. People speak loosely of science fiction, fantasy, and gothic narratives as "novels." But even though the novel is a very flexible genre and hard to define with precision, most critics seem to agree that the key characteristic of the novel is its realism, its adherence to a verifiable or at least commonly accepted understanding of the way the world is. More strictly speaking, then, the novel is a long, *realistic* fictional narrative in prose.

The term *novel* is a transliteration of the Italian *novella,* which was used in Europe for short, realistic tales like those in Boccaccio's *Decameron* (1348). *Novel,* which means "new," entered the English language in the eighteenth century to distinguish the new genre from romances, which had been in existence for centuries. In Europe the distinction between the romance and the novel seemed less clear; the term for the novel in most European countries was and still is *roman*—from *romance.*

The antecedents of the novel go back to classical antiquity. The novel has much in common, for example, with the epics of Homer and Vergil and the satirical narratives of Petronius and Apuleius. But the more immediate antecedents are the narrative forms popular in the sixteenth and seventeenth centuries: romances, biographies, memoires, travel narratives, letters, and tales. The first full-fledged novel, Cervantes's *Don Quixote* (1605, 1615), was a response to the romance. Cervantes began *Don Quixote* as a parody of the silly romances popular in Spain at the time, but he became so caught up in his characterization of Don Quixote and his companion, Sancho Panza, that the narrative transcended mere parody and became something new. The first novelists to write in English were Daniel Defoe, Samuel Richardson, and Henry Fielding. Defoe used the memoir as the model for *Robinson Crusoe* (1719) and *Moll Flanders* (1722). Richardson based *Pamela* (1740) and *Clarissa* (1747-48) on collections of letters that were used for moral instruction. Fielding claimed to model *Tom Jones* (1749) on the epic. His earlier novel, *Joseph Andrews* (1742), like *Don Quixote*, began as a parody but ended up as a novel.

The rise of the novel in the eighteenth century was accompanied by the emergence of a new readership. As economic prosperity grew in Western countries, the middle class became larger. More people learned to read and had the leisure to read. This new group of readers—often people who had risen from the lower classes—embraced the novel and established its popularity. Novels, in turn, reflected middle-class activities, aspirations, and values. Richardson's Pamela is a servant girl who, in defending her middle-class values, marries a wealthy estate owner. Robinson Crusoe is a merchant who applies sound management principles to the challenges imposed by shipwreck and isolation. Joseph Andrews, a servant, and Tom Jones, an illegitimate son on a country estate, find happiness and security in that most cherished of middle-class institutions, the family. Moll Flanders is a servant who escapes a life of crime through shrewd business practices.

After its birth in the eighteenth century, the novel rapidly became the most popular and prestigious literary form in Western countries. Authors like Jane Austen, Sir Walter Scott, Charles Dickens, Victor Hugo, James Fenimore Cooper, Nathaniel Hawthorne, George Eliot, Gustave Flaubert, and Thomas Hardy made the nineteenth century a golden age of the novel. Twentieth-century authors like Marcel Proust, James Joyce, Virginia Woolf, and William Faulkner experimented with the form of the novel, but left its fundamental characteristics intact.

The defining characteristic of the novel is realism. Novels can be realistic in many ways. Perhaps the most important is the realistic treatment of characters. To make characters seem real, novelists give them qualities we know that real people have. Realistic characters are psychologically complex. They exhibit a variety of emotions, motivations, and values. Realistic characters are morally complex. They may be destructive yet not "villains"; heroic yet flawed. Realistic characters are subject to the normal forces of nature. Time ages them. The physical and social context limits their opportunities and strength. Realistic characters can change and evolve. The lengthiness of novels makes it possible to develop characters who change in the same way that people often do in real life, slowly and in response to developing circumstances and new ideas.

A second manner in which novels are realistic is in the handling of setting. Novelists can create realistic settings in several ways. They can make the setting mirror real times and places. If we read a novel set in a place and time we know well, we can judge the accuracy of the setting from our own experience. Or if the setting is foreign to us, we can assess the novel's accuracy through research. How believably does Victor Hugo depict medieval Paris in *The Hunchback of Notre Dame?* We can answer that question by reading histories and other accounts of that place and period. Novelists also create realistic settings by using setting as a device for realistic characterization. Like real people, characters are defined by the world exterior to them. Novelists often make that world seem real by giving a detailed account of it. But more important than voluminous details is the novelist's ability to show that the setting establishes—or, at least, does not contradict—what we know to be true about real people. Conceivably, then, the setting of a novel could be totally strange to us yet could seem realistic because characters react to it as we would expect them to. If, for example, we knew nothing about the Amazon rain forest, such a setting would seem realistic if the characters exhibited "normal" patterns of behavior within it—they would eat, sleep, drink; they would get angry, feel frustration, show affection; they would protect themselves from harsh weather and from predators.

A third way in which novels are realistic is in the treatment of actions. In romances and tales, actions are often loosely connected and improbable. But actions in novels are linked by the logic of cause and effect; that is, by plot. Characters are the source of what happens in novels. Because of their circumstances, background, and genetic makeup, characters want certain things. These desires set the plot in motion. When they begin to act upon their desires, their actions generate conflict—conflict with other characters, with society, and within themselves. As the characters interact, conflicts intensify and move the plot to a crisis. The plot is realistic when the actions of the plot seem plausible. We expect the actions to be consistent with what real people would experience or do. If, for example, a character is consistently mean and miserly, we would find it implausible if that character suddenly and inexplicably became sweet and generous.

The novel's length, breadth, and realistic method give it a large capacity to teach us. Novels can immerse us in experiences, places, societies, people—"worlds"—that we have not directly experienced. By reading novels, we can feel what it was like to be a slave in the American South, to fight in Vietnam, to be a victim of the Holocaust, to cross the American plains in a covered wagon. We can feel what it is like to be a Buddhist monk, the president of the United States, an abused child, a rapist, a professional baseball player.

Novels teach us, furthermore, by embodying theories about the nature of the real world. Novels give us, not exact copies of reality, but versions of reality. No novel, even very long ones like Tolstoy's *War and Peace,* can represent every aspect of life. Novelists must select materials. While including some things, they must leave out others. Novels are in effect philosophical constructs, because the principles of selecting materials are based on theories about life. Novelists may not directly state their theories, but the details of their novels manifest them. Novelists, of course, disagree with one another about the nature of reality. We, in turn, may disagree with them. But one reason we read a novel is to experience the novelist's personal vision of life.

Willa Cather's *O Pioneers!,* the novel reprinted in this chapter, offers just such a personal vision. It gives a lyrical yet clear-sighted depiction of turn-of-the-century life on the American frontier.

WILLA CATHER

O Pioneers!

Willa Cather (1893–1947) was born and spent the first nine years of her life in the foothills of western Virginia. But the formative event of her life was her family's move to Nebraska when she was ten. Nebraska was still frontier country at that time, sparsely settled by people of many nationalities—Swedish, Bohemian, Norwegian, French, English, Russian—who had come to the prairie to farm. This rugged land embedded itself deep in Cather's consciousness. It gave her a respect for and love of nature that is a prominent feature of almost all her fiction. In *My Ántonia* she describes her first impression of the Nebraska landscape:

> There was nothing but land: not a country at all, but the material out of which countries are made. . . . I had the feeling that the world was left behind, that we had got over the edge of it, and were outside man's jurisdiction. I had never before looked up at the sky when there was not a familiar mountain ridge against it. But this was the complete dome of heaven, all there was of it. . . . Between that earth and that sky I felt erased, blotted out. I did not say my prayers that night: here, I felt, what would be would be.

Her father farmed for a year and then moved the family to the town of Red Cloud, where he worked as a banker. Until she went to high school, she received her education at home. She began studying Greek and Latin there, and continued these studies throughout her educational career. She developed an abiding appreciation for the Latin poet Vergil. His elegant style and affectionate depiction of his home in rural Italy influenced Cather's prose and her own treatment of home. She attended high school and then the University of Nebraska at Lincoln from 1891 until her graduation in 1895. She helped pay her way through college by writing newspaper articles.

For the next ten years, she worked in Pittsburgh as a journalist and high school teacher. Her first book was a collection of poems, *April Twilights* (1903). Her second book, *The Troll Garden* (1905), a collection of short stories, was published by S. S. McClure. He was so impressed with her fiction that he offered her an editorial position with *McClure's Magazine,* a national magazine headquartered in New York. She accepted his offer, moved to New York, and in time became managing editor of the magazine. Her friendship with Sarah Orne Jewett in 1909, the last year of Jewett's life, influenced the direction of

Cather's fiction. Until she met Jewett, her fiction was derivative of European fiction. Jewett, whose fiction depicts small-town and country life in Maine, encouraged Cather to write about her own country and people, the world she knew best. (One of Jewett's finest stories, "A White Heron," is reprinted on p. 401.) The success of Cather's third book (her first novel), *Alexander's Bridge* (1912), was great enough to allow her to resign from *McClure's* and devote herself full-time to writing.

In 1912 she experienced another formative event, a visit to the cliff-dweller ruins of Arizona. There she felt a profound sense of discovery, as if she had made contact with the original settlers of the Western lands. She returned again and again to the cliff-dweller country, both in person and in her fiction, using it as a way of illustrating the mysterious power she sensed in nature. Her next three novels, *O Pioneers!* (1913), *The Song of the Lark* (1915), and *My Ántonia* (1918), seem to be responses to this experience. These novels all feature female protagonists who struggle bravely against difficult circumstances but who become successful, largely because they identify with the land and derive their strength from it.

After World War I, Cather, like many other American writers, felt an emotional letdown. The world seemed driven by greed and violence. Renewal came to her through a religious conversion that led her in 1922 to join the Episcopal church. The result was another set of fine novels, all dealing with themes of religious quest and discovery. Perhaps the best-known of these are *Death Comes for the Archbishop* (1927), about a young French priest who travels to New Mexico to become archbishop of Santa Fé, and *Shadows on the Rock* (1931), about the priests and humble folk who lived in seventeenth-century Quebec. Cather felt fatigued after 1932 but continued to write fiction until her death in 1947. In her collection of essays, *Not under Forty* (1936), she talks about her methods and goals as a writer.

Cather explores many topics and themes in her work, but predominant among them is the return home. Her characters, either in person or in memory, go back to the places where they grew up. They often seem to be searching for a part of themselves that has been lost, a misplaced key to their identity. As Cather matured in her art, "home" became more than just the Nebraska prairies; home was strongly linked to the past of the original settlers in North America. Her later fiction seems not just a quest for a personal identity but a national identity as well.

Her most admirable characters maintain a close identity with their homes. She celebrates their hope, striving, shrewdness, and achievements. Her underlying optimism, however, is tempered with realism. In her prairie novels, *O Pioneers!* and *My Ántonia,* for example, she not only provides a detailed depiction of life on the prairie at the turn of the century, but also calculates the difficulties of that life. She praises the beauty of the prairie, but shows its harshness and indifference as well. In the face of nature's numbing demands, many of her characters degenerate into lethargy, mental illness, and self-destruction. Her characters, in fact, often seem like extensions of the land. Their generosity and hopefulness seem absorbed from the earth's fertility. Their cruelty and heartlessness seem at one with the instincts of the rattlesnakes that prey on the prairie dogs. Some of her characters even appear to be biological experiments, creatures that nature never quite finished. Yet they often have extraordinary gifts, as if nature overcompensated in one direction for her carelessness in another.

Cather's realism extended also to her depiction of small-town life. She shows the value of nurturing families and cooperative communities, yet as a young person she felt smothered by the narrow-mindedness of her home town. She called Red Cloud a "bitter, dead little western town." Like herself, then, her strong characters often beat their wings against the cage of convention. Nonetheless, they nearly always transcend such limitations. Their victories may include material gain—financial security—or social status, an orderly pattern of life. But their victories are also spiritual. Cather is not a preacher, but her admirable characters practice a moral responsibility and achieve a contentment that she came to associate with the religious life. They seem to recognize that the essence of life is spiritual. And this recognition gives them the strength to overcome disappointments and find peace.

To the memory of Sarah Orne Jewett in whose beautiful and delicate work there is the perfection that endures.

PRAIRIE SPRING

Evening and the flat land,
Rich and sombre and always silent;
The miles of fresh-plowed soil,
Heavy and black, full of strength and harshness;
The growing wheat, the growing weeds,
The toiling horses, the tired men;
The long empty roads,
Sullen fires of sunset, fading,
The eternal, unresponsive sky.
Against all this, Youth,
Flaming like the wild roses,

Singing like the larks over the plowed fields,
Flashing like a star out of the twilight;
Youth with its insupportable sweetness,
Its fierce necessity,
Its sharp desire,
Singing and singing,
Out of the lips of silence,
Out of the earthy dusk.

Part I: The Wild Land

I

One January day, thirty years ago, the little town of Hanover, anchored on a windy Nebraska tableland, was trying not to be blown away. A mist of fine snowflakes was curling and eddying about the cluster of low drab buildings huddled on the gray prairie, under a gray sky. The dwelling-houses were set about haphazard on the tough prairie sod; some of them looked as if they had been moved in overnight, and others as if they were straying off by themselves, headed straight for the open plain. None of them had any appearance of permanence, and the howling wind blew under them as well as over them. The main street was a deeply rutted road, now frozen hard, which ran from the squat red railway station and the grain "elevator" at the north end of the town to the lumber yard and the horse pond at the south end. On either side of this road straggled two uneven rows of wooden buildings; the general merchandise stores, the two banks, the drug store, the feed store, the saloon, the post-office. The board sidewalks were gray with trampled snow, but at two o'clock in the afternoon the shop-keepers, having come back from dinner, were keeping well behind their frosty windows. The children were all in school, and there was nobody abroad in the streets but a few rough-looking countrymen in coarse overcoats, with their long caps pulled down to their noses. Some of them had brought their wives to town, and now and then a red or a plaid shawl flashed out of one store into the shelter of another. At the hitch-bars along the street a few heavy work-horses, harnessed to farm wagons, shivered under their blankets. About the station everything was quiet, for there would not be another train in until night.

On the sidewalk in front of one of the stores sat a little Swede boy, crying bitterly. He was about five years old. His black cloth coat was much too big for him and made him look like a little old man. His shrunken brown flannel dress had been washed many times and left a long stretch of stocking between the hem of his skirt and the tops of his clumsy, copper-toed shoes. His cap was pulled down over his ears; his nose and his chubby cheeks were chapped and red with cold. He cried quietly, and the few people who hurried by did not notice him. He was afraid to stop any one, afraid to go into the store and ask for help, so he sat wringing his long sleeves and looking up a telegraph pole beside him, whimpering, "My kitten, oh, my kitten! Her will fweeze!" At the top of the pole crouched a shivering gray kitten, mewing faintly and clinging desperately to the wood with her claws. The boy had been left at the store while his sister went to the doctor's office, and in her absence a dog had chased his kitten up the pole. The little creature had never been so high before, and she was too frightened to move. Her master was sunk in despair. He was a little country boy, and this village was to him a very strange and perplexing place, where people wore fine clothes and had hard hearts. He always felt shy and awkward here, and wanted to hide behind things for fear some one might laugh at him. Just now, he was too unhappy to care who laughed. At last he seemed to see a ray of hope: his sister was coming, and he got up and ran toward her in his heavy shoes.

His sister was a tall, strong girl, and she walked rapidly and resolutely, as if she knew exactly where she was going and what she was going to do next. She wore a man's long ulster (not as if it were an affliction, but as if it were very comfortable and belonged to her; carried it like a young soldier), and a round plush cap, tied down with a thick veil. She had a serious, thoughtful face, and her clear, deep blue eyes were fixed intently on the distance, without seeming to see anything, as if she were in trouble. She did not notice the little boy until he pulled her by the coat. Then she stopped short and stooped down to wipe his wet face.

"Why, Emil! I told you to stay in the store and not to come out. What is the matter with you?"

"My kitten, sister, my kitten! A man put her out, and a dog chased her up there." His forefinger, projecting from the sleeve of his coat, pointed up to the wretched little creature on the pole.

"Oh, Emil! Did n't I tell you she'd get us into trouble of some kind, if you brought her? What made you tease me so? But there, I ought to have known better myself." She went to the foot of the pole and held out her arms, crying, "Kitty, kitty, kitty," but the kitten only mewed and faintly waved its tail. Alexandra turned away decidedly. "No, she won't come down. Somebody will have to go up after her. I saw the Linstrums' wagon in town. I'll go and see if I can find Carl. Maybe he can do something. Only you must stop crying, or I won't go a step. Where's your comforter? Did you leave it in the store? Never mind. Hold still, till I put this on you."

She unwound the brown veil from her head and tied it about his throat. A shabby little traveling man, who was just then coming out of the store on his way to the saloon, stopped and gazed stupidly at the shining mass of hair she bared when she took off her veil; two thick braids, pinned about her head in the German way, with a fringe of reddish-yellow curls blowing out from under her cap. He took his cigar out of his mouth and held the wet end between the fingers of his woolen glove. "My God, girl, what a head of hair!" he exclaimed, quite innocently and foolishly. She stabbed him with a glance of Amazonian fierceness and drew in her lower lip—most unnecessary severity. It gave the little clothing drummer such a start that he actually let his cigar fall to the sidewalk and went off weakly in the teeth of the wind to the saloon. His hand was still unsteady when he took his glass from the bartender. His feeble flirtatious instincts had been crushed before, but never so mercilessly. He felt cheap and ill-used, as if some one had taken advantage of him. When a drummer had been knocking about in little drab towns and crawling across the wintry country in dirty smoking-cars, was he to be blamed if, when he chanced upon a fine human creature, he suddenly wished himself more of a man?

While the little drummer was drinking to recover his nerve, Alexandra hurried to the drug store as the most likely place to find Carl Linstrum. There he was, turning over a portfolio of chromo "studies" which the druggist sold to the Hanover women who did china-painting. Alexandra explained her predicament, and the boy followed her to the corner, where Emil still sat by the pole.

"I'll have to go up after her, Alexandra. I think at the depot they have some spikes I can strap on my feet. Wait a minute." Carl thrust his hands into his pockets, lowered his head, and darted up the street against the north wind. He was a tall boy of fifteen, slight and narrow-chested. When he came back with the spikes, Alexandra asked him what he had done with his overcoat.

"I left it in the drug store. I could n't climb in it, anyhow. Catch me if I fall, Emil," he called back as he began his ascent. Alexandra watched him anxiously; the cold was bitter enough on the ground. The kitten would not budge an inch. Carl had to go to the very top of the pole, and then had some difficulty in tearing her from her hold. When he reached the ground, he handed the cat to her tearful little master. "Now go into the store with her, Emil, and get warm." He opened the door for the child. "Wait a minute, Alexandra. Why can't I drive for you as far as our place? It's getting colder every minute. Have you seen the doctor?"

"Yes. He is coming over to-morrow. But he says father can't get better; can't get well." The girl's lip trembled. She looked fixedly up the bleak street as if she were gathering her strength to face something, as if she were trying with all her might to grasp a situation which, no matter how painful, must be met and dealt with somehow. The wind flapped the skirts of her heavy coat about her.

Carl did not say anything, but she felt his sympathy. He, too, was lonely. He was a thin, frail boy, with brooding dark eyes, very quiet in all his movements. There was a delicate pallor in his thin face, and his mouth was too sensitive for a boy's. The lips had already a little curl of bitterness and skepticism. The two friends stood for a few moments on the windy street corner, not speaking a word, as two travelers, who have lost their way, sometimes stand and admit their perplexity in silence. When Carl turned away he said, "I'll see to your team." Alexandra went into the store to have her purchases packed in the egg-boxes, and to get warm before she set out on her long cold drive.

When she looked for Emil, she found him sitting on a step of the staircase that led up to the clothing and carpet department. He was playing with a little Bohemian girl, Marie Tovesky, who was tying her handkerchief over the kitten's head for a bonnet. Marie was a stranger in the country, having come from Omaha with her mother to visit her uncle, Joe Tovesky. She was a dark child, with brown curly hair, like a brunette doll's, a coaxing little red mouth, and round, yellow-brown eyes. Every one noticed her eyes; the brown iris had golden glints that made them look like gold-stone, or, in softer lights, like that Colorado mineral called tiger-eye.

The country children thereabouts wore their dresses to their shoe-tops, but this city child was dressed in what was then called the "Kate Greenaway" manner, and her red cashmere frock, gathered full from the yoke, came almost to the floor. This, with her poke bonnet, gave her the look of a quaint little woman. She had a white fur tippet about her neck and made no fussy objections when Emil fingered it admiringly. Alexandra had not the heart to take him away from so pretty a playfellow, and she let them tease the kitten together until Joe Tovesky came in noisily and picked up his little niece, setting her on his shoulder for every one to see. His children were all boys, and he adored this little creature. His cronies formed a circle about him, admiring and teasing the little girl, who took their jokes with great good nature. They were all delighted with her, for they seldom saw so pretty and carefully nurtured a child. They told her that she must choose one of them for a sweetheart, and each began pressing his suit and offering her bribes; candy, and little pigs, and spotted calves. She looked archly into the big, brown, mustached faces, smelling of spirits and tobacco, then she ran her tiny forefinger delicately over Joe's bristly chin and said, "Here is my sweetheart."

The Bohemians roared with laughter, and Marie's uncle hugged her until she cried, "Please don't, Uncle Joe! You hurt me." Each of Joe's friends gave her a bag of candy, and she kissed them all around, though she did not like country candy very well. Perhaps that was why she bethought herself of Emil. "Let me down, Uncle Joe," she said, "I want to give some of my candy to that nice little boy I found." She walked graciously over to Emil, followed by her lusty admirers, who formed a new circle and teased the little boy until he hid his face in his sister's skirts, and she had to scold him for being such a baby.

The farm people were making preparations to start for home. The women were checking over their groceries and pinning their big red shawls about their heads. The men were buying tobacco and candy with what money they had left, were showing each other new boots and gloves and blue flannel shirts. Three big Bohemians were drinking raw alcohol, tinctured with oil of cinnamon. This was said to fortify one effectually against the cold, and they smacked their lips after each pull at the flask. Their volubility drowned every other noise in the place, and the overheated store sounded of their spirited language as it reeked of pipe smoke, damp woolens, and kerosene.

Carl came in, wearing his overcoat and carrying a wooden box with a brass handle. "Come," he said, "I've fed and watered your team, and the wagon is ready." He carried Emil out and tucked him down in the straw in the wagon-box. The heat had made the little boy sleepy, but he still clung to his kitten.

"You were awful good to climb so high and get my kitten, Carl. When I get big I'll climb and get little boys' kittens for them," he murmured drowsily. Before the horses were over the first hill, Emil and his cat were both fast asleep.

Although it was only four o'clock, the winter day was fading. The road led southwest, toward the streak of pale, watery light that glimmered in the leaden sky. The light fell upon the two sad young faces that were turned mutely toward it: upon the eyes of the girl, who seemed to be looking with such anguished perplexity into the future; upon the sombre eyes of the boy, who seemed already to be looking into the past. The little town behind them had vanished as if it had never been, had fallen behind the swell of the prairie, and the stern frozen country received them into its bosom. The homesteads were few and far apart; here and there a windmill gaunt against the sky, a sod house crouching in a hollow. But the great fact was the land itself, which seemed to overwhelm the little beginnings of human society that struggled in its sombre wastes. It was from facing this vast hardness that the boy's mouth had become so bitter; because he felt that men were too weak to make any mark here, that the land wanted to be let alone, to preserve its own fierce strength, its peculiar, savage kind of beauty, its uninterrupted mournfulness.

The wagon jolted along over the frozen road. The two friends had less to say to each other than usual, as if the cold had somehow penetrated to their hearts.

"Did Lou and Oscar go to the Blue to cut wood to-day?" Carl asked.

"Yes. I'm almost sorry I let them go, it's turned so cold. But mother frets if the wood gets low." She stopped and put her hand to her forehead, brushing back her hair. "I don't know what is to become of us, Carl, if father has to die. I don't dare to think about it. I wish we could all go with him and let the grass grow back over everything."

Carl made no reply. Just ahead of them was the Norwegian graveyard, where the grass had, indeed, grown back over everything, shaggy and red, hiding even the wire fence. Carl realized that he was not a very helpful companion, but there was nothing he could say.

"Of course," Alexandra went on, steadying her voice a little, "the boys are strong and work hard, but we've always depended so on father that I don't see how we can go ahead. I almost feel as if there were nothing to go ahead for."

"Does your father know?"

"Yes, I think he does. He lies and counts on his fingers all day. I think he is trying to count up what he is leaving for us. It's a comfort to him that my chickens are laying right on through the cold weather and bringing in a little money. I wish we could keep his mind off such things, but I don't have much time to be with him now."

"I wonder if he'd like to have me bring my magic lantern over some evening?"

Alexandra turned her face toward him. "Oh, Carl! Have you got it?"

"Yes. It's back there in the straw. Didn't you notice the box I was carrying? I tried it all morning in the drug-store cellar, and it worked ever so well, makes fine big pictures."

"What are they about?"

"Oh, hunting pictures in Germany, and Robinson Crusoe and funny pictures about cannibals. I'm going to paint some slides for it on glass, out of the Hans Andersen book."

Alexandra seemed actually cheered. There is often a good deal of the child left in people who have had to grow up too soon. "Do bring it over, Carl. I can hardly wait to see it, and I'm sure it will please father. Are the pictures colored? Then I know he'll like them. He likes the calendars I get him in town. I wish I could get more. You must leave me here, must n't you? It's been nice to have company."

Carl stopped the horses and looked dubiously up at the black sky. "It's pretty dark. Of course the horses will take you home, but I think I'd better light your lantern, in case you should need it."

He gave her the reins and climbed back into the wagon-box, where he crouched down and made a tent of his overcoat. After a dozen trials he succeeded in lighting the lantern, which he placed in front of Alexandra, half covering it with a blanket so that the light would not shine in her eyes. "Now, wait until I find my box. Yes, here it is. Good-night, Alexandra. Try not to worry." Carl sprang to the ground and ran off across the fields toward the Linstrum homestead. "Hoo, hoo-o-o-o!" he called back as he disappeared over a ridge and dropped into a sand gully. The wind answered him like an echo, "Hoo, hoo-o-o-o-o-o!" Alexandra drove off alone. The rattle of her wagon was lost in the howling of the wind, but her lantern, held firmly between her feet, made a moving point of light along the highway, going deeper and deeper into the dark country.

II

On one of the ridges of that wintry waste stood the low log house in which John Bergson was dying. The Bergson homestead was easier to find than many another, because it overlooked Norway Creek, a shallow, muddy stream that sometimes flowed, and sometimes stood still, at the bottom of a winding ravine with steep, shelving sides overgrown with brush and cottonwoods and dwarf ash. This creek gave a sort of identity to the farms that bordered upon it. Of all the bewildering things about a new country, the absence of human landmarks is one of the most depressing and disheartening. The houses on the Divide were small and were usually tucked away in low places; you did not see them until you came directly upon them. Most of them were built of the sod itself, and were only the unescapable ground in another form. The roads were but faint tracks in the grass, and the fields were scarcely noticeable. The record of the plow was insignificant, like the feeble scratches on stone left by prehistoric races, so indeterminate that they may, after all, be only the markings of glaciers, and not a record of human strivings.

In eleven long years John Bergson had made but little impression upon the wild land he had come to tame. It was still a wild thing that had its ugly moods; and no one knew when they were likely to come, or why. Mischance hung over it. Its Genius was unfriendly to man. The sick man was feeling this as he lay looking out of the window, after the doctor had left him, on the day following Alexandra's trip to town. There it lay outside his door, the same land, the same lead-colored miles. He knew every ridge and draw and gully between him and the horizon. To the south, his plowed fields; to the east, the sod stables, the cattle corral, the pond,—and then the grass.

Bergson went over in his mind the things that had held him back. One winter his cattle had perished in a blizzard. The next summer one of his plow horses broke its leg in a prairie-dog hole and had to be shot. Another summer he lost his hogs from cholera, and a valuable stallion died from a rattlesnake bite. Time and again his crops had failed. He had lost two children, boys, that came between Lou and Emil, and there had been the cost of sickness and death. Now, when he had at last struggled out of debt, he was going to die himself. He was only forty-six, and had, of course, counted upon more time.

Bergson had spent his first five years on the Divide getting into debt, and the last six getting out. He had paid off his mortgages and had ended pretty much where he began, with the land. He owned exactly six hundred and forty acres of what stretched outside his door; his own original homestead and timber claim, making three hundred and twenty acres, and the half-section adjoining, the homestead of a younger brother who had given up the fight, gone back to Chicago to work in a fancy bakery and distinguish himself in a Swedish athletic club. So far John had not attempted to cultivate the second half-section, but used it for pasture land, and one of his sons rode herd there in open weather.

John Bergson had the Old-World belief that land, in itself, is desirable. But this land was an enigma. It was like a horse that no one knows how to break to harness, that runs wild and kicks things to pieces. He had an idea that no one understood how to farm it properly, and this he often discussed with Alexandra. Their neighbors, certainly, knew even less about farming than he did. Many of them had never worked on a farm until they took up their homesteads. They had been *handwerkers* at home; tailors, locksmiths, joiners, cigar-makers, etc. Bergson himself had worked in a shipyard.

For weeks, John Bergson had been thinking about these things. His bed stood in the sittingroom, next to the kitchen. Through the day, while the baking and washing and ironing were going on, the father lay and looked up at the roof beams that he himself had hewn, or out at the cattle in the corral. He counted the cattle over and over. It diverted him to speculate as to how much weight each of the steers would probably put on by spring. He often called his daughter in to talk to her about this. Before Alexandra was twelve years old she had begun to be a help to him, and as she grew older he had come to depend more and more upon her resourcefulness and good judgment. His boys were willing enough to work, but when he talked with them they usually irritated him. It was Alexandra who read the papers and followed the markets, and who learned by the mistakes of their neighbors. It was Alexandra who could always tell about what it had cost to fatten each steer, and who could guess the weight of a hog before it went on the scales closer than John Bergson himself. Lou and Oscar were industrious, but he could never teach them to use their heads about their work.

Alexandra, her father often said to himself, was like her grandfather; which was his way of saying that she was intelligent. John Bergson's father had been a shipbuilder, a man of considerable force and of some fortune. Late in life he married a second time, a Stockholm woman of questionable character, much younger than he, who goaded him into every sort of extravagance. On the shipbuilder's part, this marriage was an infatuation, the despairing folly of a powerful man who cannot bear to grow old. In a few years his unprincipled wife warped the probity of a lifetime. He speculated, lost his own fortune and funds entrusted to him by poor seafaring men, and died disgraced, leaving his children nothing. But when all was said, he had come up from the sea himself, had built up a proud little business with no capital but his own skill and foresight, and had proved himself a man. In his daughter, John Bergson recognized the strength of will, and the simple direct way of thinking things out, that had characterized his father in his better days. He would much rather, of course, have seen this likeness in one of his sons, but it was not a question of choice. As he lay there day after day he had to accept the situation as it was, and to be thankful that there was one among his children to whom he could entrust the future of his family and the possibilities of his hard-won land.

The winter twilight was fading. The sick man heard his wife strike a match in the kitchen, and the light of a lamp glimmered through the cracks of the door. It seemed like a light shining far away. He turned painfully in his bed and looked at his white hands, with all the work gone out of them. He was ready to give up, he felt. He did not know how it had come about, but he was quite willing to go deep under his fields and rest, where the plow could not find him. He was tired of making mistakes. He was content to leave the tangle to other hands; he thought of his Alexandra's strong ones.

"Dotter," he called feebly, *"dotter!"* He heard her quick step and saw her tall figure appear in the doorway, with the light of the lamp behind her. He felt her youth and strength, how easily she moved and stooped and lifted. But he would not have had it again if he could, not he! He knew the end too well to wish to begin again. He knew where it all went to, what it all became.

His daughter came and lifted him up on his pillows. She called him by an old Swedish name that she used to call him when she was little and took his dinner to him in the shipyard.

"Tell the boys to come here, daughter. I want to speak to them."

"They are feeding the horses, father. They have just come back from the Blue. Shall I call them?"

He sighed. "No, no. Wait until they come in. Alexandra, you will have to do the best you can for your brothers. Everything will come on you."

"I will do all I can, father."

"Don't let them get discouraged and go off like Uncle Otto. I want them to keep the land."

"We will, father. We will never lose the land."

There was a sound of heavy feet in the kitchen. Alexandra went to the door and beckoned to her brothers, two strapping boys of seventeen and nineteen. They came in and stood at the foot of the bed. Their father looked at them searchingly, though it was too dark to see their faces; they were just the same boys, he told himself, he had not been mistaken in them. The square head and heavy shoulders belonged to Oscar, the elder. The younger boy was quicker, but vacillating.

"Boys," said the father wearily, "I want you to keep the land together and to be guided by your sister. I have talked to her since I have been sick, and she knows all my wishes. I want no quarrels among my children, and so long as there is one house there must be one head. Alexandra is the oldest, and she knows my wishes. She will do the best she can. If she makes mistakes, she will not make so many as I have made. When you marry, and want a house of your own, the land will be divided fairly, according to the courts. But for the next few years you will have it hard, and you must all keep together. Alexandra will manage the best she can."

Oscar, who was usually the last to speak, replied because he was the older, "Yes, father. It would be so anyway, without your speaking. We will all work the place together."

"And you will be guided by your sister, boys, and be good brothers to her, and good sons to your mother? That is good. And Alexandra must not work in the fields any more. There is no necessity now. Hire a man when you need help. She can make much more with her eggs and butter than the wages of a man. It was one of my mistakes that I did not find that out sooner. Try to break a little more land every year; sod corn is good for fodder. Keep turning the land, and always put up more hay than you need. Don't grudge your mother a little time for plowing her garden and setting out fruit trees, even if it comes in a busy season. She has been a good mother to you, and she has always missed the old country."

When they went back to the kitchen the boys sat down silently at the table. Throughout the meal they looked down at their plates and did not lift their red eyes. They did not eat much, although they had been working in the cold all day, and there was a rabbit stewed in gravy for supper, and prune pies.

John Bergson had married beneath him, but he had married a good housewife. Mrs. Bergson was a fair-skinned, corpulent woman, heavy and placid like her son, Oscar, but there was something comfortable about her; perhaps it was her own love of comfort. For eleven years she had worthily striven to maintain some semblance of household order amid conditions that made order very difficult. Habit was very strong with Mrs. Bergson, and her unremitting efforts to repeat the routine of her old life among new surroundings had done a great deal to keep the family from disintegrating morally and getting careless in their ways. The Bergsons had a log house, for instance, only because Mrs. Bergson would not live in a sod house. She missed the fish diet of her own country, and twice every summer she sent the boys to the river, twenty miles to the southward, to fish for channel cat. When the children were little she used to load them all into the wagon, the baby in its crib, and go fishing herself.

Alexandra often said that if her mother were cast upon a desert island, she would thank God for her deliverance, make a garden, and find something to preserve. Preserving was almost a mania with Mrs. Bergson. Stout as she was, she roamed the scrubby banks of Norway Creek looking for fox grapes and goose plums, like a wild creature in search of prey. She made a yellow jam of the insipid ground-cherries that grew on the prairie, flavoring it with lemon peel; and she made a sticky dark conserve of garden tomatoes. She had experimented even with the rank buffalo-pea, and she could not see a fine bronze cluster of them without shaking her head and murmuring, "What a pity!" When there was nothing more to preserve, she began to pickle. The amount of sugar she used in these processes was sometimes a serious drain upon the family resources. She was a good mother, but she was glad when her children were old enough not to be in her way in the kitchen. She had never quite forgiven John Bergson for bringing her to the end of the earth; but, now that she was there, she wanted to be let alone to reconstruct her old life in so far as that was possible. She could still take some comfort in the world if she had bacon in the cave, glass jars on the shelves, and sheets in the press. She disapproved of all her neighbors because of their slovenly housekeeping, and the women thought her very proud. Once when Mrs. Bergson, on her way to Norway Creek, stopped to see old Mrs. Lee, the old woman hid in the haymow "for fear Mis' Bergson would catch her barefoot."

III

One Sunday afternoon in July, six months after John Bergson's death, Carl was sitting in the doorway of the Linstrum kitchen, dreaming over an illustrated paper, when he heard the rattle of a wagon along the hill road. Looking up he recognized the Bergsons' team, with two seats in the wagon, which meant they were off for a pleasure excursion. Oscar and Lou, on the front seat, wore their cloth hats and coats, never worn except on Sundays, and Emil, on the second seat with Alexandra, sat proudly in his new trousers, made from a pair of his father's, and a pink-striped shirt, with a wide ruffled collar. Oscar stopped the horses and waved to Carl, who caught up his hat and ran through the melon patch to join them.

"Want to go with us?" Lou called. "We're going to Crazy Ivar's to buy a hammock."

"Sure." Carl ran up panting, and clambering over the wheel sat down beside Emil. "I've always wanted to see Ivar's pond. They say it's the biggest in all the country. Are n't you afraid to go to Ivar's in that new shirt, Emil? He might want it and take it right off your back."

Emil grinned. "I'd be awful scared to go," he admitted, "if you big boys were n't along to take care of me. Did you ever hear him howl, Carl? People say sometimes he runs about the country howling at night because he is afraid the Lord will destroy him. Mother thinks he must have done something awful wicked."

Lou looked back and winked at Carl. "What would you do, Emil, if you was out on the prairie by yourself and seen him coming?"

Emil stared. "Maybe I could hide in a badger-hole," he suggested doubtfully.

"But suppose there was n't any badger-hole," Lou persisted. "Would you run?"

"No, I'd be too scared to run," Emil admitted mournfully, twisting his fingers. "I guess I'd sit right down on the ground and say my prayers."

The big boys laughed, and Oscar brandished his whip over the broad backs of the horses.

"He would n't hurt you, Emil," said Carl persuasively. "He came to doctor our mare when she ate green corn and swelled up most as big as the water-tank. He petted her just like you do your cats. I could n't understand much he said, for he don't talk any English, but he kept patting her and groaning as if he had the pain himself, and saying, 'There now, sister, that's easier, that's better!'"

Lou and Oscar laughed, and Emil giggled delightedly and looked up at his sister.

"I don't think he knows anything at all about doctoring," said Oscar scornfully. "They say when horses have distemper he takes the medicine himself, and then prays over the horses."

Alexandra spoke up. "That's what the Crows said, but he cured their horses, all the same. Some days his mind is cloudy, like. But if you can get him on a clear day, you can learn a great deal from him. He understands animals. Did n't I see him take the horn off the Berquist's cow when she had torn it loose and went crazy? She was tearing all over the place, knocking herself against things. And at last she ran out on the roof of the old dugout and her legs went through and there she stuck, bellowing. Ivar came running with his white bag, and the moment he got to her she was quiet and let him saw her horn off and daub the place with tar."

Emil had been watching his sister, his face reflecting the sufferings of the cow. "And then did n't it hurt her any more?" he asked.

Alexandra patted him. "No, not any more. And in two days they could use her milk again."

The road to Ivar's homestead was a very poor one. He had settled in the rough country across the county line, where no one lived but some Russians,—half a dozen families who dwelt together in one long house, divided off like barracks. Ivar had explained his choice by saying that the fewer neighbors he had, the fewer temptations. Nevertheless, when one considered that his chief business was horse-doctoring, it seemed rather short-sighted of him to live in the most inaccessible place he could find. The Bergson wagon lurched along over the rough hummocks and grass banks, followed the bottom of winding draws, or skirted the margin of wide lagoons, where the golden coreopsis grew up out of the clear water and the wild ducks rose with a whirr of wings.

Lou looked after them helplessly. "I wish I'd brought my gun, anyway, Alexandra," he said fretfully. "I could have hidden it under the straw in the bottom of the wagon."

"Then we'd have had to lie to Ivar. Besides, they say he can smell dead birds. And if he knew, we would n't get anything out of him, not even a hammock. I want to talk to him, and he won't talk sense if he's angry. It makes him foolish."

Lou sniffed. "Whoever heard of him talking sense, anyhow! I'd rather have ducks for supper than Crazy Ivar's tongue."

Emil was alarmed. "Oh, but, Lou, you don't want to make him mad! He might howl!"

They all laughed again, and Oscar urged the horses up the crumbling side of a clay bank. They had left the lagoons and the red grass behind them. In Crazy Ivar's country the grass was short and gray, the draws deeper than they were in the Bergsons' neighborhood, and the land was all broken up into hillocks and clay ridges. The wild flowers disappeared, and only in the bottom of the draws and gullies grew a few of the very toughest and hardiest: shoestring, and ironweed, and snow-on-the-mountain.

"Look, look, Emil, there's Ivar's big pond!" Alexandra pointed to a shining sheet of water that lay at the bottom of a shallow draw. At one end of the pond was an earthen dam, planted with green willow bushes, and above it a door and a single window were set into the hillside. You would not have seen them at all but for the reflection of the sunlight upon the four panes of window-glass. And that was all you saw. Not a shed, not a corral, not a well, not even a path broken in the curly grass. But for the piece of rusty stovepipe sticking up through the sod, you could have walked over the roof of Ivar's dwelling without dreaming that you were near a human habitation. Ivar had lived for three years in the clay bank, without defiling the face of nature any more than the coyote that had lived there before him had done.

When the Bergsons drove over the hill, Ivar was sitting in the doorway of his house, reading the Norwegian Bible. He was a queerly shaped old man, with a thick, powerful body set on short bow-legs. His shaggy white hair, falling in a thick mane about his ruddy cheeks, made him look older than he was. He was barefoot, but he wore a clean shirt of unbleached cotton, open at the neck. He always put on a clean shirt when Sunday morning came round, though he never went to church. He had a peculiar religion of his own and could not get on with any of the denominations. Often he did not see anybody from one week's end to another. He kept a calendar, and every morning he checked off a day, so that he was never in any doubt as to which day of the week it was. Ivar hired himself out in threshing and corn-husking time, and he doctored sick animals when he was sent for. When he was at home, he made hammocks out of twine and committed chapters of the Bible to memory.

Ivar found contentment in the solitude he had sought out for himself. He disliked the litter of human dwellings: the broken food, the bits of broken china, the old wash-boilers and tea-kettles thrown into the sunflower patch. He preferred the cleanness and tidiness of the wild sod. He always said that the badgers had cleaner houses than people, and that when he took a housekeeper her name would be Mrs. Badger. He best expressed his preference for his wild homestead by saying that his Bible seemed truer to him there. If one stood in the doorway of his cave, and looked off at the rough land, the smiling sky, the curly grass white in the hot sunlight; if one listened to the rapturous song of the lark, the drumming of the quail, the burr of the locust against that vast silence, one understood what Ivar meant.

On this Sunday afternoon his face shone with happiness. He closed the book on his knee, keeping the place with his horny finger, and repeated softly:—

> He sendeth the springs into the valleys, which run
>   among the hills;
> They give drink to every beast of the field; the wild
>   asses quench their thirst.
> The trees of the Lord are full of sap; the cedars of

Lebanon which he hath planted;
Where the birds make their nests: as for the stork, the
fir trees are her house.
The high hills are a refuge for the wild goats; and the
rocks for the conies.

Before he opened his Bible again, Ivar heard the Bergsons' wagon approaching, and he sprang up and ran toward it.

"No guns, no guns!" he shouted, waving his arms distractedly.

"No, Ivar, no guns," Alexandra called reassuringly.

He dropped his arms and went up to the wagon, smiling amiably and looking at them out of his pale blue eyes.

"We want to buy a hammock, if you have one," Alexandra explained, "and my little brother, here, wants to see your big pond, where so many birds come."

Ivar smiled foolishly, and began rubbing the horses' noses and feeling about their mouths behind the bits. "Not many birds just now. A few ducks this morning; and some snipe come to drink. But there was a crane last week. She spent one night and came back the next evening. I don't know why. It is not her season, of course. Many of them go over in the fall. Then the pond is full of strange voices every night."

Alexandra translated for Carl, who looked thoughtful. "Ask him, Alexandra, if it is true that a sea gull came here once. I have heard so."

She had some difficulty in making the old man understand.

He looked puzzled at first, then smote his hands together as he remembered. "Oh, yes, yes! A big white bird with long wings and pink feet. My! what a voice she had! She came in the afternoon and kept flying about the pond and screaming until dark. She was in trouble of some sort, but I could not understand her. She was going over to the other ocean, maybe, and did not know how far it was. She was afraid of never getting there. She was more mournful than our birds here; she cried in the night. She saw the light from my window and darted up to it. Maybe she thought my house was a boat, she was such a wild thing. Next morning, when the sun rose, I went out to take her food, but she flew up into the sky and went on her way." Ivar ran his fingers through his thick hair. "I have many strange birds stop with me here. They come from very far away and are great company. I hope you boys never shoot wild birds?"

Lou and Oscar grinned, and Ivar shook his bushy head. "Yes, I know boys are thoughtless. But these wild things are God's birds. He watches over them and counts them, as we do our cattle; Christ says so in the New Testament."

"Now, Ivar," Lou asked, "may we water our horses at your pond and give them some feed? It's a bad road to your place."

"Yes, yes, it is." The old man scrambled about and began to loose the tugs. "A bad road, eh, girls? And the bay with a colt at home!"

Oscar brushed the old man aside. "We'll take care of the horses, Ivar. You'll be finding some disease on them. Alexandra wants to see your hammocks."

Ivar led Alexandra and Emil to his little cave house. He had but one room, neatly plastered and whitewashed, and there was a wooden floor. There was a kitchen stove, a table covered with oilcloth, two chairs, a clock, a calendar, a few books on the window-shelf; nothing more. But the place was as clean as a cupboard.

"But where do you sleep, Ivar?" Emil asked, looking about.

Ivar unslung a hammock from a hook on the wall; in it was rolled a buffalo robe. "There, my son. A hammock is a good bed, and in winter I wrap up in this skin. Where I go to work, the beds are not half so easy as this."

By this time Emil had lost all his timidity. He thought a cave a very superior kind of house. There was something pleasantly unusual about it and about Ivar. "Do the birds know you will be kind to them, Ivar? Is that why so many come?" he asked.

Ivar sat down on the floor and tucked his feet under him. "See, little brother, they have come from a long way, and they are very tired. From up there where they are flying, our country looks dark and flat. They must have water to drink and to bathe in before they can go on with their journey. They look this way and that, and far below them they see something shining, like a piece of glass set in the dark earth. That is my pond. They come to it and are not disturbed. Maybe I sprinkle a little corn. They tell the other birds, and next year more come this way. They have their roads up there, as we have down here."

Emil rubbed his knees thoughtfully. "And is that true, Ivar, about the head ducks falling back when they are tired, and the hind ones taking their place?"

"Yes. The point of the wedge gets the worst of it; they cut the wind. They can only stand it there a little while—half an hour, maybe. Then they fall back and the wedge splits a little, while the rear ones come up the middle to the front. Then it closes up and they fly on, with a new edge. They are always changing like that, up in the air. Never any confusion; just like soldiers who have been drilled."

Alexandra had selected her hammock by the time the boys came up from the pond. They would not come in, but sat in the shade of the bank outside while Alexandra and Ivar talked about the birds and about his housekeeping, and why he never ate meat, fresh or salt.

Alexandra was sitting on one of the wooden chairs, her arms resting on the table. Ivar was sitting on the floor at her feet. "Ivar," she said suddenly, beginning to trace the pattern on the oilcloth with her forefinger, "I came to-day more because I wanted to talk to you than because I wanted to buy a hammock."

"Yes?" The old man scraped his bare feet on the plank floor.

"We have a big bunch of hogs, Ivar. I would n't sell in the spring, when every-body advised me to, and now so many people are losing their hogs that I am fright-ened. What can be done?"

Ivar's little eyes began to shine. They lost their vagueness.

"You feed them swill and such stuff? Of course! And sour milk? Oh, yes! And keep them in a stinking pen? I tell you, sister, the hogs of this country are put upon! They become unclean, like the hogs in the Bible. If you kept your chickens like that, what would happen? You have a little sorghum patch, maybe? Put a fence around it, and turn the hogs in. Build a shed to give them shade, a thatch on poles. Let the boys haul water to them in barrels, clean water, and plenty. Get them off the old stinking ground, and do not let them go back there until winter. Give them only grain and clean feed, such as you would give horses or cattle. Hogs do not like to be filthy."

The boys outside the door had been listening. Lou nudged his brother. "Come, the horses are done eating. Let's hitch up and get out of here. He'll fill her full of notions. She'll be for having the pigs sleep with us, next."

Oscar grunted and got up. Carl, who could not understand what Ivar said, saw that the two boys were displeased. They did not mind hard work, but they hated experiments and could never see the use of taking pains. Even Lou, who was more elastic than his older brother, disliked to do anything different from their neighbors. He felt that it made them conspicuous and gave people a chance to talk about them.

Once they were on the homeward road, the boys forgot their ill-humor and joked about Ivar and his birds. Alexandra did not propose any reforms in the care of the pigs, and they hoped she had forgotten Ivar's talk. They agreed that he was crazier than ever, and would never be able to prove up on his land because he worked it so little. Alexandra privately resolved that she would have a talk with Ivar about this and stir him up. The boys persuaded Carl to stay for supper and go swimming in the pasture pond after dark.

That evening, after she had washed the supper dishes, Alexandra sat down on the kitchen doorstep, while her mother was mixing the bread. It was a still, deep-breathing summer night, full of the smell of the hay fields. Sounds of laughter and splashing came up from the pasture, and when the moon rose rapidly above the bare rim of the prairie, the pond glittered like polished metal, and she could see the flash of white bodies as the boys ran about the edge, or jumped into the water. Alexandra watched the shimmering pool dreamily, but eventually her eyes went back to the sorghum patch south of the barn, where she was planning to make her new pig corral.

IV

For the first three years after John Bergson's death, the affairs of his family prospered. Then came the hard times that brought every one on the Divide to the brink of despair; three years of drouth and failure, the last struggle of a wild soil against the encroaching plowshare. The first of these fruitless summers the Bergson boys bore courageously. The failure of the corn crop made labor cheap. Lou and Oscar hired two men and put in bigger crops than ever before. They lost everything they spent. The whole country was discouraged. Farmers who were already in debt had to give up their land. A few foreclosures demoralized the county. The settlers sat about on the wooden sidewalks in the little town and told each other that the country was never meant for men to live in; the thing to do was to get back to Iowa, to Illinois, to any place that had been proved habitable. The Bergson boys, certainly, would have been happier with their uncle Otto, in the bakery shop in Chicago. Like most of their neighbors, they were meant to follow in paths already marked out for them, not to break trails in a new country. A steady job, a few holidays, nothing to think about, and they would have been very happy. It was no fault of theirs that they had been dragged into the wilderness when they were little boys. A pioneer should have imagination, should be able to enjoy the idea of things more than the things themselves.

The second of these barren summers was passing. One September afternoon Alexandra had gone over to the garden across the draw to dig sweet potatoes—they had been thriving upon the weather that was fatal to everything else. But when Carl Linstrum came up the garden rows to find her, she was not working. She was standing lost in thought, leaning upon her pitchfork, her sunbonnet lying beside her on the ground. The dry garden patch smelled of drying vines and was strewn with yellow seed-cucumbers and pumpkins and citrons. At one end, next the rhubarb, grew feathery asparagus, with red berries. Down the middle of the garden was a row of gooseberry and currant bushes. A few tough zenias and marigolds and a row of scarlet sage bore witness to the buckets of water that Mrs. Bergson had carried there after sundown, against the prohibition of her sons. Carl came quietly and slowly up the garden path, looking intently at Alexandra. She did not hear him. She was standing perfectly still, with that serious ease so characteristic of her. Her thick, reddish braids, twisted about her head, fairly burned in the sunlight. The air was cool enough to make the warm sun pleasant on one's back and shoulders, and so clear that the eye could follow a hawk up and up, into the blazing blue depths of the sky. Even Carl, never a very cheerful boy, and considerably darkened by these last two bitter years, loved the country on days like this, felt something strong and young and wild come out of it, that laughed at care.

"Alexandra," he said as he approached her, "I want to talk to you. Let's sit down by the gooseberry bushes." He picked up her sack of potatoes and they crossed the garden. "Boys gone to town?" he asked as he sank down on the warm, sun-baked earth. "Well, we have made up our minds at last, Alexandra. We are really going away."

She looked at him as if she were a little frightened. "Really, Carl? Is it settled?"

"Yes, father has heard from St. Louis, and they will give him back his old job in the cigar factory. He must be there by the first of November. They are taking on new men then. We will sell the place for whatever we can get, and auction the stock. We have n't enough to ship. I am going to learn engraving with a German engraver there, and then try to get work in Chicago."

Alexandra's hands dropped in her lap. Her eyes became dreamy and filled with tears.

Carl's sensitive lower lip trembled. He scratched in the soft earth beside him with a stick. "That's all I hate about it, Alexandra," he said slowly. "You've stood by us through so much and helped father out so many times, and now it seems as if we were running off and leaving you to face the worst of it. But it is n't as if we could really ever be of any help to you. We are only one more drag, one more thing you look out for and feel responsible for. Father was never meant for a farmer, you know that. And I hate it. We'd only get in deeper and deeper."

"Yes, yes, Carl, I know. You are wasting your life here. You are able to do much better things. You are nearly nineteen now, and I would n't have you stay. I've always hoped you would get away. But I can't help feeling scared when I think how I will miss you—more than you will ever know." She brushed the tears from her cheeks, not trying to hide them.

"But, Alexandra," he said sadly and wistfully, "I've never been any real help to you, beyond sometimes trying to keep the boys in a good humor."

Alexandra smiled and shook her head. "Oh, it's not that. Nothing like that. It's by understanding me, and the boys, and mother, that you've helped me. I expect that is the only way one person ever really can help another. I think you are about the only one that ever helped me. Somehow it will take more courage to bear your going than everything that has happened before."

Carl looked at the ground. "You see, we've all depended so on you," he said, "even father. He makes me laugh. When anything comes up he always says, 'I wonder what the Bergsons are going to do about that? I guess I'll go and ask her.' I'll never forget that time, when we first came here, and our horse had the colic, and I ran over to your place—your father was away, and you came home with me and showed father how to let the wind out of the horse. You were only a little girl then, but you knew ever so much more about farm work than poor father. You remember how homesick I used to get, and what long talks we used to have coming from school? We've someway always felt alike about things."

"Yes, that's it; we've liked the same things and we've liked them together, without anybody else knowing. And we've had good times, hunting for Christmas trees and going for ducks and making our plum wine together every year. We've never either of us had any other close friend. And now—" Alexandra wiped her eyes with the corner of her apron, "and now I must remember that you are going where you will have many friends, and will find the work you were meant to do. But you'll write to me, Carl? That will mean a great deal to me here."

"I'll write as long as I live," cried the boy impetuously. "And I'll be working for you as much as for myself, Alexandra. I want to do something you'll like and be proud of. I'm a fool here, but I know I can do something!" He sat up and frowned at the red grass.

Alexandra sighed. "How discouraged the boys will be when they hear. They always come home from town discouraged, anyway. So many people are trying to leave the country, and they talk to our boys and make them low-spirited. I'm afraid they are beginning to feel hard toward me because I won't listen to any talk about going. Sometimes I feel like I'm getting tired of standing up for this country."

"I won't tell the boys yet, if you'd rather not."

"Oh, I'll tell them myself, to-night, when they come home. They'll be talking wild, anyway, and no good comes of keeping bad news. It's all harder on them than it is on me. Lou wants to get married, poor boy, and he can't until times are better. See, there goes the sun, Carl. I must be getting back. Mother will want her potatoes. It's chilly already, the moment the light goes."

Alexandra rose and looked about. A golden afterglow throbbed in the west, but the country already looked empty and mournful. A dark moving mass came over the western hill, the Lee boy was bringing in the herd from the other half-section. Emil ran from the windmill to open the corral gate. From the log house, on the little rise across the draw, the smoke was curling. The cattle lowed and bellowed. In the sky the pale half-moon was slowly silvering. Alexandra and Carl walked together down the potato rows. "I have to keep telling myself what is going to happen," she said softly. "Since you have been here, ten years now, I have never really been lonely. But I can remember what it was like before. Now I shall have nobody but Emil. But he is my boy, and he is tender-hearted."

That night, when the boys were called to supper, they sat down moodily. They had worn their coats to town, but they ate in their striped shirts and suspenders. They were grown men now, and, as Alexandra said, for the last few years they had been growing more and more like themselves. Lou was still the slighter of the two, the quicker and more intelligent, but apt to go off at half-cock. He had a lively blue eye, a thin, fair skin (always burned red to the neckband of his shirt in summer), stiff, yellow hair that would not lie down on his head, and a bristly little yellow mustache, of which he was very proud. Oscar could not grow a mustache; his pale face was as bare as an egg, and his white eyebrows gave it an empty look. He was a man of powerful body and unusual endurance; the sort of man you could attach to a corn-sheller as you would an engine. He would turn it all day, without hurrying, without slowing down. But he was as indolent of mind as he was unsparing of his body. His love of routine amounted to a vice. He worked like an insect, always doing the same thing over in the same way, regardless of whether it was best or no. He felt that there was a sovereign virtue in mere bodily toil, and he rather liked to do things in the hardest way. If a field had once been in corn, he could n't bear to put it into wheat. He liked to begin his corn-planting at the same time every year, whether the season were backward or forward. He seemed to feel that by his own irreproachable regularity he would clear himself of blame and reprove the weather. When the wheat crop failed, he threshed the straw at a dead loss to demonstrate how little grain there was, and thus prove his case against Providence.

Lou, on the other hand, was fussy and flighty; always planned to get through two days' work in one, and often got only the least important things done. He liked to keep the place up, but he never got round to doing odd jobs until he had to neglect more pressing work to attend to them. In the middle of the wheat harvest, when the grain was over-ripe and every hand was needed, he would stop to mend fences or to patch the harness; then dash down to the field and overwork and be laid up in bed for a week. The two boys balanced each other, and they pulled well together. They had been good friends since they were children. One seldom went anywhere, even to town, without the other.

To-night, after they sat down to supper, Oscar kept looking at Lou as if he expected him to say something, and Lou blinked his eyes and frowned at his plate. It was Alexandra herself who at last opened the discussion.

"The Linstrums," she said calmly, as she put another plate of hot biscuit on the table, "are going back to St. Louis. The old man is going to work in the cigar factory again."

At this Lou plunged in. "You see, Alexandra, everybody who can crawl out is going away. There's no use of us trying to stick it out, just to be stubborn. There's something in knowing when to quit."

"Where do you want to go, Lou?"

"Any place where things will grow," said Oscar grimly.

Lou reached for a potato. "Chris Arnson has traded his half-section for a place down on the river."

"Who did he trade with?"

"Charley Fuller, in town."

"Fuller the real estate man? You see, Lou, that Fuller has a head on him. He's buying and trading for every bit of land he can get up here. It'll make him a rich man, some day."

"He's rich now, that's why he can take a chance."

"Why can't we? We'll live longer than he will. Some day the land itself will be worth more than all we can ever raise on it."

Lou laughed. "It could be worth that, and still not be worth much. Why, Alexandra, you don't know what you're talking about. Our place wouldn't bring now what it would six years ago. The fellows that settled up here just made a mistake. Now they're beginning to see this high land was n't never meant to grow nothing on, and everybody who ain't fixed to graze cattle is trying to crawl out. It's too high to farm up here. All the Americans are skinning out. That man Percy Adams, north of town, told me that he was going to let Fuller take his land and stuff for four hundred dollars and a ticket to Chicago."

"There's Fuller again!" Alexandra exclaimed. "I wish that man would take me for a partner. He's feathering his nest! If only poor people could learn a little from rich people! But all these fellows who are running off are bad farmers, like poor Mr. Linstrum. They could n't get ahead even in good years, and they all got into debt while father was getting out. I think we ought to hold on as long as we can on father's account. He was so set on keeping this land. He must have seen harder times than this, here. How was it in the early days, mother?"

Mrs. Bergson was weeping quietly. These family discussions always depressed her, and made her remember all that she had been torn away from. "I don't see why the boys are always taking on about going away," she said, wiping her eyes. "I don't want to move again; out to some raw place, maybe, where we'd be worse off than we are here, and all to do over again. I won't move! If the rest of you go, I will ask some of the neighbors to take me in, and stay and be buried by father. I'm not going to leave him by himself on the prairie, for cattle to run over." She began to cry more bitterly.

The boys looked angry. Alexandra put a soothing hand on her mother's shoulder. "There's no question of that, mother. You don't have to go if you don't want to. A third of the place belongs to you by American law, and we can't sell without your consent. We only want you to advise us. How did it use to be when you and father first came? Was it really as bad as this, or not?"

"Oh, worse! Much worse," moaned Mrs. Bergson. "Drouth, chince-bugs, hail, everything! My garden all cut to pieces like sauerkraut. No grapes on the creek, no nothing. The people all lived just like coyotes."

Oscar got up and tramped out of the kitchen. Lou followed him. They felt that Alexandra had taken an unfair advantage in turning their mother loose on them. The next morning they were silent and reserved. They did not offer to take the women to church, but went down to the barn immediately after breakfast and stayed there all day. When Carl Linstrum came over in the afternoon, Alexandra winked to him and pointed toward the barn. He understood her and went down to play cards with the boys. They believed that a very wicked thing to do on Sunday, and it relieved their feelings.

Alexandra stayed in the house. On Sunday afternoon Mrs. Bergson always took a nap, and Alexandra read. During the week she read only the newspaper, but on Sunday, and in the long evenings of winter, she read a good deal; read a few things over a great many times. She knew long portions of the "Frithjof Saga" by heart, and, like most Swedes who read at all, she was fond of Longfellow's verse,—the ballads and the "Golden Legend" and "The Spanish Student." To-day she sat in the wooden rocking-chair with the Swedish Bible open on her knees, but she was not reading. She was looking thoughtfully away at the point where the upland road disappeared over the rim of the prairie. Her body was in an attitude of perfect repose, such as it was apt to take when she was thinking earnestly. Her mind was slow, truthful, steadfast. She had not the least spark of cleverness.

All afternoon the sitting-room was full of quiet and sunlight. Emil was making rabbit traps in the kitchen shed. The hens were clucking and scratching brown holes in the flower beds, and the wind was teasing the prince's feather by the door.

That evening Carl came in with the boys to supper.

"Emil," said Alexandra, when they were all seated at the table, "how would you like to go traveling? Because I am going to take a trip, and you can go with me if you want to."

The boys looked up in amazement; they were always afraid of Alexandra's schemes. Carl was interested.

"I've been thinking, boys," she went on, "that maybe I am too set against making a change. I'm going to take Brigham and the buckboard to-morrow and drive down to the river country and spend a few days looking over what they've got down there. If I find anything good, you boys can go down and make a trade."

"Nobody down there will trade for anything up here," said Oscar gloomily.

"That's just what I want to find out. Maybe they are just as discontented down there as we are up here. Things away from home often look better than they are. You know what your Hans Andersen book says, Carl, about the Swedes liking to buy Danish bread and the Danes liking to buy Swedish bread, because people always think the bread of another country is better than their own. Anyway, I've heard so much about the river farms, I won't be satisfied till I've seen for myself."

Lou fidgeted. "Look out! Don't agree to anything. Don't let them fool you."

Lou was apt to be fooled himself. He had not yet learned to keep away from the shell-game wagons that followed the circus.

After supper Lou put on a necktie and went across the fields to court Annie Lee, and Carl and Oscar sat down to a game of checkers, while Alexandra read "The Swiss Family Robinson" aloud to her mother and Emil. It was not long before the two boys at the table neglected their game to listen. They were all big children together, and they found the adventures of the family in the tree house so absorbing that they gave them their undivided attention.

V

Alexandra and Emil spent five days down among the river farms, driving up and down the valley. Alexandra talked to the men about their crops and to the women about their poultry. She spent a whole day with one young farmer who had been away at school, and who was experimenting with a new kind of clover hay. She learned a great deal. As they drove along, she and Emil talked and planned. At last, on the sixth day, Alexandra turned Brigham's head northward and left the river behind.

"There's nothing in it for us down there, Emil. There are a few fine farms, but they are owned by the rich men in town, and could n't be bought. Most of the land is rough and hilly. They can always scrape along down there, but they can never do anything big. Down there they have a little certainty, but up with us there is a big chance. We must have faith in the high land, Emil. I want to hold on harder than ever, and when you're a man you'll thank me." She urged Brigham forward.

When the road began to climb the first long swells of the Divide, Alexandra hummed an old Swedish hymn, and Emil wondered why his sister looked so happy. Her face was so radiant that he felt shy about asking her. For the first time, perhaps, since that land emerged from the waters of geologic ages, a human face was set toward it with love and yearning. It seemed beautiful to her, rich and strong and glorious. Her eyes drank in the breadth of it, until her tears blinded her. Then the Genius of the Divide, the great, free spirit which breathes across it, must have bent lower than it ever bent to a human will before. The history of every country begins in the heart of a man or a woman.

Alexandra reached home in the afternoon. That evening she held a family council and told her brothers all that she had seen and heard.

"I want you boys to go down yourselves and look it over. Nothing will convince you like seeing with your own eyes. The river land was settled before this, and so they are a few years ahead of us, and have learned more about farming. The land sells for three times as much as this, but in five years we will double it. The rich men down there own all the best land, and they are buying all they can get. The thing to do is to sell our cattle and what little old corn we have, and buy the Linstrum place. Then the next thing to do is to take out two loans on our half-sections, and buy Peter Crow's place; raise every dollar we can, and buy every acre we can."

"Mortgage the homestead again?" Lou cried. He sprang up and began to wind the clock furiously. "I won't slave to pay off another mortgage. I'll never do it. You'd just as soon kill us all, Alexandra, to carry out some scheme!"

Oscar rubbed his high, pale forehead. "How do you propose to pay off your mortgages?"

Alexandra looked from one to the other and bit her lip. They had never seen her so nervous. "See here," she brought out at last. "We borrow the money for six years. Well, with the money we buy a half-section from Linstrum and a half from Crow, and a quarter from Struble, maybe. That will give us upwards of fourteen hundred acres, won't it? You won't have to pay off your mortgages for six years. By that time, any of this land will be worth thirty dollars an acre—it will be worth fifty, but we'll say thirty; then you can sell a garden patch anywhere, and pay off a debt of sixteen hundred dollars. It's not the principal I'm worried about, it's the interest and taxes. We'll have to strain to meet the payments. But as sure as we are sitting here to-night, we can sit down here ten years from now independent landowners, not struggling farmers any longer. The chance that father was always looking for has come."

Lou was pacing the floor. "But how do you *know* that land is going to go up enough to pay the mortgages and—"

"And make us rich besides?" Alexandra put in firmly. "I can't explain that, Lou. You'll have to take my word for it. I *know*, that's all. When you drive about over the country you can feel it coming."

Oscar had been sitting with his head lowered, his hands hanging between his knees. "But we can't work so much land," he said dully, as if he were talking to himself. "We can't even try. It would just lie there and we'd work ourselves to death." He sighed, and laid his calloused fist on the table.

Alexandra's eyes filled with tears. She put her hand on his shoulder. "You poor boy, you won't have to work it. The men in town who are buying up other people's land don't try to farm it. They are the men to watch, in a new country. Let's try to do like the shrewd ones, and not like these stupid fellows. I don't want you boys always to have to work like this. I want you to be independent, and Emil to go to school."

Lou held his head as if it were splitting. "Everybody will say we are crazy. It must be crazy, or everybody would be doing it."

"If they were, we wouldn't have much chance. No, Lou, I was talking about that with the smart young man who is raising the new kind of clover. He says the right thing is usually just what everybody don't do. Why are we better fixed than any of our neighbors? Because father had more brains. Our people were better people than these in the old country. We *ought* to do more than they do, and see further ahead. Yes, mother, I'm going to clear the table now."

Alexandra rose. The boys went to the stable to see to the stock, and they were gone a long while. When they came back Lou played on his *dragharmonika* and Oscar sat figuring at his father's secretary all evening. They said nothing more about Alexandra's project, but she felt sure now that they would consent to it. Just before bedtime Oscar went out for a pail of water. When he did not come back, Alexandra threw a shawl over her head and ran down the path to the windmill. She found him sitting there with his head in his hands, and she sat down beside him.

"Don't do anything you don't want to do, Oscar," she whispered. She waited a moment, but he did not stir. "I won't say any more about it, if you'd rather not. What makes you so discouraged?"

"I dread signing my name to them pieces of paper," he said slowly. "All the time I was a boy we had a mortgage hanging over us."

"Then don't sign one. I don't want you to, if you feel that way."

Oscar shook his head. "No, I can see there's a chance that way. I've thought a good while there might be. We're in so deep now, we might as well go deeper. But it's hard work pulling out of debt. Like pulling a threshing-machine out of the mud; breaks your back. Me and Lou's worked hard, and I can't see it's got us ahead much."

"Nobody knows about that as well as I do, Oscar. That's why I want to try an easier way. I don't want you to have to grub for every dollar."

"Yes, I know what you mean. Maybe it'll come out right. But signing papers is signing papers. There ain't no maybe about that." He took his pail and trudged up the path to the house.

Alexandra drew her shawl closer about her and stood leaning against the frame of the mill, looking at the stars which glittered so keenly through the frosty autumn air. She always loved to watch them, to think of their vastness and distance, and of their ordered march. It fortified her to reflect upon the great operations of nature, and when she thought of the law that lay behind them, she felt a sense of personal security. That night she had a new consciousness of the country, felt almost a new relation to it. Even her talk with the boys had not taken away the feeling that had overwhelmed her when she drove back to the Divide that afternoon. She had never known before how much the country meant to her. The chirping of the insects down in the long grass had been like the sweetest music. She had felt as if her heart were hiding down there, somewhere, with the quail and the plover and all the little wild things that crooned or buzzed in the sun. Under the long shaggy ridges, she felt the future stirring.

Part II: Neighboring Fields

I

It is sixteen years since John Bergson died. His wife now lies beside him, and the white shaft that marks their graves gleams across the wheat-fields. Could he rise from beneath it, he would not know the country under which he has been asleep. The shaggy coat of the prairie, which they lifted to make him a bed, has vanished forever.

From the Norwegian graveyard one looks out over a vast checker-board, marked off in squares of wheat and corn; light and dark, dark and light. Telephone wires hum along the white roads, which always run at right angles. From the graveyard gate one can count a dozen gayly painted farmhouses; the gilded weather-vanes on the big red barns wink at each other across the green and brown and yellow fields. The light steel wind-mills tremble throughout their frames and tug at their moorings, as they vibrate in the wind that often blows from one week's end to another across that high, active, res-olute stretch of country.

The Divide is now thickly populated. The rich soil yields heavy harvests; the dry, bracing climate and the smoothness of the land make labor easy for men and beasts. There are few scenes more gratifying than a spring plowing in that country, where the furrows of a single field often lie a mile in length, and the brown earth, with such a strong, clean smell, and such a power of growth and fertility in it, yields itself eagerly to the plow; rolls away from the shear, not even dimming the brightness of the metal, with a soft, deep sigh of happiness. The wheat-cutting sometimes goes on all night as well as all day, and in good seasons there are scarcely men and horses enough to do the harvesting. The grain is so heavy that it bends toward the blade and cuts like velvet.

There is something frank and joyous and young in the open face of the country. It gives itself ungrudgingly to the moods of the season, holding nothing back. Like the plains of Lombardy, it seems to rise a little to meet the sun. The air and the earth are curiously mated and intermingled, as if the one were the breath of the other. You feel in the atmosphere the same tonic, puissant quality that is in the tilth, the same strength and resoluteness.

One June morning a young man stood at the gate of the Norwegian graveyard, sharpening his scythe in strokes unconsciously timed to the tune he was whistling. He wore a flannel cap and duck trousers, and the sleeves of his white flannel shirt were rolled back to the elbow. When he was satisfied with the edge of his blade, he slipped the whetstone into his hip pocket and began to swing his scythe, still whistling, but softly, out of respect to the quiet folk about him. Unconscious respect, probably, for he seemed intent upon his own thoughts, and, like the Gladiator's, they were far away. He was a splendid figure of a boy, tall and straight as a young pine tree, with a hand-some head, and stormy gray eyes, deeply set under a serious brow. The space between his two front teeth, which were unusually far apart, gave him the proficiency in whistling for which he was distinguished at college. (He also played the cornet in the University band.)

When the grass required his close attention, or when he had to stoop to cut about a headstone, he paused in his lively air,—the "Jewel" song,—taking it up where he had left it when his scythe swung free again. He was not thinking about the tired pioneers over whom his blade glittered. The old wild country, the struggle in which his sister was destined to succeed while so many men broke their hearts and died, he can scarcely remember. That is all among the dim things of childhood and has been forgotten in the brighter pattern life weaves to-day, in the bright facts of being captain of the track team, and holding the interstate record for the high jump, in the all-suf-fusing brightness of being twenty-one. Yet sometimes, in the pauses of his work, the young man frowned and looked at the ground with an intentness which suggested that even twenty-one might have its problems.

When he had been mowing the better part of an hour, he heard the rattle of a light cart on the road behind him. Supposing that it was his sister coming back from one of her farms, he kept on with his work. The cart stopped at the gate and a merry contralto voice called, "Almost through, Emil?" He dropped his scythe and went toward the fence, wiping his face and neck with his handkerchief. In the cart sat a young woman who wore driving gauntlets and a wide shade hat, trimmed with red poppies. Her face, too, was rather like a poppy, round and brown, with rich color in her cheeks and lips, and her dancing yellow-brown eyes bubbled with gayety. The wind was flapping her big hat and teasing a curl of her chestnut-colored hair. She shook her head at the tall youth.

"What time did you get over here? That's not much of a job for an athlete. Here I've been to town and back. Alexandra lets you sleep late. Oh, I know! Lou's wife was telling me about the way she spoils you. I was going to give you a lift, if you were done." She gathered up her reins.

"But I will be, in a minute. Please wait for me, Marie," Emil coaxed. "Alexandra sent me to mow our lot, but I've done half a dozen others, you see. Just wait till I finish off the Kourdnas'. By the way, they were Bohemians. Why are n't they up in the Catholic graveyard?"

"Free-thinkers," replied the young woman laconically.

"Lots of the Bohemian boys at the University are," said Emil, taking up his scythe again. "What did you ever burn John Huss for, anyway? It's made an awful row. They still jaw about it in history classes."

"We'd do it right over again, most of us," said the young woman hotly. "Don't they ever teach you in your history classes that you'd all be heathen Turks if it had n't been for the Bohemians?"

Emil had fallen to mowing. "Oh, there's no denying you're a spunky little bunch, you Czechs," he called back over his shoulder.

Marie Shabata settled herself in her seat and watched the rhythmical movement of the young man's long arms, swinging her foot as if in time to some air that was going through her mind. The minutes passed. Emil mowed vigorously and Marie sat sunning herself and watching the long grass fall. She sat with the ease that belongs to persons of an essentially happy nature, who can find a comfortable spot almost anywhere; who are supple, and quick in adapting themselves to circumstances. After a final swish, Emil snapped the gate and sprang into the cart, holding his scythe well out over the wheel. "There," he sighed. "I gave old man Lee a cut or so, too. Lou's wife need n't talk. I never see Lou's scythe over here."

Marie clucked to her horse. "Oh, you know Annie!" She looked at the young man's bare arms. "How brown you've got since you came home. I wish I had an athlete to mow my orchard. I get wet to my knees when I go down to pick cherries."

"You can have one, any time you want him. Better wait until after it rains." Emil squinted off at the horizon as if he were looking for clouds.

"Will you? Oh, there's a good boy!" She turned her head to him with a quick, bright smile. He felt it rather than saw it. Indeed, he had looked away with the purpose of not seeing it. "I've been up looking at Angélique's wedding clothes," Marie went on, "and I'm so excited I can hardly wait until Sunday. Amédée will be a handsome bridegroom. Is anybody but you going to stand up with him? Well, then it will be a handsome wedding party." She made a droll face at Emil, who flushed. "Frank," Marie continued, flicking her horse, "is cranky at me because I loaned his saddle to Jan Smirka, and I'm terribly afraid he won't take me to the dance in the evening. Maybe the supper will tempt him. All Angélique's folks are baking for it, and all Amédée's twenty cousins. There will be barrels of beer. If once I get Frank to the supper, I'll see that I stay for the dance. And by the way, Emil, you must n't dance with me but once or twice. You must dance with all the French girls. It hurts their feelings if you don't. They think you're proud because you've been away to school or something."

Emil sniffed. "How do you know they think that?"

"Well, you did n't dance with them much at Raoul Marcel's party, and I could tell how they took it by the way they looked at you—and at me."

"All right," said Emil shortly, studying the glittering blade of his scythe.

They drove westward toward Norway Creek, and toward a big white house that stood on a hill, several miles across the fields. There were so many sheds and out-buildings grouped about it that the place looked not unlike a tiny village. A stranger, approaching it, could not help noticing the beauty and fruitfulness of the outlying fields. There was something individual about the great farm, a most unusual trimness and care for detail. On either side of the road, for a mile before you reached the foot of the hill, stood tall osage orange hedges, their glossy green marking off the yellow fields. South of the hill, in a low, sheltered swale, surrounded by a mulberry hedge, was the orchard, its fruit trees knee-deep in timothy grass. Any one thereabouts would have told you that this was one of the richest farms on the Divide, and that the farmer was a woman, Alexandra Bergson.

If you go up the hill and enter Alexandra's big house, you will find that it is curi-ously unfinished and uneven in comfort. One room is papered, carpeted, over-fur-nished; the next is almost bare. The pleasantest rooms in the house are the kitchen—where Alexandra's three young Swedish girls chatter and cook and pickle and preserve all summer long—and the sitting-room, in which Alexandra has brought together the old homely furniture that the Bergsons used in their first log house, the family portraits, and the few things her mother brought from Sweden.

When you go out of the house into the flower garden, there you feel again the order and fine arrangement manifest all over the great farm; in the fencing and hedg-ing, in the windbreaks and sheds, in the symmetrical pasture ponds, planted with scrub willows to give shade to the cattle in fly-time. There is even a white row of bee-hives in the orchard, under the walnut trees. You feel that, properly, Alexandra's house is the big out-of-doors, and that it is in the soil that she expresses herself best.

II

Emil reached home a little past noon, and when he went into the kitchen Alexandra was already seated at the head of the long table, having dinner with her men, as she always did unless there were visitors. He slipped into his empty place at his sister's right. The three pretty young Swedish girls who did Alexandra's housework were cutting pies, refilling coffee-cups, placing platters of bread and meat and pota-toes upon the red tablecloth, and continually getting in each other's way between the table and the stove. To be sure they always wasted a good deal of time getting in each other's way and giggling at each other's mistakes. But, as Alexandra had pointedly told her sisters-in-law, it was to hear them giggle that she kept three young things in her kitchen; the work she could do herself, if it were necessary. These girls, with their long letters from home, their finery, and their love-affairs, afforded her a great deal of entertainment, and they were company for her when Emil was away at school.

Of the youngest girl, Signa, who has a pretty figure, mottled pink cheeks, and yellow hair, Alexandra is very fond, though she keeps a sharp eye upon her. Signa is apt to be skittish at mealtime, when the men are about, and to spill the coffee or upset the cream. It is supposed that Nelse Jensen, one of the six men at the dinner-table, is courting Signa, though he has been so careful not to commit himself that no one in the house, least of all Signa, can tell just how far the matter has progressed. Nelse watches her glumly as she waits upon the table, and in the evening he sits on a bench behind the stove with his *dragharmonika,* playing mournful airs and watching her as she goes about her work. When Alexandra asked Signa whether she thought Nelse was in earnest, the poor child hid her hands under her apron and murmured, "I don't know, ma'm. But he scolds me about everything, like as if he wanted to have me!"

At Alexandra's left sat a very old man, barefoot and wearing a long blue blouse, open at the neck. His shaggy head is scarcely whiter than it was sixteen years ago, but his little blue eyes have become pale and watery, and his ruddy face is withered, like an apple that has clung all winter to the tree. When Ivar lost his land through mismanagement a dozen years ago, Alexandra took him in, and he has been a member of her household ever since. He is too old to work in the fields, but he hitches and unhitches the work-teams and looks after the health of the stock. Sometimes of a winter evening Alexandra calls him into the sitting-room to read the Bible aloud to her, for he still reads very well. He dislikes human habitations, so Alexandra has fitted him up a room in the barn, where he is very comfortable, being near the horses and, as he says, further from temptations. No one has ever found out what his temptations are. In cold weather he sits by the kitchen fire and makes hammocks or mends harness until it is time to go to bed. Then he says his prayers at great length behind the stove, puts on his buffalo-skin coat and goes out to his room in the barn.

Alexandra herself has changed very little. Her figure is fuller, and she has more color. She seems sunnier and more vigorous than she did as a young girl. But she still has the same calmness and deliberation of manner, the same clear eyes, and she still wears her hair in two braids wound round her head. It is so curly that fiery ends escape from the braids and make her head look like one of the big double sunflowers that fringe her vegetable garden. Her face is always tanned in summer, for her sunbonnet is oftener on her arm than on her head. But where her collar falls away from her neck, or where her sleeves are pushed back from her wrist, the skin is of such smoothness and whiteness as none but Swedish women ever possess; skin with the freshness of the snow itself.

Alexandra did not talk much at the table, but she encouraged her men to talk, and she always listened attentively, even when they seemed to be talking foolishly.

To-day Barney Flinn, the big red-headed Irishman who had been with Alexandra for five years and who was actually her foreman, though he had no such title, was grumbling about the new silo she had put up that spring. It happened to be the first silo on the Divide, and Alexandra's neighbors and her men were skeptical about it. "To be sure, if the thing don't work, we'll have plenty of feed without it, indeed," Barney conceded.

Nelse Jensen, Signa's gloomy suitor, had his word. "Lou, he says he would n't have no silo on his place if you'd give it to him. He says the feed outen it gives the stock the bloat. He heard of somebody lost four head of horses, feedin' 'em that stuff."

Alexandra looked down the table from one to another. "Well, the only way we can find out is to try. Lou and I have different notions about feeding stock, and that's a good thing. It's bad if all the members of a family think alike. They never get anywhere. Lou can learn by my mistakes and I can learn by his. Is n't that fair, Barney?"

The Irishman laughed. He had no love for Lou, who was always uppish with him and who said that Alexandra paid her hands too much. "I've no thought but to give the thing an honest try, mum. 'T would be only right, after puttin' so much expense into it. Maybe Emil will come out an' have a look at it wid me." He pushed back his chair, took his hat from the nail, and marched out with Emil, who, with his university ideas, was supposed to have instigated the silo. The other hands followed them, all except old Ivar. He had been depressed throughout the meal and had paid no heed to the talk of the men, even when they mentioned cornstalk bloat, upon which he was sure to have opinions.

"Did you want to speak to me, Ivar?" Alexandra asked as she rose from the table. "Come into the sitting-room."

The old man followed Alexandra, but when she motioned him to a chair he shook his head. She took up her workbasket and waited for him to speak. He stood looking at the carpet, his bushy head bowed, his hands clasped in front of him. Ivar's bandy legs seemed to have grown shorter with years, and they were completely misfitted to his broad, thick body and heavy shoulders.

"Well, Ivar, what is it?" Alexandra asked after she had waited longer than usual.

Ivar had never learned to speak English and his Norwegian was quaint and grave, like the speech of the more old-fashioned people. He always addressed Alexandra in terms of the deepest respect, hoping to set a good example to the kitchen girls, whom he thought too familiar in their manners.

"Mistress," he began faintly, without raising his eyes, "the folk have been looking coldly at me of late. You know there has been talk."

"Talk about what, Ivar?"

"About sending me away; to the asylum."

Alexandra put down her sewing-basket. "Nobody has come to me with such talk," she said decidedly. "Why need you listen? You know I would never consent to such a thing."

Ivar lifted his shaggy head and looked at her out of his little eyes. "They say that you cannot prevent it if the folk complain of me, if your brothers complain to the authorities. They say that your brothers are afraid—God forbid!—that I may do you some injury when my spells are on me. Mistress, how can any one think that?—that I could bite the hand that fed me!" The tears trickled down on the old man's beard.

Alexandra frowned. "Ivar, I wonder at you, that you should come bothering me with such nonsense. I am still running my own house, and other people have nothing to do with either you or me. So long as I am suited with you, there is nothing to be said."

Ivar pulled a red handkerchief out of the breast of his blouse and wiped his eyes and beard. "But I should not wish you to keep me if, as they say, it is against your interests, and if it is hard for you to get hands because I am here."

Alexandra made an impatient gesture, but the old man put out his hand and went on earnestly:—

"Listen, mistress, it is right that you should take these things into account. You know that my spells come from God, and that I would not harm any living creature. You believe that every one should worship God in the way revealed to him. But that is not the way of this country. The way here is for all to do alike. I am despised because I do not wear shoes, because I do not cut my hair, and because I have visions. At home, in the old country, there were many like me, who had been touched by God, or who had seen things in the graveyard at night and were different afterward. We thought nothing of it, and let them alone. But here, if a man is different in his feet or in his head, they put him in the asylum. Look at Peter Kralik; when he was a boy, drinking out of a creek, he swallowed a snake, and always after that he could eat only such food as the creature liked, for when he ate anything else, it became enraged and gnawed him. When he felt it whipping about in him, he drank alcohol to stupefy it and get some ease for himself. He could work as good as any man, and his head was clear, but they locked him up for being different in his stomach. That is the way; they have built the asylum for people who are different, and they will not even let us live in the holes with the badgers. Only your great prosperity has protected me so far. If you had had ill-fortune, they would have taken me to Hastings long ago."

As Ivar talked, his gloom lifted. Alexandra had found that she could often break his fasts and long penances by talking to him and letting him pour out the thoughts that troubled him. Sympathy always cleared his mind, and ridicule was poison to him.

"There is a great deal in what you say, Ivar. Like as not they will be wanting to take me to Hastings because I have built a silo; and then I may take you with me. But at present I need you here. Only don't come to me again telling me what people say. Let people go on talking as they like, and we will go on living as we think best. You have been with me now for twelve years, and I have gone to you for advice oftener than I have ever gone to any one. That ought to satisfy you."

Ivar bowed humbly. "Yes, mistress, I shall not trouble you with their talk again. And as for my feet, I have observed your wishes all these years, though you have never questioned me; washing them every night, even in winter."

Alexandra laughed. "Oh, never mind about your feet, Ivar. We can remember when half our neighbors went barefoot in summer. I expect old Mrs. Lee would love to slip her shoes off now sometimes, if she dared. I'm glad I'm not Lou's mother-in-law."

Ivar looked about mysteriously and lowered his voice almost to a whisper. "You know what they have over at Lou's house? A great white tub, like the stone water-troughs in the old country, to wash themselves in. When you sent me over with the strawberries, they were all in town but the old woman Lee and the baby. She took me in and showed me the thing, and she told me it was impossible to wash yourself clean in it, because, in so much water, you could not make a strong suds. So when they fill it up and send her in there, she pretends, and makes a splashing noise. Then, when they are all asleep, she washes herself in a little wooden tub she keeps under her bed."

Alexandra shook with laughter. "Poor old Mrs. Lee! They won't let her wear nightcaps, either. Never mind; when she comes to visit me, she can do all the old things in the old way, and have as much beer as she wants. We'll start an asylum for old-time people, Ivar."

Ivar folded his big handkerchief carefully and thrust it back into his blouse. "This is always the way, mistress. I come to you sorrowing, and you send me away with a light heart. And will you be so good as to tell the Irishman that he is not to work the brown gelding until the sore on its shoulder is healed?"

"That I will. Now go and put Emil's mare to the cart. I am going to drive up to the north quarter to meet the man from town who is to buy my alfalfa hay."

III

Alexandra was to hear more of Ivar's case, however. On Sunday her married brothers came to dinner. She had asked them for that day because Emil, who hated family parties, would be absent, dancing at Amédée Chevalier's wedding, up in the French country. The table was set for company in the dining-room, where highly varnished wood and colored glass and useless pieces of china were conspicuous enough to satisfy the standards of the new prosperity. Alexandra had put herself into the hands of the Hanover furniture dealer, and he had conscientiously done his best to make her dining-room look like his display window. She said frankly that she knew nothing about such things, and she was willing to be governed by the general conviction that the more useless and utterly unusable objects were, the greater their virtue as ornament. That seemed reasonable enough. Since she liked plain things herself, it was all the more necessary to have jars and punchbowls and candlesticks in the company rooms for people who did appreciate them. Her guests liked to see about them these reassuring emblems of prosperity.

The family party was complete except for Emil, and Oscar's wife who, in the country phrase, "was not going anywhere just now." Oscar sat at the foot of the table and his four tow-headed little boys, aged from twelve to five, were ranged at one side. Neither Oscar nor Lou has changed much; they have simply, as Alexandra said of them long ago, grown to be more and more like themselves. Lou now looks the older of the two; his face is thin and shrewd and wrinkled about the eyes, while Oscar's is thick and dull. For all his dullness, however, Oscar makes more money than his brother, which adds to Lou's sharpness and uneasiness and tempts him to make a show. The trouble with Lou is that he is tricky, and his neighbors have found out that, as Ivar says, he has not a fox's face for nothing. Politics being the natural field for such talents, he neglects his farm to attend conventions and to run for county offices.

Lou's wife, formerly Annie Lee, has grown to look curiously like her husband. Her face has become longer, sharper, more aggressive. She wears her yellow hair in a high pompadour, and is bedecked with rings and chains and "beauty pins." Her tight, high-heeled shoes give her an awkward walk, and she is always more or less preoccupied with her clothes. As she sat at the table, she kept telling her youngest daughter to "be careful now, and not drop anything on mother."

The conversation at the table was all in English. Oscar's wife, from the malaria district of Missouri, was ashamed of marrying a foreigner, and his boys do not understand a word of Swedish. Annie and Lou sometimes speak Swedish at home, but Annie is almost as much afraid of being "caught" at it as ever her mother was of being caught barefoot. Oscar still has a thick accent, but Lou speaks like anybody from Iowa.

"When I was in Hastings to attend the convention," he was saying, "I saw the superintendent of the asylum, and I was telling him about Ivar's symptoms. He says Ivar's case is one of the most dangerous kind, and it's a wonder he has n't done something violent before this."

Alexandra laughed good-humoredly. "Oh, nonsense, Lou! The doctors would have us all crazy if they could. Ivar's queer, certainly, but he has more sense than half the hands I hire."

Lou flew at his fried chicken. "Oh, I guess the doctor knows his business, Alexandra. He was very much surprised when I told him how you'd put up with Ivar. He says he's likely to set fire to the barn any night, or to take after you and the girls with an axe."

Little Signa, who was waiting on the table, giggled and fled to the kitchen. Alexandra's eyes twinkled. "That was too much for Signa, Lou. We all know that Ivar's perfectly harmless. The girls would as soon expect me to chase them with an axe."

Lou flushed and signaled to his wife. "All the same, the neighbors will be having a say about it before long. He may burn anybody's barn. It's only necessary for one property-owner in the township to make complaint, and he'll be taken up by force. You'd better send him yourself and not have any hard feelings."

Alexandra helped one of her little nephews to gravy. "Well, Lou, if any of the neighbors try that, I'll have myself appointed Ivar's guardian and take the case to court, that's all. I am perfectly satisfied with him."

"Pass the preserves, Lou," said Annie in a warning tone. She had reasons for not wishing her husband to cross Alexandra too openly. "But don't you sort of hate to have people see him around here, Alexandra?" she went on with persuasive smoothness. "He *is* a disgraceful object, and you're fixed up so nice now. It sort of makes people distant with you, when they never know when they'll hear him scratching about. My girls are afraid as death of him, are n't you, Milly, dear?"

Milly was fifteen, fat and jolly and pompadoured, with a creamy complexion, square white teeth, and a short upper lip. She looked like her grandmother Bergson, and had her comfortable and comfort-loving nature. She grinned at her aunt, with whom she was a great deal more at ease than she was with her mother. Alexandra winked a reply.

"Milly need n't be afraid of Ivar. She's an especial favorite of his. In my opinion Ivar has just as much right to his own way of dressing and thinking as we have. But I'll see that he does n't bother other people. I'll keep him at home, so don't trouble any more about him, Lou. I've been wanting to ask you about your new bathtub. How does it work?"

Annie came to the fore to give Lou time to recover himself. "Oh, it works something grand! I can't keep him out of it. He washes himself all over three times a week now, and uses all the hot water. I think it's weakening to stay in as long as he does. You ought to have one, Alexandra."

"I'm thinking of it. I might have one put in the barn for Ivar, if it will ease people's minds. But before I get a bathtub, I'm going to get a piano for Milly."

Oscar, at the end of the table, looked up from his plate. "What does Milly want of a pianny? What's the matter with her organ? She can make some use of that, and play in church."

Annie looked flustered. She had begged Alexandra not to say anything about this plan before Oscar, who was apt to be jealous of what his sister did for Lou's children. Alexandra did not get on with Oscar's wife at all. "Milly can play in church just the same, and she'll still play on the organ. But practising on it so much spoils her touch. Her teacher says so," Annie brought out with spirit.

Oscar rolled his eyes. "Well, Milly must have got on pretty good if she's got past the organ. I know plenty of grown folks that ain't," he said bluntly.

Annie threw up her chin. "She has got on good, and she's going to play for her commencement when she graduates in town next year."

"Yes," said Alexandra firmly, "I think Milly deserves a piano. All the girls around here have been taking lessons for years, but Milly is the only one of them who can ever play anything when you ask her. I'll tell you when I first thought I would like to give you a piano, Milly, and that was when you learned that book of old Swedish songs that your grandfather used to sing. He had a sweet tenor voice, and when he was a young man he loved to sing. I can remember hearing him singing with the sailors down in the shipyard, when I was no bigger than Stella here," pointing to Annie's younger daughter.

Milly and Stella both looked through the door into the sitting-room, where a crayon portrait of John Bergson hung on the wall. Alexandra had had it made from a little photograph, taken for his friends just before he left Sweden; a slender man of thirty-five, with soft hair curling about his high forehead, a drooping mustache, and wondering, sad eyes that looked forward into the distance, as if they already beheld the New World.

After dinner Lou and Oscar went to the orchard to pick cherries—they had neither of them had the patience to grow an orchard of their own—and Annie went down to gossip with Alexandra's kitchen girls while they washed the dishes. She could always find out more about Alexandra's domestic economy from the prattling maids than from Alexandra herself, and what she discovered she used to her own advantage with Lou. On the Divide, farmers' daughters no longer went out into service, so Alexandra got her girls from Sweden, by paying their fare over. They stayed with her until they married, and were replaced by sisters or cousins from the old country.

Alexandra took her three nieces into the flower garden. She was fond of the little girls, especially of Milly, who came to spend a week with her aunt now and then, and read aloud to her from the old books about the house, or listened to stories about the early days on the Divide. While they were walking among the flower beds, a buggy drove up the hill and stopped in front of the gate. A man got out and stood talking to the driver. The little girls were delighted at the advent of a stranger, some one from very far away, they knew by his clothes, his gloves, and the sharp, pointed cut of his dark beard. The girls fell behind their aunt and peeped out at him from among the castor beans. The stranger came up to the gate and stood holding his hat in his hand, smiling, while Alexandra advanced slowly to meet him. As she approached he spoke in a low, pleasant voice.

"Don't you know me, Alexandra? I would have known you, anywhere."

Alexandra shaded her eyes with her hand. Suddenly she took a quick step forward. "Can it be!" she exclaimed with feeling; "Can it be that it is Carl Linstrum? Why, Carl, it is!" She threw out both her hands and caught his across the gate. "Sadie, Milly, run tell your father and Uncle Oscar that our old friend Carl Linstrum is here. Be quick! Why, Carl, how did it happen? I can't believe this!" Alexandra shook the tears from her eyes and laughed.

The stranger nodded to his driver, dropped his suitcase inside the fence, and opened the gate. "Then you are glad to see me, and you can put me up overnight? I could n't go through this country without stopping off to have a look at you. How little you have changed! Do you know, I was sure it would be like that. You simply could n't be different. How fine you are!" He stepped back and looked at her admiringly.

Alexandra blushed and laughed again. "But you yourself, Carl—with that beard—how could I have known you? You went away a little boy." She reached for his suitcase and when he intercepted her she threw up her hands. "You see, I give myself away. I have only women come to visit me, and I do not know how to behave. Where is your trunk?"

"It's in Hanover. I can stay only a few days. I am on my way to the coast."

They started up the path. "A few days? After all these years!" Alexandra shook her finger at him. "See this, you have walked into a trap. You do not get away so easy." She put her hand affectionately on his shoulder. "You owe me a visit for the sake of old times. Why must you go to the coast at all?"

"Oh, I must! I am a fortune hunter. From Seattle I go on to Alaska."

"Alaska?" She looked at him in astonishment. "Are you going to paint the Indians?"

"Paint?" the young man frowned. "Oh! I'm not a painter, Alexandra. I'm an engraver. I have nothing to do with painting."

"But on my parlor wall I have the paintings—"

He interrupted nervously. "Oh, water-color sketches—done for amusement. I sent them to remind you of me, not because they were good. What a wonderful place you have made of this, Alexandra." He turned and looked back at the wide, map-like prospect of field and hedge and pasture. "I would never have believed it could be done. I'm disappointed in my own eye, in my imagination."

At this moment Lou and Oscar came up the hill from the orchard. They did not quicken their pace when they saw Carl; indeed, they did not openly look in his direction. They advanced distrustfully, and as if they wished the distance were longer.

Alexandra beckoned to them. "They think I am trying to fool them. Come, boys, it's Carl Linstrum, our old Carl!"

Lou gave the visitor a quick, sidelong glance and thrust out his hand. "Glad to see you." Oscar followed with "How d' do." Carl could not tell whether their offishness came from unfriendliness or from embarrassment. He and Alexandra led the way to the porch.

"Carl," Alexandra explained, "is on his way to Seattle. He is going to Alaska."

Oscar studied the visitor's yellow shoes. "Got business there?" he asked.

Carl laughed. "Yes, very pressing business. I'm going there to get rich. Engraving's a very interesting profession, but a man never makes any money at it. So I'm going to try the goldfields."

Alexandra felt that this was a tactful speech, and Lou looked up with some interest. "Ever done anything in that line before?"

"No, but I'm going to join a friend of mine who went out from New York and has done well. He has offered to break me in."

"Turrible cold winters, there, I hear," remarked Oscar. "I thought people went up there in the spring."

"They do. But my friend is going to spend the winter in Seattle and I am to stay with him there and learn something about prospecting before we start north next year."

Lou looked skeptical. "Let's see, how long have you been away from here?"

"Sixteen years. You ought to remember that, Lou, for you were married just after we went away."

"Going to stay with us some time?" Oscar asked.

"A few days, if Alexandra can keep me."

"I expect you'll be wanting to see your old place," Lou observed more cordially. "You won't hardly know it. But there's a few chunks of your old sod house left. Alexandra would n't never let Frank Shabata plough over it."

Annie Lee, who, ever since the visitor was announced, had been touching up her hair and settling her lace and wishing she had worn another dress, now emerged with her three daughters and introduced them. She was greatly impressed by Carl's urban appearance, and in her excitement talked very loud and threw her head about. "And you ain't married yet? At your age, now! Think of that! You'll have to wait for Milly. Yes, we've got a boy, too. The youngest. He's at home with his grandma. You must come over to see mother and hear Milly play. She's the musician of the family. She does pyrography, too. That's burnt wood, you know. You would n't believe what she can do with her poker. Yes, she goes to school in town, and she is the youngest in her class by two years."

Milly looked uncomfortable and Carl took her hand again. He liked her creamy skin and happy, innocent eyes, and he could see that her mother's way of talking distressed her. "I'm sure she's a clever little girl," he murmured, looking at her thoughtfully. "Let me see—Ah, it's your mother that she looks like, Alexandra. Mrs. Bergson must have looked just like this when she was a little girl. Does Milly run about over the country as you and Alexandra used to, Annie?"

Milly's mother protested. "Oh, my, no! Things has changed since we was girls. Milly has it very different. We are going to rent the place and move into town as soon as the girls are old enough to go out into company. A good many are doing that here now. Lou is going into business."

Lou grinned. "That's what she says. You better go get your things on. Ivar's hitching up," he added, turning to Annie.

Young farmers seldom address their wives by name. It is always "you," or "she."

Having got his wife out of the way, Lou sat down on the step and began to whittle. "Well, what do folks in New York think of William Jennings Bryan?" Lou began to bluster, as he always did when he talked politics. "We gave Wall Street a scare in ninety-six, all right, and we're fixing another to hand them. Silver was n't the only issue," he nodded mysteriously. "There's a good many things got to be changed. The West is going to make itself heard."

Carl laughed. "But, surely, it did do that, if nothing else."

Lou's thin face reddened up to the roots of his bristly hair. "Oh, we've only begun. We're waking up to a sense of our responsibilities, out here, and we ain't afraid, neither. You fellows back there must be a tame lot. If you had any nerve you'd get together and march down to Wall Street and blow it up. Dynamite it, I mean," with a threatening nod.

He was so much in earnest that Carl scarcely knew how to answer him. "That would be a waste of powder. The same business would go on in another street. The street does n't matter. But what have you fellows out here got to kick about? You have the only safe place there is. Morgan himself could n't touch you. One only has to drive through this country to see that you're all as rich as barons."

"We have a good deal more to say than we had when we were poor," said Lou threateningly. "We're getting on to a whole lot of things."

As Ivar drove a double carriage up to the gate, Annie came out in a hat that looked like the model of a battleship. Carl rose and took her down to the carriage, while Lou lingered for a word with his sister.

"What do you suppose he's come for?" he asked, jerking his head toward the gate.

"Why, to pay us a visit. I've been begging him to for years."

Oscar looked at Alexandra. "He did n't let you know he was coming?"

"No. Why should he? I told him to come at any time."

Lou shrugged his shoulders. "He does n't seem to have done much for himself. Wandering around this way!"

Oscar spoke solemnly, as from the depths of a cavern. "He never was much account."

Alexandra left them and hurried down to the gate where Annie was rattling on to Carl about her new dining-room furniture. "You must bring Mr. Linstrum over real soon, only be sure to telephone me first," she called back, as Carl helped her into the carriage. Old Ivar, his white head bare, stood holding the horses. Lou came down the path and climbed into the front seat, took up the reins, and drove off without saying anything further to any one. Oscar picked up his youngest boy and trudged off down the road, the other three trotting after him. Carl, holding the gate open for Alexandra, began to laugh. "Up and coming on the Divide, eh, Alexandra?" he cried gayly.

IV

Carl had changed, Alexandra felt, much less than one might have expected. He had not become a trim, self-satisfied city man. There was still something homely and wayward and definitely personal about him. Even his clothes, his Norfolk coat and his very high collars, were a little unconventional. He seemed to shrink into himself as he used to do; to hold himself away from things, as if he were afraid of being hurt. In short, he was more self-conscious than a man of thirty-five is expected to be. He looked older than his years and not very strong. His black hair, which still hung in a triangle over his pale forehead, was thin at the crown, and there were fine, relentless lines about his eyes. His back, with its high, sharp shoulders, looked like the back of an overworked German professor off on his holiday. His face was intelligent, sensitive, unhappy.

That evening after supper, Carl and Alexandra were sitting by the clump of castor beans in the middle of the flower garden. The gravel paths glittered in the moonlight, and below them the fields lay white and still.

"Do you know, Alexandra," he was saying, "I've been thinking how strangely things work out. I've been away engraving other men's pictures, and you've stayed at home and made your own." He pointed with his cigar toward the sleeping landscape. "How in the world have you done it? How have your neighbors done it?"

"We had n't any of us much to do with it, Carl. The land did it. It had its little joke. It pretended to be poor because nobody knew how to work it right; and then, all at once, it worked itself. It woke up out of its sleep and stretched itself, and it was so big, so rich, that we suddenly found we were rich, just from sitting still. As for me, you remember when I began to buy land. For years after that I was always squeezing and borrowing until I was ashamed to show my face in the banks. And then, all at once, men began to come to me offering to lend me money—and I did n't need it! Then I went ahead and built this house. I really built it for Emil. I want you to see Emil, Carl. He is so different from the rest of us!"

"How different?"

"Oh, you'll see! I'm sure it was to have sons like Emil, and to give them a chance, that father left the old country. It's curious, too; on the outside Emil is just like an American boy,—he graduated from the State University in June, you know,—but underneath he is more Swedish than any of us. Sometimes he is so like father that he frightens me; he is so violent in his feelings like that."

"Is he going to farm here with you?"

"He shall do whatever he wants to," Alexandra declared warmly. "He is going to have a chance, a whole chance; that's what I've worked for. Sometimes he talks about studying law, and sometimes, just lately, he's been talking about going out into the sand hills and taking up more land. He has his sad times, like father. But I hope he won't do that. We have land enough, at last!" Alexandra laughed.

"How about Lou and Oscar? They've done well, have n't they?"

"Yes, very well; but they are different, and now that they have farms of their own I do not see so much of them. We divided the land equally when Lou married. They have their own way of doing things, and they do not altogether like my way, I am afraid. Perhaps they think me too independent. But I have had to think for myself a good many years and am not likely to change. On the whole, though, we take as much comfort in each other as most brothers and sisters do. And I am very fond of Lou's oldest daughter."

"I think I liked the old Lou and Oscar better, and they probably feel the same about me. I even, if you can keep a secret,"—Carl leaned forward and touched her arm, smiling,—"I even think I liked the old country better. This is all very splendid in its way, but there was something about this country when it was a wild old beast that has haunted me all these years. Now, when I come back to all this milk and honey, I feel like the old German song, 'Wo bist du, wo bist du, mein geliebtest Land?'—Do you ever feel like that, I wonder?"

"Yes, sometimes, when I think about father and mother and those who are gone; so many of our old neighbors." Alexandra paused and looked up thoughtfully at the stars. "We can remember the graveyard when it was wild prairie, Carl, and now—"

"And now the old story has begun to write itself over there," said Carl softly. "Is n't it queer: there are only two or three human stories, and they go on repeating themselves as fiercely as if they had never happened before; like the larks in this country that have been singing the same five notes over for thousands of years."

"Oh, yes! The young people, they live so hard. And yet I sometimes envy them. There is my little neighbor, now; the people who bought your old place. I would n't have sold it to any one else, but I was always fond of that girl. You must remember her, little Marie Tovesky, from Omaha, who used to visit here? When she was eighteen she ran away from the convent school and got married, crazy child! She came out here a bride, with her father and husband. He had nothing, and the old man was willing to buy them a place and set them up. Your farm took her fancy, and I was glad to have her so near me. I've never been sorry, either. I even try to get along with Frank on her account."

"Is Frank her husband?"

"Yes. He's one of these wild fellows. Most Bohemians are good-natured, but Frank thinks we don't appreciate him here, I guess. He's jealous about everything, his farm and his horses and his pretty wife. Everybody likes her, just the same as when she was little. Sometimes I go up to the Catholic church with Emil, and it's funny to see Marie standing there laughing and shaking hands with people, looking so excited and gay, with Frank sulking behind her as if he could eat everybody alive. Frank's not a bad neighbor, but to get on with him you've got to make a fuss over him and act as if you thought he was a very important person all the time, and different from other people. I find it hard to keep that up from one year's end to another."

"I should n't think you'd be very successful at that kind of thing, Alexandra." Carl seemed to find the idea amusing.

"Well," said Alexandra firmly, "I do the best I can, on Marie's account. She has it hard enough, anyway. She's too young and pretty for this sort of life. We're all ever so much older and slower. But she's the kind that won't be downed easily. She'll work all day and go to a Bohemian wedding and dance all night, and drive the hay wagon for a cross man next morning. I could stay by a job, but I never had the go in me that she has, when I was going my best. I'll have to take you over to see her to-morrow."

Carl dropped the end of his cigar softly among the castor beans and sighed. "Yes, I suppose I must see the old place. I'm cowardly about things that remind me of myself. It took courage to come at all, Alexandra. I would n't have, if I had n't wanted to see you very, very much."

Alexandra looked at him with her calm, deliberate eyes. "Why do you dread things like that, Carl?" she asked earnestly. "Why are you dissatisfied with yourself?"

Her visitor winced. "How direct you are, Alexandra! Just like you used to be. Do I give myself away so quickly? Well, you see, for one thing, there's nothing to look forward to in my profession. Wood-engraving is the only thing I care about, and that had gone out before I began. Everything's cheap metal work nowadays, touching up miserable photographs, forcing up poor drawings, and spoiling good ones. I'm absolutely sick of it all." Carl frowned. "Alexandra, all the way out from New York I've been planning how I could deceive you and make you think me a very enviable fellow, and here I am telling you the truth the first night. I waste a lot of time pretending to people, and the joke of it is, I don't think I ever deceive any one. There are too many of my kind; people know us on sight."

Carl paused. Alexandra pushed her hair back from her brow with a puzzled, thoughtful gesture. "You see," he went on calmly, "measured by your standards here, I'm a failure. I couldn't buy even one of your cornfields. I've enjoyed a great many things, but I've got nothing to show for it all."

"But you show for it yourself, Carl. I'd rather have had your freedom than my land."

Carl shook his head mournfully. "Freedom so often means that one is n't needed anywhere. Here you are an individual, you have a background of your own, you would be missed. But off there in the cities there are thousands of rolling stones like me. We are all alike; we have no ties, we know nobody, we own nothing. When one of us dies, they scarcely know where to bury him. Our landlady and the delicatessen man are our mourners, and we leave nothing behind us but a frock-coat and a fiddle, or an easel, or a typewriter, or whatever tool we got our living by. All we have ever managed to do is to pay our rent, the exorbitant rent that one has to pay for a few square feet of space near the heart of things. We have no house, no place, no people of our own. We live in the streets, in the parks, in the theatres. We sit in restaurants and concert halls and look about at the hundreds of our own kind and shudder."

Alexandra was silent. She sat looking at the silver spot the moon made on the surface of the pond down in the pasture. He knew that she understood what he meant. At last she said slowly, "And yet I would rather have Emil grow up like that than like his two brothers. We pay a high rent, too, though we pay differently. We grow hard and heavy here. We don't move lightly and easily as you do, and our minds get stiff. If the world were no wider than my cornfields, if there were not something beside this, I would n't feel that it was much worth while to work. No, I would rather have Emil like you than like them. I felt that as soon as you came."

"I wonder why you feel like that?" Carl mused.

"I don't know. Perhaps I am like Carrie Jensen, the sister of one of my hired men. She had never been out of the cornfields, and a few years ago she got despondent and said life was just the same thing over and over, and she did n't see the use of it. After she had tried to kill herself once or twice, her folks got worried and sent her over to Iowa to visit some relations. Ever since she's come back she's been perfectly cheerful, and she says she's contented to live and work in a world that's so big and interesting. She said that anything as big as the bridges over the Platte and the Missouri reconciled her. And it's what goes on in the world that reconciles me."

V

Alexandra did not find time to go to her neighbor's the next day, nor the next. It was a busy season on the farm, with the corn-plowing going on, and even Emil was in the field with a team and cultivator. Carl went about over the farms with Alexandra in the morning, and in the afternoon and evening they found a great deal to talk about. Emil, for all his track practice, did not stand up under farmwork very well, and by night he was too tired to talk or even to practise on his cornet.

On Wednesday morning Carl got up before it was light, and stole downstairs and out of the kitchen door just as old Ivar was making his morning ablutions at the pump. Carl nodded to him and hurried up the draw, past the garden, and into the pasture where the milking cows used to be kept.

The dawn in the east looked like the light from some great fire that was burning under the edge of the world. The color was reflected in the globules of dew that sheathed the short gray pasture grass. Carl walked rapidly until he came to the crest of the second hill, where the Bergson pasture joined the one that had belonged to his father. There he sat down and waited for the sun to rise. It was just there that he and Alexandra used to do their milking together, he on his side of the fence, she on hers. He could remember exactly how she looked when she came over the close-cropped grass, her skirts pinned up, her head bare, a bright tin pail in either hand, and the milky light of the early morning all about her. Even as a boy he used to feel, when he saw her coming with her free step, her upright head and calm shoulders, that she looked as if she had walked straight out of the morning itself. Since then, when he had happened to see the sun come up in the country or on the water, he had often remembered the young Swedish girl and her milking pails.

Carl sat musing until the sun leaped above the prairie, and in the grass about him all the small creatures of day began to tune their tiny instruments. Birds and insects without number began to chirp, to twitter, to snap and whistle, to make all manner of fresh shrill noises. The pasture was flooded with light; every clump of ironweed and snow-on-the-mountain threw a long shadow, and the golden light seemed to be rippling through the curly grass like the tide racing in.

He crossed the fence into the pasture that was now the Shabatas' and continued his walk toward the pond. He had not gone far, however, when he discovered that he was not the only person abroad. In the draw below, his gun in his hands, was Emil, advancing cautiously, with a young woman beside him. They were moving softly, keeping close together, and Carl knew that they expected to find ducks on the pond. At the moment when they came in sight of the bright spot of water, he heard a whirr of wings and the ducks shot up into the air. There was a sharp crack from the gun, and five of the birds fell to the ground. Emil and his companion laughed delightedly, and Emil ran to pick them up. When he came back, dangling the ducks by their feet, Marie held her apron and he dropped them into it. As she stood looking down at them, her face changed. She took up one of the birds, a rumpled ball of feathers with the blood dripping slowly from its mouth, and looked at the live color that still burned on its plumage.

As she let it fall, she cried in distress, "Oh, Emil, why did you?"

"I like that!" the boy exclaimed indignantly. "Why, Marie, you asked me to come yourself."

"Yes, yes, I know," she said tearfully, "but I did n't think. I hate to see them when they are first shot. They were having such a good time, and we've spoiled it all for them."

Emil gave a rather sore laugh. "I should say we had! I'm not going hunting with you any more. You're as bad as Ivar. Here, let me take them." He snatched the ducks out of her apron.

"Don't be cross, Emil. Only—Ivar's right about wild things. They're too happy to kill. You can tell just how they felt when they flew up. They were scared, but they did n't really think anything could hurt them. No, we won't do that any more."

"All right," Emil assented. "I'm sorry I made you feel bad." As he looked down into her tearful eyes, there was a curious, sharp young bitterness in his own.

Carl watched them as they moved slowly down the draw. They had not seen him at all. He had not overheard much of their dialogue, but he felt the import of it. It made him, somehow, unreasonably mournful to find two young things abroad in the pasture in the early morning. He decided that he needed his breakfast.

VI

At dinner that day Alexandra said she thought they must really manage to go over to the Shabatas' that afternoon. "It's not often I let three days go by without seeing Marie. She will think I have forsaken her, now that my old friend has come back."

After the men had gone back to work, Alexandra put on a white dress and her sun-hat, and she and Carl set forth across the fields. "You see we have kept up the old path, Carl. It has been so nice for me to feel that there was a friend at the other end of it again."

Carl smiled a little ruefully. "All the same, I hope it has n't been *quite* the same."

Alexandra looked at him with surprise. "Why, no, of course not. Not the same. She could not very well take your place, if that's what you mean. I'm friendly with all my neighbors, I hope. But Marie is really a companion, some one I can talk to quite frankly. You would n't want me to be more lonely than I have been, would you?"

Carl laughed and pushed back the triangular lock of hair with the edge of his hat. "Of course I don't. I ought to be thankful that this path has n't been worn by—well, by friends with more pressing errands than your little Bohemian is likely to have." He paused to give Alexandra his hand as she stepped over the stile. "Are you the least bit disappointed in our coming together again?" he asked abruptly. "Is it the way you hoped it would be?"

Alexandra smiled at this. "Only better. When I've thought about your coming, I've sometimes been a little afraid of it. You have lived where things move so fast, and everything is slow here; the people slowest of all. Our lives are like the years, all made up of weather and crops and cows. How you hated cows!" She shook her head and laughed to herself.

"I did n't when we milked together. I walked up to the pasture corners this morning. I wonder whether I shall ever be able to tell you all that I was thinking about up there. It's a strange thing, Alexandra; I find it easy to be frank with you about every-thing under the sun except—yourself!"

"You are afraid of hurting my feelings, perhaps." Alexandra looked at him thoughtfully.

"No, I'm afraid of giving you a shock. You've seen yourself for so long in the dull minds of the people about you, that if I were to tell you how you seem to me, it would startle you. But you must see that you astonish me. You must feel when people admire you."

Alexandra blushed and laughed with some confusion. "I felt that you were pleased with me, if you mean that."

"And you've felt when other people were pleased with you?" he insisted.

"Well, sometimes. The men in town, at the banks and the county offices, seem glad to see me. I think, myself, it is more pleasant to do business with people who are clean and healthy-looking," she admitted blandly.

Carl gave a little chuckle as he opened the Shabatas' gate for her. "Oh, do you?" he asked dryly.

There was no sign of life about the Shabatas' house except a big yellow cat, sun-ning itself on the kitchen doorstep.

Alexandra took the path that led to the orchard. "She often sits there and sews. I did n't telephone her we were coming, because I did n't want her to go to work and bake cake and freeze ice-cream. She'll always make a party if you give her the least excuse. Do you recognize the apple trees, Carl?"

Linstrum looked about him. "I wish I had a dollar for every bucket of water I've carried for those trees. Poor father, he was an easy man, but he was perfectly merci-less when it came to watering the orchard."

"That's one thing I like about Germans; they make an orchard grow if they can't make anything else. I'm so glad these trees belong to some one who takes comfort in them. When I rented this place, the tenants never kept the orchard up, and Emil and I used to come over and take care of it ourselves. It needs mowing now. There she is, down in the corner. Maria-a-a!" she called.

A recumbent figure started up from the grass and came running toward them through the flickering screen of light and shade.

"Look at her! Is n't she like a little brown rabbit?" Alexandra laughed.

Marie ran up panting and threw her arms about Alexandra. "Oh, I had begun to think you were not coming at all, maybe. I knew you were so busy. Yes, Emil told me about Mr. Linstrum being here. Won't you come up to the house?"

"Why not sit down there in your corner? Carl wants to see the orchard. He kept all these trees alive for years, watering them with his own back."

Marie turned to Carl. "Then I'm thankful to you, Mr. Linstrum. We'd never have bought the place if it had n't been for this orchard, and then I would n't have had Alexandra, either." She gave Alexandra's arm a little squeeze as she walked beside her. "How nice your dress smells, Alexandra; you put rosemary leaves in your chest, like I told you."

She led them to the northwest corner of the orchard, sheltered on one side by a thick mulberry hedge and bordered on the other by a wheatfield, just beginning to yellow. In this corner the ground dipped a little, and the bluegrass, which the weeds had driven out in the upper part of the orchard, grew thick and luxuriant. Wild roses were flaming in the tufts of bunchgrass along the fence. Under a white mulberry tree there was an old wagon-seat. Beside it lay a book and a workbasket.

"You must have the seat, Alexandra. The grass would stain your dress," the hostess insisted. She dropped down on the ground at Alexandra's side and tucked her feet under her. Carl sat at a little distance from the two women, his back to the wheatfield, and watched them. Alexandra took off her shade-hat and threw it on the ground. Marie picked it up and played with the white ribbons, twisting them about her brown fingers as she talked. They made a pretty picture in the strong sunlight, the leafy pattern surrounding them like a net; the Swedish woman so white and gold, kindly and amused, but armored in calm, and the alert brown one, her full lips parted, points of yellow light dancing in her eyes as she laughed and chattered. Carl had never forgotten little Marie Tovesky's eyes, and he was glad to have an opportunity to study them. The brown iris, he found, was curiously slashed with yellow, the color of sunflower honey, or of old amber. In each eye one of these streaks must have been larger than the others, for the effect was that of two dancing points of light, two little yellow bubbles, such as rise in a glass of champagne. Sometimes they seemed like the sparks from a forge. She seemed so easily excited, to kindle with a fierce little flame if one but breathed upon her. "What a waste," Carl reflected. "She ought to be doing all that for a sweetheart. How awkwardly things come about!"

It was not very long before Marie sprang up out of the grass again. "Wait a moment. I want to show you something." She ran away and disappeared behind the low-growing apple trees.

"What a charming creature," Carl murmured. "I don't wonder that her husband is jealous. But can't she walk? does she always run?"

Alexandra nodded. "Always. I don't see many people, but I don't believe there are many like her, anywhere."

Marie came back with a branch she had broken from an apricot tree, laden with pale-yellow, pink-cheeked fruit. She dropped it beside Carl. "Did you plant those, too? They are such beautiful little trees."

Carl fingered the blue-green leaves, porous like blotting-paper and shaped like birch leaves, hung on waxen red stems. "Yes, I think I did. Are these the circus trees, Alexandra?"

"Shall I tell her about them?" Alexandra asked. "Sit down like a good girl, Marie, and don't ruin my poor hat, and I'll tell you a story. A long time ago, when Carl and I were, say, sixteen and twelve, a circus came to Hanover and we went to town in our wagon, with Lou and Oscar, to see the parade. We had n't money enough to go to the circus. We followed the parade out to the circus grounds and hung around until the show began and the crowd went inside the tent. Then Lou was afraid we looked foolish standing outside in the pasture, so we went back to Hanover feeling very sad. There was a man in the streets selling apricots, and we had never seen any before. He had driven down from somewhere up in the French country, and he was selling them twenty-five cents a peck. We had a little money our fathers had given us for candy, and I bought two pecks and Carl bought one. They cheered us a good deal, and we saved all the seeds and planted them. Up to the time Carl went away, they had n't borne at all."

"And now he's come back to eat them," cried Marie, nodding at Carl. "That *is* a good story. I can remember you a little, Mr. Linstrum. I used to see you in Hanover sometimes, when Uncle Joe took me to town. I remember you because you were always buying pencils and tubes of paint at the drug store. Once, when my uncle left me at the store, you drew a lot of little birds and flowers for me on a piece of wrapping-paper. I kept them for a long while. I thought you were very romantic because you could draw and had such black eyes."

Carl smiled. "Yes, I remember that time. Your uncle bought you some kind of a mechanical toy, a Turkish lady sitting on an ottoman and smoking a hookah, was n't it? And she turned her head backwards and forwards."

"Oh, yes! Was n't she splendid! I knew well enough I ought not to tell Uncle Joe I wanted it, for he had just come back from the saloon and was feeling good. You remember how he laughed? She tickled him, too. But when we got home, my aunt scolded him for buying toys when she needed so many things. We wound our lady up every night, and when she began to move her head my aunt used to laugh as hard as any of us. It was a music-box, you know, and the Turkish lady played a tune while she smoked. That was how she made you feel so jolly. As I remember her, she was lovely, and had a gold crescent on her turban."

Half an hour later, as they were leaving the house, Carl and Alexandra were met in the path by a strapping fellow in overalls and a blue shirt. He was breathing hard, as if he had been running, and was muttering to himself.

Marie ran forward, and, taking him by the arm, gave him a little push toward her guests. "Frank, this is Mr. Linstrum."

Frank took off his broad straw hat and nodded to Alexandra. When he spoke to Carl, he showed a fine set of white teeth. He was burned a dull red down to his neckband, and there was a heavy three-days' stubble on his face. Even in his agitation he was handsome, but he looked a rash and violent man.

Barely saluting the callers, he turned at once to his wife and began, in an outraged tone, "I have to leave my team to drive the old woman Hiller's hogs out-a my wheat. I go to take dat old woman to de court if she ain't careful, I tell you!"

His wife spoke soothingly. "But, Frank, she has only her lame boy to help her. She does the best she can."

Alexandra looked at the excited man and offered a suggestion. "Why don't you go over there some afternoon and hog-tight her fences? You'd save time for yourself in the end."

Frank's neck stiffened. "Not-a-much, I won't. I keep my hogs home. Other peoples can do like me. See? If that Louis can mend shoes, he can mend fence."

"Maybe," said Alexandra placidly; "but I've found it sometimes pays to mend other people's fences. Good-bye, Marie. Come to see me soon."

Alexandra walked firmly down the path and Carl followed her.

Frank went into the house and threw himself on the sofa, his face to the wall, his clenched fist on his hip. Marie, having seen her guests off, came in and put her hand coaxingly on his shoulder.

"Poor Frank! You've run until you've made your head ache, now have n't you? Let me make you some coffee."

"What else am I to do?" he cried hotly in Bohemian. "Am I to let any old woman's hogs root up my wheat? Is that what I work myself to death for?"

"Don't worry about it, Frank. I'll speak to Mrs. Hiller again. But, really, she almost cried last time they got out, she was so sorry."

Frank bounced over on his other side. "That's it; you always side with them against me. They all know it. Anybody here feels free to borrow the mower and break it, or turn their hogs in on me. They know you won't care!"

Marie hurried away to make his coffee. When she came back, he was fast asleep. She sat down and looked at him for a long while, very thoughtfully. When the kitchen clock struck six she went out to get supper, closing the door gently behind her. She was always sorry for Frank when he worked himself into one of these rages, and she was sorry to have him rough and quarrelsome with his neighbors. She was perfectly aware that the neighbors had a good deal to put up with, and that they bore with Frank for her sake.

VII

Marie's father, Albert Tovesky, was one of the more intelligent Bohemians who came West in the early seventies. He settled in Omaha and became a leader and adviser among his people there. Marie was his youngest child, by a second wife, and was the apple of his eye. She was barely sixteen, and was in the graduating class of the Omaha High School, when Frank Shabata arrived from the old country and set all the Bohemian girls in a flutter. He was easily the buck of the beer-gardens, and on Sunday he was a sight to see, with his silk hat and tucked shirt and blue frock-coat, wearing gloves and carrying a little wisp of a yellow cane. He was tall and fair, with splendid teeth and close-cropped yellow curls, and he wore a slightly disdainful expression, proper for a young man with high connections, whose mother had a big farm in the

Elbe valley. There was often an interesting discontent in his blue eyes, and every Bohemian girl he met imagined herself the cause of that unsatisfied expression. He had a way of drawing out his cambric handkerchief slowly, by one corner, from his breast-pocket, that was melancholy and romantic in the extreme. He took a little flight with each of the more eligible Bohemian girls, but it was when he was with little Marie Tovesky that he drew his handkerchief out most slowly, and, after he had lit a fresh cigar, dropped the match most despairingly. Any one could see, with half an eye, that his proud heart was bleeding for somebody.

One Sunday, late in the summer after Marie's graduation, she met Frank at a Bohemian picnic down the river and went rowing with him all the afternoon. When she got home that evening she went straight to her father's room and told him that she was engaged to Shabata. Old Tovesky was having a comfortable pipe before he went to bed. When he heard his daughter's announcement, he first prudently corked his beer bottle and then leaped to his feet and had a turn of temper. He characterized Frank Shabata by a Bohemian expression which is the equivalent of stuffed shirt.

"Why don't he go to work like the rest of us did? His farm in the Elbe valley, indeed! Ain't he got plenty brothers and sisters? It's his mother's farm, and why don't he stay at home and help her? Have n't I seen his mother out in the morning at five o'clock with her ladle and her big bucket on wheels, putting liquid manure on the cabbages? Don't I know the look of old Eva Shabata's hands? Like an old horse's hoofs they are—and this fellow wearing gloves and rings! Engaged, indeed! You are n't fit to be out of school, and that's what's the matter with you. I will send you off to the Sisters of the Sacred Heart in St. Louis, and they will teach you some sense, *I* guess!"

Accordingly, the very next week, Albert Tovesky took his daughter, pale and tearful, down the river to the convent. But the way to make Frank want anything was to tell him he could n't have it. He managed to have an interview with Marie before she went away, and whereas he had been only half in love with her before, he now persuaded himself that he would not stop at anything. Marie took with her to the convent, under the canvas lining of her trunk, the results of a laborious and satisfying morning on Frank's part; no less than a dozen photographs of himself, taken in a dozen different love-lorn attitudes. There was a little round photograph for her watch-case, photographs for her wall and dresser, and even long narrow ones to be used as book-marks. More than once the handsome gentleman was torn to pieces before the French class by an indignant nun.

Marie pined in the convent for a year, until her eighteenth birthday was passed. Then she met Frank Shabata in the Union Station in St. Louis and ran away with him. Old Tovesky forgave his daughter because there was nothing else to do, and bought her a farm in the country that she had loved so well as a child. Since then her story had been a part of the history of the Divide. She and Frank had been living there for five years when Carl Linstrum came back to pay his long deferred visit to Alexandra. Frank had, on the whole, done better than one might have expected. He had flung himself at the soil with savage energy. Once a year he went to Hastings or to Omaha, on a spree. He stayed away for a week or two, and then came home and worked like a demon. He did work; if he felt sorry for himself, that was his own affair.

VIII

On the evening of the day of Alexandra's call at the Shabatas', a heavy rain set in. Frank sat up until a late hour reading the Sunday newspapers. One of the Goulds was getting a divorce, and Frank took it as a personal affront. In printing the story of the young man's marital troubles, the knowing editor gave a sufficiently colored account of his career, stating the amount of his income and the manner in which he was supposed to spend it. Frank read English slowly, and the more he read about this divorce case, the angrier he grew. At last he threw down the page with a snort. He turned to his farm-hand who was reading the other half of the paper.

"By God! if I have that young feller in de hayfield once, I show him something. Listen here what he do wit his money." And Frank began the catalogue of the young man's reputed extravagances.

Marie sighed. She thought it hard that the Goulds, for whom she had nothing but good will, should make her so much trouble. She hated to see the Sunday newspapers come into the house. Frank was always reading about the doings of rich people and feeling outraged. He had an inexhaustible stock of stories about their crimes and follies, how they bribed the courts and shot down their butlers with impunity whenever they chose. Frank and Lou Bergson had very similar ideas, and they were two of the political agitators of the county.

The next morning broke clear and brilliant, but Frank said the ground was too wet to plough, so he took the cart and drove over to Sainte-Agnes to spend the day at Moses Marcel's saloon. After he was gone, Marie went out to the back porch to begin her butter-making. A brisk wind had come up and was driving puffy white clouds across the sky. The orchard was sparkling and rippling in the sun. Marie stood looking toward it wistfully, her hand on the lid of the churn, when she heard a sharp ring in the air, the merry sound of the whetstone on the scythe. That invitation decided her. She ran into the house, put on a short skirt and a pair of her husband's boots, caught up a tin pail and started for the orchard. Emil had already begun work and was mowing vigorously. When he saw her coming, he stopped and wiped his brow. His yellow canvas leggings and khaki trousers were splashed to the knees.

"Don't let me disturb you, Emil. I'm going to pick cherries. Is n't everything beautiful after the rain? Oh, but I'm glad to get this place mowed! When I heard it raining in the night, I thought maybe you would come and do it for me to-day. The wind wakened me. Did n't it blow dreadfully? Just smell the wild roses! They are always so spicy after a rain. We never had so many of them in here before. I suppose it's the wet season. Will you have to cut them, too?"

"If I cut the grass, I will," Emil said teasingly. "What's the matter with you? What makes you so flighty?"

"Am I flighty? I suppose that's the wet season, too, then. It's exciting to see everything growing so fast,—and to get the grass cut! Please leave the roses till last, if you must cut them. Oh, I don't mean all of them, I mean that low place down by my tree, where there are so many. Are n't you splashed! Look at the spider-webs all over the grass. Good-bye. I'll call you if I see a snake."

She tripped away and Emil stood looking after her. In a few moments he heard the cherries dropping smartly into the pail, and he began to swing his scythe with that long, even stroke that few American boys ever learn. Marie picked cherries and sang softly to herself, stripping one glittering branch after another, shivering when she caught a shower of raindrops on her neck and hair. And Emil mowed his way slowly down toward the cherry trees.

That summer the rains had been so many and opportune that it was almost more than Shabata and his man could do to keep up with the corn; the orchard was a neglected wilderness. All sorts of weeds and herbs and flowers had grown up there; splotches of wild larkspur, pale green-and-white spikes of hoarhound, plantations of wild cotton, tangles of foxtail and wild wheat. South of the apricot trees, cornering on the wheatfield, was Frank's alfalfa, where myriads of white and yellow butterflies were always fluttering above the purple blossoms. When Emil reached the lower corner by the hedge, Marie was sitting under her white mulberry tree, the pailful of cherries beside her, looking off at the gentle, tireless swelling of the wheat.

"Emil," she said suddenly—he was mowing quietly about under the tree so as not to disturb her—"what religion did the Swedes have away back, before they were Christians?"

Emil paused and straightened his back. "I don't know. About like the Germans', was n't it?"

Marie went on as if she had not heard him. "The Bohemians, you know, were tree worshipers before the missionaries came. Father says the people in the mountains still do queer things, sometimes,—they believe that trees bring good or bad luck."

Emil looked superior. "Do they? Well, which are the lucky trees? I'd like to know."

"I don't know all of them, but I know lindens are. The old people in the mountains plant lindens to purify the forest, and to do away with the spells that come from the old trees they say have lasted from heathen times. I'm a good Catholic, but I think I could get along with caring for trees, if I had n't anything else."

"That's a poor saying," said Emil, stooping over to wipe his hands in the wet grass.

"Why is it? If I feel that way, I feel that way. I like trees because they seem more resigned to the way they have to live than other things do. I feel as if this tree knows everything I ever think of when I sit here. When I come back to it, I never have to remind it of anything; I begin just where I left off."

Emil had nothing to say to this. He reached up among the branches and began to pick the sweet, insipid fruit,—long ivory-colored berries, tipped with faint pink, like white coral, that fall to the ground unheeded all summer through. He dropped a handful into her lap.

"Do you like Mr. Linstrum?" Marie asked suddenly.

"Yes. Don't you?"

"Oh, ever so much; only he seems kind of staid and school-teachery. But, of course, he is older than Frank, even. I'm sure I don't want to live to be more than thirty, do you? Do you think Alexandra likes him very much?"

"I suppose so. They were old friends."

"Oh, Emil, you know what I mean!" Marie tossed her head impatiently. "Does she really care about him? When she used to tell me about him, I always wondered whether she was n't a little in love with him."

"Who, Alexandra?" Emil laughed and thrust his hands into his trousers pockets. "Alexandra's never been in love, you crazy!" He laughed again. "She would n't know how to go about it. The idea!"

Marie shrugged her shoulders. "Oh, you don't know Alexandra as well as you think you do! If you had any eyes, you would see that she is very fond of him. It would serve you all right if she walked off with Carl. I like him because he appreciates her more than you do."

Emil frowned. "What are you talking about, Marie? Alexandra's all right. She and I have always been good friends. What more do you want? I like to talk to Carl about New York and what a fellow can do there."

"Oh, Emil! Surely you are not thinking of going off there?"

"Why not? I must go somewhere, must n't I?" The young man took up his scythe and leaned on it. "Would you rather I went off in the sand hills and lived like Ivar?"

Marie's face fell under his brooding gaze. She looked down at his wet leggings. "I'm sure Alexandra hopes you will stay on here," she murmured.

"Then Alexandra will be disappointed," the young man said roughly. "What do I want to hang around here for? Alexandra can run the farm all right, without me. I don't want to stand around and look on. I want to be doing something on my own account."

"That's so," Marie sighed. "There are so many, many things you can do. Almost anything you choose."

"And there are so many, many things I can't do." Emil echoed her tone sarcastically. "Sometimes I don't want to do anything at all, and sometimes I want to pull the four corners of the Divide together,"—he threw out his arm and brought it back with a jerk,—"so, like a table-cloth. I get tired of seeing men and horses going up and down, up and down."

Marie looked up at his defiant figure and her face clouded. "I wish you were n't so restless, and did n't get so worked up over things," she said sadly.

"Thank you," he returned shortly.

She sighed despondently. "Everything I say makes you cross, don't it? And you never used to be cross to me."

Emil took a step nearer and stood frowning down at her bent head. He stood in an attitude of self-defense, his feet well apart, his hands clenched and drawn up at his sides, so that the cords stood out on his bare arms. "I can't play with you like a little boy any more," he said slowly. "That's what you miss, Marie. You'll have to get some other little boy to play with." He stopped and took a deep breath. Then he went on in a low tone, so intense that it was almost threatening: "Sometimes you seem to understand perfectly, and then sometimes you pretend you don't. You don't help things any by pretending. It's then that I want to pull the corners of the Divide together. If you *won't* understand, you know, I could make you!"

Marie clasped her hands and started up from her seat. She had grown very pale and her eyes were shining with excitement and distress. "But, Emil, if I understand, then all our good times are over, we can never do nice things together any more. We shall have to behave like Mr. Linstrum. And, anyhow, there's nothing to understand!" She struck the ground with her little foot fiercely. "That won't last. It will go away, and things will be just as they used to. I wish you were a Catholic. The Church helps people, indeed it does. I pray for you, but that's not the same as if you prayed yourself."

She spoke rapidly and pleadingly, looked entreatingly into his face. Emil stood defiant, gazing down at her.

"I can't pray to have the things I want," he said slowly, "and I won't pray not to have them, not if I'm damned for it."

Marie turned away, wringing her hands. "Oh, Emil, you won't try! Then all our good times are over."

"Yes; over. I never expect to have any more."

Emil gripped the hand-holds of his scythe and began to mow. Marie took up her cherries and went slowly toward the house, crying bitterly.

IX

On Sunday afternoon, a month after Carl Linstrum's arrival, he rode with Emil up into the French country to attend a Catholic fair. He sat for most of the afternoon in the basement of the church, where the fair was held, talking to Marie Shabata, or strolled about the gravel terrace, thrown up on the hillside in front of the basement doors, where the French boys were jumping and wrestling and throwing the discus. Some of the boys were in their white baseball suits; they had just come up from a Sunday practice game down in the ball-grounds. Amédée, the newly married, Emil's best friend, was their pitcher, renowned among the country towns for his dash and skill. Amédée was a little fellow, a year younger than Emil and much more boyish in appearance; very lithe and active and neatly made, with a clear brown and white skin, and flashing white teeth. The Sainte-Agnes boys were to play the Hastings nine in a fortnight, and Amédée's lightning balls were the hope of his team. The little Frenchman seemed to get every ounce there was in him behind the ball as it left his hand.

"You'd have made the battery at the University for sure, 'Médée," Emil said as they were walking from the ball-grounds back to the church on the hill. "You're pitching better than you did in the spring."

Amédée grinned. "Sure! A married man don't lose his head no more." He slapped Emil on the back as he caught step with him. "Oh, Emil, you wanna get married right off quick! It's the greatest thing ever!"

Emil laughed. "How am I going to get married without any girl?"

Amédée took his arm. "Pooh! There are plenty girls will have you. You wanna get some nice French girl, now. She treat you well; always be jolly. See,"—he began checking off on his fingers,—"there is Séverine, and Alphosen, and Joséphine, and Hectorine, and Louise, and Malvina—why, I could love any of them girls! Why don't you get after them? Are you stuck up, Emil, or is anything the matter with you? I never did know a boy twenty-two years old before that did n't have no girl. You wanna be a priest, maybe? Not-a for me!" Amédée swaggered. "I bring many good Catholics into this world, I hope, and that's a way I help the Church."

Emil looked down and patted him on the shoulder. "Now you're windy, 'Médée. You Frenchies like to brag."

But Amédée had the zeal of the newly married, and he was not to be lightly shaken off. "Honest and true, Emil, don't you want *any* girl? Maybe there's some young lady in Lincoln, now, very grand,"—Amédée waved his hand languidly before his face to denote the fan of heartless beauty,—"and you lost your heart up there. Is that it?"

"Maybe," said Emil.

But Amédée saw no appropriate glow in his friend's face. "Bah!" he exclaimed in disgust. "I tell all the French girls to keep 'way from you. You gotta rock in there," thumping Emil on the ribs.

When they reached the terrace at the side of the church, Amédée, who was excited by his success on the ball-grounds, challenged Emil to a jumping-match, though he knew he would be beaten. They belted themselves up, and Raoul Marcel, the choir tenor and Father Duchesne's pet, and Jean Bordelau, held the string over which they vaulted. All the French boys stood round, cheering and humping themselves up when Emil or Amédée went over the wire, as if they were helping in the lift. Emil stopped at five-feet-five, declaring that he would spoil his appetite for supper if he jumped any more.

Angélique, Amédée's pretty bride, as blonde and fair as her name, who had come out to watch the match, tossed her head at Emil and said:—

"'Médée could jump much higher than you if he were as tall. And anyhow, he is much more graceful. He goes over like a bird, and you have to hump yourself all up."

"Oh, I do, do I?" Emil caught her and kissed her saucy mouth squarely, while she laughed and struggled and called, "'Médée! 'Médée!"

"There, you see your 'Médée is n't even big enough to get you away from me. I could run away with you right now and he could only sit down and cry about it. I'll show you whether I have to hump myself!" Laughing and panting, he picked Angélique up in his arms and began running about the rectangle with her. Not until he saw Marie Shabata's tiger eyes flashing from the gloom of the basement doorway did he hand the disheveled bride over to her husband. "There, go to your graceful; I have n't the heart to take you away from him."

Angélique clung to her husband and made faces at Emil over the white shoulder of Amédée's ball-shirt. Emil was greatly amused at her air of proprietorship and at Amédée's shameless submission to it. He was delighted with his friend's good fortune. He liked to see and to think about Amédée's sunny, natural, happy love.

He and Amédée had ridden and wrestled and larked together since they were lads of twelve. On Sundays and holidays they were always arm in arm. It seemed strange that now he should have to hide the thing that Amédée was so proud of, that the feeling which gave one of them such happiness should bring the other such despair. It was like that when Alexandra tested her seed-corn in the spring, he mused. From two ears that had grown side by side, the grains of one shot up joyfully into the light, projecting themselves into the future, and the grains from the other lay still in the earth and rotted; and nobody knew why.

X

While Emil and Carl were amusing themselves at the fair, Alexandra was at home, busy with her account-books, which had been neglected of late. She was almost through with her figures when she heard a cart drive up to the gate, and looking out of the window she saw her two older brothers. They had seemed to avoid her ever since Carl Linstrum's arrival, four weeks ago that day, and she hurried to the door to welcome them. She saw at once that they had come with some very definite purpose. They followed her stiffly into the sitting room. Oscar sat down, but Lou walked over to the window and remained standing, his hands behind him.

"You are by yourself?" he asked, looking toward the doorway into the parlor.

"Yes. Carl and Emil went up to the Catholic fair."

For a few moments neither of the men spoke.

Then Lou came out sharply. "How soon does he intend to go away from here?"

"I don't know, Lou. Not for some time, I hope." Alexandra spoke in an even, quiet tone that often exasperated her brothers. They felt that she was trying to be superior with them.

Oscar spoke up grimly. "We thought we ought to tell you that people have begun to talk," he said meaningly.

Alexandra looked at him. "What about?"

Oscar met her eyes blankly. "About you, keeping him here so long. It looks bad for him to be hanging on to a woman this way. People think you're getting taken in."

Alexandra shut her account-book firmly. "Boys," she said seriously, "don't let's go on with this. We won't come out anywhere. I can't take advice on such a matter. I know you mean well, but you must not feel responsible for me in things of this sort. If we go on with this talk it will only make hard feeling."

Lou whipped about from the window. "You ought to think a little about your family. You're making us all ridiculous."

"How am I?"

"People are beginning to say you want to marry the fellow."

"Well, and what is ridiculous about that?"

Lou and Oscar exchanged outraged looks. "Alexandra! Can't you see he's just a tramp and he's after your money? He wants to be taken care of, he does!"

"Well, suppose I want to take care of him? Whose business is it but my own?"

"Don't you know he'd get hold of your property?"

"He'd get hold of what I wished to give him, certainly."

Oscar sat up suddenly and Lou clutched at his bristly hair.

"Give him?" Lou shouted. "Our property, our homestead?"

"I don't know about the homestead," said Alexandra quietly. "I know you and Oscar have always expected that it would be left to your children, and I'm not sure but what you're right. But I'll do exactly as I please with the rest of my land, boys."

"The rest of your land!" cried Lou, growing more excited every minute. "Did n't all the land come out of the homestead? It was bought with money borrowed on the homestead, and Oscar and me worked ourselves to the bone paying interest on it."

"Yes, you paid the interest. But when you married we made a division of the land, and you were satisfied. I've made more on my farms since I've been alone than when we all worked together."

"Everything you've made has come out of the original land that us boys worked for, has n't it? The farms and all that comes out of them belongs to us as a family."

Alexandra waved her hand impatiently. "Come now, Lou. Stick to the facts. You are talking nonsense. Go to the county clerk and ask him who owns my land, and whether my titles are good."

Lou turned to his brother. "This is what comes of letting a woman meddle in business," he said bitterly. "We ought to have taken things in our own hands years ago. But she liked to run things, and we humored her. We thought you had good sense, Alexandra. We never thought you'd do anything foolish."

Alexandra rapped impatiently on her desk with her knuckles. "Listen, Lou. Don't talk wild. You say you ought to have taken things into your own hands years ago. I suppose you mean before you left home. But how could you take hold of what wasn't there? I've got most of what I have now since we divided the property; I've built it up myself, and it has nothing to do with you."

Oscar spoke up solemnly. "The property of a family really belongs to the men of the family, no matter about the title. If anything goes wrong, it's the men that are held responsible."

"Yes, of course," Lou broke in. "Everybody knows that. Oscar and me have always been easy-going and we've never made any fuss. We were willing you should hold the land and have the good of it, but you got no right to part with any of it. We worked in the fields to pay for the first land you bought, and whatever's come out of it has got to be kept in the family."

Oscar reinforced his brother, his mind fixed on the one point he could see. "The property of a family belongs to the men of the family, because they are held responsible, and because they do the work."

Alexandra looked from one to the other, her eyes full of indignation. She had been impatient before, but now she was beginning to feel angry. "And what about my work?" she asked in an unsteady voice.

Lou looked at the carpet. "Oh, now, Alexandra, you always took it pretty easy! Of course we wanted you to. You liked to manage round, and we always humored you. We realize you were a great deal of help to us. There's no woman anywhere around that knows as much about business as you do, and we've always been proud of that, and thought you were pretty smart. But, of course, the real work always fell on us. Good advice is all right, but it don't get the weeds out of the corn."

"Maybe not, but it sometimes puts in the crop, and it sometimes keeps the fields for corn to grow in," said Alexandra dryly. "Why, Lou, I can remember when you and Oscar wanted to sell this homestead and all the improvements to old preacher Ericson for two thousand dollars. If I'd consented, you'd have gone down to the river and scraped along on poor farms for the rest of your lives. When I put in our first field of alfalfa you both opposed me, just because I first heard about it from a young man who had been to the University. You said I was being taken in then, and all the neighbors said so. You know as well as I do that alfalfa has been the salvation of this country. You all laughed at me when I said our land here was about ready for wheat, and I had to raise three big wheat crops before the neighbors quit putting all their land in corn. Why, I remember you cried, Lou, when we put in the first big wheat-planting, and said everybody was laughing at us."

Lou turned to Oscar. "That's the woman of it; if she tells you to put in a crop, she thinks she's put it in. It makes women conceited to meddle in business. I shouldn't think you'd want to remind us how hard you were on us, Alexandra, after the way you baby Emil."

"Hard on you? I never meant to be hard. Conditions were hard. Maybe I would never have been very soft, anyhow; but I certainly did n't choose to be the kind of girl I was. If you take even a vine and cut it back again and again, it grows hard, like a tree."

Lou felt that they were wandering from the point, and that in digression Alexandra might unnerve him. He wiped his forehead with a jerk of his handkerchief. "We never doubted you, Alexandra. We never questioned anything you did. You've always had your own way. But you can't expect us to sit like stumps and see you done out of the property by any loafer who happens along, and making yourself ridiculous into the bargain."

Oscar rose. "Yes," he broke in, "everybody's laughing to see you get took in; at your age, too. Everybody knows he's nearly five years younger than you, and is after your money. Why, Alexandra, you are forty years old!"

"All that does n't concern anybody but Carl and me. Go to town and ask your lawyers what you can do to restrain me from disposing of my own property. And I advise you to do what they tell you; for the authority you can exert by law is the only influence you will ever have over me again." Alexandra rose. "I think I would rather not have lived to find out what I have to-day," she said quietly, closing her desk.

Lou and Oscar looked at each other questioningly. There seemed to be nothing to do but to go, and they walked out.

"You can't do business with women," Oscar said heavily as he clambered into the cart. "But anyhow, we've had our say, at last."

Lou scratched his head. "Talk of that kind might come too high, you know; but she's apt to be sensible. You had n't ought to said that about her age, though, Oscar. I'm afraid that hurt her feelings; and the worst thing we can do is to make her sore at us. She'd marry him out of contrariness."

"I only meant," said Oscar, "that she is old enough to know better, and she is. If she was going to marry, she ought to done it long ago, and not go making a fool of herself now."

Lou looked anxious, nevertheless. "Of course," he reflected hopefully and inconsistently, "Alexandra ain't much like other women-folks. Maybe it won't make her sore. Maybe she'd as soon be forty as not!"

XI

Emil came home at about half-past seven o'clock that evening. Old Ivar met him at the windmill and took his horse, and the young man went directly into the house. He called to his sister and she answered from her bedroom, behind the sitting-room, saying that she was lying down.

Emil went to her door.

"Can I see you for a minute?" he asked. "I want to talk to you about something before Carl comes."

Alexandra rose quickly and came to the door. "Where is Carl?"

"Lou and Oscar met us and said they wanted to talk to him, so he rode over to Oscar's with them. Are you coming out?" Emil asked impatiently.

"Yes, sit down. I'll be dressed in a moment."

Alexandra closed her door, and Emil sank down on the old slat lounge and sat with his head in his hands. When his sister came out, he looked up, not knowing whether the interval had been short or long, and he was surprised to see that the room had grown quite dark. That was just as well; it would be easier to talk if he were not under the gaze of those clear, deliberate eyes, that saw so far in some directions and were so blind in others. Alexandra, too, was glad of the dusk. Her face was swollen from crying.

Emil started up and then sat down again. "Alexandra," he said slowly, in his deep young baritone, "I don't want to go away to law school this fall. Let me put it off another year. I want to take a year off and look around. It's awfully easy to rush into a profession you don't really like, and awfully hard to get out of it. Linstrum and I have been talking about that."

"Very well, Emil. Only don't go off looking for land." She came up and put her hand on his shoulder. "I've been wishing you could stay with me this winter."

"That's just what I don't want to do, Alexandra. I'm restless. I want to go to a new place. I want to go down to the City of Mexico to join one of the University fellows who's at the head of an electrical plant. He wrote me he could give me a little job, enough to pay my way, and I could look around and see what I want to do. I want to go as soon as harvest is over. I guess Lou and Oscar will be sore about it."

"I suppose they will." Alexandra sat down on the lounge beside him. "They are very angry with me, Emil. We have had a quarrel. They will not come here again."

Emil scarcely heard what she was saying; he did not notice the sadness of her tone. He was thinking about the reckless life he meant to live in Mexico.

"What about?" he asked absently.

"About Carl Linstrum. They are afraid I am going to marry him, and that some of my property will get away from them."

Emil shrugged his shoulders. "What nonsense!" he murmured. "Just like them."

Alexandra drew back. "Why nonsense, Emil?"

"Why, you've never thought of such a thing, have you? They always have to have something to fuss about."

"Emil," said his sister slowly, "you ought not to take things for granted. Do you agree with them that I have no right to change my way of living?"

Emil looked at the outline of his sister's head in the dim light. They were sitting close together and he somehow felt that she could hear his thoughts. He was silent for a moment, and then said in an embarrassed tone, "Why, no, certainly not. You ought to do whatever you want to. I'll always back you."

"But it would seem a little bit ridiculous to you if I married Carl?"

Emil fidgeted. The issue seemed to him too far-fetched to warrant discussion. "Why, no. I should be surprised if you wanted to. I can't see exactly why. But that's none of my business. You ought to do as you please. Certainly you ought not to pay any attention to what the boys say."

Alexandra sighed. "I had hoped you might understand, a little, why I do want to. But I suppose that's too much to expect. I've had a pretty lonely life, Emil. Besides Marie, Carl is the only friend I have ever had."

Emil was awake now; a name in her last sentence roused him. He put out his hand and took his sister's awkwardly. "You ought to do just as you wish, and I think

Carl's a fine fellow. He and I would always get on. I don't believe any of the things the boys say about him, honest I don't. They are suspicious of him because he's intelligent. You know their way. They've been sore at me ever since you let me go away to college. They're always trying to catch me up. If I were you, I wouldn't pay any attention to them. There's nothing to get upset about. Carl's a sensible fellow. He won't mind them."

"I don't know. If they talk to him the way they did to me, I think he'll go away."

Emil grew more and more uneasy. "Think so? Well, Marie said it would serve us all right if you walked off with him."

"Did she? Bless her little heart! *She* would." Alexandra's voice broke.

Emil began unlacing his leggings. "Why don't you talk to her about it? There's Carl, I hear his horse. I guess I'll go upstairs and get my boots off. No, I don't want any supper. We had supper at five o'clock, at the fair."

Emil was glad to escape and get to his own room. He was a little ashamed for his sister, though he had tried not to show it. He felt that there was something indecorous in her proposal, and she did seem to him somewhat ridiculous. There was trouble enough in the world, he reflected, as he threw himself upon his bed, without people who were forty years old imagining they wanted to get married. In the darkness and silence Emil was not likely to think long about Alexandra. Every image slipped away but one. He had seen Marie in the crowd that afternoon. She sold candy at the fair. *Why* had she ever run away with Frank Shabata, and how could she go on laughing and working and taking an interest in things? Why did she like so many people, and why had she seemed pleased when all the French and Bohemian boys, and the priest himself, crowded round her candy stand? Why did she care about any one but him? Why could he never, never find the thing he looked for in her playful, affectionate eyes?

Then he fell to imagining that he looked once more and found it there, and what it would be like if she loved him,—she who, as Alexandra said, could give her whole heart. In that dream he could lie for hours, as if in a trance. His spirit went out of his body and crossed the fields to Marie Shabata.

At the University dances the girls had often looked wonderingly at the tall young Swede with the fine head, leaning against the wall and frowning, his arms folded, his eyes fixed on the ceiling or the floor. All the girls were a little afraid of him. He was distinguished-looking, and not the jollying kind. They felt that he was too intense and preoccupied. There was something queer about him. Emil's fraternity rather prided itself upon its dances, and sometimes he did his duty and danced every dance. But whether he was on the floor or brooding in a corner, he was always thinking about Marie Shabata. For two years the storm had been gathering in him.

XII

Carl came into the sitting-room while Alexandra was lighting the lamp. She looked up at him as she adjusted the shade. His sharp shoulders stooped as if he were very tired, his face was pale, and there were bluish shadows under his dark eyes. His anger had burned itself out and left him sick and disgusted.

"You have seen Lou and Oscar?" Alexandra asked.

"Yes." His eyes avoided hers.

Alexandra took a deep breath. "And now you are going away. I thought so."

Carl threw himself into a chair and pushed the dark lock back from his forehead with his white, nervous hand. "What a hopeless position you are in, Alexandra!" he exclaimed feverishly. "It is your fate to be always surrounded by little men. And I am no better than the rest. I am too little to face the criticism of even such men as Lou and Oscar. Yes, I am going away; to-morrow. I cannot even ask you to give me a promise until I have something to offer you. I thought, perhaps, I could do that; but I find I can't."

"What good comes of offering people things they don't need?" Alexandra asked sadly. "I don't need money. But I have needed you for a great many years. I wonder why I have been permitted to prosper, if it is only to take my friends away from me."

"I don't deceive myself," Carl said frankly. "I know that I am going away on my own account. I must make the usual effort. I must have something to show for myself. To take what you would give me, I should have to be either a very large man or a very small one, and I am only in the middle class."

Alexandra sighed. "I have a feeling that if you go away, you will not come back. Something will happen to one of us, or to both. People have to snatch at happiness when they can, in this world. It is always easier to lose than to find. What I have is yours, if you care enough about me to take it."

Carl rose and looked up at the picture of John Bergson. "But I can't, my dear, I can't! I will go North at once. Instead of idling about in California all winter, I shall be getting my bearings up there. I won't waste another week. Be patient with me, Alexandra. Give me a year!"

"As you will," said Alexandra wearily. "All at once, in a single day, I lose everything; and I do not know why. Emil, too, is going away." Carl was still studying John Bergson's face and Alexandra's eyes followed his. "Yes," she said, "if he could have seen all that would come of the task he gave me, he would have been sorry. I hope he does not see me now. I hope that he is among the old people of his blood and country, and that tidings do not reach him from the New World."

Part III: Winter Memories

I

Winter has settled down over the Divide again; the season in which Nature recuperates, in which she sinks to sleep between the fruitfulness of autumn and the passion of spring. The birds have gone. The teeming life that goes on down in the long grass is exterminated. The prairie-dog keeps his hole. The rabbits run shivering from one frozen garden patch to another and are hard put to it to find frost-bitten cabbage-stalks. At night the coyotes roam the wintry waste, howling for food. The variegated fields are all one color now; the pastures, the stubble, the roads, the sky are the same leaden gray. The hedgerows and trees are scarcely perceptible against the bare earth, whose slaty hue they have taken on. The ground is frozen so hard that it bruises the foot to walk in the roads or in the ploughed fields. It is like an iron country, and the spirit is oppressed by its rigor and melancholy. One could easily believe that in that dead landscape the germs of life and fruitfulness were extinct forever.

Alexandra has settled back into her old routine. There are weekly letters from Emil. Lou and Oscar she has not seen since Carl went away. To avoid awkward encounters in the presence of curious spectators, she has stopped going to the Norwegian Church and drives up to the Reform Church at Hanover, or goes with Marie Shabata to the Catholic Church, locally known as "the French Church." She has not told Marie about Carl, or her differences with her brothers. She was never very communicative about her own affairs, and when she came to the point, an instinct told her that about such things she and Marie would not understand one another.

Old Mrs. Lee had been afraid that family misunderstandings might deprive her of her yearly visit to Alexandra. But on the first day of December Alexandra telephoned Annie that to-morrow she would send Ivar over for her mother, and the next day the old lady arrived with her bundles. For twelve years Mrs. Lee had always entered Alexandra's sitting-room with the same exclamation, "Now we be yust-a like old times!" She enjoyed the liberty Alexandra gave her, and hearing her own language about her all day long. Here she could wear her nightcap and sleep with all her windows shut, listen to Ivar reading the Bible, and here she could run about among the stables in a pair of Emil's old boots. Though she was bent almost double, she was as spry as a gopher. Her face was as brown as if it had been varnished, and as full of wrinkles as a washerwoman's hands. She had three jolly old teeth left in the front of her mouth, and when she grinned she looked very knowing, as if when you found out how to take it, life was n't half bad. While she and Alexandra patched and pieced and quilted, she talked incessantly about stories she read in a Swedish family paper, telling the plots in great detail; or about her life on a dairy farm in Gottland when she was a girl. Sometimes she forgot which were the printed stories and which were the real stories, it all seemed so far away. She loved to take a little brandy, with hot water and sugar, before she went to bed, and Alexandra always had it ready for her. "It sends good dreams," she would say with a twinkle in her eye.

When Mrs. Lee had been with Alexandra for a week, Marie Shabata telephoned one morning to say that Frank had gone to town for the day, and she would like them to come over for coffee in the afternoon. Mrs. Lee hurried to wash out and iron her new cross-stitched apron, which she had finished only the night before; a checked gingham apron worked with a design ten inches broad across the bottom; a hunting scene, with fir trees and a stag and dogs and huntsmen. Mrs. Lee was firm with herself at dinner, and refused a second helping of apple dumplings. "I ta-ank I save up," she said with a giggle.

At two o'clock in the afternoon Alexandra's cart drove up to the Shabatas' gate, and Marie saw Mrs. Lee's red shawl come bobbing up the path. She ran to the door and pulled the old woman into the house with a hug, helping her to take off her wraps while Alexandra blanketed the horse outside. Mrs. Lee had put on her best black satine dress—she abominated woolen stuffs, even in winter—and a crocheted collar, fastened with a big pale gold pin, containing faded daguerreotypes of her father and mother. She had not worn her apron for fear of rumpling it, and now she shook it out and tied it round her waist with a conscious air. Marie drew back and threw up her hands, exclaiming, "Oh, what a beauty! I've never seen this one before, have I, Mrs. Lee?"

The old woman giggled and ducked her head. "No, yust las' night I ma-ake. See dis tread; verra strong, no wa-ash out, no fade. My sister send from Sveden. I yust-a ta-ank you like dis."

Marie ran to the door again. "Come in, Alexandra. I have been looking at Mrs. Lee's apron. Do stop on your way home and show it to Mrs. Hiller. She's crazy about cross-stitch."

While Alexandra removed her hat and veil, Mrs. Lee went out to the kitchen and settled herself in a wooden rocking-chair by the stove, looking with great interest at the table, set for three, with a white cloth, and a pot of pink geraniums in the middle. "My, a-an't you gotta fine plants; such-a much flower. How you keep from freeze?"

She pointed to the window-shelves, full of blooming fuchsias and geraniums.

"I keep the fire all night, Mrs. Lee, and when it's very cold I put them all on the table, in the middle of the room. Other nights I only put newspapers behind them. Frank laughs at me for fussing, but when they don't bloom he says, 'What's the matter with the darned things?'—What do you hear from Carl, Alexandra?"

"He got to Dawson before the river froze, and now I suppose I won't hear any more until spring. Before he left California he sent me a box of orange flowers, but they did n't keep very well. I have brought a bunch of Emil's letters for you." Alexandra came out from the sitting-room and pinched Marie's cheek playfully. "You don't look as if the weather ever froze you up. Never have colds, do you? That's a good girl. She had dark red cheeks like this when she was a little girl, Mrs. Lee. She looked like some queer foreign kind of a doll. I've never forgot the first time I saw you in Mieklejohn's store, Marie, the time father was lying sick. Carl and I were talking about that before he went away."

"I remember, and Emil had his kitten along. When are you going to send Emil's Christmas box?"

"It ought to have gone before this. I'll have to send it by mail now, to get it there in time."

Marie pulled a dark purple silk necktie from her workbasket. "I knit this for him. It's a good color, don't you think? Will you please put it in with your things and tell him it's from me, to wear when he goes serenading."

Alexandra laughed. "I don't believe he goes serenading much. He says in one letter that the Mexican ladies are said to be very beautiful, but that don't seem to me very warm praise."

Marie tossed her head. "Emil can't fool me. If he's bought a guitar, he goes serenading. Who would n't, with all those Spanish girls dropping flowers down from their windows! I'd sing to them every night, would n't you, Mrs. Lee?"

The old lady chuckled. Her eyes lit up as Marie bent down and opened the oven door. A delicious hot fragrance blew out into the tidy kitchen. "My, somet'ing smell good!" She turned to Alexandra with a wink, her three yellow teeth making a brave show, "I ta-ank dat stop my yaw from ache no more!" she said contentedly.

Marie took out a pan of delicate little rolls, stuffed with stewed apricots, and began to dust them over with powdered sugar. "I hope you'll like these, Mrs. Lee; Alexandra does. The Bohemians always like them with their coffee. But if you don't, I have a coffee-cake with nuts and poppy seeds. Alexandra, will you get the cream jug? I put it in the window to keep cool."

"The Bohemians," said Alexandra, as they drew up to the table, "certainly know how to make more kinds of bread than any other people in the world. Old Mrs. Hiller told me once at the church supper that she could make seven kinds of fancy bread, but Marie could make a dozen."

Mrs. Lee held up one of the apricot rolls between her brown thumb and forefinger and weighed it critically. "Yust like-a fedders," she pronounced with satisfaction. "My, ain't dis nice! she exclaimed as she stirred her coffee. "I yust ta-ake a liddle yelly now, too, I ta-ank."

Alexandra and Marie laughed at her forehandedness, and fell to talking of their own affairs. "I was afraid you had a cold when I talked to you over the telephone the other night, Marie. What was the matter, had you been crying?"

"Maybe I had," Marie smiled guiltily. "Frank was out late that night. Don't you get lonely sometimes in the winter, when everybody has gone away?"

"I thought it was something like that. If I had n't had company, I'd have run over to see for myself. If you get down-hearted, what will become of the rest of us?" Alexandra asked.

"I don't, very often. There's Mrs. Lee without any coffee!"

Later, when Mrs. Lee declared that her powers were spent, Marie and Alexandra went upstairs to look for some crochet patterns the old lady wanted to borrow. "Better put on your coat, Alexandra. It's cold up there, and I have no idea where those patterns are. I may have to look through my old trunks." Marie caught up a shawl and opened the stair door, running up the steps ahead of her guest. "While I go through the bureau drawers, you might look in those hat-boxes on the closet-shelf, over where Frank's clothes hang. There are a lot of odds and ends in them."

She began tossing over the contents of the drawers, and Alexandra went into the clothes-closet. Presently she came back, holding a slender elastic yellow stick in her hand.

"What in the world is this, Marie? You don't mean to tell me Frank ever carried such a thing?"

Marie blinked at it with astonishment and sat down on the floor. "Where did you find it? I did n't know he had kept it. I have n't seen it for years."

"It really is a cane, then?"

"Yes. One he brought from the old country. He used to carry it when I first knew him. Is n't it foolish? Poor Frank!"

Alexandra twirled the stick in her fingers and laughed. "He must have looked funny!"

Marie was thoughtful. "No, he did n't, really. It did n't seem out of place. He used to be awfully gay like that when he was a young man. I guess people always get what's hardest for them, Alexandra." Marie gathered the shawl closer about her and still looked hard at the cane. "Frank would be all right in the right place," she said reflectively. "He ought to have a different kind of wife, for one thing. Do you know, Alexandra, I could pick out exactly the right sort of woman for Frank—now. The trouble is you almost have to marry a man before you can find out the sort of wife he needs; and usually it's exactly the sort you are not. Then what are you going to do about it?" she asked candidly.

Alexandra confessed she did n't know. "However," she added, "it seems to me that you get along with Frank about as well as any woman I've ever seen or heard of could."

Marie shook her head, pursing her lips and blowing her warm breath softly out into the frosty air. "No; I was spoiled at home. I like my own way, and I have a quick tongue. When Frank brags, I say sharp things, and he never forgets. He goes over and over it in his mind; I can feel him. Then I'm too giddy. Frank's wife ought to be timid, and she ought not to care about another living thing in the world but just Frank! I did n't, when I married him, but I suppose I was too young to stay like that." Marie sighed.

Alexandra had never heard Marie speak so frankly about her husband before, and she felt that it was wiser not to encourage her. No good, she reasoned, ever came from talking about such things, and while Marie was thinking aloud, Alexandra had been steadily searching the hat-boxes. "Are n't these the patterns, Maria?"

Marie sprang up from the floor. "Sure enough, we were looking for patterns, were n't we? I'd forgot about everything but Frank's other wife. I'll put that away."

She poked the cane behind Frank's Sunday clothes, and though she laughed, Alexandra saw there were tears in her eyes.

When they went back to the kitchen, the snow had begun to fall, and Marie's visitors thought they must be getting home. She went out to the cart with them, and tucked the robes about old Mrs. Lee while Alexandra took the blanket off her horse. As they drove away, Marie turned and went slowly back to the house. She took up the package of letters Alexandra had brought, but she did not read them. She turned them over and looked at the foreign stamps, and then sat watching the flying snow while the dusk deepened in the kitchen and the stove sent out a red glow.

Marie knew perfectly well that Emil's letters were written more for her than for Alexandra. They were not the sort of letters that a young man writes to his sister. They were both more personal and more painstaking; full of descriptions of the gay life in the old Mexican capital in the days when the strong hand of Porfirio Diaz was still strong. He told about bull-fights and cock-fights, churches and *fiestas,* the flower-markets and the fountains, the music and dancing, the people of all nations he met in the Italian restaurants on San Francisco Street. In short, they were the kind of letters a young man writes to a woman when he wishes himself and his life to seem interesting to her, when he wishes to enlist her imagination in his behalf.

Marie, when she was alone or when she sat sewing in the evening, often thought about what it must be like down there where Emil was; where there were flowers and street bands everywhere, and carriages rattling up and down, and where there was a little blind bootblack in front of the cathedral who could play any tune you asked for by dropping the lids of blacking-boxes on the stone steps. When everything is done and over for one at twenty-three, it is pleasant to let the mind wander forth and follow a young adventurer who has life before him. "And if it had not been for me," she thought, "Frank might still be free like that, and having a good time making people admire him. Poor Frank, getting married was n't very good for him either. I'm afraid I do set people against him, as he says. I seem, somehow, to give him away all the time. Perhaps he would try to be agreeable to people again, if I were not around. It seems as if I always make him just as bad as he can be."

Later in the winter, Alexandra looked back upon that afternoon as the last satisfactory visit she had had with Marie. After that day the younger woman seemed to shrink more and more into herself. When she was with Alexandra she was not spontaneous and frank as she used to be. She seemed to be brooding over something, and holding something back. The weather had a good deal to do with their seeing less of each other than usual. There had not been such snowstorms in twenty years, and the path across the fields was drifted deep from Christmas until March. When the two neighbors went to see each other, they had to go round by the wagon-road, which was twice as far. They telephoned each other almost every night, though in January there was a stretch of three weeks when the wires were down, and when the postman did not come at all.

Marie often ran in to see her nearest neighbor, old Mrs. Hiller, who was crippled with rheumatism and had only her son, the lame shoemaker, to take care of her; and she went to the French Church, whatever the weather. She was a sincerely devout girl. She prayed for herself and for Frank, and for Emil, among the temptations of that gay, corrupt old city. She found more comfort in the Church that winter than ever before. It seemed to come closer to her, and to fill an emptiness that ached in her heart. She tried to be patient with her husband. He and his hired man usually played California Jack in the evening. Marie sat sewing or crocheting and tried to take a friendly interest in the game, but she was always thinking about the wide fields outside, where the snow was drifting over the fences; and about the orchard, where the snow was falling and packing, crust over crust. When she went out into the dark kitchen to fix her plants for the night, she used to stand by the window and look out at the white fields, or watch the currents of snow whirling over the orchard. She seemed to feel the weight of all the snow that lay down there. The branches had become so hard that they wounded your hand if you but tried to break a twig. And yet, down under the frozen crusts, at the roots of the trees, the secret of life was still safe, warm as the blood in one's heart; and the spring would come again! Oh, it would come again!

II

If Alexandra had had much imagination she might have guessed what was going on in Marie's mind, and she would have seen long before what was going on in Emil's. But that, as Emil himself had more than once reflected, was Alexandra's blind side, and her life had not been of the kind to sharpen her vision. Her training had all been toward the end of making her proficient in what she had undertaken to do. Her personal life, her own realization of herself, was almost a subconscious existence; like an underground river that came to the surface only here and there, at intervals months apart, and then sank again to flow on under her own fields. Nevertheless, the underground stream was there, and it was because she had so much personality to put into her enterprises and succeeded in putting it into them so completely, that her affairs prospered better than those of her neighbors.

There were certain days in her life, outwardly uneventful, which Alexandra remembered as peculiarly happy; days when she was close to the flat, fallow world about her, and felt, as it were, in her own body the joyous germination in the soil. There were days, too, which she and Emil had spent together, upon which she loved to look back. There had been such a day when they were down on the river in the dry year, looking over the land. They had made an early start one morning and had driven a long way before noon. When Emil said he was hungry, they drew back from the road, gave Brigham his oats among the bushes, and climbed up to the top of a grassy bluff to eat their lunch under the shade of some little elm trees. The river was clear there, and shallow, since there had been no rain, and it ran in ripples over the sparkling sand. Under the overhanging willows of the opposite bank there was an inlet where the water was deeper and flowed so slowly that it seemed to sleep in the sun. In this little bay a single wild duck was swimming and diving and preening her feathers, disporting herself very happily in the flickering light and shade. They sat for a long time, watching the solitary bird take its pleasure. No living thing had ever seemed to Alexandra as beautiful as that wild duck. Emil must have felt about it as she did, for afterward, when they were at home, he used sometimes to say, "Sister, you know our duck down there—" Alexandra remembered that day as one of the happiest in her life. Years afterward she thought of the duck as still there, swimming and diving all by herself in the sunlight, a kind of enchanted bird that did not know age or change.

Most of Alexandra's happy memories were as impersonal as this one; yet to her they were very personal. Her mind was a white book, with clear writing about weather and beasts and growing things. Not many people would have cared to read it; only a happy few. She had never been in love, she had never indulged in sentimental reveries. Even as a girl she had looked upon men as work-fellows. She had grown up in serious times.

There was one fancy indeed, which persisted through her girlhood. It most often came to her on Sunday mornings, the one day in the week when she lay late abed listening to the familiar morning sounds; the windmill singing in the brisk breeze, Emil whistling as he blacked his boots down by the kitchen door. Sometimes, as she lay thus luxuriously idle, her eyes closed, she used to have an illusion of being lifted up bodily and carried lightly by some one very strong. It was a man, certainly, who carried her, but he was like no man she knew; he was much larger and stronger and swifter, and he carried her as easily as if she were a sheaf of wheat. She never saw him, but, with eyes closed, she could feel that he was yellow like the sunlight, and there was the smell of ripe cornfields about him. She could feel him approach, bend over her and lift her, and then she could feel herself being carried swiftly off across the fields. After such a reverie she would rise hastily, angry with herself, and go down to the bath-house that was partitioned off the kitchen shed. There she would stand in a tin tub and prosecute her bath with vigor, finishing it by pouring buckets of cold well-water over her gleaming white body which no man on the Divide could have carried very far.

As she grew older, this fancy more often came to her when she was tired than when she was fresh and strong. Sometimes, after she had been in the open all day, overseeing the branding of the cattle or the loading of the pigs, she would come in chilled, take a concoction of spices and warm home-made wine, and go to bed with her body actually aching with fatigue. Then, just before she went to sleep, she had the old sensation of being lifted and carried by a strong being who took from her all her bodily weariness.

Part IV: The White Mulberry Tree

I

The French Church, properly the Church of Sainte-Agnes, stood upon a hill. The high, narrow, red-brick building, with its tall steeple and steep roof, could be seen for miles across the wheatfields, though the little town of Sainte-Agnes was completely hidden away at the foot of the hill. The church looked powerful and triumphant there on its eminence, so high above the rest of the landscape, with miles of warm color lying at its feet, and by its position and setting it reminded one of some of the churches built long ago in the wheat-lands of middle France.

Late one June afternoon Alexandra Bergson was driving along one of the many roads that led through the rich French farming country to the big church. The sunlight was shining directly in her face, and there was a blaze of light all about the red church on the hill. Beside Alexandra lounged a strikingly exotic figure in a tall Mexican hat, a silk sash, and a black velvet jacket sewn with silver buttons. Emil had returned only the night before, and his sister was so proud of him that she decided at once to take him up to the church supper, and to make him wear the Mexican costume he had brought home in his trunk. "All the girls who have stands are going to wear fancy costumes," she argued, "and some of the boys. Marie is going to tell fortunes, and she sent to Omaha for a Bohemian dress her father brought back from a visit to the old country. If you wear those clothes, they will all be pleased. And you must take your guitar. Everybody ought to do what they can to help along, and we have never done much. We are not a talented family."

The supper was to be at six o'clock, in the basement of the church, and afterward there would be a fair, with charades and an auction. Alexandra had set out from home early, leaving the house to Signa and Nelse Jensen, who were to be married next week. Signa had shyly asked to have the wedding put off until Emil came home.

Alexandra was well satisfied with her brother. As they drove through the rolling French country toward the westering sun and the stalwart church, she was thinking of that time long ago when she and Emil drove back from the river valley to the still unconquered Divide. Yes, she told herself, it had been worth while; both Emil and the country had become what she had hoped. Out of her father's children there was one who was fit to cope with the world, who had not been tied to the plow, and who had a personality apart from the soil. And that, she reflected, was what she had worked for. She felt well satisfied with her life.

When they reached the church, a score of teams were hitched in front of the basement doors that opened from the hillside upon the sanded terrace, where the boys wrestled and had jumping-matches. Amédée Chevalier, a proud father of one week, rushed out and embraced Emil. Amédée was an only son,—hence he was a very rich young man,—but he meant to have twenty children himself, like his uncle Xavier. "Oh, Emil," he cried, hugging his old friend rapturously, "why ain't you been up to see my boy? You come to-morrow, sure? Emil, you wanna get a boy right off! It's the greatest thing ever! No, no, no! Angel not sick at all. Everything just fine. That boy he come into this world laughin', and he been laughin' ever since. You come an' see!" He pounded Emil's ribs to emphasize each announcement.

Emil caught his arms. "Stop, Amédée. You're knocking the wind out of me. I brought him cups and spoons and blankets and moccasins enough for an orphan asylum. I'm awful glad it's a boy, sure enough!"

The young men crowded round Emil to admire his costume and to tell him in a breath everything that had happened since he went away. Emil had more friends up here in the French country than down on Norway Creek. The French and Bohemian boys were spirited and jolly, liked variety, and were as much predisposed to favor any-thing new as the Scandinavian boys were to reject it. The Norwegian and Swedish lads were much more self-centred, apt to be egotistical and jealous. They were cautious and reserved with Emil because he had been away to college, and were prepared to take him down if he should try to put on airs with them. The French boys liked a bit of swagger, and they were always delighted to hear about anything new: new clothes, new games, new songs, new dances. Now they carried Emil off to show him the club room they had just fitted up over the post-office, down in the village. They ran down the hill in a drove, all laughing and chattering at once, some in French, some in English.

Alexandra went into the cool, whitewashed basement where the women were setting the tables. Marie was standing on a chair, building a little tent of shawls where she was to tell fortunes. She sprang down and ran toward Alexandra, stopping short and looking at her in disappointment. Alexandra nodded to her encouragingly.

"Oh, he will be here, Marie. The boys have taken him off to show him some-thing. You won't know him. He is a man now, sure enough. I have no boy left. He smokes terrible-smelling Mexican cigarettes and talks Spanish. How pretty you look, child. Where did you get those beautiful earrings?"

"They belonged to father's mother. He always promised them to me. He sent them with the dress and said I could keep them."

Marie wore a short red skirt of stoutly woven cloth, a white bodice and kirtle, a yellow silk turban wound low over her brown curls, and long coral pendants in her ears. Her ears had been pierced against a piece of cork by her great-aunt when she was seven years old. In those germless days she had worn bits of broomstraw, plucked from the common sweeping-broom, in the lobes until the holes were healed and ready for little gold rings.

When Emil came back from the village, he lingered outside on the terrace with the boys. Marie could hear him talking and strumming on his guitar while Raoul Marcel sang falsetto. She was vexed with him for staying out there. It made her very nervous to hear him and not to see him; for, certainly, she told herself, she was not going out to look for him. When the supper bell rang and the boys came trooping in to get seats at the first table, she forgot all about her annoyance and ran to greet the tallest of the crowd, in his conspicuous attire. She did n't mind showing her embarrassment at all. She blushed and laughed excitedly as she gave Emil her hand, and looked delightedly at the black velvet coat that brought out his fair skin and fine blond head. Marie was incapable of being lukewarm about anything that pleased her. She simply did not know how to give a half-hearted response. When she was delighted, she was as likely as not to stand on her tip-toes and clap her hands. If people laughed at her, she laughed with them.

"Do the men wear clothes like that every day, in the street?" She caught Emil by his sleeve and turned him about. "Oh, I wish I lived where people wore things like that! Are the buttons real silver? Put on the hat, please. What a heavy thing! How do you ever wear it? Why don't you tell us about the bull-fights?"

She wanted to wring all his experiences from him at once, without waiting a moment. Emil smiled tolerantly and stood looking down at her with his old, brooding gaze, while the French girls fluttered about him in their white dresses and ribbons, and Alexandra watched the scene with pride. Several of the French girls, Marie knew, were hoping that Emil would take them to supper, and she was relieved when he took only his sister. Marie caught Frank's arm and dragged him to the same table, managing to get seats opposite the Bergsons, so that she could hear what they were talking about. Alexandra made Emil tell Mrs. Xavier Chevalier, the mother of the twenty, about how he had seen a famous matador killed in the bull-ring. Marie listened to every word, only taking her eyes from Emil to watch Frank's plate and keep it filled. When Emil finished his account,—bloody enough to satisfy Mrs. Xavier and to make her feel thankful that she was not a matador,—Marie broke out with a volley of questions. How did the women dress when they went to bull-fights? Did they wear mantillas? Did they never wear hats?

After supper the young people played charades for the amusement of their elders, who sat gossiping between their guesses. All the shops in Sainte-Agnes were closed at eight o'clock that night, so that the merchants and their clerks could attend the fair. The auction was the liveliest part of the entertainment, for the French boys always lost their heads when they began to bid, satisfied that their extravagance was in a good cause. After all the pincushions and sofa pillows and embroidered slippers were sold, Emil precipitated a panic by taking out one of his turquoise shirt studs, which every one had been admiring, and handing it to the auctioneer. All the French girls clamored for it, and their sweethearts bid against each other recklessly. Marie wanted it, too, and she kept making signals to Frank, which he took a sour pleasure in disregarding. He did n't see the use of making a fuss over a fellow just because he was dressed like a clown. When the turquoise went to Malvina Sauvage, the French banker's daughter, Marie shrugged her shoulders and betook herself to her little tent of shawls, where she began to shuffle her cards by the light of a tallow candle, calling out, "Fortunes, fortunes!"

The young priest, Father Duchesne, went first to have his fortune read. Marie took his long white hand, looked at it, and then began to run off her cards. "I see a long journey across water for you, Father. You will go to a town all cut up by water; built on islands, it seems to be, with rivers and green fields all about. And you will visit an old lady with a white cap and gold hoops in her ears, and you will be very happy there."

"Mais, oui," said the priest, with a melancholy smile. "C'est L'Isle-Adam, chez ma mère. Vous êtes très savante, ma fille." He patted her yellow turban, calling, "Venez donc, mes garçons! Il y a ici une véritable clairvoyante!"

Marie was clever at fortune-telling, indulging in a light irony that amused the crowd. She told old Brunot, the miser, that he would lose all his money, marry a girl of sixteen, and live happily on a crust. Sholte, the fat Russian boy, who lived for his stomach, was to be disappointed in love, grow thin, and shoot himself from despondency. Amédée was to have twenty children, and nineteen of them were to be girls. Amédée slapped Frank on the back and asked him why he did n't see what the fortune-teller would promise him. But Frank shook off his friendly hand and grunted, "She tell my fortune long ago; bad enough!" Then he withdrew to a corner and sat glowering at his wife.

Frank's case was all the more painful because he had no one in particular to fix his jealousy upon. Sometimes he could have thanked the man who would bring him evidence against his wife. He had discharged a good farm-boy, Jan Smirka, because he thought Marie was fond of him; but she had not seemed to miss Jan when he was gone, and she had been just as kind to the next boy. The farm-hands would always do anything for Marie; Frank could n't find one so surly that he would not make an effort to please her. At the bottom of his heart Frank knew well enough that if he could once give up his grudge, his wife would come back to him. But he could never in the world do that. The grudge was fundamental. Perhaps he could not have given it up if he had tried. Perhaps he got more satisfaction out of feeling himself abused than he would have got out of being loved. If he could once have made Marie thoroughly unhappy, he might have relented and raised her from the dust. But she had never humbled herself. In the first days of their love she had been his slave; she had admired him abandonedly. But the moment he began to bully her and to be unjust, she began to draw away; at first in tearful amazement, then in quiet, unspoken disgust. The distance between them had widened and hardened. It no longer contracted and brought them suddenly together. The spark of her life went somewhere else, and he was always watching to surprise it. He knew that somewhere she must get a feeling to live upon, for she was not a woman who could live without loving. He wanted to prove to himself the wrong he felt. What did she hide in her heart? Where did it go? Even Frank had his churlish delicacies; he never reminded her of how much she had once loved him. For that Marie was grateful to him.

While Marie was chattering to the French boys, Amédée called Emil to the back of the room and whispered to him that they were going to play a joke on the girls. At eleven o'clock, Amédée was to go up to the switchboard in the vestibule and turn off the electric lights, and every boy would have a chance to kiss his sweetheart before Father Duchesne could find his way up the stairs to turn the current on again. The only difficulty was the candle in Marie's tent; perhaps, as Emil had no sweetheart, he would oblige the boys by blowing out the candle. Emil said he would undertake to do that.

At five minutes to eleven he sauntered up to Marie's booth, and the French boys dispersed to find their girls. He leaned over the cardtable and gave himself up to looking at her. "Do you think you could tell my fortune?" he murmured. It was the first word he had had alone with her for almost a year. "My luck has n't changed any. It's just the same."

Marie had often wondered whether there was anyone else who could look his thoughts to you as Emil could. To-night, when she met his steady, powerful eyes, it was impossible not to feel the sweetness of the dream he was dreaming; it reached her before she could shut it out, and hid itself in her heart. She began to shuffle her cards furiously. "I'm angry with you, Emil," she broke out with petulance. "Why did you give them that lovely blue stone to sell? You might have known Frank would n't buy it for me, and I wanted it awfully!"

Emil laughed shortly. "People who want such little things surely ought to have them," he said dryly. He thrust his hand into the pocket of his velvet trousers and brought out a handful of uncut turquoises, as big as marbles. Leaning over the table he dropped them into her lap. "There, will those do? Be careful, don't let any one see them. Now, I suppose you want me to go away and let you play with them?"

Marie was gazing in rapture at the soft blue color of the stones. "Oh, Emil! Is everything down there beautiful like these? How could you ever come away?"

At that instant Amédée laid hands on the switchboard. There was a shiver and a giggle, and every one looked toward the red blur that Marie's candle made in the dark. Immediately that, too, was gone. Little shrieks and currents of soft laughter ran up and down the dark hall. Marie started up,—directly into Emil's arms. In the same instant she felt his lips. The veil that had hung uncertainly between them for so long was dissolved. Before she knew what she was doing, she had committed herself to that kiss that was at once a boy's and a man's, as timid as it was tender; so like Emil and so unlike any one else in the world. Not until it was over did she realize what it meant. And Emil, who had so often imagined the shock of this first kiss, was surprised at its gentleness and naturalness. It was like a sigh which they had breathed together; almost sorrowful, as if each were afraid of wakening something in the other.

When the lights came on again, everybody was laughing and shouting, and all the French girls were rosy and shining with mirth. Only Marie, in her little tent of shawls, was pale and quiet. Under her yellow turban the red coral pendants swung against white cheeks. Frank was still staring at her, but he seemed to see nothing. Years ago, he himself had had the power to take the blood from her cheeks like that. Perhaps he did not remember—perhaps he had never noticed! Emil was already at the other end of the hall, walking about with the shoulder-motion he had acquired among the Mexicans, studying the floor with his intent, deep-set eyes. Marie began to take down and fold her shawls. She did not glance up again. The young people drifted to the other end of the hall where the guitar was sounding. In a moment she heard Emil and Raoul singing:—

> Across the Rio Grand-e
> There lies a sunny land-e,
> My bright-eyed Mexico!

Alexandra Bergson came up to the card booth. "Let me help you, Marie. You look tired."

She placed her hand on Marie's arm and felt her shiver. Marie stiffened under that kind, calm hand. Alexandra drew back, perplexed and hurt.

There was about Alexandra something of the impervious calm of the fatalist, always disconcerting to very young people, who cannot feel that the heart lives at all unless it is still at the mercy of storms; unless its strings can scream to the touch of pain.

II

Signa's wedding supper was over. The guests, and the tiresome little Norwegian preacher who had performed the marriage ceremony, were saying good-night. Old Ivar was hitching the horses to the wagon to take the wedding presents and the bride and groom up to their new home, on Alexandra's north quarter. When Ivar drove up to the gate, Emil and Marie Shabata began to carry out the presents, and Alexandra went into her bedroom to bid Signa good-bye and to give her a few words of good counsel. She was surprised to find that the bride had changed her slippers for heavy shoes and was pinning up her skirts. At that moment Nelse appeared at the gate with the two milk cows that Alexandra had given Signa for a wedding present.

Alexandra began to laugh. "Why, Signa, you and Nelse are to ride home. I'll send Ivar over with the cows in the morning."

Signa hesitated and looked perplexed. When her husband called her, she pinned her hat on resolutely. "I ta-ank I better do yust like he say," she murmured in confusion.

Alexandra and Marie accompanied Signa to the gate and saw the party set off, old Ivar driving ahead in the wagon and the bride and groom following on foot, each leading a cow. Emil burst into a laugh before they were out of hearing.

"Those two will get on," said Alexandra as they turned back to the house. "They are not going to take any chances. They will feel safer with those cows in their own stable. Marie, I am going to send for an old woman next. As soon as I get the girls broken in, I marry them off."

"I've no patience with Signa, marrying that grumpy fellow!" Marie declared. "I wanted her to marry that nice Smirka boy who worked for us last winter. I think she liked him, too."

"Yes, I think she did," Alexandra assented, "but I suppose she was too much afraid of Nelse to marry any one else. Now that I think of it, most of my girls have married men they were afraid of. I believe there is a good deal of the cow in most Swedish girls. You high-strung Bohemians can't understand us. We're a terribly practical people, and I guess we think a cross man makes a good manager."

Marie shrugged her shoulders and turned to pin up a lock of hair that had fallen on her neck. Somehow Alexandra had irritated her of late. Everybody irritated her. She was tired of everybody. "I'm going home alone, Emil, so you need n't get your hat," she said as she wound her scarf quickly about her head. "Good-night, Alexandra," she called back in a strained voice, running down the gravel walk.

Emil followed with long strides until he overtook her. Then she began to walk slowly. It was a night of warm wind and faint starlight, and the fireflies were glimmering over the wheat.

"Marie," said Emil after they had walked for a while, "I wonder if you know how unhappy I am?"

Marie did not answer him. Her head, in its white scarf, drooped forward a little.

Emil kicked a clod from the path and went on:—

"I wonder whether you are really shallow-hearted, like you seem? Sometimes I think one boy does just as well as another for you. It never seems to make much difference whether it is me or Raoul Marcel or Jan Smirka. Are you really like that?"

"Perhaps I am. What do you want me to do? Sit round and cry all day? When I've cried until I can't cry any more, then—then I must do something else."

"Are you sorry for me?" he persisted.

"No, I'm not. If I were big and free like you, I would n't let anything make me unhappy. As old Napoleon Brunot said at the fair, I would n't go lovering after no woman. I'd take the first train and go off and have all the fun there is."

"I tried that, but it did n't do any good. Everything reminded me. The nicer the place was, the more I wanted you." They had come to the stile and Emil pointed to it persuasively. "Sit down a moment, I want to ask you something." Marie sat down on the top step and Emil drew nearer. "Would you tell me something that's none of my business if you thought it would help me out? Well, then, tell me, *please* tell me, why you ran away with Frank Shabata!"

Marie drew back. "Because I was in love with him," she said firmly.

"Really?" he asked incredulously.

"Yes, indeed. Very much in love with him. I think I was the one who suggested our running away. From the first it was more my fault than his."

Emil turned away his face.

"And now," Marie went on, "I've got to remember that Frank is just the same now as he was then, only then I would see him as I wanted him to be. I would have my own way. And now I pay for it."

"You don't do all the paying."

"That's it. When one makes a mistake, there's no telling where it will stop. But you can go away; you can leave all this behind you."

"Not everything. I can't leave you behind. Will you go away with me, Marie?"

Marie started up and stepped across the stile. "Emil! How wickedly you talk! I am not that kind of a girl, and you know it. But what am I going to do if you keep tormenting me like this!" she added plaintively

"Marie, I won't bother you any more if you will tell me just one thing. Stop a minute and look at me. No, nobody can see us. Everybody's asleep. That was only a firefly. Marie, *stop* and tell me!"

Emil overtook her and catching her by the shoulders shook her gently, as if he were trying to awaken a sleepwalker.

Marie hid her face on his arm. "Don't ask me anything more. I don't know anything except how miserable I am. And I thought it would be all right when you came back. Oh, Emil," she clutched his sleeve and began to cry, "what am I to do if you don't go away? I can't go, and one of us must. Can't you see?"

Emil stood looking down at her, holding his shoulders stiff and stiffening the arm to which she clung. Her white dress looked gray in the darkness. She seemed like a troubled spirit, like some shadow out of the earth, clinging to him and entreating him to give her peace. Behind her the fireflies were weaving in and out over the wheat. He put his hand on her bent head. "On my honor, Marie, if you will say you love me, I will go away."

She lifted her face to his. "How could I help it? Did n't you know?"

Emil was the one who trembled, through all his frame. After he left Marie at her gate, he wandered about the fields all night, till morning put out the fireflies and the stars.

III

One evening, a week after Signa's wedding, Emil was kneeling before a box in the sitting-room, packing his books. From time to time he rose and wandered about the house, picking up stray volumes and bringing them listlessly back to his box. He was packing without enthusiasm. He was not very sanguine about his future. Alexandra sat sewing by the table. She had helped him pack his trunk in the afternoon. As Emil came and went by her chair with his books, he thought to himself that it had not been so hard to leave his sister since he first went away to school. He was going directly to Omaha, to read law in the office of a Swedish lawyer until October, when he would enter the law school at Ann Arbor. They had planned that Alexandra was to come to Michigan—a long journey for her—at Christmas time, and spend several weeks with him. Nevertheless, he felt that this leavetaking would be more final than his earlier ones had been; that it meant a definite break with his old home and the beginning of something new—he did not know what. His ideas about the future would not crystallize; the more he tried to think about it, the vaguer his conception of it became. But one thing was clear, he told himself; it was high time that he made good to Alexandra, and that ought to be incentive enough to begin with.

As he went about gathering up his books he felt as if he were uprooting things. At last he threw himself down on the old slat lounge where he had slept when he was little, and lay looking up at the familiar cracks in the ceiling.

"Tired, Emil?" his sister asked.

"Lazy," he murmured, turning on his side and looking at her. He studied Alexandra's face for a long time in the lamplight. It had never occurred to him that his sister was a handsome woman until Marie Shabata had told him so. Indeed, he had never thought of her as being a woman at all, only a sister. As he studied her bent head, he looked up at the picture of John Bergson above the lamp. "No," he thought to himself, "she did n't get it there. I suppose I am more like that."

"Alexandra," he said suddenly, "that old walnut secretary you use for a desk was father's, was n't it?"

Alexandra went on stitching. "Yes. It was one of the first things he bought for the old log house. It was a great extravagance in those days. But he wrote a great many letters back to the old country. He had many friends there, and they wrote to him up to the time he died. No one ever blamed him for grandfather's disgrace. I can see him now, sitting there on Sundays, in his white shirt, writing pages and pages, so carefully. He wrote a fine, regular hand, almost like engraving. Yours is something like his, when you take pains."

"Grandfather was really crooked, was he?"

"He married an unscrupulous woman, and then—then I'm afraid he was really crooked. When we first came here father used to have dreams about making a great fortune and going back to Sweden to pay back to the poor sailors the money grandfather had lost."

Emil stirred on the lounge. "I say, that would have been worth while, would n't it? Father was n't a bit like Lou or Oscar, was he? I can't remember much about him before he got sick."

"Oh, not at all!" Alexandra dropped her sewing on her knee. "He had better opportunities; not to make money, but to make something of himself. He was a quiet man, but he was very intelligent. You would have been proud of him, Emil."

Alexandra felt that he would like to know there had been a man of his kin whom he could admire. She knew that Emil was ashamed of Lou and Oscar, because they were bigoted and self-satisfied. He never said much about them, but she could feel his disgust. His brothers had shown their disapproval of him ever since he first went away to school. The only thing that would have satisfied them would have been his failure at the University. As it was, they resented every change in his speech, in his dress, in his point of view; though the latter they had to conjecture, for Emil avoided talking to them about any but family matters. All his interests they treated as affectations.

Alexandra took up her sewing again. "I can remember father when he was quite a young man. He belonged to some kind of a musical society, a male chorus, in Stockholm. I can remember going with mother to hear them sing. There must have been a hundred of them, and they all wore long black coats and white neckties. I was used to seeing father in a blue coat, a sort of jacket, and when I recognized him on the platform, I was very proud. Do you remember that Swedish song he taught you, about the ship boy?"

"Yes. I used to sing it to the Mexicans. They like anything different." Emil paused. "Father had a hard fight here, did n't he?" he added thoughtfully.

"Yes, and he died in a dark time. Still, he had hope. He believed in the land."

"And in you, I guess," Emil said to himself. There was another period of silence; that warm, friendly silence, full of perfect understanding, in which Emil and Alexandra had spent many of their happiest half-hours.

At last Emil said abruptly, "Lou and Oscar would be better off if they were poor, would n't they?"

Alexandra smiled. "Maybe. But their children would n't. I have great hopes of Milly."

Emil shivered. "I don't know. Seems to me it gets worse as it goes on. The worst of the Swedes is that they're never willing to find out how much they don't know. It was like that at the University. Always so pleased with themselves! There's no getting behind that conceited Swedish grin. The Bohemians and Germans were so different."

"Come, Emil, don't go back on your own people. Father was n't conceited, Uncle Otto was n't. Even Lou and Oscar were n't when they were boys."

Emil looked incredulous, but he did not dispute the point. He turned on his back and lay still for a long time, his hands locked under his head, looking up at the ceiling. Alexandra knew that he was thinking of many things. She felt no anxiety about Emil. She had always believed in him, as she had believed in the land. He had been more like himself since he got back from Mexico; seemed glad to be at home, and talked to her as he used to do. She had no doubt that his wandering fit was over, and that he would soon be settled in life.

"Alexandra," said Emil suddenly, "do you remember the wild duck we saw down on the river that time?"

His sister looked up. "I often think of her. It always seems to me she's there still, just like we saw her."

"I know. It's queer what things one remembers and what things one forgets." Emil yawned and sat up. "Well, it's time to turn in." He rose, and going over to Alexandra stooped down and kissed her lightly on the cheek. "Good-night, sister. I think you did pretty well by us."

Emil took up his lamp and went upstairs. Alexandra sat finishing his new night-shirt, that must go in the top tray of his trunk.

IV

The next morning Angélique, Amédée's wife, was in the kitchen baking pies, assisted by old Mrs. Chevalier. Between the mixing-board and the stove stood the old cradle that had been Amédée's, and in it was his black-eyed son. As Angélique, flushed and excited, with flour on her hands, stopped to smile at the baby, Emil Bergson rode up to the kitchen door on his mare and dismounted.

"'Médée is out in the field, Emil," Angélique called as she ran across the kitchen to the oven. "He begins to cut his wheat to-day; the first wheat ready to cut anywhere about here. He bought a new header, you know, because all the wheat's so short this year. I hope he can rent it to the neighbors, it cost so much. He and his cousins bought a steam thresher on shares. You ought to go out and see that header work. I watched it an hour this morning, busy as I am with all the men to feed. He has a lot of hands, but he's the only one that knows how to drive the header or how to run the engine, so he has to be everywhere at once. He's sick, too, and ought to be in his bed."

Emil bent over Hector Baptiste, trying to make him blink his round, bead-like black eyes. "Sick? What's the matter with your daddy, kid? Been making him walk the floor with you?"

Angélique sniffed. "Not much! We don't have that kind of babies. It was his father that kept Baptiste awake. All night I had to be getting up and making mustard plasters to put on his stomach. He had an awful colic. He said he felt better this morning, but I don't think he ought to be out in the field, overheating himself."

Angélique did not speak with much anxiety, not because she was indifferent, but because she felt so secure in their good fortune. Only good things could happen to a rich, energetic, handsome young man like Amédée, with a new baby in the cradle and a new header in the field.

Emil stroked the black fuzz on Baptiste's head. "I say, Angélique, one of 'Médée's grandmothers, 'way back, must have been a squaw. This kid looks exactly like the Indian babies."

Angélique made a face at him, but old Mrs. Chevalier had been touched on a sore point, and she let out such a stream of fiery *patois* that Emil fled from the kitchen and mounted his mare.

Opening the pasture gate from the saddle, Emil rode across the field to the clearing where the thresher stood, driven by a stationary engine and fed from the header boxes. As Amédée was not on the engine, Emil rode on to the wheatfield, where he recognized, on the header, the slight, wiry figure of his friend, coatless, his white shirt puffed out by the wind, his straw hat stuck jauntily on the side of his head. The six big work-horses that drew, or rather pushed, the header, went abreast at a rapid walk, and as they were still green at the work they required a good deal of management on Amédée's part; especially when they turned the corners, where they divided, three and three, and then swung round into line again with a movement that looked as complicated as a wheel of artillery. Emil felt a new thrill of admiration for his friend, and with it the old pang of envy at the way in which Amédée could do with his might what his hand found to do, and feel that, whatever it was, it was the most important thing in the world. "I'll have to bring Alexandra up to see this thing work," Emil thought; "it's splendid!"

When he saw Emil, Amédée waved to him and called to one of his twenty cousins to take the reins. Stepping off the header without stopping it, he ran up to Emil who had dismounted. "Come along," he called. "I have to go over to the engine for a minute. I gotta green man running it, and I gotta to keep an eye on him."

Emil thought the lad was unnaturally flushed and more excited than even the cares of managing a big farm at a critical time warranted. As they passed behind a last year's stack, Amédée clutched at his right side and sank down for a moment on the straw.

"Ouch! I got an awful pain in me, Emil. Something's the matter with my insides, for sure."

Emil felt his fiery cheek. "You ought to go straight to bed, 'Médée, and telephone for the doctor; that's what you ought to do."

Amédée staggered up with a gesture of despair. "How can I? I got no time to be sick. Three thousand dollars' worth of new machinery to manage, and the wheat so ripe it will begin to shatter next week. My wheat's short, but it's gotta grand full berries. What's he slowing down for? We haven't got header boxes enough to feed the thresher, I guess."

Amédée started hot-foot across the stubble, leaning a little to the right as he ran, and waved to the engineer not to stop the engine.

Emil saw that this was no time to talk about his own affairs. He mounted his mare and rode on to Sainte-Agnes, to bid his friends there good-bye. He went first to see Raoul Marcel, and found him innocently practising the "Gloria" for the big confirmation service on Sunday while he polished the mirrors of his father's saloon.

As Emil rode homewards at three o'clock in the afternoon, he saw Amédée staggering out of the wheatfield, supported by two of his cousins. Emil stopped and helped them put the boy to bed.

V

When Frank Shabata came in from work at five o'clock that evening, old Moses Marcel, Raoul's father, telephoned him that Amédée had had a seizure in the wheatfield, and that Doctor Paradis was going to operate on him as soon as the Hanover doctor got there to help. Frank dropped a word of this at the table, bolted his supper, and rode off to Sainte-Agnes, where there would be sympathetic discussion of Amédée's case at Marcel's saloon.

As soon as Frank was gone, Marie telephoned Alexandra. It was a comfort to hear her friend's voice. Yes, Alexandra knew what there was to be known about Amédée. Emil had been there when they carried him out of the field, and had stayed with him until the doctors operated for appendicitis at five o'clock. They were afraid it was too late to do much good; it should have been done three days ago. Amédée was in a very bad way. Emil had just come home, worn out and sick himself. She had given him some brandy and put him to bed.

Marie hung up the receiver. Poor Amédée's illness had taken on a new meaning to her, now that she knew Emil had been with him. And it might so easily have been the other way—Emil who was ill and Amédée who was sad! Marie looked about the dusky sitting-room. She had seldom felt so utterly lonely. If Emil was asleep, there was not even a chance of his coming; and she could not go to Alexandra for sympathy. She meant to tell Alexandra everything, as soon as Emil went away. Then whatever was left between them would be honest.

But she could not stay in the house this evening. Where should she go? She walked slowly down through the orchard, where the evening air was heavy with the smell of wild cotton. The fresh, salty scent of the wild roses had given way before this more powerful perfume of midsummer. Wherever those ashes-of-rose balls hung on their milky stalks, the air about them was saturated with their breath. The sky was still red in the west and the evening star hung directly over the Bergsons' windmill. Marie crossed the fence at the wheatfield corner, and walked slowly along the path that led to Alexandra's. She could not help feeling hurt that Emil had not come to tell her about

Amédée. It seemed to her most unnatural that he should not have come. If she were in trouble, certainly he was the one person in the world she would want to see. Perhaps he wished her to understand that for her he was as good as gone already.

Marie stole slowly, flutteringly, along the path, like a white night-moth out of the fields. The years seemed to stretch before her like the land; spring, summer, autumn, winter, spring; always the same patient fields, the patient little trees, the patient lives; always the same yearning, the same pulling at the chain—until the instinct to live had torn itself and bled and weakened for the last time, until the chain secured a dead woman, who might cautiously be released. Marie walked on, her face lifted toward the remote, inaccessible evening star.

When she reached the stile she sat down and waited. How terrible it was to love people when you could not really share their lives!

Yes, in so far as she was concerned, Emil was already gone. They couldn't meet any more. There was nothing for them to say. They had spent the last penny of their small change; there was nothing left but gold. The day of love-tokens was past. They had now only their hearts to give each other. And Emil being gone, what was her life to be like? In some ways, it would be easier. She would not, at least, live in perpetual fear. If Emil were once away and settled at work, she would not have the feeling that she was spoiling his life. With the memory he left her, she could be as rash as she chose. Nobody could be the worse for it but herself; and that, surely, did not matter. Her own case was clear. When a girl had loved one man, and then loved another while that man was still alive, everybody knew what to think of her. What happened to her was of little consequence, so long as she did not drag other people down with her. Emil once away, she could let everything else go and live a new life of perfect love.

Marie left the stile reluctantly. She had, after all, thought he might come. And how glad she ought to be, she told herself, that he was asleep. She left the path and went across the pasture. The moon was almost full. An owl was hooting somewhere in the fields. She had scarcely thought about where she was going when the pond glittered before her, where Emil had shot the ducks. She stopped and looked at it. Yes, there would be a dirty way out of life, if one chose to take it. But she did not want to die. She wanted to live and dream—a hundred years, forever! As long as this sweetness welled up in her heart, as long as her breast could hold this treasure of pain! She felt as the pond must feel when it held the moon like that; when it encircled and swelled with that image of gold.

In the morning, when Emil came downstairs, Alexandra met him in the sitting-room and put her hands on his shoulders. "Emil, I went to your room as soon as it was light, but you were sleeping so sound I hated to wake you. There was nothing you could do, so I let you sleep. They telephoned from Sainte-Agnes that Amédée died at three o'clock this morning."

VI

The Church has always held that life is for the living. On Saturday, while half the village of Sainte-Agnes was mourning for Amédée and preparing the funeral black for his burial on Monday, the other half was busy with white dresses and white veils for the great confirmation service to-morrow, when the bishop was to confirm a class of one hundred boys and girls. Father Duchesne divided his time between the living and the dead. All day Saturday the church was a scene of bustling activity, a little hushed by the thought of Amédée. The choir were busy rehearsing a mass of Rossini, which they had studied and practised for this occasion. The women were trimming the altar, the boys and girls were bringing flowers.

On Sunday morning the bishop was to drive overland to Sainte-Agnes from Hanover, and Emil Bergson had been asked to take the place of one of Amédée's cousins in the cavalcade of forty French boys who were to ride across country to meet the bishop's carriage. At six o'clock on Sunday morning the boys met at the church. As they stood holding their horses by the bridle, they talked in low tones of their dead comrade. They kept repeating that Amédée had always been a good boy, glancing toward the red brick church which had played so large a part in Amédée's life, had been the scene of his most serious moments and of his happiest hours. He had played and wrestled and sung and courted under its shadow. Only three weeks ago he had proudly carried his baby there to be christened. They could not doubt that that invisible arm was still about Amédée; that through the church on earth he had passed to the church triumphant, the goal of the hopes and faith of so many hundred years.

When the word was given to mount, the young men rode at a walk out of the village; but once out among the wheatfields in the morning sun, their horses and their own youth got the better of them. A wave of zeal and fiery enthusiasm swept over them. They longed for a Jerusalem to deliver. The thud of their galloping hoofs interrupted many a country breakfast and brought many a woman and child to the door of the farmhouses as they passed. Five miles east of Sainte-Agnes they met the bishop in his open carriage, attended by two priests. Like one man the boys swung off their hats in a broad salute, and bowed their heads as the handsome old man lifted his two fingers in the episcopal blessing. The horsemen closed about the carriage like a guard, and whenever a restless horse broke from control and shot down the road ahead of the body, the bishop laughed and rubbed his plump hands together. "What fine boys!" he said to his priests. "The Church still has her cavalry."

As the troop swept past the graveyard half a mile east of the town,—the first frame church of the parish had stood there,—old Pierre Séguin was already out with his pick and spade, digging Amédée's grave. He knelt and uncovered as the bishop passed. The boys with one accord looked away from old Pierre to the red church on the hill, with the gold cross flaming on its steeple.

Mass was at eleven. While the church was filling, Emil Bergson waited outside, watching the wagons and buggies drive up the hill. After the bell began to ring, he saw Frank Shabata ride up on horseback and tie his horse to the hitch-bar. Marie, then, was not coming. Emil turned and went into the church. Amédée's was the only empty pew, and he sat down in it. Some of Amédée's cousins were there, dressed in black and weeping. When all the pews were full, the old men and boys packed the open space at the back of the church, kneeling on the floor. There was scarcely a family in town that was not represented in the confirmation class, by a cousin, at least. The new communicants, with their clear, reverent faces, were beautiful to look upon as they entered in a body and took the front benches reserved for them. Even before the Mass began, the air was charged with feeling. The choir had never sung so well and Raoul Marcel, in the "Gloria," drew even the bishop's eyes to the organ loft. For the offertory he sang Gounod's "Ave Maria,"°—always spoken of in Sainte-Agnes as "the Ave Maria."

Emil began to torture himself with questions about Marie. Was she ill? Had she quarreled with her husband? Was she too unhappy to find comfort even here? Had she, perhaps, thought that he would come to her? Was she waiting for him? Overtaxed by excitement and sorrow as he was, the rapture of the service took hold upon his body and mind. As he listened to Raoul, he seemed to emerge from the conflicting emotions which had been whirling him about and sucking him under. He felt as if a clear light broke upon his mind, and with it a conviction that good was, after all, stronger than evil, and that good was possible to men. He seemed to discover that there was a kind of rapture in which he could love forever without faltering and without sin. He looked across the heads of the people at Frank Shabata with calmness. That rapture was for those who could feel it; for people who could not, it was non-existent. He coveted nothing that was Frank Shabata's. The spirit he had met in music was his own. Frank Shabata had never found it; would never find it if he lived beside it a thousand years; would have destroyed it if he had found it, as Herod slew the innocents, as Rome slew the martyrs.

San—cta Mari-i-i-a,

wailed Raoul from the organ loft;

O—ra pro no-o-bis!

And it did not occur to Emil that any one had ever reasoned thus before, that music had ever before given a man this equivocal revelation.

The confirmation service followed the Mass. When it was over, the congregation thronged about the newly confirmed. The girls, and even the boys, were kissed and embraced and wept over. All the aunts and grandmothers wept with joy. The housewives had much ado to tear themselves away from the general rejoicing and hurry back to their kitchens. The country parishioners were staying in town for dinner, and nearly every house in Sainte-Agnes entertained visitors that day. Father Duchesne, the bishop, and the visiting priests dined with Fabien Sauvage, the banker. Emil and Frank Shabata were both guests of old Moïse Marcel. After dinner Frank and old Moïse retired to the rear room of the saloon to play California Jack and drink their cognac, and Emil went over to the banker's with Raoul, who had been asked to sing for the bishop.

At three o'clock, Emil felt that he could stand it no longer. He slipped out under cover of "The Holy City," followed by Malvina's wistful eye, and went to the stable for his mare. He was at that height of excitement from which everything is foreshortened, from which life seems short and simple, death very near, and the soul seems to soar like an eagle. As he rode past the graveyard he looked at the brown hole in the earth

---

Gounod's "Ave Maria." Usually referred to as composed by Bach-Gounod. In this version of the Ave Maria, the French composer Charles Gounod (1818-93) overlaid a melody onto another composition by the German composer J. S. Bach (1685-1750).

where Amédée was to lie, and felt no horror. That, too, was beautiful, that simple door-way into forgetfulness. The heart, when it is too much alive, aches for that brown earth, and ecstasy has no fear of death. It is the old and the poor and the maimed who shrink from that brown hole; its wooers are found among the young, the passionate, the gallant-hearted. It was not until he had passed the graveyard that Emil realized where he was going. It was the hour for saying good-bye. It might be the last time that he would see her alone, and today he could leave her without rancor, without bitterness.

Everywhere the grain stood ripe and the hot afternoon was full of the smell of the ripe wheat, like the smell of bread baking in an oven. The breath of the wheat and the sweet clover passed him like pleasant things in a dream. He could feel nothing but the sense of diminishing distance. It seemed to him that his mare was flying, or run-ning on wheels, like a railway train. The sunlight, flashing on the window-glass of the big red barns, drove him wild with joy. He was like an arrow shot from the bow. His life poured itself out along the road before him as he rode to the Shabata farm.

When Emil alighted at the Shabatas' gate, his horse was in a lather. He tied her in the stable and hurried to the house. It was empty. She might be at Mrs. Hiller's or with Alexandra. But anything that reminded him of her would be enough, the orchard, the mulberry tree . . . When he reached the orchard the sun was hanging low over the wheatfield. Long fingers of light reached through the apple branches as through a net; the orchard was riddled and shot with gold; light was the reality, the trees were merely interferences that reflected and refracted light. Emil went softly down between the cherry trees toward the wheatfield. When he came to the corner, he stopped short and put his hand over his mouth. Marie was lying on her side under the white mulberry tree, her face half hidden in the grass, her eyes closed, her hands lying limply where they had happened to fall. She had lived a day of her new life of perfect love, and it had left her like this. Her breast rose and fell faintly, as if she were asleep. Emil threw himself down beside her and took her in his arms. The blood came back to her cheeks, her amber eyes opened slowly, and in them Emil saw his own face and the orchard and the sun. "I was dreaming this," she whispered, hiding her face against him, "don't take my dream away!"

VII

When Frank Shabata got home that night, he found Emil's mare in his stable. Such an impertinence amazed him. Like everybody else, Frank had had an exciting day. Since noon he had been drinking too much, and he was in a bad temper. He talked bitterly to himself while he put his own horse away, and as he went up the path and saw that the house was dark he felt an added sense of injury. He approached quietly and listened on the doorstep. Hearing nothing, he opened the kitchen door and went softly from one room to another. Then he went through the house again, upstairs and down, with no better result. He sat down on the bottom step of the box stairway and tried to get his wits together. In that unnatural quiet there was no sound but his own heavy breathing. Suddenly an owl began to hoot out in the fields. Frank lifted his head. An idea flashed into his mind, and his sense of injury and outrage grew. He went into his bedroom and took his murderous 405 Winchester from the closet.

When Frank took up his gun and walked out of the house, he had not the faintest purpose of doing anything with it. He did not believe that he had any real grievance. But it gratified him to feel like a desperate man. He had got into the habit of seeing himself always in desperate straits. His unhappy temperament was like a cage; he could never get out of it; and he felt that other people, his wife in particular, must have put him there. It had never more than dimly occurred to Frank that he made his own unhappiness. Though he took up his gun with dark projects in his mind, he would have been paralyzed with fright had he known that there was the slightest probability of his ever carrying any of them out.

Frank went slowly down to the orchard gate, stopped and stood for a moment lost in thought. He retraced his steps and looked through the barn and the hayloft. Then he went out to the road, where he took the footpath along the outside of the orchard hedge. The hedge was twice as tall as Frank himself, and so dense that one could see through it only by peering closely between the leaves. He could see the empty path a long way in the moonlight. His mind traveled ahead to the stile, which he always thought of as haunted by Emil Bergson. But why had he left his horse?

At the wheatfield corner, where the orchard hedge ended and the path led across the pasture to the Bergsons', Frank stopped. In the warm, breathless night air he heard a murmuring sound, perfectly inarticulate, as low as the sound of water coming from a spring, where there is no fall, and where there are no stones to fret it. Frank strained his ears. It ceased. He held his breath and began to tremble. Resting the butt of his gun on the ground, he parted the mulberry leaves softly with his fingers and peered through the hedge at the dark figures on the grass, in the shadow of the mulberry tree. It seemed to him that they must feel his eyes, that they must hear him breathing. But they did not. Frank, who had always wanted to see things blacker than they were, for once wanted to believe less than he saw. The woman lying in the shadow might so easily be one of the Bergsons' farm-girls. . . . Again the murmur, like water welling out of the ground. This time he heard it more distinctly, and his blood was quicker than his brain. He began to act, just as a man who falls into the fire begins to act. The gun sprang to his shoulder, he sighted mechanically and fired three times without stopping, stopped without knowing why. Either he shut his eyes or he had vertigo. He did not see anything while he was firing. He thought he heard a cry simultaneous with the second report, but he was not sure. He peered again through the hedge, at the two dark figures under the tree. They had fallen a little apart from each other, and were perfectly still—No, not quite; in a white patch of light, where the moon shone through the branches, a man's hand was plucking spasmodically at the grass.

Suddenly the woman stirred and uttered a cry, then another, and another. She was living! She was dragging herself toward the hedge! Frank dropped his gun and ran back along the path, shaking, stumbling, gasping. He had never imagined such horror. The cries followed him. They grew fainter and thicker, as if she were choking. He dropped on his knees beside the hedge and crouched like a rabbit, listening; fainter, fainter; a sound like a whine; again—a moan—another—silence. Frank scrambled to his feet and ran on, groaning and praying. From habit he went toward the house, where he was used to being soothed when he had worked himself into a frenzy, but at the sight of the black, open door, he started back. He knew that he had murdered somebody, that a woman was bleeding and moaning in the orchard, but he had not realized before that it was his wife. The gate stared him in the face. He threw his hands over his head. Which way to turn? He lifted his tormented face and looked at the sky. "Holy Mother of God, not to suffer! She was a good girl—not to suffer!"

Frank had been wont to see himself in dramatic situations; but now, when he stood by the windmill, in the bright space between the barn and the house, facing his own black doorway, he did not see himself at all. He stood like the hare when the dogs are approaching from all sides. And he ran like a hare, back and forth about that moonlit space, before he could make up his mind to go into the dark stable for a horse. The thought of going into a doorway was terrible to him. He caught Emil's horse by the bit and led it out. He could not have buckled a bridle on his own. After two or three attempts, he lifted himself into the saddle and started for Hanover. If he could catch the one o'clock train, he had money enough to get as far as Omaha.

While he was thinking dully of this in some less sensitized part of his brain, his acuter faculties were going over and over the cries he had heard in the orchard. Terror was the only thing that kept him from going back to her, terror that she might still be she, that she might still be suffering. A woman, mutilated and bleeding in his orchard—it was because it was a woman that he was so afraid. It was inconceivable that he should have hurt a woman. He would rather be eaten by wild beasts than see her move on the ground as she had moved in the orchard. Why had she been so careless? She knew he was like a crazy man when he was angry. She had more than once taken that gun away from him and held it, when he was angry with other people. Once it had gone off while they were struggling over it. She was never afraid. But, when she knew him, why had n't she been more careful? Did n't she have all summer before her to love Emil Bergson in, without taking such chances? Probably she had met the Smirka boy, too, down there in the orchard. He did n't care. She could have met all the men on the Divide there, and welcome, if only she had n't brought this horror on him.

There was a wrench in Frank's mind. He did not honestly believe that of her. He knew that he was doing her wrong. He stopped his horse to admit this to himself the more directly, to think it out the more clearly. He knew that he was to blame. For three years he had been trying to break her spirit. She had a way of making the best of things that seemed to him a sentimental affectation. He wanted his wife to resent that he was wasting his best years among these stupid and unappreciative people; but she had seemed to find the people quite good enough. If he ever got rich he meant to buy her pretty clothes and take her to California in a Pullman car, and treat her like a lady; but in the mean time he wanted her to feel that life was as ugly and as unjust as he felt it. He had tried to make her life ugly. He had refused to share any of the little pleasures she was so plucky about making for herself. She could be gay about the least thing in the world; but she must be gay! When she first came to him, her faith in him, her adoration—Frank struck the mare with his fist. Why had Marie made him do this thing; why had she brought this upon him? He was overwhelmed by sickening misfortune. All at once he heard her cries again—he had forgotten for a moment. "Maria," he sobbed aloud, "Maria!"

When Frank was halfway to Hanover, the motion of his horse brought on a violent attack of nausea. After it had passed, he rode on again, but he could think of nothing except his physical weakness and his desire to be comforted by his wife. He wanted to get into his own bed. Had his wife been at home, he would have turned and gone back to her meekly enough.

VIII

When old Ivar climbed down from his loft at four o'clock the next morning, he came upon Emil's mare, jaded and lather-stained, her bridle broken, chewing the scattered tufts of hay outside the stable door. The old man was thrown into a fright at once. He put the mare in her stall, threw her a measure of oats, and then set out as fast as his bow-legs could carry him on the path to the nearest neighbor.

"Something is wrong with that boy. Some misfortune has come upon us. He would never have used her so, in his right senses. It is not his way to abuse his mare," the old man kept muttering, as he scuttled through the short, wet pasture grass on his bare feet.

While Ivar was hurrying across the fields, the first long rays of the sun were reaching down between the orchard boughs to those two dew-drenched figures. The story of what had happened was written plainly on the orchard grass, and on the white mulberries that had fallen in the night and were covered with dark stain. For Emil the chapter had been short. He was shot in the heart, and had rolled over on his back and died. His face was turned up to the sky and his brows were drawn in a frown, as if he had realized that something had befallen him. But for Marie Shabata it had not been so easy. One ball had torn through her right lung, another had shattered the carotid artery. She must have started up and gone toward the hedge, leaving a trail of blood. There she had fallen and bled. From that spot there was another trail, heavier than the first, where she must have dragged herself back to Emil's body. Once there, she seemed not to have struggled any more. She had lifted her head to her lover's breast, taken his hand in both her own, and bled quietly to death. She was lying on her right side in an easy and natural position, her cheek on Emil's shoulder. On her face there was a look of ineffable content. Her lips were parted a little; her eyes were lightly closed, as if in a day-dream or a light slumber. After she lay down there, she seemed not to have moved an eyelash. The hand she held was covered with dark stains, where she had kissed it.

But the stained, slippery grass, the darkened mulberries, told only half the story. Above Marie and Emil, two white butterflies from Frank's alfalfa-field were fluttering in and out among the interlacing shadows; diving and soaring, now close together, now far apart; and in the long grass by the fence the last wild roses of the year opened their pink hearts to die.

When Ivar reached the path by the hedge, he saw Shabata's rifle lying in the way. He turned and peered through the branches, falling upon his knees as if his legs had been mowed from under him. "Merciful God!" he groaned; "merciful, merciful God!"

Alexandra, too, had risen early that morning, because of her anxiety about Emil. She was in Emil's room upstairs when, from the window, she saw Ivar coming along the path that led from the Shabatas'. He was running like a spent man, tottering and lurching from side to side. Ivar never drank, and Alexandra thought at once that one of his spells had come upon him, and that he must be in a very bad way indeed. She ran downstairs and hurried out to meet him, to hide his infirmity from the eyes of her household. The old man fell in the road at her feet and caught her hand, over which he bowed his shaggy head. "Mistress, mistress," he sobbed, "it has fallen! Sin and death for the young ones! God have mercy upon us!"

Part V. Alexandra

I

Ivar was sitting at a cobbler's bench in the barn, mending harness by the light of a lantern and repeating to himself the 101st Psalm. It was only five o'clock of a mid-October day, but a storm had come up in the afternoon, bringing black clouds, a cold wind and torrents of rain. The old man wore his buffalo-skin coat, and occasionally stopped to warm his fingers at the lantern. Suddenly a woman burst into the shed, as if she had been blown in, accompanied by a shower of rain-drops. It was Signa, wrapped in a man's overcoat and wearing a pair of boots over her shoes. In time of trouble Signa had come back to stay with her mistress, for she was the only one of the maids from whom Alexandra would accept much personal service. It was three months now since the news of the terrible thing that had happened in Frank Shabata's orchard had first run like a fire over the Divide. Signa and Nelse were staying on with Alexandra until winter.

"Ivar," Signa exclaimed as she wiped the rain from her face, "do you know where she is?"

The old man put down his cobbler's knife. "Who, the mistress?"

"Yes. She went away about three o'clock. I happened to look out of the window and saw her going across the fields in her thin dress and sun-hat. And now this storm has come on. I thought she was going to Mrs. Hiller's, and I telephoned as soon as the thunder stopped, but she had not been there. I'm afraid she is out somewhere and will get her death of cold."

Ivar put on his cap and took up the lantern. "*Ja, ja,* we will see. I will hitch the boy's mare to the cart and go."

Signa followed him across the wagon-shed to the horses' stable. She was shivering with cold and excitement. "Where do you suppose she can be, Ivar?"

The old man lifted a set of single harness carefully from its peg. "How should I know?"

"But you think she is at the graveyard, don't you?" Signa persisted. "So do I. Oh, I wish she would be more like herself! I can't believe it's Alexandra Bergson come to this, with no head about anything. I have to tell her when to eat and when to go to bed."

"Patience, patience, sister," muttered Ivar as he settled the bit in the horse's mouth. "When the eyes of the flesh are shut, the eyes of the spirit are open. She will have a message from those who are gone, and that will bring her peace. Until then we must bear with her. You and I are the only ones who have weight with her. She trusts us."

"How awful it's been these last three months." Signa held the lantern so that he could see to buckle the straps. "It don't seem right that we must all be so miserable. Why do we all have to be punished? Seems to me like good times would never come again."

Ivar expressed himself in a deep sigh, but said nothing. He stooped and took a sandburr from his toe.

"Ivar," Signa asked suddenly, "will you tell me why you go barefoot? All the time I lived here in the house I wanted to ask you. Is it for a penance, or what?"

"No, sister. It is for the indulgence of the body. From my youth up I have had a strong, rebellious body, and have been subject to every kind of temptation. Even in age my temptations are prolonged. It was necessary to make some allowances; and the feet, as I understand it, are free members. There is no divine prohibition for them in the Ten Commandments. The hands, the tongue, the eyes, the heart, all the bodily desires we are commanded to subdue; but the feet are free members. I indulge them without harm to any one, even to trampling in filth when my desires are low. They are quickly cleaned again."

Signa did not laugh. She looked thoughtful as she followed Ivar out to the wagon-shed and held the shafts up for him, while he backed in the mare and buckled the hold-backs. "You have been a good friend to the mistress, Ivar," she murmured.

"And you, God be with you," replied Ivar as he clambered into the cart and put the lantern under the oilcloth lap-cover. "Now for a ducking, my girl," he said to the mare, gathering up the reins.

As they emerged from the shed, a stream of water, running off the thatch, struck the mare on the neck. She tossed her head indignantly, then struck out bravely on the soft ground, slipping back again and again as she climbed the hill to the main road. Between the rain and the darkness Ivar could see very little, so he let Emil's mare have the rein, keeping her head in the right direction. When the ground was level, he turned her out of the dirt road upon the sod, where she was able to trot without slipping.

Before Ivar reached the graveyard, three miles from the house, the storm had spent itself, and the downpour had died into a soft, dripping rain. The sky and the land were a dark smoke color, and seemed to be coming together, like two waves. When Ivar stopped at the gate and swung out his lantern, a white figure rose from beside John Bergson's white stone.

The old man sprang to the ground and shuffled toward the gate calling, "Mistress, mistress!"

Alexandra hurried to meet him and put her hand on his shoulder. *"Tyst!* Ivar. There's nothing to be worried about. I'm sorry if I've scared you all. I did n't notice the storm till it was on me, and I could n't walk against it. I'm glad you've come. I am so tired I did n't know how I'd ever get home."

Ivar swung the lantern up so that it shone in her face. *"Gud!* You are enough to frighten us, mistress. You look like a drowned woman. How could you do such a thing!"

Groaning and mumbling he led her out of the gate and helped her into the cart, wrapping her in the dry blankets on which he had been sitting.

Alexandra smiled at his solicitude. "Not much use in that, Ivar. You will only shut the wet in. I don't feel so cold now; but I'm heavy and numb. I'm glad you came."

Ivar turned the mare and urged her into a sliding trot. Her feet sent back a continual spatter of mud.

Alexandra spoke to the old man as they jogged along through the sullen gray twilight of the storm. "Ivar, I think it has done me good to get cold clear through like this, once. I don't believe I shall suffer so much any more. When you get so near the dead, they seem more real than the living. Worldly thoughts leave one. Ever since Emil died, I've suffered so when it rained. Now that I've been out in it with him, I shan't dread it. After you once get cold clear through, the feeling of the rain on you is sweet. It seems to bring back feelings you had when you were a baby. It carries you back into the dark, before you were born; you can't see things, but they come to you, somehow, and you know them and are n't afraid of them. Maybe it's like that with the dead. If they feel anything at all, it's the old things, before they were born, that comfort people like the feeling of their own bed does when they are little."

"Mistress," said Ivar reproachfully, "those are bad thoughts. The dead are in Paradise."

Then he hung his head, for he did not believe that Emil was in Paradise.

When they got home, Signa had a fire burning in the sitting-room stove. She undressed Alexandra and gave her a hot footbath, while Ivar made ginger tea in the kitchen. When Alexandra was in bed, wrapped in hot blankets, Ivar came in with his tea and saw that she drank it. Signa asked permission to sleep on the slat lounge outside her door. Alexandra endured their attentions patiently, but she was glad when they put out the lamp and left her. As she lay alone in the dark, it occurred to her for the first time that perhaps she was actually tired of life. All the physical operations of life seemed difficult and painful. She longed to be free from her own body, which ached and was so heavy. And longing itself was heavy: she yearned to be free of that.

As she lay with her eyes closed, she had again, more vividly than for many years, the old illusion of her girlhood, of being lifted and carried lightly by some one very strong. He was with her a long while this time, and carried her very far, and in his arms she felt free from pain. When he laid her down on her bed again, she opened her eyes, and, for the first time in her life, she saw him, saw him clearly, though the room was dark, and his face was covered. He was standing in the doorway of her room. His white cloak was thrown over his face, and his head was bent a little forward. His shoulders seemed as strong as the foundations of the world. His right arm, bared from the elbow, was dark and gleaming, like bronze, and she knew at once that it was the arm of the mightiest of all lovers. She knew at last for whom it was she had waited, and where he would carry her. That, she told herself, was very well. Then she went to sleep.

Alexandra wakened in the morning with nothing worse than a hard cold and a stiff shoulder. She kept her bed for several days, and it was during that time that she formed a resolution to go to Lincoln to see Frank Shabata. Ever since she last saw him in the courtroom, Frank's haggard face and wild eyes had haunted her. The trial had lasted only three days. Frank had given himself up to the police in Omaha and pleaded guilty of killing without malice and without premeditation. The gun was, of course, against him, and the judge had given him the full sentence,—ten years. He had now been in the State Penitentiary for a month.

Frank was the only one, Alexandra told herself, for whom anything could be done. He had been less in the wrong than any of them, and he was paying the heaviest penalty. She often felt that she herself had been more to blame than poor Frank. From the time the Shabatas had first moved to the neighboring farm, she had omitted no opportunity of throwing Marie and Emil together. Because she knew Frank was surly about doing little things to help his wife, she was always sending Emil over to spade or plant or carpenter for Marie. She was glad to have Emil see as much as possible of an intelligent, city-bred girl like their neighbor; she noticed that it improved his manners. She knew that Emil was fond of Marie, but it had never occurred to her that Emil's feeling might be different from her own. She wondered at herself now, but she had never thought of danger in that direction. If Marie had been unmarried,—oh, yes! Then she would have kept her eyes open. But the mere fact that she was Shabata's wife, for Alexandra, settled everything. That she was beautiful, impulsive, barely two years older than Emil, these facts had had no weight with Alexandra. Emil was a good boy, and only bad boys ran after married women.

Now, Alexandra could in a measure realize that Marie was, after all, Marie; not merely a "married woman." Sometimes, when Alexandra thought of her, it was with an aching tenderness. The moment she had reached them in the orchard that morning, everything was clear to her. There was something about those two lying in the grass, something in the way Marie had settled her cheek on Emil's shoulder, that told her everything. She wondered then how they could have helped loving each other; how she could have helped knowing that they must. Emil's cold, frowning face, the girl's content—Alexandra had felt awe of them, even in the first shock of her grief.

The idleness of those days in bed, the relaxation of body which attended them, enabled Alexandra to think more calmly than she had done since Emil's death. She and Frank, she told herself, were left out of that group of friends who had been overwhelmed by disaster. She must certainly see Frank Shabata. Even in the courtroom her heart had grieved for him. He was in a strange country, he had no kinsmen or friends, and in a moment he had ruined his life. Being what he was, she felt, Frank could not have acted otherwise. She could understand his behavior more easily than she could understand Marie's. Yes, she must go to Lincoln to see Frank Shabata.

The day after Emil's funeral, Alexandra had written to Carl Linstrum; a single page of notepaper, a bare statement of what had happened. She was not a woman who could write much about such a thing, and about her own feelings she could never write very freely. She knew that Carl was away from post-offices, prospecting somewhere in the interior. Before he started he had written her where he expected to go, but her ideas about Alaska were vague. As the weeks went by and she heard nothing from him, it seemed to Alexandra that her heart grew hard against Carl. She began to wonder whether she would not do better to finish her life alone. What was left of life seemed unimportant.

II

Late in the afternoon of a brilliant October day, Alexandra Bergson, dressed in a black suit and traveling-hat, alighted at the Burlington depot in Lincoln. She drove to the Lindell Hotel, where she had stayed two years ago when she came up for Emil's Commencement. In spite of her usual air of sureness and self-possession, Alexandra felt ill at ease in hotels, and she was glad, when she went to the clerk's desk to register, that there were not many people in the lobby. She had her supper early, wearing her hat and black jacket down to the dining-room and carrying her handbag. After supper she went out for a walk.

It was growing dark when she reached the university campus. She did not go into the grounds, but walked slowly up and down the stone walk outside the long iron fence, looking through at the young men who were running from one building to another, at the lights shining from the armory and the library. A squad of cadets were going through their drill behind the armory, and the commands of their young officer rang out at regular intervals, so sharp and quick that Alexandra could not understand them. Two stalwart girls came down the library steps and out through one of the iron gates. As they passed her, Alexandra was pleased to hear them speaking Bohemian to each other. Every few moments a boy would come running down the flagged walk and dash out into the street as if he were rushing to announce some wonder to the world. Alexandra felt a great tenderness for them all. She wished one of them would stop and speak to her. She wished she could ask them whether they had known Emil.

As she lingered by the south gate she actually did encounter one of the boys. He had on his drill cap and was swinging his books at the end of a long strap. It was dark by this time; he did not see her and ran against her. He snatched off his cap and stood bareheaded and panting. "I'm awfully sorry," he said in a bright, clear voice, with a rising inflection, as if he expected her to say something.

"Oh, it was my fault!" said Alexandra eagerly. "Are you an old student here, may I ask?"

"No, ma'am. I'm a Freshie, just off the farm. Cherry County. Were you hunting somebody?"

"No, thank you. That is—"" Alexandra wanted to detain him. "That is, I would like to find some of my brother's friends. He graduated two years ago."

"Then you'd have to try the Seniors, would n't you? Let's see; I don't know any of them yet, but there'll be sure to be some of them around the library. That red building, right there," he pointed.

"Thank you, I'll try there," said Alexandra lingeringly.

"Oh, that's all right! Good-night." The lad clapped his cap on his head and ran straight down Eleventh Street. Alexandra looked after him wistfully.

She walked back to her hotel unreasonably comforted. "What a nice voice that boy had, and how polite he was. I know Emil was always like that to women." And again, after she had undressed and was standing in her nightgown, brushing her long, heavy hair by the electric light, she remembered him and said to herself: "I don't think I ever heard a nicer voice than that boy had. I hope he will get on well here. Cherry County; that's where the hay is so fine, and the coyotes can scratch down to water."

At nine o'clock the next morning Alexandra presented herself at the warden's office in the State Penitentiary. The warden was a German, a ruddy, cheerful-looking man who had formerly been a harness-maker. Alexandra had a letter to him from the German banker in Hanover. As he glanced at the letter, Mr. Schwartz put away his pipe.

"That big Bohemian, is it? Sure, he's gettin' along fine," said Mr. Schwartz cheerfully.

"I am glad to hear that. I was afraid he might be quarrelsome and get himself into more trouble. Mr. Schwartz, if you have time, I would like to tell you a little about Frank Shabata, and why I am interested in him."

The warden listened genially while she told him briefly something of Frank's history and character, but he did not seem to find anything unusual in her account.

"Sure, I'll keep an eye on him. We'll take care of him all right," he said, rising. "You can talk to him here, while I go to see to things in the kitchen. I'll have him sent in. He ought to be done washing out his cell by this time. We have to keep 'em clean, you know."

The warden paused at the door, speaking back over his shoulder to a pale young man in convicts' clothes who was seated at a desk in the corner, writing in a big ledger.

"Bertie, when 1037 is brought in, you just step out and give this lady a chance to talk."

The young man bowed his head and bent over his ledger again.

When Mr. Schwartz disappeared, Alexandra thrust her black-edged handkerchief nervously into her handbag. Coming out on the streetcar she had not had the least dread of meeting Frank. But since she had been here the sounds and smells in the corridor, the look of the men in convicts' clothes who passed the glass door of the warden's office, affected her unpleasantly.

The warden's clock ticked, the young convict's pen scratched busily in the big book, and his sharp shoulders were shaken every few seconds by a loose cough which he tried to smother. It was easy to see that he was a sick man. Alexandra looked at him timidly, but he did not once raise his eyes. He wore a white shirt under his striped jacket, a high collar, and a necktie, very carefully tied. His hands were thin and white and well cared for, and he had a seal ring on his little finger. When he heard steps approaching in the corridor, he rose, blotted his book, put his pen in the rack, and left the room without raising his eyes. Through the door he opened a guard came in, bringing Frank Shabata.

"You the lady that wanted to talk to 1037? Here he is. Be on your good behavior, now. He can set down, lady," seeing that Alexandra remained standing. "Push that white button when you're through with him, and I'll come."

The guard went out and Alexandra and Frank were left alone.

Alexandra tried not to see his hideous clothes. She tried to look straight into his face, which she could scarcely believe was his. It was already bleached to a chalky gray. His lips were colorless, his fine teeth looked yellowish. He glanced at Alexandra sullenly, blinked as if he had come from a dark place, and one eyebrow twitched continually. She felt at once that this interview was a terrible ordeal to him. His shaved head, showing the conformation of his skull, gave him a criminal look which he had not had during the trial.

Alexandra held out her hand. "Frank," she said, her eyes filling suddenly, "I hope you'll let me be friendly with you. I understand how you did it. I don't feel hard toward you. They were more to blame than you."

Frank jerked a dirty blue handkerchief from his trousers pocket. He had begun to cry. He turned away from Alexandra. "I never did mean to do not'ing to dat woman," he muttered. "I never mean to do not'ing to dat boy. I ain't had not'ing ag'in' dat boy. I always like dat boy fine. An' then I find him—" He stopped. The feeling went out of his face and eyes. He dropped into a chair and sat looking stolidly at the floor, his hands hanging loosely between his knees, the handkerchief lying across his striped leg. He seemed to have stirred up in his mind a disgust that had paralyzed his faculties.

"I have n't come up here to blame you, Frank. I think they were more to blame than you." Alexandra, too, felt benumbed.

Frank looked up suddenly and stared out of the office window. "I guess dat place all go to hell what I work so hard on," he said with a slow, bitter smile. "I not care a damn." He stopped and rubbed the palm of his hand over the light bristles on his head with annoyance. "I no can t'ink without my hair," he complained. "I forget English. We not talk here, except swear."

Alexandra was bewildered. Frank seemed to have undergone a change of personality. There was scarcely anything by which she could recognize her handsome Bohemian neighbor. He seemed, somehow, not altogether human. She did not know what to say to him.

"You do not feel hard to me, Frank?" she asked at last.

Frank clenched his fist and broke out in excitement. "I not feel hard at no woman. I tell you I not that kind-a man. I never hit my wife. No, never I hurt her when she devil me something awful!" He struck his fist down on the warden's desk so hard that he afterward stroked it absently. A pale pink crept over his neck and face. "Two, t'ree years I know dat woman don' care no more 'bout me, Alexandra Bergson. I know she after some other man. I know her, oo-oo! An' I ain't ever hurt her. I never would-a done dat, if I ain't had dat gun along. I don' know what in hell make me take dat gun. She always say I ain't no man to carry gun. If she been in dat house, where she ought-a been— But das a foolish talk."

Frank rubbed his head and stopped suddenly, as he had stopped before. Alexandra felt that there was something strange in the way he chilled off, as if something came up in him that extinguished his power of feeling or thinking.

"Yes, Frank," she said kindly. "I know you never meant to hurt Marie."

Frank smiled at her queerly. His eyes filled slowly with tears. "You know, I most forgit dat woman's name. She ain't got no name for me no more. I never hate my wife, but dat woman what make me do dat— Honest to God, but I hate her! I no man to fight. I don' want to kill no boy and no woman. I not care how many men she take under dat tree. I no care for not'ing but dat fine boy I kill, Alexandra Bergson. I guess I go crazy sure 'nough."

Alexandra remembered the little yellow cane she had found in Frank's clothes-closet. She thought of how he had come to this country a gay young fellow, so attractive that the prettiest Bohemian girl in Omaha had run away with him. It seemed unreasonable that life should have landed him in such a place as this. She blamed Marie bitterly. And why, with her happy, affectionate nature, should she have brought destruction and sorrow to all who had loved her, even to poor old Joe Tovesky, the uncle who used to carry her about so proudly when she was a little girl? That was the strangest thing of all. Was there, then, something wrong in being warm-hearted and impulsive like that? Alexandra hated to think so. But there was Emil, in the Norwegian graveyard at home, and here was Frank Shabata. Alexandra rose and took him by the hand.

"Frank Shabata, I am never going to stop trying until I get you pardoned. I'll never give the Governor any peace. I know I can get you out of this place."

Frank looked at her distrustfully, but he gathered confidence from her face. "Alexandra," he said earnestly, "if I git out-a her, I not trouble dis country no more. I go back where I come from; see my mother."

Alexandra tried to withdraw her hand, but Frank held on to it nervously. He put out his finger and absently touched a button on her black jacket. "Alexandra," he said in a low tone, looking steadily at the button, "you ain' t'ink I use dat girl awful bad before—"

"No, Frank. We won't talk about that," Alexandra said, pressing his hand. "I can't help Emil now, so I'm going to do what I can for you. You know I don't go away from home often, and I came up here on purpose to tell you this."

The warden at the glass door looked in inquiringly. Alexandra nodded, and he came in and touched the white button on his desk. The guard appeared, and with a sinking heart Alexandra saw Frank led away down the corridor. After a few words with Mr. Schwartz, she left the prison and made her way to the street-car. She had refused with horror the warden's cordial invitation to "go through the institution." As the car lurched over its uneven roadbed, back toward Lincoln, Alexandra thought of how she and Frank had been wrecked by the same storm and of how, although she could come out into the sunlight, she had not much more left of her life than he. She remembered some lines from a poem she had liked in her schooldays:—

> Henceforth the world will only be
> A wider prison-house to me,—

and sighed. A disgust of life weighed upon her heart; some such feeling as had twice frozen Frank Shabata's features while they talked together. She wished she were back on the Divide.

When Alexandra entered her hotel, the clerk held up one finger and beckoned to her. As she approached his desk, he handed her a telegram. Alexandra took the yellow envelope and looked at it in perplexity, then stepped into the elevator without opening it. As she walked down the corridor toward her room, she reflected that she was, in a manner, immune from evil tidings. On reaching her room she locked the door, and sitting down on a chair by the dresser, opened the telegram. It was from Hanover, and it read:—

> Arrived Hanover last night. Shall wait here until you come. Please hurry.
> CARL LINSTRUM.

Alexandra put her head down on the dresser and burst into tears.

III

The next afternoon Carl and Alexandra were walking across the fields from Mrs. Hiller's. Alexandra had left Lincoln after midnight, and Carl had met her at the Hanover station early in the morning. After they reached home, Alexandra had gone over to Mrs. Hiller's to leave a little present she had bought for her in the city. They stayed at the old lady's door but a moment, and then came out to spend the rest of the afternoon in the sunny fields.

Alexandra had taken off her black traveling-suit and put on a white dress; partly because she saw that her black clothes made Carl uncomfortable and partly because she felt oppressed by them herself. They seemed a little like the prison where she had worn them yesterday, and to be out of place in the open fields. Carl had changed very little. His cheeks were browner and fuller. He looked less like a tired scholar than when he went away a year ago, but no one, even now, would have taken him for a man of business. His soft, lustrous black eyes, his whimsical smile, would be less against him in the Klondike than on the Divide. There are always dreamers on the frontier.

Carl and Alexandra had been talking since morning. Her letter had never reached him. He had first learned of her misfortune from a San Francisco paper, four weeks old which he had picked up in a saloon, and which contained a brief account of Frank Shabata's trial. When he put down the paper, he had already made up his mind that he could reach Alexandra as quickly as a letter could; and ever since he had been on the way; day and night, by the fastest boats and trains he could catch. His steamer had been held back two days by rough weather.

As they came out of Mrs. Hiller's garden they took up their talk again where they had left it.

"But could you come away like that, Carl, without arranging things? Could you just walk off and leave your business?" Alexandra asked.

Carl laughed. "Prudent Alexandra! You see, my dear, I happen to have an honest partner. I trust him with everything. In fact, it's been his enterprise from the beginning, you know. I'm in it only because he took me in. I'll have to go back in the spring. Perhaps you will want to go with me, then. We have n't turned up millions yet, but we've got a start that's worth following. But this winter I'd like to spend with you. You won't feel that we ought to wait longer, on Emil's account, will you, Alexandra?"

Alexandra shook her head. "No, Carl; I don't feel that way about it. And surely you need n't mind anything Lou and Oscar say now. They are much angrier with me about Emil, now, than about you. They say it was all my fault. That I ruined him by sending him to college."

"No, I don't care a button for Lou or Oscar. The moment I knew you were in trouble, the moment I thought you might need me, it all looked different. You've always been a triumphant kind of person." Carl hesitated, looking sidewise at her strong, full figure. "But you do need me now, Alexandra?"

She put her hand on his arm. "I needed you terribly when it happened, Carl. I cried for you at night. Then everything seemed to get hard inside of me, and I thought perhaps I should never care for you again. But when I got your telegram yesterday, then—then it was just as it used to be. You are all I have in the world, you know."

Carl pressed her hand in silence. They were passing the Shabatas' empty house now, but they avoided the orchard path and took one that led over by the pasture pond.

"Can you understand it, Carl?" Alexandra murmured. "I have had nobody but Ivar and Signa to talk to. Do talk to me. Can you understand it? Could you have believed that of Marie Tovesky? I would have been cut to pieces, little by little, before I would have betrayed her trust in me!"

Carl looked at the shining spot of water before them. "Maybe she was cut to pieces, too, Alexandra. I am sure she tried hard; they both did. That was why Emil went to Mexico, of course. And he was going away again, you tell me, though he had only been home three weeks. You remember that Sunday when I went with Emil up to the French Church fair? I thought that day there was some kind of feeling, something unusual, between them. I meant to talk to you about it. But on my way back I met Lou and Oscar and got so angry that I forgot everything else. You must n't be hard on them, Alexandra. Sit down here by the pond a minute. I want to tell you something."

They sat down on the grass-tufted bank and Carl told her how he had seen Emil and Marie out by the pond that morning, more than a year ago, and how young and charming and full of grace they had seemed to him. "It happens like that in the world sometimes, Alexandra," he added earnestly. "I've seen it before. There are women who spread ruin around them through no fault of theirs, just by being too beautiful, too full of life and love. They can't help it. People come to them as people go to a warm fire in winter. Do you remember how all the Bohemians crowded round her in the store that day, when she gave Emil her candy? You remember those yellow sparks in her eyes?"

Alexandra sighed. "Yes. People could n't help loving her. Poor Frank does, even now, I think; though he's got himself in such a tangle that for a long time his love has been bitterer than his hate. But if you saw there was anything wrong, you ought to have told me, Carl."

Carl took her hand and smiled patiently. "My dear, it was something one felt in the air, as you feel the spring coming, or a storm in summer. I did n't *see* anything. Simply, when I was with those two young things, I felt my blood go quicker, I felt— how shall I say it?—an acceleration of life. After I got away, it was all too delicate, too intangible, to write about."

Alexandra looked at him mournfully. "I try to be more liberal about such things than I used to be. I try to realize that we are not all made alike. Only, why could n't it have been Raoul Marcel, or Jan Smirka? Why did it have to be my boy?"

"Because he was the best there was, I suppose. They were both the best you had here."

The sun was dropping low in the west when the two friends rose and took the path again. The straw-stacks were throwing long shadows, the owls were flying home to the prairie-dog town. When they came to the corner where the pastures joined, Alexandra's twelve young colts were galloping in a drove over the brow of the hill.

"Carl," said Alexandra, "I should like to go up there with you in the spring. I have n't been on the water since we crossed the ocean, when I was a little girl. After we first came out here I used to dream sometimes about the shipyard where father worked, and a little sort of inlet, full of masts." Alexandra paused. After a moment's thought she said, "But you would never ask me to go away for good, would you?"

"Of course not, my dearest. I think I know how you feel about this country as well as you do yourself." Carl took her hand in both his own and pressed it tenderly.

"Yes, I still feel that way, though Emil is gone. When I was on the train this morning, and we got near Hanover, I felt something like I did when I drove back with Emil from the river that time, in the dry year. I was glad to come back to it. I've lived here a long time. There is great peace here, Carl, and freedom. . . . I thought when I came out of that prison, where poor Frank is, that I should never feel free again. But I do, here." Alexandra took a deep breath and looked off into the red west.

"You belong to the land," Carl murmured, "as you have always said. Now more than ever."

"Yes, now more than ever. You remember what you once said about the graveyard, and the old story writing itself over? Only it is we who write it, with the best we have."

They paused on the last ridge of pasture, overlooking the house and the windmill and the stables that marked the site of John Bergson's homestead. On every side the brown waves of the earth rolled away to meet the sky.

"Lou and Oscar can't see those things," said Alexandra suddenly. "Suppose I do will my land to their children, what difference will that make? The land belongs to the future, Carl; that's the way it seems to me. How many of the names on the county clerk's plat will be there in fifty years? I might as well try to will the sunset over there to my brother's children. We come and go, but the land is always here. And the people who love it and understand it are the people who own it—for a little while."

Carl looked at her wonderingly. She was still gazing into the west, and in her face there was that exalted serenity that sometimes came to her at moments of deep feeling. The level rays of the sinking sun shone in her clear eyes.

"Why are you thinking of such things now, Alexandra?"

"I had a dream before I went to Lincoln—But I will tell you about that afterward, after we are married. It will never come true, now, in the way I thought it might." She took Carl's arm and they walked toward the gate. "How many times we have walked this path together, Carl. How many times we will walk it again! Does it seem to you like coming back to your own place? Do you feel at peace with the world here? I think we shall be very happy. I have n't any fears. I think when friends marry, they are safe. We don't suffer like—those young ones." Alexandra ended with a sigh.

They had reached the gate. Before Carl opened it, he drew Alexandra to him and kissed her softly, on her lips and on her eyes.

She leaned heavily on his shoulder. "I am tired," she murmured. "I have been very lonely, Carl."

They went into the house together, leaving the Divide behind them, under the evening star. Fortunate country, that is one day to receive hearts like Alexandra's into its bosom, to give them out again in the yellow wheat, in the rustling corn, in the shining eyes of youth!

Questions for Study

1. What is the point of view of the novel? Why does Cather choose this point of view? What would the novel be like if she had used a different point of view?

2. How does the epigraph, the poem "Prairie Spring," relate to the contents of the novel?

3. Cather gives a title to each of the five parts of the novel. How do these titles reflect the contents of their parts? What does the title of the novel—O Pioneers!—seem to mean?

4. How does the opening scene establish the key relationships and situations of the novel?

5. What are the different moods and qualities of the prairie? What effect does the land have on the major characters? What senses does Cather appeal to in her description of the land?

6. What characterizes Alexandra? Does she change during the novel? What challenges or tests her? Who or what influences her? How is she different from her brothers? What is her brothers' attitude toward her?

7. Who are the people who inhabit this land? How are the different national groups portrayed? What is the narrator's attitude toward them?

8. What characterizes Ivar? Why do Alexandra and Ivar have such a strong attachment to each other? Why do Alexandra's brothers, among others, resent and disapprove of this attachment?

9. What is the nature of Alexandra's relationship to Carl Linstrum? Why do Alexandra's brothers disapprove of this relationship?

10. Emil's story parallels Alexandra's. How are the two stories interrelated? How are Alexandra and Emil similar and different? What kinds of "love" does each experience? Why is Emil so important to Alexandra?

11. What characterizes Marie? What are the circumstances of her marriage? Why is Alexandra drawn to her? What characterizes Frank Shabata?

12. What are the various characters' attitudes toward Emil and Marie's relationship? What is Alexandra's? What is Carl's? What attitude toward this relationship does the narrator seem to have? What might people's attitude be today? What is your attitude?

13. What is the significance of Alexandra's dream (first described at the end of chapter II, part III (Winter Memories)? Who or what is the man? What does this dream seem to mean?

14. How is the cycle of seasons important in Cather's handling of characters and events?

15. Why does Alexandra visit Frank Shabata? What is Frank's attitude toward Marie? What is Frank and Alexandra's attitude toward each other? What seems to be the result of this scene?

16. What is the meaning of the final paragraph of the novel?

17. What oppositions does Cather establish in this novel?

FOR FURTHER READING

Allen, Walter. *The English Novel: A Short Critical History.* New York: E. P. Dutton, 1954. Allen's history of the novel is readable and, up through the early modern period, is thorough.

Forster, E. M. *Aspects of the Novel.* New York: Harcourt Brace and Co., 1927. Forster, an important English novelist and short story writer, provides an eloquent discussion of the nature of the novel.

Goldknopf, David. *The Life of the Novel.* Chicago: U of Chicago P, 1972. Goldknopf gives a brief history of the novel and discusses its conventions. In one of his chapters, he argues that realism is the essential ingredient of the novel.

Hemmings, F. W. J., ed. *The Age of Realism.* Baltimore: Penguin, 1974. The authors of the essays in this book deal with literary realism in the eighteenth and nineteenth centuries. They devote much of their attention to the novel and the prevalence of artistic realism in modern society.

Madden, David. *A Primer of the Novel: For Readers and Writers.* Metuchen: Scarecrow Press, 1980. Madden reviews basic information about the novel.

Milligan, Ian. *The Novel in English: An Introduction.* New York: St. Martin's Press, 1983. Milligan gives an overview of the novel, including discussions of the appeal, nature, and structure of the novel.

Price, Martin. *Forms of Life: Character and Moral Imagination in the Novel.* New Haven: Yale UP, 1983. Price discusses the importance of characters in the novel. His first two chapters consider the relationship between novel and reader and the realistic qualities of the novel.

Stevick, Philip, ed. *The Theory of the Novel.* New York: Free Press, 1967. This anthology includes essays on the elements of the novel.

Van Ghent, Dorothy. *The English Novel: Form and Function.* New York: Harper & Row, 1953. Van Ghent's introduction is a penetrating analysis of the relationship between the form and meaning of a novel. She follows the introduction with a series of trenchant essays about classic English novels.

Watson, George. *The Story of the Novel.* New York: Barnes and Noble, 1979. Watson discusses the history and use of the conventions of the novel. His first chapter treats the importance of realism in the novel.

Watt, Ian. *The Rise of the Novel: Studies in Defoe, Richardson, and Fielding.* Berkeley: U of California P, 1957. Watt investigates the origins of the English novel. He speculates that the form and subject matter of the novel evolved in the seventeenth and eighteenth centuries because of the interests of a new middle-class audience.

Glossary of Terms

Page numbers refer to discussion in the text, which in most cases is more detailed and provides context for the use of these terms.

allegory   A narrative whose characters, settings, and actions symbolize ideas. Allegories function on two levels of meaning: literal and thematic. **238**

alliteration   The repetition of like consonant sounds at the beginning of words. **306**

analogy   A comparison between things that may seem dissimilar at first glance but that have underlying similarities. **306**

anapest   Poetic meter in which two unaccented syllables are followed by one accented syllable. **305**

animal fable   Fables that feature animals as characters who act like human beings and whose actions often expose certain unpleasant realities of human experience. Fables may point out a moral, merely be explanatory, or may be intended to elicit laughter. Whatever their purpose, most animal fables contain some commentary on human life. **167**

antagonist   A person or persons in conflict with a protagonist, or other things (a force of nature, a hostile divinity, or a psychological trait) that causes physical, emotional, or intellectual conflicts for the protagonist. **8**

archetype   A convention—a character type, plot pattern, image, symbol, etc.—that recurs in many works of literature. **24–25**

assonance   A sound pattern similar to rhyme in which only like vowel sounds are linked. **306**

atmosphere   The emotional reaction that we or the characters have to the world of the narrative; how we feel about the narrative. **14, 306**

binary opposition   A rhetorical device employing two opposing or contradictory forces or ideas. **5**

blank verse   Metrical pattern of iambic pentameter verse with no end rhyme. **307**

characterization   The author's presentation and development of characters. **10–12**

characters   The actors in a narrative. **10**

complex (or round) characters   Characters with numerous, sometimes conflicting, personality traits. **10**

connotation   The subjective, emotional association a word has for one person or for a group of people. **306**

consonance   A sound pattern linking consonant sounds at the end of words. **306**

convention   Any aspect of literature—a plot pattern, a character type, a particular setting, a poetic form, or a set of words—that through repeated use has become recognized as a means of literary expression, as "literary." **4, 19–21**

dactyl   Poetic meter in which an accented syllable is followed by two unaccented syllables. **306**

denotation   The object or idea—the referent—that a word represents; the denotative meaning of a word is usually equivalent to the definition in a dictionary. **306**

diction   The poet's choice of words, not just for their sound qualities but for their meaning. **306**

dramatic point of view   See *objective point of view*

dynamic characters   Characters who change—who alter their beliefs and patterns of behavior. **11** (See *static characters*)

epic   A long narrative poem that gives an account of heroic deeds. **73–75**

epiphany   A character's recognition of the truth about himself or herself and about the nature of his or her circumstances; a moment of discovery in which a character achieves a new understanding about the nature of reality; often the climax of the plot and usually a trigger for change in the protagonist. **11, 372**

fable   A brief, simple story that usually makes some point about the human condition. A widespread and popular kind of narrative. **167**

first-person point of view   Point of view in which the story is told by one of the characters in it. **16–17**

fixed forms   Already established poetic structures, such as the sonnet, ballad stanza, and Spenserian stanza. **307**

flat characters   See *simple characters*

folk epic   Epics that originate as oral forms—they may at some point be written down but they first exist in oral form. **73–75**

folktale   A short, usually fictional narrative that belongs to an oral tradition and that is told for entertainment. **74, 165–66, 182, 205**

foot   A single rhythmical unit in poetry. **305**

free verse   A metrical pattern that contains no end rhyme, no regular metrical patterns, and no lines of fixed lengths. **308**

genre   A kind of literature defined by conventions that mark it as distinct from other genres. **19–25**

gothic romance   A romance that includes "gothic" conventions, such as a mysterious and threatening atmosphere, gloomy locales, supernatural events, grotesque characters, emotionally tormented protagonists, and satanic villains. **236**

iamb   The most common meter in the English language, consisting of an unaccented syllable followed by an accented syllable. **305**

iambic pentameter   A frequently used meter in English poetry, consisting of five iambic feet per line. **305**

imagery   In literature, an appeal to one or more of the senses that establishes the physical world of a work of literature. **306**

incremental repetition   A convention often used in medieval ballads in which a phrase or stanza is repeated with slight but meaningful changes of phrasing. **308**

intertextuality   The borrowing from and reference to conventions of other genres by which authors let readers know that the qualities and meanings usually associated with one genre are now applicable within another genre. **24**

legend   A story about historical beings who lived in the distant past; may include exaggerations and fictional material, but the characters are thought to have actually lived and to have performed many of the deeds described in the legend. **74**

limited omniscient point of view   A point of view like the omniscient point of view except that the narrator provides access to the mind of only one character. Readers experience a story told from the limited omniscient point of view from one of two positions: that of one of the characters or that of the narrator. **16**

literary epic   Written imitations of folk epics. **73–75**

medieval ballads (Scottish border ballads)   Poems of anonymous authorship from England, Scotland, and especially the border region of the two countries that were first written down in the eighteenth century but are much older (possibly going back to the Middle Ages, then passed from generation to generation by folk artists) and that are characterized by short, relatively simple stanzas that may or may not conform to a metrical pattern.   308–9

metaphor   Generally, any analogy or comparison between things that may seem dissimilar at first glance but that have underlying similarities. Specifically, a particular kind of analogy that is contrasted with the *simile;* a comparison that eliminates the words *like* and *as* and directly equates compared items.   306–7

meter   In poetry, a rhythmical unit.   305

metrical pattern   The repetition of a rhythmical unit.   305

myth   An anonymous story, emerging from the beliefs of a race or nation, that contains elements of the supernatural and attempts to explain or represent fundamental realities of existence. Myths are usually religious in origin and nature.   26–29, 74

narrative   A telling of a story, a recounting of events in a temporal sequence.   2

narrative fiction   A recounting of events that have not happened, or that some people, at least, believe have not happened.   2

novel   In its broadest sense, any relatively long fictional narrative written in prose; more strictly, a long, *realistic* fictional narrative in prose.   546–48

novella   A short novel, like Joseph Conrad's *Heart of Darkness* and Thomas Mann's *Death in Venice.*   546

novelle   Italian term from which the term *novel* was transliterated; originally used for short, realistic tales like those in Boccaccio's *Decameron.*   546

objective (or dramatic) point of view   Point of view in which the narrator remains outside the characters' minds and refrains from commenting about the meaning of the events.   17

omniscient point of view   Position from which the narrator seems to have complete knowledge of everything that happens in the narrative, including facts about the physical location, the history of the society, and the characters' actions and thoughts.   16

onomatopoeia   The use of words that sound like what they mean.   306

parable   A less playful form of fable than animal fables, and one that is more severely restricted in its theme; almost always features human beings as characters. Teaches personal morality and proper attitude. Nearly every detail in a parable is tied to a message, and parables are virtually never comic.   167

parody   A kind of literature that makes fun of other works or genres, usually by imitating the form of the work or genre to treat silly or trivial subject matter.   24

plot   The events in a narrative and the author's selection and arrangement of them, typically by a logical relationship of cause and effect.   7–10

point of view   The position from which the story is told and the position from which the reader or hearer experiences the story.   15–19

protagonist   The main character in a narrative; frequently in conflict with one or more *antagonists.*   8

rhetoric   The art of speaking or writing effectively. An implicit aim of rhetoric is persuasion.   5

rhyme   The repetition of accented vowels and the sounds that follow; a linking of both vowel and consonant sounds that can occur both within lines of poetry and at the ends of lines.   306

rhyme scheme   The pattern established by the end rhymes of lines of poetry. **307**

romance   During the Middle Ages, stories about knights and chivalry. More generally, any long narrative in either poetry or prose featuring idealized characters who experience surprising and improbable events in an idealized setting. **235–39**

round characters   See *complex characters*

scansion   A method of determining the meter of a poem by marking the accented and unaccented syllables of one or more lines and dividing the lines into feet. **305**

scenic narration   Narration in which the narrator describes an event in so much detail that the account takes about as long to read as it would to occur in real life. **13–14**

setting   The physical, temporal, and cultural details of the world of the narrative. **12–15**

shope   A bard who accompanied his recital with the rhythmic strumming of a lyre. **79**

simile   A comparison that is signaled by the use of the words *like* and *as*. **306**

simple (or **flat**) **characters**   Characters that have only one or two personality traits and that are easily identifiable as stereotypes. **10**

Spenserian stanza   A fixed stanzaic form named after its creator, Edmund Spenser. The form is characterized by nine lines rhyming *ababbcbcc,* of which the first eight lines are iambic pentameter and the ninth is iambic hexameter. **307, 318**

spondee   Poetic meter in which there are two accented syllables together. **306**

stanza   A repeated grouping of two or more lines of poetry separated from other stanzas by spaces. **307**

static characters   Characters who remain the same throughout a work. **11** (See *dynamic characters*)

story   A series of events that occur in time; the chronological sequence in which events occur. **2, 7**

subject   Something a work of literature is about. **5**

summary narration   Narration in which the narrator briefly relates (sums up) events and directly states how much time is passing. **13–14**

symbol   Broadly speaking, something that represents something else; in literature, an object that has meaning beyond itself—the object is concrete and the meanings are abstract. **6**

tale   A relatively short story whose main purpose is to entertain and whose material and form are usually traditional. **165–66**

theme   The ideas in a work of literature; what the work says about a particular subject. **5–7**

tone   The narrator's attitude toward the narrative's subject matter. **4**

trochee   Poetic meter in which an accented syllable is followed by an unaccented syllable. **305**

Credits and Acknowledgments

Index of Authors and Works